PEARSON   ALWAYS LEARNING

A Brief Guide to Writing from Readings
Selected Readings Included

Second Custom Edition for Ivy Tech Community College Bloomington

Taken from:
A Brief Guide to Writing from Readings,
Seventh Edition
by Stephen Wilhoit

Pearson Education, Inc., 330 Hudson Street, New York, New York 10013
A Pearson Education Company
www.pearsoned.com

Printed in the United States of America

1   17

000200010272092713

KR/JL

ISBN 10: 1-323-64968-9
ISBN 13: 978-1-323-64968-8

COPYRIGHT ACKNOWLEDGMENTS

Grateful acknowledgment is made to the following sources for permission to reprint material copyrighted or controlled by them:

"On Freedom of Expression and Campus Speech Codes," (1992), reprinted by permission from the American Association of University Professors.

"Hate-Speech Codes That Will Pass Constitutional Muster," by Lawrence White, reprinted by permission from the *Chronicle of Higher Education* (1994).

"Fairness to All: Free Speech and Civility in Conflict–For Narrowly Tailored Limitations on Gender-Based Discriminatory Speech," by Ann Browning Masters, reprinted from the *Journal for a Just and Caring Education* 1, no. 4 (1995), by permission of Sage Publications.

"Only Speech Codes Should Be Censored," by Gary Pavela, reprinted by permission from the *Chronicle of Higher Education*, (2006).

"The Real Impact of Virtual Words: How Digital Culture Shapes Students' Minds," by Thomas A. Workman, reprinted by permission from the *Chronicle of Higher Education*, (2008).

"Generation Text," by Mark Bauerlein, reprinted by permission from *America*, October 12, 2009.

"Online Social Networks and Learning," by Christine Greenhow, reprinted from *On the Horizon* 19, no.1 (2011), by permission of Emerald Group Publishing Limited.

"Why Pop Culture in Education Matters," by William Reynolds, reprinted from *Popular Culture*, by permission of Intellect Ltd.

"Small Change: Why the Revolution Will Not be Tweeted," by Malcolm Gladwell, reprinted from *The New Yorker*, 2010, by permission of the author.

"Parenting and Popular Culture," by Jim Taylor, reprinted from *Psychology Today: The Power of Prime*, February 6, 2012, Carol Mann Literary Agency.

"Watching TV Makes You Smarter," by Steven Johnson, reprinted from *New York Times Magazine*, April 25, 2005, by permission of Lydia Wills LLC.

CONTENTS

Chapter 8   RHETORICAL ANALYSIS OF VISUAL TEXTS   145

Chapter 9   INFORMATIVE SYNTHESIS   *167*

Chapter 10   ARGUMENTATIVE SYNTHESIS   *197*

Chapter 11 PLAGIARISM   *233*

Anthology of Readings **289**

PREFACE

In the seventh edition of *A Brief Guide to Writing from Readings*, my goal remains unchanged from the earlier editions: to help students master one of the most common academic genres—writing from readings. Toward this end, and based on responses from students and faculty using the book, I have made several significant changes to the seventh edition. The changes include the following:

- a new chapter on analyzing readings and composing analytical essays
- new coverage of literary analysis and the inclusion of a short story
- eight new academic readings: two on controversies surrounding academic freedom, three on the ethics of human genetic enhancement, and three on leadership
- readings drawn from a wider range of academic sources than in previous editions
- four new sample essays
- expanded coverage of how to include electronic sources of information on APA reference lists and MLA works cited lists

To accommodate these changes, I have dropped the appendix, which offered instruction on peer review of writing, but which reviewers indicated was not widely used.

With these changes to the seventh edition, *A Brief Guide* extends its coverage of source-based writing, most notably through the inclusion of a new chapter with instruction on analyzing texts, the addition of a short story (Kate Chopin's "The Story of an Hour"), and an examination of how to write literary analysis essays. This new chapter compliments the instruction on analyzing arguments already included in the chapter on writing critiques and the chapter on analyzing visual texts. However, much remains the same in this new edition. Faculty and students have long noted the collegial tone of the book and the utility of the summary charts located at the end of most chapters, in addition to the revision checklists. These features have all been retained. From the first edition, I have tried to maintain a clear, process-oriented approach to writing instruction, laying out for writers a series of steps they can follow or modify as needed when composing commonly assigned source-based essays.

As in previous editions of the textbook, the sample readings are drawn from a range of disciplines with an emphasis on academic sources. Readings vary in length and in difficulty, but all are intended to pique student interest and serve as prompts for class discussion. Each sample student essay I include in the text can serve as a model for students to follow in terms of its thesis, organization, and use of sources, but none of them is perfect. Students should be encouraged to read the sample essays in this textbook as critically as they read any other material in college. They may identify several ways each essay can be improved. In fact, instructors might consider asking their students to do just that: to use the instruction offered in *A Brief Guide* to critique and revise these sample essays.

In the end, my hope, as always, is that the instruction offered in this textbook will help students develop the skills they need to successfully complete source-based college writing assignments, to read texts honestly and critically, and to explore connections they find between the material they read and their own knowledge, experience, and beliefs.

SUPPLEMENTS

MYWRITINGLAB: NOW AVAILABLE FOR COMPOSITION

MyWritingLab is an online homework, tutorial, and assessment program that provides engaging experiences to today's instructors and students. By incorporating rubrics into the writing assignments, faculty can create meaningful assignments, grade them based on their desired criteria, and analyze class performance through advanced reporting. For students who enter the course under-prepared, MyWritingLab offers a diagnostic test and personalized remediation so that students see improved results and instructors spend less time in class reviewing the basics. Rich multimedia resources, including a text-specific ebook in many courses, are built in to engage students and support faculty throughout the course. Visit www.mywritinglab.com for more information.

INSTRUCTOR'S MANUAL

An Instructor's Manual is available for *A Brief Guide to Writing from Readings.* The Instructor's Manual includes a brief introduction to each chapter, an examination of problems students commonly face when writing each type of source-based essay, and a series of exercises and assignments designed to help students improve their writing.

ACKNOWLEDGMENTS

I would like to thank the following reviewers for their helpful suggestions as I prepared each new edition of *A Brief Guide to Writing from Readings:* Curtis R. Burdette, Central Michigan University; Jennifer Campbell, University of Denver; Jacqueline E. Cason, University of Alaska, Anchorage; Tim Catalano, Marietta College; Jane Creighton, University of Houston–Downtown; Sally Ebest, University of Missouri, St. Louis; Daniel P. Galvin, Clemson University; Karen Gardiner, University of Alabama; Monica E. Hogan, Johnson County Community College; Wesley Jones, University of Mary; David D. Knapp,

Front Range Community College; Greg Luthi, Johnson County Community College; Raj Mohan, Cleveland State University; Anne Pici, University of Dayton; Kathy Overhulse Smith, Indiana University–Bloomington; and Mary Trachsel, University of Iowa. Reviewers of the seventh edition include Nathan A. Breen, College of Lake County; Sarah K. Cantrell, University of Alabama; David M. Higgins, Inver Hills Community College; Brooke Parks, University of West Georgia; Kari Vara, Cleveland State University; and Carmaletta M. Williams, Johnson County Community College.

Stephen Wilhoit

Chapter 1

....

CRITICAL READING

In this chapter you will learn how to

1. Read closely and critically

2. Highlight and annotate readings

3. Take notes while you read

DEFINITION AND PURPOSE

Most successful college writers are also sophisticated, critical readers. They assume a skeptical attitude toward texts: instead of believing whatever they read, they critically examine the author's ideas and their own responses to the reading. They are active, reflective readers who ask questions about the words on the page, mark passages, take notes, and draw connections between the author's ideas and their own experiences and knowledge. They are open to new ideas, but do not accept them without serious, reflective consideration. Unreflective readers, however, tend to accept unquestioningly what they see in print. In their view, if something has been published, it must be accurate. Instead of asking questions about what they read, they tend to accept the author's words at face value.

A major difference, then, between reflective and unreflective readers is the way they try to learn from what they read. Unreflective readers usually believe that the meaning of a text can be found in the words on the page: to understand a text, all a reader has to do is understand the meaning of the author's words. For them, reading is a rather simple, straightforward process: they read through a text, look up any words they do not know, isolate the author's main ideas, perhaps take some notes, and then move on to the next reading. They also tend to believe that because the meaning of a text resides in the author's words, students reading the same material ought to come away with the same information; the text should mean roughly the same thing to any competent reader who studies it.

Reflective, critical readers, however, tend to adopt a different view of reading. They believe that the meaning of a text resides in the *interaction* between the reader and the words on the page: to understand a text, readers must be aware of how their own knowledge, feelings, and experience influence their *interpretation* of the words on the page. For them, reading is a rather dynamic, fluid process: they read through a text skeptically, assess the author's words and ideas in light of their own knowledge and experience, jot down some notes that capture their questions and responses, reread the text after they have had some time to consider what the author had to say, and then move on.

Viewing reading as an interactive process can help you better understand the complex nature of writing from sources and the need to be an active, critical reader. For example, it helps you understand why a story you read during your first year in high school means something different to you when you read it again in your first year in college. The words on the page have not changed—you have, and because you have changed, the "meaning" of the story has changed for you as well. This interactive view of reading also helps explain how twenty students in an introductory philosophy class can read the same meditation by Descartes and come away with twenty slightly different interpretations of the piece. Active, critical readers understand that for any given person, the meaning of a text results from the interaction between the words on the page and that reader's knowledge, feelings, and expertise; reading involves more than a simple transfer of information from the words on the page to the mind of the reader.

Does this mean that all interpretations of a reading are equally valid? No. Although every person forms his or her own understanding of a reading, people can and often do misread texts: they may not read carefully, they may not understand certain terms or ideas, or they may lack the knowledge and experience they need to form an adequate interpretation of the text. As a safeguard against misinterpretation, critical readers discuss the material with others who have read it. Comparing their own reading of a text with a teacher's or a peer's reading can help clarify the material and prevent misunderstanding.

In addition, the author of the piece plays an important role in reading. Good writers try to influence their readers' understanding of and response to a text. When writing, authors manipulate the language, structure, and content of their prose to achieve a certain effect on their audience. Success is never guaranteed, but good writers know that they can at least influence how readers might respond to their work through the choices they make while composing. Critical readers take this into account when approaching a text—they try to be aware not only of what they bring to the reading, but also of the choices the writer has made to achieve a certain goal.

Learning to read material actively and critically can be difficult. However, critical readers tend to understand course material more fully, prepare for class more efficiently, and write from readings more effectively. Following are a number of suggestions aimed at helping you become a more active, critical reader. Central to this process is the ability and willingness to ask good questions about your reading of a text and to keep a written record of your responses. Critical readers refuse to sit back passively while they read; they actively question and respond to texts in light of their own knowledge, feelings, and experience.

ASKING QUESTIONS ABOUT WHAT YOU READ

Instead of passively accepting the ideas an author presents, a critical reader attempts to engage in a dialogue with the text, posing and working out answers to tough questions concerning the material's purpose, audience, language, and content.

The most productive critical questions center on the connections that exist between a text's author and his or her audience, subject, and language. Everything you read has been written by someone for someone about something using certain words on a page. Learning how to identify and question the relationship between these various aspects of a reading can help you understand the material more fully and determine its meaning and importance.

Typical questions you should ask of a reading include:

- Who is the author of the piece?
- What is her stand on the issue she is addressing?
- What are her interests, qualifications, or possible biases?
- What was her intent when writing this piece?
- Who is the intended audience?
- How does the author support her contentions?
- What language has she used to convey her ideas on this topic to this audience for this purpose?
- Based on my own knowledge and experience, what do I think about her ideas, intent, language, and support?
- How well does the author achieve her goal?

When you are confronted with conflicting sources of information on a topic (as is frequently the case in college), asking questions such as these is a particularly important way to sort out the authors' different positions, evaluate the worth of each source, and decide who presents the clearer, more convincing case.

Forming a full, critical understanding of a reading requires asking the right kinds of questions about the author, subject, audience, and language of the piece. Following you will find a series of questions to ask before, during, and after your reading. However, these questions are merely suggestive, not exhaustive; they indicate only starting points for your critical assessment of a text. Your teacher and peers may suggest other questions to ask as well. Finally, it is a good idea to write out your answers to these questions. Do not rely on your memory alone to keep track of your responses.

QUESTIONS TO ASK BEFORE YOU BEGIN A CLOSE READING OF A TEXT

Whether you are assigned to read material in history or art, biology or sociology, before you begin you need to ask yourself a series of questions concerning the author and publication in which the piece appeared as well as your own knowledge of and attitude toward the topic. Answering these questions may help you determine any biases present in the reading and ensure that you remain open to any new perspectives or information the author has to offer.

Questions Concerning the Author

- Who is the author?
- What are his credentials?
- What else has he written on the topic?
- What possible biases might have influenced his work?

Before you begin to read a text, try to assess the credibility and expertise of the person who wrote the piece. Who is the author, and what are his or her qualifications for writing on this topic? If, for instance, you are writing a paper about global warming for your English class and find an article you want to use in your essay, note whether you are reading a research report produced by a scientist who conducted her own studies on the topic, an informative article composed by a reporter who interviewed that scientist, or an opinion piece written by a television star who has no particular expertise in climatology. The first author is probably well qualified to offer expert opinion; the second author, while less qualified than the first, may still be a legitimate source of information. However, approach the third author skeptically: good actors are rarely good scientists. If you plan to use any of these readings to support a position of your own in an essay, understand that academic readers will tend to believe authors with solid, professional credentials and demonstrated expertise in the topic.

Also determine, as best you can, any biases operating in the authors' work. Note who the writers work for, who supported their research, and who publishes their results. Writers are never completely objective; all writers bring to their work certain biases or preferences, whether political, religious, or methodological. These biases may influence the type of study authors conduct, the type of evidence they use to support their contentions, the language they employ, and the conclusions they draw. When researching a paper on abortion, for instance, it would be important to note whether the author of a piece is a member of the National Abortion Rights Action League or Operation Life, even if the writer claims to be presenting the results of an objective study. In college you will often read expert testimony that presents conflicting views and interpretations of the same topic, data, or event. Often your job as a *writer* is to examine these different perspectives, compare their quality or worth, and use them to form and defend a position of your own. However, recognizing potential authorial bias in a reading does not disqualify it as a legitimate source of information: it simply puts you in a better position to read the work skeptically and to ask better, more critical questions.

Most academic journals include brief biographical entries on the authors at the beginning or end of each article or in a separate section of the journal typically labeled "Contributor Notes" or "Contributors." Many popular magazines also include some information on the author of each article they publish. (If you cannot find this information, see a reference librarian for help locating biographical dictionaries. Later, including in your essay the credentials of the authors whose work you are quoting or paraphrasing can help increase the credibility of your assertions.)

Questions Concerning the Publication

- In what regard is the publication held by professionals in the field?
- Toward what type of readership is the publication aimed?
- How long ago was the piece published?
- What, generally, is the editorial stance of the publication?

When assessing the quality of a publication, your first questions ought to address its credibility and audience. Do members of the profession or the academy consider this a reputable journal? Does it publish scholarly work or general interest features? What type of reader is this publication trying to reach: scholars or the general public? Answering these questions can help you determine whether work published in this journal or magazine is appropriate for inclusion in an essay of your own.

To answer these questions about the publication, first consult your teacher. He or she can probably tell you in what regard a particular journal is held by professionals in the field. Also, if you want to consult only scholarly sources of information, you may want to limit your research to specialized scholarly indexes and databases—drawing information from *The Applied Science and Technology Index* rather than from *Academic Search Complete*. Again, your teacher or a reference librarian can help you identify scholarly reference works.

Just as individual authors have certain biases or preferences that may influence their writing, publications have certain editorial slants that may influence what they print. Some publications will have definite political or ideological agendas. For example, *The New Republic* and *The National Review* are not likely to publish the same article on gun control. Other publications may exhibit certain methodological biases: they prefer to publish only historical studies or empirical studies or Marxist studies of a topic. Determining the editorial or methodological slant of a publication can be difficult: if you have not read widely in a field, you may not know a great deal about its principal publications. Often, your best recourse in gathering this type of information is to scan the titles and abstracts of other articles in the journal to determine its political or methodological preferences or, if you are reading newspaper or magazine articles, to read the editorials.

However, a particular periodical's political or methodological slant does not necessarily make it any more or less valid a source of information. Recognizing these preferences, though, should help you read material more skeptically. A publication's biases may affect the content of the articles it publishes, its authors' interpretations of statistics, even the nature of the graphics and illustrations accompanying the text. When you are thoroughly researching a topic, gathering information from several different sources is one way to guard against one-sided, unbalanced treatments of a topic.

Questions Concerning Your Own Views of the Topic

- What are my beliefs about the issue addressed in the reading?
- How open am I to new ideas on this topic?

Just as every author and publication presents material from a particular perspective, readers, too, bring their own prejudices and preferences to a text. Though absolute objectivity may be impossible for readers and writers to attain, knowing your own predispositions toward the topic an author addresses can help you guard against unfairly judging someone else's arguments or shutting yourself off from potentially helpful ideas.

Author Peter Elbow suggests two frames of mind students ought to assume when reading material. First, he advises students to play the "believing game"—that is, to assume that what the writer has to say is correct. If the author of the piece is right in what he says, how do his ideas influence your current views on the topic? What are the implications of the author's ideas? Can you draw any connections between what the author has to say and what you already know? Next, Elbow suggests that students play the "doubting game"—that is, assume a more critical stance toward the author's ideas. What are the weaknesses in the writer's arguments? What are the limitations of his ideas? In what ways are the author's ideas incompatible with what you already know about the topic?

Being aware of your own stance on an issue *before* you begin to read something for the first time can help you play the believing and doubting games more effectively. First, reading with your own beliefs firmly in mind can help you recognize which ideas are hard for you to accept or even to consider fairly. We all resist ideas that run counter to our beliefs: giving them legitimacy forces us to question our own positions. However, being a critical reader means you are willing to do just that, to consider ideas that you might otherwise ignore or reject. When you dismiss an idea in a source text, consider why: if it is only because that idea runs counter to your views, try playing the believing game before moving on.

Second, reading with your beliefs firmly in mind can help you recognize which ideas are hard for you to question and criticize. We all like to read material that confirms our present positions, because such reinforcement is comforting and reassuring. However, as a critical reader you must be willing to question authors who voice opinions you endorse, to criticize fairly and thoroughly ideas you are predisposed to accept unquestioningly. If you accept information without question, consider why: if it is only because you agree with the author, try playing the doubting game before moving on.

QUESTIONS TO ASK WHILE YOU READ AND REREAD MATERIAL

After you have read material with these questions in mind, reread it. If necessary, read it a third or fourth time—very few of us truly understand a text the first time we read it. When rereading material, though, you should consider another set of questions that focus your attention on the audience, purpose, content, and organization of the piece, along with your response to the author's ideas.

Questions about the Audience of the Piece

- What audience does the author seem to be trying to reach?
- What type of reader would be attracted to the author's writing, and what type would be alienated by it?
- How does your sense of the text's audience influence your reading of the piece?

Audience is one of the most important concepts in writing: an author's sense of audience will greatly affect, among other things, the language she uses, the material she includes, and the organizational strategy she employs. However, *audience* can be a difficult term to define. In one sense, it refers to actual people a writer may know. When composing a letter to a friend, for instance, a writer can make fairly accurate predictions about the way her reader will react to what she says or the language she uses.

In another sense, though, *audience* can have very little to do with specific people the author has in mind as he writes a text. Much of what you read in college, for example, was written by people who possessed a much more nebulous sense of audience as they wrote. They knew the *type* of reader they were trying to address (for example, a first-year student taking an introductory geology course) or perhaps the *type* of reader they wanted to interest (for example, people curious about feminist interpretations of literature). When writing, they did not have in mind as their audience a specific, individual reader. Instead, they were trying to produce prose that would attract or interest a particular type of reader.

Therefore, as you read and reread material, try to determine the audience the author is trying to address: how is she attempting to interest or appeal to that type of reader? How successful is she in achieving that goal? Pay attention to the language, content, and organization of the piece as you try to answer questions such as these:

- Was the author trying to reach a general reader, an educated reader, or a specialist?
- What language does the author use to try to reach this audience? What examples? What graphics?
- What type of reader would actually find the work helpful, informative, valuable, or difficult?
- Would any readers be alienated by the material in the piece? Why?

Answering these questions will help you better understand how the text you are reading came to assume its present form. When writing, authors choose language, examples, and a structure they believe will help them achieve their desired effect on an audience. Part of reading a text critically is determining in your mind how successful each writer has been in making these choices.

Realize, too, that when you read something, you become a member of that writer's audience. *Your* response to what you read is extremely important to note as you try to understand what the author has to say. Is the writer communicating his ideas effectively to you? Do you find the material in the piece interesting or boring, helpful or irrelevant, engaging, or alienating? What choices has the writer made that led to these responses? What knowledge or experience do you bring to the text that contributes to your reaction? Understanding the complex relationship between the audience and the writer of a piece can help you become a more sensitive, critical reader.

Questions about Purpose

- What was the author's purpose in writing the piece?
- What is the author's thesis?
- Does the author successfully achieve his or her goals?

Generally, when writing a text, an author will have one of three aims: to entertain, to inform, or to persuade his readers. Many times a work will serve multiple purposes—it will both entertain and inform, or inform and persuade. However, as a critical reader, you ought to identify the primary purpose of the piece you are reading. To criticize an article for failing to present an effective argument on a topic would be unproductive and unfair if all the author intended was to write an informative essay.

However, determining an author's purpose or goal can be difficult. In social science and natural science journals, look for the author's stated purpose in his abstract or thesis ("The purpose of this article is . . ." and "The authors seek to prove that . . ."). The conventions of most humanities journals, however, require authors to be less straightforward or declaratory in stating their purpose, but again thesis statements and abstracts are good places to start your search. Even if the author states his or her goal somewhere in the paper or abstract, be wary. When you finish rereading the piece, ask yourself, "Given the content, language, and structure of this piece, what do *I* believe to be the writer's primary goal or purpose?"

Questions about Content

- What are the author's major assertions or findings?
- How does the author support these assertions or findings?

When examining the content of any reading, try first to locate the author's thesis and paraphrase it. A thesis statement will be either stated or implied. If it is stated, you will be able to point to a sentence or two in the reading that serves as the thesis. If it is implied, a general idea or argument unites and guides the writing, but the author never explicitly puts it into words. When you paraphrase or recognize this general idea or argument, you have identified the thesis. In either case, as a first step in analyzing a reading's content, state the author's thesis in your own words to form a clear idea of what the author is trying to accomplish in the piece.

Next, note how the author supports her thesis—identify her primary ideas, arguments, or findings and the evidence, reasons, or examples she offers to support them. As you reread the piece, ask yourself what empirical, philosophical, theoretical, or other type of evidence or reasoning the author has provided to support her thesis and achieve her goal.

Finally, be sure to examine what you already know about the topic—what you have learned in the past and what you are learning now by reading *this* piece. Has the author left out any important information or arguments? Has she neglected certain interpretations of evidence others have offered? If so, why do you think that is? How can the reading's content be explained by its author, audience, or purpose?

Questions about Organization

- How is the material organized?
- What headings and subheadings does the author provide?
- What does the organization of the essay tell you about the author's view of the material?
- What gets stressed as a result of the organization?

As a writer composes his piece, he has to make a series of decisions about organization: he needs to determine the order in which he will present his findings, ideas, or arguments. Good writers organize their material purposefully—to make their article clear, to make their book more persuasive, or to make their findings more accessible. Through the order in which they present their material and through their use of paragraph breaks, headings, and subheadings, they try to help the reader understand or accept their views.

As you read a source text, think critically about its organization. First, form at least a rough idea of how the writer has organized his ideas. What are the major sections of the text? In what order are the ideas, arguments, or findings presented? You might want to produce a scratch outline or list that captures the reading's organization. Also, use the headings and subheadings the author provides to get a better understanding of how he views his material and how he sets priorities among his findings. For example, what ideas, arguments, or findings get emphasized through the author's selection of headings? How do the headings and subheadings guide you through the piece? Are there any instances in which you think a heading or subheading is misleading or poorly stated? Why?

Questions about the Author's Sources

- How does the author use other people's ideas or findings?
- How credible are the sources the author uses to support his ideas or findings?

As you analyze the content of a reading, examine the sources the author relied on when writing. What is documented? Flip back to the works cited list or bibliography at the end of the piece. Where does the author's information come from? Is the paper based on library research, primary research, or interviews? If much of the text's material comes from previously published work, how credible are the sources the author used to support her claims? For example, is the author relying on scholarly sources of information? Is there any apparent bias in the author's use of source material: is most of her material taken from journals that share similar editorial stances, or has the writer tried to draw information from sources representing a variety of political, theoretical, or methodological perspectives? Answering questions such as these can help you determine the credibility and utility of the author's ideas, arguments, or findings.

Questions about Graphics

- How clear are the charts, graphs, tables, or illustrations the author provides?
- How well does the author explain the graphics?
- How well do the graphics support or explain what the author has to say?

Graphics include charts, tables, graphs, drawings, and pictures. Although authors may add graphics to entertain readers, most include them to support arguments, summarize findings, or illustrate ideas. As you read a text, try to determine how the author is using graphics in her work and how clear, helpful, or informative you find them.

Questions about Your Reactions and Responses

- How do I feel about the topic, issues, or findings addressed in the reading?
- What is convincing? What is unclear?
- What ideas in the piece contradict my understanding of the topic?
- What ideas in the piece are new to me? Which ones do I accept and which ones do I reject?

People's beliefs and knowledge influence how they read material—what they take note of, what they understand the author to be saying, what they remember after they read the piece. Understanding your response to the material you read can help you become a more critical reader and a more effective writer in several ways. First, honestly assessing your response can help you be balanced and fair. As a skeptical reader you need to be both critical of ideas you at first enthusiastically support and open to ideas you at first strongly reject.

Second, examining your response to what you read can help you decide on and develop effective paper topics—your responses may help you identify an interest or question you can later pursue more thoroughly in an essay. Especially consider what you learn from a reading. What information is new? How do the author's ideas or findings confirm or contradict what you have come to think? Examining your answers to questions such as these can result in some interesting essays.

MARKING TEXTS

Look at the books of active, critical readers and you will see pages filled with underlined passages, marginal comments, questions, and reactions. Because they have recognized the close link between reading and writing, they rarely read without a pencil in hand. They underline the reading's thesis statement and any important passages they find. As they question the material they are reading, they annotate the text and write down the answers to the questions they ask so that when they return to the material later, they can recall the author's purpose and findings, remember how they responded to the author's ideas, and locate the information they want to use in their papers.

The two most common ways of marking texts are highlighting and annotating. Highlighting typically involves underlining, circling, bracketing, or color coding passages, while annotating involves writing comments or questions in the margin or at the end of the text.

HIGHLIGHTING TEXTS

Highlighting involves underlining, color coding, or in some other way marking important passages in a reading. Most students tend to highlight too little or too much. Some never make a mark in their books. Perhaps they were trained in high school not to mark up readings, or maybe they are concerned about the resale value of their books. Whatever their reason, these students rarely, if ever, highlight material they read. Other students highlight too many passages in a reading—practically every sentence is underlined, and almost every paragraph is shaded yellow or pink. You have to be selective in what you highlight: you mark up a reading in order to understand it more clearly and to identify important passages you may return to later when you write your paper.

In order to highlight a reading effectively, you need to develop your own marking system, a kind of code that helps you locate certain types of information in a text. Good writers usually develop unique ways of highlighting readings: they underline certain kinds of passages, place brackets around specific types of information, and circle other parts of the text. Later, when they return to the reading to write their paper, they can easily find the information they need. Following are some suggestions about what to mark in a text:

1. Mark an author's thesis, primary assertions, and supporting evidence.
2. Mark the names of authors, dates of studies, locations of research projects, and other important facts mentioned in the reading.
3. Mark key passages you might want to reread, quote, or paraphrase later as you write your paper.
4. Mark words or terms you do not know so you can look up their definitions.

Establish your own way of highlighting a text: circle authors' names, bracket dates, use a yellow highlighting pen to mark any passages you may want to quote and blue ink to indicate questionable statements, or whatever variations make sense to you. When you establish your own highlighting system, writing from readings will become much easier for you.

ANNOTATING TEXTS

While you are highlighting a reading, you should also annotate it—that is, *write out* your responses, questions, observations, or conclusions. Generally, there are two types of annotations you will use: marginal and end comments. Marginal annotations are notes that you make to yourself in the top, bottom, or side margins of the page; end annotations are notes that you make at the end of the text.

Marginal Annotations

Marginal annotations are typically short and in many cases may make sense only to the person who wrote them. Generally, they can be divided into content notes, organization notes, connection notes, questions, and responses.

Content notes typically identify the meaning or purpose of the marked passage. For example, after bracketing an author's first argument—that eliminating a particular government program may have negative consequences on the poor, for instance—you may write in the margin, "Argument 1—consequences for poor." When you review a reading to find material you want to use in your paper, content notes help you easily locate what you need, which is particularly important if you are completing a research project involving multiple readings.

Organization notes identify the major sections of a source text. After underlining an article's thesis, you may write *thesis* in the margin in order to find it more easily later, then bracket the first few paragraphs and write *introduction* in the margin. You might draw a line down the margin beside the next few paragraphs and write *first argument* in the margin, then highlight the next section and write *refutation of first argument*. Organization notes help you understand how the author has structured the piece and may help you locate particular sections of the text you would like to review.

Connection notes identify the links you see between an author's ideas and those offered by other writers or between ideas an author develops in different sections of a reading: "this idea echoes Weber's argument," "illustrates first point," or "contradicts teacher's position." As you read an article, you should note how the author's ideas confirm or refute ideas developed by other writers. Note the connections in the margin of the essay you are reading in case you want to examine the link more closely later: do not rely on your memory. If you are reading multiple sources on the same topic, distinctions between the texts can quickly blur; you may have a difficult time remembering who wrote what if you do not write good connection notes. Also, use connection notes to trace the development of each writer's thesis. Note in the margin of the reading the link between the various ideas, arguments, or findings the writer offers and his or her thesis.

Questions can serve several purposes. First, they can identify passages you find confusing: in a question, try to capture *precisely* what you find confusing in a passage, especially if you will have a chance to discuss the reading in class. Second, questions can help you identify in a reading the material you want to dispute. Try to capture in a critical question or two why you disagree with what the author has written. Finally, questions can identify where the author has failed to consider important information or arguments. These are typically "what about" questions: "What about the theory proposed by Smith?" "What about people who can't afford day care?" Your goal is to indicate with a question possible limitations to an author's ideas or arguments.

Response notes record your reactions to what you read. These notes may indicate which ideas you accept, which ones you reject, and which ones you doubt. They can range from a simple "yes!" or "huh?" to more elaborate and detailed reactions that allow you to explore your response in some detail.

Remember to keep your marginal notes brief. Their purpose is to help you read the text more critically and recall your responses and questions when you reread the material.

End Annotations

End annotations typically make some type of comment on the source as a whole and can assume different forms, including summaries, responses, and questions.

Summaries offer brief, objective overviews of a reading. You may want to write a one- or two-sentence summary at the end of a reading, especially if you are reading several source texts for your paper. The purpose of these summaries is to jog your memory about the reading's content or thesis so you don't have to reread the entire text. These summaries are especially helpful if you have to read several texts with similar titles: it is easy to confuse these readings, and the summaries can often help you find the particular text you need.

Responses capture your reaction to the work as a whole. Try to capture in your note your response to the author's ideas, argument, writing style, or any other aspect of the reading that strikes you as important. These responses can help you form comments to offer in class when you discuss the piece and often they serve as a good starting point for developing a topic for a paper: you may want to investigate and develop your response more thoroughly and formally in an essay.

Questions written at the end of a reading typically address the source's clarity, purpose, or effectiveness. Your questions might address the reading's claims, evidence, or reasoning; its syntax, tone, or structure. Other questions might address the reading's relationship to what you already know about the topic or what you have already read. These questions help you draw connections between the readings and your own knowledge and experience. Still other questions might indicate specific aspects of a topic you still need to investigate ("I wonder how his ideas might have an impact on part two of my paper—need to reconsider?") or links between two or more authors' claims that need further consideration ("Do her arguments refute the textbook's claims?").

You will usually jot down several different types of endnotes when you finish reading a text. You may write out a brief one- or two-sentence summary, a few questions, and a response. These endnotes can prove very helpful when you return to the material later: they indicate your assessment of the source text's content, strengths, weaknesses, and worth.

Together, highlighting and annotating can help you fully understand a reading and determine the best way to use it in your own writing. A word of warning, though: do not be blinded by your own annotations and highlights. When you review a source text you have already marked and annotated and are now planning to use in your paper, be critical of your *own* highlighting and annotations. Be sure to question whether your highlighting and annotations *really* capture the source's key points. As you review your comments and marked passages, ask yourself whether you feel the same way now about the reading. If you have been engaged in researching a topic, are you now in a better position to assess the value and meaning of the reading before you? Have your views changed? Also, try to answer the questions you asked in the margins or at the end of the article. Reassess your original reactions.

SAMPLE ANNOTATED READING

Review the following sample annotated reading. Your system for marking a reading will likely be different from the system used here. Note, though, how the reader used highlighting and annotations to gain a better understanding of the author's content, structure, language, and purpose.

Hard Choices

Patrick Moore, Ph.D.

[annotation: founded Greenpeace]
[annotation: Check bio. notes— who is this person?]

More than 20 years ago, I was one of a dozen or so activists who founded Greenpeace in the basement of the Unitarian Church in Vancouver, British Columbia. The Vietnam War was raging and nuclear holocaust seemed closer every day. We linked peace, ecology and a talent for media communications and went on to build the world's largest environmental activist organization. By 1986, Greenpeace was established in 26 countries and had an annual income of more than $100 million.

[annotation: open w/ personal information]

In its early years, the environmental movement specialized in confronting polluters and others who were damaging public lands and resources. Groups such as Greenpeace played a valuable role by ringing an eco-logical fire alarm, wakening mass consciousness to the true dimensions of our global predicament.

[annotation: Brief history of environ movement]
[annotation: ecological movement wins?]

By the 1980s, the battle for public opinion had been won: Virtually everyone inside and outside politics and industry expressed a commitment to environmental protection and good stewardship. Environmentalists were invited to the table in boardrooms and caucuses around the world to help design solutions to pressing ecological problems.

[annotation: Are companies environ friendly now?]

Rather than accept this invitation to be part of the solution, many environmentalists chose instead to radi-calize their message. They demanded restrictions on human activity and the uses of natural resources that

[annotation: Thesis?]

too "radical"

anti-science ?

not build on earlier successes

far exceed any scientific justification. That tactical decision created an atmosphere in which many environmentalists today must rely on sensational rhetoric and
misinformation rather than good science. Programs
have gone forward without input from more knowledgeable environmentalists and other experts; the public debate has been needlessly polarized as a result of
the movement's unwillingness to collaborate with others less radical.

environ. not work w/others ?

In addition to choosing a dubious tactic, the environmental movement also changed its philosophy
along the way. It once prided itself on subscribing to a
philosophy that was "transpolitical, transideological,
and transnational" in character. Non-violent direct action and peaceful disobedience were the hallmarks of
the movement. Truth mattered and science was respected for the knowledge it brought to the debate.

says current movement rejects truth & science

Thesis →

That tradition was abandoned by many environmental groups during the 1990s. A new brand of environmental extremism has emerged that rejects science, diversity of opinion, and even democracy. These
eco-extremists tend to be:

*Anti-technology and anti-science. Eco-extremists
entirely reject machinery and industry; they invoke
science as a means of justifying the adoption of beliefs
that have no basis in science to begin with.

anti-science

note headings

*Anti-free enterprise. Although communism and
state socialism have failed to protect the environment,
eco-extremists are basically anti-business. They have
not put forward an alternative system of organization
that would meet the material needs of society.

anti-business

point not developed well

*Anti-democratic. Eco-extremists do not tolerate
dissent and do not respect the opinions and beliefs of
the general public. In the name of "speaking for the
trees and other species," we are faced with a movement that would usher in an era of eco-fascism.

anti-democratic

The international debate over clearcutting offers a
case study of eco-extremism in action. Groups such as
Greenpeace and the Sierra Club have mounted major

example of clearcutting

need clearcutting

campaigns against clearcutting, claiming that it is responsible for "deforestation" on a massive scale in Canada and elsewhere. In fact, no such deforestation is taking place in Canada or the United States, and a ban on clearcutting could do more harm than good.

It is an ecological fact that many types of forest ecosystems thrive most successfully when they are periodically cleared and allowed to regenerate. Fire, volcanic eruptions, windstorms, insect attacks, disease and climate change (ice ages) destroy massive areas of forests, part of a natural cycle of forest destruction and renewal that has existed since long before modern humans arrived on the scene.

[margin note: ignores diversity— usually replanted w/ only one type of tree]

The use of hype and myths by Greenpeace and the Sierra Club is symptomatic of the larger problems facing the modern environmental movement. Confrontation too often is preferred over collaboration, and eco-extremism has shoved aside the earlier spirit of tolerance and concern for the fate of humanity. The results have been harmful to the movement as well as to the environment we seek to protect.

[margin note: hype and myths of Green & Sierra]

As an environmentalist in the political center, I now find myself branded a traitor and a sellout by this new breed of saviors. My name appears in Greenpeace's "Guide to Anti-Environmental Organizations." But surely the shoe belongs on the other foot: The eco-extremists who have taken control of the nation's leading environmental organizations must shoulder the blame for the anti-environmental backlash now taking place in the United States and elsewhere. Unless they change their philosophy and tactics, the prospects for a protected environment will remain dim.

[margin note: founder now an enemy ?]

[margin note: he is in political center— how defined ?]

[margin note: why a backlash ?]

Patrick Moore earned a Ph.D. in ecology from the University of British Columbia in 1972. He was a founding member of Greenpeace and for seven years served as director of Greenpeace International.

[margin note: credentials but who does he work for ?]

[margin note: Summary— "Eco-extremists" reject science, truth, alternative views → why lose pop. support ?]

NOTE TAKING

Especially when working on an extended writing project, you may want to take notes on a source text after carefully reading and annotating it. If you are working on a research paper for a class, check with your instructor about any requirements he or she might have concerning your notes. Some teachers, for example, require their students to take notes on index cards following rather specific guidelines. Other teachers set no guidelines concerning notes. It is always a good idea to check with your instructor concerning his or her requirements.

If you take notes on index cards, be sure you indicate somewhere on each card the title and/or author of the work you are reading. If your cards get out of order, you need some way of identifying the source of the information on each card. If you are more comfortable taking notes on paper, try to use only one side of each sheet. Using your notes to write your essay is easier if you are not constantly flipping over sheets of paper to find the information you need.

Some writers like their notes to consist only of quotes; others mix quoted, paraphrased, and summarized material. Some write notes in complete sentences; some use a combination of sentences, sentence fragments, and even single words or diagrams. As with annotations, you will need to work out your own system for taking notes, one that helps you sort out and organize the useful material you find in the sources you read.

Keep in mind the guidelines that follow as you take your notes. Following them can help you avoid problems later as you use your notes to write your paper.

BEFORE JOTTING DOWN ANY NOTES, ALWAYS WRITE DOWN THE SOURCE TEXT'S FULL BIBLIOGRAPHIC INFORMATION

Whenever you take notes on a reading, be sure to write down the author's full name, the exact title of the piece, the full title of the publication, all the publication information, and the inclusive page numbers. Often students will be completing a paper the night before it is due and realize they used material that needs to be documented. Without having the full bibliographic information with their notes, they have to make a frantic last-minute dash back to the library. If you are careful to write down this information before you take your notes, you can avoid some problems later.

IN YOUR NOTES, CAREFULLY DISTINGUISH BETWEEN MATERIAL YOU QUOTE AND MATERIAL YOU PARAPHRASE

One of the major sources of unintentional plagiarism is faulty note taking. This problem occurs when you copy down a passage word for word from a source text into your notes but fail to enclose that passage in quotation marks. If you then copy that material directly from your notes into your paper—thinking you originally paraphrased the passage—and fail to place quotation marks around it in your essay, you will be guilty of plagiarism. You can avoid this problem if you carefully indicate with quotation marks which passages in your notes are exact quotations and which are paraphrases of an author's ideas.

CAREFULLY LIST PAGE NUMBERS

In your notes, be sure to indicate the exact page number of the source text that contains the material you are quoting, paraphrasing, or summarizing. You will need this information later for proper documentation.

PAY ATTENTION TO THE PUNCTUATION IN THE SOURCE TEXT

If you are quoting material in your notes, reproduce the original punctuation exactly as it appears on the page. Many times students misquote material because they incorrectly copied the original punctuation into their notes.

IN YOUR NOTES, CLEARLY DIFFERENTIATE BETWEEN THE AUTHOR'S IDEAS AND YOUR OWN

Again, failing to differentiate between what an author says about a topic and what you have to say is a major source of unintentional plagiarism. As you take your notes, you may want to jot down some observations or ideas of your own—reading other people's ideas will often lead you to new insights of your own. However, if you do not make the distinction clear in your notes—if, when reviewing your notes, you cannot tell which ideas were yours and which were the other writer's—you might attribute ideas to authors who never suggested them or take credit for ideas that were originally developed by someone else. To make this distinction clear in your notes, perhaps you could place your ideas and reflections in brackets.

BE CONSISTENT WITH YOUR NOTE-TAKING SYSTEM

Whether you use a notebook, looseleaf paper, index cards, or a personal computer for taking notes, be consistent in how and where you note bibliographic information, page numbers, and your responses to the material. Adhering to a system will make it easier for you to find material in your notes and will help you avoid making mistakes.

Additional Reading

Getting Serious about Eradicating Binge Drinking

Henry Wechsler

Henry Wechsler *directs the College Alcohol Studies program at Harvard's School of Public Health.*

Most of us are aware that binge drinking is a major problem on many college campuses. Since the Harvard School of Public Health's first College Alcohol Study used that term, in 1994, to describe the drinking pattern of significant numbers of American college students, the problem has drawn media attention across the nation. Despite this, the problem has not declined over the past four years. In fact, our latest research findings, released in September, showed little change in the proportion of college students who binge. Among more than 14,500 students surveyed at 116 institutions, 43 percent reported that they had binged at least once in the preceding two weeks, compared with 44 percent in the earlier study.

Although the number of students who abstain from alcohol grew to 19 percent this year from 15.6 percent in the first study, among students who drink we found an increase in drunkenness, in drinking deliberately to get drunk, and in alcohol-related problems—including injuries, drunk driving, violence, and academic difficulties. For example, among students who drink, 52 percent said a major motivation was "to get drunk," compared with 39 percent in the first study. Thus, despite a spate of widely publicized student deaths in alcohol-related incidents, the binge goes on.

Why isn't this behavior decreasing? For one thing, binge drinking has been so deeply entrenched for so long at colleges that it can't be expected to disappear overnight. However, the more important reason that change eludes us is that some colleges have relied too much on one approach to solve the problem—trying to get the binge drinkers themselves to stop, rather than focusing equal attention on factors that make it easy for students to drink too much.

Of course, some campuses use multiple approaches to attack the problem, but many focus most of their energies on educational efforts directed at drinkers, particularly during events such as the recent Alcohol

Awareness Week. Such educational efforts are an important way to teach some students the facts about alcohol abuse. But those efforts overlook the environment around binge drinkers that condones and supports and often even encourages their behavior.

So what are the factors that promote binge drinking at colleges? One is that students who binge tend to think they represent the norm; they argue that they're just doing what most of their peers do. Most binge drinkers don't think they have a problem. They think they are only having fun, and most consider themselves to be moderate drinkers. Doing research into actual behavior and then informing students about how many students actually binge—generally fewer than binge drinkers believe—can help to reduce the behavior.

Another approach to changing student norms is to focus on the disruptive behavior of binge drinkers. Colleges are civic communities, and all too frequently they are disrupted by the behavior of students who drink excessively. Rather than search for contraband alcohol, a college would be wise to engage student leaders in helping administrators work out a clearly worded code of conduct that penalizes drunken behavior—and then to enforce it consistently.

Students who become drunk and disorderly should be made to take responsibility for the messes that they have created: They should have to clean up vomit in the bathrooms made unusable on weekends, help care for drunken students at the college health center, repair damage from vandalism, and pick up litter. The punishment should fit the crime.

But with repeat offenders, colleges need to consider enforcing a "three strikes and you're out" policy for alcohol-related violations of the student conduct code.

At the center of binge drinking on many campuses are fraternities and sororities. While they attract only a small percentage of students nationally, they continue to play a prominent role in campus life at many institutions. Our data shows that in fraternity houses, four of five residents binge, and more than half are frequent binge drinkers. And fraternity parties are attended by many more students than just members. They attract even some high-school seniors—future college students who are introduced to binge drinking as a social norm. Not surprisingly, most of the alcohol-related deaths of college students recently reported in the media involved fraternity parties.

While some colleges have begun to address the drinking culture created by fraternities, many administrators are still hesitant to move strongly against fraternities, for fear of angering alumni donors who fondly remember their own college years of partying. But administrators have a responsibility to protect all of their students against alcohol-related disruptions and injuries, and should not wait for tragedy to strike before they revoke official recognition of fraternities that consistently cause problems. Colleges also can require all first-year students who live on campus to reside in dormitories, and not in fraternity or sorority houses. Of course, then those colleges must work to create interesting alcohol-free activities centered in the residence halls, to show students that out-of-control drinking need not be the focus of social life.

A third impetus for binge drinking on college campuses—one rarely mentioned publicly—involves alumni at tailgate parties during homecoming activities and sporting events. Any alcohol-control measures adopted for students must also apply to visiting alumni. Banning alcohol at home sporting events for everyone except alumni who contribute more than $50, as one college did recently, is not a good way to win students' support for new alcohol-control policies. I would hope that most alumni, if informed that an institution is trying to cope with a serious problem, would cooperate. Colleges that base their decision making on fund-raising concerns must ask themselves: What will cost the college more money—alumni who might decrease their contributions if they're cut off from alcohol at sporting events, or a few large jury awards of damages to families of injured or deceased students?

Another center of college binge drinking is found in athletics programs. Athletes binge more than other students, according to our data. In fact, involvement in athletics—compared with time spent in other activities—increases rather than decreases a student's propensity for binge drinking. Students involved in athletics are one and a half times as likely to be binge drinkers as are other students. This tradition is kept alive through the beer-advertising blitz that surrounds sports. After all, Mark McGwire's 70th home run was hit at Busch Stadium.

As a first step, college athletics officials should stay clear of alcohol-industry promotions and advertising. Further, although coaches at some colleges require team members to abstain from alcohol during the competitive season, relatively few coaches are involved in campus-wide programs to reduce alcohol abuse. Colleges should make it a priority to enlist their coaches and athletics directors in programs designed to reach all students with the message that binge drinking interferes with performance in every area of their lives. The National Collegiate Athletic Association should encourage this. Colleges also should press coaches to stress the institution's commitment to preventing alcohol abuse when they recruit high-school athletes.

Another important point of intervention is at the high-school level. Half of college binge drinkers start in high school. Colleges should begin to address this problem at high schools that send a large number of freshmen to their campuses, by sending college students from those high schools back to talk to the younger students about alcohol and other substance abuse. The volunteers should stress that one in five college students nationally abstains from alcohol, and that another two in five drink, but not to excess.

High-school students are more likely to believe the messages of college students than those of teachers and other adults. Let future freshmen get their first view of college life from these volunteers, rather than from attending fraternity parties or tailgate events. Once freshmen have unpacked and settled in, it may be too late to tell them about college rules on alcohol use. That message should be sent before they even apply.

Colleges also need to focus more attention a block or two away from the campus—on the ring of bars and liquor stores that encircles many institutions. Colleges need to map the density of those establishments; many institutions have more than 50 such alcohol outlets surrounding them. These are formidable competitors for students' attention, and cannot be coped with by the college alone; community leaders must be enlisted to help, particularly in barring the low-price specials that the outlets use to compete with each other: two-for-one offers, cut-rate drinks and free food during happy hours, and free drinks for women on certain nights. Some states and communities already have laws that ban those types of sales. Remember, the problem is not alcohol itself; it is the availability of a large volume of alcohol at a low price, usually to be consumed in a short period of time.

All of the problem areas that I've cited cannot be attacked by every college at once. Some issues may be more pressing than others on particular campuses, and the solutions must be fashioned to fit local circumstances.

Some important actions are being taken by colleges and universities across the country. Many are trying to sever the connection between alcohol and sports by banning advertising in the programs for sporting events and prohibiting alcohol at college stadiums. Some colleges are discontinuing the practice of not holding classes or exams on Fridays, and are no longer allowing local bars to advertise drink specials in campus publications. And some colleges are experimenting with new student-housing arrangements, such as living–learning centers that take faculty members and classes into the dorms, to try to completely change the environments there.

Institutions also are trying to give students more alcohol-free entertainment options. Some are working with neighborhood groups, as well as community and state officials, to find legal and other means of controlling students' behavior off campus. Other colleges are imposing stricter sanctions on students who break the rules—notifying parents after a certain number of infractions, and suspending or expelling repeat offenders.

What institutions need to avoid are one-dimensional programs that focus on particular students but ignore the ways in which colleges help enable some students to continue binging for four years. Not holding classes or exams on Fridays, for example, enables students to binge from Thursday to Sunday without interruption. Making new rules, but not enforcing even the old ones—for example, banning alcohol in the dormitories, but allowing it to be carried in unmarked cups—tells students that the college is not serious about eradicating the problem.

To anyone who thinks that binge drinking is behavior that cannot be changed, I offer the following challenge. At the next meeting you attend, look around and count how many people are smoking. Not many years ago, the room would have been filled with smoke. Today, because of the wide recognition that smoking hurts both the smoker and people nearby, through secondhand effects, the air is clear. Binge drinking can become equally unacceptable on college campuses.

Summary Chart

CRITICAL READING: ASKING QUESTIONS

---

1. **Questions to Ask Before You Begin a Close Reading of a Text**

   Questions concerning the author:
   - *Who is the author?*
   - *What are her credentials?*
   - *What else has she written on the topic?*
   - *What possible biases might have influenced her work?*

   Questions concerning the publication:
   - *In what regard is the publication held by professionals in the field?*
   - *Toward what type of readership is the publication aimed?*
   - *How long ago was the piece published?*
   - *What, generally, is the editorial stance of the publication?*

   Questions concerning your own views of the topic:
   - *What are my beliefs about the issue addressed in the reading?*
   - *How open am I to new ideas on this topic?*

2. **Questions to Ask While You Read and Reread Material**

   Questions concerning the audience of the piece:
   - *What audience does the author seem to be trying to reach?*
   - *What type of reader would be attracted to the author's writing, and what type would be alienated by it?*
   - *How does your sense of the text's audience influence your reading of the piece?*

   Questions concerning the purpose of the piece:
   - *What was the author's purpose in writing the piece?*
   - *What is the author's thesis?*
   - *Does the author successfully achieve his or her goals?*

   Questions concerning the content of the piece:
   - *What are the author's major assertions or findings?*
   - *How does the author support these assertions or findings?*

   Questions concerning the organization of the piece:
   - *How is the material organized?*
   - *What headings and subheadings does the author provide?*

- *What does the organization of the essay tell you about the author's view of the material?*
- *What gets stressed as a result of the organization?*

Questions concerning the author's sources:
- *How does the author use other people's ideas or findings?*
- *How credible are the sources the author uses to support his ideas or findings?*

Questions concerning graphics in the piece:
- *How clear are the charts, graphs, tables, or illustrations the author provides?*
- *How well does the author explain the graphics?*
- *How well do the graphics support or explain what the author has to say?*

Questions concerning your reactions and responses to the piece:
- *How do I feel about the topic, issues, or findings addressed in the reading?*
- *What is convincing? What is unclear?*
- *What ideas in the piece contradict my understanding of the topic?*
- *What ideas in the piece are new to me? Which ones do I accept and which ones do I reject?*

Summary Chart

CRITICAL READING: MARKING TEXTS

1. **Highlighting Texts**

   Highlight the text's thesis, primary assertions, and supporting evidence.

   Highlight the names of authors, specific dates mentioned, and principal sources cited.

   Highlight key passages you may want to reread, quote, or paraphrase later.

   Highlight terms you do not understand or want to discuss in class.

2. **Annotating Texts**

   Marginal annotations
   - *Content notes: identify the meaning or purpose of the marked passages.*
   - *Organization notes: identify the major sections of the text.*
   - *Connection notes: identify links between readings and within a reading.*
   - *Questions: identify confusing, controversial, or questionable passages.*
   - *Response notes: identify your reactions to the reading.*

   End annotations
   - *Summaries: convey a brief overview of the reading.*
   - *Responses: convey your overall reaction to the piece.*
   - *Questions: convey your assessment of the reading's clarity, purpose, or effectiveness.*

Summary Chart

CRITICAL READING: NOTE TAKING

1. Before jotting down any notes, always write down the source text's full bibliographic information.
2. In your notes, carefully distinguish between material you quote and material you paraphrase.
3. Carefully list page numbers in your notes.
4. Pay attention to the punctuation in the source text.
5. In your notes, clearly differentiate between the author's ideas and your own.
6. Be consistent with your note-taking system.

Chapter 2

QUOTATION

In this chapter you will learn how to

1. Quote material properly
2. Integrate quoted material into your own writing
3. Avoid misquoting material
4. Document quoted material

DEFINITION AND PURPOSE

When you use someone else's words in your paper, you have to place them in quotation marks and supply proper documentation. Quoting and documenting material tells your readers where they can find that *exact* language in the source text. If you make any significant changes in a passage you are quoting, you need to indicate the alterations in your text with ellipses, brackets, or an explanation.

Generally, if you take more than three words in a row from a source text and incorporate them word for word in your essay, you need to place quotation marks around the passage. However, there are several exceptions to this general guideline. For example, if you repeat in your paper someone's official title as it appears in the source text (e.g., president of the school board), you do not need to quote the title, even if it is longer than three words. Also, if you use in your paper a *single* word or term from a source text that is significant or unusual, you *may* need to quote it. Learning what to quote and when to quote takes some time, practice, and thought. Making good decisions about quoting can be easier, though, if you keep in mind one of the main reasons for quoting material: you want to acknowledge an author's distinctive language.

When employed properly and judiciously, quotations can add color and credibility to your writing; they can help make your papers clearer, more entertaining, and more persuasive. If used improperly, quotations can give the impression that you cannot think through a topic for yourself or cannot articulate ideas in your own words. Therefore, knowing how to quote material properly is an extremely important part of writing from readings.

GUIDELINES ON WHEN TO QUOTE MATERIAL

You ought to have a good reason for quoting material in your paper. Do not quote material just to fill up space or to avoid thinking about your topic. Instead, consider how quoting material will help you support your thesis or explain important ideas to your reader. The following guidelines will help you decide when to quote a word or passage and offer suggestions on how to use that material in your paper. As you plan and draft a source-based paper, consider ways to integrate *a few* carefully selected quotations with your own writing to present your ideas as clearly and effectively as possible.

QUOTE PASSAGES WHEN THE AUTHOR HAS WRITTEN SOMETHING IN A DISTINCTIVE OR ESPECIALLY INSIGHTFUL OR INTERESTING WAY

Often an author will express an idea so well it is difficult or impossible for you to express it better by paraphrasing it. The author may have expressed the idea succinctly, employed especially effective adjectives or metaphors, or supplied an especially interesting example. In such cases, quote the word or passage—it may help make your paper more entertaining or persuasive.

QUOTE MATERIAL THAT LENDS SUPPORT TO A POSITION YOU ARE TRYING TO MAKE IN YOUR PAPER

Letting your readers see for themselves that an expert agrees with a position you are advocating can help persuade them to accept your argument or can help them better understand your position. You must be sure, though, that in your effort to find support for your position, you do not misrepresent an author's thoughts or findings. By leaving words out of a quotation or by adding language to it, you should not misrepresent what the author actually had to say. For example, several years ago a student of mine quoted an editorial writer as saying, "President Reagan's proposed budget cuts will . . . double the number of people living in poverty." I checked the original editorial; the actual sentence read, "President Reagan's proposed budget cuts will not double the number of people living in poverty." By leaving out the word *not,* this student clearly misrepresented the author's intended meaning. Such changes to a quotation are unethical.

Also, in an effort to find support for your thesis, do not limit your research to those authors who agree with the position you are advancing. For several reasons, this strategy is a mistake. First, in doing research, you should learn about a topic by studying many different views. Quite often writers change their position as they write and rewrite their papers; sifting through the material they have read frequently leads them to rethink and restate their thesis.

Second, you may want to quote authors who present ideas that challenge your thesis: doing so can increase your credibility in the eyes of many readers. Finally, by seeking out alternative perspectives and learning more about the topic, you place yourself in a better position to defend your assertions, improving the likelihood that your readers will value what you have to say on the topic because of your expertise. Therefore, do not neglect opposing viewpoints when searching for material to quote in your paper.

When you use expert testimony to support a position in your paper, it is a good idea to mention the person's credentials in your paper:

> According to Helen Carter, former president of the First National Bank, ". . . "
> Milton Friedman, noted economist and winner of the Nobel Prize, contends that ". . ."

Citing the credentials of the experts you quote may help convince your readers to accept or at least seriously consider what they have to say. Again, you do not need to cite the credentials of every author every time you quote from his or her work. You also do not want to cite so many credentials that the sentence is hard to read. Variety is the key to using quotations well—cite the credentials when you think they are significant, and do so in a way that fits the overall tone of your paper.

QUOTE AUTHORITIES WHO DISAGREE WITH A POSITION YOU ARE ADVOCATING OR WHO OFFER ALTERNATIVE EXPLANATIONS OR CONTRADICTORY DATA

Often it is a good idea to quote authors who offer views or data that call into question the position you are advocating in your paper. Many beginning authors balk at this idea. They believe that introducing opposing views will only weaken the impact of their thesis. However, when you include in your paper a variety of perspectives, your readers are more likely to perceive you to be fair and thorough in your treatment of the subject: these quotations demonstrate that you recognize and understand alternative points of view. Second, such quotations allow you the opportunity to examine critically the other person's position, acknowledging its worth or value when needed and criticizing it when appropriate.

If you decide to quote authors who challenge your thesis, you must somehow address their ideas or findings, usually in one of four ways. You need to explain in your own words:

- how that author's ideas do not seriously damage your thesis,
- how that author's ideas or findings may actually support your contentions,
- how your thesis may be altered slightly to accommodate the author's ideas, or
- how that author's ideas are incorrect or at least questionable.

If you do not somehow address the opposing ideas you quote in your paper, your reader will likely be confused, wondering how that material fits your paper's thesis.

GUIDELINES ON WHEN NOT TO QUOTE MATERIAL

When writing from sources, students often rely too heavily on quoted material: their essays are a string of quotations. These papers more accurately represent the ideas and language of the source texts than they do the ideas and language of the student. To avoid producing a paper like this, consider these guidelines outlining when you should *not* quote material. Use quotations *selectively;* they should never make up the bulk of your paper.

DO NOT QUOTE PASSAGES MERELY TO FILL SPACE

Too often when writing from sources, students try to pad their essays with extensive quotations, and their final papers end up being a patchwork of quoted material. This is especially true when students are writing to meet a length requirement. If a teacher wants a paper eight to ten pages long, some students think the easiest way to reach that length is to keep piling on quotations. However, in college your readers will usually want to know what *you* think about your subject, what conclusions *you* have reached through your research, and how *you* understand material. Do not substitute other people's views and voices for your own; use theirs to *support* your own.

DO NOT QUOTE PASSAGES AS A SUBSTITUTE FOR THINKING

In addition to using quotations to fill space, too often students rely on quotations alone to clarify, defend, or substantiate a finding or position. They may introduce an idea in a topic sentence, then string together two or three quotations to substantiate the point they want to make. Instead of presenting their own ideas in their own language, they rely on quoted material to present and defend their case.

The better course to follow is to integrate selected quotations into your essay carefully: their purpose is to advance your argument or support your conclusions or findings. Do not expect a quotation alone to convince your readers to accept some contention you want to make. As you work through a writing assignment, find language that reflects and communicates the conclusions you have drawn and the assertions you want to make. When appropriate, support or illustrate your position with quoted material. Also remember that when you do quote material, in most cases you will need to comment on it, explaining in your own words the quotation's meaning, relevance, or importance.

Do Not Quote Passages Because You Do Not Understand the Author's Ideas Well Enough to Paraphrase Them

As you read material in college, you will often run into words you do not know, ideas that seem strange, arguments that are hard to follow, and research methodologies and discussions of findings that seem to be written in a language of their own. If you have to write papers based on these readings, do not rely on quotations as a way to avoid thought. You need to understand the material you quote. As a general guideline, if you cannot paraphrase the material, do not quote it. That is, if you cannot convey that information in your own words, quoting it is probably a bad idea.

INTEGRATING QUOTATIONS INTO YOUR WRITING

There are several ways to place quoted material in your papers. You should study and practice several of these techniques because varying the way you integrate quotations into your writing can make your papers more interesting.

One of the real difficulties in learning to write from readings in college is the fact that different disciplines follow different rules concerning the proper way to document and punctuate quotations. Two primary style manuals used in your college courses are those published by the Modern Language Association (MLA), primarily used in humanities classes such as English and history, and by the American Psychological Association (APA), primarily used in social science classes such as psychology and sociology. Because each of these manuals offers its own set of rules concerning the proper punctuation and documentation of quotations, when you receive an assignment, always ask your instructor which style manual he or she expects you to follow. (See Chapters 12 and 13 for a complete discussion of the documentation guidelines suggested by each.)

Two Basic Types of Quotations

When you quote material, you will either set it off in a block quotation or integrate it into the body of your essay. Your choice depends on length: longer passages must be block quoted, while shorter quotations should be integrated.

Properly punctuating quotations can be tricky: again, the rules you follow depend on the academic stylebook your teacher wants you to follow. Although the two major style manuals generally agree on how to punctuate integrated quotations, they offer different guidelines for formatting, punctuating, and documenting block quotations. Pay close attention to how the following sample quotations are punctuated. All of the sample quotations will draw on passages from the following essay published in *America*.

Generation Text

The Dark Digital Ages: 13 to 17

Mark Bauerlein

Mark Bauerlein *is a professor of English at Emory University and author of* The Dumbest Generation: How the Digital Age Stupefies Young Americans and Jeopardizes Our Future.

Children between the ages of 13 and 17 who have a mobile phone average 1,742 text messages each month, according to a report by the Nielsen Company in September 2008. That comes to nearly 60 per day. They also make 231 voice calls each month, close to eight per day. They play games on the device as well, and browse the Web, take pictures and log hours of social networking.

No wonder so many of them consider the cellphone (for some it is a BlackBerry or an iPhone) an essential part of their lives. Half of all young people between the ages of 8 and 12 own one such device, according to a Harris Interactive poll conducted in July 2008. The rate rises to around four out of five for teenagers; that's a 36 percent increase over the previous three years, which means that these tools have swept into young people's lives with the dispatch and coerciveness of a youth fad (like Pokemon and Harry Potter). The devices are more than just consumer goods. They are signs and instruments of status.

The age-old force of peer pressure bears down hard. Indeed, 45 percent of the teens that sport one agree that "Having a cellphone is the key to my social life"—not just helpful or useful, but "the key." If you don't own a cellphone, if you can't text, game, network and chat, then you are out of the loop. It is like not being picked to play kickball back in the primitive days of neighborhood sandlot gatherings. If a 16-year-old runs up 3,000 text messages in one month (and does not have a flat payment plan), mom and dad take the phone away. It's just a silly, expensive toy, they think. But the 16-year-old thinks, "You have destroyed my life!" And for them, this seems true. Digital tools are the primary means of social contact. When they lose them, kids feel excluded and unpopular, and nothing hits a 16-year-old harder than the disregard of other 16-year-olds. They do not care what 40-year-olds think, and they do not worry about what happened at Thermopylae or what

Pope John Paul II said about the "splendor of truth." They care about what other students in biology class think, what happened last week at the party and what so-and-so said about them.

It is an impulse long preceding the advent of the microchip, but digital devices have empowered that impulse as never before. Think about the life stage of adolescence. Teenagers stand at a precarious threshold, no longer children and not yet adults, eager to be independent but lacking the equipment and composure. They have begun to leave the home and shed the influence of parents, but they don't know where they are headed, and most of them find meager materials beyond the home out of which to build their characters. So they look to one another, emulating dress and speech, forming groups of insiders and outsiders, finding comfort in boyfriends and girlfriends, and deflecting more or less tenuously the ever-present risk of embarrassment.

Everyone passes through this phase, but this generation's experience marks a crucial change in the process. In the past, social life proceeded intermittently, all day at school and for a few hours after school. Kids hung out for an afternoon over the weekend and enjoyed a movie or party on Friday or Saturday night. Other than that, social life pretty much ended. They went home for dinner and entered a private space with only a "landline" as a means of contact (which appears to young people today a restricted connection—show them a rotary phone and watch them scowl). Teenage social life and peer-to-peer contact had a limit.

Teenagers did not like it. I certainly didn't want to listen to my parents when I turned 16. But the limit was healthy and effectual. Adolescents needed then and need now a reprieve from the tribal customs and peer fixations of middle school and high school. Wounds from lunchroom gossip and bullying, as well as the blandishments of popularity and various niche-crowd memberships, disable the maturing process. These form a horizon of adolescent triumphs and set the knowledge of history, civics, religion, fine art and foreign affairs beyond the pale of useful and relevant acquisitions. If a sophomore sat down on a bus with the gang and said, "Hey, did you see the editorial on school funding in *The Times* this morning?" the rest would scrunch up their faces as if an alien being sat among them.

Youthful mores screen out such things, which is all the more reason for parents to offer an alternative. A home and leisure life separate from teen stuff exposes youths to heroes and villains that surpass the idols of the senior class, to places beyond the food court and Apple Store, to times well before the glorious day they got their driver's license. It acquaints them with adult duties, distant facts and values and truths they will not fully comprehend until much later. They don't like them and rarely find them meaningful, but in pre-digital times teens had nowhere else to go after they entered the front door. They had to sit at the dining table and listen to parents talk about grocery shopping, vacation plans, Nixon, gas prices and the news.

No longer. In 1980, when an angry parent commanded, "Go to your room—you're grounded!" the next few hours meant isolation for the teen. Today, the bedroom is not a private space. It's a social hub. For many kids, the bedroom at midnight provides a rich social life that makes daytime face-to-face conversations seem tame and slow. Amid the pillows with laptop or BlackBerry, they chat with buddies in 11th grade and in another state. Photos fly back and forth while classmates sleep, revelations spill forth in tweets ("OMG, Billy just called Betty his ——"), and Facebook pages gain flashier graphics.

In this dynamic 24/7 network, teen activity accrues more and more significance. The events of the day carry greater weight as they are recorded and circulated. The temptation for teens to be self-absorbed and self-project, to consider the details of their lives eminently memorable and share-able, grows and grows. As they give in online, teenagers' peer consciousness expands while their historical understanding, civic awareness and taste go dormant before they have even had much chance to develop. This is the hallmark of what I have called the Dumbest Generation. These kids have just as much intelligence and ambition as any previous cohort, but they exercise them too much on one another. They are building youth culture into a ubiquitous universe, and as ever, youth culture is a drag on maturity. This time it has a whole new arsenal.

THE BLOCK QUOTATION

The APA and MLA style manuals both agree that longer quotations must be set off from the rest of the text, but they differ in how they define "longer":

- APA states that quotations of forty words or more must be block quoted.
- MLA says to block quote passages that would be more than four typed lines in your paper.

Regardless of the style manual you follow, you should introduce a block quotation with a colon. You do not add quotation marks at the beginning or end of the passage, and all the punctuation in the source text stays the same in the block quotation.

APA Guidelines

According to the APA style manual, you should start a block quotation on a new line in your paper, setting the left margin of the quotation one-half inch in from the original left margin. Subsequent lines of the quotation align on that indent. (If you are quoting additional paragraphs in the source text, indent the first line of each an additional half inch.) The right margin stays the same, and the whole passage is double-spaced.

Example 1

In "Generation Text," Mark Bauerlein (2009) describes how the nature of "being grounded" has changed due to advances in technology:

> In 1980, when an angry parent commanded, "Go to your room—you're grounded!" the next few hours meant isolation for the teen. Today, the bedroom is not a private space. It's a social hub. For many kids, the bedroom at midnight provides a rich social life that makes daytime face-to-face conversations seem tame and slow. Amid the pillows with laptop or BlackBerry, they chat with buddies in 11th grade and in another state. Photos fly back and forth while classmates sleep, revelations spill forth in tweets ("OMG, Billy just called Betty his ——"), and Facebook pages gain flashier graphics. (p. 36)

Kids sent to their bedroom today do not face isolation. Thanks to modern technology, they can stay in constant contact with their friends.

Analysis

Notice that the period at the end of the quotation precedes the parenthetical citation. (If the quotation runs longer than one page in the source text, use "pp." to introduce the inclusive page numbers.) There are no quotation marks added at the beginning or end of the block quote. The words "Go to your room—you're grounded!" are quoted because they have quotation marks around them in the source text. If any words are italicized in the source text, they remain italicized in your block quote. Note also that the left-hand margin of the block quotation is indented a half inch.

MLA Guidelines

MLA says to begin a block quotation on a new line, indent the left margin one-half inch (and a quarter inch more for new paragraphs within the block quote), leave the right margin unchanged, and double-space the block quotation.

Example 2

In "Generation Text," Mark Bauerlein describes how the nature of "being grounded" has changed due to advances in technology:

> In 1980, when an angry parent commanded, "Go to your room—you're grounded!" the next few hours meant isolation for the teen. Today, the bedroom is not a private space. It's a social hub. For many kids, the bedroom at midnight provides a rich social life that makes daytime face-to-face conversations seem tame and slow. Amid the pillows with laptop or BlackBerry, they chat with buddies in 11th grade and in another state. Photos fly back and forth while classmates sleep, revelations spill forth in tweets ("OMG, Billy just called Betty his ——"), and Facebook pages gain flashier graphics. (36)

>Kids sent to their bedroom today do not face isolation. Thanks to modern technology, they can stay in constant contacts with their friends.

Analysis

Note how the parenthetical documentation follows the period at the end of the quotation. No quotation marks are added to the block quote. The words quoted from the original passage retain their punctuation. There is a new left margin, but the right margin remains unchanged.

Example 3

Bauerlein introduces "Generation Text" by citing some interesting, and perhaps startling, statistics concerning children's use of technology:

>Children between the ages of 13 and 17 who have a mobile phone average 1,742 text messages each month, according to a report by the Nielsen Company in September 2008. That comes to nearly 60 per day. They also make 231 voice calls each month, close to eight per day. They play games on the device as well, and browse the Web, take pictures and log hours of social networking.
>
>No wonder so many of them consider the cellphone (for some it is a BlackBerry or an iPhone) an essential part of their lives. Half of all young people between the ages of 8 and 12 own one such device, according to a Harris Interactive poll conducted in July 2008. The rate rises to around four out of five for teenagers; that's a 36 percent increase over the previous three years, which means that these tools have swept into young people's lives with the dispatch and coerciveness of a youth fad (like Pokemon and Harry Potter). (34)

According to Bauerlein, this technology has spread quickly in the culture like so many other fads.

Analysis

Since this block quotation runs longer than one paragraph, note how the first line of the second paragraph is indented an additional quarter inch.

THE INTEGRATED QUOTATION

Short quotations should be integrated in the body of your essay rather than set off in a block quotation. As you will see, you have several ways to integrate quoted material into your paper. Try to use several of these techniques when writing an essay—such variety can help make your paper more interesting to read.

The APA and MLA style manuals generally agree on where to place quotation marks, how to use single and double quotation marks, and how to otherwise punctuate integrated quotations. Remember that all quotations must be documented. Again, see Chapter 12 for a detailed discussion on how to document quotations. In the following samples, I alternate between APA and MLA documentation conventions.

Introduce a Quotation with a Verb

Probably the most common way of introducing a quotation is to give the author's name, perhaps his or her credentials, maybe even the title of the work, followed by an appropriate verb—*says, notes, comments, contends, asserts,* and so on. Place a comma after the verb of saying.

Example 4 (MLA Documentation)

> Bauerlein, believing that owning a cellphone is a sign of social status and inclusion, writes, "Indeed, 45 percent of the teens that sport one agree that 'Having a cellphone is the key to my social life'—not just helpful or useful, but 'the key'" (34).

When you integrate material from a source text that already contains quotation marks, the regular quotation marks in the original (" ") are changed to single quotation marks (' ') in your paper.

Note the punctuation at the end of the sentence; the final period follows the parenthetical citation. If the last sentence of the quotation ends with an exclamation point or a question mark, include it before the closing quotation mark and place a period after the parenthetical citation. This punctuation guideline holds true for the APA and MLA style manuals.

Example 5 (APA Documentation)

> Bauerlein (2009) states that this generation of students, unlike others, expect to use only modern technology to communicate. In the past, he writes, children ". . . went home for dinner and entered a private space with only a 'landline' as a means of contact (which appears to young people today a restricted connection—show them a rotary phone and watch them scowl) (p. 35).

Again, note how a comma follows the verb (in this case, "writes"), how the material quoted in the source text is placed in single quotation marks, how the ellipsis indicates part of the passage was left out of the quote, and how the final period follows the documentation.

Example 6 (MLA Documentation)

> Bauerlein claims, "Children between the ages of 13 and 17 who have a mobile phone average 1,742 text messages each month . . . " (34).

Introduce a Quotation without a Verb

A more formal way of integrating a quotation into your paper is to introduce it with a colon. Commonly, quotations used as illustrations or elaborations of a point you have just made are introduced this way. Make sure that the colon comes at the end of a complete sentence; leave one space between the colon and the opening quotation mark.

Example 7 (APA Documentation)

> Toward the end of his essay, Bauerlein (2009) assumes a darker tone: "This is the hallmark of what I have called the Dumbest Generation. These kids have just as much intelligence and ambition as any previous cohort, but they exercise them too much on one another" (p. 36).

Example 8 (MLA Documentation)

> In generations past, teens needed a place to escape their peers: "Adolescents needed then and need now a reprieve from the tribal customs and peer fixations of middle school and high school" (Bauerlein 35).

Note that in this last example, because I did not use Bauerlein's name in the passage, I had to include it in the citation.

Run Your Sentence and the Quotation Together

This particular technique can be hard to master. Instead of separating your words from the quoted passage with a comma or colon, you run the two together seamlessly, relying on the quotation marks to let your reader know when you begin using someone else's language. Integrating quotations in this way, while sophisticated stylistically, can also lead you to misquote material if you are not careful. As students first learn to run their sentence and the quotation together, they tend to alter the quotation to fit the sentence they are writing rather than to alter their sentence to fit the quotation. As you practice this method of quoting material, try to craft your sentence so it runs smoothly into the quotation. If you have to change the quoted passage in any substantive way, you must indicate the changes (see the section on "Altering Quoted Material and Avoiding Misquotations," which follows).

When you employ this technique properly and read your essay aloud, a listener would not be able to tell where the quotation started and ended. Note that you do not need to place a comma before the quoted material or insert an ellipsis if you are picking up the quotation in midsentence.

Example 9 (APA Documentation)

> Bauerlein (2009) believes that "the age-old force of peer pressure bears down hard" (p. 34).

In this example, note that the capital *T* in *The* can be changed to lowercase without the addition of brackets. Also, when using this approach, you do not need to include an ellipsis if you begin a quotation in midsentence.

Example 10 (MLA Documentation)

> Changes in education and technology have "set the knowledge of history, civics, religion, fine art and foreign affairs beyond the pale of useful and relevant acquisitions" (Bauerlein 35).

Pick Out Only Certain Words to Quote in Your Sentence

You do not always have to quote entire passages or sentences in your paper. Often you want to quote only a few key words or phrases. Be sure, though, to include proper documentation even if you quote only one word.

Example 11 (MLA Documentation)

> Bauerlein believes teens "stand at a precarious threshold" and that they are "eager to be independent" (35).

This particular example needs only one parenthetical citation because all the quoted material comes from the same page in the source text. If it came from different pages in the source text, parenthetical citations would follow each quoted word or phrase.

Example 12 (APA Documentation)

> According to Bauerlein (2009), because "peer pressure bears down hard" (p. 34), the children's use of social technologies "accrues more and more significance" (p. 36).

ALTERING QUOTED MATERIAL AND AVOIDING MISQUOTATIONS

When you place quotation marks around material in your essay and document that passage, you are telling your readers that if they turn to that page of that source text, they will find that passage as it appears in your paper: the words and punctuation have not been changed. If that is not the case—if you have made any substantive changes to material you are quoting—then you need to acknowledge those alterations. Especially important is learning how to indicate that you left words out of a quotation, added words to a quotation, or changed the emphasis given words in a quotation.

LEAVING WORDS OUT OF A QUOTATION

Use an ellipsis (. . .) to indicate that you left material out of a quotation. Add a fourth dot to act as a period if you omit the end of a sentence or leave out an entire sentence when block quoting. When you introduce a quotation with a colon, include an ellipsis if you pick up a quotation in the middle of a sentence in the source text.

Example 13 (MLA Documentation)

> Bauerlein observes, "No wonder so many of them consider the cellphone. . . an essential part of their lives" (34).

Example 14 (APA Documentation)

> Escaping the detrimental effects of social technologies, students will better learn adult behaviors: ". . . adult duties, distant facts and values and truths they will not fully comprehend until much later" (Bauerlein, 2009, p. 35).

ADDING WORDS TO A QUOTATION

When you add words to a quotation, use square brackets, not parentheses, around the words. Add material to quotations sparingly. Do it only when absolutely necessary to avoid confusing your readers.

Example 15 (MLA Documentation)

> Home life is devalued, "So they [teenagers] look to one another, emulating dress and speech. . . " (Bauerlein 35).

NOTING EMPHASIS ADDED TO A QUOTATION

If you want to emphasize a word or passage in a quotation, put it in italics. The stylebooks offer different guidelines on how to indicate the addition of emphasis to a quotation:

- APA style: immediately after the emphasized words, place in square brackets the words "emphasis added."
- MLA style: after the quotation itself, place in parentheses the words "emphasis added," after the page number (if any). Or place "emphasis added" in square brackets immediately after the emphasized words.

If you do not indicate otherwise, readers will assume any words italicized in a quotation appear in italics in the source text.

Example 16 (APA Documentation)

> Bauerlein (2009) notes that "everyone passes through this phase, but this generation's experience marks a *crucial change* [emphasis added] in the process" (p. 35)

Example 17 (MLA Documentation)

> English Professor Mark Bauerlein observes that "everyone passes through this phase, but this generation's experience marks a *crucial change* in the process" (35, emphasis added).

Summary Chart

GUIDELINES ON QUOTATIONS

---

1. When to Quote Material

Quote passages when the author has said something in a distinctive or especially insightful or interesting way.

Quote material that supports the assertions you make in your paper.

Quote authorities who disagree with a position you are advocating or who offer alternative explanations or contradictory data.

2. When Not to Quote Material

Do not quote passages merely to fill in space.

Do not quote passages as a substitute for thinking.

Do not quote passages because you do not understand the author's ideas well enough to paraphrase them.

Summary Chart

INTEGRATING QUOTATIONS INTO YOUR WRITING

1. **Block Quotations**

   Employ this method with longer quotations.

   Follow guidelines established by the style manual your instructor requires.

2. **Integrated Quotations**

   Introduce the quotation with an appropriate verb.
   - *precede with a comma*
   - *employ a verb of saying that fits the overall tone of your essay, such as:*

says	holds
states	maintains
asserts	contends
claims	explains

   Introduce the quotation without a verb.
   - *a more formal way of introducing the quotation*
   - *precede with a colon*

   Run your sentence and the quotation together.
   - *edit your sentence so it fits the tone and syntax of the quoted passage*

   Pick out only certain words to quote.
   - *quote interesting uses of language such as coined or controversial terms*
   - *quote terms to draw attention to them*

QUOTATION REVISION CHECKLIST

	Yes	No
1. Did you check your quoted passages against the original to make sure the wording is accurate?	____	____
2. Is the capitalization of words in the quotation proper and accurate?	____	____
3. Is the punctuation in the quotation proper and accurate?	____	____
4. Do you need to add italics, underline certain words, or use single quotation marks in the quotation?	____	____
5. Did you check the punctuation you employed to introduce the quotation?	____	____
6. Did you check the format of your block quotations?	____	____
7. If you added words to or deleted words from the source passage, did you confirm that you have not misrepresented the author?	____	____
8. Is the format of your documentation at the end of the quotation in the correct style?	____	____
9. Did you list the right page number or numbers in your documentation?	____	____

Chapter 3

....

PARAPHRASE

In this chapter you will learn how to

1. Paraphrase material accurately and effectively

2. Vary the way you paraphrase material

3. Integrate paraphrased material into your own writing

4. Document paraphrased material

DEFINITION AND PURPOSE

When you paraphrase a passage, you express an author's arguments, findings, or ideas in your own words. Much of the writing you do in college will require you to paraphrase material. Some of these assignments will simply ask you to gather and convey information. To write this type of paper, you study the work of various authors, then paraphrase what they have written, trying to convey to your readers as clearly and accurately as possible what each has to say about the topic.

In other assignments you will rely on paraphrased material to help you develop and defend an argument. Paraphrasing the work of experts who agree with your position in a paper can be quite persuasive. Even paraphrasing the work of authors who *disagree* with a position you have assumed in your essay can be helpful: after you objectively present that opposing view, you can examine its strengths and weaknesses and adjust your position to accommodate ideas you can neither discredit nor dismiss. However, when paraphrasing information as a part of an argument you are advancing, you must fairly represent an author's views. It is always tempting to misrepresent what people say, especially when you disagree with them, either by oversimplifying their position or by employing misleading language. Try to resist these temptations; always try to be fair to an author when you paraphrase his or her work.

Finally, paraphrasing allows you to convey your unique understanding of a reading. Paraphrases of the same material written by different students are not likely to be exactly the same because writing a paraphrase involves a series of choices: each writer decides what information to include, what language to use, and what organization to employ. Though you should attempt to be objective in your paraphrase of a reading, the details you choose to include and the language you choose to substitute for the author's will be communicating your unique view of the passage.

QUALITIES OF A GOOD PARAPHRASE

Generally, a good paraphrase of a passage exhibits four characteristics. It is thorough, accurate, fair, and objective:

* *Thorough*—it will include all of the author's primary ideas or findings.
* *Accurate*—it will reflect what the author actually wrote.
* *Fair*—your choice of language will be as evenhanded as possible.
* *Objective*—you will avoid voicing your own opinion on the topic or on the quality of the source text.

THOROUGH

A paraphrase of a passage differs from a summary of a passage in its comprehensiveness. In a summary, you try to reduce the source material to its most essential message; in a paraphrase, you try to capture the entire content of the passage. Because you change words and sentence structure when paraphrasing material, your paraphrase of a passage may actually be longer than the original text. Summaries, however, will always be shorter than the original passage. Even though your goal is to be thorough, writing a paraphrase involves making some choices concerning content: you may leave out what you believe to be insignificant details, examples, or explanations found in the source text. Guiding these decisions, though, should be your desire to produce as complete a paraphrase as possible.

ACCURATE

Because you are not quoting authors when you paraphrase their work—because you are substituting your words for theirs—you must take care to be accurate in what you write. Your paraphrase should offer your reader a precise restatement of what the author wrote: though the language is different, your paraphrase should convey the same information or arguments found in the source text. However, accuracy can be hard to achieve. Even slight changes in language can drastically alter the meaning of a passage. Therefore, when writing and revising a paraphrase, check your work against your understanding of the source text. Have you at all misrepresented the *content* of the other writer's piece? Would the author read your paraphrase and agree that you have indeed captured what he or she wrote?

FAIR

Being fair in your paraphrase is related to being accurate. Writing a paraphrase involves putting into your own words someone else's ideas, arguments, or findings. When doing so, first you want to be fair to the author whose work you are paraphrasing. In exchanging your words for his or hers, you want to be as evenhanded as possible. Avoid language, for example, that implies a judgment on your part or makes an author's work appear more sophisticated or more simplistic than it actually is. Second, you want to be fair to your readers. When people read your paraphrase of an author's work, they expect you to give them a fair and accurate understanding of that material. They do not expect you to censure or praise the source text—that's the function of a critique, not a paraphrase.

For a number of reasons, paraphrases are often inaccurate or unfair. First, students often *misread source texts* and make flatly incorrect assertions about the author's work. This type of problem can be avoided through a careful, critical reading of the source text before you try to paraphrase it and by discussing the reading with others. Second, students often *paraphrase material out of context.* Their paraphrase of a passage is misleading because in the larger context of the work the passage has an entirely different meaning from the one reflected in the student's essay. This type of error frequently occurs if the author of the source text is summarizing opposing views in his work. Students who paraphrase this material out of context will frequently misrepresent the author's views, making it appear the author actually agrees with his critics. When you paraphrase someone else's ideas, be sensitive to the relationship between the passage you are working with and the meaning of source text as a whole. Finally, students often produce unfair paraphrases of a source text by *relying on emotionally charged or heavily connotative language.* If an article talks about "presidential aides" and you substitute "presidential cronies," "presidential lackeys," or "presidential co-conspirators," you probably are not being entirely fair in your paraphrase.

OBJECTIVE

A good paraphrase does not take sides. Students often fail to be objective in one of three ways. First, as discussed above, they may employ language that clearly editorializes. In writing a paraphrase, try to use language that fairly and accurately captures the meaning and intent of the source text, not language that reflects your views of the topic or the quality of the source text itself. Second, in writing a paraphrase, sometimes students want to comment directly on the topic the author is addressing. When paraphrasing an author's views on abortion rights, for instance, they may want to articulate their stand on the issue. That material does not belong in a paraphrase, where your goal is to communicate someone else's views. Finally, students sometimes want to include in their paraphrase comments on the quality of the author's work—that they found the argument convincing or faulty, that the author's style was cumbersome or flowing, that the article was "good" or "bad." These types of comments are appropriate for a critique, not for a paraphrase. Your goal in a paraphrase is to be as objective in your content and language as possible.

Before you try to paraphrase someone else's ideas, though, be sure you understand what he or she has written. Again, one of the most common causes of inadequate paraphrasing is failing to grasp the meaning of the source text. Therefore, whether you are paraphrasing a sentence, paragraph, chapter, or essay, you need to understand fully what the author has written before you attempt to put that person's ideas into your own words. Your paraphrase of that person's ideas or findings must be complete, accurate, fair, and objective. It cannot meet these standards if you are confused or at all uncertain about what the author has written.

However, paraphrasing a passage can also be an effective way of determining its meaning. If you are not sure what a passage means, try paraphrasing it. Putting someone else's ideas into your own words is often the best way for you to understand what the author has written. Always reread your paraphrase and the source text to be sure you have been thorough and fair, especially if the paraphrased material is going to be a part of a paper you are turning in.

HOW TO PARAPHRASE MATERIAL

Generally, you paraphrase material by changing words, changing sentence structures, or changing the order of ideas in a passage. More often than not, you will make all three types of changes each time you paraphrase someone's ideas.

CHANGING WORDS

One way to paraphrase a passage is to substitute your words for the author's. However, finding appropriate synonyms for words in the source text can often be challenging. Many students are tempted to turn immediately to a thesaurus for a list of possible replacement words. However, it is usually better to try to come up with appropriate synonyms on your own. Remember, writing a paraphrase involves putting someone else's ideas into *your* own words. If you can come up with replacement words that are fair, accurate, and appropriate for the tone of your paper, use them. If you cannot come up with a new word on your own, then turn to a thesaurus. However, after you look up a possible substitute word in the thesaurus, check its definition in a dictionary to see if the word accurately reflects the meaning you want to convey. The words you find in a thesaurus are not always interchangeable; there are often subtle differences in meaning that you can determine by checking the definition of each term in a good dictionary.

Whether you rely on your own resources or on a thesaurus, using synonyms in a paraphrase raises similar concerns:

- Does the new word convey the author's original idea accurately and objectively?
- Does the new word fit the overall tone of the rest of your essay? Is it too formal or informal? Too technical or too general?

Often, it may be impossible to find an adequate substitute for a word or phrase in a passage: perhaps the author coined a phrase or used an unusual or shocking term. In such cases, it is appropriate for you to quote the language found in the source text (see Chapter 2 for guidelines on quoting material). When paraphrasing material, however, try to keep the number of quotations to a minimum. Also, remember that *all* paraphrased passages you include in your papers must be documented—even though you change the language of the source text when you paraphrase, you need to acknowledge through your documentation the source of the *ideas* you are discussing.

Below are examples of passages paraphrased primarily through word substitution. You will find the original passage, a rough-draft paraphrase, and a final paraphrase. The original passages in all of the following examples are drawn from the readings included in Chapters 1 and 2.

Example 1

A. Original

"Teenagers stand at a precarious threshold, no longer children and not yet adults, eager to be independent but lacking the equipment and composure."

B. Rough-Draft Paraphrase

Teenagers stand at a dangerous moment in their lives, between childhood and adulthood, wanting to be independent but not possessing the ability and maturity to do so.

C. Final Paraphrase (APA Documentation)

Teens face a dangerous time in their lives, between childhood and adulthood, wanting desperately to live on their own but not possessing the skills and maturity they need to enter the next phase of their lives (Bauerlein, 2009, p. 35).

Discussion: In my rough draft, I changed a few words: "precarious threshold" became "dangerous moment in their lives," "no longer children and not yet adults" became "between childhood and adulthood," and "lacking the equipment and composure" became "not possessing the ability and maturity to do so." In places, my first attempt was still too close to the wording in the original passage, and I wasn't sure I captured the connotative meaning of several words. I liked "between childhood and adulthood," but I retained the word "independent" (which I thought I needed to change), "ability" did not seem like the right word to replace "equipment," "moment" wasn't the right word to replace "threshold," and I did not think the end of my paraphrase captured what the author meant in the context of the original. So in my next draft, I changed "moment in their lives" to "time in their lives," changed "ability" to "skills" (which I think comes closer to the author's word—"equipment"), and added the last part of the sentence to clarify what I think the author meant in the original. The basic sentence structure has remained the same; I've only tried to change some of the words.

Example 2

A. Original

"For many kids, the bedroom at midnight provides a rich social life that makes daytime face-to-face conversations seem tame and slow."

B. Rough-Draft Paraphrase

Many kids, even in their bedrooms in the middle of the night, have a richer social life electronically than they do talking one-on-one to their friends during the day.

C. Final Paraphrase (MLA Documentation)

Thanks to technology, many kids have a more exciting life electronically with friends overnight in their bedrooms than they have talking with them one-on-one during the day (Bauerlein 36).

Discussion: This was a difficult text to paraphrase out of context. In the original work, the author is clearly discussing the impact of technology on teenagers' social lives, but that word, "technology," does not appear in the passage. In my rough draft, I added the word "electronically" after "social life" to capture this meaning. The word "midnight" became "middle of the night," and "daytime face-to-face conversations" became "talking one-on-one to their friends during the day." I switched "rich social life" for "richer social life," which clearly needed to be changed or quoted. In my final draft, I opened the sentence with "Thanks to technology" to place the passage in context, changed "richer social life" to "more exciting life electronically." Again, I'm still not entirely happy with this paraphrase because I've only substituted words—it would be a better paraphrase if I also employed the techniques described below.

CHANGING SENTENCE STRUCTURE

Besides changing words, when composing a good paraphrase of material, you may also need to alter the sentence structure employed in the source text. Often such changes involve rearranging the order of ideas in a sentence or altering the order of dependent and independent clauses.

Example 3

A. Original

"Although communism and state socialism have failed to protect the environment, eco-extremists are basically anti-business."

B. Rough-Draft Paraphrase

"Eco-extremists" oppose business interests even though communism and state socialism have failed to protect the environment.

C. Final Paraphrase (MLA Documentation)

"Eco-extremists" oppose business even though communist and socialist governments have permitted environmental degradation (Moore 16).

Discussion: In my rough draft, I first changed the order of the ideas in the sentence. I could not think of an appropriate substitution for "eco-extremist" so I quoted it and changed "anti-business" to "oppose business." In my final draft, I had to find a better way of addressing the second half of my paraphrase. I started by changing "communism and state socialism" to "communist and socialist governments" and reworded the idea about failing to protect the environment to "have permitted environmental degradation." Looking at it now, I think "degradation" may not be the best word—some additional changes might be needed.

COMBINING SENTENCES

When you paraphrase longer passages, you will often have to "combine" sentences in the source text to paraphrase the material adequately. After you read the entire passage, you may feel that you can condense the information into fewer sentences while still being thorough and fair in your paraphrase. By changing words, altering sentence structures, and combining information found in two or more source sentences into one sentence of your own, you can often achieve a smooth, effective paraphrase of material.

Example 4

A. Original

"In addition to choosing a dubious tactic, the environmental movement also changed its philosophy along the way. It once prided itself on subscribing to a philosophy that was 'transpolitical, transideological, and transnational' in character. Non-violent direct action and peaceful disobedience were the hallmarks of the movement. Truth mattered and science was respected for the knowledge it brought to the debate."

B. Rough-Draft Paraphrase

In recent years the environmental movement has adopted a new philosophy. It once believed its philosophy cut across political, ideological, and national lines. While its adherents believed in direct action and peaceful disobedience, truth also mattered, as did science, which brought knowledge to the debate.

C. *Final Paraphrase (APA Documentation)*

According to Patrick Moore (1995), the environmental movement has changed its guiding philosophy. They used to believe their ideas cut across political, ideological, and national lines. They also believed in peaceful protests, respected the truth, and valued science for the information it brought them.

Discussion: In my rough draft, I condensed the four sentences found in the source text into three sentences in my paraphrase. I was especially interested in combining the last two sentences. At the same time, I was trying to change some of the words. For example, I altered "transpolitical, transideological, and transnational" but let stand much of the language in those last two sentences. To begin my final draft, I added the author's name and dropped "in recent years," which I had added in the rough draft. In the next two sentences I tried to echo the term "philosophy" with the word "believed" and achieve parallel structure by using "They" twice. I continued to change some of the terms, substituting "peaceful" for "non-violent" and again tried to achieve some sense of parallel structure in my last sentence (which combines two sentences in the source text).

"Unpacking" Sentences

Sometimes a sentence in a reading may be so densely written, so full of ideas, that in your paraphrase you may need two or three sentences to convey the same information. When "unpacking" a sentence like this, your goal remains to convey the author's ideas fairly and thoroughly in your own language. Be sure first, however, that you fully understand the source passage—densely written material is often hard to read.

Example 5

A. *Original*

"So they look to one another, emulating dress and speech, forming groups of insiders and outsiders, finding comfort in boyfriends and girlfriends, and deflecting more or less tenuously the ever-present risk of embarrassment."

B. *Rough-Draft Paraphrase*

Because many teenagers are still trying to define themselves, they look to each other for support. They end up dressing alike. They define who their friends are. They look to boyfriends or girlfriends. All the time, though, they are trying not to embarrass themselves.

C. *Final Paraphrase (MLA Documentation)*

Many teenagers look beyond their home and parents to define themselves. Instead, they look to each other for support. Ironically, in an effort to define their individuality, they end up dressing like their peers, forming cliques, and devoting themselves to girlfriends or boyfriends. All the time, though, they try, more or less successfully, to keep from embarrassing themselves (Bauerlein 35).

Discussion: This was a difficult passage to paraphrase. First, the original sentence makes little sense out of context, so in my rough draft, I paraphrased the sentence that leads up to this one in the source text: "Because many teenagers are still trying to define themselves." I then broke up the original sentence into five sentences, each covering one of the main ideas in the source text. This passage, however, was choppy and repetitive; I needed to combine them for better coherence. The final version has four sentences, and in the third sentence I added "Ironically" to capture the tone and intent of the original sentence as I interpreted it. Even at this stage, though, I think the first two sentences could be combined to make the paraphrase even more concise—perhaps going back to the syntax I used in the rough draft.

COMBINING STRATEGIES: PARAPHRASING LONGER PASSAGES IN SOURCE TEXTS

There may be times when you have to paraphrase passages from a source text that are several sentences or even several paragraphs long. When this is the case, you will likely need to employ all of the strategies discussed in this chapter.

Example 6

A. Original

"At the center of binge drinking on many campuses are fraternities and sororities. While they attract only a small percentage of students nationally, they continue to play a prominent role in campus life at many institutions. Our data shows that in fraternity houses, four of five residents binge, and more than half are frequent binge drinkers. And, fraternity parties are attended by many more students than just members. They attract even some high-school seniors— future college students who are introduced to binge drinking as a social norm. Not surprisingly, most of the alcohol-related deaths of college students recently reported in the media involved fraternity parties.

"While some colleges have begun to address the drinking culture created by fraternities, many administrators are still hesitant to move strongly against fraternities, for fear of angering alumni donors who fondly remember their own college years of partying. But administrators have a responsibility to protect all of their students against alcohol-related disruptions and injuries, and should not wait for tragedy to strike before they revoke official recognition of fraternities that consistently cause problems. Colleges also can require all first-year students who live on campus to reside in dormitories, and not in fraternity or sorority houses. Of course, then those colleges must work to create interesting alcohol-free activities centered in the residence halls, to show students that out-of-control drinking need not be the focus of social life."

B. *Rough-Draft Paraphrase*

Even though only a small number of students join fraternities and sororities in college, they are responsible for much of the binge drinking on U.S. campuses. In fact, one study showed that four of five fraternity and sorority members binge drink, more than half, frequently. In addition, high-school students sometimes attend Greek parties, introducing them to binge drinking even before they enroll in college. Recently, several students have even died after becoming drunk at fraternity parties.

Although they know fraternities are often the site of binge drinking, college administrators are often reluctant to crack down on them because they are afraid of angering alumni donors who themselves were Greeks. However, in doing so, administrators fail to uphold their responsibility to protect all students. One way to attack the problem would be to require all freshmen to live in dorms, but schools would then also have to provide alcohol-free recreational opportunities to demonstrate that students do not have to get drunk to have fun.

C. *Final Paraphrase (MLA Documentation)*

In the United States, while only a small number of students join fraternities and sororities in college, they are responsible for much of the binge drinking. One study showed that four out of five fraternity and sorority members binge drink (over 50 percent, frequently) and often introduce binge drinking to high-school students who attend their parties. Although administrators know that fraternities are often the site of binge drinking (and that some students have died after getting drunk at fraternity parties), they are reluctant to crack down on them—many potential alumni donors were Greeks and may object to such action. To address the problem, administrators could prohibit freshmen from living in Greek housing, but they would also have to provide alcohol-free recreational opportunities to demonstrate that students do not have to get drunk to have fun (Wechsler 21–22).

Discussion: As I moved through the rough draft into the final paraphrase, I tried to condense and simplify the sentences in the source text while remaining comprehensive. I ended up with one paragraph instead of two, although the order of the ideas in my paraphrase still follows the order of ideas presented in the original. I'm still not sure that I like substituting "Greek" for "fraternities and sororities" in the paraphrase of the expression "crack down on them" (it may be too informal). To condense the material, I used parentheses twice to enclose material I thought was of secondary importance. Also note that I need to provide documentation only once, at the end of the paraphrased passage.

BLENDING YOUR WRITING WITH PARAPHRASED MATERIAL

Often in academic writing you will be blending your writing with material you're paraphrasing from source texts. Through documentation and attribution, you will guide your readers through the passage, clarifying which prose is yours and which is paraphrased. I have numbered the sentences in Example 7 below to make it easier to discuss the passage.

Example 7 (Using APA Documentation)

> [1]Clearly, binge drinking is a problem on many college campuses, but who is to blame? [2]Author Henry Wechsler (1998) lays part of the responsibility at the feet of fraternities and sororities. [3]According to Wechsler, although only a small number of college students actually "go Greek," fraternity and sorority members account for a disproportionate number of binge drinkers. [4]Fraternities, in particular, seem to promote binge drinking, since four out of five students living in a fraternity house report that they binge drink (p. 21). [5]If college administrators know that fraternities and sororities are a major site of binge drinking on their campuses, why don't they act to stop that behavior? [6]Wechsler believes it comes down to money. [7]They are afraid to offend alumni donors who were themselves Greeks by cracking down on fraternities and sororities (p. 21). [8]If these alumni feel that the administration is unfairly targeting Greeks, they will be less likely to donate money to the school.

Discussion: In this example, sentences 3, 4, and 7 are paraphrased from the source text and are therefore documented. Sentences 1, 2, 5, 6, and 8 are ones I wrote and therefore do not need to be documented. Note how citing the source text at the end of sentence 4 provides sufficient documentation for sentences 3 and 4.

DOCUMENTATION

Remember that any material you paraphrase from a source must be properly documented. Failing to document paraphrased material is a form of plagiarism. Although the various forms of documentation you will encounter in college are discussed in Chapter 12, remember that every discipline expects writers to document all paraphrased material properly.

Summary Chart

HOW TO PARAPHRASE MATERIAL

1. **Read, reread, and annotate the material.**
   - *Use a dictionary to find the meaning of any words you do not know.*
   - *Form your own opinion about the meaning of the passage.*

2. **Change words in the passage.**
   - *Substitute synonyms for key terms in the passage.*
   - *Substitute pronouns for nouns when appropriate.*
   - *Change the verbs.*

3. **Change the sentence structure in the passage.**
   - *Rearrange the order of ideas presented in the source text.*

4. **Combine sentences found in the source text.**
   - *Combine into single sentences ideas presented in two or more sentences in the source text.*

5. **Unpack sentences found in the source text.**
   - *Convey in two or more sentences ideas presented in one sentence in the source text.*

PARAPHRASE REVISION CHECKLIST

	Yes	No
1. Have you provided the full title of the source and identified its author?	_____	_____
2. Have you employed a variety of methods to paraphrase the material?	_____	_____
3. Have you checked to be sure your paraphrase accurately captures the author's ideas?	_____	_____
4. Have you remained as objective as possible in choosing language for your paraphrase?	_____	_____
5. Have you avoided offering your opinions on the topic of the reading or on the writer's style?	_____	_____
6. Have you checked your language to make sure each word you have chosen means what you think it means, has the connotation you want it to have, and fits the general tone of your paraphrase?	_____	_____
7. Have you reviewed your sentence structure for clarity and variety?	_____	_____
8. Have you provided appropriate transitions between the ideas you paraphrase?	_____	_____
9. Have you provided proper and accurate documentation?	_____	_____
10. Have you properly punctuated your documentation?	_____	_____

Chapter 4

SUMMARY

In this chapter you will learn how to

1. Differentiate among various forms of summary

2. Write effective informative and explanatory summaries

3. Write abstracts

4. Document summarized material

DEFINITION AND PURPOSE

Summarizing a reading involves two separate processes: (1) identifying the important material in the text and (2) restating the material in your own words. Because part of your job when writing a summary is deciding what to include from the reading and what to leave out, summaries are always shorter than the source text. Like paraphrases, summaries are always written in your own words (you can use quotations in a summary, but only sparingly), and they should be as objective as possible (you do not include in a summary your own opinions, beliefs, or judgments, and you try to use neutral language).

The ability to summarize readings is fundamental to academic, source-based writing. You will likely be summarizing information when you prepare a lab report, review a movie, write a research paper, or take an essay test. Instructors will often ask you to summarize articles or book chapters to be sure you can read carefully and critically, identify key ideas and important supporting evidence or arguments, and express that information clearly in your own words.

Sometimes summaries are part of a longer work. In a history research paper, for example, you may summarize the work of several different theorists while presenting an argument of your own. Other times, however, summaries will be "freestanding"—graded as independent formal essays. Your goal in writing them is to convey in your own words only the most important ideas, arguments, or findings in a reading. To write these types of assignments, you need to form a clear understanding of the source text, decide what to include in your summary and what to leave out, and choose language that clearly and objectively conveys the author's ideas.

Other times, though, you will use summaries to support a larger argument you are advancing in an essay. First, you may summarize the arguments or findings of experts who agree with the position you have assumed in your thesis; readers may accept your position if they see that other authorities support it as well. Second, you may summarize the work of experts who call into question your thesis. Doing so will help your work appear informed and balanced, again improving your credibility in the eyes of many academic readers. Be sure, however, that if you do summarize opposing views in your essay, you then somehow address them. For example, following your summary, you can critique that information—pointing out its strengths and weaknesses—and explain how the opposing ideas affect the validity of your thesis.

Whether your summary is part of a longer work or stands on its own, it must make sense to someone who has not read the source text. If, for example, you are working as a loan officer in a bank and your boss hands you a financial report to summarize, she wants to be able to understand your summary without having to read the report herself. She wants *you* to read the report carefully and distill from it the information she needs to know.

TYPES OF SUMMARIES

In college you will probably write two different types of summaries: informative and explanatory. An informative summary simply conveys the author's main ideas, data, arguments, and supporting material; an explanatory summary conveys this information as well, but also indicates the overall structure of the source text, explaining how the author develops his or her assertions. Informative summaries are shorter than explanatory summaries and are usually incorporated into longer works or take the form of an **abstract**. Explanatory summaries are longer than informative summaries, follow the organizational scheme of the source text, frequently refer to the name of the source text's author, and usually serve as independent, freestanding essays.

Below are two different summaries of the opening lines of the Gettysburg Address, one informative and one explanatory. As you read them, note the differences in content, structure, and word choice.

Example 1

Source Text

"Four score and seven years ago our fathers brought forth on this continent, a new nation, conceived in Liberty and dedicated to the proposition that all men are created equal. Now we are engaged in a great civil war, testing whether that nation, or any nation so conceived and so dedicated, can long endure. We are met on a great battlefield of that war. We have come to dedicate a portion of that field, as a final resting place for those who here gave their lives that that nation might live."

Informative Summary

> Eighty-seven years ago the United States was founded on the idea that all people are created equal. Currently a civil war is testing whether such a nation can survive. A portion of this battlefield is to be designated as a cemetery for those who fought in the war.

Explanatory Summary

> Lincoln opens the Gettysburg Address by remarking that eighty-seven years ago the United States was founded on the idea that all people are created equal. He next points out how the country is engaged in a civil war that will determine whether such a nation can survive, then acknowledges the occasion of the speech: to dedicate part of a great battlefield as a cemetery for the combatants.

Notice that the point of the informative summary is simply to capture in your own words the important ideas found in the source text. In an explanatory summary, though, you repeatedly refer to the author of the work and indicate how the piece was organized through your choice of verbs ("opens," "points out") and transition words ("next," "then").

QUALITIES OF A GOOD SUMMARY

Informative and explanatory summaries need to be comprehensive, brief, accurate, neutral, and independent.

- *Comprehensive*—it conveys all the important information in the reading.
- *Brief*—it conveys this information concisely.
- *Accurate*—it correctly conveys the author's ideas, findings, or arguments.
- *Neutral*—it avoids judgments concerning the reading's topic or style.
- *Independent*—it makes sense to someone who has not read the source text.

COMPREHENSIVE

Your summary needs to include all of the important ideas, assertions, or findings contained in the source text as well as the most significant information or arguments the author provides to support them. When you paraphrase a passage, you try to capture in your own language everything the author has written. However, when you summarize that same passage, you have to be more selective in choosing material to include. You need to identify what you believe to be the most important material in the passage and include only that in your summary. In this way your summary is comprehensive—you have not left out any important information.

Does that mean that if a number of people were summarizing the same article, all of their essays would be identical, at least in content?

No. Determining what to include in a summary requires judgment. Each individual writer must decide what is most important in the source text. Some writers will make good choices; some will make poor choices. Even those making good choices may decide to include different information. Consequently, students assigned to summarize the same reading will likely produce slightly different essays. If you carefully and critically read the source text before you begin to write your summary, and if you check your work against the source text before you turn it in to be sure you have included all of the important information, you will probably produce a comprehensive summary.

BRIEF

In writing a summary, you have to balance two concerns: you want your summary to be comprehensive, but you also want it to be brief. The point of writing a summary is to *reduce* a text to its most essential information. In a summary, brevity is usually achieved through carefully selecting your content and words. First you need to include (1) the reading's primary ideas, arguments, or findings and (2) the primary means of support the author offers for his or her contentions. Second, you must always be concerned about word count: if you can say something gracefully in four words rather than five, say it in four; if you can condense material by cutting unnecessary prepositions or adjectives, cut them. Composing a good summary requires disciplined writing.

ACCURATE

Your readers depend on you to be accurate in your summary. You have to be careful not to misrepresent—purposefully or accidentally—what the author wrote. Instead of reading the source text, your readers are depending on you to provide them with a thorough, accurate, and fair overview of the piece. Misrepresenting an author in your summary is unfair to both your reader and the original author. However, accuracy can be hard to maintain. Because in a summary you are substituting your language for the author's, even slight changes in words can drastically alter the meaning of a passage. Therefore, when you review your summary, check it against the source to be sure you have accurately represented what the author wrote. Make sure you have not misrepresented the author's ideas or findings either by omitting some important information or by using inaccurate, slanted, or vague language.

NEUTRAL

Summaries should be objective. No matter how much you would like to praise or criticize an author's argument, interpretation of data, or style of writing, such comments do not belong in a summary. In a summary you do not present your views on the topic the author is addressing, you do not comment on the quality of the author's argument or writing, and you do not voice any of your opinions at all. Instead, you try to present what the author has written accurately and objectively. When reviewing your summary, make sure you have not included your own opinions and that you have used objective language. By avoiding highly charged or judgmental terms, you can help ensure that your summary is neutral, balanced, and fair.

When there are problems with objectivity in a summary, more often than not they appear in one of three places: at the beginnings of paragraphs, in the middle of long paragraphs, and at the very end of the piece. At the beginnings of paragraphs, students sometimes react to the material contained in the previous paragraph; instead of moving on to summarize the author's next point, they respond to the previous one. In the middle of paragraphs, students sometimes begin to debate the author. They may notice that the author has presented a weak argument, for example, and feel compelled to point that out. Such criticisms are appropriate for a critique, but not for a summary. Finally, at the ends of summaries, students sometimes add the kind of concluding line commonly found in high school book reports, "Overall, I really liked this book because . . ." or "Although I found the author convincing, sometimes I had a hard time. . . ." Such statements do not belong in an objective, neutral summary.

INDEPENDENT

Your summary ought to make sense to someone who has not read the source text. Keep in mind the purpose of a summary. If, for instance, your employer asks you to summarize a report, she wants to learn from your summary the main points of the report without having to read the original text. Your summary must be able to stand on its own—read independently, it has to make sense. To achieve this goal, you need to pay special attention to word choice when drafting your summary. For example, are there any terms that, taken from the context of the source text, will need to be defined in your summary? Have you included in your summary any pronouns that refer to an antecedent in the source, not to an antecedent in your summary? Have you referred to people who were identified in the source but are not identified in your summary?

To make sure your summary is independent, let someone read it who has not read the source text before you turn it in for a grade. Ask that person to mark any words or passages he or she finds confusing.

HOW TO SUMMARIZE A TEXT

READ, REREAD, AND ANNOTATE THE SOURCE TEXT

Obviously, the first step in writing a summary is to read the material you are summarizing. As you read through it for the first time, try to get a sense of the passage's main ideas and structure—a sense of what the author covers and the order in which the ideas are presented. Next, read the material again, only more slowly this time. As you reread, carefully mark the passage, highlighting important material and taking notes in the margin that identify the main points, key supporting information, and the structure of the piece.

If you are summarizing a paragraph, locate and mark the topic sentence. If there is no topic sentence, paraphrase the main point of the paragraph in the margin. If you are summarizing an entire essay or article, locate the thesis. If the author states the thesis, underline it and make a note in the margin. If the thesis is implied rather than stated, paraphrase the main point of the piece at the end of the passage. If the source text has headings and subheadings, note how they help structure the piece.

SUMMARIZE EACH SECTION OF THE SOURCE TEXT

Identify the major sections of the piece—where the author discusses one idea or develops one argument or explores one finding. These sections may consist of a single paragraph or a group of paragraphs. In the margin of the passage or on a separate sheet of paper, briefly summarize each section of the text. Using your own words, note the primary idea, assertion, or finding being developed in each section along with the primary supporting material the author provides—the most effective example, the most telling statistic, the most important authority cited.

CHECK THE SECTION SUMMARIES AGAINST THE SOURCE TEXT

The brief summaries you produce of each section of the source text will help you incorporate the material into a longer essay you are writing, compose an abstract of the source text, or produce an explanatory summary of the reading. Now is a good time to check these brief summaries against the source text to ensure they are accurate, neutral, comprehensive, and clear.

HOW TO WRITE AN ABSTRACT

As stated earlier, the goal of an informative summary is to convey as briefly and accurately as possible the primary content of a source text or perhaps just a certain section of that text. When you incorporate summarized material into a longer essay you are writing—a report or research paper, for example—you may introduce the material by referring to the author's name and/or the title of the piece before you add it to your essay. A special form of an informative summary in academic writing is an abstract. Abstracts are usually paragraph-long informative summaries of a reading and frequently accompany scholarly texts. Most often located under the title of the text, an abstract provides a succinct overview of the reading, informing readers of the text's primary assertions, findings, or arguments. When you are engaged in a research project, abstracts can be invaluable: when you locate a source text that looks interesting, by reading the abstract alone you can decide whether to read the entire piece or move on to the next one.

After you draft your abstract, be sure to check it against the original to ensure that the abstract is comprehensive and independent—it ought to make the main points of the reading clear to someone who has not read the text. Also be sure that you are paraphrasing the source text throughout your abstract: the language you use should be yours. Sometimes you might have to quote specific terms the author has used if they are particularly important or novel.

HOW TO WRITE AN INFORMATIVE SUMMARY ESSAY

An informative summary is longer and more detailed than an abstract, covering the author's primary assertions, findings, and arguments, as well as how they are supported. Informative summaries frequently follow the source text's organization—summarizing the text's first main point first, the second main point next, and so on. This is not necessary, however, if using a different organizational strategy would make your summary stronger. In the end, your informative summary should be comprehensive, brief, accurate, neutral, and independent.

In the *opening section* of your essay, introduce the topic or context of the reading, provide the source text's full title and the full names of its authors, and state your thesis. You might also want to provide the author's credentials or the publication information of the source text (where and when it was originally published). Your thesis will be a paraphrase of the source text's thesis.

In the *body* of your informative summary, paraphrase the primary content of the source text. You may want to use the one-sentence summaries of each section you composed earlier as a guide. Just paraphrase the content of the readings—do not embellish or editorialize. Your goal is to write a thorough summary of the source text that is both clear and neutral. Do not comment on the text's content, style, or structure. Plagiarism can be a problem with summarizing a text: be sure you paraphrase the material properly. You may quote material in an informative summary, but you should use quotations sparingly.

Informative summaries do not have conclusions like other forms of source-based essays. Instead, you close your paper by summarizing the source text's last key assertion, finding, or argument. Do not editorialize at the end of your summary—do not include any judgmental statements like "Overall, the author did a good job of presenting her ideas" or "The piece was extremely interesting and easy to read." Your summary should be neutral and objective.

As always, review your rough draft against the source text as you revise to ensure that your summary is comprehensive and that you have adequately covered the source text's primary content.

HOW TO WRITE AN EXPLANATORY SUMMARY ESSAY

As with an informative summary, an explanatory summary conveys the primary content of a text. However, it describes not only what the reading says but also how it is put together through frequent references to the author's organizational strategy. When a teacher asks you to write a summary of a text, this is the type of document he or she usually has in mind: an explanatory summary of the reading that is comprehensive, brief, accurate, neutral, and independent.

In the *opening section* of your summary—usually the first paragraph or two—introduce the topic of the source text, give the title of the piece you are summarizing, mention the name and credentials of the person who wrote the piece, and include your thesis. In a summary, your thesis will likely be a paraphrase of the source text's thesis.

In the *body* of your summary, present in your own words the author's primary assertions, conclusions, or findings, as well as the supporting examples or statistics you believe your readers will need to know to understand and appreciate the author's contentions. Use as a guide the brief summaries of each section of the text you wrote earlier. An explanatory summary is different from an informative summary because in the body of your essay you will make frequent references to the author of the piece and explain how the source text is structured through your use of transitions. Assume you are working with an article by Alice Smith. Your explanatory summary will include many passages such as these: "Smith opens her essay by . . . ," "Next, Smith discusses . . . ," "Smith's third main argument is . . . ," and "Smith concludes her essay with. . . ." All of these example passages include the author's name and some listing or transition word (e.g., "first," "next," "then"). You do not have to use the author's name in every sentence, just when you are moving from your summary of one section of the source text to another section so your reader has a clear sense of the source text's structure.

Generally, summaries do not need a *conclusion*; simply end your essay with a summary of the author's last point. If you want or need a formal conclusion, make it a brief restatement of the author's thesis.

When you have finished the rough draft of your explanatory summary essay, reread the source text to ensure that you have captured all of the important content of the reading. To be sure that your summary is clear, ask someone who has not read the source text to read your summary and identify any passages he or she finds confusing. Remember: unless you are told otherwise by your teacher, assume your audience has not read the source text. Also check the tone of your summary. It ought to be objective and neutral.

DOCUMENTATION

Summarized material should be documented. Many students do not feel they need to document summarized material that is part of a larger essay because they are using their own language to convey the author's ideas. However, you still need to give the author credit for those ideas, arguments, or findings. Documentation also tells your readers where they can locate the source text if they want to read the whole piece themselves.

READING

After the following article, "From *Animal House* to *Big Brother:* Student Privacy and Campus Security in an Age of Accountability," by Ron Chesbrough, you will find three summaries—an abstract, an informative summary, and an explanatory summary. The article originally appeared in *Student Affairs Leader.*

From *Animal House* to *Big Brother:* Student Privacy and Campus Safety in an Age of Accountability

Ron Chesbrough

Ron Chesbrough is the vice president of student affairs at Hastings College in Nebraska. He is also a member of Student Affairs Leader's editorial board.

Two Scenarios: A student at a large university spots a gun on the desk of a fellow student during class. Frightened, the student sends a text message to someone outside of the classroom, who in turn contacts the University Police Department. Members of the University Police respond immediately, going to the classroom and removing the student and the gun. In the process, they learn that the gun is a toy gun used in the popular game "Assassin." They seek out the other students engaged in the game and confiscate their toy guns. A notice is sent to the university community describing the incident in detail and announcing the prohibition of this game on university property.

A student at a small private college reports to the dean of students that she has read disturbing poems on the Facebook page of another student. The dean reviews the postings, which contain references to being unhappy and questioning the purpose of life. The dean calls the student in and requires that he undergo a full psychiatric evaluation based on the poems.

Background

We have learned recently many times over, and with crushing severity, what we have long known—that college campuses are risk-inherent environments. We have also been tragically reminded of a corollary fact—that one of our greatest challenges in creating and preserving safe environments on our campuses is the ability to find and strike a proper balance between our students' rights to privacy and their rights to a safe and healthy living and learning community. This is not a new imperative for us; it is simply one that has gained importance in recent years and with recent events on our campuses.

In the wake of the tragedy of the Virginia Tech shootings of nearly a year ago and those that have followed, the intersection of student privacy rights and community safety is, now more than ever, one where the traffic light is changing erratically. With the lights blinking red, green, and yellow on all sides, institutions and professionals are left largely to their own interpretations and intuitions about when to go, stop, or proceed with caution when it comes to student privacy rights.

From emergency alert text messaging systems to patrols of Facebook and MySpace and all things in between, colleges and universities are searching for the new right relationship with students in the interest of campus safety.

Take, for example, a recent article in the *Wall Street Journal*, featured in the February 1 issue of *Student Affairs Leader*, [that] described Cornell University's new "alert team" and related university-wide training to recognize and report signs of student emotional distress and behavioral concerns ("Bucking Privacy Concerns, Cornell Acts as Watchdog," *WSJ*, December 28, 2007). These practices place Cornell "squarely in the center of a debate over the rights of American college students," according to the article. Just what is the debate, we should ask, and how have we arrived here?

FERPA in Transition

The Family Education Rights and Privacy Act (FERPA) has long governed the treatment of student privacy rights in higher education. Its protections and allowances are familiar enough by now to not bear detailed repeating here, although a refresher on the various amendments to FERPA, particularly over the past decade, is not a bad idea.

It is also useful to gain some familiarity with the shifting ground of case law in matters concerning student privacy rights and our duty to protect students from harm—whether from themselves or others.

Two recent cases worth reading again in this regard are *Shin v. Massachusetts Institute of Technology* and *Schieszler v. Ferrum College*. In both cases the courts found a special duty to care (in these cases to prevent self-harm) based on the unique relationship between students and their academic institutions.

If we set aside the legitimate and compelling question of an institution's ability to "prevent" harm to all students at all times, we can see that the real central issue here is one of discernment and disclosure.

In other words, how do we maximize our ability to detect or discern threats to safety on our campuses? And once a possible or plausible threat is discerned, to what end and to whom do we disclose this information? And finally, what are the implications of this discernment/disclosure puzzle for our relationships with students?

Disclosure

To begin, we might begin to rethink our definition of "privacy" in this scenario. We might also question the original intent of FERPA—asking who and what it was originally intended to protect, and from whom. Here it seems clear that the original and ongoing intent of FERPA is to provide reasonable protections against undue intrusions into the education records of students by those not determined under law to have legal rights to such access, and to provide students with their own due process rights to the same information pertaining to them and being held by the institution.

Where institutions keep information of a disciplinary nature, and where such records do not constitute criminal records, the same protections and rights have applied, with notable recent amendments allowing disclosure of information to certain others (e.g., parents, victims) when in relation to certain types of potentially noncriminal records (e.g., campus drug/alcohol violations, sexual violence).

Similarly, allowances exist for disclosure of certain medical or treatment records held by the college to both parents and others as directed by FERPA. Finally, the Jeanne Clery Act not only allows but also requires both annual reporting and timely warning (in cases of an ongoing threat) of criminal activity on our campuses.

Given these provisions for disclosures under FERPA and what some would argue is a gross historic misunderstanding of more general parental disclosure rights of the institution under FERPA, it is fair to say that we have often overstated protections afforded to students under this law.

It is safe to say, historically speaking, that we have often erred on the side of overprotecting these rights, especially in the grey areas of FERPA, that many would argue still exist after more than four decades and numerous amendments to the legislation. But are we moving too far, too fast into this new intersection of student privacy rights and campus safety?

Who Bears Responsibility—and to Whom

In their recent look at critical issues for student affairs professionals, Arthur Sandeen and Margaret J. Barr had this to say about the rising complexity of the question of student safety on our campuses: "Legal requirements, institutional missions, parental expectations, chronic psychological problems of students, and student behaviors require both the profession and institutions to answer this fundamental question" (Sandeen & Barr, 2006, p. xii). Their chapter entitled "Who Has the Responsibility for the Lives of Students?" is an attempt to answer this question.

I would argue, as perhaps they would, that this is not a new question, but an old one posed in a new context, with new and literal meaning imbued by recent events on our campuses nationwide. It is not the "who" in this question that has changed, but the "how."

How are we differently responsible for the lives of our students in the current era, and as importantly, how do we best fulfill that responsibility when faced with the kinds of scenarios posed at the outset? Put differently, how do we begin to rebalance the right of all students to a safe learning environment with the rights of those whom Sandeen and Barr refer to as our "disturbed" students, students whom they suggest are coming to us in increasing numbers (Sandeen & Barr, pp. 155–180)?

A Beginning Attempt

To begin, we need to revisit this concept of the disturbed student, first coined by Ursula Delworth, two decades ago in a definition that has almost eerie accuracy in today's environment of high-stakes disturbance on campus. These students, according to Delworth, can demonstrate an outward (anger and lashing out) or inward (depression and withdrawal) focus, and hold the potential to harm themselves or others (Delworth, 1989). Of particular importance, according to Delworth, is our recognition and response to those students who are both disturbed and disturbing of the campus environment.

We should refresh ourselves in the clear communication roles and responsibilities among campus administrators and health professionals established by Hollingsworth and Dunkle (2005) in our coordinated response to these students. And in this we should heed Arthur Sandeen's (1989) reminder that "an institution that decides it can not afford the resources required to address the problems of the disturbed and disturbing student may discover the costs of ignoring them are too great" (p. 61).

We should set clear behavioral expectations of our students in the classroom, in residence halls, and in the campus community at large. These are simply those norms that we insist should exist for the emotional and physical comfort of all members of the learning community, and they should be indexed to those instances where a certain behavior might reasonably be seen as imposing on or limiting the rights of other members of the community to a safe, healthy, and positive living and learning environment.

We should anticipate both the reasonable accommodations that might be made to students unable to meet certain behavioral requirements consistently or in all settings, and the absolute limits of behaviors that fall outside of the pale of the learning community. And we should clearly state what our responses would be in either case.

If we intend to not allow play guns on campus, or if concerning posts to a Facebook page are cause for college response, then students should be aware of this and the consequences of behaving in these ways. This takes hard and deliberate thought and imagination, and ought to involve a hearty dose of student and faculty input. It will lead to debate, discussion, and disagreement—but it is precisely this debate that needs to occur, in anticipation of difficult campus events rather than in response to them.

Students, and their parents, should be made to understand that college officials will exercise their full rights under FERPA to share information deemed necessary between college health officials and administrators; between administrators and parents or appropriate outside officials; and between members of the faculty, staff, and administration of the college or university as allowed by law—to ensure the safety of all members of the community to the best of their ability. And the mechanisms for said sharing should be transparent and readily understood by all members of the learning community and its constituents.

Implications

Some will point to a chilling effect of a learning environment so characterized. I would argue the opposite. What is chilling in the present environment is the relative lack of these types of safeguards in the face of clear and repeated evidence of our need for them. What is discomforting is the unease we feel at the intersection of student privacy rights and community safety—and it is discomforting not just for student affairs practitioners, but also for students, staff, faculty, and parents alike.

In this environment, it falls most logically to student affairs professionals to take the steps necessary to police this intersection and to work with others to develop the proper new traffic signals for this new environment.

It can also be said that this new posture poses new legal liability threats to institutions that may be claiming, by making such clear statements of intent, to be able to prevent bad things from happening on their campuses. Arguably, due diligence does in fact take on a new meaning in light of commitments like those described to attempt to discern and report potential threats to safety.

At the same time, we enter an environment wherein the lack of such stepped-up attempts may soon be discerned as a failure of due diligence, particularly as institutions move individually in these directions and as findings from various reports raise the question for legislators, parents, and others as to what our due diligence ought to, in fact, entail.

Still others may find such measures to have a discriminatory or dampening effect on admission for those students disclosing in that process a pre-existing diagnosis that may make them more prone to "concerning" exhibitions of behavior. All the better that college officials have more knowledge about the support needs of incoming students from the outset in order to put in place appropriate accommodations and to take the "handoff" from those who have provided supports and accommodations up to that point.

We might ask ourselves which student with special needs has the better chance of success in a college environment: the student who has disclosed what has helped him or her to succeed, or the student with special needs who is silent?

Finally, to those who herald this as a return to an even more extreme version of *in loco parentis* in our relationships with our students than we have so recently congratulated ourselves on shedding, I would say not quite, and perhaps the opposite. If we look closely at the legal doctrine of *in loco parentis*, we find that it describes a circumstance in which one assumes responsibility for a child without formally adopting the child. Applied to schools and colleges, this has typically meant that, by our actions, policies, and formal statements we agree to accept responsibility for our students "in the place of" their parents. Here I am arguing for something different.

I am arguing that we find new ways to hold our students accountable for their own actions, and that we involve parents as active partners and appropriate outside professionals whenever the need is evident. Staying with the Latin, we might call this the doctrine of *modestus pateo*, or, loosely translated, orderly openness. More simply, we might think of where we have arrived in higher education in this and many other regards as the *age of accountability*—to our students, their parents, our colleagues, and our many constituencies—in all that we do.

If campus safety at your institution is still something that the student affairs professionals are left to figure out and stew over, then it is time for change. The issues raised here about student privacy, campus safety, and our right relationship with our students in this age are not student affairs issues; they are issues of concern and importance to every member of the college community. Everyone must join the conversation. We are all standing at the same intersection, and the lights are still flashing red, green, and yellow.

References

Delworth, D., (1989). *Dealing with the Behavioral and Psychological Problems of Students*. New Directions for Student Services, no. 45. San Francisco: Jossey-Bass.

Hollingsworth, K., and Dunkle, J. "Dealing with Disturbed and Disturbing Students: Best Practices and Their Implications." Paper presented at the National Association of Student Affairs Personnel Administrators Annual Conference, Tampa, FL, 2005.

Sandeen, A., (1989). "A Chief Student Affairs Officer's Perspective on the AISP Model," in U. Oelworth (Ed.), *Dealing with the Behavioral and Psychological Problems of Students*. New Directions for Student Services, no. 45. San Francisco: Jossey-Bass.

Sandeen, A., and Barr, M. J., (2006). *Critical Issues for Student Affairs: Challenges and Opportunities*. San Francisco: Jossey-Bass.

Schieszler v. Ferrum College, 233 F.Supp.2d 796 (W.D.Va. 2002).

Shin v. MIT, 2005 Mass. Super. LEXIS 333, *32.

Wall Street Journal, "Bucking Privacy Concerns: Cornell Acts as 'Watchdog,'" 12/28/2007.

SAMPLE ABSTRACT

The author discusses a dilemma facing campus administrators: keeping students safe while protecting their privacy rights. The author argues that administrators may be reading FERPA restrictions too narrowly, failing to collect and share information that might protect students. He states that student safety is the responsibility of the entire campus community and that students' parents may play a more expanded role in forming a viable solution to the problem.

SAMPLE INFORMATIVE SUMMARY ESSAY

Ron Chesbrough's "From *Animal House* to *Big Brother*: Student Privacy and Campus Safety in an Age of Accountability" examines the tension that exists between college administrators' desire to keep students safe while at the same time protecting their privacy rights. After the fatal shootings at Virginia Tech, administrators have had to reconsider their existing policies.

Difficulties arise due to the Family Education Rights and Privacy Act (FERPA), legislation that has long served to protect student privacy. FERPA may prevent college authorities from addressing potential threats because doing so might violate a student's right to privacy. On the other hand, courts have held that colleges have a special obligation to protect the safety of students.

To address this dilemma, school administrators need to revisit the intention of FERPA, which was to ensure the privacy of student academic records and provide students due process rights. Allowances in the law enable schools to contact parents and other appropriate authorities about student health or disciplinary problems. In the past, schools have erred on the side of caution and have generally not communicated their concerns about particular students to off-campus authorities.

Particular attention needs to be paid to how schools address "disturbed" students who for medical or non-medical reasons pose a possible threat to other students. Schools must employ health care professionals who can help these students, convey to all students the school's standards of behavior, develop plans for accommodating students who need extra help coping with school, ban firearms from campus, and inform parents and students that school administrators will use all the powers FERPA provides to protect the safety of everyone on campus.

Some may find these actions too severe or opening colleges up to litigation should a tragedy occur. However, proper due diligence on the school's part is required to ensure student safety and privacy. Central to this effort is holding students accountable for their actions and enlisting the help of students and parents when formulating new school policies.

SAMPLE EXPLANATORY SUMMARY ESSAY

In "From *Animal House* to *Big Brother*: Student Privacy and Campus Safety in an Age of Accountability," author Ron Chesbrough explores how to make college campuses safer. Reacting to recent tragedies such as the killings at Virginia Tech, Chesbrough questions how best to balance the needs for student safety and student privacy, especially in light of safeguards guaranteed by the Family Education Rights and Privacy Act (FERPA). He argues that college administrators may need to operate out of a more liberal reading of FERPA regulations and enlist the aid of parents to meet the needs of students who may pose safety issues for a school.

Chesbrough opens his essay by defining a problem all college administrators face: how to ensure student safety while maintaining the privacy rights of students who may exhibit threatening or concerning behavior or actions. Central to the debate is how administrators interpret the restrictions placed on colleges through FERPA. While agreeing that FERPA has many benefits, Chesbrough notes how two recent court cases have redefined schools' responsibilities to protect students from themselves and their peers. He then poses an additional question to consider: under these new interpretations of FERPA, how do college administrators know when to release information about students who might pose a risk to the school and when to keep such information confidential?

To answer this question, Chesbrough examines the original intent of FERPA: who was it intended to protect and from what? He concludes that the act was passed primarily to protect student academic records and to ensure students due process rights concerning the release of those records. However, Chesbrough notes, FERPA allows for the release of some student medical information to parents while the Clery Act compels college administrators to act in a timely manner and with due diligence to address campus threats.

Chesbrough then offers a number of initial steps that might be taken to improve campus safety within FERPA restrictions: better define what a school means by a "disturbed" student, establish a clear communication protocol across campus to respond to any dangerous situations, share with students what constitutes acceptable and unacceptable behavior, and clarify university policy regarding firearms and Facebook postings.

Closing his essay, Chesbrough contends that taking these steps will make campuses safer while still maintaining student privacy rights. While there is a threat to privacy in identifying students who have potentially harmful mental or emotional conditions, administrators can enlist the aid of parents to help ensure that these students receive the assistance they need and that the safety of other students is protected.

Summary Chart

HOW TO SUMMARIZE TEXTS

---

1. **Read, reread, and annotate the material.**

   Carefully read the material, paying particular attention to the content and structure of the piece.

   Reread and annotate the material, being sure to note:
   * *the thesis;*
   * *the primary assertions, arguments, or findings; and*
   * *the primary means of support for each point.*

2. **Write one-sentence summaries of each section of the text.**

   Identify the major sections of the reading, in which the writer develops one idea before moving on to the next.

   In your own words, restate the main point developed in each section of the text and primary means of support the author provides.

3. **Write the first draft of your summary.**

   Introduce the topic of the reading.

   Include, early in your essay, the author's full name and the full title of the piece.

   In the body of your summary, elaborate on the one-sentence summaries, clearly explaining the important content of the reading.

4. Check the rough draft of your summary against the source text. As you review your work, make sure your summary is:

Brief—you have written your summary to be both clear and concise.

Comprehensive—you have included in your summary all of the author's important ideas, assertions, or findings.

Accurate—in choosing words and selecting material for your summary, you have not misrepresented the author's positions or findings.

Neutral—in choosing words and selecting material for your summary, you have attempted to be objective and fair.

Independent—your summary will make sense to someone who has not read the source text.

5. Rewrite your summary.

Based on your evaluation of your rough draft, make any needed changes in the content, organization, or language of your summary.

If you are writing an explanatory summary, include any transition words you need to guide your reader through your work.

SUMMARY REVISION CHECKLIST

	Yes	No
1. In the opening section of your summary have you:		
• introduced the topic of the essay?	_____	_____
• given the full title of the source text?	_____	_____
• given the full name of the author?	_____	_____
• included your thesis?	_____	_____
2. In the body of your essay do you summarize only one point at a time?	_____	_____
3. Have you accurately and fairly put into your own words all of the author's important findings, arguments, or ideas?	_____	_____
4. Have you identified the primary means of support the author provides for each finding, argument, or idea?	_____	_____
5. By cutting material or words, have you tried to make your summary as brief as possible while still being comprehensive?	_____	_____
6. To be neutral, have you avoided comments on:		
• the topic of the piece?	_____	_____
• the author's ideas?	_____	_____
• the author's style?	_____	_____
7. To help ensure that your summary will make sense to someone who has not read the original work, have you:		
• defined any unusual or technical terms?	_____	_____
• identified any people you refer to in your work?	_____	_____
• provided a sufficient context for understanding the author's assertions or findings?	_____	_____
8. Do you have adequate paragraph breaks and transitions?	_____	_____
9. Have you supplied proper documentation?	_____	_____

Chapter 5

RESPONSE ESSAYS

In this chapter you will learn how to

1. Differentiate response from summary and analysis
2. Identify and articulate your responses to a text
3. Write effective response essays

DEFINITION AND PURPOSE

Response essays ask you to examine, explain, and often defend your personal reaction to a reading. In this type of essay you explore why you liked the reading, agreed with the author, found the piece informative or confusing—whatever your response might be. There are not necessarily any "right" or "wrong" reactions to material; instead, response essays are usually evaluated on the basis of how well you demonstrate an understanding of the reading and how clearly you explain your reactions.

Sometimes teachers grade response essays the same way they grade any other assignment. Other times they assign ungraded response essays—usually as a way to help students develop material for graded essays. Still other teachers combine response essays with other types of papers; for example, they might ask students to summarize and then respond to a reading, or to respond to a reading and then critique it. Sometimes teachers will specify which aspects of the text they would like you respond to in your essay (for example, the author's thesis or use of figurative language); other times they will leave the choice of content up to you. In short, the response essay is a very flexible assignment employed widely by teachers in college. Writing this type of paper helps you understand your personal reaction to what you read: what you think about the topic, how you judge the author's ideas, and how the words on the page affect you as a reader.

Effective response essays demonstrate a strong connection between the source text and your reaction. Your responses are triggered by what you read, by certain words on the page. It is important to keep that connection strongly in mind as you compose your response essay. First, you need to put into words your responses to the source text. Second, you need to identify which words on the page triggered those responses. Third, you need to determine—and then explain for your reader—why and how those words triggered those responses.

In writing this type of essay, you cannot simply state your response and move on: "I liked this. I didn't like that." "This interested me; that puzzled me." Instead, you must develop and explain your response: what, *exactly*, is your response; what part of the text triggered it; what, *exactly*, is the relationship between the words on the page and your reactions to them? Although the idea of "developing" your response may seem odd, remember that you are writing for a reader, not just for yourself. You want your reader to be able to understand and appreciate both your response and what led you to have it. Clearly, writing a response essay is more difficult than it might first appear.

QUALITIES OF A GOOD RESPONSE ESSAY

Part of what makes a good response essay difficult to write is that it must be honest, informed, clear, and well supported.

- *Honest*—it reflects your true responses.
- *Informed*—it reflects an accurate and thorough understanding of the source text.
- *Clear*—it makes sense to your readers.
- *Well supported*—it demonstrates a close link between your responses and the source text itself.

HONEST

A response essay should focus on your sincere, thoughtful reactions to what you read. You want to identify your responses to the material and explore their relationship to the text itself: What gives rise to your reactions? How do they affect your reading of the author's work? These essays are highly subjective—you focus on *your* reactions to the text. Consequently, you should not pretend your responses are other than what they truly are. If you found a work boring, for example, do not claim that you found it intriguing simply because you think that is the way you are *supposed* to respond.

INFORMED

Can your responses, then, ever be "wrong"? In one sense, they cannot—your responses are your responses. That does not mean, however, that all responses to a reading are equally informed. For example, if your response is based on a misunderstanding of the source text—if you criticize an author for saying something she never said—then your response is misguided. Responses can also be naïve, shortsighted, or biased. These responses are not, in a sense, "wrong," but neither are they very insightful. Informed response essays are based on a clear understanding of the source text: the more you know about a topic, author, or reading, the more likely your response will be informed.

Take, for example, an experience I had a few years ago. I asked a group of students to respond to a satirical political essay before we discussed the piece in class. The students who recognized the satire produced fine response essays. However, the students who did not understand that the author was being satirical terribly misread the piece and produced misguided essays. Their responses were honest—the responses accurately reflected their reading of the text—but they were not informed.

CLEAR

When your readers finish your response essay, they should understand (1) how you reacted to the reading and (2) how your reactions are tied to the source text. Problems with clarity often arise from weak content, weak organization, or poor word choice.

Problems with clarity involving **content** occur when the person writing the response essay fails to state clearly the nature of his or her response, fails to identify which aspect of the source text gave rise to that response, or fails to explain the relationship between his or her response and those aspects of the text. Unless all three are clearly stated and explored, readers can be left confused about the nature of your response to the reading.

Other problems with clarity involve **organization**. Be sure that your essay has a fully developed opening and closing section and a clearly stated thesis. A good response essay also explores only one reaction at a time and provides clear transitions between the various sections of the paper. Problems with clarity can occur when you shift too quickly from discussing one response to discussing another— without a good transition, the change of focus might not be clear to your reader.

Finally, problems with clarity often involve the **language** used in response essays. Too often students use vague language to explore their reactions— words that mean something to them but nothing to their readers. Though response essays are highly subjective, when you turn them in for a grade, they must be addressed to a more public audience. Good response essays can be difficult to write for just this reason: you have to find language that clearly and efficiently communicates to others your subjective responses to a reading.

WELL SUPPORTED

In good response essays, students support and explain their reactions to the text with specific, elaborated examples. For example, if a student claims that she was offended by an author's illogical assertions, she should quote some of those passages and explain why she finds them illogical. If another student reads the same work and finds the same passages convincing because they match his experiences, he should also quote some examples and explain why he finds them convincing. In either case, the student supports her or his responses by citing from the source text examples that gave rise to them and then clearly explaining the relationship between those examples and their responses.

WRITING THE RESPONSE ESSAY

CAREFULLY READ THE MATERIAL

The problem with many response essays is that the students have not *fully* understood the source text before they begin to write. Some students respond to only part of the reading, without indicating they understand how the material fits into the author's overall thesis. As a result, their responses often seem limited or even biased; their work tends to ignore important issues raised in the source text. Other students simply misread the source text—basing their response on something the author neither wrote nor intended.

Therefore, when you are assigned to respond to a reading, read it several times and briefly summarize it before you write your essay (see Chapter 4 for advice on writing summaries). Summarizing the piece first can help ensure that your response will be based on a full and accurate understanding of the text's content, structure, tone, and thesis.

Explore Your Responses to the Reading as You Annotate the Text

To develop material for your response essay, as you read and annotate the text, note your responses briefly in the margin of the piece. Sometimes just jotting down a key word or two will do; other times you may need to write out a question you have. Even punctuation marks, such as exclamation points or question marks, can help you keep track of your reactions. When you are finished, expand on these notes at the end of the reading or on a separate sheet of paper. Your goal is to capture in a few sentences your overall response to what you have just read. These notes will form the basis of your response essay. In deciding what to mark and what kinds of comments to write as you read the source text, try answering the following questions.

How Do You React Emotionally to What the Author Has Written?

Your subjective, emotional reaction to a reading is a good place to start generating material for a response essay. Does the text make you angry? Excited? Bored? To explore these reactions, ask yourself several questions:

1. What, exactly, has the author written that makes you feel this way?
2. At what point in your reading did you have these reactions?
3. Which words on the page or ideas caused this response?
4. In short, what has the author done to make you respond this way? Examine the choices the writer made concerning content, organization, and style. What aspects of the text contribute to your response?

As you try to capture your responses in writing, carefully examine your reactions and, when possible, tie them to specific words, passages, or graphics in the text.

How Do the Ideas Offered in the Reading Compare with Your Experience or Your Sense of Reality?

We have all had the experience of hearing or reading something that has a ring of truth or falsehood. Something in a reading makes sense to us because it squares with our experience; it sits right with what we have come to understand about the world. As you reread and annotate a reading, note which of the author's ideas you tend to agree with or question based on how they match your own experience.

There is a real danger, though, in judging what others say by the standards of our experience alone. All of us bring to a reading important but limited experiences. When an author's statements do not match our sense of reality, we should not act defensively and immediately dismiss her ideas. Likewise, simply because we tend to agree with an author does not mean we ought to accept her ideas uncritically. Writing a response essay will give you the chance to question what you believe in light of what the author writes and to understand how your experiences influence the way you react to new ideas.

How Do the Ideas Offered in the Source Match What Others Have Had to Say on the Topic?

When you read a source, you bring with you not only what you think and feel based on your own experience, but also what you know, what you have already learned from your reading and education. There is no reason to ignore this knowledge when you write your response essay. In fact, whether the source text confirms or contradicts what you already know about the topic may be one of the reasons for your reaction to the piece. Be sure to note any reactions you have based on the match between the author's ideas and those proposed by other authors you have read.

COMPOSE YOUR ROUGH DRAFT

When you write your response essay, you will need to introduce the source text, provide your reader with a brief summary of its content, and then develop and clarify your reactions.

Introduce Your Topic, Source Text, and Thesis

When composing the opening of your response essay, you have four goals: introduce the topic of your essay, introduce your source text, state your thesis, and capture reader interest. After you introduce the source text's topic, provide its title and its author's full name. Your thesis for this type of essay will be a statement of your overall response to the reading and, if you like, an indication of how you will develop or explore that response in the body of your paper.

If you employ an "open" thesis statement for your essay, you will indicate your overall response to the piece:

- I found parts of the essay confusing.
- Reading this essay proved to be an emotional challenge.

If you employ a "closed" thesis statement for your essay, you will indicate your overall response to the source text and also indicate how you will develop that response in the body of your paper:

- I found parts of the essay confusing, especially its structure and many of its allusions.
- Because members of my family have been touched by the issues the author discusses, reading this essay proved to be an emotional challenge.

Either type of thesis can work equally well.

Finally, to capture reader interest you may want to use one of the following strategies:

- Open your essay with a provocative or interesting question raised by the reading or your response to it.
- Open your essay with an interesting quotation from the reading.
- Open your essay with a personal anecdote or hypothetical story related to the topic of the reading.
- Open your essay with a reference to a current controversy or public issue related to the topic of the reading.

Summarize the Source Text

After introducing the source and stating your thesis, give a brief summary of the reading. Generally, this summary will be only a paragraph or two long, highlighting the reading's most important findings, conclusions, or arguments. In the summary, anticipate what you will address in the body of your response. For example, if you know you will be questioning the validity of some of the author's claims, summarize his claims in this part of your essay. When they come up again in the body of your response, your reader will remember them and will be able to follow your assertions more easily.

State and Explain Your Responses Clearly and Concisely

In the body of your essay, you explore your responses, clearly and thoroughly, one at a time. This process might sound simple, but clearly and thoroughly stating and explaining your response to a reading can be difficult primarily because it is *your* response. The language you use when describing your reaction may make perfect sense to you but might well be unclear to your reader. For instance, if you were reading someone else's response essay and the writer complained that the source text made her feel "wheezy," would you really know what the person meant? Perhaps her explanation would make it clear, but the language she uses to characterize her response may hinder her readers' ability to understand her reaction. Therefore, a first step in clarifying your response for a reader is to choose language that others can understand. Likewise, explain the terms you use. For example, if you contend that a source is "confusing," explain whether you had difficulty understanding the writer's language, findings, structure, or some other aspect of the text.

Next, be sure to provide specific examples from the source text to help your reader understand each response. When you have a particular response to a reading, something on the page triggered it. In your essay, identify those "triggering" passages before you explain the dynamics of your response. For example, if you contend that a source text is confusing, identify and perhaps quote a passage that you cannot understand, then explain what it is about the writing you find difficult to follow (the logic of the passage? the wording? the structure?).

WRITE YOUR CONCLUSION

With a response essay, your conclusion should restate your overall response to the source text, echoing your thesis. To give a sense of closure to your essay, you should also try to mirror the strategy you employed to capture reader interest in the opening of your essay. For example, if you opened your essay with a question, return to that question in your conclusion and provide an answer. If you opened with an anecdote or story, refer back to it in your conclusion, perhaps indicating how that anecdote or story turned out. If you opened with a quotation from the source text, consider closing with a quotation as well.

REVISE YOUR ROUGH DRAFT

As you revise the rough draft of your response, pay particular attention to your assertions, organization, language, and support.

Review Your Assertions

When you review the assertions you make in your response essay, your primary concern is accuracy:

- Have you truly captured your reactions to the reading?
- Have you openly, honestly, and thoroughly explored your response to the material?
- Does your essay offer an accurate representation of your reaction?
- When other people read your essay, will they be able to understand and appreciate your reaction?

To check your assertions, first reread the source text and see whether you still feel the same way about it. Even a short time away from a reading may enable you to reconsider your reactions—maybe your views have changed. If they have changed, revise your essay. Also, in reviewing the source text, be sure you reread the annotations you originally made. Have you addressed the concerns, questions, and reactions you noted as you earlier annotated the piece?

Review Your Support and Explanations

As you revise your response, examine the way you illustrate and explain each of your responses. Remember that your responses should be tied to specific aspects of the source text, such as words, images, and graphics. When you compose your response, you need to explain for your reader the link between the source text and your reaction. In the body of your essay, you should state a response, point out what aspect of the reading led to that reaction (perhaps quoting the passage), and then explain clearly and thoroughly how that material led you to that response. As you revise your draft, make sure you accomplish all three goals in each section of your essay.

Review Your Organization

Next, when you review the organization of your rough draft, check to be sure you have fully developed opening and closing sections and have a clearly stated thesis. In the body of your essay, be sure that you are developing only one response at a time. Often when you write your rough draft, examining one reaction will lead you to a new response, one you have not previously considered. That is one of the real powers of writing: it not only helps you capture ideas in words but often will help you generate new ideas as well. When this happens, some writers will follow that new idea even if it does not belong in that part of the essay, knowing that in the next draft they can place it elsewhere. Other writers prefer to write a note to themselves to explore that new idea later, not wanting to lose track of the idea they are currently exploring. When you review your rough draft, check to see that you are developing only one response at a time in your essay.

Finally, be sure you indicate to your reader—through paragraph breaks and transition words—when you shift focus from one response to the next. Adding these signals to your paper makes it easier for your reader to follow your line of thought. Since you are writing about *your* responses, you know when you have changed focus; your readers, though, may have a harder time recognizing the structure of your essay. Adding appropriate paragraph breaks and transitions can help.

Review Your Language

As indicated earlier, word choice—finding and choosing appropriate terms to express your reactions—can be truly problematic when you are writing response essays. First, your initial reactions to what you read may be so emotional or so abstract that you cannot put them into words. You may struggle to find appropriate language. Second, your first efforts at finding words may result in highly "private" writing; since they arise from your own knowledge and experience, the terms you use may make sense only to you. In this case, you need to find terms that can communicate your responses to others. Before you turn in the final draft of your response essay, be sure to have someone else read your work, someone you trust to give you an honest appraisal of your language. Ask that person to indicate any part of the response he or she does not understand because of the words you are using.

SAMPLE RESPONSE ESSAY

This sample essay is responding to the article "From *Animal House* to *Big Brother*: Student Privacy and Campus Safety in an Age of Accountability" by Ron Chesbrough, found in Chapter 4 of this text. If you are unfamiliar with the article, read it before you read the following response essay.

A RESPONSE TO "FROM *ANIMAL HOUSE* TO BIG BROTHER: STUDENT PRIVACY AND CAMPUS SAFETY IN AN AGE OF ACCOUNTABILITY"

As Ron Chesbrough notes in his essay "From *Animal House* to *Big Brother*: Student Privacy and Campus Safety in an Age of Accountability," violent episodes, like the shootings at Virginia Tech a few years ago, have raised serious concerns about campus safety. Though my roommates and I have discussed this issue a few times and we had a floor meeting to talk about emergency evacuation plans at the beginning of the term, Chesbrough's essay offers a perspective on the problem I hadn't considered: what policies can the administration at a school adopt to keep students safe? As a first-year college student, I found Chesbrough's essay informative but not very helpful. In the end, he fails to offer very satisfying answers to the problems he raises.

Campus safety happens to be an issue I deeply care about. When the shootings took place at Virginia Tech, my sister was attending Radford College, which is not far from Blacksburg. When I saw the news coverage on television, I started texting my sister immediately to be sure she was safe. She told me the students at her school were also keeping up with the story and were a little nervous, but that I shouldn't worry because nothing like that had ever happened at her school. I felt better, but when I thought about it, what happened at Virginia Tech could happen at any college in the country.

In his article, Chesbrough explores why the violence erupted at Tech and offers a few explanations I had not considered. For example, I had not realized the kinds of restrictions administrators face due to FERPA (the Family Education Rights and Privacy Act). From orientation, I knew that my school could not release my grades to anyone without my permission, even to my parents. I was surprised to learn that FERPA regulations might have kept the administrators at Virginia Tech from acting to prevent the attack. According to news reports, the shooter, Seung-Hui Cho, had a history of mental illness and had received treatment while a high school student. Virginia Tech officials were not informed of Cho's past problems, and when they started to emerge on campus, FERPA regulations kept administrators from telling his teachers or others because Cho did not authorize the release of that information.

This whole scenario is just frustrating, especially for college students like me who could be facing similar dangers and not know it. Respecting a student's privacy is important, but should privacy concerns override safety concerns? I think they should not, but Chesbrough explains why Tech officials did not act. "Due diligence" requirements would seem to mandate that school officials step in to restrain students whose behavior is dangerous. Not acting could open them to lawsuits should something terrible happen. However, if the officials act and nothing happens, they can be sued for violating the student's privacy. I agree with Chesbrough that parents should inform the administration of any pre-existing emotional problems a student has when he or she enters school. Instead of using this information to keep these students from enrolling at the school, administrators can use it to provide the students the help and support they need.

Chesbrough's ideas all seem reasonable, but I do not think they offer a satisfying response to the problem. When balancing the privacy needs of potentially dangerous students against the safety of the entire student body, schools should take greater action to protect the campus. Simply knowing up front which entering students have emotional and psychological problems does not guarantee that the students will seek appropriate treatment on campus. Instead, schools should consider provisional admission for these students—they can stay enrolled on campus as long as they verify that they are getting appropriate treatment. The treatment can remain private, but the administration has to make sure it is taking place. The campus health center could be charged with monitoring the students' treatment, ensuring that they are taking the medicines or receiving the counseling they need. If these students do not keep up with the treatments prescribed by their physician or therapist, they are expelled from school. This solution is not perfect because treatments are not perfect, but it would help ensure that troubled students are receiving help while maintaining their privacy.

Most of the time I do not worry about campus safety. If students take the right precautions on our campus (like never going out alone at night, staying with groups of people, locking doors and windows at night), they can avoid problems. After reading this article though, I am more concerned. How many students on campus have severe emotional or psychological problems? How many of them are getting help so that our school does not become another Virginia Tech?

Summary Chart

HOW TO WRITE A RESPONSE ESSAY

---

1. Carefully read the material.

Your goal is to form a clear understanding of what the writer has to say.

Identify and be able to paraphrase the writer's thesis and main assertions or findings.

2. Reread and annotate the text.

As you reread the material, begin to examine your responses by asking yourself the following questions:
- *How do I react emotionally to what the author has written?*
- *How do the ideas offered in the source text match my experience and my sense of reality?*
- *How do the ideas offered in the text match what others have had to say about the topic?*

Note in the margin your responses to these questions using some combination of the following:
- *key words*
- *questions*
- *statements*
- *punctuation marks*

When you are finished, write out in a few sentences your response to the material.

3. Compose your rough draft.

Introduce the topic, your source text, and the full name of the author or authors.

Summarize the source text.

State and explain your responses clearly and concisely one at a time.
- *State your response. (For example, the material made you angry.)*
- *Explain the terms you are using. (What do you mean by "angry"?)*
- *Tie that response to some aspect of the source text.*

  What material in the reading made you feel that way?
- *Explain how that material gave rise to that response.*

  Why or how did that material make you feel angry?
- *Write your conclusion.*

  What was your overall response to the material?

SUMMARY CHART: HOW TO WRITE A RESPONSE ESSAY *(CONTINUED)*

4. **Revise your rough draft.**

   Review your assertions about your reactions.
   - *Are they honest?*
   - *Are they informed?*
   - *Are they clear?*
   - *Are they well supported?*

   Review your organization.
   - *Are your opening and closing sections constructed well?*
   - *Are you addressing one response at a time?*
   - *Are there clear transitions between the responses you explore?*
   - *Are your responses tied to some guiding thesis?*

   Review your language.
   - *Are you using terms your readers are likely to understand?*
   - *Are you invoking a consistent tone, not becoming too informal, too angry, or too satiric when that does not match the tone of your response as a whole?*

   Review your support.
   - *Have you tied each response to some aspect of the text?*
   - *Have you added enough textual references to make clear the connections between the reading and your response?*
   - *Have you attempted to explain those connections?*

RESPONSE ESSAY REVISION CHECKLIST

	Yes	No
1. In the introductory section of your essay, have you:		
• introduced the topic of the reading?	_____	_____
• included the full and exact title of the reading?	_____	_____
• included the full name of the author?	_____	_____
2. Have you included a thesis statement that captures your overall response to the reading, a response you develop in the body of your essay?	_____	_____
3. Have you considered the accuracy and honesty of the responses you include in your essay?	_____	_____
4. Have you clearly stated each of these responses?	_____	_____
5. Have you explained the terms you used to characterize each of your responses?	_____	_____
6. Have you tied each of your responses to some aspect of the source that gave rise to it?	_____	_____
7. Have you explained how the material in the source text gave rise to your response?	_____	_____
8. Have you developed only one response at a time in each section of your essay?	_____	_____
9. Have you used language that helps your reader understand when you are moving from your discussion of one response to the next?	_____	_____
10. Have you explained the connection between each response you explore and your overall thesis?	_____	_____
11. Have you reviewed the language you use to make sure your word choice is clear and accurate?	_____	_____

Chapter 6

CRITIQUE

In this chapter you will learn how to

1. Identify appropriate evaluative criteria and standards
2. Apply those criteria and standards to evaluate a reading
3. Write an effective critique essay

DEFINITION AND PURPOSE

While response essays focus on your personal reactions to a reading, critiques offer a more formal evaluation. Instead of responding to a reading in light of your experience and feelings, in a critique you evaluate a source text's quality or worth according to a set of established criteria. Based on your evaluation, you then assert some judgment concerning the text—whether the reading was effective, ineffective, valuable, or trivial. Critiques, then, are usually argumentative. Your goal is to convince your readers to accept your judgments concerning the quality of the reading.

These judgments will be based on certain criteria and standards. **Criteria** are certain aspects of a reading that serve as the basis of your assessment—for example, the text's style or use of evidence. **Standards** serve as the basis for evaluating a criterion—what makes a certain "style" good or bad, acceptable or unacceptable? What counts as "valid" evidence in a reading? When you critique a reading, you will employ either **general** academic criteria and standards (those used to evaluate source material in many fields) or **discipline-specific** criteria and standards (those used by scholars in a particular field of study and generally not applicable to material studied in other disciplines).

In college composition courses you may learn how to critique a source text using general evaluative criteria—for example, how to assess the quality of a reading based on its structure, style, or evidence. These criteria can help you evaluate source material in a variety of classes. In your other college courses you may learn discipline-specific evaluative criteria typically used to assess source material in that field of study. For example, in an English literature course you may learn the criteria used by scholars to critique a poem or a play; in an accounting class, you may learn to employ the criteria and standards experts in that discipline use to critique a financial report or prospectus.

Students often find the idea of writing a critique intimidating: they are not sure what the assignment is asking them to do, how to generate material for their paper, what to include in their essay, how to support their assertions, or what tone to assume. However, you are probably more familiar with this type of writing than you realize since you are often exposed to one special form of critique: the movie review. If you ever listened to movie critics argue over a film, you are familiar with the basic structure of a critique. If you ever discussed the strengths and weaknesses of a movie and tried to get a friend to go see it (or to avoid it), then you have already engaged in critique. Examining how a film critic writes a review of a movie can help you understand how to write a critique of a reading.

THE FILM REVIEW AS CRITIQUE

First, consider the nature of a movie critic's job: he watches a film, analyzes and evaluates what he sees, forms some judgment based on that analysis and evaluation, then writes his review, trying to clarify and defend his judgments with specific references to the film and clear explanations of his assertions. In writing his review, the critic does not address every aspect of the film; he addresses only those aspects of the movie that best support his judgment of it. If, for instance, he thought a film was wonderful, he would address in his review only the aspects of the film that, in his opinion, made it exceptional— for example, the direction, the photography, and the acting. If he thought the film was uneven—some parts good, other parts weak—he would offer in his review examples of what made the film effective (maybe the plot or the lighting) and examples of what made it ineffective (maybe the musical score and the special effects).

Think about the way you discuss a film with someone. Maybe the conversation runs something like this:

"So, did you like the movie?"

"Yeah, pretty much. I wasn't too sure about some of the dialogue— sounded pretty lame sometimes—but the special effects were good and the acting was ok."

"The acting was just 'ok'? What didn't you like? I thought the acting was great."

"Well, there was that scene early in the film, right before he shot the guy; I just didn't buy it when he . . ."

In this conversation, one friend asserts a position about the film, is challenged, then begins to defend or explain her view. To convince her friend to accept her judgment, she will likely discuss specific aspects of the film she believes best illustrate her views.

Most of us are accustomed to talking about movies, television shows, or music this way—we form and defend judgments about what we see, hear, and read all the time. However, we are usually more comfortable evaluating movies than we are critiquing arguments, book chapters, or lab reports. First, when it comes to movies, we are probably familiar with many of the source texts—we have seen lots of films—and most of us feel we can knowledgeably discuss what we have seen. We can generate, fairly easily, lots of examples from a movie to support our views. Second, we know *how* to talk about films: we know how to identify and discuss particular aspects of a movie—certain criteria—that influence our judgment. We know that when we analyze a movie we can address the dialogue, the acting, the special effects, and so forth. Finally, we know the standards usually applied to evaluate various aspects of a film; we know what passes for good dialogue, good acting, good special effects, and so on. In short, when we discuss a movie, we know how to *analyze* it (what parts to focus on for review), *evaluate* it (what kinds of questions to ask of each part when assessing its quality), and *defend* our assertions (how to examine specific scenes from the film that support our judgments).

These are the same basic skills you employ to critique readings in college. To critique readings, you need to engage in:

- *Analysis*—break readings down into their essential parts.
- *Evaluation*—assess the quality of those various parts.
- *Explanation*—link your judgments to specific aspects of the readings and make those connections clear and convincing to your reader.

Even though you have probably engaged in this process quite often when discussing movies or television shows, you may have a hard time using these skills to critique readings. First, you are probably less familiar with how critiques look and sound than you are with how movie reviews look and sound. When you are assigned to write a critique, no model may come to mind. Second, the readings you are asked to critique in college can be hard to understand. You cannot critique a reading until you are certain you know what it has to say. Finally, you are probably less familiar with the criteria and standards used in college to analyze and critique readings than you are with the criteria and standards used to review films. When you are asked to critique a philosophical essay on the nature of knowledge, do you know how to break that reading down into its key parts and what kinds of questions to ask of each part to determine its quality? When asked to critique a chapter of your history book, do you know what to look for, what questions to ask? Learning how to critique readings such as these is a central goal of your college education, a skill you will obtain through practice in many different disciplines.

Examining how a movie critic organizes a review can also help you understand how to structure a critique. For example, a critic typically opens her review with a "thesis" that captures her overall assessment of the film. This thesis may take the form of a statement early in the review, a graphic placed beside the review—for example, five stars or two stars—or frequently a comment at the end of the review. Sometimes the critic will love the film; she will give it five stars and a rave review. Sometimes she will hate the movie; she will give it one star and a terrible review. Still other times she will have a split decision; she will give it two and a half stars and in her review acknowledge the strengths and weaknesses of the movie. Next, the critic will typically offer a brief summary of the film so her readers can follow what she has to say in the review. Then, in the body of the review, she will address only the aspects of the film that best illustrate or defend her thesis: she will introduce a particular element of the film (for example, the special effects), comment on its quality (claim they were especially effective), describe a specific example or two from the film (perhaps the climactic battle scene), and explain how that specific example illustrates or supports her judgment (what made the special effects in that battle scene especially good).

Writing a critique involves much the same process. After reading the text, you'll form a judgment of its quality or worth based on some set of criteria and standards. This judgment will form the thesis of your critique, which you will explain or defend in the body of your essay, with specific references to the reading. As you draft your thesis, keep in mind the range of judgments open to the film critic. To critique a reading does not necessarily mean only to criticize it. If you honestly think a reading is weak, based on your evaluation of its various parts, then say so in your thesis. If, however, you think the writing is quite strong, say that. If your judgments fall somewhere in the middle—some parts are strong while others are weak—reflect *that* in your thesis. Your thesis should reflect your carefully considered opinion of the reading's overall quality or worth, whatever that judgment may be.

Next, you will offer a brief summary of the text so your reader can follow what you later have to say about the piece. In the body of your critique, you will choose for examination only the parts of the reading that best illustrate or defend your thesis: you will introduce a particular aspect of the reading (for example, its use of statistical evidence), describe a specific example or two from the reading (perhaps the way statistics are used to support the author's second argument), and explain how that specific example illustrates or supports your judgment (what makes the statistical evidence especially compelling in this section of the text).

Your goal, then, in writing a critique mirrors in many ways the goal you would have in writing a movie review. Your task is to analyze and evaluate a reading according to a set of established criteria and standards, pass judgment on the reading's quality or worth, then assert, explain, and defend that judgment with specific references to the reading.

WRITING A CRITIQUE

Writing a critique typically involves five steps:

1. Read and annotate the text.
2. Analyze and evaluate the piece: break it down into its primary parts and judge the quality of each part.

3. Write your thesis and decide which aspects of the reading you will focus on in your essay.
4. Compose your rough draft.
5. Rewrite your critique.

This is only a general guide. Throughout college you will learn much more specific, specialized ways to critique readings.

STEP 1—CAREFULLY READ AND ANNOTATE THE SOURCE TEXT

Before you start to write a critique, you first need to develop a clear understanding of the reading you are about to analyze and evaluate. The material you read in college is often challenging; you have to work hard to understand exactly what the author is asserting. However, this work is unavoidable; it makes little sense to evaluate a piece of writing when you are not completely sure what point the author is attempting to make. As you annotate a reading for a critique, keep in mind the following suggestions.

Note the Author's Thesis, Primary Assertions, and Primary Means of Support

Be sure that you mark the author's thesis, highlight and summarize each major point the author makes, and highlight and summarize how the author supports each idea, argument, or finding. Are the thesis and primary assertions clearly stated? Does the thesis direct the development of the paper? Are the assertions supported?

Note the Author's Use of Graphics, Headings, and Subheadings

What graphics does the author provide? What is their function? How do the headings and subheadings organize the piece? Are the headings and graphics effective? How so?

Note the Author's Diction and Word Choice

Consider the kind of language the writer is employing. Is it formal or informal? Is it overly technical? Is it appropriate? Do you notice any shifts in diction? Are some sections of the text more complicated or jargon laden than others? Note any strengths or weaknesses you see in the author's language.

Note the Author's Tone

What seems to be the author's attitude toward the topic? Is he being serious, comical, or satiric? Does the tone seem appropriate, given the writer's topic and thesis? Are there any places in the text where the tone shifts? Is the shift effective?

Note the Author's Audience

When you finish the piece, determine what the writer seemed to assume about his readers. For example, is the writer addressing someone who knows something about the topic or someone likely reading about it for the first time? Is the author assuming readers agree or disagree with the position being forwarded in the piece? Judging from the content, organization, diction, and tone of the piece, which type of reader would tend to accept the author's position and which would tend to reject it?

Note the Author's Purpose

Decide, in your own mind, the primary aim of the piece. Is the author attempting to entertain, inform, or persuade readers? Where in the text has the author attempted to achieve this aim? How successful are those attempts? Note at the beginning or end of the reading your comments concerning the author's purpose.

Summarize the Piece

After you have read and studied the text, write a brief summary of the piece, either at the end of the reading or on a separate sheet of paper (see Chapter 4 for tips on summarizing a reading).

When you have finished reading, rereading, and annotating the source text, you should have a clear understanding of its content, organization, purpose, and audience. Try to clear up any questions you have about the reading before you attempt to critique it. You want your critique to be based on a thorough and clear understanding of the source text.

STEP 2—ANALYZE AND EVALUATE THE READING

Think back to the process of putting together a movie review. When a movie critic watches a film, she forms a judgment of its quality based on certain things she sees or hears. As she watches the movie, she will examine and judge certain aspects of the film, including its

acting	scenery	lighting
direction	costuming	plot
special effects	dialogue	action
theme	pacing	makeup
cinematography	stunts	music

Her evaluation of these various elements of the film, either positive or negative, will form her overall judgment of the movie—her thesis.

What, then, should you look for when analyzing a reading? What parts of a text should you be isolating for evaluation as you read and reread the piece? In part, the answer depends on the course you are taking: each discipline has generally agreed-on ways of analyzing a reading. As you take courses in anthropology or physical education, you will learn how experts in those fields analyze readings. However, analyzing certain general aspects of a reading can help you better understand material in a wide variety of classes. Regardless of the course you are taking, you might start to analyze a reading by identifying its

- thesis and primary assertions or findings,
- evidence and reasoning,
- organization, and
- style.

After you have analyzed a reading, isolating for consideration its essential elements, your next task in writing a critique is to evaluate the quality of each element. Here, writing a critique differs from writing a response essay. In a response essay, your goal is to articulate your personal, subjective reaction to what you have read. In a critique, though, you are expected to evaluate the reading according to an established set of standards. Think about the movie critic's job again. Most reviewers employ similar criteria and standards when evaluating a film. If a reviewer decides to critique the musical score of a film, she knows the types of evaluative questions one usually asks about this aspect of a movie: How did the music contribute to the overall mood of the film? Was it too intrusive? Did it add humor or depth to the scenes? Did it heighten drama? Was it noteworthy because of the performers who recorded it? Her answers to these questions will lead to her final assessment of this particular aspect of the film. (Of course, another reviewer employing the same criteria and applying the same standards could come to a different judgment concerning the quality of the music in the film; for example, one reviewer might think it heightened the drama in a particular scene while another might think that it did not.)

In college, you will quickly discover that the criteria and standards used to evaluate readings vary from discipline to discipline. Teachers often employ evaluative criteria unique to their field of study, especially in upper-level courses in which the professor is preparing students to enter a profession. In lower-level courses designed to introduce you to a field of study, you may encounter a different sort of problem. Teachers in different fields may be asking you to employ the same or similar criteria, but their standards are very different. Suppose, for example, you are asked to evaluate the style of a particular reading in both an education and an English course. Your job is the same—determine, stylistically, whether this is a well-written essay. Your answer might be different in each class. According to the stylistic standards advocated by the school of education, you might have before you a well-written essay. According to the standards advocated by the English department, however, the same piece of writing might not fare so well. As always, work closely with your teacher when evaluating a reading to be sure you are applying an appropriate set of criteria and standards.

Following is a series of questions you can ask to begin your analysis and evaluation of a reading's thesis, assertions, evidence, reasoning, organization, and style. The questions are meant to serve only as general guidelines. Your teacher may have much more specific questions he would like you to ask of a reading or evaluative criteria he would like you to employ. Together, analysis and evaluation enable you to critique a reading. After breaking a reading into its essential parts and judging their effectiveness, you will form the thesis of your critique—a judgment of the reading's quality or worth—which you will develop and defend in your essay.

Analyzing and Evaluating a Reading's Thesis and Primary Assertions or Findings

Sometimes identifying an author's thesis can be relatively easy—you can point to a specific sentence or two in the text. Other times, though, an author will not state his thesis. Instead, the thesis is implied: some controlling idea is directing the development of the piece even though the author never puts it into words. If this is the case, you will need to identify and paraphrase this controlling idea yourself and evaluate it as if it were the thesis.

Many times, identifying the author's primary assertions or findings can be easy, too. For example, if the author has made effective use of paragraph breaks, topic sentences, headings, or graphics, you can usually locate his primary assertions fairly easily. However, do not rely on these means alone to identify the author's main ideas. Not every source text is well written. Often, important assertions get buried in an article; key findings may be glossed over. As you analyze a reading, make up your mind about its primary assertions or findings independently of what the author may indicate. Also, be sure to distinguish between primary assertions and their evidence or support. Often a student will identify as a primary argument of a reading some statistic or quotation that the author is using only as a piece of evidence, something to support the actual assertion he is trying to make. In short, to analyze a reading's thesis and primary assertions, consider the following questions:

- What is the author's thesis? Is it stated or unstated? If stated, highlight it; if unstated, paraphrase it.
- What are the primary assertions in the reading? Highlight each one and paraphrase it in the margin of the text.
- What is the primary means of support offered to illustrate or defend each assertion? Again, highlight this material.

In determining the quality of a reading's thesis and primary assertions or findings, you can begin by questioning their clarity, effectiveness, and organization. The thesis, whether stated or implied, should direct the development of the piece. Each major finding or assertion should be clearly stated and linked to that thesis through the effective use of transitions, repetition of key terms, or headings. To evaluate an author's thesis and findings, you might begin by asking the following questions. If your answers are positive, you can likely claim that the author has effectively presented and developed his thesis; if your answers are negative, be sure to articulate exactly where the problems exist.

- Is the thesis clearly stated? Does it control the organization of the piece? Is it consistently held or does the author shift positions in the essay?
- If the thesis is implied rather than stated, does it still serve to direct the organization of the piece? Are you able to paraphrase a comprehensive thesis on your own, or does the material included in the piece preclude that?
- Are the author's assertions or findings clearly stated?
- Are the author's assertions or findings somehow tied to the thesis?

Analyzing and Evaluating a Reading's Evidence and Reasoning

Here you identify two separate, but related, aspects of a reading: (1) the evidence an author provides to support or illustrate her assertions and (2) the author's reasoning process or line of argument.

First, try to identify the types of **evidence** the author uses to support her thesis. (At this point do not try to evaluate the effectiveness of the evidence—that comes later.) The types of evidence used to support a thesis vary greatly in academic writing, so again be cautious when using these guidelines to analyze the readings in any particular course. However, to begin your analysis of the evidence an author employs, you might try asking yourself this series of questions:

- In supporting her assertions or findings, what kinds of evidence has the author employed? Has the author used any of these forms of evidence:

  statistics   empirical data   precedent
  expert testimony   emotional appeals   case histories
  personal experience historical analysis analogies

- Where in the article is each type of evidence employed?
- Is there a pattern? Are certain types of evidence used to support certain types of claims?
- Where has the author combined forms of evidence as a means of support?

Analyzing an author's **reasoning process** is more difficult because it is more abstract. First, you identify how the author uses evidence to support her thesis and how she develops and explains her ideas, her line of reasoning. Second, you examine the assumptions an author makes concerning her topic and readers. As she wrote the piece, which aspects of the text did she decide needed more development than others? Which terms needed clarification? Which argument or explanation needed the most support? In analyzing the author's reasoning process, these are the kinds of questions you might ask:

- In what order are the ideas, arguments, or findings presented?
- What are the logical connections between the major assertions being made in the piece? How does one idea lead to the next?

- What passages in the text explain these connections?
- What assumptions about the topic or the reader is the author making?
- Where in the text are these assumptions articulated, explained, or defended?

Standards used to assess the quality of an author's evidence and reasoning will vary greatly across the disciplines. For example, you might want to determine whether an author offers "adequate" support for his or her thesis. However, what passes for adequate support of a claim will be quite different in an English class from what it will be in a physics course or a statistics course: these fields of study each look at "evidence" and the notion of "adequacy" very differently. In other words, a good general strategy to employ when critiquing a reading is to determine the adequacy of its evidence; however, how that strategy is implemented and what conclusions you reach employing it can vary depending on the course you are taking. Part of learning any subject matter is coming to understand how scholars in that field evaluate evidence; therefore, answer the following questions thoughtfully:

- Does the author support her contentions or findings?
- Is this support adequate? Does the author offer enough evidence to support her contentions?
- Is the evidence authoritative? Does it come from legitimate sources? Is it current?
- Does the author explain *how* the evidence supports or illustrates her assertions?
- Has the author ignored evidence, alternative hypotheses, or alternative explanations for the evidence she offers?
- In developing her position, are there any problems with unstated assumptions? Does the author assume something to be the case that she needs to clarify or defend?
- Are there problems with logical fallacies such as hasty generalizations, false dilemmas, or appeals to false authorities?
- Has the author addressed the ethical implications of her position?
- Is the author's reasoning a notable strength in the piece? Is it clear and convincing?

Your answers to these questions will help you determine whether there are serious problems with the evidence and reasoning employed in the reading.

Analyzing and Evaluating a Reading's Organization

At this point you want to identify how the author orders the material contained in the reading. As the author develops a set of findings or ideas, lays out his reasoning for the reader, and offers examples and explanations, what comes first? Second? Third? How has the author attempted to mold these parts into a coherent whole? When analyzing the organization of a reading, you might begin by considering the following questions:

- In what order are the ideas or findings presented?
- How has the author indicated that he is moving from a discussion of one point to the discussion of another point?
- What is the relationship between the thesis of the piece (stated or unstated) and the order in which the assertions or findings are presented?
- How has the author tried to help the reader understand the organization of the reading? Identify where in the text the author has used any of the following to help guide his readers through the text:

headings and subheadings	repetition of key terms
transition words or phrases	repetition of names or titles
transition paragraphs	repetition of language from the thesis

If any aspect of a reading's organization makes it difficult for you to understand the author's message, you may want to examine it in your critique. Clearly explain the nature of the problem and how it damages the reading's effectiveness. Likewise, if the organization is especially strong—if it significantly enhances the reading's clarity or effectiveness—you can point that out in your critique and explain how it helps the text. Here are some questions to consider when evaluating the source text's organization:

- Is there a clear connection between the major assertions of the essay? Does there seem to be some reason why one idea precedes or follows another?
- Are all the assertions clearly related to the overall thesis of the piece?
- Has the author provided headings or subheadings to help readers follow his line of thought? How effective are they?
- Has the author provided adequate transitions to help readers move through the writing and see the logical connection between the assertions he is making? How effective are they?

Analyzing and Evaluating a Reading's Style

Stylistic analysis is a complicated process—an academic specialty in and of itself within the field of English studies. In most of your college courses, though, when analyzing style you will likely focus on issues of clarity and convention. First, when you critique a reading, you might comment on its clarity. You will want to identify which aspects of the writer's word choice and sentence structure help you understand what she has to say or which serve to complicate your reading of the text. Other times, you may ask a different set of questions concerning style, especially in upper-division courses. Your assignment will be to assess how well an author adheres to the stylistic conventions of a discipline. For example, you might explore whether the author's language, tone, and syntax are appropriate for a particular type of writing or field of study. To begin your analysis of style, here are some questions you might ask about a reading:

- What level of diction is the writer employing (how formal is the prose)?

  formal   conversational
  informal   a mixture

  Identify which words or passages lead you to this conclusion.
- What is the tone of the piece (what is the author's apparent attitude toward the topic)?

  serious   satiric   involved
  humorous   angry   detached

  Identify which words or passages lead you to this conclusion.
- What kind of language is used in the piece? Identify any passages using specialized language, emotional language, or jargon.
- What types of sentences are used in the reading?

  simple, compound, complex, complex-compound
  long or short
  active or passive
  a mixture of types

When critiquing a reading's style, you evaluate elements of the author's prose such as diction, tone, word choice, and syntax. Again, stylistic standards vary greatly across the disciplines. Although teachers in various disciplines may use similar terms when describing "good" style in writing—that it should be clear and concise, for example—how they define their criteria is likely to vary. Clear and concise writing in a chemistry lab report may have little in common, stylistically, with clear and concise writing in a philosophy research report. Below are some questions that might help you begin to evaluate certain aspects of an author's style. Remember, though, that your answers may well depend on the stylistic standards accepted by a particular discipline:

- How would you characterize the diction of the piece: formal, informal, or somewhere in the middle? Is it consistently maintained? Is it appropriate? Does it contribute to the effectiveness of the piece?
- How would you characterize the tone of the piece? Is it inviting, satiric, or humorous? Is it appropriate, given the topic and intent of the piece? Does the tone enhance or damage the effect of the writing?
- Is the author's word choice clear and effective? Or does the writer rely too heavily on jargon, abstractions, or highly technical terms?
- Is the author's word choice needlessly inflammatory or emotional? Or do the words convey appropriate connotations?

- Are the sentences clearly written? Are any of the sentences so poorly structured that the source is difficult to read and understand?
- Are the sentence types varied? Is the syntax appropriate given the audience and intent of the piece?

STEP 3—WRITE YOUR THESIS AND DECIDE WHICH ASPECTS OF THE READING WILL BE THE FOCUS OF YOUR ESSAY

At this point you need to develop your thesis and decide which aspects of the reading you will use to develop your critique. To formulate your thesis, you need to decide which elements of the source text best illustrate or defend your judgment. You want your reader to understand and accept your thesis, but this acceptance can come about only if you clearly explain each claim you make about the reading and offer convincing examples from the text to illustrate and defend your contentions.

In your critique, you do not need to address every aspect of the source text. Remember how the movie critic supports her assertions about a film. No review addresses every aspect of a movie. Instead, the critic chooses to discuss in her review only those elements of the movie she thinks most clearly and effectively illustrate her judgment. Maybe she will address only the acting and direction, perhaps only the dialogue, plot, and special effects. Perhaps she will choose to mention, only briefly, the costuming and musical score, then concentrate more attention on the film's cinematography.

Follow the same line of thinking when you decide which aspects of the reading to address in your critique. To illustrate and defend your thesis, you may choose to look only at the logic of the piece and its structure. However, you may choose to ignore both of these and concentrate, instead, on the writer's style. Maybe you will decide to look briefly at the evidence the author offers, and then concentrate most of your attention on the organization of the piece. Your decisions should be based on two fairly simple questions: (1) Which aspects of the reading most influenced your judgment of its quality and worth? (2) Which aspects will best illustrate and support your thesis? Choose only those aspects of the reading for examination in your critique.

Your thesis in a critique is a brief statement of what you believe to be the overall value or worth of the source text based on your analysis and evaluation of its parts. In stating your thesis, you have several options. You can say only positive things about the reading, only negative things, or some mixture of the two. Your main concern at this point is that your thesis honestly and accurately reflects your judgment.

Also, your thesis statement can be either open or closed. In an open thesis statement, you offer your overall judgment of the piece and nothing else. In a closed thesis statement, you offer your judgment and indicate which aspects of the reading you will examine when developing your essay. Following are some sample open and closed thesis statements for a critique—positive, negative, and mixed.

Positive Thesis Statement

Open

Jones presents a clear, convincing argument in favor of increased funding for the school district.

Closed

Through his use of precise examples and his accessible style, Jones presents a clear and convincing argument in favor of increased funding for the school district.

Negative Thesis Statement

Open

Jones's argument in favor of increased funding is not convincing.

Closed

Due to numerous lapses in reasoning and problems with the organization, Jones's argument in favor of increased funding is not convincing.

Mixed Thesis Statement

Open

Although uneven in its presentation, Jones's argument in favor of increased funding for the school district is, ultimately, convincing.

Closed

Even though there are some problems with the organization Jones employs in his report, his use of expert testimony makes his argument for increased funding for the schools convincing.

STEP 4—WRITE YOUR ROUGH DRAFT

Although there are many ways to structure a critique, the suggestions that follow can serve as a general guide.

Introductory Section

- Introduce the topic of the reading.
- Give the title of the piece and the name of its author.
- Give your thesis.
- Summarize the source text.

In the opening section of your critique, you should introduce the topic of the reading and give your reader its exact title and the full name of its author. You will also include here your thesis and a brief summary of the reading (one or two paragraphs long). The exact order you choose to follow when covering this material is up to you. Some writers like to begin with the summary of the source text before giving the thesis; some prefer to give the thesis first. Overall, though, your introductory section should only be two or three paragraphs long.

Body

- Examine one element of the reading at a time.
- Cite specific examples of this element from the reading.
- Explain your evaluation of each example you offer.

State the Criteria and Your Judgments

In the body of your critique, you will explain and defend the judgment you made in your thesis, focusing on one aspect of the reading at a time. Topic sentences in a critique usually indicate the element of the reading you will be examining in that part of the essay and whether you found it to be a strength or liability—for example, "One of the real strengths of the essay is the author's use of emotional language."

Offer Examples

Whatever aspect of the reading you are examining—logic, word choice, structure—give your readers specific examples from the source text to clarify your terms and demonstrate that your judgment is sound. For example, the student who hopes to prove that the author's use of emotional language is one of the reading's strengths will need to quote several examples of language from the text he believes are emotional. Offering only one example might not be convincing; readers might question whether the student isolated the single occurrence of that element in the text for praise or criticism.

Explain Your Judgments

After you have specified the aspect of the reading you are examining in that part of your critique and have offered your readers examples from the text, you need to explain and defend your judgment. After the student mentioned above cites a few specific examples of the author's emotional language, he will need to explain clearly and convincingly *how* that language strengthens the author's writing. Simply saying it does is not good enough. The student will have to explain how this type of language helps make the author's article clearer or more convincing.

In this section of the critique you will likely develop and explain your unique perspective on the reading. Suppose you and your friend are critiquing the same reading. You could both agree that it is effective and could even choose to focus on the same elements of the reading to defend and illustrate this judgment; for example, you could both choose to focus on the author's use of evidence. The two of you will probably differ, though, in your explanation of how and why the author's use of evidence is strong. You will offer your individual assessments of how the writer effectively employed evidence to support his thesis.

Conclusion

- Wrap up the paper.
- Reassert the thesis.

In your concluding section, try to give your reader a sense of closure. Consider mirroring in your conclusion the strategy you used to open your critique. For example, if you opened your essay with a question, consider closing it by answering that question; if you began with a quotation, end with a quotation; if you opened with a story, finish the story. You might also consider restating your thesis—your overall assessment of the piece—to remind your readers of the judgments you developed in the body of your essay.

STEP 5—REWRITE YOUR CRITIQUE

In rewriting your critique, check to make sure your work is accurate, thorough, organized, and clear.

- *Accurate*—it reflects your true assessment of the source text.
- *Thorough*—you completely explain your assertions.
- *Organized*—readers can easily follow the development of your critique.
- *Clear*—you have explained all the terms you need to explain and supported any assumptions that might reasonably be questioned.

Check for Accuracy

When reviewing your work, first check for accuracy. You want to be sure that your essay reflects your honest assessment of the source text. Starting with your thesis, look through your essay to make sure the assertions you make, the supporting material you employ, and the explanations you offer accurately reflect your point of view.

Check the Development of Your Assertions

Next, make sure you have been thorough in developing your critique. Check to be sure you have offered examples from the source text to support and illustrate your claims and that you have explained your reasoning clearly and completely. Add material—quotations, examples, and explanations—where you think it is needed.

Check the Organization

As you review the organization of your critique, make sure your thesis guides the development of your essay. Are you examining only one aspect of the reading at a time? If not, move material around to improve the organization in your essay. Have you provided adequate transitions to help your reader move through the piece? Do you repeat key terms or provide transition words that remind your reader of your thesis or signal the relationship between the various assertions you make?

Check for Clarity

Check your critique for clarity. Have you used any terms that need to be defined? Have you made any assertions that readers would find unclear? Have you made any assumptions that need to be explained or defended? When necessary, change the content, word choice, or sentence structure of your essay to make your ideas more accessible to your readers.

READINGS

The essay "The Doctrine of Academic Freedom" by Sandra Y. L. Korn was published in *The Harvard Crimson*. Michael LaBrossiere critiques Korn's argument in "Academic Freedom vs. Academic Justice" which appeared on *The Philosopher's Blog*. Following both readings is a sample critique essay that also examines Korn's argument.

The Doctrine of Academic Freedom

Sandra Y. L. Korn

Sandra Y. L. Korn is an editorial writer for The Harvard Crimson.

In July 1971, Harvard psychology professor Richard J. Herrnstein penned an article for *Atlantic Monthly* titled "I.Q." in which he endorsed the theories of UC Berkeley psychologist Arthur Jensen, who had claimed that intelligence is almost entirely hereditary and varies by race. Herrnstein further argued that because intelligence was hereditary, social programs intended to establish a more egalitarian society were futile—he wrote that "social standing [is] based to some extent on inherited differences among people."

When he returned to campus for fall semester 1971, Herrnstein was met by angry student activists. Harvard-Radcliffe Students for a Democratic

Society protested his introductory psychology class with a bullhorn and leaflets. They tied up Herrnstein's lectures with pointed questions about scientific racism. SDS even called for Harvard to fire Herrnstein, along with another of his colleagues, sociologist Christopher Jencks.

Herrnstein told *The Crimson*, "The attacks on me have not bothered me personally. . . . What bothers me is this: Something has happened at Harvard this year that makes it hazardous for a professor to teach certain kinds of views." This, Herrnstein seems not to have understood, was precisely the goal of the SDS activists—they wanted to make the "certain kinds of views" they deemed racist and classist unwelcome on Harvard's campus.

Harvard's deans were also unhappy. They expressed concerns about student activists' "interference with the academic freedom and right to speak of a member of the Harvard faculty." Did SDS activists at Harvard infringe on Herrnstein's academic freedom? The answer might be that yes, they did—but that's not the most important question to ask. Student and faculty obsession with the doctrine of "academic freedom" often seems to bump against something I think much more important: academic justice.

In its oft-cited Statement of Principles on Academic Freedom and Tenure, the American Association of University Professors declares that "Teachers are entitled to full freedom in research and in the publication of the results." In principle, this policy seems sound: It would not do for academics to have their research restricted by the political whims of the moment.

Yet the liberal obsession with "academic freedom" seems a bit misplaced to me. After all, no one ever has "full freedom" in research and publication. Which research proposals receive funding and what papers are accepted for publication are always contingent on political priorities. The words used to articulate a research question can have implications for its outcome. No academic question is ever "free" from political realities. If our university community opposes racism, sexism, and heterosexism, why should we put up with research that counters our goals simply in the name of "academic freedom"?

Instead, I would like to propose a more rigorous standard: one of "academic justice." When an academic community observes research promoting or justifying oppression, it should ensure that this research does not continue.

The power to enforce academic justice comes from students, faculty, and workers organizing together to make our universities look as we want them to do. Two years ago, when former summer school instructor Subramanian Swamy published hateful commentary about Muslims in India, the Harvard community organized to ensure that he would not return to teach on campus. I consider that sort of organizing both appropriate and commendable. Perhaps it should even be applied more broadly. Does Government Professor Harvey Mansfield have the legal right to publish a book in which he claims that "to resist rape a woman needs . . . a certain ladylike modesty?" Probably. Do I think he should do that? No, and I would happily organize with other feminists on campus to stop him from publishing further sexist commentary under the authority of a Harvard faculty position.

"Academic freedom" might permit such an offensive view of rape to be published; academic justice would not.

Over winter break, Harvard published a statement responding to the American Studies Association's resolution to boycott Israeli academic institutions until Israel ends its occupation of Palestine. Much of the conversation around this academic boycott has focused on academic freedom. Opponents of the boycott claim that it restricts the freedom of Israeli academics or interrupts the "free flow of ideas." Proponents of the boycott often argue that the boycott is intended to, in the end, increase, not restrict, academic freedom—the ASA points out that "there is no effective or substantive academic freedom for Palestinian students and scholars under conditions of Israeli occupation."

In this case, discourse about "academic freedom" obscures what should fundamentally be a political argument. Those defending the academic boycott should use a more rigorous standard. The ASA, like three other academic associations, decided to boycott out of a sense of social justice, responding to a call by Palestinian civil society organizations for boycotts, divestment, and sanctions until Israel ends its occupation of Palestine. People on the right opposed to boycotts can play the "freedom" game, calling for economic freedom to buy any product or academic freedom to associate with any institution. Only those who care about justice can take the moral upper hand.

It is tempting to decry frustrating restrictions on academic research as violations of academic freedom. Yet I would encourage student and worker organizers to instead use a framework of justice. After all, if we give up our obsessive reliance on the doctrine of academic freedom, we can consider more thoughtfully what is just.

Academic Freedom vs. Academic Justice

Michael LaBossiere

Michael LaBossiere is a philosophy professor at Florida A&M University.

Sandra Y. L. Korn has proposed dispensing with academic freedom in favor of academic justice. Korn begins by presenting the example of Harvard psychology Professor Richard Herrnstein's 1971 article for *Atlantic Monthly*.

In this article, Herrnstein endorsed the view that intelligence is primarily hereditary and linked to race. Herrnstein was attacked for this view, but defended himself and was defended by others via appeals to academic freedom. Korn seems to agree with Herrnstein that the attacks against him infringed on academic freedom. However, Korn proposes that academic justice is more important than academic freedom.

Korn makes use of the American Association of University Professors view of academic freedom: "Teachers are entitled to full freedom in research and in the publication of the results." However, Korn regards the "liberal obsession" with this freedom as misplaced.

Korn's first argument seems to be as follows. Korn notes that there is not "full freedom" in research and publication. As Korn correctly notes, which proposals get funded and which papers get published is largely a matter of academic politics. Korn then notes that no academic question is free from the realities of politics. From this, Korn draws a conditional conclusion: "If our university community opposes racism, sexism, and heterosexism, why should we put up with research that counters our goals simply in the name of 'academic freedom'?"

It might be suspected that there is a false dilemma lurking here: either there is full academic freedom or restricting it on political values is acceptable. There is not full academic freedom. Therefore restricting it on political values is acceptable. The reason why this would be a false dilemma is that there is a considerable range of options between full academic freedom (which seems to be complete freedom) and such restrictions. As such, one could accept the obvious truth that there is not full (complete) freedom while also legitimately rejecting that academic freedom should be restricted on the proposed grounds.

To use the obvious analogy to general freedom of expression, the fact that people do not possess full freedom of expression (after all, there are limits on expression) does not entail that politically based restrictions should thus be accepted. After all, there are many alternatives between full freedom and the specific restrictions being proposed.

To be fair to Korn, no such false dilemma might exist. Instead, Korn might be reasoning that because the reality is such that political values restrict academic expression it follows that adding additional restrictions is not problematic. To re-use the analogy to general free expression, the reasoning would [be] that since there are already limits on free expression, more restrictions are acceptable. This could be seen as a common practice fallacy, but perhaps it could be justified by showing that the additional restrictions are warranted. Sorting this out requires considering what Korn is proposing.

In place of the academic freedom standard, Korn proposes "a more rigorous standard: one of 'academic justice.' When an academic community observes research promoting or justifying oppression, it should ensure that this research does not continue."

While Korn claims that this is a more rigorous standard, it merely seems to be more restrictive. There is also the rather obvious problem of presenting an account of what it is for research to promote or justify oppression in a way that is rigorous and, more importantly, accurate. After all, "oppression" gets thrown around with some abandon in academic contexts and can be a rather vague notion. In order to decide what is allowed and what is not, Korn proposes that students, faculty and workers should organize in order to "to make our universities look as we want them to do." While that sounds somewhat democratic, there is still the rather important concern about what standards will be used.

While there are paradigm cases (like the institutionalized racism of pre-civil rights America), people do use the term "oppression" to refer to what merely offends them. In fact, Korn makes reference to the offensiveness of a person's comment as grounds for removing a professor from a faculty position.

The obvious danger is that the vagueness of this principle could be used to suppress and oppress research that vocal or influential people find offensive. There is also the obvious concern that such a principle would yield a political hammer with which to beat down those who present dissenting or unpopular views. For example, suppose a researcher finds legitimate evidence that sexual orientation is strongly influenced by choice and is accused of engaging research that promotes oppression because her research runs counter to an accepted view among certain people. As another example, imagine a faculty member who holds conservative views that some might find offensive, such as the view that people should work for their government support. This person could be seen as promoting oppression of the poor and thus be justly restricted by this principle.

Interestingly, Korn does present an example of a case in which a Harvard faculty member was asked not to return on the basis of objections against remarks that had been made. This would seem to indicate that Korn's proposal might not be needed. After all, if academic freedom does not provide protection against being removed or restricted on these grounds, then there would seem to be little or no need to put in place a new principle. To use an analogy, if people can already be silenced for offensive speech, there is no need to restrict freedom of speech with a new principle—it is already restricted. At least at Harvard.

In closing, I am certainly in favor of justice and even more in favor of what is morally good. As such, I do endorse holding people morally accountable for their actions and statements. However, I do oppose restrictions on academic freedom for the same reason I oppose restrictions on the general freedom of expression (which I have written about elsewhere). In the case of academic freedom, what should matter is whether the research is properly conducted and whether or not the claims are well-supported. To explicitly adopt a principle for deciding what is allowed and what is not based on ideological views would, as history shows, have a chilling effect on research and academics. While the academic system is far from perfect, flawed research and false claims do get sorted out—at least fairly often. Adding in a political test would not seem to help with reaching the goal of truth.

As far as when academic freedom should be restricted, I also go with my general view of freedom of expression: when an action creates enough actual harm to warrant limiting the freedom. So, merely offending people is not enough to warrant restrictions—even if people are very offended. Actually threatening people or engaging in falsification of research results would be rather different matters and obviously not protected by academic freedom.

As such, I am opposed to Korn's modest proposal to impose more political restrictions on academic freedom. As Korn notes, there are already many restrictions in place—and there seem to be no compelling reasons to add more.

SAMPLE CRITIQUE

AN UNCONVINCING ARGUMENT CONCERNING ACADEMIC FREEDOM

Academic freedom is a cornerstone of American higher education. Under the protection of academic freedom, faculty are free to conduct their research and publish their results without fear of retaliation from the college or university even if the topics they investigate are controversial. In a recent article published in *The Harvard Crimson*, student and editorial writer Sandra Korn argues that academic freedom should be abolished in favor of "academic justice." Under a policy of academic justice, colleges and universities could fire or otherwise punish faculty who conduct research concerning topics the institution, its students, or its other faculty deem inappropriate, immoral, or counter to the stated school's stated goals. Korn's argument, though interesting and provocative, is unconvincing due to numerous flaws in her reasoning.

One of the ways Korn supports her argument is by citing precedent. In 2012, Subramanian Swamy, an economics professor who taught summer courses at Harvard, published what Korn describes as "hateful commentary about Muslims in India" (128). Harvard did not rehire him. For Korn, disciplining Swamy demonstrated "the power to enforce academic justice" (128). She states that the same standard ought to have been applied in 1971 when a Harvard psychologist, Richard Herrnstein, published an essay in support of research on intelligence and heredity that Korn asserts was racist. It should also be applied today to discipline a Harvard government professor, Harvey Mansfield, whose recent book contained comments about rape that Korn characterizes as sexist. Korn argues that "'Academic freedom' might permit such an offensive view of rape to be published; academic justice would not" (129).

Korn implies that the same standard used to punish Swamy ought to apply to faculty like Herrnstein and Mansfield. Korn's argument by precedent is unconvincing. First, she fails to establish that the actions taken again Swamy were fair and just, which is crucial since she presenting an argument in favor of academic "justice." She assumes that Harvard took the correct action in not rehiring Swamy, but does not present any support for or explanation of that assertion. She simply assumes that the justice of Harvard's action is self-evident. However, without establishing that Harvard acted properly and justly with Swamy, no precedent is set to serve as a basis for claiming that Jensen and Mansfield ought to have been dealt with similarly. It could be that in not rehiring Swamy, Harvard acted unjustly, in violation of academic freedom, and does not want to repeat that mistake.

Korn also argues that academic freedom can be curtailed for political reasons because academic freedom is never absolute and academic work is always political in nature. In Korn's view, "no one ever has 'full freedom' in research and publication. Which research proposals receive funding and what papers are accepted for publication are always contingent on political priorities" (128). In other words, research funding and publication are always political decisions. If this is true, then political criteria are used to make these decisions, and adding "academic justice" as one of those criteria is not a significant change. Also for Korn, "no academic question is ever 'free' from political realities" (128). That is, the criteria of academic justice applies not just to what research gets funded and published but also which research questions ought to be asked.

Korn's reasoning in this argument is not convincing. Decisions about what research might get funded or published could involve politics, but may not be exclusively or predominately political. Other factors may come into play (lack of funds, for example, or fundamental problems with the research methodology or writing). To reduce all issues to politics oversimplifies reality. Korn's assertion that all academic questions are political is tenuous as well. They may, in part, be political, but that does not mean they are exclusively political or that political concerns ought to determine what academic questions are asked. That gives far too much power to one, possible inconsequential, motivation for asking the question. Korn privileges politics to support her argument. If politics rules all academic questions, research, and publication, the pursuit of knowledge at the heart of higher education would be stifled. In fact, Korn contradicts her own argument in the piece. She acknowledges, "It would not do for academics to have their research restricted by the political whims of the moment" (128). Yet this is exactly what would result under Korn's proposal to prioritize political considerations in the name of academic justice.

In fact, the very term "academic justice" poses a major problem for Korn's argument. She asserts that this standard should replace "academic freedom" in higher education, but she does not define what she means by "justice" or indicate who would decide whether particular research questions or publications are just. A few defining criteria are offered: research should be stopped that is oppressive (128), "racist" (128), or "sexist" (128), yet Korn assumes that these terms are not in dispute. Do students or faculty at a university decide? How many students or faculty are must deem a research project "oppressive" for it to be censored? Which students or faculty? If research projects are permitted one year at a university then stopped the next because the student population changes or faculty changed their minds, all research would cease. No faculty would commit to a project that might get him or her fired if someone at some time at the institution deemed it unjust. These questions do no not come into play when research is protected under academic freedom.

Academic freedom does not protect faculty or students at a university from being offended by someone's research. Yet, such offense can be the justifying reason for some research to take place: challenging accepted wisdom, pushing against political constraints, or asking uncomfortable questions is essential to knowledge making mission of a university. Korn states that shifting to a standard of academic justice may result in "frustrating restrictions" (129) for some researchers, but the consequences would be much more serious. In her essay, Korn does not present a convincing argument to abandon academic freedom at universities for academic justice—an ill-defined, ill-conceived restriction on the pursuit of knowledge.

Summary Chart

HOW TO WRITE A CRITIQUE

1. **Carefully read and annotate the source text.**
   - *Read and reread the text.*
   - *Identify the author's intent, thesis, and primary assertions or findings.*
   - *Write an informal summary of the piece.*

2. **Analyze and evaluate the reading, breaking it down into its parts and judging the quality of each element.**

   Identify and evaluate the author's logic and reasoning.
   - *Is the thesis clearly stated, and does it direct the development of the text?*
   - *Are the author's primary assertions reasonable and clearly tied to the thesis?*
   - *Are there problems with logical fallacies?*
   - *Are the author's positions or findings logically presented?*

   Identify and evaluate the text's evidence.
   - *Does the author support his or her assertions or findings?*
   - *Is the support offered adequate to convince readers?*
   - *Is the evidence authoritative?*
   - *Is the evidence current?*
   - *Does the author explain how the evidence supports his or her assertions or findings?*
   - *Has the author ignored evidence or alternative hypotheses?*

   Identify and evaluate the text's organization.
   - *Is there a clear connection between the assertions developed in the essay?*
   - *Are the assertions or findings tied to a guiding thesis?*
   - *Does there seem to be a reason for one assertion following another, or do they seem randomly organized?*

   Identify and evaluate the text's style.
   - *Is the author's diction consistently maintained?*
   - *Is the author's word choice clear and effective?*
   - *Is the author's tone consistent and effective?*
   - *Are the author's sentences clear?*

SUMMARY CHART: HOW TO WRITE A CRITIQUE *(CONTINUED)*

3. **Formulate your thesis and choose the criteria you will include in your essay.**
   - *Draft a thesis, a brief statement concerning the overall value or worth of the source text.*
   - *Choose which elements of the reading you will focus on in your critique.*

4. **Write your rough draft.**
   - *Introduce the topic, source text, and your thesis.*
   - *Establish your evaluative criteria and your judgments of them.*
   - *Offer examples to substantiate each of your criteria and judgments.*
   - *Explain your judgments, clarifying how the examples you provide support your assertions.*

5. **Rewrite your critique.**

   Check to make sure your writing is accurate.
   - *Does your writing honestly reflect your judgment?*
   - *Does your writing misrepresent the author?*

   Check to make sure your writing is thorough.
   - *Do you cover all the aspects of the source text you need to cover?*
   - *Do you clearly and thoroughly explain and support your assertions?*

   Check to make sure your writing is organized.
   - *Does your thesis statement guide the development of your essay?*
   - *Have you provided transitional devices to help lead your reader through your work?*

   Check to make sure your writing is clear.
   - *Is your terminology clear?*
   - *Are your sentences clear?*
   - *Are your examples and explanations clear?*

CRITIQUE REVISION CHECKLIST

	Yes	No
1. Have you included the title of the reading and the author's name in your introduction?	_____	_____
2. Does your thesis make clear your overall assessment of the reading?	_____	_____
3. Toward the beginning of your critique, have you provided a brief summary of the reading?	_____	_____
4. In the body of your critique, do you examine only one element of the reading at a time?	_____	_____
5. Do you clearly state a judgment concerning each element of the reading you explore?	_____	_____
6. Do you provide examples from the reading to support and illustrate your judgment of each element you examine?	_____	_____
7. Do you clearly and thoroughly explain your judgments concerning each example you provide from the reading?	_____	_____
8. Have you employed proper evaluative criteria and standards?	_____	_____
9. Have you provided clear transitions between the major sections of your paper?	_____	_____
10. Is there a clear relationship between each section of your paper and your thesis?	_____	_____
11. Have you provided proper documentation for all quoted, paraphrased, and summarized material?	_____	_____
12. Have you revised your paper for accuracy? In other words, does the final draft reflect your honest appraisal of the reading?	_____	_____

CRITIQUE REVISION CHECKLIST *(CONTINUED)*

	Yes	No
13. Have you reviewed the language in your paper to make sure your words adequately capture and communicate your judgments?	_____	_____
14. As you review your work, do your judgments still stand? Do you need to change your thesis or any part of your paper?	_____	_____

Chapter 7

....

RHETORICAL ANALYSIS OF WRITTEN TEXTS

In this chapter you will learn how to

1. Identify a reading's rhetorical situation

2. Identify a reading's core rhetorical strategies

3. Evaluate a reading in terms of its rhetorical situation and rhetorical strategies

4. Compose an effective rhetorical analysis of a written text

DEFINITION AND PURPOSE

A rhetorical analysis essay is a special form of critique (see Chapter 6). In a critique essay, you determine a source text's overall value or worth by critically examining a set of relevant criteria; in a rhetorical analysis essay, you determine a source text's rhetorical effectiveness by examining how the author employs language and/or visual images to achieve a particular effect on an audience. This chapter addresses how to compose a rhetorical analysis of a written text; the following chapter offers instruction on how to compose a rhetorical analysis of a visual text.

Writing a rhetorical analysis of a reading requires you to answer three related questions:

- What response is the author of the reading trying to elicit from his or her readers?
- How does the author employ language to elicit that response?
- How well does the author succeed in achieving this response?

Composing a rhetorical analysis requires you to examine a source text from the perspective of both a reader and a writer, assessing how well an author achieves certain rhetorical goals in a text.

Rhetorical analysis of print texts is based on certain assumptions about how writers write and the way writing works. First is the assumption that writing is purposeful, that every text is written by someone who directs it toward some audience to achieve some purpose. To accomplish their ends, writers make a series of strategic choices—they choose this approach to the topic instead of that approach, this set of arguments rather than that set of arguments, this evidence instead of that evidence, this thesis rather than that one, this organizational plan in place of another, this word rather than that word. In a rhetorical analysis essay, you critically examine this series of choices, identifying and critiquing the strategies a writer employs to achieve his or her rhetorical goals.

A second assumption is that text and context are intimately connected, that text is fundamentally influenced by the context in which it is written. Writers work within a set of givens, a rhetorical context or situation that includes their reasons for writing the text, their purpose or aim, their audience's needs or interests, and their knowledge of the topic they are addressing. To be effective, writers must adapt their writing to meet the needs of the given rhetorical situation. If they ignore or misconstrue any element of the rhetorical situation, their writing will be less effective than it might otherwise be. Because writers typically want to produce the most effective text possible, they take particular efforts to ensure that their language suits the text's audience, purpose, message, and occasion. Therefore, to evaluate a text's rhetorical effectiveness, you must understand the context in which it was written.

A final assumption is that no rhetorical analysis is definitive. Readers often disagree about a text's purpose, intended audience, rhetorical strategies, and effectiveness. Because readers always bring their own knowledge, experiences, sensitivities, and biases to a text, they will form unique, individualized responses to even the most fundamental questions concerning how a reading communicates its meaning. Consequently, when you write a rhetorical analysis essay, you must explain your conclusions as clearly as you can, supporting them with thorough explanations and specific references to the source text.

THE RHETORICAL SITUATION

When you compose a rhetorical analysis essay of a written text, you must examine how an author uses language to achieve a particular response from readers. However, your task is a little more complicated than it might appear at first. You will actually be examining how an author uses language to achieve a particular response from readers *given the specific context in which the writer produced the text*. This "specific context" is called the text's **rhetorical situation**, which includes the author's audience, subject matter, purpose, and occasion for writing. In your paper, you will assess how the writer manipulates language to meet the needs of the rhetorical situation and achieve his or her goals for the text.

A brief example may help explain why understanding the rhetorical situation of a source text is essential to composing an effective rhetorical analysis essay. Suppose your source text is a set of instructions for installing a new hard drive on a computer. Your task is to evaluate how well the instructions achieve their intended purpose. The first thing you notice is that the instructions are full of undefined technical terms—IDE cables, jumper selectors, drive rails, boot drives. Are the instructions effective? Upon consideration, you would have to conclude that the answer is, "It depends." If the instructions are written for someone who is already well versed in computer technology, they may be fine; if they are written for a novice computer owner, they may not be so effective. Composing an effective rhetorical analysis of the instructions requires that you evaluate the writing in light of its purpose and intended audience, two crucial elements of the text's rhetorical situation.

Because understanding a text's rhetorical situation is so fundamental to writing this type of essay, it is worthwhile to examine each element in isolation. The following section contains definitions of various elements of a text's rhetorical situation and a series of questions writers frequently ask of each element as they prepare to write a rhetorical analysis essay.

ELEMENTS OF THE RHETORICAL SITUATION

Author—the person or people who wrote the text

- Who wrote the piece?
- What is the author's background in terms of race, sex, education, political affiliation, economic status, or religion?
- What are the author's possible or likely biases?
- What perspective does the author bring to the topic?
- How does the author "sound" on the page—angry, detached, confused, funny?
- What has the author written about the topic in the past?

Topic—what the text is about

- What is the person writing about?
- Is the author addressing a particular aspect of the topic or the topic as a whole?
- Which aspects of the topic receive the most attention and which receive the least?
- What, exactly, is the author stating about the topic?
- What have others said about this subject matter?
- What is the relationship between what others have written about the topic and what the author is writing about it?

Audience—whom the writer is addressing

- To whom is the text addressed?
- If the text is not written to a specific person or group of people, what kind of reader did the author seem to have in mind when writing the piece? For example, does the author seem to be assuming he or she is

addressing a friendly audience or a hostile audience? An expert audience or a novice audience? An academic audience or a popular audience?

- What is the audience's likely knowledge of or attitude toward the author and/or subject matter?
- What assumptions does the author make about the audience? Are these assumptions accurate?

Purpose or Aim—what the author is trying to accomplish in writing the text

- If the author states a purpose or aim for the piece, what is it? To inform, persuade, entertain, educate, provoke to action, draw attention, ridicule, shock?
- If it is not stated, what is the author's implied purpose or aim for the text?
- Is there more than one purpose or aim for the text? If so, what are they? Does one purpose seem more dominant than the others? Which one?
- How does the author's purpose influence the text's content, structure, or language?

Occasion—what prompted the writer to write the piece

- Why did the author feel compelled to write this text?
- What is the historical context of the piece?
- Is the author adding to a debate over a particular political issue or social question? Is the author responding to another writer or text? Is the author responding to a particular historical event or cultural phenomenon?

Writing a rhetorical analysis essay usually requires you to examine the complex interrelationships that exist among these elements. For example, how does the author's audience influence what she writes about the topic or the language she employs? What is the relationship between a text's purpose and the time or place it was written? How effective is the author in producing a text that is appropriate for both the audience and the occasion?

RHETORICAL STRATEGIES

After you understand the text's rhetorical situation, you are ready to turn your analysis to the author's rhetorical strategies—the way the author manipulates the text's content, structure, or style to achieve his or her aim. **Content** concerns the material an author includes in the text, **structure** concerns the order in which the author presents that material, and **style** concerns the language and sentence structure an author uses to convey that material. A rhetorical analysis essay is unlikely to address every aspect of a text's content, structure, or style. In fact, it may address just one or two of the author's rhetorical strategies.

As the person writing the analysis, you will determine which strategies you wish to examine. They will likely be the ones that you think are most essential to the author achieving his or her aim.

CONTENT

When composing a rhetorical analysis essay, most writers analyze a text's content in one or two related ways: by examining its arguments, evidence, and reasoning or by examining its persuasive appeals. Because both approaches are closely related, writers will often examine aspects of each in their essays. Both are discussed here.

Arguments, Evidence, and Reasoning

When analyzing a text's rhetorical strategies in terms of its arguments, evidence, and reasoning, you are primarily concerned with examining the claims or assertions a writer makes, the way that writer supports those claims, and the way he or she explains them. You need to ask yourself, given the text's rhetorical situation, why the writer would choose those particular arguments. Are they the best arguments for the writer to make? Why did the writer choose to support those claims the way he or she did? Again, was this the best choice of evidence? How effective were the writer's decisions? Does the writer explain his or her reasoning in the piece, exploring or defending the link between his or her claims and supporting evidence? Are there certain assumptions or leaps of reasoning the writer leaves unstated? Why might the writer have made that choice? Was it a good decision? Following are some questions that can help you analyze and evaluate a text's rhetorical strategies in terms of its arguments, evidence, and reasoning.

Arguments or Assertions

- What arguments or assertions does the author make and how are they related to the rhetorical situation?
- How does the audience, purpose, and occasion of the text influence the author's arguments or assertions?
- Given the audience and purpose of the text, are these the most effective arguments? If so, what makes them effective? If not, why not? What arguments might be more effective?
- What arguments or assertions are emphasized the most? Why did the author decide to emphasize those assertions instead of others?
- What relevant arguments or assertions are ignored or slighted? Why do you think the author chose not to address them?
- How might the intended audience respond to the arguments offered? How well does the author seem to anticipate and perhaps address these likely responses?

Evidence or Examples

- How does the author support his or her assertions? Are they supported by primary or secondary research? By personal experience? By statistics or expert testimony?
- What is the source of the author's evidence for each assertion or argument? Are they particularly effective sources, given the text's rhetorical situation?
- Is the evidence offered appropriate, given the text's rhetorical situation? Does the evidence offered effectively support each claim?
- How might the intended audience respond to the evidence or examples offered? How well does the author seem to anticipate and perhaps address these likely responses?
- Is the presentation balanced or one-sided? In either case, is that choice appropriate given the rhetorical situation?
- How does the author address possible counterarguments or evidence that does not support his or her assertions?
- Are there obvious arguments the author chooses to ignore or gloss over? What are the effects of these omissions? How might they be explained, given the text's rhetorical situation?

Reasoning

- Does the author present a clear and cogent line of reasoning in the text?
- How well does the author move from one assertion to the next?
- How compelling is the connection the author makes among assertions? Between assertions and their supporting evidence?
- Does the text lead logically and convincingly to its conclusion?
- Are there clear connections between the text's thesis and its primary assertions?
- Are there any important assumptions that the author leaves unstated? Does leaving them unstated and undefended make the text any less successful?
- Is the reasoning fair and balanced? Should it be, given the text's rhetorical situation?
- Are there any logical fallacies or flaws in reasoning that might hinder the text's effectiveness, given its audience, purpose, and occasion?

Persuasive Appeals

Another set of strategies authors often employ to achieve their rhetorical goals involves appealing to their readers' rationality (logos) or emotions (pathos) or establishing their own credibility as an authority on the topic (ethos). Though one of the three appeals may dominate a particular reading, most effective persuasive texts use elements of all three. In brief, when authors try to persuade readers by presenting a reasonable series of arguments supported by evidence and examples, they are relying on **logos** to achieve their goal; when they try to persuade readers through emotional language or examples or by appealing to the reader's needs or interests, they are relying on **pathos**; when they try to persuade readers by appearing fair, balanced, and informed or by establishing their own credibility and authority on the subject, they are relying on **ethos**. Below are some questions you can ask about a text's persuasive appeals if you are analyzing its rhetorical effectiveness.

Logos

- How reasonable and appropriate are the author's claims, given the rhetorical situation?
- How clear are the author's claims?
- Are the author's claims broad and sweeping or does the author limit or qualify them?
- How well does the author use facts, statistics, and expert testimony to support his or her claims?
- Are the author's claims adequately explained?
- Does the author avoid lapses in reasoning or logical fallacies?
- Does the author address opposing or alternative viewpoints?
- Are there relevant claims the author fails to address?
- Are the author's claims convincing?

Pathos

- Does the author attempt to convince his or her readers through appeals to their emotions?
- To which emotions is the author appealing? To the readers' personal fears or concerns? To the readers' economic or social self-interests? To the readers' desires for acceptance, love, or beauty? To the readers' sense of justice or social responsibility?
- Does the author appeal to his readers' emotions through his choice of arguments, evidence, language, or some combination of the three?
- How are appeals to emotion balanced with other appeals in the text?
- Does the author try too hard to appeal to readers' emotions? Are the appeals to emotion too clumsy or awkward to be effective?
- Is an appeal to the readers' emotions an effective strategy to employ given the rhetorical situation?

Ethos

- How does the author attempt to establish her credibility or authority?
- What level of expertise does the author demonstrate when writing about the topic of her text?
- Does the author's own experience or expertise lend credibility to the text?
- Does the author demonstrate or document the validity of the source texts used to support her assertions?

- Does the author present a balanced or a one-sided argument? Is that approach appropriate, given the rhetorical situation?
- Does the author demonstrate a sufficient understanding of the topic's complex or controversial nature?
- Does the text's tone or the author's voice contribute to or detract from her credibility?

STRUCTURE

Although many rhetorical strategies are related to a text's content, others involve its structure. After writers decide what information or arguments they will include in their essays, they need to decide the order in which to present them. Structure also involves the way a writer introduces and concludes a text and draws connections among parts of the text. Following are some questions you can ask about a text's structure as you evaluate its rhetorical effectiveness.

- In what order does the author present information or claims?
- What purpose might lie behind this order?
- How might the text's structure influence an audience's response to the author's ideas, findings, or assertions?
- Does the text present a clear and consistent line of reasoning?
- Are there clear connections between the text's stated or implied thesis and its topic sentences?
- Does the text's structure enhance its appeal to logic? Does the author draw clear, logical connections among the text's ideas, findings, or assertions?
- Does the structure of the piece enhance its appeal to emotion, particularly in its introduction or conclusion?
- Does the structure of the piece enhance its appeal to credibility? Does the author seem in control of the writing? Does the text hold together as a whole? Are there any obvious flaws in structure that might damage the author's credibility?

STYLE

Finally, when analyzing an author's rhetorical strategies, consider his or her style. Among other elements of writing, style concerns the text's sentence structure, word choice, punctuation, voice, tone, and diction. Here are some questions that can help you assess how style contributes to a text's rhetorical effectiveness:

- What type of syntax does the author employ? How does the author vary sentence length (long or short) and sentence type (simple, compound, complex, and compound-complex; cumulative, periodic, and balanced)? How is syntax related to the audience, purpose, or occasion of the text?
- What types of figurative language does the author employ (for example, metaphors, similes, or analogies)? Are the choices of figurative language appropriate and effective given the text's rhetorical situation?

- What types of allusions does the author employ? Are they appropriate and effective?
- How appropriate and effective is the author's voice, given the text's rhetorical situation?
- How appropriate and effective is the author's tone, given the text's rhetorical situation?
- How appropriate and effective is the author's diction, given the text's rhetorical situation?

ANALYZING A TEXT'S RHETORICAL STRATEGIES—AN EXAMPLE

To better understand how to analyze a text's rhetorical strategies in terms of its content, structure, and style, carefully read the following speech, Abraham Lincoln's Second Inaugural Address. Lincoln delivered this speech on March 4, 1865, in Washington, D.C. Though the Civil War was not yet over, the struggle had turned in the Union's favor, and the end of the conflict was in sight. In this address, Lincoln acknowledges the price the nation has paid for the war and argues that lasting peace and reconciliation will come only through mercy and forgiveness. Many historians and rhetoricians consider this Lincoln's greatest speech.

Lincoln's Second Inaugural Address

Fellow-Countrymen:

At this second appearing to take the oath of the Presidential office there is less occasion for an extended address than there was at the first. Then a statement somewhat in detail of a course to be pursued seemed fitting and proper. Now, at the expiration of four years, during which public declarations have been constantly called forth on every point and phase of the great contest which still absorbs the attention and engrosses the energies of the nation, little that is new could be presented. The progress of our arms, upon which all else chiefly depends, is as well known to the public as to myself, and it is, I trust, reasonably satisfactory and encouraging to all. With high hope for the future, no prediction in regard to it is ventured.

On the occasion corresponding to this four years ago all thoughts were anxiously directed to an impending civil war. All dreaded it, all sought to avert it. While the inaugural address was being delivered from this place, devoted altogether to *saving* the Union without war, urgent agents were in the city seeking to *destroy* it without war; seeking to dissolve the Union and divide effects by negotiation. Both parties deprecated war, but one of them would *make* war rather than let the nation survive, and the other would *accept* war rather than let it perish, and the war came.

One-eighth of the whole population were colored slaves, not distributed generally over the Union, but localized in the southern part of it. These slaves constituted a peculiar and powerful interest. All knew that this interest was somehow the cause of the war. To strengthen, perpetuate, and extend this interest was the object for which the insurgents would rend the Union even by war, while the Government claimed no right to do more than to restrict the territorial enlargement of it. Neither party expected for the war the magnitude or the duration which it has already attained. Neither anticipated that the *cause* of the conflict might cease with or even before the conflict itself should cease. Each looked for an easier triumph, and a result less fundamental and astounding. Both read the same Bible and pray to the same God, and each invokes His aid against the other. It may seem strange that any men should dare to ask a just God's assistance in wringing their bread from the sweat of other men's faces, but let us judge not, that we be not judged. The prayers of both could not be answered. That of neither has been answered fully. The Almighty has His own purposes. "Woe unto the world because of offenses; for it must needs be that offenses come, but woe to that man by whom the offense cometh." If we shall suppose that American slavery is one of those offenses which, in the providence of God, must needs come, but which, having continued through His appointed time, He now wills to remove, and that He gives to both North and South this terrible war as the woe due to those by whom the offense came, shall we discern therein any departure from those divine attributes which the believers in a living God always ascribe to Him? Fondly do we hope, fervently do we pray, that this mighty scourge of war may speedily pass away. Yet, if God wills that it continue until all the wealth piled by the bondsman's two hundred and fifty years of unrequited toil shall be sunk, and until every drop of blood drawn with the lash shall be paid by another drawn with the sword, as was said three thousand years ago, so still it must be said "the judgments of the Lord are true and righteous altogether."

With malice toward none, with charity for all, with firmness in the right as God gives us to see the right, let us strive on to finish the work we are in, to bind up the nation's wounds, to care for him who shall have borne the battle and for his widow and his orphan, to do all which may achieve and cherish a just and lasting peace among ourselves and with all nations.

A RHETORICAL ANALYSIS OF LINCOLN'S SPEECH

In terms of the speech's content, notice how Lincoln makes several related arguments designed to persuade his audience that after the Civil War ends, the North must treat the South with charity and compassion. He opens his address by asserting that he will not detail the current state of the conflict—clearly everyone in the nation has been and continues to be consumed by the war. Next, Lincoln asserts that the primary cause of the war was slavery. Four years earlier, the Union sought to halt the spread of slavery peacefully. However, the Confederacy, he asserts, would not accept this position and turned to armed conflict instead. Neither side, though, anticipated the duration and ferocity of the war. Although both sides in the conflict call on God for victory, Lincoln questions whether any divine power would support the perpetuation of slavery. Interestingly, he sees *both* sides in the war being chastised for their involvement with slavery and hopes that the suffering all are undergoing can purge their collective guilt and set the stage for a more just nation. Lincoln closes his speech by asserting that reconciliation will only succeed if it is based on mercy, forgiveness, and justice, not revenge and recrimination.

Both Lincoln's position as president and the occasion of the speech lend credibility to his address. However, Lincoln enhances his credibility by articulating the North's perspective on the war's causes, a position most of his audience would presumably endorse. Making numerous references to God and God's will also serves to enhance his ethos but serves as an emotional appeal as well: Lincoln hopes the citizens of the North will be swayed to extend mercy to the South after the war by ascribing such a position to divine will. By speaking mercifully and understandingly about the suffering of the South during the war, Lincoln models the behavior and attitudes he hopes the members of his audience will adopt themselves.

Structurally, Lincoln opens his address by commenting on the previous four years of his presidency and acknowledging the country's current struggle before laying out the North's view of the war's cause. Having articulated a position his audience would accept, Lincoln then changes the direction of the speech. Instead of attacking the Confederacy for its secession from the Union, he speaks about the suffering the war has brought to *all* Americans, how neither side in the conflict accurately anticipated the terrible nature of the war, and how the South has already suffered severely for its actions. Audience members might expect Lincoln to call for revenge against the South; instead, he argues that both sides have suffered enough. At the end of his speech, he urges his audience to treat the South with charity.

Stylistically, the speech is remarkable for its somber tone. Though this is an inaugural speech, Lincoln is not celebrating. Instead, his tone reflects the suffering the nation has endured over the previous four years and the hard work that lies ahead of it. Syntactically, he employs balanced sentences to create memorable phrases—"All dreaded it, all sought to avert it," "Fondly do we hope, fervently do we pray," "With malice toward none, with charity for all"—and to emphasize the balanced view he takes concerning the war's consequences. The North and South have both suffered, and Reconstruction must be based on an understanding of their shared humanity. Lincoln repeatedly employs language from the Old Testament to emphasize his view of the war as a form of divine judgment against the nation for its past offenses. Underlying this argument is the notion that justice lies in the hands of God: if God has scourged the nation for its transgressions, there is no need for humans to further the South's punishment following the war.

This brief rhetorical analysis of Lincoln's speech gives you some idea of how an author can manipulate a text's content, structure, and style to achieve a particular aim.

WRITING A RHETORICAL ANALYSIS ESSAY

STEP 1—CAREFULLY READ THE ASSIGNMENT

As you read the assignment, be sure you understand who *your* audience is for your essay. What can you assume your reader knows about the source text, its author, or the context in which it was written? How much information do you need to provide so your reader will understand your analysis of the text? Also, what can you assume your reader knows about rhetoric? What terms, if any, will you need to define in your essay?

STEP 2—ESTABLISH THE SOURCE TEXT'S RHETORICAL SITUATION

First, establish the rhetorical situation of the source text (see "The Rhetorical Situation" previously). Following are some of the questions you should answer either before or as you carefully read the source text:

- Who is the author?
- What is the writer's message?
- Who is the writer addressing?
- What is the writer's purpose or goal?
- Why is the writer composing this text?
- When was the text produced?
- Where was the text published?

To establish the text's rhetorical situation you might need to do a little research, but writing a rhetorical analysis essay requires that you understand the context in which the text was produced.

STEP 3—DETERMINE THE AUTHOR'S GOAL

In a sentence or two, paraphrase what you think the author is trying to accomplish in the text. What effect does she want to have on the audience? Is the author trying to persuade her readers to adopt a particular position? Does the author want to influence what her readers believe? Is the author trying to elicit a particular emotional response from people who read the text? State the author's purpose or goal, as you understand it, as clearly and specifically as you can.

STEP 4—IDENTIFY AND EVALUATE THE TEXT'S RHETORICAL STRATEGIES

When you have a clear sense of the text's rhetorical situation, read through it again to identify the strategies the author employed to achieve his goal. Examine the text's content, structure, and style in relation to its rhetorical situation. How has the author manipulated various elements of the text to achieve a particular response from his readers? Spend as much time on this step in the process as you need—the ideas and insights you develop now will help you form a thesis for your essay. Remember that in your essay, you will not address every rhetorical strategy the writer employed. Instead, you will focus on the strategies you think most significantly contribute to the text's ability or inability to achieve its rhetorical goal. As you reread the text, make a list of the ways the author employs content, structure, and style to achieve his purpose, noting specific examples of each from the reading. Based on this list, decide which strategies help the writer achieve his goals and which do not, given the text's audience, topic, purpose, and occasion. State in one or two sentences what makes each strategy successful or unsuccessful.

STEP 5—DETERMINE YOUR THESIS

In your thesis, you will state how successful you think the author is in achieving his or her rhetorical goal and indicate which of the author's rhetorical strategies you will examine in your essay. Your thesis may indicate that the author succeeds in achieving his or her rhetorical goals, fails to achieve them, or succeeds in some ways but fails in others. Whatever your assessment, state it clearly in your thesis, along with the rhetorical strategies you will examine to explain and defend your judgment.

Sample Thesis Statement 1: Author succeeds in achieving his or her rhetorical purpose

> Lincoln's Second Inaugural Address effectively establishes the North's moral imperative for successful Reconstruction by making repeated appeals to authority and emotion.

Sample Thesis Statement 2: Author fails to achieve his or her rhetorical purpose

> Lincoln's Second Inaugural Address fails to establish the North's moral imperative for successful Reconstruction because he relies too heavily on religious allusions and does not adequately address the North's desire for revenge after the war.

Sample Thesis Statement 3: Author has mixed success in achieving his or her rhetorical purpose

> Lincoln's attempts to establish the North's moral imperative for successful Reconstruction in his Second Inaugural Address are aided by his repeated appeals to authority, but they are hindered by his overreliance on religious allusions.

Whatever stand you assume, your thesis statement should establish the purpose and focus of your essay.

STEP 6—WRITE YOUR ROUGH DRAFT

Although every rhetorical analysis essay will be structured a little differently, the following outline may help you determine how to organize your paper.

Introductory Section

- Indicate the topic of the source text.
- Introduce the text you are analyzing or evaluating.
- State your thesis.
- Capture reader interest.

In this part of your paper, you need to indicate the topic of your essay, introduce the source text (provide the author's full name and the title of the reading), and state your thesis. One of the real challenges in writing the introductory section of a rhetorical analysis essay is to capture reader interest as well. You may be able to develop reader interest in your essay by opening with a question raised by the source text, starting with an exciting quotation from the reading or providing some interesting information about the reading's author or historical significance.

Summary of Source Text and Overview of the Rhetorical Situation

- Briefly summarize the source text.
- Explain the source text's rhetorical situation.

In one or two paragraphs, summarize the reading and its rhetorical situation. In addition to stating what the author wrote, explain the audience, purpose, and occasion of the piece. Your analysis will depend on readers understanding the source text's rhetorical situation, so explain it carefully in this part of the paper. You will be making frequent reference back to this information in the body of your essay.

Body Paragraphs

- Examine the text one rhetorical strategy at a time (content, structure, or style).
- Cite specific examples from the source text to support any assertion you make.
- Explain the link between the examples you provide and the assertions you make.

As you draft the body of your rhetorical analysis essay, carefully critique the text one rhetorical strategy at a time, explaining whether employing that strategy helps the author achieve his or her rhetorical goal. You will need to illustrate and support your assertions with specific examples from the source text. Generally, each of your body paragraphs will contain (1) an assertion regarding whether a particular rhetorical strategy helps the author achieve his or her rhetorical goal, (2) examples from the source text that illustrate that particular rhetorical strategy, and (3) an explanation of how each example you cite supports your assertion.

Do not make the mistake of thinking that the examples you cite will "speak for themselves"—that you do not need to explain how the examples support your assertion because the link will be obvious to anyone who has read the text. Instead, always explain the link between your evidence and your assertion. In fact, the success of your rhetorical analysis essay often depends on the clarity and logic of this explanation: your readers need to understand how the examples you cite support your assertion.

Conclusion

- Wrap up the essay.
- Remind readers of your thesis.
- Maintain reader interest.

In the conclusion of your rhetorical analysis essay, provide your readers with a sense of closure and remind them of your thesis. The conclusion should flow naturally from the body of your essay and recapture your readers' interest. One strategy you might employ is to echo your paper's introduction. For example, if you open your essay with a question, you might want to come back to it in your conclusion; if you open with a quotation, consider concluding your essay with one. This repetition will help give your essay a sense of balance and closure.

STEP 7—REVISE YOUR ESSAY

When revising your rhetorical analysis essay, make sure your work is accurate, developed, organized, clear, and documented.

- *Accurate*—your essay accurately captures your analysis and accurately represents the source text.
- *Developed*—you thoroughly develop and explain your assertions.
- *Organized*—the assertions in your essay are easy to follow and are interconnected.
- *Clear*—you have provided your readers with the information they need to understand your essay and have presented your ideas using clear, accessible language and sentences.
- *Documented*—all quoted and paraphrased material is documented as needed and your readers can easily discern which information comes from the source texts and which information you provide.

Check the Accuracy of Your Assertions and Examples

As you revise, start by checking your essay's content. First, make sure you have covered everything you intended to cover in your paper and that your essay accurately reflects your views. Second, be sure you have not misrepresented the author of the source text—any material you quote or paraphrase from the source text must accurately capture what the author actually wrote. Finally, be sure you fairly and accurately represent the text's rhetorical situation.

Check the Development of Your Essay

All of your assertions need to be fully explained and supported. Because your rhetorical analysis essay will reflect your individual response to and evaluation of the source text, you have to explain all of your assertions thoroughly. Readers need to know not only what you think but also why you think it. Do not expect readers to draw connections between your assertions and evidence on their own.

Check the Organization

First, be sure your thesis statement offers an accurate overview of your essay. The thesis statement should help guide your reader through your rhetorical analysis, previewing assertions you will develop in the body of your essay. Next, check the topic sentences in the body of your essay. Each topic sentence should relate back to the thesis statement, introduce a new idea, and provide a transition from the previous section of your essay. Be sure that you employ effective transitions within your body paragraphs as well, highlighting the logical relationship of one sentence to the next. Finally, check the opening and closing sections of your essay to be sure each accomplishes what it is supposed to accomplish.

Check for Clarity

Are there any terms that need to be defined? Any references drawn from the source text that need to be explained? Any sentences that could be more clear? Check to see that all quoted and paraphrased material will make sense to someone who has not read the source text and that any technical terms that need to be defined are defined.

Check Your Documentation

Because you are working with a source text, be sure that all quoted and paraphrased material is properly documented.

SAMPLE RHETORICAL ANALYSIS ESSAY

The following is a rhetorical analysis of Lincoln's Second Inaugural Address.

RHETORICAL ANALYSIS OF LINCOLN'S SECOND INAUGURAL ADDRESS

When President Lincoln stepped up to the podium to deliver his second inaugural address, he knew the Civil War was reaching its end. Though victory was not certain, events on the battlefield suggested that Union forces would soon put down the Southern rebellion and reunite the country. Lincoln knew he would soon be presiding over a deeply divided country, with many in the North demanding revenge against the Southern states, including the arrest and execution of the Confederacy's leaders. A close analysis of Lincoln's address makes clear, however, that he envisioned a Reconstruction based on mercy and forgiveness rather than vengeance, a message he forcefully conveys though the somber tone of the speech and its many religious allusions.

Since the Union forces were nearing victory after four years of brutal warfare, one might assume that Lincoln would deliver a joyful second inaugural address. Instead, the speech's tone is somber and reserved. While he states that the war's progress has been "reasonably satisfactory and encouraging to all" (147), Lincoln makes no prediction about its final outcome. He asserts that both sides in the conflict "deprecated" (148) war and that neither "expected for the war the magnitude or duration which it has already obtained" (148). Lincoln claims that "American slavery" (148) was the primary cause of the war, and though he states that the South was at fault for maintaining and spreading the practice, Lincoln claims that God "gives to both North and South this terrible war as the woe due to those by whom the offense came . . ." (148). Instead of celebrating the North's impending victory in the war, Lincoln claims that both the North and the South are paying a terrible price for their moral transgressions.

In his speech, Lincoln soberly assesses the causes and consequences of the war and indicates how the nation should proceed once peace comes. The final paragraph of his speech begins with the famous phrase "With malice toward none, with charity for all" (148), summing up Lincoln's message of mercy and forgiveness. The needed course of action now, Lincoln contends, is "to bind up the nation's wounds, to care for him who shall have borne the battle and for his widow and orphan" (148). This statement embraces both sides in the conflict: the nation's obligation is to care for both Yankee and Rebel soldiers, for all widows and orphans. Such mercy is the only way to obtain "a just and lasting peace among ourselves and with all nations" (148). Again, "ourselves" is inclusive: Lincoln is including the people of both the North and South in this statement, pointing the way to a reunited country. Lincoln's reflective, restrained tone in this speech indicates how he would like every citizen of the United States to respond to war's conclusion: with forgiveness, introspection, and understanding.

Lincoln's message of mercy and forgiveness is also furthered by his many religious allusions. Rather than claiming that the North's coming victory in the war has been ordained by God, Lincoln believes that God is neutral in the conflict, that the North and South are united by a common religious heritage: "Both read the same Bible and pray to the same God . . ." (148). Though Lincoln doubts that any deity would support human slavery, he warns his listeners, "judge not, that we be not judged" (148). Lincoln's repeated invocations of God strike a note of humility, reminding his audience that their fate is not in their own hands, that Providence dictates the course of history. The North has no reason to gloat in its victory or to judge the South severely after the war. Both sides have suffered judgment already; now is the time to act "with firmness in the right as God gives us to see the right . . ." (148).

Lincoln's Second Inaugural Address establishes a somber, reflective tone and employs numerous religious allusions to convey successfully his central message that, in victory, the North must act with mercy, forgiveness, and humility during Reconstruction. Revenge and retaliation is not the path to reestablishing a peaceful, united, just nation. "With malice toward none, with charity for all," the nation could be reunited. Unfortunately, one of those attending the speech that day was John Wilkes Booth, who would soon assassinate the president at Ford's Theater. Lincoln never had the chance to put his philosophy of merciful Reconstruction to the test.

Summary Chart

HOW TO WRITE A RHETORICAL ANALYSIS ESSAY

1. **Carefully read the assignment.**
   - *Who is your audience?*
   - *What can you assume your audience knows about the source text and rhetoric?*

2. **Establish the source text's rhetorical situation.**
   - *Who is the source text's author?*
   - *What is the source text's topic?*
   - *Who is the source text's audience?*
   - *What is the source text's purpose?*
   - *What was the occasion for writing the source text?*

3. **Determine the author's goal.**
   - *In a sentence or two, state clearly and specifically what you think the author is trying to accomplish in the source text.*

4. **Identify and evaluate the source text's rhetorical strategies.**
   - *strategies involving the text's content*
   - *use of arguments, evidence, and reasoning*
   - *use of logos, pathos, and ethos*
   - *strategies involving the text's structure*
   - *strategies involving the text's style*

5. **Determine your thesis.**
   - *State how successful the author is in achieving his or her rhetorical goal.*
   - *State which rhetorical strategies you will examine in your essay.*

SUMMARY CHART: HOW TO WRITE A RHETORICAL ANALYSIS ESSAY *(CONTINUED)*

6. Write your rough draft.

- *Write the introductory section of your essay, indicating the topic of the source text, its title and author, and your thesis. Capture reader interest as well.*
- *Summarize the source text and its rhetorical situation.*
- *Draft the body of your essay, examining one rhetorical strategy at a time and supporting your judgment with specific examples from the source text. Explain how each example you cite supports your claim.*
- *Write the concluding section of your essay, reminding readers of your thesis and maintaining reader interest.*

7. Revise your essay.

- *Make sure your writing is developed.*
- *Make sure your essay thoroughly develops and explains your assertions.*
- *Make sure your writing is organized.*
- *Make sure the assertions in your essay are easy to follow.*
- *Make sure the assertions in your essay are connected logically.*
- *Make sure your essay accurately reflects your thesis.*
- *Make sure your writing is clear.*
- *Make sure you have provided your readers with the information they need to understand your essay.*
- *Make sure you have checked to be sure all of your sentences are clear.*
- *Make sure your essay accurately represents the source text.*
- *Make sure all of the material in your essay that needs to be documented is documented.*
- *Make sure readers can tell which information in your essay came from your source text and which information comes from you.*

RHETORICAL ANALYSIS OF WRITTEN TEXTS REVISION CHECKLIST

	Yes	No
1. Have you analyzed the assignment to determine who *your* audience is?	_____	_____
2. Have you established the source text's rhetorical situation?	_____	_____
3. Have you paraphrased the author's goal?	_____	_____
4. Have you evaluated the author's rhetorical strategies in light of his or her goal?	_____	_____
5. Have you determined which of the author's rhetorical strategies you will evaluate in your essay?	_____	_____
6. Check the introductory section of your essay. Do you:		
• introduce the topic of your source text?	_____	_____
• introduce your source text?	_____	_____
• capture reader interest?	_____	_____
7. Examine the wording of your thesis. Do you:		
• state whether the author successfully achieves his or her goal?	_____	_____
• indicate which rhetorical strategies you will examine in your essay?	_____	_____
8. Do you summarize the source text and describe its rhetorical situation?	_____	_____
9. Check each section in the body of your essay. Do you:		
• examine one rhetorical strategy at a time?	_____	_____
• support your judgments with specific examples from the source text?	_____	_____
• explain the link between your assertions and their supporting evidence?	_____	_____

RHETORICAL ANALYSIS OF WRITTEN TEXTS REVISION CHECKLIST *(CONTINUED)*

	Yes	No
10. Have your revised your essay for:		
• accuracy?	_____	_____
• development?	_____	_____
• organization?	_____	_____
• clarity?	_____	_____
• documentation?	_____	_____

Chapter 8

RHETORICAL ANALYSIS OF VISUAL TEXTS

In this chapter you will learn how to

1. Identify the rhetorical situation of visual texts

2. Identify a visual text's rhetorical strategies

3. Evaluate a visual text in terms of its rhetorical situation and rhetorical strategies

4. Compose an effective rhetorical analysis of a visual text

DEFINITION AND PURPOSE

Consider for a moment the power of images—how photographs, drawings, or graphics affect the way you experience texts. Images can add emotional punch to a reading, illustrate an assertion, or make a text more entertaining. Images can even make an argument, either alone or in combination with written text. In our daily lives, we are constantly surrounded by visual images. Which ones grab your attention? How do writers manipulate the visual aspects of a text to achieve their desired effects? By analyzing these images, what lessons can you learn about effectively using visual images in your own texts?

The ability to critically read and rhetorically analyze visual texts is becoming an increasingly important skill. Although visual texts have long been a part of human communication (think about the prehistoric cave drawings found throughout the world), they have become more central to communication over the last century. Since the advent of television, our culture has become more centered on visual images, and advances in computer technology have made it increasingly possible for students to incorporate visual images in their own texts. In fact, at some schools, visual presentations—films, streaming video, PowerPoint presentations, and posters—have replaced traditional print-based assignments like term papers and reports. In many majors, students are expected to develop the same kind of fluency in manipulating visual images as they are in manipulating the written word.

This chapter offers advice and instruction on how to read, interpret, and rhetorically analyze different types of visual texts. Although you may not have had much experience thinking about visual texts the way you will be instructed to do in this chapter, remember that the processes you will employ and the types of questions you will ask closely resemble those you commonly use to read, analyze, and interpret written texts.

READING VISUAL TEXTS CRITICALLY

You might find it odd to consider how you "read" visual texts like photographs, drawings, cartoons, or advertisements. People often draw a distinction between written and visual texts: they "read" words, not pictures. However, as discussed in Chapter 1, reading a text—any text—involves understanding, analyzing, and interpreting it. Similar processes apply to both written and visual texts.

Following are a series of questions you can consider to help you read visual texts critically. Answering them will give you a clearer sense of a visual text's content, creator, purpose, and audience, as well as your response to the image.

QUESTIONS CONCERNING THE VISUAL TEXT ITSELF

- What image does the visual represent?
- What are the various parts of the visual?
- What written text, if any, accompanies the visual?

As with written texts, start your reading of a visual text by forming a clear understanding of its literal meaning—what is it in and of itself, what are its parts, and what is its relationship to any accompanying written text? Although this first step may sound easy, it can actually be difficult to examine a visual text objectively, to identify its constituent parts, and to find language that accurately describes what you see. Your first step is to summarize and paraphrase the visual text: state in your own words what you think the visual is depicting. At this point, you are not concerned with the visual's intention or purpose, only with its literal meaning. Pay particular attention to the details of the image. Your eye may immediately be drawn to only one or two aspects of the visual text, but don't stop your analysis there. Examine every aspect of the image—note what is in the background and in the foreground, in light and in shadow, in color and in black and white.

Next, identify the various parts of the visual text. When analyzing a written text, you may discuss its thesis, claims, examples, explanations, structure, and so forth. When analyzing a visual text, you will focus your attention on elements such as these:

Images: What images are contained in the visual? How many
               are there in the text? Which ones seem to command the
               most attention? Are there images of people in the text?

	If so, who? What are they doing? Are particular objects included in the text? Which ones? What type of setting is depicted in the text: interior or exterior, urban or natural, realistic or fantastic?
Layout:	How are the images arranged in the visual? How are they grouped? Which aspects of the images are emphasized in the layout? Which aspects are deemphasized? If there are people in the image, where do they appear in relation to the other images in the text? What appears in the foreground, and what appears in the background? What appears in light, and what appears in shadows?
Color:	How is color used in the visual text? What colors are used? What is highlighted by the text's use of color, and what is not? If you are examining a black-and-white image, how is shading used to highlight or emphasize particular elements? If there is written text, what color is it? How does color influence the way you respond to the writing?
Appeals:	What elements of the visual text are intended to appeal to the reader's emotions, values, or needs? How does the author of the text manipulate its content and/or layout to elicit a particular emotional response from readers? What elements of the text are included to appeal to the reader's intellect or reason? Which elements, if any, are intended to establish the author's credibility or authority?

Note: Carefully examine any written text included in the visual. What does the text say? What is the relationship between the written and visual elements of the text? For example, does the text comment on the images or draw the reader's attention to particular visual elements of the text? How is the writing placed in the text, and where does it appear? Is the placement of the written text significant? Does it impact how you read the visual text?

QUESTIONS CONCERNING THE VISUAL TEXT'S CREATOR OR SOURCE

- Who created the visual text?
- What is the source of the visual text?
- In what publication or website does the visual appear?
- Toward what readership is the publication or website aimed?
- What, generally, is the editorial stance of that publication or website?

Although finding answers to these questions might prove difficult, you should try. As with written texts, identifying the authorship of a visual text is central to understanding and evaluating it. Authorial bias can affect visual texts just as it can written texts. If possible, identify who created the visual text. Who was the artist or photographer? What can you learn about that person's previous work and his or her credentials or affiliations? Approach visual texts as skeptically as you would written texts. We tend to trust visual texts more readily than we do written texts. After all, who hasn't heard the saying, "Pictures don't lie"? Of course, we know that pictures can lie—visual texts can be manipulated as easily as written texts. Visual texts can communicate truths, untruths, or half-truths. Understanding who created a visual text can help you establish its credibility.

Also consider the visual text's source. In what periodical did it appear? On what website? On what television show? In what film? In what advertisement? You need to understand the agenda of the visual text's source. What is the publication or website attempting to accomplish through its use of this particular visual text? Is its intention to inform, persuade, or entertain readers? What biases or agendas might influence the types of visuals a source employs or how it uses those sources? As noted in the chapter on critical reading (Chapter 1), if you are investigating the topic of abortion rights, it would be important to note whether a visual text you are examining was published by the National Abortion Rights Action League or by Operation Life. Each group has its own agenda on this issue, which may well influence how each designs and employs visual texts in its publications or on its website. Again, the possible bias does not disqualify or discredit a visual text. You simply need to take that bias into account when you read, analyze, or evaluate the text.

To better understand a publication's or website's general editorial stance, read some of the articles it publishes or posts and examine other visual texts it provides. Although you may not be able to conclude definitively that the particular visual text you are examining reflects the publication's or website's general editorial stance, you will be in a better position to read that material in context. You will be able to conclude whether the particular visual text you are examining is typical of that publication or website.

QUESTIONS CONCERNING THE VISUAL TEXT'S PURPOSE

- What is the intended purpose of the visual?
- How does the creator attempt to achieve that purpose?

Purpose can be difficult to determine when analyzing a text—visual or written—because any text may be serving multiple purposes. Broadly speaking, a visual text may be attempting to inform, persuade, or entertain readers. Although it may be difficult to determine a visual text's exact intent, making an effort to do so is important. You can misread a visual text if you fail to understand its intended purpose.

For example, imagine an advertisement placed in a news magazine by the Sierra Club, one of the nation's largest environmental groups. The full-page ad consists of a black-and-white picture of a mountainside recently cleared of trees by a logging company. All that is left is a seemingly endless string of stumps, charred tree limbs, and muddy pits. In the lower left-hand corner of the page is a single message, printed in white type against the gray background: "The Sierra Club: *www.sierraclub.org.*" What is the purpose of this advertisement? Is it informative, persuasive, or both? Is it trying to inform readers about the Sierra Club's work, encourage them to find out more about the organization, or persuade them to join? While the picture itself may be striking, is the intention of the advertisement to entertain? How do you know? What if the text were different; that is, what if it read: "Help Us Fight Homelessness, *www .sierraclub.org*"? How would this new text change your interpretation of the advertisement's purpose?

Students sometimes run into problems when they read persuasive visual texts as if the texts were merely informative. We tend to read informative texts as if they were objective and factual; after all, that's what makes them different from persuasive texts. From experience, we know we need to read persuasive texts more skeptically than we do informative texts, because the author is actively attempting to sway our opinion about something or move us to act in a particular way. Our defenses are up when we read texts that we believe are persuasive in ways they are not when we read texts we think are primarily informative. In other words, our interpretation of a text's purpose influences how we read that text, how open we are to its message, and how critical we are as readers. Clarifying the purpose of the visual texts you read can help you read them more effectively and accurately.

QUESTIONS CONCERNING THE VISUAL TEXT'S AUDIENCE

- What audience is the visual text's creator trying to reach?
- How has the creator manipulated the visual text to successfully reach that audience?
- How does your understanding of the visual text's intended audience influence the way you read that text?

When you read a visual text, consider the type of reader its author or creator is attempting to reach. Sometimes you can base your conclusion on the publication in which the visual text appears: certain publications cater to certain types of readers. The general readership of *Inside Wrestling* magazine is likely different from the general readership of *Opera Aficionado* (although there may well be people who subscribe to both). Consider the interests and backgrounds of the people who would likely read the periodical or visit the website in which the visual text appeared. How might the author's interest in appealing to that type of reader influence the visual text he or she creates?

Another approach to analyzing audience is to consider the elements of the visual text itself: how did the author's view of his or her audience influence the way he or she constructed the visual text? Put another way, if you did not know the publication or website in which the visual text appeared, how could you determine the writer's or creator's sense of audience by carefully analyzing various elements of the text itself? Consider these questions:

- What types of images are included in the text? Would they appeal to a wide range of readers or to just certain types of readers?
- What examples are included in the text? Would they appeal to a popular or to a specialized audience?
- If there are human models in the text, who are they? What types of people are they? Who might identify with these models? Who might not?
- If there is written text, how formal is it? What cultural references does the written text include? What types of figurative language does it employ? Which readers would likely understand and appreciate this use of language?

Forming an understanding of the visual text's intended audience is important because it will guide the way you analyze that text. Central to analysis is a deceivingly simple question: why did the author/creator construct the text this way? Assuming a rhetorical intent for all texts—that they are produced to have a particular effect on a particular audience—identifying the intended audience can guide the way you analyze the text itself. In other words, your analysis of the text will be based on your understanding of its intended audience.

QUESTIONS CONCERNING YOUR RESPONSE TO THE VISUAL TEXT

- What is my response to the visual text?
- Which aspects of the visual text elicit that response?
- What are the sources of my response?
- How does my response influence my understanding of the text?

Authors often incorporate visuals into their texts because they know readers are likely to respond to them in ways they will not respond to words alone. Visuals can stir our imagination, move us to anger or sympathy, attract us or alienate us, and cause us to laugh or to cringe. However, we often don't stop to consider our responses to visual texts: we are so wrapped up in responding to them that we don't consider the nature or cause of the response itself. The first step, then, is to recognize and articulate your reaction to a visual text. How does it make you feel? What is your response? Although it might prove difficult, find language that captures your reaction.

Next, identify which elements of the text evoke those responses. People looking at the same visual text may have very different emotional reactions to it, even if they are focusing on the exact same elements. Likewise, two people may have the same emotional response to a text even if they are focusing on different elements: one may be responding to a particular image included in the text and another to the text's layout. As you consider your response to a visual text, try to identify the specific elements that give rise to it. Encountering that text, you felt a particular way—what was in the text, exactly, that gave rise to your response?

Finally, consider why you respond to particular elements of the text the way you do. What knowledge, experience, or values do you have that cause you to react that way? Examining this link can be difficult, but doing so is extremely important, especially if you are going to discuss your response with someone else. For example, you and a classmate may have similar reactions to the same elements of a visual, but why you respond to those elements in a certain way may be very different. Articulating the link between the elements of the text and your responses can help you more fully understand your reactions and how they differ from the responses of others.

READING A VISUAL TEXT—AN EXAMPLE

The following example of a visual text (see the next page) is an advertisement produced by the National Center for Family Literacy and published in the April 2008 edition of *Black Enterprise* magazine. Take a few minutes to carefully study the advertisement, then answer the following questions to get a better sense of how you are reading the visuals and text.

QUESTIONS CONCERNING THE VISUAL TEXT

- What images does the advertisement contain? How would you describe them?
- What do you assume is the relationship between the two people photographed in the advertisement? Why do you assume that? How does the photograph lead you to that conclusion?
- What else does the advertisement contain besides a photograph of the two people? For example, there's copy, but what else is there?
- What does the copy say? What words or ideas stand out in the copy? Why?
- Notice the National Center for Family Literacy name and logo at the bottom of the advertisement. Why are they included? What copy appears below the logo?
- Examine how the images and words on the page are arranged. What purpose might their arrangement serve?
- Notice how the copy employs two shades of gray. What purpose does that alternation serve?
- Which words stand out because they are flush with the margin? Which stand out because they are in dark type?
- What emotional appeals is the advertisement making? Examine how the people are posed for the picture. What appeal is the photographer making? Read the copy carefully. Point out instances in which particular words or phrases are included to appeal to readers in specific ways.

Because I can read,
 I can understand. I can write a letter.
 I can fill out a job application.
 I can finally get off welfare.

Because I can read,
 I can learn. I can help my daughter
 with her homework.
 I can inspire her to be better.
 I can be a role model.

Because I can read,
 I can succeed, I can
 contribute. I can live
 my life without fear,
 without shame.
 I can be whatever
 I want to be.

Because I can read.

 National Center for Family Literacy

Literacy can make the difference between poverty and progress.
Visit **www.famlit.org** to help us write more success stories.

©2005 Photographer: Marvin Young

Source: National Center for Family Literacy

QUESTIONS CONCERNING THE VISUAL TEXT'S CREATOR OR SOURCE

- This advertisement appeared in *Black Enterprise* magazine. What do you assume or know about this publication?
- The advertisement was placed by the National Center for Family Literacy. What do you assume or know about this organization?
- Which types of people are likely to read *Black Enterprise*? What can you assume about their backgrounds and interests?
- How has the National Center for Family Literacy used images and copy to appeal to this type of reader?
- Why does the advertisement include copy like the following:
    - "Because I can read, I can understand. I can write a letter. I can fill out a job application. I can finally get off welfare."
    - "Because I can read, I can succeed, I can contribute."
    - "Literacy can make the difference between poverty and progress."

QUESTIONS CONCERNING THE VISUAL TEXT'S PURPOSE

- What is the advertisement's intended purpose? How do you know?
- Is the advertisement primarily a call to action ("Visit www.famlit.org to help us write more success stories"), or does it serve other purposes as well? If it serves other purposes, what are they?
- How has the National Center for Family Literacy attempted to achieve their purpose with this advertisement? How are their efforts related to the publication in which the advertisement appears?
- If the goal of the advertisement is primarily to inform readers, what do its creators intend for them to learn? How does the advertisement attempt to do this?
- If the advertisement is primarily a call to action, what is the action its creators want readers to take? How do they attempt to convince or move readers to act in this way?

QUESTIONS CONCERNING THE VISUAL TEXT'S AUDIENCE

- What audience is this advertisement attempting to reach?
- If the advertisement is a call to action, who is supposed to act? How do you know?
- How has the National Center for Family Literacy attempted to reach its intended audience? How has it manipulated the elements of the advertisement—for example, images, copy, layout, color—to reach its audience?
- Who do you assume is the speaker in the advertisement? Who is the first-person narrator? How do you know this? Why might the advertisement be written this way?

- What are the race, gender, and age of the people shown in the advertisement? Why do you think they were chosen as models for this advertisement? How might that choice be related to the intended audience?

QUESTIONS CONCERNING YOUR RESPONSE TO THE VISUAL TEXT

- How do you respond to the advertisement?
- Do you find it interesting? If so, why? If not, why not?
- Are you moved to take any action as a result of reading the advertisement? If so, what action and why? If not, why not?
- Do you respond one way to the photograph of the people and another way to the copy? Why?
- What personal experience or knowledge might influence the way you respond to this advertisement? What is the link between that experience or knowledge and your response?

WRITING A RHETORICAL ANALYSIS OF A VISUAL TEXT

Although on occasion you may be asked to write essays in which you just describe visual texts, you will more commonly be required to analyze and evaluate them rhetorically as well. When you write this type of essay, you will identify how the text's author attempts to achieve a particular rhetorical goal and assess his or her success.

STEP 1—CAREFULLY READ THE ASSIGNMENT

As always, be sure you understand the assignment's intent and requirements. The words *analysis* or *evaluation* may never appear in the assignment. Instead, you might be asked to "assess" or "critique" the text, to decide "how effective" it is, or to argue "how well" it achieves its goal. If you have any questions regarding the goals of the essay you are being asked to write, talk to your teacher.

Also be sure you understand whether you will be evaluating a visual text you locate on your own or if you will be working with an assigned text. If you are free to choose your own visual text for rhetorical analysis, clarify whether there are any restrictions on your choice. For example, does your teacher want you to work with a particular type of visual text (i.e., an advertisement, a political cartoon, a photograph, a sign, or a painting)? Are particular types of visual texts excluded from the analysis? Finally, if the choice of source texts is up to you, have your teacher approve your selection before you begin to write your essay.

STEP 2—ANALYZE AND DESCRIBE THE TEXT

Although this step sounds simple, in some ways it is the most difficult. You need to carefully and objectively examine the text, finding language to describe exactly what you see and read. In several chapters, this textbook discusses the issue of bias when it comes to writing and reading texts—readers need to understand and take into account possible authorial bias when they read texts and acknowledge the biases they themselves bring to the texts they read and write. The same concerns hold true for visual texts as well.

Although you need to consider the biases that may have influenced the visual text's creation, you also need to be aware of any biases that could cloud or color your reading of it. Bias can lead you to misinterpret a visual image or actually fail to "see" what is on the page or computer screen because you are not looking for it. Therefore, when you analyze and describe a visual text, try to put aside as best you can any prejudices or assumptions you have concerning the text's content, message, creator, or source. Just as when you write a summary of a print text, your goal here is to be as objective as possible. Try to describe the visual text as objectively and accurately as you can, using language that is neutral and clear.

STEP 3—ESTABLISH THE TEXT'S RHETORICAL SITUATION

To establish the visual text's rhetorical situation, consider your answers to the following questions. Be sure to draw on the insights you gained through your earlier critical reading of the text:

- Who is the text's author or creator?
- Where was the text published, or where does it appear?
- What is the text's message? If there is more than one message, what are they? Does one message dominate?
- Who is the text's intended audience?
- How does the text want to affect that audience? What is the text's purpose?

If you have a hard time answering any of these questions, consider asking someone else—a classmate, roommate, parent, or friend—to examine the text and discuss it with them. Sometimes talking about a visual text with someone is the best way of determining its rhetorical situation.

STEP 4—DETERMINE HOW THE TEXT ATTEMPTS TO ACHIEVE ITS RHETORICAL GOALS

After you have determined the text's rhetorical goals, identify how its creator manipulates its images and/or text to achieve those ends. Here you would examine how the various elements of the text you identified earlier work separately and together to achieve the text's purpose. Your goal is to find language to describe how the visual text "works," how it communicates its message, and how it accomplishes its goals. The various elements of the text you focus on at this stage in the writing process are the ones you will likely write about in your essay.

STEP 5—DETERMINE YOUR THESIS

Your thesis statement can be either open or closed. An open thesis statement would indicate how successfully you believe the visual text achieved its rhetorical goal. Using the National Center for Family Literacy ad on page 152, an open thesis statement may read something like this:

> The National Center for Family Literacy produced an advertisement that successfully encourages readers to support their organization.

This thesis identifies what the writer believes to be the advertisement's goal or purpose (to encourage readers to support the sponsoring organization) and asserts a judgment concerning its success.

A closed thesis statement would indicate both your judgment of how well the visual text achieved its goals and the elements of the text you will examine to support your conclusion. Again, using the ad presented on page 152, a closed thesis statement could resemble this:

> Through its copy and its depiction of a mother and her daughter, the National Center for Family Literacy advertisement successfully encourages readers to support their organization.

This thesis still indicates the writer's judgment concerning how successfully the advertisement achieves its goal but also indicates how she will support her claim (by examining the advertisement's use of copy and its portrayal of a mother and her daughter).

STEP 6—WRITE A ROUGH DRAFT

Although the content and structure of the essays you write will vary by the type of visual text you are analyzing and evaluating, the following guidelines will help you write an effective rough draft.

Introductory Section

- Introduce the topic of your essay.
- Introduce the source text you will be working with.
- State your thesis.
- Capture reader interest.

You might consider opening your essay by introducing the topic that the visual text addresses, discussing the specific genre of visual text you will be working with (for example, an advertisement or a web page), or paraphrasing the assignment you've been given. Next, introduce the specific visual text you will be working with in your essay, indicating its authorship, source, and perhaps its date of publication. You should also include your thesis statement, typically placed toward the end of your introduction.

Description of the Visual Text and Overview of the Rhetorical Situation

- Describe the visual text.
- Explain the text's rhetorical situation.

In this section of your essay, describe and summarize the visual text you will be working with. Students sometimes understandably question why this section of the paper is needed, especially if the visual text is going to accompany the essay they write: why describe the text when readers will have access to it? Keep in mind that your description is preparing your readers for the argument you are going to make concerning the text's effectiveness. Through your description, you will bring to your readers' attention the aspects and elements of the text you will discuss in the body of your essay. You will introduce those aspects and elements in this section of your essay and evaluate them later.

The same advice holds true for explaining the visual text's rhetorical situation. You need to tell your reader where and in what context the visual text appeared, who created it, when it was created, and why it was produced. Identify what you believe to be the text's intended audience and purpose. If you believe your readers might interpret the text's purpose differently than you do in your essay, address those concerns here, acknowledging them and defending your own interpretation. The more clearly you explain the text's rhetorical situation in this part of your essay, the easier it will be to write a convincing argument in the body of your paper.

Body Paragraphs

- Develop your thesis one criterion or one example at a time.
- Cite specific examples from the visual text to support your assertions.
- Explain how those examples support the assertions you are making.
- Address possible objections or alternatives to your interpretations, as needed.

As you explain and develop the assertion(s) you put forward in your thesis, examine one evaluative criterion or example from the visual text at a time. For example, if you are basing your evaluation of a text on its use of color, examine one use of color in the text at a time, explaining how it supports the assertion you are making. Afterward, move on to your next example. If you are basing your evaluation on the text's use of color and layout, don't jump back and forth between the two—develop one criterion at a time.

Also, do not assume that the examples you cite speak for themselves or that your readers will understand on their own how the examples you draw from the visual text support the assertion you are making. Instead, carefully explain the link as you see it, and explain how each example lends credibility to your assertion.

Finally, be aware that any conclusions you have reached regarding the visual text are based on your interpretation of that text. Your judgments reflect the way you have interpreted and responded to the images and/or writing. Other readers could legitimately interpret the text differently. As you develop and explain your particular interpretation, note likely objections to your assertions or viable alternative interpretations, when necessary. Acknowledging and addressing these objections or alternatives increases your credibility as a writer and strengthens your assertions.

Conclusion

- Wrap up your essay in an interesting way.
- Remind readers of your thesis.

As with other types of source-based essays, you want to wrap up your analysis/ evaluation of a visual text in a way that reminds readers of the primary assertions you've made and that maintains interest. One way to reassert your primary claims is to simply restate your thesis; however, this approach does little to sustain reader interest. Instead, consider closing your essay with an interesting question or provocative assertion, to either challenge other readers' interpretations of the visual text or to predict the future, perhaps speculating on how successful the visual text will be in achieving its desired goals.

STEP 7—REVISE YOUR ESSAY

When revising your analysis/evaluation of a visual text, make sure your writing is clear, developed, and well organized.

- *Clear*—your readers understand the assertions you are making and the link between your evaluations and the source text.
- *Developed*—you have thoroughly explained your assertions and have examined alternative interpretations when needed.
- *Organized*—your assertions are logically connected, and your evaluation is guided by an overarching thesis.

Check for Clarity

When you revise your essay, at some point try to switch roles: you are no longer the author of your paper but someone reading it for the first time. Are there any assertions a reader might have a difficult time understanding? Are there any terms that need to be more clearly defined? Is the connection between your analysis/evaluation and the source text itself always clear? In other words, would readers understand exactly what aspects or elements of the source text you are analyzing, evaluating, or responding to? Have you explained your assertions thoroughly? Revise your essay as necessary to improve clarity.

Check the Development of Your Essay

Have you supported each of your assertions with references to the source text? Have you explained the connection between your assertions and the source text? The examples you cite from the source text cannot speak for themselves; do not expect your readers to understand the link between your assertions and the evidence you cite. Instead, clearly explain your reasoning.

Check the Organization

First, check your thesis statement. Does it accurately reflect and predict your essay's content and structure? If not, revise it. Second, check your topic sentences. Does each one introduce a new idea, provide a transition from the previous section of your essay, and, in some way, echo your thesis statement? Check the quality of the opening and closing sections of your essay—do they accomplish their intended goals? Finally, add transitions within paragraphs where needed to help guide your readers through your essay.

SAMPLE RHETORICAL ANALYSIS OF A VISUAL TEXT

The following sample essay analyzes and evaluates the National Center for Family Literacy advertisement on page 152.

AN EFFECTIVE ADVERTISEMENT FOR LITERACY SUPPORT

The idea of an organization devoted to the promotion of literacy paying for a magazine advertisement may seem odd. After all, if people can read the ad, they are already literate and have no need of the organization's services. If they are illiterate, they cannot read the ad at all. So what would be the purpose of such an advertisement? Judging by the ad placed by the National Center for Family Literacy in the April 2008 edition of *Black Enterprise* magazine, the purpose would be to garner support for the organization's programs and services. Through its use of copy, layout, and models, the National Center for Family Literacy demonstrates just how effective such an ad can be.

Unlike many other advertisements in *Black Enterprise*, the one sponsored by the National Center for Family Literacy is simple—using shades of black and white rather than color. Most of the ad consists of copy printed on a white background with two models—seemingly a mother and her daughter—appearing in the bottom right-hand corner. The bottom left-hand corner contains the National Center for Family Literacy name and logo, the message "Literacy can make the difference between poverty and progress," and an appeal to "Visit www.famlit.org to help us write more success stories."

The copy consists of the phrase "Because I can read" repeated four times in boldface print. Below three of these phrases—which serve as headings—are first-person statements (presumably from the mother in the ad) printed in a lighter typeface to finish the sentence. Under the first heading, the copy explains how becoming literate helped her find a job and get off welfare. Under the second heading, the copy focuses on how becoming literate helped her become a better mother and role model for her daughter. Under the third, the copy explains how being able to read has enabled the mother to live without fear and shame, allowing her to achieve economic success.

One reason this advertisement works well is that its copy appeals to the type of person likely to read *Black Enterprise* magazine. *Black Enterprise* is aimed primarily at African-American businesspeople, entrepreneurs, and philanthropists, people who have established or work for successful companies, who are looking for business opportunities, or who seek charitable opportunities. Those who read this magazine are aware of how important it is to have a trained, literate workforce and may have a greater understanding of and sympathy for people who must overcome obstacles to succeed.

Consequently, the copy under the first heading reads, "Because I can read, I can understand. I can write a letter. I can fill out a job application. I can finally get off welfare." Many readers of *Black Enterprise* would want to support an organization that helps potential workers learn how to fill out a job application, join the workforce, and move off of welfare. The copy under the second heading appeals to the readers' emotions. Supporting the work of the National Center for Family Literacy will improve the life of the family pictured in the ad—thanks to the organization, the mother can now "help my daughter with her homework," "inspire her to be better," and be a better "role model." Supporting the National Center for Family Literacy is not just in the economic interest of those who read *Black Enterprise*, it is also a humanitarian act.

The copy under the third heading combines elements of the first two. It opens with an echo of the first: "Because I can read, I can succeed. I can contribute." The copy indicates that the National Center for Family Literacy can help women like the one in the advertisement enter the workforce and achieve economic success. The next two statements, however, return to emotional appeals: "I can live my life without fear, without shame. I can be whatever I want to be." The copy is designed to build a bridge between the readers' experiences and the National Center's mission by stressing the need to help people overcome fears and obstacles and by working hard, to succeed.

Also making the National Center for Family Literacy's ad effective is its use of layout—how the copy and visuals are arranged on the page. The phrase "Because I can read," is repeated four times, printed in boldface along the left-hand margin of the page. Because of their placement and appearance, these words catch the reader's eye first. This repeated phrase dominates the ad, leading the reader's eye down the page to the National Center for Family Literacy's logo. The lighter-colored text underneath each heading catches the reader's eye because of its appearance and the repetition of "I": nine of the thirteen lines under the headings begin with "I." The use of first person in these lines makes the advertisement's copy personal, encouraging readers to identify with the mother and daughter pictured in the lower right-hand corner. People are more likely to support a charitable organization if they can identify and empathize with those who will be receiving the aid.

In fact, the depiction of the people in the advertisement also makes it effective. The copy surrounds and frames the two people, a mother and her child. Reading the headings left to right leads the reader's eye directly toward them. The mother is squatting down and her daughter is standing behind her, leaning in, a hand on each of her mother's shoulders. The mother's right hand is on her knee; her left hand rests on top of her daughter's right hand. The mother has a slight, proud grin on her face, while the daughter shows a full-toothed smile. These are average people—the mother appears to be wearing a sweatsuit of some sort and the daughter a polo shirt. The mother and her daughter are quite ordinary people, people whom the readers of *Black Enterprise* might know or see every day on the street. The message of the ad is clear: the National Center for Family Literacy helps average families like this one.

Finally, the facial expressions and race of the mother and daughter are crucial elements of the advertisement. The daughter seems overjoyed with the fact that her mother can now read, while the mother is brimming with confidence. Who wouldn't want to support an organization that would improve the life of such a cute little girl? Significant, too, is the fact that the mother is white while her daughter is biracial. Although *Black Enterprise* magazine primarily attracts African-American readers, the advertisement makes clear that the National Center for Family Literacy works to improve the lives of all people, regardless of race.

The National Center for Family Literacy advertisement that appeared in *Black Enterprise* magazine is not aimed at recruiting people who need the center's services. Instead, it is intended to attract possible donors and supporters. Beneath the center's logo at the bottom of the ad is copy that reads, "Literacy can make the difference between poverty and progress," and an appeal to "Visit www.famlit.org to help us write more success stories." Readers with a charitable heart may well consider supporting the organization after reading this successful ad.

Summary Chart

HOW TO WRITE A RHETORICAL ANALYSIS OF A VISUAL TEXT

1. **Carefully read the assignment.**
   - *Clarify your purpose.*
   - *Clarify the degree of freedom you have to select a visual text to evaluate.*

2. **Analyze and describe the text.**
   - *Examine every aspect of the text.*
   - *Attempt to put aside any biases you bring to the text.*

3. **Establish the text's rhetorical situation.**
   - *Who is the text's author or creator?*
   - *Where was the text published or where does it appear?*
   - *What is the text's message?*
   - *Who is the text's intended audience?*
   - *What is the text's purpose?*

4. **Determine how the text attempts to achieve its rhetorical goals.**
   - *How do the various elements of the text work separately and together to achieve the text's purpose or goal?*

5. **Determine your thesis.**
   - *Identify what you think the text's goal is and assert a judgment concerning how well it succeeds in achieving that goal.*
   - *Decide if you will use an open or closed thesis.*
   - *If you use a closed thesis, indicate which elements of the text you will examine in your essay.*

6. **Write a rough draft.**
    - *Write the introductory section of your essay, indicating the topic of your essay, identifying the source text you will be working with, stating your thesis, and capturing reader interest.*
    - *Provide a brief but thorough description of the text and explain its rhetorical situation.*
    - *Draft the body of your evaluation in a manner that is consistent with your thesis, examining one element at a time of the visual text, citing specific examples from the text to support any assertions you make, explaining how those examples support your claims, and addressing possible objections to or questions concerning your interpretation.*
    - *Write the concluding section of your essay, writing up your evaluation, reminding readers of your thesis, and maintaining reader interest.*

7. **Revise your essay.**
    - *Make sure your writing is clear.*
    - *Make sure your writing is well developed.*
    - *Make sure your writing is organized.*

RHETORICAL ANALYSIS OF A VISUAL TEXT REVISION CHECKLIST

	Yes	No
1. Have you carefully analyzed the assignment to determine whether you are supposed to describe, analyze, and/or evaluate the text?	_____	_____
2. Have you carefully examined every aspect of the source text?	_____	_____
3. Have you established the visual text's rhetorical situation?	_____	_____
4. Have you established how the creators of the visual text attempt to achieve their rhetorical goal?	_____	_____
5. Have you determined how well they achieve their goal?	_____	_____
6. Have you expressed your findings in a clear thesis statement that can guide the development of your essay?	_____	_____
7. In the introductory section of your essay, do you:		
• introduce the topic?	_____	_____
• introduce the source text?	_____	_____
• state your thesis?	_____	_____
• attempt to capture reader interest?	_____	_____
8. In the body of your essay, do you:		
• provide an overview or description of the visual text?	_____	_____
• develop your essay one criterion at a time?	_____	_____
• cite specific examples from the text to support your claims?	_____	_____
• explain how those examples support your assertions?	_____	_____
• address possible objections to your interpretation?	_____	_____

	Yes	No
9. In the concluding section of your essay, do you:		
• wrap up your essay in an interesting way?	_____	_____
• remind readers of your thesis?	_____	_____
10. Have you revised your essay for:		
• clarity?	_____	_____
• development?	_____	_____
• organization?	_____	_____
11. Have you proofread your essay?	_____	_____

Chapter 9

INFORMATIVE SYNTHESIS

In this chapter you will learn how to

1. Read critically to identify similarities and differences among texts

2. Combine information from multiple readings

3. Develop an effective thesis and organizational plan

4. Support assertions with appropriate evidence and examples

5. Document multi-source informative essays

DEFINITION AND PURPOSE

In a synthesis, you combine information from two or more readings to support a position of your own. Your aim in the paper can be expository (to convey information) or argumentative (to convince readers that your thesis concerning the readings is correct). In either case, when writing a synthesis, you combine material from two or more readings with your own knowledge and reasoning to explain or support your thesis.

College writing assignments often require you to synthesize material. In some courses the assignment will be direct and clear: "Compare what author A and author B have to say about topic X. How are their views alike and how are they different?" Other times the assignment might be more subtle: "Authors A, B, and C all address topic X. Which do you find most convincing?" Completing either assignment would require you to form and defend a thesis by drawing information from two or more readings.

To write a synthesis, you first need to sort through the readings to find information you can use in your paper. Being able to annotate readings thoroughly is essential. Second, you need to find the best way to organize this material around your own thesis and the demands of the assignment. Third, you need to find a place in the essay for your own ideas, findings, or arguments. Composing a synthesis usually involves more than just stringing together quoted and paraphrased material from other writers. Fourth, as you write your paper, you need to keep straight who receives credit for which ideas. Through proper documentation, you need to clarify for your readers when you are drawing on the work of a particular author and when you are developing material yourself. Finally, as you revise your work, you need to keep clearly in mind the rhetorical situation of the assignment. In your efforts to work with other people's ideas, you cannot afford to lose sight of your readers' needs and the purpose of the assignment.

TYPES OF SYNTHESIS ESSAYS

Synthesis essays can assume many different forms in college, some rather specialized and sophisticated. One way to begin sorting through all this variety is to recognize that for the most part the assignments you receive will ask you to compose either an **informative** or an **argumentative** synthesis (see Chapter 10).

The goal of an informative synthesis is to clearly and efficiently communicate the information you have gathered from two or more readings. You do not defend a position of your own or critique the source texts in this type of paper. Your primary aim is to summarize the material in the readings and convey the information to your readers in a clear, concise, organized fashion, often comparing and contrasting the texts. In contrast, the goal of an argumentative synthesis is to convince your reader to accept an argument you are presenting on either the quality of the readings or the topic they address. You use the material in the source texts to support your thesis, sometimes summarizing the readings and sometimes critiquing them.

Either type of synthesis can be organized in a variety of ways. Often writers will choose to employ either a **block** or an **alternating** format. When you use a block format to structure your synthesis, you discuss only one source text at a time. With an alternating format, you switch back and forth between readings as you develop your thesis point by point.

Before examining each type of synthesis in more detail, read the following arguments concerning the relationship between television viewing and childhood violence. What is each author's stance on the topic? What aspects of the topic most capture the author's interest? How convincing is each author's argument?

Humanity 2.0?

Enhancement, Evolution and the Possible Futures of Humanity

Sarah Chan

Sarah Chan is a Research Fellow at the Institute for Science, Ethics, and Innovation at the University of Manchester, UK.

Particular concern about human enhancement often seems to focus on genetic manipulation and the undesirability of using it to enhance our children or ourselves. As I have argued . . . there is nothing wrong with enhancement *per se*. Opponents of genetic enhancements, therefore, must show that there is something particular about the use of genetic technologies that renders these enhancements unacceptable, whereas the use of chemical or mechanical enhancements is not.

Genetic manipulation might be perceived as less acceptable because it is a relatively new procedure—at least when applied to human beings— and therefore carries the possibility of unforeseen risks. Gene therapy, in particular, has received bad press after a few cases in which potential dangers did manifest. Examples include the gene-therapy trials to treat severe defects of the immune system that resulted in leukaemia (Cavazzana-Calvo et al., 2000) and the death of Jesse Gelsinger, who suffered an adverse reaction to the virus used as a vector in gene therapy against ornithine transcarbamylase deficiency (Savulescu, 2001).

The presence of risk is not a factor unique to genetic enhancement— it is also likely that other types of enhancement technology have risks associated with their application, as do current drug therapeutics. Every new treatment involves some amount of risk; this, in itself, does not render it unethical. If we were to avoid every activity that carried any amount of risk, no matter how small, then we would never drive motor cars, cross the road or even get out of bed in the morning. The most ethical course of action in the face of risk is to evaluate the balance of risk and benefit, and attempt to minimize the risks where they must be faced. This might not be an easy thing to do in the case of new technologies, but it is better done than not.

So is there anything intrinsically wrong with genetic manipulation? There certainly cannot be a moral proscription against modifying the somatic genome: we are at liberty to make changes to our physical bodies in terms of their appearance, condition or health, and DNA is simply a part of that—in fact, somatic mutation occurs all the time.

Arguments against human genetic modification have therefore concentrated in particular on the ethical unacceptability of germ-line gene therapy. The distinguishing feature of germ-line genetic modification—as opposed to somatic genetic modification—is that any changes made to the genome will be heritable and therefore affect not only the individuals treated, but also their descendants—and by extension, the future human race as a whole.

The argument invoked is that it is wrong to make genetic choices for our descendants. One reason given for this is sometimes expressed in terms of the "right to an open future" (Feinberg, 1980): that is, by predetermining the genes of our children, we are somehow limiting their own right to choose. Choosing the genes of our children, so the argument goes, deprives them of the right to make their own choices about their lives and thereby infringes their autonomy (Buchanan et al., 2000; Davis, 2001; Habermas, 2003; Mameli, 2007).

Yet children can never exert a choice over the genes that they are born with, regardless of whether their parents do. Those who believe in genetic determinism must realize that abandoning our children to the mercy of the 'genetic lottery' does not free them from the tyranny of their genes, rather, it merely removes any element of choice on the part of anyone as to what those genes are. Those of us, by contrast, who look beyond genetic determinism to see that it is far more than genes that determine the future of our children, will probably also realize that—to the extent that genes do determine some aspects of our lives, in particular our health and associated quality of life—it is surely far better to have a predisposition to a healthy life than to risk a higher chance of suffering and disease.

The corollary to the above argument is that parents themselves should not seek to make such choices and that attempting to enhance children represents "a kind of hyperagency—a Promethean aspiration to remake nature, including human nature, to serve our purposes and satisfy our desires" (Sandel, 2004, 2007). According to this argument, parental virtue requires acceptance rather than control and an "openness to the unbidden", rather than the "hubris [of] an excess of mastery"—that is, an appreciation of the 'gifted' nature of human achievement, rather than an aspiration to increase these achievements. Choosing to enhance is therefore wrong both because it violates the principles of good parenting and because of the negative social consequences that will follow the abandonment of such principles.

In each case, however, it is not clear whether the availability or use of genetic enhancements will result in the predicted disintegration of social values, or if allowing parents to make choices about their children contravenes the requirements of parental responsibility. It is true that the use of genetic-enhancement technologies will involve parents making decisions about the genetic heritage of their children. However, once the technology exists and has been proven to be safe, to refrain from using it is likewise to make a decision about the genetic inheritance of our descendants—specifically: that they will not receive such enhancements and will be denied the consequent benefits. If we were to have the choice of eradicating a serious disease for future generations and decided against doing so, I doubt that our descendants would thank us for it. Abdicating choice is not the action of a responsible parent; exercising choice wisely is.

Of course, this applies equally to both genetic and non-genetic interventions. Every parent wants to have a healthy child and there is nothing wrong with this. Indeed, we might look askance at a parent who did not claim to want the best for their children. Yet what do we mean by healthy? The only logical answer to this question is 'as healthy as possible'. For example, we know that certain maternal behaviours during pregnancy can have adverse consequences for child health: the use of alcohol and tobacco increase the risk of low birth weight and associated developmental delay, and poor maternal diet can increase the chances of developing type 2 diabetes in later life. We encourage mothers-to-be to improve the health of their children by avoiding these things; indeed, we consider them to be irresponsible if they fail to do so. Similarly, we advocate folate supplements as a positive measure to decrease the risk of spina bifida. Therefore, we see it as a strong obligation on parents to use the available knowledge and medical technology to maximize the health of their children. We also encourage the use of vaccination and other choices for children that protect and benefit them.

Surely, then, this argument also applies to genetic enhancement. If we could, with safety and certainty, engineer our children to have immunity to viral infection, protection from heart disease and reduced susceptibility to cancer, we should do so. In other words, not only is genetic enhancement morally acceptable, but, if and when it becomes safe and affordable, there will be a moral imperative to use it for the benefit of future generations (Chan & Harris, 2007).

More general concerns about genetic manipulations focus on the consequences of genetic enhancement for the future of the human race. These concerns include worries about the loss of genetic diversity: that we will become a race of clones—either literally, through the use of reproductive cloning to create armies of identical beings, or because our uniform desire for enhancements will result in overall genetic uniformity. Others seem to have the opposite fear: that changing our genome and creating genetic differences will lead to the fragmentation and destruction of the human race. The American bioethicist George Annas, for example, has described genetic engineers as "potential bioterrorists" because of the possibility of genocide based on engineered genetic differences (Annas, 2001). The United Nations Educational, Scientific and Cultural Organization (UNESCO) Universal

Declaration on the Human Genome states that, "the human genome must be preserved as the common heritage of humanity" (UNESCO, 1997). However, the only way to eradicate all genetic differences that might lead to genocide, and the only way to preserve the human genome exactly as it is today, is universal human reproductive cloning—a course of action that neither Annas nor UNESCO would be likely to favour.

These arguments, then, are confusing and contradictory, yet they strike a note of concern with many. Even if this concern is misplaced or misdirected, we might well wonder what the consequences of enhancement will be for humanity as a whole.

We are familiar with the idea of Darwinian evolution: natural selection acting on genetic variation to produce long-term changes in our genetic make-up. There is also a sense in which human society and culture can be said to undergo evolution, as ideas that are more successful—whether because they are correct or intuitively attractive or both—will propagate themselves: a process known as meme evolution. This, of course, includes the progression of technological ideas.

It is reasonable to say that the relationship between humans and technology has probably influenced the course of our genetic and cultural evolution in the past. For example, it seems likely that the technological developments since pre-history have changed the selection pressures acting on human beings—one can plausibly suppose, for example, that the transition from hunter–gatherer to agricultural societies would have altered the environment to allow different genes to be favoured. Moreover, technology has undeniably influenced the course of social development.

It is often said, with reference to the human race, that we have halted evolution by doing away with natural selection. It is true that modern medicine allows many individuals to survive and reproduce when they might not otherwise have done so; yet, we must remember that the marked reductions in infant mortality, deaths from disease and so on are only a product of the past century or so—a mere few generations. In the context of the roughly three billion year history of life on Earth, it seems to be a little premature to declare victory over natural selection—although we are probably the first and only species that understands evolution and might be in a position to influence its course deliberately.

Even if we were to remove the influence of natural selection entirely, it would not necessarily mean the end of evolution—if by evolution we mean social change or cultural evolution—or the end of genetic change. In fact, although the collective human genome is not changing appreciably faster than it has in the past, the development of human society as a whole—that is, evolution in the cultural sense—is progressing faster than ever, and is constantly accelerating. What we want to do and what we dream of doing is rapidly outpacing what we can do with the genomes and the bodies that we are presently born with. Hans Moravec, who is a robotics expert at Carnegie Mellon University (Pittsburgh, PA, USA), has expressed this as, "the drag of the flesh on the spirit . . . the problem is that cultural development proceeds much faster than biological evolution" (Moravec, 1989). Interestingly, he noted this in the context of artificial intelligence and wondered whether machines might overcome the "drag of the flesh" from which humans suffer. With the new biological technologies offered to us, we might be able to overcome the drag in our own bodies.

Modifying the human genome might be one way of doing this. Some see it as tampering with the process of natural evolution that produced the human genome in its current form. True enough, our present genome is, by definition, a successful one: it is still around today. However, evolution so far has operated somewhat in the dark. The happenstance of natural evolution has also bequeathed us a legacy of genetic failings: susceptibility to disease, cancer and the depredations of old age, to name but a few. We are, as the British evolutionary scientist Richard Dawkins might put it, stranded on our own particular peak of 'Mount Improbable' (Dawkins, 1996), lumbered with all the genetic encumbrances of our evolutionary history, good and bad.

We have, almost within our reach, the power to transcend this situation: to change our genotypes, much as we can already change our phenotypes to improve health and quality of life. There might be no guarantee of success; however, in comparison to natural evolution, any genetic modifications aimed at improving the human condition will at least be evidence-based rather than random, and unless blind watch-making is to be the new gold standard in scientific research, that is as good as it gets with current technology (Chan & Harris, 2006).

How will this new "enhancement evolution" (Harris, 2007) be mediated? The prospect of genetic enhancement is always haunted by the spectre of eugenics—the state-coerced use of technology to change us whether we will or no. To this point, we should emphasize once again the importance of individual choice. Yet, enhancements might also limit individual choices through the so-called genetic arms race, in which everyone is forced to use enhancements to 'keep up with the Joneses'. Is this a bad thing? Evolution, again, has always been a genetic arms race: we are designed to compete. The end point in this case, however, is not the threat of mutually assured destruction, but rather the survival of our species. Of course, we should have the option not to participate, to refuse enhancements. Yet why would we want to? If the ultimate result of these technologies is better lives for all humans, then their use is probably a good thing. Put another way, we currently engage in a type of educational arms race of enhancements. Reading and writing was once the province of a few privileged scholars; now it is almost mandatory to equip children with these skills, if they are to keep up with their peers. The result of this educational arms race has been almost ubiquitous literacy—surely a benefit?

Even these sort of claims, however, really only apply to the developed and industrialized world. The 'ubiquitous' benefits that we enjoy are often not readily available to those in developing nations—and in this sense, enhancements raise crucial questions of justice. Will the ultimate result of human enhancement be better lives for everyone, or will it be better lives for a few at the expense of the disadvantaged many?

The issue of how to address the aims of justice with respect to enhancement technologies is a complex one, and I have scope only to note two brief points here. The first is that concerns about justice do not warrant turning our backs entirely on enhancement technologies—"it is doubtful ethics to deny a benefit to some unless and until it can be provided to all" (Harris, 2007). Certainly, that is not the position we take on most new technologies. Allowing access to expensive technologies to those who can afford them will, in all likelihood, speed their development to become more readily available to everyone. The second point is that this process might need a helping hand: if we see injustice, we should move to address it in a positive way, to 'level up', so that the same opportunities are available to all, rather than 'levelling down' and reducing everyone to the same level.

A few last words, then, on what enhancement might mean for humanity. Enhancement technologies, provided their application is correctly managed, will ultimately be of benefit to humankind and, as such, we have good moral reasons to pursue them. They will not, as some fear, destroy humanity by turning us into something other—something more—than what we are. We have always wanted—and will probably always want—to be more than we are. Yet by the same token, we will always remain 'what we are'—in the sense of that which really matters to us, that which makes us human. Surely, being human and the definition of 'humanness' should not depend arbitrarily on a particular combination of abilities and limitations—to run no faster than 25 miles per hour, to live no longer than a century. Indeed, logically it cannot depend on such limitations, or we would be forced to admit that we ourselves are no longer human compared to our predecessors who had more limited abilities and life spans.

Instead, what make us human are our aspirations, our awareness of ourselves as beings in the world (including our limitations), our ability for self-contemplation and reflection, and the desire to attempt to change what we see. We are not designed to remain "passive, inert players in the game of life" (Chan & Harris, 2007). What makes us uniquely human is the ability to shape our own destinies according to our desires—and genetic and other enhancement technologies provide further means for us to do so. In this sense, enhancements and the desire to avail ourselves of them are an expression of our essential humanity.

The advent of new forms of human enhancement on our technological horizon does not therefore signify, as some have warned, the end of humanity. Rather, it is just the next step in a continuing process: that of human evolution, which stretches far back into the dim past and, we might hope, will continue into the future for many thousands of years to come.

References

Annas G (2001) Genism, racism and the prospect of genetic genocide. Presentation at UNESCO 21st Century Talks: World Conference Against Racism, Racial Discrimination, Xenophobia and Related Intolerance in Durban, South Africa, September 3rd. www.thehumanfuture.org

Buchanan A, Brock DW, Daniels N, Wikler D (2000) *From Chance to Choice: Genetics and Justice.* Cambridge, UK: Cambridge University Press

Cavazzana-Calvo M et al. (2000) Gene therapy of human severe combined immunodeficiency (SCID)-X1 disease. *Science* **288**: 669–672

Chan S, Harris J (2006) The ethics of gene therapy. *Curr Opin Mol Ther* **8**: 377–383

Chan S, Harris J (2007) In support of enhancement. *Studies in Ethics Law and Technology* 1: Article 10

Davis DS (2001) *Genetic Dilemmas.* New York, NY, USA: Routledge

Dawkins R (1996) *Climbing Mount Improbable.* London, UK: Penguin Books

Feinberg J (1980) The child's right to an open future. In *Whose Child? Children's Rights, Parental Authority and State Power,* W Aiken, H LaFollette (eds), pp 124–153. Totowa, NJ, USA: Rowman and Litlefield

Habermas J (2003) *The Future of Human Nature.* Cambridge, UK: Polity

Harris J (2007) *Enhancing Evolution.* Princeton, NJ, USA: Princeton University Press

Mameli M (2007) Reproductive cloning, genetic engineering and the autonomy of the child: the moral agent and the open future. *J Med Ethics* **33**: 87–93

Moravec H (1989) Human culture: A genetic takeover underway. In *Artificial Life,* CG Langton (ed). Indianapolis, IN, USA: Addison-Wesley

Sandel MJ (2004) The case against perfection: What's wrong with designer children, bionic athletes, and genetic engineering. *Atl Mon* **292**: 50–54, 56–60, 62

Sandel MJ (2007) *The Case Against Perfection: Ethics in the Age of Genetic Engineering.* Cambridge, MA, USA: Belknap

Savulescu J (2001) Harm, ethics committees and the gene therapy death. *J Med Ethics* **27**: 148–150

UNESCO (1997) *Universal Declaration on the Human Genome and Human Rights.* Paris, France: UNESCO

On Designer Babies: Genetic Enhancement of Human Embryos Is Not a Practice for Civil Societies

Sheldon Krimsky

Sheldon Krimsky is Lenore Stern Professor of Humanities and Social Sciences at Tufts University.

You may remember a short period in the 1990s when a broad consensus emerged among biologists about the ethics of human genetic engineering. Somatic cell gene therapy was considered an acceptable biomedical research program, whereas germ line genetic modification was treated as unethical. By the new millennium, that moral boundary had eroded.

A recent debate in New York City in which I was a participant highlighted the cultural change. Our topic: "Babies Should Not Be Genetically Engineered." I argued in support of the proposition to prohibit the genetic modification of human reproductive cells prior to gestation in the womb.

Two compelling reasons to genetically alter human reproductive cells in preparation for childbirth, I argued, are for curing or preventing a disease or for the "enhancement" of a child. With respect to the former, there are safer and more dependable methods for preventing the birth of a child with a severe genetic abnormality than by genetic modification of the germ cells. The use of prenatal screening or preimplantation embryo diagnosis will suffice in most cases to prevent the birth of a genetically abnormal embryo.

Accordingly, the only remaining rationale for engaging in the genetic modification of human reproductive cells is for enhancement of the child to achieve such traits as heightened intelligence, resistance to disease, muscle strength, appealing personality or longevity, to cite a few common examples. I believe that pursuit of this goal represents the greatest scientific folly and moral failure.

First, for whatever enhancement is sought, the only method for determining efficacy is to engage in a clinical trial with a few dozen fertilized human eggs or embryos, where half would be genetically modified, all would be carried to term, and the development of the children would be followed throughout their lives to determine whether the genetic modification worked and worked safely. No animal studies can answer these questions.

It is unimaginable that any humane society would permit such a trial where the potential risks so outweigh the social benefits.

The second reason to shun genetic enhancement is that it makes no sense from a biological and developmental perspective. The human traits typically cited for enhancement, such as intelligence, personality or musicianship, are complex and not only involve dozens if not hundreds of genes, but are the result of a complex mix of determinants, including nutrition, social and environmental factors, gene-to-gene interactions and epigenetic switches that are outside the reductive chemistry of the DNA code.

Even for height, one of the most heritable traits known, scientists have discovered at least 50 genes that can account for 2 to 3 percent of the variance in the samples. There could be hundreds of genes associated with height. If you want a tall child, then marry tall.

Finally, the idea of genetic enhancement grows out of a eugenics ideology that human perfection can be directed by genetics. I am all for human enhancement, but it must start after an egg is fertilized beginning in utero—by protecting the fetus from neurotoxins and other endocrine-disrupting substances and continuing after birth with nutritional and cognitive enrichment and moral education, for example.

The greatest danger of a belief in genetics engineering lies in its likely social impact. Eugenics will inevitably be used by those with wealth and power to make others believe that to be prenatally genetically modified makes you better. This would be as much a myth as believing that the sperm from Nobel Laureates will produce a genius child.

A Moderate Approach to Enhancement

Michael Selgelid

Michael Selgelid is Director of the Centre for Human Bioethics at Monash University in Melbourne.

Revolutionary developments in biomedical science, particularly in genetics, may lead to new cures or preventative therapies for a wide variety of human diseases. Just about everyone agrees that this would be a good thing.

However, the very same kinds of developments that may be used to combat disease might also be used for the purpose of human enhancement—that is, to make people "better than well".

Consider genetic testing, for example. Genetic testing of embryos produced by *in vitro* fertilization (IVF) can allow us to detect genetic sequences known to be associated with a wide variety of diseases before embryos are implanted in the mother's uterus. Couples can thus increase the likelihood of having healthy offspring by choosing to implant only those embryos that test negative for genetic diseases. As knowledge about the relationship between genes and human traits increases, we will be able to detect genetic sequences associated with a wide variety of positively desired characteristics too. Many parents might then want to select *for* traits such as increased height, intelligence, strength, beauty, and so on, with the aim of giving their children higher-quality lives. The limits would depend on the extent to which a genetic basis for such traits is eventually demonstrated by genetic science. We can imagine a future where each embryo produced via IVF receives a "genetic report card", indicating predispositions to a large number of advantageous as well as disadvantageous human traits.

Similar possibilities may arise via genetic engineering. When diseases are caused by an individual lacking an important genetic sequence, or having a disease-causing genetic sequence, it might eventually become possible to insert the missing sequence, or replace the pathogenic sequence with a normal sequence, via "genetic therapy". If and when such procedures are perfected, it might also be possible to alter an individual's genome purely for enhancement purposes. Genetic sequences associated with normal stature, for example, might be replaced by those associated with greater than average, or even exceptional, height; genetic sequences associated with normal cognitive capacity might be replaced by those associated with greater than average, or even exceptional, cognitive capacity, and so on. The limits will depend again on the extent to which relationships between genes and human traits are eventually demonstrated by genetic science, and in this case, also on the extent to which it becomes technically possible to make precise changes to human genomes.

This of course raises questions about whether or not non-therapeutic enhancement-oriented genetic interventions are morally permissible, and whether or not they should be permitted legally. Most people agree that using such procedures to reduce disease would be relatively non-problematic, at least if these procedures can be shown to be safe and effective. On the other hand, many object to the idea of using biomedical technology for the purpose of enhancement. But why should this be so?

The Good of Individuals Versus the Good of Society

Advocates of enhancement often point out that enhancement is, by definition, a good thing. "To enhance" *means* "to make better". So when we are talking about true enhancements, we are necessarily talking about making people better off than they otherwise would have been in terms of their overall wellbeing. In the case of genetic screening in the context of IVF, we are talking about parents choosing embryos that, based on the best available information, they expect to have the healthiest or happiest lives. What, one wonders, could possibly be wrong with that?

The best objection to true human enhancement appeals to potential adverse social consequences. In other words, it might be good for enhanced individuals, but bad for society as a whole. In particular, the practice of human enhancement would be expected to lead to increased social inequality. If the kinds of genetic technologies discussed above are indeed developed, then they will presumably only be available to those with the money to pay for them. It is hard to imagine that they would be made freely available to all via universal healthcare systems, which, due to resource constraints, are often unable to provide even medically necessary services to all who need them. So the relatively wealthy will then be able to enhance themselves and their children while the relatively poor and their children will remain unenhanced, or at least less enhanced. The (more) enhanced richfolk will then have even greater competitive advantages than previously. The divide between the haves and have-nots will inevitably increase, and become more intractable. Or so the argument goes.

This kind of appeal to equality is routinely made by those opposed to genetic enhancement. Advocates of genetic enhancement routinely reply by pointing out that we already tolerate a wide variety of inequality-promoting non-genetic enhancements. The wealthy send their children to special schools, sports camps, music lessons, and so on—and these things increase the advantages of those children who are already advantaged in other ways. What, genetic enhancement advocates ask, could be so different about genetic enhancements that they would be wrong, while other non-genetic kinds of enhancements are perfectly acceptable? Given that it is hard to imagine what could be so special and different about (true, safe and effective) genetic enhancement *per se*, they conclude that genetic enhancement must be acceptable too. They often appear to think this should be an argument stopper.

However, this argument in defense of enhancement is not altogether convincing. It might be true that there is no inherent moral difference between genetic enhancement and the other kinds of enhancements enumerated above. But there could very well turn out to be important *differences in scale*. If enough genetic enhancements become available, their use becomes sufficiently widespread, and they turn out to be especially powerful in their effects on people's capacities, then *the extent of their impact on equality* could turn out to be much greater than that which results from currently available non-genetic means of enhancement. According to some authors, the threat to equality posed by genetic enhancement may be unprecedented. Existing kinds of enhancements might be tolerable because we value the liberty of individuals to pursue them, and because the inequalities that result are not bad enough to justify our infringing on this liberty. On the other hand, if the consequences of the inequalities were bad enough, then liberty considerations might be outweighed by equality considerations.

In addition to being unjust, deep inequality can compromise democracy and social stability. Severe inequality can thus make everyone significantly worse off. And the use of genetic enhancements could have adverse effects on society in other ways. One less frequently discussed concern about the social consequences of enhancement is that if it becomes especially profitable to develop and offer genetic enhancement services, then this will drain medical research and healthcare provision resources away from disease treatment and prevention.

We are already faced with a situation known as the "10/90 divide": 90 per cent of medical research resources focus on diseases that account for 10 per cent of the global burden of disease. This is because the majority of medical research focuses on developing the drugs and other interventions expected to make the most profits, rather than those that are most important from a global public health perspective. We can imagine that this situation will only be exacerbated if the provision of genetic enhancement services turns out to be highly profitable. If a drain of resources thus occurs, the quality of life improvements *overall* made by enhancement may turn out to be less than would have been achieved if those resources had instead focused on disease reduction and the prevention of suffering.

Conflicting Values

Questions about the ethics of genetic enhancement thus turn both on unresolved empirical questions and on unresolved philosophical questions.

There are unresolved empirical questions about (1) the extent of inequality that would likely result from an unrestricted practice of human enhancement, and (2) the overall impact that an unrestricted practice of human enhancement would have on human wellbeing. We cannot predict such consequences with certainty, of course, but interdisciplinary social science research, including sophisticated modeling and so on, could shed some light on the potential impact of genetic enhancement under various scenarios—that is, depending on the kinds of genetic enhancements projected to become possible. In the meantime, it is surprising and unfortunate that so many philosophers have spilt so much ink on speculative discussion about what the social consequences of genetic enhancement are likely to be—telling just-so stories about why the impact of genetic enhancement on social equality or welfare will or won't turn out to be problematic. These philosophers should more often admit that questions about the likely impact of enhancement ultimately require empirical research by those with the appropriate expertise for conducting it. They should refrain from pretending that these empirical questions are really philosophical questions.

The spectre of genetic enhancement does, however, also raise important and difficult philosophical questions—but these have received insufficient attention, being only very rarely explicitly addressed in the burgeoning literature. The key unresolved philosophical questions concern how the value of personal liberty should be weighed against social equality and welfare in cases where these values conflict.

Liberty is an important value, and there are widely-accepted presumptions in favour of its protection unless there are very good reasons for interfering with it. Liberty is rightly considered especially important in the context of reproduction in particular. Insofar as we place an especially high value on reproductive liberty, we should be reluctant to restrict parents' choices regarding the genetic enhancement of their offspring.

However, liberty should not be thought to have absolute priority over all other values. Liberty, equality and welfare all matter, so none should have absolute priority over the others. Thus if the social costs of the unrestricted practice of genetic enhancement are sufficiently great (i.e., disastrous) for welfare or equality, then the importance of individual liberty might be outweighed by the importance of these other values. The unresolved philosophical question is thus: How socially damaging would enhancement need to be in order for personal liberty to be justly overridden? This points to a need for theoretical development in the fields of ethics and political philosophy.

At present there are three main approaches on the table. First, utilitarians argue that aggregate benefit is the only thing that ultimately matters to society, and so "utility", the greatest benefit for the greatest number of people, should always be promoted, even at the expense of liberty and equality. By contrast, egalitarians often place extreme weight on the value of equality; and libertarians place extreme weight on the value of liberty. Each of these perspectives gets something right, because the values they respectively emphasize each matter. But they each arguably get something wrong too, insofar as they each tend to place absolute or overriding weight on the values they emphasize. In this latter respect they are out of line with commonsense ethical thinking and what is generally considered to be good policy-making. To resolve questions about genetic enhancement, and many other difficult issues in practical ethics, we need a fourth approach that provides a principled way of striking a balance or making trade-offs between liberty, equality, and utility in cases of conflict. Development of a "moderate pluralist" theory such as this would be necessary to determine how great the costs of enhancement would need to be for us to be justified in denying people the freedom to enhance themselves and their offspring, and to what extent.

INFORMATIVE SYNTHESIS

DEFINITION

Your goal in writing an informative synthesis is to combine material on some topic you have gathered from two or more readings into a clear, organized essay. After finishing your essay, a reader should have a better understanding of the topic and should know the position of the various authors whose work you include. You are not trying to show how one author is correct in what she says and another is wrong. Neither are you trying to advocate a position of your own on the topic. Instead, you are trying to present other people's ideas or findings as clearly and concisely as you can, highlighting key similarities and differences. Teachers also commonly refer to these papers as "reports" or "comparison-contrast essays."

For example, if you were writing an informative synthesis of the essays included in this chapter, you would want to summarize what each writer had to say about the genetic enhancement of human beings. In fact, a good way to write this paper would be to isolate for examination certain aspects of the topic that all of the writers address—that way you could draw direct comparisons among the pieces. As you point out for your reader important similarities or differences you see in the various essays, you would not argue that one author is correct in his or her position on the topic and that the others are misguided, nor would you comment on the quality of the writing or argument in any particular essay.

To compose an informative synthesis, you employ many of the same skills needed to write summaries. As with writing summaries, you may encounter a number of problems when composing an informative synthesis:

1. Because of their content, language, or structure, the source texts themselves might be hard for you to understand. Because you need to form a clear understanding of the readings before you write about them, you need strong critical reading skills to write a successful synthesis.

2. You will often be looking for subtle differences among readings—not just different arguments or findings that the authors put forward, but slightly different interpretations of data, slightly different uses of terminology, slightly different emphases. Because a synthesis involves multiple source texts, when you examine a reading you plan to use in your paper, you also have to keep in mind the material contained in the readings you have already read. The more readings you are working with, the harder it is to keep track of the material contained in each and the easier it is to overlook the subtle differences between them.

3. You need to stay as objective as possible when examining the source texts and writing your essay. You do not editorialize in an informative synthesis: your goal is *not* to comment on the topic of the readings or on the quality of their writing. Instead, you need to be open-minded when reading them,

to pull out from them material relevant to your thesis, and to present that material as clearly, concisely, and fairly as possible. As when you are writing a summary, remaining neutral can be difficult, especially when you feel strongly about a topic and must include in your informative synthesis ideas that disturb or anger you.

4. Organizing an informative synthesis can also be challenging. You need to decide how to construct your thesis so it adequately guides your reader through your work, how to order the information you include in your paper, and how to employ transitions within the body of your essay.

5. Supplying proper documentation in an informative synthesis can be problematic. One paragraph of your paper may contain information you have drawn from several different authors. Learning how to document such passages properly can be trying; remembering to do it is crucial. Improper documentation can lead to problems with clarity and plagiarism.

WRITING AN INFORMATIVE SYNTHESIS

Because writing an informative synthesis can be challenging, it is best to break the process down into a series of more manageable steps:

1. Analyze the assignment.
2. Review and annotate the readings.
3. Formulate a thesis and organizational plan.
4. Write your rough draft.
5. Revise your draft.
6. Check your quotations and documentation.

Remember that this method of writing a synthesis will not work for everybody. We all have our preferred way of writing papers, which can vary according to the type of essay we are composing and the time we have to complete the assignment. For example, some writers like to complete a rough draft before they write their thesis, while others must have a thesis in hand before they begin to write; some will rewrite a paper several times before they turn it in for a grade, while others revise very little. Use these directions as a rough guide for writing an informative synthesis. The important principle to keep in mind is to complete your paper in a series of steps, no matter the nature or order of those steps.

Step 1—Analyze the Assignment

Read the assignment carefully to make sure your instructor is asking you to write an informative rather than an argumentative synthesis. If you have any doubt, ask your teacher to clarify the assignment. Make sure you understand how many sources you are required to consult when researching the topic or to include when writing your paper. Also, check on the type of source texts your teacher expects you to use if you are required to collect the readings yourself. Some instructors will want you to use only "academic" sources—material written by experts in the field.

Step 2—Review and Annotate the Readings

After you have assembled the readings that will serve as the basis of your synthesis, read through them several times with your assignment in mind. In most cases, you will look for specific information in each reading, passages that address the topic of your paper. Thoroughly annotate the reading and then summarize it. As you work with the material, remember to be fair and open-minded. Consider how the author's perspective on the topic is similar to or different from what other authors have written and decide whether you think it should be included in your essay.

Step 3—Formulate a Thesis and an Organizational Plan

Your thesis in an informative synthesis serves an important function. More likely than not, it will indicate the topic of your essay and indicate how you will structure your synthesis—what you will discuss and in what order you will discuss it. Always keep in mind the rhetorical function of your thesis statement. When people read your paper, they need to know early on what you will be discussing and will look to your thesis as a guide.

Your thesis for an informative synthesis can be either open or closed. In an open thesis you indicate the topic and general structure of your paper:

> Chan, Krimsky, and Selgelid offer a range of opinions on the ethics of human genetic enhancement.

or

> While both Chan and Selgelid support human genetic enhancement, Krimsky disagrees.

With a closed thesis you list the specific issues you will address in your essay. However, you have to be careful not to put too much information in your thesis—doing so will only lead to cluttered prose. A possible closed thesis statement for the paper described above might read something like this:

> Chan, Krimsky, and Selgelid offer a range of opinions on the ethics of human genetic enhancement, primarily focusing on how it might impact social stability and individual liberty.

Either type of thesis can be effective, but in general, the longer your paper will be, the more likely you are to use an open thesis.

When writing an informative synthesis, you can employ either a block or alternating format to organize your essay. With a **block format,** you discuss what one source says about the topic in relation to your thesis before moving on to what the next source says. However, instead of just summarizing each source text, you also compare and contrast them, pointing out their key similarities and differences. Suppose, for example, that you are writing an essay with the thesis, "Chan, Krimsky, and Selgelid offer a range of opinions on the ethics of human genetic enhancement." In outline form, your paper might look something like this:

Opening Section

Introduce the topic of your essay

Give your thesis

Section on Chan Essay

Summarize Chan's position on the topic

Discuss its relationship to the other two readings

Section on Krimsky Essay

Summarize Krimsky's position on the topic

Discuss its relationship to the other two readings

Section on Selgelid Essay

Summarize Selgelid's position on the topic

Discuss its relationship to the other two readings

Conclusion

You might, though, choose to use an **alternating format** to organize your essay, especially if you use a closed thesis. Remember that with a closed thesis, you list the specific issues you will address in your essay. Using an alternating format allows you to discuss what each source says about these specific issues in order. For example, suppose you are writing an essay with this thesis: "Chan, Krimsky, and Selgelid offer a range of opinions on the ethics of human genetic enhancement, primarily focusing on how it might impact social stability and individual liberty." Using an alternating format, your paper might be organized like this:

Opening Section

Introduce the topic of your essay

Give your thesis

Effect of Human Genetic Enhancement on Social Stability

Chan's views and their relation to the other authors' views

Krimsky's views and their relation to the other authors' views

Selgelid's views and their relation to the other authors' views

Effect of Human Genetic Enhancement on Individual Liberty

Chan's views and their relation to the other authors' views

Krimsky's views and their relation to the other authors' views

Selgelid's views and their relation to the other authors' views

Conclusion

Of course, you could write the same paper using a block format. If you did, it might be organized like this:

Opening Section

Introduce the topic of your essay

Give your thesis

Chan Essay

Her views on how human genetic enhancement might impact social stability and how they are similar to and/or different from the views of the other authors on the topic

Her views on how human genetic enhancement might impact individual liberty and how they are similar to and/or different from the views of the other authors

Krimsky Essay

His views on how human genetic enhancement might impact social stability and how they are similar to and/or different from the views of the other authors on the topic

His views on how human genetic enhancement might impact individual liberty and how they are similar to and/or different from the views of the other authors

Selgelid Essay

His views on how human genetic enhancement might impact social stability and how they are similar to and/or different from the views of the other authors on the topic

His views on how human genetic enhancement might impact individual liberty and how they are similar to and/or different from the views of the other authors

Conclusion

Alternating and block formats have their particular strengths and weaknesses. The alternating format allows you to compare and contrast the views of different writers fairly easily. In this paper, for example, you would be able to present each author's position on how human genetic enhancement might impact social stability in its own section of your own essay before moving on to discuss its impact on individual liberty. If you were using a block format, you might discuss Chan's views on page one of your paper and might not get to Selgelid's views until page six or seven. Your reader might have a hard time remembering Chan's views by the time you reached Selgelid's views. Using a block format, however, allows you to give your readers a good sense of the general argument presented by each author in sequential order. Yet the block format often results in repetitive prose and frequently discourages students from discussing similarities and differences among the readings, simply summarizing each author's views instead.

Regardless of the structure you employ, your job in writing an informative synthesis involves more than summarizing what each critic has to say. In writing this paper, you would not be arguing a position of your own concerning the effects of human genetic enhancement. Instead, you would point out for your readers important similarities and differences among the views advanced by the source texts' authors.

After you have designed your thesis, you need to go back through the readings, consult your annotations, and locate material you want to include in your essay. Preparing an informal outline can be quite helpful at this point. In your outline, indicate the focus for each part of your paper, the material you will draw from the readings to develop that section of the essay, and the ideas you will contribute.

Step 4—Write Your Rough Draft

The introductory section of an informative thesis should, first, capture your readers' interest. You might consider opening your paper with an interesting anecdote, a case history, an important statistic, or a telling quotation from one of the readings. Writing an effective opening gives you the chance to be imaginative and creative. A second goal of the opening section of your synthesis is to introduce the topic of your essay. The title of the synthesis should give your readers some indication of your essay's topic, but you want to be sure to clarify the topic in your opening section. Finally, the introduction to your essay should contain your thesis statement. Whether your thesis is open or closed, you need to include it in your introduction to serve as a guide to the rest of your synthesis.

In the body of your essay, you will follow the structure supplied by your thesis, explaining ideas one author or issue at a time. If you were writing an informative synthesis using the three articles on human genetic enhancement as your source texts, in the body of your paper you would summarize, paraphrase, and quote what each author has to say about the topic, including in your essay material that best captures each writer's views and illustrates your thesis. However, not all the material in your informative synthesis will come from the readings. You have significant contributions to make, too. Besides quoting, paraphrasing, and summarizing what various authors have to say, you will contribute transitions, elaborations, clarifications, and connections.

For example, in one paragraph of your essay, you may introduce the issue to be discussed, introduce a reading by giving the author's name and qualifications as well as the title of the article, quote a relevant passage from the piece, restate the author's ideas in your own words to clarify them, point out how the author's stance differs from the author you discussed in the previous paragraph, and provide a transition to your next paragraph. If you devote a sentence to each of these tasks, your paragraph will be six sentences long, with only one sentence coming directly from the reading. The rest of the material in the paragraph comes from you.

When concluding your informative synthesis, you want to reiterate the main issues or findings you have covered in the body of your essay and give your work a sense of closure. You might want to look back at your opening strategy and reemploy it in your conclusion, if possible. For example, if you opened your paper with a quotation, consider ending it with a quotation. If you began with a question, conclude with the same question, perhaps answering it this time. If you began with a story, come back to the story in your conclusion.

Step 5—Revise Your Draft

Revising a synthesis takes time. In fact, it is probably best to revise your paper in several stages. Initially, you might check the **content** of your essay. Here you have two concerns. First, reread what you have written to make sure you are being true to your own intentions. You might ask the following questions of your manuscript:

- Does my thesis accurately reflect my understanding of the readings?
- Have I said in my paper what I wanted to say?
- Have I covered all of the material I hoped to cover when annotating the readings?
- Have I covered the ideas I discovered as I wrote the essay, ideas I did not plan on addressing but developed as I wrote?

A related goal is to review the content of your essay in light of the assignment. Here the questions you ask might include:

- Have I met the demands of the assignment?
- Have I adequately covered the ideas contained in the reading?
- Have I avoided editorializing or arguing a particular position?
- Have I kept my reader in mind? Would this essay make sense to someone who knows little or nothing about the readings? Do any ideas need more development or explanation?

Next, you might review the **organization** of your essay. Here you are concerned with the quality of your thesis statement, topic sentences, and transitions. These are some of the questions you should be asking:

- Does my thesis guide the development of the essay? Put another way, does my essay follow the format suggested or outlined by my thesis?
- Do I have clearly stated topic sentences introducing the major sections of my essay? Are these topic sentences tied to the thesis?
- Have I supplied enough transitional devices to guide my reader through my synthesis, especially when I move from discussing one author to discussing another?

Finally, revise with an eye toward **accuracy** and **clarity.** Here your concerns are word choice, sentence structure, and documentation. Again, you need to ask yourself a series of questions as you review your work, making needed changes when any of your answers are no:

- In choosing words, have I remained as fair and objective as possible?
- Have I successfully avoided jargon and highly technical terms when such language would not be appropriate for my audience?
- Are my sentences easy to read?
- Have I varied the type and length of my sentences?
- Have I quoted material accurately and properly?
- Have I paraphrased material accurately, properly, and fairly?
- Have I documented material thoroughly and properly?

You may need to revise your informative synthesis several times to address all of these concerns adequately.

Step 6—Check Quotations and Documentation

Before you turn in your final draft for a grade, be sure to check the accuracy of your quotations and documentation. Take the time to check any material you quoted against the source text to be sure you have accurately transcribed the information. Pay special attention to any passages in which you have added language to or taken language out of a quotation: these changes should not alter the meaning of the source text. Also, check to be sure that you have documented all of the material in your paper that needs to be documented and that you have employed the proper form of documentation in each instance. Remember that all paraphrased and quoted material in your paper should be documented. Because you are combining information from two or more sources in your synthesis, be sure it is always clear to your reader which source text you are referring to in your documentation.

SAMPLE INFORMATIVE SYNTHESIS

Following is a sample informative synthesis of the three articles on genetic enhancement provided earlier in this chapter. Notice how the writer structures the essay and employs material from the readings.

The Ethical Debate over Human Enhancement and Designer Babies

Advances in modern genetics have been astounding. What used to be dreamed of only in science fiction is becoming reality today. Scientists have discovered how to manipulate human genes to help eradicate disease and will soon be able to alter embryonic genes to enhance certain traits, such as a person's height, intelligence, or musical ability. All of these advances, however, raise serious ethical questions: Is it right to alter a person's genetic makeup? Are treatments to prevent disease more acceptable than those to enhance personal characteristics? Not surprisingly, scientists and philosophers addressing these questions have yet to reach consensus.

An important distinction in the debate is the difference between therapeutic and non-therapeutic genetic modification—whether the manipulation is undertaken to prevent disease or deformity (therapeutic) or whether its aim is to enhance certain desirable physical traits or abilities (non-therapeutic). Currently, when *in vitro* fertilization methods are used to have children, embryos can be tested for a range of genetic disorders or illnesses and parents can choose to implant only healthy embryos, a process known as genetic screening. To a growing degree, though, doctors are able to alter the genetic makeup of the embryo to correct the disorder or cure the illness prior to implantation—a process known as genetic therapy. Sarah Chan, a Research Fellow at the Institute for Science, Ethics, and Innovation at England's University of Manchester, argues that genetic therapy is a moral imperative: "If we could, with safety and certainly, engineer our children to have immunity to viral infection, protection from heart disease and reduced susceptibility to cancer, we should do so. . . . there would be a moral imperative to use it for the benefit of future generations" (187).

Michael Selgelid, a professor of human bioethics, generally agrees with at least part of Chan's argument. In "A Moderate Approach to Enhancement," Selgelid notes that current genetic screening enables parents to implant only healthy embryos, a process he also believes is morally acceptable: "Most people agree that using such procedures to reduce disease would be relatively non-problematic, at least if these procedures can be shown to be safe and effective" (194). Selgelid does not take up the issue of genetic therapy.

However, in his essay "On Designer Babies: Genetic Enhancement of Human Embryos Is Not a Practice for Civil Societies," Sheldon Krimsky does address the issue of genetic therapy and strongly disagrees with Chan. Krimsky argues that "the genetic modification of human reproductive cells prior to gestation in the womb" (192) is immoral because "there are safer and more dependable methods for preventing the birth of a child with a severe genetic abnormality" (192), namely, genetic selection.

The greatest disagreement among these authors concerns the question of non-therapeutic genetic enhancement. Selgelid summarizes what will soon be possible:

> As knowledge about the relationship between genes and human traits increases, we will be able to detect genetic sequences associated with a wide variety of positively desired characteristics too. Many parents might then want to select *for* traits such as increased height, intelligence, strength, beauty, and so on, with the aim of giving their children higher-quality lives. (194)

Selgelid then addresses a major objection to non-therapeutic genetic enhancement: the procedures might promote greater social inequality. Those with enough money to pay for enhancement will be greatly advantaged over those who cannot pay for them. If genetic enhancement becomes widespread and limited to the rich, equality and democracy may be threatened. As a result, the right to choose enhancement may need to be curtailed due to the adverse social consequences.

Krimsky unambiguously opposes non-therapeutic genetic modification, stating that the "pursuit of this goal represents the greatest scientific folly and moral failure" (192). First, Krimsky argues that even testing whether such genetic engineering can work is immoral: in a clinical trial, scientists would have to enhance some embryos and not others, then study the resulting children for the rest of their lives to determine whether the procedure worked and whether unforeseen negative consequences resulted. Society would not accept using children as lab rats in this way. Second, the characteristics parents may seek to enhance in their children are only moderately determined by genetics—attempting to make a child more musical through genetic manipulation, for example, fails to account for the environment the child is raised in, the child's exposure to music, the impact of teachers and peers, and so on. In addition, no single gene accounts for a particular human characteristic. According to Krimsky, "Even for height, one of the most heritable traits known, scientists have discovered at least 50 genes that can account for 2 to 3 percent of the variance in the sample" (193). Attempting to identify and alter all of the genes involved "makes no sense from a biological and developmental perspective" (193). Finally, Krimsky raises the same objection Selgelid noted: non-therapeutic gene therapy will favor the wealthy over the poor, promoting social inequality.

Chan, who supports non-therapeutic genetic enhancement, addresses many of the concerns Selgelid and Krimsky raise. First, Chan believes in the primary importance of people being able to lead good lives. Diseases inhibit one's ability to lead a good life; therefore, genetic therapy is acceptable: "to the extent that genes do determine some aspects of our lives, in particular our health and associated quality of life—it is surely far better to have a predisposition to a healthy life than to risk a higher chance of suffering and disease" (186).

Yet, leading a good life goes beyond just being free of illness. Human lives can actually be enhanced through genetic engineering—children can be made stronger, taller, faster, smarter, more beautiful, more musical, and so on (Chan 190; Krimsky 192; Selgelid 194). What's more, these traits will be passed along to future generations (Chan 186). In fact, Chan argues that genetically enhancing one's children would be an act of responsible parenting:

> . . . once the technology exists and has been proven to be safe, to refrain from using it is likewise to make a decision about the genetic inheritance of our descendants—specifically: that they will not receive such enhancements and will be denied the consequent benefits. . . . Abdicating choice is not the action of a responsible parent; exercising choice wisely is. (187)

In other words, as this technology becomes more widely available and safe, the question will become how parents choose to enhance their children genetically, not whether they will.

Chan largely discounts the social impact of genetic enhancement, believing that although at first the technology will be expensive, over time it will become available to all (190). She also maintains that once humans start to become enhanced, justice will dictate that everyone should have the opportunity to "level up" (190). In the conflict between individual liberty and social obligation that Selgelid discussed, Chan comes down firmly on the side of the individual. She states that all decisions about enhancement should be based on "individual choice" (189).

Human enhancement is already here: sports stars use steroids to get bigger and stronger, college student drink coffee to help them study, children get vaccinated, people with mental or physical illnesses take medications to improve the quality of their lives. Of course, these types of enhancements influence only the individual; they are not passed on to future generations through genetic manipulation. Together, Chan, Selgelid, and Krimsky offer a glimpse of the benefits genetic enhancement can offer but also raise serious ethical questions that at some point humans will have to answer.

Summary Chart

HOW TO WRITE AN INFORMATIVE SYNTHESIS

1. **Analyze the assignment.**
   - *Determine whether you are being asked to write an informative or argumentative synthesis.*
   - *Determine the number and types of readings you are expected to use in your paper.*

2. **Review and annotate the readings.**
   - *Review the readings with your assignment in mind, looking for and marking information related to the topic of your paper.*
   - *Briefly summarize each reading.*

3. **Formulate a thesis and organizational plan.**
   - *Determine what stance you will assume in your essay.*
   - *Determine whether you will use an open or closed thesis statement.*
   - *Decide how you will order the ideas you will develop in your essay.*
   - *Decide whether you will present your ideas using a block or alternating format.*

4. **Write your rough draft.**
   - *Follow the organization plan implied or stated by your thesis.*
   - *Summarize and combine (synthesize) material from the source texts to support your thesis.*
   - *Both paraphrase and quote material as necessary.*
   - *Add transitions, elaborations, clarifications, and connections where needed.*
   - *Include a concluding paragraph.*

SUMMARY CHART: HOW TO WRITE AN INFORMATIVE SYNTHESIS *(CONTINUED)*

5. **Revise your draft.**

   Revise to improve the content of your essay.
   - *Does your thesis accurately reflect your position and intention?*
   - *Have you communicated in your paper what you want to communicate?*
   - *Will your paper give your reader a thorough understanding of the source texts and your thesis?*
   - *Have you avoided editorializing in your paper?*
   - *Would your essay make sense to someone who has not read the source texts?*

   Revise to improve the organization of your essay.
   - *Does your thesis guide the development of your essay?*
   - *Do you provide topic sentences to introduce major sections of your essay?*
   - *Have you provided transitions that help lead your reader through your paper?*

   Revise to improve the accuracy and clarity of your essay.
   - *Have you used language that is as fair and impartial as possible?*
   - *Have you avoided jargon and overly technical language when they would not be appropriate?*
   - *Have you checked for sentence variety and clarity?*
   - *Have you proofread for spelling, punctuation, and usage errors?*

6. **Check your quotations and documentation.**
   - *Have you quoted and paraphrased material properly, accurately, and fairly?*
   - *Have you documented all the material that needs to be documented?*
   - *Have you documented material employing the proper format?*

INFORMATIVE SYNTHESIS REVISION CHECKLIST

	Yes	No
1. Have you checked your assignment to be sure you have written the proper kind of synthesis essay: informative or argumentative?	____	____
2. In your introduction do you:		
• introduce the topic of the paper?	____	____
• offer your thesis?	____	____
• capture your readers' interest?	____	____
3. Examine the wording of your thesis. Does it clearly indicate what stance you will assume in your essay?	____	____
4. Examine the structure of your essay. Does it follow the organizational plan indicated by your thesis?	____	____
5. Check each section in the body of your essay. Do you:		
• examine just one issue at a time?	____	____
• combine information from your source texts?	____	____
• explain the link between the examples you cite and the assertion you are making?	____	____
• make clear the relationship you see among your source texts?	____	____
6. Examine your transitions. Have you provided adequate signals to help guide your readers through your work?	____	____
7. The first time you introduce a source text, do you give the full title of the piece and the author's full name?	____	____
8. Have you properly documented all quoted, summarized, and paraphrased material?	____	____

INFORMATIVE SYNTHESIS REVISION CHECKLIST *(CONTINUED)*

	Yes	No
9. Have you reviewed your quotations for accuracy and variety?	____	____
10. Is your works cited or reference list correct?	____	____
11. Have you reviewed your essay to be sure the content accurately communicates your position and intention?	____	____
12. Have you reviewed your word choice for clarity and accuracy?	____	____

Chapter 10

ARGUMENTATIVE SYNTHESIS

In this chapter you will learn how to

1. Recognize the elements of argument and persuasion in readings
2. Compare readings in terms of the arguments they present
3. Develop and state an argumentative thesis
3. Employ material from readings to support an argument
4. Document multi-source argumentative essays

DEFINITION AND PURPOSE

In an argumentative synthesis, you use material from various readings to support and illustrate an argument of your own, usually concerning the quality of writing in the source texts or an issue they address. If your argument centers on the quality of the readings, you might argue that one text is better written or more convincing than the others. If, however, your teacher asks you to present an argument on the issue the readings address, you will draw on the material in the readings to support your thesis.

For a number of reasons, writing an argumentative synthesis can be challenging:

1. As with the informative synthesis, the sources you consult when gathering information for this type of essay can be difficult to read. They will often present complex arguments themselves or employ terminology or research methodologies new to you. Being able to read this material critically is essential if you hope to write a successful argumentative synthesis.
2. As you read these source texts, you will need to critique them. For example, if you are arguing that one is better written than another, you will have to critique both to determine the relative strengths and weaknesses of each. If you are using the readings to develop an argument of your own on the topic they address, again you will have to critique the source texts to determine the quality of the arguments and information in each. You want to base your argument on the best available material.

3. When you compose your argumentative synthesis, you have to be concerned, first, with the content and quality of *your* argument. You need to decide if the material you are including in your paper will achieve the desired effect on your reader—will your audience be convinced by your argument? At the same time, since you are working with source texts, you have to pay close attention to the way you are using other people's findings or arguments to be sure you are fairly representing their work.
4. Part of composing an argumentative synthesis is deciding how best to order the claims, evidence, findings, or arguments you present. You need to decide which ideas or arguments you will present in which order and to provide effective transitions between and within the major sections of your argument.
5. In supporting your argument with source material, you will need to quote, summarize, and paraphrase other people's ideas, arguments, and findings. As a result, documentation becomes a challenge. You will need to be explicit and clear in acknowledging the source of the information you use to support your assertions.

THE ELEMENTS OF ARGUMENT

As you develop, draft, and revise your argumentative synthesis, pay particular attention to the three basic elements of any argument: **claims**, **grounds**, and **warrants**. According to British philosopher Stephen Toulmin in *The Uses of Argument* (Cambridge University Press, 1958), every argument involves an assertion (claim) that is supported by evidence (grounds) and rests on a particular set of assumptions or line of reasoning (warrant). Effective arguments employ clear, limited claims; reliable, appropriate grounds; and fully developed, explicit warrants. Understanding each of these elements can help you compose more effective argumentative synthesis essays.

CLAIMS

A **claim** is an assertion that you want your readers to accept. In an argumentative synthesis essay, your thesis statement is a claim, one you will develop and support with other claims in the body of your essay. Suppose, for example, you are writing an argumentative synthesis using the articles on human genetic enhancement in Chapter 9 and decide on the following thesis: "Due to her analogies, examples, and reasoning, Chan's argument that human genetic enhancement is ethical proves more persuasive than Krimsky's argument that it is not ethical." Your thesis is a claim: Chan's argument is stronger than Krimsky's argument. You will support this assertion with three other claims or "because" statements: Chan's argument is stronger because she employs more effective analogies, better examples, and a clearer line of reasoning. In the body of your essay you will develop these three claims with valid grounds and warrants if you want readers to accept your thesis.

When you compose an essay from source texts, most of your claims will be based on what you read and can include:

- claims concerning the source text's topic;
- claims concerning the source text's content, organization, or style;
- claims concerning the quality of the source text's writing; and
- claims concerning your response or reaction to the source texts.

Your teacher may give you several readings to study or require you to collect material on your own outside of class. In either case, you will be expected to critique the readings, form an argumentative thesis or claim, and explain or defend that assertion in your essay.

Well-written claims are **accurate, clear**, and **limited**. Any claim you make about a reading should be accurate: you should not misrepresent what an author writes. Claims should also be clear and unambiguous. "There are several good things about Chan's argument" is not a clear claim. What does the writer mean by "good" or by "things"? When forming claims, be as specific as you can, using language that precisely captures the assertion you want to make. Also, avoid broad, unlimited claims because such assertions are usually inaccurate and difficult to support. Claims like "Chan's essay is the best piece of writing ever produced" or "There is absolutely no value at all to Chan's argument" are not sufficiently limited. In writing limited claims, you may find yourself using words like "most" instead of "all," "often" instead of "always," or "likely" instead of "certainly." Limited claims (including limited thesis statements) are easier to explain and defend than unlimited, sweeping claims.

GROUNDS

Grounds is another name for the evidence you use to support a claim. As with claims, when you compose a source-based argumentative synthesis essay, you will draw most of your grounds from readings, though many teachers will allow you to use relevant personal experience to support a claim as well. Source-based grounds can include facts, statistics, testimony, and opinions. Each type of evidence has its own strengths and limitations. When deciding how to employ each in support of a claim, consider the questions that follow. Remember: the quality of your essay often depends on the quality of the grounds you employ to support your claims. If you rely on weak, questionable, or irrelevant grounds to support your claims, your writing is unlikely to convince thoughtful readers.

Facts: information the author of the source text presents as verifiably true

- Is the information up to date?
- Does the information come from a reliable source?

- Is the information documented?
- Is the information clear and unambiguous in its meaning?
- Is the information relevant to the claim you are making?
- Is the information consistent with your understanding, knowledge, or experience?
- Is the information consistent with what other source texts contend?

Examples: illustrations drawn from the source text to support your claim

- Are the examples relevant to the claim you are making?
- How much background information do you need to provide so that your reader will understand the examples you incorporate from the source text?
- Are the examples true or fictional? Is either acceptable given your assignment?
- Do the examples come from a reliable source?
- Are the examples timely?
- Are the examples representative and typical or limited and unique?

Statistics: data the author of the source text employs to support his or her claims

- Do you understand the statistics, what they mean, and their limitations?
- Do the statistics come from a reliable, trustworthy source?
- What are the possible biases of the source text? How might those biases affect the statistics offered in the piece?
- How do the statistics compare with evidence found in other source texts?
- Does the author of the source text acknowledge the limitations of the statistics?
- Are the statistics relevant to the claim you are trying to support in your essay?
- Can you adequately explain the link between the statistics you cite and the claim you are supporting?

Testimony: personal experiences offered by the author of the source text in support of his or her claims

- Does the testimony come from a reliable, qualified source?
- Is the testimony firsthand or secondhand?
- How is the testimony relevant to the claim you are trying to support?
- What background information from the source text will you need to provide so that your reader will understand the meaning and nature of the testimony?
- Does the author of the source text acknowledge the limitations of the testimony?
- How does the testimony complement (or contradict) other grounds provided in the essay?

Opinions: what the author of a source text believes to be true

- Is this the opinion of the source text's author or is the author offering someone else's opinion?
- Is the person sufficiently qualified to offer an opinion worth citing in your essay?
- How will you make clear in the body of your essay that this opinion comes from a reliable source?
- Does the author sufficiently explain and clarify his or her opinion?
- Does the author support that opinion with evidence?
- Is the opinion sufficiently qualified?
- Is the opinion supported by other types of evidence in the source text or by evidence you have gathered from other sources?

Whatever grounds you employ in your essay, be sure they are **relevant**, **reliable**, and **appropriate**. As you defend or illustrate a claim, first be sure the evidence you use is relevant to the assertion you are making. Writing an argumentative synthesis can be confusing because you are working with multiple texts and multiple claims. As you select the grounds you will use to support a particular claim, be sure they clearly relate to that claim and not to some other assertion you are making in your essay. Also, be sure the grounds are reliable—examine the credentials and possible biases of the source text's author, the publication's or website's credibility, and the date of publication. Finally, be sure your grounds are appropriate for the assignment and audience. As you write papers in classes across the curriculum, you will discover that what counts as valid grounds in one class may not count as valid grounds in another. Learning what grounds are appropriate for arguments in a field of study is part of learning how to reason like a member of that discipline. Analyze the texts you read in class to determine the kinds of evidence successful authors in that field of study utilize in their arguments and ask your instructor for help if you have doubts about the appropriateness of evidence you plan to use in any essay.

One final note about grounds: most writers know that they can support a claim in an argumentative synthesis essay by quoting, paraphrasing, or otherwise alluding to the work of authors who agree with the position they are advancing. Citing authorities who support the claims you make improves your work's credibility. However, there are other ways to use source material to support an argument. For example, consider citing authorities who *disagree* with the claim you are making. Incorporating counterexamples into your argumentative synthesis can be effective if you employ them correctly. First, acknowledging alternative positions increases your credibility as a writer. It demonstrates your knowledge of the subject matter, your fairness, and the confidence you have in your own position. However, citing counterexamples alone will not help you achieve these benefits; instead, you must integrate them into your essay by refuting them, conceding to them, or accommodating them.

When you **refute** counterexamples, you offer a fair summary of the opposing view, then demonstrate how that position is wrong, problematic, or otherwise flawed. You can then explain how your position is better. When you **concede** to an opposing view, you acknowledge how and when the opposition might be right in its assertions. However, you then demonstrate how that fact does not seriously damage your own position or thesis. Finally, when you **accommodate** an opposing view, you explain how that position and your own may be equally correct and how, by combining them, one might gain a better, more comprehensive understanding of the issue. In short, be imaginative in your use of source material as grounds in an argumentative synthesis. Just be sure the grounds you use are linked to your claims with strong warrants.

WARRANTS

Warrants are a little harder to understand than claims or grounds because they tend to be more abstract. Simply stated, though, a warrant is a line of reasoning, a set of assumptions, or an explanation that links a claim to its grounds. When writing an argumentative synthesis, remember that in most cases the grounds will not speak for themselves: you need to explain how they support the claim you are making. For instance, suppose you wrote the following passage, a claim supported by an example:

> Chan's argument is stronger than Krimsky's, in part, due to the analogies she employs to support and illustrate many of her claims. For example, she compares human genetic enhancement to the widely accepted practice of vaccinating children for diseases or providing children the best possible education after they are born.

Are you ready to move on to your next claim now? Have you sufficiently supported your claim by citing an example or two from the text? No. What's missing here is your warrant—before you move on to your next claim, you have to *explain how* the analogies you cite make Chan's argument more convincing than Krimsky's. What is it about citing statistics or citing *these* analogies that makes Chan's argument more convincing? Why might readers be more convinced by Chan's argument than the one put forth by Krimsky because Chan includes these analogies in her essay? As you explain the link between your assertion and the evidence you provide for it, you are articulating your warrant.

When you draft and revise your argumentative synthesis, you need to ask yourself a series of questions concerning the nature and effectiveness of your warrants.

1. **Is my warrant stated or unstated? If unstated, will the link between my claims and my grounds be sufficiently clear for my readers?**
   In everyday conversation, many warrants go unstated: the link between a claim and its grounds is so clear or so readily accepted that no warrant is needed. In academic writing, however, warrants usually need to be stated and explained. The aim of an academic argument is to let your reader know where you stand on an issue (your claim), to convince your reader

to accept this position as reasonable or correct by supporting it with evidence (your grounds), and to explain how this evidence makes the case for the claim (your warrant). Two writers may make the same assertion in their papers and may even support those assertions with similar evidence, but how they explain the link they see between the evidence and the claim will likely differ. In academic writing, warrants can help make your essay distinctive. Therefore, examine your essay for any unstated warrants and decide whether they need to be made explicit. If you think there is any chance your readers may question the link between a claim and its grounds, state your warrant.

2. **Is my warrant logical and reasonable?**
How *do* the grounds you employ actually support your claim? What assumptions are you making about the link between your grounds and claims? Are you assuming that your readers will recognize and accept the connection you see between your claims and grounds? Is the connection you see between them logical and reasonable? Will your readers see the connection as logical and reasonable?

3. **Is my warrant clear, fully explained, and supported?**
Underdeveloped warrants are a common problem with argumentative synthesis essays: writers, understanding that they need to state their warrants, simply fail to explain them adequately. Clear, well-developed warrants are crucial to successful arguments, especially if you believe your audience will question the validity of your claim or grounds. In these cases, you may need to explain your warrant at length, perhaps even acknowledging alternative readings of your grounds as you clarify your own interpretation. Determining whether your warrants are sufficiently explained and supported can be difficult, which is why you should have other people read and critique drafts of your writing. Specifically ask them to read your essay skeptically; to question the validity of your claims, grounds, and warrants; and to indicate any weaknesses they note or questions they have. Sometimes the warrants themselves rest on unstated assumptions that need to be explained and defended.

ARGUMENT AND PERSUASION

Rhetoricians often draw a distinction between argument and persuasion. Argument, they maintain, involves demonstrating the credibility of a position; persuasion involves moving readers to accept or act on that position. The most commonly acknowledged agents of persuasion are logos (logic), pathos (emotion), and ethos (character): writers can often persuade readers to accept or act on an argument by appealing to the readers' logic or emotions or by sufficiently establishing their own credibility or character (see Chapter 7 for a further discussion of logos, pathos, and ethos).

APPEALS BASED ON REASON

In an argumentative synthesis, successful appeals to **logos** largely depend on the quality of your claims, grounds, and warrants. Clear, qualified claims supported by valid grounds and clear, reasonable warrants will go a long way toward persuading a reader that your position is reasonable enough to accept and act on. Such writing, however, rarely happens by accident. It results from careful, critical drafting and revision. Here are a few steps you can take to improve the logical appeal of your argumentative synthesis essay:

1. **Make clear, limited claims.**
   Be sure all of your claims are clear, reasonable, and limited. Vague claims will not be convincing and neither will unreasonable assertions or sweeping generalizations. The claims you make—including your thesis—form the framework around which you will build your argumentative synthesis. If your claims are unclear, unreasonable, or unconnected to one another, the logical appeal of your essay will be diminished.

2. **Employ grounds that are relevant, credible, and timely.**
   As you decide what evidence or examples to offer in support of a claim, choose the material that is most relevant to your assertion. First, avoid using grounds that are only tangentially related to your claim. Second, be sure the grounds you employ come from credible sources. If you use reliable sources in your essay, readers are more likely to see your assertions as reasonable. Basing your paper on material drawn from questionable sources will bring into question the legitimacy of your own assertions. Finally, be sure the material you use in your paper is timely. As a rule, draw on the most recent research you can find when writing your paper—employing out-of-date source texts may hamper your efforts to sway readers' opinions.

3. **Explain your reasoning process.**
   One of the best ways to improve the logical appeal of your essay is to explain your reasoning process on the page. Lay bare for your readers the reasoning process that led you to your conclusions: elaborate on the meaning of your claims, explain connections among your assertions, explore alternative arguments, and discuss the links you see between your claims and their grounds. Most academic audiences will expect to find this type of discussion and explanation in your essay.

APPEALS BASED ON EMOTION

Successful persuasive appeals to **pathos** can be difficult to achieve but can also be very effective. Employing pathos to persuade readers is tricky because it can have the opposite effect if used incorrectly or clumsily. Pathos can quickly turn into bathos, or unintentionally comic appeals to emotion. However, when used sparingly and appropriately, emotionally charged grounds or language can prove very persuasive. Here are a few suggestions on how to employ pathos effectively in an argumentative synthesis essay.

1. **Include in your essay material that might appeal to your readers' interests.**

   Although it is often difficult to know with any degree of certainty what material might appeal to your readers' interests, it may be possible to make some educated guesses. For example, what might interest them given their economic, political, educational, or religious backgrounds? What can you assume they know or may want to know about the topic of your essay? What aspects of the topic interest you? How similar are you to your audience—can you assume they might have similar interests? Though it is very difficult to make completely accurate assessments of what material might interest your readers, the closer you come to hitting the mark, the more likely you are to obtain a positive emotional response to your writing.

2. **Include in your essay material that might appeal to your readers' needs or fears.**

   As you consider what material to include in your argumentative synthesis, can you identify examples, arguments, testimonials, statistics, or other material that might appeal to your readers' needs or address their concerns? Your goal is not to play on your readers' emotions. Instead, you want to connect emotionally with readers, to construct a bridge between your essay and reader needs or concerns, thus helping them see the relevancy of your essay to their lives. Is there material, for example, that might appeal to your readers' concerns about their physical, psychological, or financial safety; need for self-affirmation; or desires for joy or happiness? Successfully employing this type of material in your argumentative synthesis greatly increases the chances that readers will find your essay persuasive.

3. **Employ language that is evocative or captivating.**

   Another way to improve the emotional appeal of your argumentative synthesis is to use especially evocative or captivating language. Words have both denotative (literal) and connotative (emotional) meanings. You will often face instances when you can choose among words that have roughly the same denotative meaning but vary widely in their connotative implications. In these cases, consider using language that more effectively appeals to your reader's emotions. Also consider your use of figurative language. Although most academic writers employ extended metaphors sparingly, the use of analogies, allusions, and other figurative language is more common. Your goal is not to produce flowery prose. Instead, your aim is to employ language that persuades readers to accept or act on your arguments by developing in them an emotional understanding of your topic.

APPEALS BASED ON CHARACTER AND CREDIBILITY

In one sense, **ethos** is closely linked to logos because it has to do with the credibility of the claims, grounds, and warrants that you employ in your essay. Ethos involves trust and character: do you demonstrate through the quality of the claims, grounds, and warrants you employ in your writing that you are a trustworthy, knowledgeable, fair-minded individual? If you do, then you may persuade some readers to accept your position through your own ethos as a writer. Ethos, though, also has to do with the quality of your own prose. Even if you compose a synthesis with strong claims, grounds, and warrants, you will lose credibility if your prose is marred by misspellings, grammatical problems, typos, or other surface errors. Readers may feel that they cannot trust authors who are careless with their writing; if an author is so sloppy with word choice, syntax, spelling, or punctuation, how sloppy has the author been with his or her research, reasoning, and documentation? Persuasion depends on trust, and you may lose the trust of your readers—and your credibility as a writer—if your writing is full of easily correctable errors. Here are a few steps you can take to improve ethos in your argumentative synthesis:

1. **Present informed, balanced arguments.**
   You will enhance your credibility as a writer if you present a balanced argument in your essay, examining the strengths and weaknesses of your assertions and exploring alternative points of view. Presenting a balanced argument requires you to research and consider a range of perspectives on your essay's topic. Examining this range of perspectives in your essay increases the likelihood of readers seeing you as a knowledgeable, fair-minded writer, and readers are more likely to consider and perhaps adopt arguments presented by writers they perceive as informed and fair.

2. **Demonstrate the credibility of your source texts.**
   Another way to enhance your ethos is by demonstrating the credibility of the source texts you use in your essay. Readers are more likely to accept or act on your arguments if they perceive that your claims are supported by authoritative sources. In-text documentation is one way to demonstrate that your arguments are supported by credible sources. You can also establish the authority of your source texts by including in your essay the full name of the person who wrote the text and a summary of his or her credentials when you first quote or paraphrase material from him or her.

3. **Employ fair, balanced language.**
   Just as you want the content of your argumentative synthesis to be fair and balanced, you also want to avoid language that might make you appear narrow-minded or uninformed. Although on occasion you will want to employ emotionally evocative language (see the discussion of pathos earlier in this chapter), consistently employing words that make you sound shrill, sarcastic, or hostile will usually hinder your efforts to persuade readers to consider or accept your arguments, especially if you are addressing

a neutral or possibly antagonistic audience. In these cases, you might be better served using language that is more judicious and fair.

4. **Proofread your work carefully.**
Finally, remember that the quality of your own prose influences whether your readers perceive you as a credible authority. Argumentative synthesis essays that are full of surface-level errors are unlikely to persuade many readers. Rightly or wrongly, most readers will judge the quality of your argument by the quality of your prose: in their minds, error-laden writing is likely to reflect error-laden thinking. You can help ensure that your writing is persuasive simply by proofreading your essay thoroughly before you submit your final draft for review.

WRITING AN ARGUMENTATIVE SYNTHESIS

Because argumentative syntheses are so complex, writing them in a number of steps or stages is often helpful. Here are some of the steps you might consider following when writing an argumentative synthesis:

1. Analyze the assignment.
2. Annotate and critique the readings.
3. Formulate a thesis.
4. Choose an organizational plan.
5. Write your rough draft.
6. Revise your draft.
7. Check quotations and documentation.

STEP I—ANALYZE THE ASSIGNMENT

Some teachers will not specify the type of argument they want you to present in your synthesis. If this is the case, you will need to decide for yourself whether you want to focus on the quality of the writing in the readings or on the issue they address. However, if a teacher specifically asks you to focus your argument on the quality of the source texts, his assignment might include directions such as these:

> Review the readings in Chapter 5 of the textbook. Which author do you believe presents the most convincing case? Why?

* * * * *

> Review the readings in Chapter 5 of the textbook. Which piece is better written? How so?

In the first assignment, the teacher wants you to analyze, evaluate, then compare the **arguments** presented by the various writers, arguing that one presents the best case. In the second assignment, the teacher wants you to analyze, evaluate, then compare the **styles** of the various writers, arguing that one produces the best-written text.

However, when a teacher wants you to take a stand on the topic the readings address, her directions may read something like this:

> Review the readings in Chapter 5 of the textbook. Where do you stand on the issue? Present an argument in favor of your position using the readings for support.

Here the teacher wants you to read the articles, think about the arguments presented by each author, reflect on your own knowledge and feelings concerning the topic, and then present an argument in which you assume and defend a position of your own on the issue.

After you have determined the type of argument the teacher wants you to write, check the assignment to determine the number and types of sources the teacher wants you to use in your paper. Sometimes instructors specify a certain number of readings you must use in your paper, asking you, for example, to base your paper on four to six sources. Other times teachers specify the types of readings you have to use: those provided in class, those you find on your own in the library, academic sources only, and so on. If you have any questions about the number or type of readings you need to use in your synthesis, be sure to check with your instructor.

STEP 2—ANNOTATE AND CRITIQUE THE READINGS

As you begin to collect the readings you plan to use when writing your argumentative synthesis, you need to annotate and critique them (see Chapter 6 for advice on critiquing readings). First, annotate each reading, identifying its thesis, primary assertions, and evidence. Next, analyze and critique the content and structure of each reading. If you base your argument on other authors' faulty writing or reasoning, your essay will likely reflect their weaknesses; likewise, if you base your argument on solid, well-written sources, your argument will likely be stronger. The questions you want to ask of a reading include:

- What, exactly, is the main point of this reading?
- How has the author supported his ideas, arguments, or findings?
- How well has the author explained or supported his ideas, arguments, or findings?
- Do I find the reading convincing? Why or why not?
- How have the structure and tone of the piece influenced my reaction?
- What is the quality of the writing?
- How do the author's ideas, arguments, or findings compare with those found in the other sources I have read?

Place your annotations in the margins of the reading, on sheets of paper, or on index cards. If you use paper or index cards, be sure you copy all the bibliographic information you will need to complete a reference list entry on the source, in case you use any of that material in your paper.

In an argumentative synthesis, all quoted, paraphrased, or summarized material needs to be documented.

STEP 3—FORMULATE A THESIS

Formulating a clear thesis statement is an essential step in writing a successful argumentative synthesis. Your thesis statement tells your readers the position you plan to advance in your paper and will likely indicate the structure of your essay. Put another way, your thesis statement establishes in your readers' minds certain expectations concerning the content and form of your paper. When you satisfy those expectations, your readers will have an easier time following your argument; if you do not, however, readers may feel your work is confusing and disorganized. So you need to spend some time forming and refining your thesis statement.

In an argumentative synthesis you advance a position of your own concerning the quality and/or topic of the readings. If you are focusing on the quality of the readings themselves, you can assume a number of different positions. For example, suppose you are writing an argumentative synthesis using the readings on genetic human enhancement in Chapter 9. You may argue that one essay is more convincing than another:

> While both Chan and Selgelid argue that human genetic enhancement is ethical, Chan offers the more persuasive argument.

Or you may argue that one work is better written than another:

> While both Chan and Selgelid argue that human genetic enhancement is ethical, Chan's essay is more clearly written.

In either case, the thesis sets out the position you will be developing in your paper.

As with other types of essays, thesis statements for argumentative syntheses can be either open or closed. Although both of the examples above are open thesis statements, they could easily be modified to give the reader a better indication of what exactly will be covered in the paper:

> While both Chan and Selgelid argue that human genetic enhancement is ethical, Chan offers the more persuasive argument through her use of analogies and compelling examples.

* * * * *

> While both Chan and Selgelid argue that human genetic enhancement is ethical, Chan's essay is more clearly written because she avoids unnecessary jargon and employs a more casual style of writing.

If, however, your goal in composing an argumentative synthesis is to assert a position of your own on the topic of the readings, your thesis will read a little differently, something like this (employing an open thesis):

> Although philosophers and scientists offer varying assessments and positions, human genetic enhancement is ethical.

Or perhaps this (employing a closed thesis):

> Although philosophers and scientists offer varying assessments and positions, human genetic enhancement is ethical because it helps to prevent disabilities, secures individual liberty, and promotes the general welfare of society.

STEP 4—CHOOSE AN ORGANIZATIONAL PLAN

If you use a **block format** to organize your essay, you would critique in turn what each author has to say about the topic, and then advance your own position. Suppose you were working with this thesis: "Although philosophers and scientists offer varying assessments and positions, human genetic enhancement is ethical because it helps to prevent disabilities, secures individual liberty, and promotes the general welfare of society." In outline form, your paper might look like this:

Argumentative Synthesis—Block Format

Opening Section

Capture reader interest

Introduce the topic

Give your thesis

Discussion of Chan Article

Introduce the article—title, author, publication information

Summarize the article—Chan's argument

Critique the article—strengths and weaknesses of her argument

    Tie criticisms to specific passages in the article

    Fully explain or defend your criticism

    Draw links with other source texts

Discussion of Krimsky Article

Introduce the article—title, author, publication information

Summarize the article—Krimsky's argument

Critique the article—strengths and weaknesses of his argument

    Tie criticisms to specific passages in the article

    Fully explain or defend your criticism

    Draw links with other source texts

Discussion of Selgelid Article

Introduce the article—title, author, publication information

Summarize the article—Selgelid's argument

Critique the article—strengths and weaknesses of his argument

Tie criticisms to specific passages in the article

Fully explain or defend your criticism

Draw links with other source texts

Your Argument Concerning the Ethics of Human Genetic Enhancement

How human genetic enhancement helps to prevent disabilities

Tie arguments to specific examples from the articles

Fully explain and defend your assertions

Refer back to other authors' opinions to bolster your position

How human genetic enhancement secures individual liberty

Tie arguments to specific examples from the articles

Fully explain and defend your assertions

Refer back to other authors' opinions to bolster your position

How human genetic enhancement promotes the general welfare of society

Tie arguments to specific examples from the articles

Fully explain and defend your assertions

Refer back to other authors' opinions to bolster your position

Conclusion

In the opening section of your paper, you would introduce the topic of your essay, capture reader interest, and offer your thesis. In the body of your paper, you would critique the arguments offered by each of your source texts, focusing your attention on what they have to say about the ethics of human genetic enhancement. Finally, you would present your own argument, supporting your position with specific references to the source texts to help support or explain your thesis.

If you prefer, you could organize the paper using an **alternating format**, structuring your essay around the aspects of the topic you have chosen as your focus rather than each source text. In this case, your paper might be organized like this:

Argumentative Synthesis—Alternating Format

Opening Section

Capture reader interest

Introduce the topic

Give your thesis

Discuss how human genetic enhancement prevents disabilities

Explain your assertion

Support your argument with convincing grounds, including material from the source texts

Explain how your position differs from the positions presented in the source texts

Discuss how human genetic enhancement secures individual liberty

Explain your assertion

Support your argument with convincing grounds, including material from the source texts

Explain how your position differs from the positions presented in the source texts

Discuss how human genetic enhancement promotes the general welfare of society

Explain your assertion

Support your argument with convincing grounds, including material from the source texts

Explain how your position differs from the positions presented in the source texts

Conclusion

In the opening of your paper, you would again introduce the topic of your essay, capture reader interest, and state your thesis. In the body of your essay, you would argue, in order, that human genetic enhancement helps to prevent disabilities, secures individual liberty, and promotes the general welfare of society. In developing your argument, you would explain your claims or assertions, support them with grounds (e.g., evidence, examples, reasons) and include material from the source texts when appropriate, and discuss how your position differs from the ones presented in those texts.

After you have drafted at least a preliminary thesis for your paper and have some sense of the assertions that will serve as the focus of your synthesis, you will need to return to the readings to locate material to include in your essay. Remember that the focus of an argumentative synthesis should be the argument you are advancing, not the material from the readings. In other words, your first responsibility is to develop a sound argument; the source material serves to illustrate or support *your* assertions.

STEP 5—WRITE YOUR ROUGH DRAFT

When you feel you are ready to begin writing your rough draft, be sure you have in front of you all of your source texts and notes. Some students like to begin writing immediately—they need to see some of their ideas in writing before they can decide on a final thesis or organize their paper. Other students have to begin with a clear thesis and outline in hand. Follow the method of composing that is most comfortable and successful for you.

When writing your essay, you will support your argument with material from the readings. You can use source material to give your readers background information on the topic (quote or paraphrase material you think your reader needs to know to understand your argument), to support your assertions (quote or paraphrase material that substantiates or illustrates your claims), or to acknowledge opposing views (quote or paraphrase material that calls into question your assertions; you then must decide whether to refute, accommodate, or concede to these different perspectives).

STEP 6—REVISE YOUR DRAFT

Revising your argumentative synthesis to make it ready for others to read is a time-consuming process again best approached in a series of steps. First, revise to improve the **content** of your paper, focusing on the quality and clarity of the argument you are advancing. Here are some questions you might ask about your draft as you revise to improve its content:

- Have I clearly indicated the point I want to prove?
- Have I clearly indicated the reasons I believe others should accept my position?
- Have I supported each of those reasons with expert testimony, statistics, or some other means of support as well as with clear explanations?
- Have I acknowledged opposing views in my paper when necessary? Have I found ways of refuting, accommodating, or conceding to them?

Next, review the **organization** of your essay, asking these questions:

- Is the thesis statement clearly worded, and does it control the structure of the essay?
- Have I provided clear transitions between the major sections of my essay?
- Are there clear connections between the material I draw from the readings and my own elaborations and explanations?

Finally, when checking the **accuracy** and **clarity** of your work, ask yourself:

- Have I chosen words that are clear yet contribute to the effect I wanted to elicit from my readers?
- Are my sentences clearly structured with adequate variety?
- Have I quoted and paraphrased material accurately and properly?

- When incorporating quoted or paraphrased material in my synthesis, have I supplied enough background information on the source text so the material makes sense to my readers?
- Have I defined all the terms I need to define?
- Have I documented all the material that needs to be documented?

STEP 7—CHECK QUOTATIONS AND DOCUMENTATION

Before you turn in your final draft for a grade, set aside time to check the accuracy of your quotations and documentation. First, make sure that you have quoted material accurately by comparing your text against the source text. Second, be sure that you have documented all of the material in your paper that needs to be documented, including all paraphrased information. Because you are combining information from several source texts in your synthesis and presenting your own argument as well, be sure your readers can always tell through your documentation the source of the material you include in your paper.

SAMPLE ARGUMENTATIVE SYNTHESIS

Following is an argumentative synthesis essay drawing on the readings found in Chapter 9. As you read the essay, consider how it is structured, how it uses material from the source texts, and how the writer develops the paper's argument.

MAKE HUMAN ENHANCEMENT AVAILABLE TO ALL

Thanks to groundbreaking work in genetics, the definition of what it means to be human has come into question. As the twenty-first century unfolds, scientists will gain a better understanding of and ability to manipulate the genes that dictate not only our height and weight, the color of our eyes and hair, but also our sex, our susceptibility to certain diseases, and perhaps even our intelligence and emotional disposition. Genetic research has undoubtedly improved the lives of countless people by helping them avoid disease and birth defects, but the next stage of research is more troubling. Genetic engineering makes human enhancement possible, real, and affordable. Parents may soon be able to "design" their future children—manipulating their children's genes to insure they grow up to be strong or smart, tall or musical, assertive or beautiful. These advances have the potential to improve the human condition, but they raise serious ethical questions that must be addressed before the technology is made available to everyone.

The current debate over human enhancement centers around embryonic genetic manipulation and involves only children born through *in vitro* fertilization (IVF). With IVF, numerous embryos are created and several implanted in the mother's uterus. Currently, these embryos can undergo genetic testing before implantation to determine if any of them have genetic abnormalities that could lead to conditions like Down syndrome or to diseases like cancer. Parents can choose to have implanted only those embryos shown to have no genetic problems. This process is termed "genetic screening" and is widely employed (Krimsky 192).

Scientists will soon have the ability to take this process one step further and perfect genetic engineering. With genetic engineering, scientists change the genetic makeup of an embryo prior to implantation to help insure that the resulting child possesses certain physical characteristics (such as height), skills (such as music ability), or dispositions (such as patience), all according to the parents' wishes. As scientists discover which genes control which characteristics, they can modify them prior to implantation. Michael Selgelid, Director of the Centre for Human Bioethics at Monash University, puts it this way:

> As knowledge about the relationship between genes and human traits increases, we will be able to detect genetic sequences associated with a wide variety of positively desired characteristics . . . Many parents might then want to select *for* traits such as increased height, intelligence, strength, beauty, and so on, with the aim of giving their children higher-quality lives. The limits would depend on the extent to which a genetic basis for such traits is eventually demonstrated by genetic science. (194)

Non-therapeutic genetic enhancement—or the creation of "designer babies"—is controversial. It raises some serious ethical concerns that need to be addressed. However, it can also greatly enhance human potential and happiness and must be made available to everyone, not just a select few.

Some argue that embryonic enhancement techniques should never be employed because they interfere with nature: human reproduction should not be tampered with, and parents must love and accept their children no matter what problems or limitations accompany them at birth. In "Humanity 2.0? Enhancement, Evolution and the Possible Futures of Humanity," Professor Sarah Chan offers a different perspective. She acknowledges that genetic engineering technologies challenge natural selection and current conceptions of human evolution. However, in the past, evolution "operated somewhat in the dark" (189) but can be guided by reason. Science, not random luck, can guide the genetic fate of children: "in comparison to natural evolution, any genetic modifications aimed at improving the human condition will at least be evidence-based rather than random . . . " (189).

Sheldon Krimsky, Lenore Stern Professor of Humanities and Social Sciences at Tufts University, believes that genetic enhancement is never morally acceptable. In fact, he believes that the "pursuit of this goal represents the greatest scientific folly and moral failure" (192). Krimsky argues that holding clinical tests of human enhancement technologies are inherently immoral—some embryos must be altered and others not and the results tracked over time. In such a case, the children are laboratory rats bred to serve scientific investigation, fundamentally demeaning their humanity. In his view, human enhancement should take place after the embryo is implanted and take the form of proper nutrition, protection from harm, and moral education following birth.

Krimsky's arguments are logical—clinical testing as he describes it raises serious moral questions—but that is not, in fact, how the technology is progressing. Krimsky is arguing against a procedure that is not being employed and likely will not be. Instead, as genetic engineering becomes increasingly common, no clinical trials will be run—the technology will simply be used, for better or worse.

More serious objections to genetic engineering focus on its societal implications. First, these therapies are expensive. The wealthy in any society are more likely to have access to this type of medical care than are the poor—rich people will be able to enhance their children's lives in ways the poor simply cannot. As Michael Selgelid explains in "A Modest Approach to Enhancement," genetic therapy could lead to "increased social inequality" (195) because the "enhanced richfolk will then have even greater competitive advantages than previously" (195). The rich could afford treatments to help ensure that their children are stronger, smarter, and more competitive than children born without such enhancements, giving them even greater social advantages beyond the wealth they will inherit. If there is not equal access to these therapies, then their use cannot be just, yet it is hard to imagine how universal health care plans will pay for treatments like these when these plans have a hard time covering basic health needs.

Arguments over the ethics of genetic engineering may come down to the balance between society's needs and individual liberty. Selgelid argues that unequal access to these treatments could lead to social instability and even threaten democracy (196) if a wide gulf develops between the genetic haves and the genetic have-nots. As Krimsky notes, genetic engineering "will inevitably be used by those with wealth and power to make others believe that to be prenatally genetically modified makes you better" (193).

Yet social concerns need to be balanced by respect for individual liberty: "The key unresolved philosophical questions concern how the value of personal liberty should be weighed against social equality and welfare in cases where these values conflict" (Selgelid 197). Individual liberty would dictate that people have the right to make decisions concerning their genetic makeup or that of their children. Society ought not interfere with a person's desire to ensure that his or her children are free of genetic abnormalities and possess traits that will help them be happy and successful. For Sarah Chan, the ultimate questions surrounding genetic engineering involve matters of individual choice: "What makes us uniquely human is the ability to shape our destinies according to our desires—and genetic and other enhancement technologies provide further means for us to do so" (190). For Michael Selgelid, the ultimate question genetic engineering must face is this: "How socially damaging would enhancement need to be in order for personal liberty to be justly overridden" (197).

To override personal liberty, the social damage caused by genetic engineering would have to be substantial and real, not just theoretical. Scientists know with growing certainty that genetic engineering can enhance the quality of human life; ethicists can only speculate about possible negative social consequences. Yet this type of philosophical questioning is valuable. Knowing what social consequences might arise from genetic engineering increases the chances that they can be avoided.

Another objection to genetic engineering seems more well founded—the procedures will be expensive and will, initially, be limited to those who can afford them. However, there is every reason to believe that in terms of cost and availability, genetic engineering will follow the same path as other scientific breakthroughs like laser eye surgery or cardiac stents. Initially medical treatments like these are rare and expensive, but over time they become more accessible and affordable. Genetic engineering procedures will undergo the same transformation. "Allowing access to expensive technologies to those who can afford them will, in all likelihood, speed their development to become more readily available to everyone" (Chan 190).

If genetic engineering has the potential to improve human health and well-being, protect people from disease, and improve the general welfare of society by producing more intelligent and more caring children, then policies must be implemented to make it available to everyone. Reserving this technology for only those who can afford it is unjust, unethical, and, as Selgelid argues, could have devastating social consequences. The technologies of human enhancement must be available to all humans and likely will be over time.

Additional Readings

A New Definition of Leadership

Josh Misner

Josh Misner holds a doctorate degree in communication and leadership studies.

Sheryl Sandberg, the chief operating officer of Facebook, recently proposed that we ban the word "bossy." Her reasoning?

> When a little boy asserts himself, he's called a "leader." Yet when a little girl does the same, she risks being branded "bossy." Words like bossy send a message: don't raise your hand or speak up. By middle school, girls are less interested in leading than boys—a trend that continues into adulthood.

A little over a month ago, I posted a quote from Sandberg on my website's Facebook page: "I want every little girl who is told she is bossy to be told she has leadership skills." The post ignited a firestorm of commentary. However, my reasoning behind the post was for my daughters. I want them to grow up in a world that values their leadership skills, especially considering the level of time and effort I am investing in teaching them these skills. As a professor whose doctorate is in leadership studies, it was only a matter of time before I waded into the issue.

In the four weeks that followed my post, and Sandberg's movement to ban the word, the media backlash has been stunning. Most of this backlash states the same thing: that we should call out bossiness for what it is, and leadership for what it is.

I, for one, agree—with BOTH!

In a day and age when we are mostly told to pick a side and that we have to lean one way or another, I propose a new definition of leadership, but one that clearly takes the best of both worlds, without compromising each other.

Let me begin with Sandberg's ideas. She wants to break down the barriers preventing women from having leadership roles, as well as pave the way for women leaders of tomorrow, and rightfully so.

According to catalyst.org, women comprise slightly less than 15 percent of the executive leadership of the Fortune 500, a number that has become stagnant and unchanging over the last four years. Women hold a mere 17 percent of the seats in both houses of Congress. Throughout the U.S., men continue to hold 82 percent of leadership positions, across all sectors.

This is the world in which we live, men and women alike, and it is the world from which Sandberg writes. There is clearly a problem somewhere, and I don't fault Sandberg one bit for trying to do something about it.

Perhaps she's right, at least, to an extent. She cites research that states, between elementary school and high school, girls' self-esteem drops an average of 3.5 times more than boys' self-esteem. Being the father of one teenage girl and one preteen girl, I can vouch for this, on a gut level. Is it because young girls are taught that being assertive is "bossy" or inappropriate behavior for a young lady? When we take a look at the b-word that "bossy" is eventually replaced with once girls become women, we can intuitively see this phenomenon for ourselves being evident in b-words that are both used for the same purpose.

However, we also need to look at the other side of the argument.

There are times when bossy means bossy, whether for a boy or a girl. There are certainly times when authoritative crosses the line into authoritarian, and a child, regardless of gender, needs to be taught the art of leadership. Looking deeper into this point, we can see that "banning bossy" could create myriad problems for future generations.

This is where I propose a new conception of leadership.

The English language, as most of us know, borrows words from many other cultures, and from these cultures, there are many choices we could use to describe leadership. We could use the French "*chief*," meaning the ruler or head of something. We could use the Dutch "*baas*," meaning master. We could use the Italian "*maneggiare*," meaning to control.

But we don't.

Instead, we use the Old English word "*leader*," which is derived from "*laedan*," meaning to guide.

Why guide? Deep down in our hearts, we know that to lead **is** to guide, which implies a symbiotic, side-by-side, mutual relationship in which leader and follower benefit equally.

To equate qualities like "bossiness" or assertiveness with being the hallmark of great leaders is a categorical mistake, and this is where I think Sandberg gets it wrong. If a boy or a girl is acting in accordance with words like chief, boss or manager, trying to suppress others' opinions and make decisions in a vacuum, decisions that affect everyone without their input—a.k.a. being bossy—then they should be corrected.

After all, do we want to raise a future generation of managers by allowing such behavior to continue unchecked? Or, would we rather raise a generation of leaders by teaching them to know the difference?

Sandberg's heart is in the right place, and although her critics are now trying to silence her, what they need to realize is the value in what she is trying to accomplish. To raise up a generation of leaders, we cannot continue defining leadership solely from a traditionally male perspective. We need to embrace a new definition of leadership that combines the best of all possible worlds.

Traditionally, an annual performance review at any given U.S. organization will assess an employee based on some or all of the following criteria: *Activities, tasks, objectives, goals, initiative, time and stress management, etc.*

These criteria are what we consider to be task-oriented, and are easily quantified, which coincides with the positivist movement of the Industrial Revolution. This movement was sparked by thinkers such as Max Weber and Henri Fayol, people who saw humans as cogs in a machine and eventually started treating them as such. This movement was responsible for much of the stark, emotionless landscape of the American workplace that existed for many generations beyond the industrial era.

These criteria are also inherently associated with masculinity, which should come as no surprise, because when the idea of performance reviews first emerged, the workplace was dominated by men, so the measure of success was set up by men, for men. As women began flooding the workplace, these women quickly learned that what would help them succeed was to reprogram themselves to live up to inherently male standards.

This was a benign practice five decades ago, but today, with more than half of our workforce comprised of women, it is profoundly wrong.

Leadership for tomorrow must be infused with a new set of qualities—qualities that are traditionally associated with the feminine, and are often too abstract to be measured. These qualities include:

- **Empathy**—The ability to become aware of the thoughts, opinions and feelings of others, as well as to be able to identify with them.
- **Vulnerability**—The ability to remain accountable, accurately assess one's limits and seek out help when needed.
- **Humility**—The drive to serve others through leadership and to offer up credit to others when credit is due.
- **Work-Life Balance**—While giving one's life to work was once admirable, today we know that maintaining a solid work-life balance is critical to mental and emotional well-being.
- **Inclusiveness**—The desire to gain others' perspectives and to make decisions based on the good of the group, rather than the individual alone.
- **Patience**—The greatest leaders do not need it all, nor do they need it now. They are visionary and willing to invest time and energy to achieve a long-term set of goals.

Unlike the assessment criteria for leaders from last century, these are not easily quantified. There are no reliable assessments to assign numerical values to these qualities, so how can we recognize when somebody exhibits leadership as defined by this new perspective?

The answer to this is simple. We need not quantify everything. For the quantifiable, traditionally masculine characteristics of leadership, let's run a report and assess it.

But that must not be the end of the leader's assessment.

For the abstract, relationally based characteristics of leadership that we need to promote as beneficial, let us be more observant and take note. While these qualities are not necessarily measurable, they are most definitely *felt,* so when someone exhibits these qualities, let us nurture them, let us promote them, and most importantly, let us encourage them in all aspects of the new leadership.

Qualities of leadership can no longer continue to be gendered as feminine vs. masculine. These are now necessary to balance leadership. More importantly, these qualities, when taken together as a whole, are needed to take leadership from being a *managerial* conception to that which more closely resembles the *guidance* from which leadership derives its namesake.

To Sandberg and her critics: I will be raising my children as leaders, but not according to a narrow, traditional view of leadership. The problem this leadership professor has with "Ban Bossy" is not the view of leadership where girls are called bossy whenever they assert themselves. The problem I have is with the view of leadership where boys who are bossy are used to define what it means to lead.

My children—both sons *and* daughters—will be raised with balance, knowing how to temper ambition and drive with compassion, and when to pause to listen to others for the good of the group, rather than push forward for their own sake.

Understanding Your Leadership Balance

Lee Ellis

Lee Ellis *is president of Leadership Forum, a leadership and team development company.*

Abraham Lincoln is frequently cited as our most popular president, probably because he achieved great results in the face of incredibly difficult circumstances. Did you ever stop to think, how did he do it? What was his secret and what are the keys to success for great leadership? I have a good idea after posing this question to hundreds of managers and supervisors. A survey I conducted while facilitating leadership development at several large corporations revealed more than 120 attributes of great leaders.

These attributes fell into four areas: trust, relationships, results, and emotional intelligence. The best leaders exhibit qualities from all levels; however, results and relationship behaviors were mentioned more often than all others. Relationship-oriented and results-oriented attributes correlate very closely with our naturally motivated behaviors (personalities). These behaviors are absolutely critical to success, and they are excellent areas for potential growth in almost all leaders.

After working with thousands of people over the years, I have discovered a natural seesaw effect between relationships and results; that is, most people tend to be good at (and inclined toward) one and struggle with (neglect or avoid) the other. If, therefore, you are naturally good at setting standards and holding people accountable (results oriented), you are likely to struggle with relationship-oriented behaviors like listening, encouraging, and showing empathy. If you are relationship oriented, then the opposite is likely to be true.

Results-oriented Behaviors

Results-oriented behaviors typically garner a great deal of attention because they are obviously necessary for success. Without them, you can't achieve goals or stay in business. It's only natural that organizations have very sophisticated ways of keeping score on how effective leaders are at achieving results. In most companies, there seems to be a constant mantra coming from the top that "results count." Results-oriented behaviors begin with vision and include the energy and drive to challenge people to do their best.

Shown below are the top ranked results-oriented behaviors in my survey on attributes of great leaders:

- Big picture, visionary, strategic
- Straightforward, sets clear expectations
- Strong focus on tasks
- Good problem solver
- Decisive, gives direction, firm (but flexible)
- High standards/goals for self and others

It was interesting to note that of the people surveyed, regardless of whether they were results oriented or relationship oriented, both types valued leaders who set and enforced high standards. Furthermore, they wanted clear expectations, accountability, decisiveness, and challenging work.

President Lincoln experienced great frustration early in the Civil War because there was little action and not many results on the battlefield. His top generals would not initiate the fight, delaying action to "recruit more soldiers," or "get more training," or "rest the horses." He kindly and patiently tried to encourage them, but with little success. Ultimately, he had to fire three successive generals before discovering Ulysses S. Grant, a leader who took the initiative and achieved results.

Relationship-oriented Behaviors

The ability to build good relationships is one of the most powerful leadership assets. Believing that someone else—especially your leader—cares about you and believes in you is a potent motivator. That's why the following relationship-oriented behaviors are so powerful for leading, managing, mentoring, and coaching.

Pause for a moment and reflect on your greatest leader. No matter how results oriented you may be, it's likely that the relationship attributes listed next were evident in that leader's style and played a key role in your personal development and success:

- Good listener
- Cared, concerned about me
- Encouraging, gave positive feedback
- Trusted me to do the job

- Supportive, lent a helping hand
- Respected others and me

The Dilemma of the Relationships—Results Seesaw

Leaders must achieve results to stay in business and be competitive, but they also must build relationships because it's people (with motivations and emotions) who do the work. Both, therefore, are essential to good leadership, but the dilemma is that most leaders are good at one and struggle with the other.

The struggle comes because these attributes are highly correlated to a person's "go to" behavioral style. By nature, some people are relationship oriented and some are results oriented. Typically, one is easy and one is a struggle. The side of the seesaw that's a struggle may not be a weakness, but it will require a conscious (and usually stretching) effort to carry out those behaviors. They are a struggle because it goes against the grain of our natural behaviors.

As already noted, organizational survival and success logically dictate a strong push for results. Consequently, companies are more likely to select results-oriented people for leadership roles. In most organizations, therefore, it's the relationship side of the seesaw that is light and not in balance.

Results Count, and Relationship Behaviors Enhance Results

The good news is that good relationships get better results. Twenty years of research by the Gallup Organization indicates that good relationships improve productivity and retention. This body of evidence provided the central theme for the highly popular business book, *First, Break All the Rules: What the World's Greatest Managers Do Differently.* In it, the authors point out that "The talented employee may join a company because of its charismatic leaders, its generous benefits, and its world-class training programs, but how long that employee stays and how productive he is while he is there is determined by his relationship with his immediate supervisor."[1]

Exit interviews conducted by corporations typically provide similar evidence—that talented people leave because of poor relationships with their immediate boss.

Leading through relationship behaviors is often a challenge for results-oriented people because it "feels" soft. Also, it's not natural for them to think or operate this way. As one highly results-oriented leader said, "It doesn't occur to me to encourage people because I don't need it. I can just look at the numbers and see how we are doing. That's enough for me."

He was missing that many of his people were starving for positive feedback—especially his more extroverted people who needed a regular dose of approval to stay at their peak. In reality, everyone needs encouragement and even the "tough" leaders admit that they admired the leaders who listened to them, supported them, and communicated high regard for their talents and efforts.

What Can You Do to Become a Better Leader?

Results-oriented Leader

Slow down, listen, and soften your tone. Realize that your natural inclination is probably to avoid the relationship behaviors because on the surface they do not appear to contribute to results. Also, since those "people" behaviors may not "feel" natural, you will need to push yourself to stretch and adapt behaviors outside of your comfort zone.

Adapting your normal behavioral style will be easier if you remind yourself frequently of two things:

- It is your responsibility as a leader to take a genuine interest in the growth and development of your people.
- When you value (care about) people you increase their confidence and inspire them to perform at a higher level and, therefore, produce better results with less turnover.

Of course, when your people are feeling better about their relationship with you, they are more confident and thus empowered to be better leaders and teammates themselves. Your investment has a positive multiplier effect that cascades down through the organization. Furthermore, you are modeling the very behaviors you need to coach.

Relationship-oriented Leader

Tighten up, toughen up, and deal proactively with necessary conflict. If you are naturally amiable and people oriented, acknowledge that your desire for harmony has its down side, too. Delaying unpopular decisions and avoiding creative conflict does not help the cause on either side of the leadership seesaw. Resolve to stand up for your beliefs and deal with difficult issues regardless of how it feels to you.

Remember that people want a leader who leads, so initiate, make decisions, and direct others to get results. Set and enforce reasonable boundaries, holding people accountable in a caring but firm way. Doing so will bring you into balance and win the respect of those on both sides of this seesaw. The normally amiable Lincoln succeeded because he adapted his behaviors to the needs of the situation.

In *Presidential Temperament,* the authors say Lincoln "was predisposed to restrain himself . . . But when he was faced with Southern secession, he acted boldly and vigorously . . . When the crisis of the Civil War finally broke . . . the non-directive, rational Lincoln became ceaselessly active and persistently commanding."[2]

The secret of great leaders like Lincoln and so many others is their ability to do what needs to be done even when it doesn't "feel" natural.

Psychologist William James has remarked that it's difficult to feel our way into a new way of acting, so we have to act our way into a new way of feeling. This is the test of true courage—will a person do what is appropriate for the situation, even when it feels unnatural and uncomfortable?

For some, it will take courage to coach themselves into becoming an empathic listener. For others, it will take courage to confront individuals and hold them accountable. Regardless of your tilt, the question is, "Do you have the courage to adapt your behaviors as needed?" Although adapting to new and unnatural behaviors is not the same as attacking a machine gun nest or going into a burning building to rescue someone, it does take emotional courage, and that is an essential quality of great leadership.

The bottom line is that regardless of where we are in our leadership balance we all can improve by developing some of those areas we would rather ignore. To be a great leader, it's not an option to be either results oriented or relationships oriented—we need skills for both. Lincoln learned to do both, and we can, too.

References

1. Marcus and Curt Coffman, *First, Break All the Rules*, Gallup Organization, 1999, pp. 11–12.
2. Ray Choiniere, David Keirsey, *Presidential Temperament*, Promethus Nemesis, 1992.

A Question of Leadership

Gene Klann and Talula Cartwright

Gene Klann *and* **Talula Cartwright** *are both senior program associates at the Center for Creative Leadership.*

Gene Klann

Traditionally, management has been viewed as a science because it encompasses rules and principles that appear to be consistent in all situations. Leadership, however, has traditionally been viewed as an art, the reasoning being that it does not have fixed principles and requires greater creativity in its practical application than management does—primarily because no two leadership situations are the same.

But the notion that leadership can also be a science deserves a closer look. Having lived and led in seven countries on four continents, I believe a case can be made that leadership is a science, with rules and principles that can apply to every situation.

One principle to follow is that each person is unique and the population as a whole is diverse. Consequently leaders, to maximize the potential of the people they lead, must deal with each person as a distinct and exclusive personality.

Second, despite this uniqueness and diversity, there is also an element of uniformity and consistency among people. They all have emotions and feelings such as love, hate, fear, anger, joy, and grief. These emotions might be expressed in different ways in different cultures, but the fact remains that they exist in all individuals everywhere. In view of this, leaders should always take the emotional response of their followers into consideration. This is particularly important in difficult, stressful, or crisis situations. Emotions drive behaviors, and leaders should lead in a way that ensures negative emotions are relieved anpd their harmful effects are reduced.

A third principle is that most people want to be treated with respect, trust, and dignity. No normal person wants to be abused, marginalized, or disrespected. This is why systems such as serfdom, slavery, and fascism have never succeeded over the long term—the human spirit has not allowed it. The concept of treating others as you want to be treated is universal, found in every major religion. People also have a strong need for communication, so they want their leaders to give them timely, accurate, and complete information about things that affect them. They also want their leaders to listen to and respond their ideas.

A fourth scientific principle of leadership is that character matters. People want their leaders to tell the truth, to do what they say they will do, and to be consistent in their words and actions. Leaders' willingness and ability to fulfill these desires largely determines their level of moral authority—an important attribute for effective leadership.

So leadership is really a combination of science and art. It is a science because it encompasses universal, consistent rules and principles. However, these rules and principles must be creatively applied to the leadership situation at hand, making leadership a form of art.

Talula Cartwright

Merriam-Webster's Collegiate Dictionary offers some interesting insights into the meanings of the words *art* and *science*. Among the definitions of *art* are "skill acquired by experience, study, or observation"; "an occupation requiring knowledge or skill"; and "the conscious use of skill and creative imagination esp. in the production of aesthetic objects." According to the dictionary the term *skill* stresses technical knowledge and proficiency, whereas *art* implies a personal, unanalyzable creative power.

This is quite different from what the dictionary has to say about *science*, including "knowledge or a system of knowledge covering general truths or the operation of general laws esp. as obtained and tested through scientific method," and "a system or method reconciling practical ends with scientific laws."

So which of these definitions—of art or of science—applies more to leadership?

Leaders may look for general and universal laws that affect specific actions and decisions. People count on their leaders to know how some of these broad principles will bear on leadership actions and decisions so that the organization will not be caught by detrimental surprises as a natural result of those actions and decisions. This aspect of leadership appears to be scientific. Leaders try to apply universal patterns to their specific, local situations, thereby avoiding huge, costly errors. For instance, a leader in the United States who learns of an environment-damaging error by a leader in a different industry and a different country can draw on that experience to avoid making a similar misstep.

Leadership becomes an art, however, when leaders are able to benchmark not only against the lessons drawn from other organizations but also against the many other models leaders have in their lives—childhood stories, the beauty and tragedy of nature, lessons from their hearts and souls, the wisdom contained in literature and the arts, hunches from intuition, and the insights that come from experience and the wisdom of the ages.

Great leaders all have this deep storehouse to draw from, so they are able to create rich metaphors from the stuff of everyday life, ennobling and lending integrity to their decisions even when there are no scientific benchmarks against which to measure those choices. The greatest leaders build their leadership from universal stories that cross not only continents but also space and time. They benchmark not only against other organizations but also against the legends of King Arthur, the paintings of Eugène Delacroix, and the parables from the Bible.

Leadership is not something that stops at the company door. People who are driven to lead are hungry for the kind of stories that inspire them to think ahead about their own future decisions. In even the most everyday circumstances—a Little League game, a movie, a family disagreement, a tennis match—they can find substance that inspires their thoughts about leadership. They are always pondering the stuff of everyday life and making decisions about it that will inform their future choices and help them hold the high ground when they have to think quickly. In this sense their leadership ability is a continually developing skill that is honed and improved consciously and deliberately by study and observation. The result is aesthetic in that it doesn't merely conform with natural and universal laws but is also elegant and of high quality. This continually developing proficiency and production of elegant results is what makes leadership an art.

Summary Chart

HOW TO WRITE AN ARGUMENTATIVE SYNTHESIS

1. **Analyze the assignment.**
   - *Determine whether you are being asked to write an informative or argumentative synthesis.*
   - *Determine the number and types of readings you are expected to use in your paper.*

2. **Review and annotate the readings.**
   - *Review the readings with your assignment in mind, looking for and marking information related to the topic of your paper.*
   - *Briefly summarize and critique each reading.*

3. **Formulate a thesis.**
   - *Determine what stance you will assume in your essay.*
   - *Determine whether you will use an open or closed thesis statement.*

4. **Choose an organizational plan.**
   - *Decide how you will order the ideas you will develop in your essay.*
   - *Decide whether you will present your ideas using a block or alternating format.*

5. **Write your rough draft.**
   - *Follow the organization plan implied or stated by your thesis.*
   - *Combine your insights, ideas, arguments, and findings with material in the source texts to develop and support your thesis.*
   - *Both paraphrase and quote material as necessary.*
   - *Add transitions, elaborations, clarifications, and connections where needed.*
   - *Include a concluding paragraph.*

6. **Revise your draft.**

    Revise to improve the content of your essay.
    - *Have you clearly indicated the point you want to prove?*
    - *Have you clearly indicated the reasons you believe others should accept your position?*
    - *Have you supported each of those reasons with expert testimony, statistics, or some other means of support as well as with clear explanations?*
    - *Have you acknowledged opposing views in your paper when necessary? Have you found ways of refuting, accommodating, or conceding to them?*

    Revise to improve the organization of your essay.
    - *Is the thesis statement clearly worded and does it control the structure of the essay?*
    - *Have you provided clear transitions between the major sections of your essay?*
    - *Are there clear connections between the material drawn from the readings and your own elaborations and explanations?*

    Revise to improve the accuracy and clarity of your essay.
    - *Have you chosen words that are clear and contribute to the effect you want to elicit from your readers?*
    - *Are your sentences clearly structured with adequate variety?*
    - *Have you defined all the terms you need to define?*
    - *Have you proofread for spelling, punctuation, or usage errors?*

7. **Check your quotations and documentation.**
    - *Have you quoted and paraphrased material properly, accurately, and fairly?*
    - *When incorporating quoted or paraphrased material in your synthesis, have you supplied enough background information on the source text so that the material makes sense to your readers?*
    - *Have you documented all the material that needs to be documented?*
    - *Have you documented material employing the proper format?*

ARGUMENTATIVE SYNTHESIS REVISION CHECKLIST

	Yes	No
1. Have you checked your assignment to be sure you have written the proper kind of synthesis essay: informative or argumentative?	____	____
2. Have you carefully read, annotated, and critiqued all of the source texts you will use in your essay?	____	____
3. Examine the wording of your thesis statement. Does it clearly state the stance you will assume in your essay?	____	____
4. Check the opening section of your essay. Does it:		
• introduce the topic of your paper?	____	____
• capture reader interest?	____	____
• include your thesis statement?	____	____
5. Examine each section in the body of your essay. Do you:		
• focus on just one issue at a time?	____	____
• make clear assertions?	____	____
• support your assertions with evidence?	____	____
• explain the link between each assertion and its supporting evidence?	____	____
6. Check the organization of your essay. Do you:		
• follow the organizational plan indicated by your thesis?	____	____
• provide transitions to help guide your reader through your essay?	____	____
7. Have you supported your assertions with some combination of quoted, summarized, and paraphrased source material?	____	____
8. Have you documented all the material that needs to be documented?	____	____

	Yes	No
9. Have you checked the content of your essay to be sure it accurately communicates your position and intention?	____	____
10. Have you reviewed your sentences for accuracy and variety?	____	____
11. Have you reviewed your word choice for clarity and accuracy?	____	____
12. Is your works cited or reference list correct?	____	____

Chapter 11

PLAGIARISM

In this chapter you will learn how to

1. Define plagiarism
2. Recognize common forms of plagiarism
3. Avoid plagiarism in your own writing

DEFINITION

Plagiarism occurs when writers take credit for work that is not really theirs. Because it encompasses a wide range of errors in academic writing, from improper citation to calculated fraud, plagiarism is an especially common problem for writers unfamiliar with the conventions of source-based writing. These writers often do not realize that any material they quote or paraphrase from a reading must be documented to avoid plagiarism.

Penalties for plagiarism vary from school to school, department to department, even instructor to instructor. They can range from a warning, to a failing grade on a paper, to a failing grade for a course, to expulsion from school. The academic community takes plagiarism seriously, but with care and honesty you can avoid problems and give the authors of the readings you use the credit they deserve for their work.

FORMS OF PLAGIARISM

Plagiarism is a difficult problem to address because it can assume so many different forms and involves so many different types of errors, some more serious than others. Understanding the various forms that plagiarism can assume will help you avoid problems.

PURCHASING A PAPER

Sometimes students will decide to purchase a paper rather than write one themselves. Whether you buy one from a fellow student or from a commercial vendor, purchasing a paper and turning it in as if it were your own is clearly a form of plagiarism. You are purposely taking credit for work that is not truly yours. Your teachers expect you to do your own work. Sometimes they may ask you to work with other students to write an essay, but even then you will be expected to do your own work in the group. Purchasing a paper—or even part of a paper—from someone and turning it in as if were your own is never acceptable.

TURNING IN A PAPER SOMEONE ELSE HAS WRITTEN FOR YOU

This form of plagiarism, related to the first, occurs when two students decide to let one take credit for work the other has actually completed—a student may ask his roommate to write a paper for him, then turn it in for a grade. If caught, both students may face some sort of penalty for plagiarism. In other cases, roommates taking different sections of the same class may hand in the same paper to their instructors without permission. In this case, both students have committed plagiarism. Finally there are instances in which a student retrieves a paper from the "fraternity" or "sorority" file, collections of papers written for various courses kept for students to copy and turn in (high-tech versions of this file are the collections of student papers kept on university computer systems). These papers may have been written by people the student has never known; however, if the student represents it as her own work, that student is guilty of plagiarism.

TURNING IN ANOTHER STUDENT'S WORK WITHOUT THAT STUDENT'S KNOWLEDGE

This form of plagiarism has increased over the past few years as more and more students write their papers on computers. Here a student searches another student's computer files for a paper, copies the paper, and then turns it in as if it were his own work. This is clearly a form of plagiarism.

IMPROPER COLLABORATION

More and more teachers are asking students to work together on class projects. If a teacher asks you to collaborate with others on a project, be sure to clarify exactly what she expects you to do individually when preparing the final essay. Sometimes a teacher will want a group of students to produce a single paper. The members of the group decide among themselves how they will divide the labor, and all group members get equal credit for the final essay. Though the group members should help each other complete the essay, if you are asked to complete a certain task as part of the larger project, make sure you give credit to others, when appropriate, for any material that was not originally your own. Other times a teacher will want the members of the group to work individually on their own papers; the other group members serve as each other's consultants and peer editors rather than as coauthors. In this case, you should acknowledge at the beginning of your essay or through documentation in the body of your paper any ideas or material that you did not develop yourself.

COPYING A PAPER FROM A SOURCE TEXT WITHOUT PROPER ACKNOWLEDGMENT

This form of plagiarism occurs when a student consults a website, an encyclopedia, book, or journal article, copies the information directly from the reading into his paper, puts his name on the essay, and turns it in for a grade. Sometimes a student will compose an entire essay this way; sometimes he will copy only part of his paper directly from a source. In either case, copying from a reading without proper quotation and documentation is a form of plagiarism. So is copying material directly from a computerized encyclopedia. Even though your computer may come with a subscription to a well-respected online encyclopedia, you cannot copy material from it and turn it in as your own work without proper documentation and acknowledgment.

CUTTING AND PASTING MATERIAL FROM SOURCES

Instead of copying all of the material for a paper from a single source text and passing the work off as their own, students increasingly lift material from several source texts and weave it together to construct a paper. This form of plagiarism is especially common when students gather information from the Web. Copying chunks of text from several websites into an essay and passing it off as your own work is unacceptable. All of the material drawn from websites must be properly documented.

LIFTING IMAGES FROM THE WEB OR OTHER SOURCES

If you copy photographs, pictures, charts, artwork, cartoons, or any other type of visual image from the Web or any other source, you need to document its source and give proper credit to its creator. Normally you would cite its source in a caption below the image or include the information as a way of introducing the image in your essay. Include a works cited or reference list entry for it at the end of your essay.

COPYING STATISTICS

Properly cite and document any statistics you use in your paper. If they come from a source text, including a website, they need to be documented. The same holds true if you include statistics from your own research in an essay you write. Indicate in your essay the source of these statistics and include a proper works cited or reference entry for them.

COPYING MATERIAL FROM A SOURCE TEXT, SUPPLYING PROPER DOCUMENTATION, BUT LEAVING OUT QUOTATION MARKS

Many students have a hard time understanding this form of plagiarism. The student has copied material directly from a source and has supplied proper documentation. However, if the student does not properly quote the passage, the student is guilty of plagiarism. The documentation a student provides acknowledges the writer's debt to another for the ideas she has used in the paper, but by failing to supply quotation marks, the writer is claiming credit for the language of the passage, language originally employed by the author of the source text. To properly credit the author for both the ideas and the language of the source text, the student needs to supply both proper quotation marks and proper documentation.

PARAPHRASING MATERIAL FROM A READING WITHOUT PROPER DOCUMENTATION

Suppose a student takes material from a source, paraphrases it, and includes it in his paper. Has this student committed an act of plagiarism? The student has if he fails to document the passage properly. The language is the student's own, but the original ideas were not. Adding proper documentation ensures that the author of the source text will receive proper credit for his ideas.

SELF-PLAGIARISM

The concept of self-plagiarism is difficult for many students to grasp: How is it possible to plagiarize or "copy" my own work? Self-plagiarism is considered an act of academic dishonesty for one primary reason: when teachers give students a writing assignment, they expect the student will turn in original work. If a student simply "recycles" an earlier paper—turns in a paper she or he had written in the past or for another class—the teacher is not receiving original work. Plagiarism also occurs if a student uses parts of an earlier paper in a current assignment without acknowledging the source of the recycled material. Keep in mind that unless otherwise indicated, teachers expect original work in the papers they assign—properly acknowledge and document material that comes from any outside source, including your own prior writing.

WHY STUDENTS PLAGIARIZE WORK

Students plagiarize work for many reasons—to boost their course grade, to meet an impending deadline, or to avoid the hard work of writing. It's easier for them to have a friend write the paper, to "borrow" a roommate's essay, or to purchase a paper from an online paper mill. Clearly these are all instances of fraud—the students are intentionally passing off someone else's work as their own.

Other times, though, plagiarism can be unintentional. For example, students may plagiarize work because they do not fully understand the rules and conventions governing citation practices in academic writing. They may not know what material needs to be cited. Plagiarism can also result from weak paraphrasing skills—though students provide in-text documentation for a paraphrased passage, its language and/or syntax is still too close to the original and parts of it should have been placed in quotation marks as well. It can even result from faulty note taking. Students may copy passages from source texts in their notes but not place quotation marks around them. When they write their essay, they copy the passage from their notes into their paper, and though they might document the passage correctly, they still commit plagiarism because the passage is not also placed in quotation marks. Understanding why students plagiarize work can help both instructors and students avoid the problem. However, whether committed intentionally or unintentionally, plagiarism is never acceptable.

HOW TO AVOID PLAGIARISM

DO YOUR OWN WORK

Obviously, the first way to avoid plagiarism is to do your own work when composing papers—do your own research and write your own essay. This suggestion does not mean, however, that collaborating with others when you write or getting needed help from your teacher, tutor, or classmates is wrong. Many instructors will suggest or even require you to work with others on some writing projects—classmates, writing center tutors, friends. Just be sure the paper you turn in fairly and accurately represents, acknowledges, and documents the efforts you and others have put into the essay. If you get help on a paper you are writing, make sure that you can honestly take credit for the unacknowledged ideas and language it contains. If important or substantial ideas or words in the paper came from someone else, be sure to document those contributions properly. When you turn in a paper with your name on the title page, you are taking credit for the material in the essay. You are also, though, taking responsibility for that material—you are, in effect, telling your reader that you compiled this information, developed these arguments, or produced these findings and will stand behind what you have written. Taking that responsibility seriously, doing the hard work of writing yourself and composing papers that represent your best efforts, can help you avoid problems with plagiarism.

TAKE GOOD NOTES

One common source of unintentional plagiarism is poor note taking. Here is what can happen: a student goes to the library and looks up an article she thinks will help her write her paper. She reads the piece and, taking notes, copies down information and passages she thinks she might use in her essay.

However, if she is not careful to put quotation marks around passages she takes word for word from the source, she can be in trouble when she writes her essay. If she later consults her notes when drafting her paper, she may not remember that the passage in her notes should be quoted in her paper—she may believe she paraphrased the material when taking notes. If she copies the passage exactly as she has it written in her notes and fails to place it in quotation marks in her paper, she has plagiarized the material, even if she documents it. Remember, to avoid plagiarism, passages taken word for word from a source must be quoted *and* documented. Therefore, be very careful when taking notes to place quotation marks around material you are copying directly from a reading. If you later incorporate that material in your essay, you will know to place the passage in quotation marks and document it.

To avoid problems, consider developing a consistent system for taking notes. In many high schools, students are required to write their notes on index cards with the source text's full bibliographic information on each card. If you find this system of note taking helpful, you can continue it in college. If you found this method too repetitive and time consuming, you can make a few alterations. For example, you can take notes on lined paper, citing the bibliographic information at the top and the source text's page numbers along the left margin. Consider writing on only one side of the paper, though, so you're not flipping sheets around when you write your essay. You might consider using a research journal as a place to keep all of your notes for an assignment. One common practice among academics is to keep content notes from source texts on the left-hand side of the journal and their own responses, insights, and questions on the right-hand side so as not to confuse the two (these are frequently referred to as "dual entry" journals). Whatever system you use, employ it consistently and be sure to indicate in your notes what material is copied verbatim from a source and what is paraphrased.

PARAPHRASE PROPERLY

Another source of unintentional plagiarism is improper paraphrasing. When you paraphrase material, you have to be sure to change substantially the language of the source passage (see Chapter 3 for guidelines on paraphrasing material). If you do not do a good job paraphrasing a passage, you can be guilty of plagiarism even if you document the material. If in your paraphrase there are phrases or clauses that should be quoted (because they appear in your paper exactly as they appear in the source), you will be guilty of plagiarism if you do not place quotation marks around them, even if the whole passage is properly documented.

SUPPLY PROPER DOCUMENTATION

When you proofread a source-based essay, set aside time to look for problems involving documentation before you turn it in. Problems like these can be hard to detect; you need to pay close attention to finding them as you review your work. Make sure everything that should be documented is properly cited. If you ever have any questions about whether to document a particular passage or word, see your instructor. Because instructors know the documentation conventions of their particular fields of study, they can often give you the best advice. If you have a question about whether to document a passage and you cannot reach your teacher for advice, you should probably err on the side of documentation. When responding to your work, your teacher can indicate whether the documentation was absolutely necessary.

Remember, whenever you quote *or* paraphrase material, you need to supply proper documentation, indicating the source of those words or ideas. Most students remember to document quotations. Remembering to document paraphrased material can be more problematic, especially if you have been told *not* to document "common knowledge." Though this may appear to be a fairly simple guideline, in practice it can be confusing and vague. What is **common knowledge**? What qualifies as common knowledge varies from discipline to discipline in college, as well as from audience to audience. Information that does not need to be documented in a history research paper may need to be documented in a philosophy research paper—the information is common knowledge for readers in history but not for readers in philosophy. Among one group of readers, certain facts, references, statistics, claims, or interpretations may be well known and generally accepted; among other readers, the same material may be new or controversial. For the first group of readers, documentation may not be necessary; for the second, it probably is. Again, if you ever have a question concerning whether something should or should not be documented, ask your instructor, who has expert knowledge about the discipline.

Many students express dismay over this guideline because it means that if they are writing a paper on a topic relatively new to them, they will have to document almost everything. When you are writing certain kinds of papers in certain classes, there may be no way to avoid having documented material in almost every paragraph. However, this situation is not "bad"; in fact, it is to be expected when you are writing on a subject new to you. There are ways to consolidate your documentation so the citations do not take up too much space in your essay (see the two "Consolidating References" sections in Chapter 12).

ONLINE PLAGIARISM CHECK

Many professors employ online plagiarism detection services like TurnItIn. com. These services search electronic versions of your paper to detect strings of words that match strings in the vast collection of source texts and prior student papers the company maintains on its server. At many schools, professors ask students to turn in the final drafts of their papers electronically so they can use a service like this. Other professors ask students to run rough drafts of their papers through the service in order to detect and fix passages that might be plagiarized. Check with your instructor or school librarian to see if you can take advantage of a service like this as you draft your essay.

CLARIFY COLLABORATION GUIDELINES

If you are asked to collaborate with others on a project, be sure to clarify the guidelines your teacher wants you to follow. You want to be sure you know what your teacher expects of each student in the group. Are the individual members of the group supposed to work together to produce a single essay? Are the group members supposed to help each individual member of the group write his or her own paper? How much help is acceptable? Can another student supply you with the material or arguments you will use in your essay? Can others help you with the organization, perhaps suggesting how you should structure your work? Can other students write part of your paper for you? Can others revise your paper for you, changing the language when needed? Be sure you know what your teacher expects before you begin work on a collaborative project, and be sure to ask your teacher to clarify how she expects you to acknowledge and document the help you receive from others.

Summary Chart

PLAGIARISM

1. **Forms of plagiarism**
   Purchasing a paper
   Turning in a paper someone else has written for you
   Turning in another student's work without that student's knowledge
   Improper collaboration
   Copying a paper from a source text without proper acknowledgment
   Cutting and pasting material from multiple sources
   Lifting images from the Web or other sources
   Copying statistics
   Copying material from a source text and supplying proper
   documentation, but leaving out quotation marks
   Paraphrasing material from a reading without proper documentation
   Self-plagiarism

2. **How to avoid plagiarism**
   Do your own work.
   Take good notes.
   Paraphrase properly.
   Supply proper documentation.
   Use an online plagiarism check.
   Clarify collaboration guidelines.

PLAGIARISM CHECKLIST

	Yes	No
1. Are all of your quotations properly documented?	____	____
2. Is all paraphrased material properly documented?	____	____
3. Have you acknowledged or documented the help you have received in writing your paper?	____	____
4. If this is a group project, have you checked the original assignment to be sure your work conforms to the teacher's guidelines?	____	____
5. Does the paper truly represent your own original work and effort?	____	____

Chapter 12

....

DOCUMENTATION

In this chapter you will learn how to

1. Recognize when you need to document material in your writing

2. Apply APA documentation guidelines

3. Apply MLA documentation guidelines

DEFINITION AND PURPOSE

Proper documentation for your papers serves several functions. First, it allows your readers to know exactly where to find specific information if they want to check the accuracy of what you have written or if they want to learn more about the subject. When combined with a reference list or bibliography, proper documentation enables readers to locate information easily and efficiently. Second, documentation gives credit to others for their ideas, arguments, findings, or language. When you write from readings, you are joining an ongoing conversation—people have likely written on the topic before you began your research and will likely write on it after you have finished your essay. With documentation, you acknowledge the work of those previous authors and locate your work clearly in that conversation. Finally, as a practical matter, proper documentation helps you avoid plagiarism. Many instances of unintentional plagiarism result from improper documentation. You can avoid these problems if you take a few minutes to check the accuracy of your documentation before you turn your papers in for a grade.

TYPES OF DOCUMENTATION

In college, you will encounter two primary methods of documentation: (1) in-text parenthetical documentation and (2) footnotes or endnotes. When you use in-text parenthetical documentation, you indicate where that information can be found in the original source by placing a citation in parentheses right after the quoted or paraphrased material. With footnotes or endnotes, you place a raised (superscript) number after the quoted or paraphrased material and then indicate where in the source text that information can be found.

Your citation will be placed either at the bottom of your page (in a footnote) or at the end of your paper (in an endnote). Over the past few years, parenthetical methods of documentation have largely replaced footnotes and endnotes. You may still find professors, though, who prefer those older forms of documentation. Always check with your teacher if you have any questions about the type of documentation you should be using in a class.

PRIMARY ACADEMIC STYLE MANUALS

The biggest problem you will face when documenting papers in college is lack of uniform practice, as styles of documentation will vary from class to class. When you write papers in college, your teacher will expect you to follow the guidelines set out in the style manual commonly used in that field of study—a set of directions that writers in that discipline follow when composing and documenting papers.

Teachers in humanities classes (English, history, philosophy, art) often follow the guidelines established by the Modern Language Association (MLA), as published in the *MLA Handbook* (8th ed., Modern Language Association, 2016). Teachers in the social sciences (sociology, anthropology, psychology, criminal justice) tend to follow the rules set by the American Psychological Association (APA), which appear in *Publication Manual of the American Psychological Association* (6th ed., Washington, DC: American Psychological Association, 2010). However, you may have a class with a sociology teacher who prefers that you follow MLA rules or a philosophy teacher who wants you to use APA style. Also, teachers within a given field may want their students to follow different style manuals. During the same term, for example, you may be taking two communication courses, with one teacher asking you to use MLA documentation and the other wanting you to follow APA guidelines. If teachers do not specify the format they want you to follow, always ask them which style manual they want you to use when writing your paper. If a teacher voices no preference, then choose one format and follow it consistently.

The APA and MLA style manuals agree that writers should employ in-text parenthetical documentation and explanatory footnotes; however, they disagree over the exact form this documentation should assume. Though differences between the formats dictated by these style manuals may seem minor, knowing how to properly document your work helps mark you as a member of a particular academic or research community. Not knowing how may mark you as a novice or outsider.

The following are guidelines for using APA and MLA styles of documentation. The examples offered are not comprehensive. They may be sufficient for some of the papers you write, but you may have to use types of source texts not covered here. If you do, you can find each of the major style manuals in your college library; consult them if the following examples do not answer your questions.

APA GUIDELINES

IN-TEXT DOCUMENTATION

The APA recommends an author-date-page method of in-text documentation. When you quote material, note parenthetically the last name of the author whose work you are using, the year that work was published, and the page number in the reading where that material can be found. When you paraphrase material, you need to note the last name of the author whose work you are using and the year that work was published, but you do not need to include a specific page number in the documentation. What you include in a parenthetical citation can change, however, depending on the information you have already included in your text. For example, if the author's name has already been used to introduce the material, you do not repeat the name in the parenthetical citation.

Source with One Author

When you quote a passage from a source that has only one author, place the author's last name in parentheses, followed by the year the work was published and the page number where the passage can be found in the source text, all separated by commas. Precede the page reference with "p." if the passage is located on one page in the source text ("p. 12") and with "pp." if the passage runs on more than one page ("pp. 12–13"):

Example 1

> "Drug-using women may be in a position to capitalize most on the advantages of women-inspired prevention methods, and be hindered the least by the disadvantages, as compared with other groups of at-risk women" (Gollub, 2008, p. 108).

If you were to paraphrase that passage, following APA guidelines, you would not include a specific page number in the documentation, only the author and year of publication:

Example 2 Paraphrase

> Prevention methods designed and inspired by women may offer more help to drug-using women than to other similar at-risk groups (Gollub, 2008).

Note the space between the end of the paraphrased passage and the parenthetical citation. Also, the period for the sentence follows the documentation (which is not the case with block quotations). Remember not to repeat information in your parenthetical citation that is included in the body of your essay. For example, if you mention the author's name to introduce a quotation or paraphrase, that information does not need to be repeated in the parenthetical citation. The year of publication should be in parentheses (preferably right after the author's name), and the page number, also in parentheses, should be after any quoted source material:

Example 3

> According to Erica L. Gollub (2008), "Drug-using women may be in a position to capitalize most on the advantages of women-inspired prevention methods, and be hindered the least by the disadvantages, as compared with other groups of at-risk women" (p. 108).

Source with Two Authors

If a work has two authors, cite the last names of both authors when you refer to their work. Separate the names with an ampersand (&) if you are citing them parenthetically, but use "and" if they appear in the body of your text:

Example 4

> "At the beginning of the AIDS epidemic, the large size of high-risk groups, and their lack of organization around public health issues virtually guaranteed that high levels of collective action to combat AIDS would be extremely low" (Broadhead & Heckathorn, 1994, p. 475).

Example 5 Paraphrase

> According to Broadhead and Heckathorn (1994), because the group of people most likely to be affected by AIDS was so large and tended not to focus on health issues, a poor response to the epidemic was almost certain.

Source with Three to Five Authors

The first time you refer to work from a source with three to five authors, list the last names of all the authors in the order in which they appear in the source. Again, use an ampersand before the last name when citing the authors parenthetically. In subsequent references to the work, cite the last name of the first author followed by "et al." (which means "and others"):

Example 6

> A recent study has shown that people who are infected with the HIV virus live longer and healthier lives when they receive various combinations of antiretroviral treatments (Kalichman, Eaton, Cain, Cherry, & Pope, 2006).

Example 7

> A recent study by Kalichman, Eaton, Cain, Cherry, and Pope (2006) has shown that people who are infected with the HIV virus live longer and healthier lives when they receive various combinations of antiretroviral treatments.

Example 8

> Kalichman et al. (2006) found that . . .

If shortening a citation through the use of "et al." will cause any confusion (that is, if two or more citations become identical when shortened), include as many names as necessary to distinguish the works.

Source with Six or More Authors

If a work has six or more authors, cite only the last name of the first author followed by "et al." and the year of publication:

Example 9

> A recent study in Africa confirms that among sexually active people, regular condom use helps prevent the spread of HIV and AIDS (Laga et al., 1994).

Example 10

> A recent study in Africa by Laga et al. (1994) confirms that among sexually active people, regular condom use helps prevent the spread of HIV and AIDS.

As in the previous examples, if shortening a citation through the use of "et al." will cause any confusion, list as many authors' last names as needed to differentiate the works, and then replace the remaining names with "et al."

Source with No Author

When a work has no author, cite the first word or two of the title and the year of publication. If the source text is a journal article or book chapter, the shortened title will appear in quotation marks; if the work is a pamphlet or a book, the shortened title should be italicized:

Example 11

> "The world has recognized that an adult with AIDS in Zambia has as much right to treatment as one in Norway. Children should not be left to die simply because they cannot pay" ("Children," 2005, p. 16).

Example 12

> In "Children and AIDS" (2005), the editors of the *New York Times* argue, "The world has recognized that an adult with AIDS in Zambia has as much right to treatment as one in Norway. Children should not be left to die simply because they cannot pay" (p. 16).

Because the title of the article is used to introduce the quotation in Example 12, it is not repeated in the parenthetical citation.

Sources Whose Authors Have the Same Last Name

If two authors have the same last name, differentiate them by their first initials:

Example 13

> Surveys have found that many people avoid discussing AIDS because they feel they know too little about the topic (J. Brown, 1991); consequently, a number of companies are beginning to develop programs to educate their workers (L. Brown, 1991).

Two or More Sources by the Same Author

If you are referring to two or more works by the same author, differentiate them by date of publication separated by commas. If both are included in the same parenthetical citation, order them by year of publication:

Example 14

> Because AZT has proved to be ineffective in controlling the effects of AIDS (Brown, 1993), scientists have been working hard to develop a vaccine against the virus, especially in developing countries where the epidemic is spreading quickly (Brown, 1994).

Example 15

> A series of articles in *New Scientist* by Phillida Brown (1993, 1994) traces efforts to develop adequate treatments to combat AIDS.

Two or More Sources by the Same Author Published the Same Year

If you are referring to two or more works by the same author published in the same year, differentiate them by adding lowercase letters after the dates:

Example 16

> Two recent articles (Brown, 1994a, 1994b) trace the efforts to improve AIDS treatment in developing countries.

The "a" article is the reference that appears first in the reference list, the "b" second, and so on.

Electronic Sources of Information

If you refer to the work as a whole, include the author's last name and the year of publication. If, instead, you are citing specific information in the source text, include the author's last name, the year of publication, and the page number. If the pages are not numbered, include the paragraph or section number in the source text where the material can be found, preceded by "para.":

Example 17

> According to one expert, AIDS has killed 14 million people over the past 20 years (Underwood, 1999, para. 1).

As always, do not repeat information in the citation that is already present in your essay.

Consolidating APA-Style References

If you want to include references to two or more sources in one parenthetical citation, arrange them alphabetically by the last name of the authors and separate them with semicolons:

Example 18

> Many recent studies have examined the best treatment options for women who suffer from HIV infection (Gollub, 2008; Kalichman et al., 2006; Wanjama, Kimani, & Lodiaga, 2007).

FOOTNOTES AND ENDNOTES

Some style manuals still advocate using footnotes or endnotes as the primary means of documenting source-based essays, but the APA suggests they be used sparingly, only to supply commentary or information you do not want to include in the body of your paper. These notes are numbered consecutively in the text with superscript numerals.

Example 19

> A survey of recent articles published on AIDS shows a growing interest in developing reliable research methods to test high-risk groups, such as drug abusers and prostitutes.[1]

The notes may be placed at the bottom of the page on which they appear or on a separate page at the end of the paper with the word "Footnotes" centered at the top. The footnotes are double-spaced in numerical order, preceded by superscript numerals. The first line of every note is indented five to seven spaces.

MLA GUIDELINES

IN-TEXT DOCUMENTATION

MLA style uses an author-page system of in-text documentation. When you quote or paraphrase material, you tell your reader parenthetically the name of the author whose work you are using and where in that reading the passage or information can be found. If your reader wants more information on this source text (for instance, whether it is a book or an article, when it was published, or what journal it appeared in), she will refer to the works cited list at the end of your paper, where you provide this information.

The exact form of the parenthetical documentation—what information goes into the parentheses and in what order—varies depending on the type of source you are referring to and what you have already mentioned about the source in the body of your essay.

Source with One Author

When you quote or paraphrase information from a reading that has just one author, place the author's last name in parentheses, leave a space, and then indicate the page number or numbers in the source where the passage or information can be found. Whether you are quoting or paraphrasing material, the period follows the parentheses. In the following examples, pay particular attention to spacing and the proper placement of quotation marks:

Example 20

> "Drug-using women may be in a position to capitalize most on the advantages of women-inspired prevention methods, and be hindered the least by the disadvantages, as compared with other groups of at-risk women" (Gollub 108).

Example 21 Paraphrase

> Prevention methods designed and inspired by women may offer more help to drug-using women than to other similar at-risk groups (Gollub 108).

When using the MLA format, do *not* include "p." or "pp." before the page number or numbers. Again, notice that the final period is placed *after* the documentation. The only exception to this punctuation rule occurs when you block quote information, in which case the period comes before the parenthetical documentation.

Do not repeat in the parentheses information that is already included in the text itself. For example, if you mention the author's name leading up to the quotation or believe your reader will know who the author is from the context of the quotation, you do not need to repeat the author's name in parentheses:

Example 22

> According to Erica L. Gollub, "Drug-using women may be in a position to capitalize most on the advantages of women-inspired prevention methods, and be hindered the least by the disadvantages, as compared with other groups of at-risk women" (108).

MLA style requires you to record specific page references for material directly quoted or paraphrased. If you are quoting or paraphrasing a passage that runs longer than one page in a reading, indicate all the page numbers where that information can be found:

Example 23

According to Gollub, many recent studies have investigated the sexual practices of drug users who are infected with the HIV virus (107-8).

Source with Two Authors

If a work has two authors, list the last names of the authors in the order they appear in the source, joined by "and." If you mention the authors in the body of your essay, include only the page number or numbers in parentheses:

Example 24

"At the beginning of the AIDS epidemic, the large size of high-risk groups, and their lack of organization around public health issues virtually guaranteed that high levels of collective action to combat AIDS would be extremely low" (Broadhead and Heckathorn 475).

Example 25 Paraphrase

According to Broadhead and Heckathorn, because the group of people most likely to be affected by AIDS was so large and tended not to focus on health issues, a poor response to the epidemic was almost certain (475).

Source with Three or More Authors

If a work has three or more authors, list the last name of the first author followed by the abbreviation *et al.*, Latin for *and others.*

Example 26

Recently, researchers have begun to examine the AIDS epidemic by combining a wide range of scientific and social perspectives and methodologies (Fan et al).

Since this citation refers to the entire work, no specific page reference is provided.

Example 27

A recent study has shown that people who are infected with the HIV virus live longer and healthier lives when they receive various combinations of antiretroviral treatments (Kalichman et al. 401).

Since this citation refers to a specific page, the page number is included.

Source with No Author

If a work has no author, parenthetically cite the first word or two of the title. If the work is a journal article or book chapter, the shortened title will appear in quotation marks. If the work is longer, the shortened title should be italicized. If you mention the title of the work in the body of your essay, you will need to include only the page number or numbers in parentheses:

Example 28

> "The world has recognized that an adult with AIDS in Zambia has as much right to treatment as one in Norway. Children should not be left to die simply because they cannot pay" ("Children" 16).

Example 29

> In "Children and AIDS," the editors of the *New York Times* argue, "The world has recognized that an adult with AIDS in Zambia has as much right to treatment as one in Norway. Children should not be left to die simply because they cannot pay" (16).

Sources Whose Authors Have the Same Last Name

If two different authors have the same last name, differentiate them in your documentation by including their first initials:

Example 30

> Surveys have found that many people avoid discussing AIDS because they feel they know too little about the topic (J. Brown 675); consequently, a number of companies are beginning to develop programs to educate their workers (L. Brown 64).

Two or More Sources by the Same Author

If you are referring to two or more works by the same author, differentiate them in your documentation by putting a comma after the last name of the author and adding a shortened version of the title before citing the specific page reference:

Example 31

> Because AZT has proved to be ineffective in controlling the effects of AIDS (Brown, "Drug" 4), scientists have been working hard to develop a vaccine against the virus, especially in developing countries where the epidemic is spreading quickly (Brown, "AIDS" 10).

Again, the shortened title of an article or chapter is placed in quotation marks; the shortened title of a longer work would be italicized.

Electronic Sources of Information

If the pages in the electronic source text are numbered, include the author's last name and the page number. If, instead, the paragraphs or sections in the source text are numbered, include the author's last name and the paragraph or section number or numbers (use "par." for one paragraph, "pars." for more than one paragraph). *Separate the author's last name and the paragraph numbers with a comma.* If the source text does not number pages, paragraphs, or sections, include only the author's last name.

Consolidating MLA-Style References

Many times in papers, you will include in one paragraph information you gathered from several different sources. When you document this passage, arrange the references alphabetically by the last names of the authors and separate them with semicolons:

Example 32

> Many recent studies have examined the best treatment options for women who suffer from HIV infection (Gollub; Kalichman et al.; Wanjama, Kimani, and Lodiaga).

No page numbers are included here because the passage refers to the general topic of the articles, not to specific information in them.

FOOTNOTES AND ENDNOTES

The MLA suggests that footnotes or endnotes be used only to supply commentary or information you do not want to include in the body of your paper. Whether you are adding content notes (explanations of or elaborations on ideas you have discussed in the body of your paper) or bibliographic notes (a list of sources your readers might want to consult if they are interested in learning more about the topic you are discussing), try to keep them to a minimum because they can be distracting.

Number footnotes and endnotes consecutively in the body of your essay with superscript numerals:

> A survey of recent articles published on AIDS shows a growing interest in developing reliable research methods to test high-risk groups, such as drug abusers and prostitutes.[1]

If you are using footnotes, the citation appears at the bottom of the page on which the corresponding number appears. If you are using endnotes, all the citations appear in numerical order at the end of your paper on a separate page with the heading "Notes" centered one inch from the top margin. Double-space after typing this heading and then begin the citations. All the citations are double-spaced and begin with the corresponding full-size number followed by a space. Indent the first line of each note five spaces or one-half inch from the left margin.

Chapter 13

REFERENCE LISTS AND WORKS CITED ENTRIES

In this chapter you will learn how to

1. Explain the role reference lists and works cited play in academic writing
2. Apply APA reference list guidelines
3. Apply MLA works cited guidelines

DEFINITION AND PURPOSE

A reference or works cited list comes at the end of your paper. In it you provide all of the bibliographic information for the sources you used when writing your essay. You have one entry for every source you refer to in the body of your paper, an entry that lists for your readers the information they would need to locate the source and read it themselves.

With in-text documentation you indicate where you found the specific information or language you used in your paper, usually including only the last name of the author and the page number on which the material is located. In your reference list you will give your reader much more information concerning this reading: the author's full name, the full title of the piece, and the place and year of publication. Also, while in-text documentation indicates a specific page where the material can be found, a reference list citation indicates all the page numbers of the source.

A works cited or reference list is sometimes also called a *bibliography*, but the two may not be the same, depending on the style you are following. While the entry format for each is the same, in a bibliography you might include an entry for every source you *consulted* when researching your paper; in a works cited list you include an entry only for the sources you actually *included* in your paper. Suppose you consulted ten books or articles when researching a topic for a paper but used only seven of them in your final draft. If your teacher asked you to put together an APA bibliography for your essay, you would have ten entries. If she asked you for a works cited or reference list, you would have only seven entries. If you are unsure what to include in your list of references, consult with your teacher.

Putting together a works cited or reference list can be tedious and time-consuming because there are specific forms you have to follow. These forms are dictated by the type of source you are using and the style manual you are following. Your job is to follow these forms exactly. There is an important reason for this uniformity. When you put together a works cited list in the proper form, you are providing a valuable service for your readers: when writers in a discipline agree to follow the same format for reference lists, readers can easily determine where to locate the sources that interest them because they know how to read the entries.

Complicating your efforts to put together a proper reference list is the fact that each field of study has its preferred ways of structuring entries. Although the information in the entries generally stays the same across the disciplines, the order in which you present that information varies widely. As explained in the previous chapter, teachers in the humanities tend to follow the guidelines established by the Modern Language Association (MLA) and those in the social sciences typically employ the guidelines established by the American Psychological Association (APA). When putting together a works cited or reference list, your best approach is to follow the guidelines and sample entries as closely as you can, placing the information from your source exactly where it appears in the model. Pay very close attention to capitalization, spacing, and punctuation.

The samples provided in this chapter follow the guidelines of the major style manuals, but they are not comprehensive. As you write a paper, you may use types of readings not covered in these examples. If this occurs, you can obtain a copy of each style manual at your library and follow the sample entry it contains for the type of text you are employing.

APA FORMAT

SAMPLE REFERENCE LIST ENTRIES

In an APA reference list, you include the name of the author, the publication date, the title, and the publishing information for all of the readings you use in the body of your essay. You include each author's last name, followed by a comma and the initials of the first and middle names. If a source has more than one author, list their last names first, followed by their initials and a comma, then use an ampersand (&) to introduce the final name. The date of publication appears in parentheses, followed by a period. Book and journal titles are italicized; article titles are not (neither are they placed in quotation marks). In the titles of books and articles, you capitalize only the first word of the title and subtitle (if any) and any proper nouns and proper adjectives. The format for listing the publishing information varies by the type of source, so follow the sample entries precisely. The first line of every entry is flush with the left margin; all other lines are indented, and all entries end with a period except where they end with a DOI or a URL.

Journal Article, One Author

Gollub, E. L. (2008). A neglected population: Drug-using women and women's methods of HIV/STI prevention. *AIDS Education & Prevention, 20*(2), 107–120.

- Note how the author's first and middle initials are used.
- Note where the year of publication is listed.
- Note how the title of the article is not placed in quotation marks.
- Note which words are capitalized and which are not in the title of the article.
- Note how the journal title and volume numbers are italicized.

Journal Article, Two Authors

Broadhead, R. S., & Heckathorn, D. D. (1994). AIDS prevention outreach among injection drug users: Agency problems and new approaches. *Social Problems, 41*(3), 473–495.

- Note the order of the names: last name first followed by initials. The names are separated by a comma and the second name is introduced by an ampersand.
- The year of publication comes next, noted parenthetically.
- Note that the "A" in "Agency" is capitalized because it is the first word in the subtitle.
- Note that the volume number follows the title of the journal; it is also italicized.

Journal Article, Three to Seven Authors

Kalichman, S., Eaton, L., Cain, D., Cherry, C., Pope, H., & Kalichman, M. (2006). HIV treatment beliefs and sexual transmission risk behaviors among HIV positive men and women. *Journal of Behavioral Medicine, 29*(5), 401–410.

- When there are three to seven authors, list all of their names.

Journal Article, More Than Seven Authors

Laga, M., Alary, M., Nzila, N., Manoka, A. T., Tuliza, M., Behets, F., . . . Pilot, P. (1994). Condom promotion, sexually transmitted diseases treatment, and declining incidence of HIV-1 infection in female Zairian sex workers. *The Lancet, 344,* 246–248.

- When there are eight or more authors, list the first six, then include an ellipsis and the last author's name.
- When you cite an article like this in the body of your essay, you will use the first author's surname followed by "et al." (Laga et al., 1994).

Article from a Monthly Periodical

Minkel, J. R. (2006, July). Dangling a carrot for vaccines. *Scientific American,* *295*, 39–40.

- For a monthly periodical, indicate the month of publication after the year, separating the two with a comma.
- Be sure to include the volume number as well, after the journal title.

Article from a Weekly Periodical

Clinton, B. (2006, May 15). My quest to improve care. *Newsweek, 147,* 50–52.

- Indicate the month and day of publication after the year, separating the year and month with a comma.
- Include the volume number after the journal title.

Newspaper Article

Chase, M. (2005, April 20). Panel suggests a "Peace Corps" to fight AIDS. *The Wall Street Journal,* pp. B1, B5.

Dugger, C. W. (2008, March 9). Rift over AIDS treatment lingers in South Africa. *The New York Times,* p. 8.

- Note the placement of the date: year followed by month and day, with a comma separating the year and month.
- The title of the newspaper is capitalized and italicized.
- Precede the page number with "p." if the article is on one page, and with "pp." if it runs longer than one page.
- If the newspaper is divided into sections, indicate the section along with the page number.

Newspaper Article, No Author

Children and AIDS. (2005, February 16). *The New York Times,* p. 16.

- When there is no author, begin the citation with the title.

Book with One Author

Hinds, M. J. (2008). *Fighting the AIDS and HIV epidemic: A global battle.* Berkeley Heights, NJ: Enslow.

- Note that the order of information for citing a book parallels the order of information for citing an article.
- Book titles are italicized. The first word in the title is capitalized and so are all proper nouns and proper adjectives and the first word in the subtitle.
- Following the title, indicate the city of publication and the publisher.

Books with Multiple Authors

Douglas, P. H., & Pinsky, L. (1991). *The essential AIDS fact book*. New York: Pocket Books.

Wanjama, L. N., Kimani, E. N., & Lodiaga, M. L. (2007). *HIV and AIDS: The pandemic*. Nairobi: Jomo Kenyatta Foundation.

- List multiple authors by their last names and initials, separating them with commas, and using an ampersand to introduce the final author.
- If a book has up to seven authors, list all of their names in your reference citation. For more than seven authors, see the previous guideline for periodicals. In the body of your paper, when you parenthetically cite a source with six or more authors, use only the first author's name followed by "et al." and the year of publication.

Two or More Works by the Same Person

Squire, C. (1997). *AIDS panic*. New York: Routledge.

Squire, C. (2007). *HIV in South Africa: Talking about the big thing*. London: Routledge.

- Arrange the citations in chronological order, with the earliest first.

Book, Corporate Author

National Gay and Lesbian Task Force. (1987). *Anti-gay violence: Victimization and defamation in 1986*. New York: Author.

- If the publisher is the same as the corporate author, simply write "Author" after the city where the work was published.

Book, Later Edition

Fan, H. Y., Conner, R. F., & Villarreal, L. (2007). *AIDS: Science and society* (5th ed.). Sudbury, MA: Jones and Bartlett.

- If you are using a later edition of a book, list the edition number parenthetically after the title.

Edited Book

Cohen, A., & Gorman, J. M. (Eds.). (2008). *Comprehensive textbook of AIDS psychiatry*. New York: Oxford University Press.

- If one person edited the book, place "(Ed.)." after his name. If more than one person edited the work, place "(Eds.)." after their names.
- Pay particular attention to the periods in this citation. It is easy to leave some of them out.

Book, No Author or Editor

Corporate responses to HIV/AIDS: Case studies from India. (2007). Washington, DC: World Bank.

- When the title page of a book lists no author, begin your citation with the title.
- Note that in this type of entry, an edition number would precede the year of publication.

Multivolume Book

Daintith, J., Mitchell, S., & Tootill, E. (Eds.). (1981). *A biographical encyclopedia of scientists* (Vols. 1–2). New York: Facts on File.

- Indicate for your reader how many volumes comprise the work. This information follows the title.

One Volume of a Multivolume Book

Daintith, J., Mitchell, S., & Tootill, E. (Eds.). (1981). *A biographical encyclopedia of scientists* (Vol. 1). New York: Facts on File.

- When you use just one volume of a multivolume work, indicate the volume number parenthetically after the title.

English Translation of a Book

Jager, H. (Ed.). (1988). *AIDS phobia: Disease pattern and possibilities of treatment* (J. Welch, Trans.). New York: Halsted Press.

- Open the citation with the name of the author or editor.
- Following the title, give the translator's name followed by a comma and "Trans."
- Note that in giving the translator's name, you begin with her initials, followed by the last name.
- Again, pay attention to all the periods included in this citation.

Article or Chapter from an Anthology

Many times in writing a source-based paper you will use a work contained in an anthology of readings. When this is the case, follow this format in your reference list:

Bethell, T. (2006). The African AIDS epidemic is exaggerated. In D. A. Leone (Ed.), *Responding to the AIDS epidemic* (pp. 18–22). Detroit: Greenhaven Press.

Patton, C. (1993). "With champagne and roses": Women at risk from/in AIDS discourse. In C. Squire (Ed.), *Women and AIDS* (pp. 165–187). London: Sage.

- Open your citation with the name of the author whose ideas or language you included in your paper.
- Next, give the title of the specific reading you referred to in the body of your essay.
- Next, give the name of the author or editor of the anthology and the larger work's title (the title of the book is italicized). Precede this information with the word "In" (note capitalization).
- Follow the title with the specific page numbers on which the article can be found. In this case, Patton's article can be found on pages 165–187 of Squire's book; Bethell's article can be found on pages 18–22 of Leone's book.
- Close the entry with the publishing information.

Article in a Reference Work

Acquired immune deficiency syndrome. (1990). In *The new Encyclopaedia Britannica* (Vol. 1, p. 67). Chicago: Encyclopaedia Britannica.

Haseltine, W. A. (1992). AIDS. In *Encyclopedia Americana* (Vol. 1, pp. 365–366). Danbury, CT: Grolier.

- When the entry in the reference work is signed, begin the citation with the author's name; when it is not signed, begin the citation with the title of the entry.
- Include the year the reference work was published, the title of the work (italicized), the volume number and inclusive page numbers of the entry (noted parenthetically), followed by the publishing information.

Personal Interview

Under APA guidelines, all personal communications are to be cited in the text only. Include the name of the person you interviewed (first and middle initials, full last name), the words "personal communication," and the date of the interview (month, day, year), all separated by commas:

(F. Smith, personal communication, June 24, 1995)

Electronic Sources of Information

The latest set of guidelines published by the American Psychological Association (www.apa.org) stipulates that writers include in their reference list entries specific information concerning where the material can be found online. The APA requires writers to include either the document's digital object identifier (DOI) number or to write "Retrieved from" followed by the Uniform Resource Locator (URL). Include the URL for a site's home page, not for the source text itself. If the source text cannot be reached from the site's home page, then include the source text's URL. Give preference to the DOI—include that number if available and not the URL.

Entire Website

APA recommends incorporating bibliographic information for an entire website parenthetically in the body of the text, not as a separate reference list entry:

One source of current information on the worldwide threats posed by AIDS is the United Nations' website UNAIDS (http://www.unaids.org/en/).

- The APA recommends that writers check the links they include in their work to ensure they function.
- To avoid mistakes in typing, copy and paste the URL from the website itself.

Page on a Website

Bonsor, K. (n.d.). How AIDS works. howstuffworks. Retrieved from http://www.howstuffworks.com

- This particular website had no date of publication, indicated by "n.d."
- The URL is for the website itself, not for the particular page on that website.
- Do not include a period at the end of the entry—readers may believe it is part of the URL.

Article in an Online Publication

If the text exists only electronically, use this format:

Ambinder, M. (2007, December 8). Huck and AIDS. Retrieved from http://theatlantic.com

- Note how the date of publication is listed.

Article in a Scholarly Journal

Honer, P., & Nassir, R. (2013). Social cultural stressors in Dominican Republic HIV/AIDS prevention and treatment. *Journal of AIDS & Clinical Research 4*(10). doi:10.4172/2155-6113.1000242

- Note that "doi" is followed by a colon with no space after it.
- Note that you do not add a period at the end of the DOI.

Jacobson, S. (2011). HIV/AIDS interventions in an aging population. *Health & Social Work 36*(2), 149–156. Retrieved from http://www.naswpress.org/publications/journals/hsw.html

- This article does not have a DOI number, so "Retrieved from" is used instead.

Baligh, Y., & Frank, I. (2011). Battling AIDS in America: An evaluation of the national HIV/AIDS strategy. *American Journal of Public Health 10*(9), 4–8. doi:10.2105/AJPH.2011.300259

- If you need to break a DOI number or a URL at the end of your line, do so in front of a punctuation mark (a slash or a period).

Article from an Online Database

Harris, A. (2013). Framing AIDS facts. *Black Theology: An International Journal 11*(3), 305–322. Retrieved from Academic Search Complete database.

Book on the Web

Fan, H. Y., Connor, R. F., & Villarreal, L. P. (2011). *AIDS: Science and society*. Retrieved from http://books.google.com/books/about/AIDS. html?id=wyfWRd6k2lAC

Pepin, J. (2011). *The origin of AIDS*. Retrieved from http://ebooks.-cambridge.org/ebook.jsf?bid=CBO9781139005234

- Publication information for the print edition of the book is not required.

Newspaper on the Web

Holland, J. (2001, December 15). Delivering hope by another route: H.I.V. activists collect drugs for the needy outside the U.S. *The New York Times*. Retrieved from http://www.nytimes.com

Movers and shakers in the AIDS community. (2006, August 13). *The Toronto Star*. Retrieved from http://www.thestar.com

- If the newspaper article is unsigned, begin the entry with the title.

An Image

Dillon, T. (2012, February 13). AIDS quilt [Photograph]. Retrieved from http://www.huffingtonpost.com/012/02/13/aids-memorial-quilt-san-francisco_n_1274035.html

- Note how the type of image (in this case a photograph) is listed in brackets.
- Provide the URL for the image.

Video

Swoope, T. (2013, May 7). Famous people who have died from Aids [Video file]. Retrieved from http://www.youtube.com/watch?v=BTYP03DuVH4

- Note how to format the date the video was posted: year, month day.
- The type of file is included in brackets.

E-mail

APA considers e-mails to be a form of personal communication that should not be included on your reference page. Instead, include the reference information parenthetically in the text: author of the e-mail, nature of the communication, and date it was received:

(J. Edwards, personal communication, July 31, 2011)

Blog Entry

Gordon, N. (2013, December 11). New Senate bill would help end HIV discrimination [Blog post]. Retrieved from http://www.hrc.org/blog

- Begin the entry with the name of the author.
- Note how the date of the blog post is provided: year, month day.
- In brackets indicate the nature of the entry.
- Provide the URL for the blog, not for the specific blog entry.

Online Reference Work

AIDS. (2011). In *Encyclopaedia Britannica*. Retrieved from http://www. britannica.com

- If the source text is signed, begin the entry with the author's name.
- If the text is unsigned, begin the entry with the title.

SAMPLE APA-STYLE REFERENCE LIST

List all of your references at the end of your paper, beginning the list on a new page. At the top of the page, center the word "References." After the heading, double-space and list your citations in alphabetical order according to the last name of the author or first key word in the title if there is no author. The first line of every citation should be set flush left. Indent subsequent lines.

References

AIDS. (2011). In *Encyclopaedia Britannica*. Retrieved from http:// www.britannica.com

Bethell, T. (2006). The African AIDS epidemic is exaggerated. In D. A. Leone (Ed.), *Responding to the AIDS epidemic* (pp. 18–22). Detroit: Greenhaven Press.

Chase, M. (2005, April 20). Panel suggests a "Peace Corps" to fight AIDS. *The Wall Street Journal*, pp. B1, B5.

Children and AIDS. (2005, February 16). *The New York Times*, p. 16.

Clinton, B. (2006, May 15). My quest to improve care. *Newsweek, 147,* 50–52.

Cohen, A., & Gorman, J. M. (Eds.). (2008). *Comprehensive textbook of AIDS psychiatry.* New York: Oxford University Press.

Corporate responses to HIV/AIDS: Case studies from India. (2007). Washington, DC: World Bank.

Douglas, P. H., & Pinsky, L. (1991). *The essential AIDS fact book.* New York: Pocket Books.

Dugger, C. W. (2008, March 9). Rift over AIDS treatment lingers in South Africa. *The New York Times,* p. 8.

Fan, H. Y., Conner, R. F., & Villarreal, L. (2007). *AIDS: Science and society* (5th ed.). Sudbury, MA: Jones and Bartlett.

Gollub, E. L. (2008). A neglected population: Drug-using women and women's methods of HIV/STI prevention. *AIDS Education & Prevention, 20*(2), 107–120.

Hinds, M. J. (2008). *Fighting the AIDS and HIV epidemic: A global battle.* Berkeley Heights, NJ: Enslow.

Honer, P., & Nassir, R. (2013). Social cultural stressors in Dominican Republic HIV/AIDS prevention and treatment. *Journal of AIDS & Clinical Research 4*(10). doi:10.4172/2155-6113.1000242

Laga, M., Alary, M., Nzila, N., Manoka, A. T., Tuliza, M., Behets, F., . . . Pilot P. (1994). Condom promotion, sexually transmitted diseases treatment, and declining incidence of HIV-1 infection in female Zairian sex workers. *The Lancet, 344,* 246–248.

Minkel, J. R. (2006, July). Dangling a carrot for vaccines. *Scientific American*, 295, 39–40.

Squire, C. (1997). *AIDS panic*. New York: Routledge.

Squire, C. (2007). *HIV in South Africa: Talking about the big thing*. London: Routledge.

Wanjama, L. N., Kimani, E. N., & Lodiaga, M. L. (2007). *HIV and AIDS: The pandemic*. Nairobi: Jomo Kenyatta Foundation.

MLA FORMAT

SAMPLE WORKS CITED ENTRIES

When you are asked to employ MLA style when writing a paper, follow the guidelines published in the eighth edition of the *MLA Handbook* (2016). MLA states that every works cited entry should contain five core elements—the source text's author(s), title, publisher, location, and publication dates—in a prescribed order detailed below. When listing the primary author, include the full name, last name first. Titles of sources that are parts of larger works—articles in journals or pages on web sites—are placed in quotation marks; titles of "stand-alone" sources—books or web sites—are italicized. All words in titles are capitalized except prepositions and conjunctions. Journal titles are italicized, and you should list all the pages in the source text, preceded by "p." if it is only one page long and by "pp." if it is two or more pages long. Finally, MLA style employs hanging indentation: begin the first line of each entry at the left margin and indent all subsequent lines one-half inch. Place a period at the end of each works cited entry.

   In their guidelines for composing works cited entries, MLA stresses both flexibility and adherence to certain principles. Along with the core elements of each entry, in some cases you can add additional information (such as the city in which a book was published) if you think it will help readers locate material they would like to examine themselves. Your goal—make the entries useful for your readers by including needed information in an accessible, understandable format. For more information, visit the MLA website: https://style.mla.org/.

Journal Article, One Author

Gollub, Erica L. "A Neglected Population: Drug-Using Women and Women's Methods of HIV/STI Prevention." *AIDS Education and Prevention*, vol. 20, no. 2, Apr. 2008, pp. 107–20.

- Give the full name of the author as it is printed in the article, last name first.

- The title of the article is placed in quotation marks and all key words are capitalized. A period comes at the end of the title, inside the closing quotation mark.
- The title of the journal is italicized.
- Indicate the volume and issue number of the journal (using "vol." and "no." separated by commas) along with the month and year of publication.
- The inclusive page numbers of the article are preceded by "pp."

Journal Article, Two Authors

Broadhead, Robert S., and Douglas D. Heckathorn. "AIDS Prevention Outreach among Injection Drug Users: Agency Problems and New Approaches." *Social Problems*, vol. 41, no. 3, Aug. 1994. pp. 473–95.

- When there are two authors, list both in the order they appear in the article. Start with the first author's last name, then his or her first name. The other author's name goes in normal order. Separate the authors' names with a comma and the word "and."

Journal Article, Three or More Authors

Kalichman, Seth, et al. "HIV Treatment Beliefs and Sexual Transmission Risk Behaviors among HIV Positive Men and Women." *Journal of Behavioral Medicine*, vol. 29, no. 5, Oct. 2006. pp. 401–10.

- When there are three or more authors, list only the first author, last name first. Follow that name with "et al." (which means "and others"). Note the comma preceding "et al."

Article from a Monthly Periodical

Minkel, J. R. "Dangling a Carrot for Vaccines." *Scientific American*, July 2006, pp. 39–40.

- Include the month of publication after the title, separated by a comma. Months are abbreviated except for May, June, and July.
- Note that you do not include the volume number of the work, only the month and year of publication.

Article from a Weekly Periodical

Clinton, Bill. "My Quest to Improve Care." *Newsweek*, 15 May 2006, pp. 50–52.

- After the title of the publication, list the day, month, and year of publication, in that order. Note the lack of punctuation between day, month, and year.

Newspaper Article

Chase, Marilyn. "Panel Suggests a 'Peace Corps' to Fight AIDS." *The Wall Street Journal*, 20 Apr. 2005, pp. B1+.

Dugger, Celia W. "Rift over AIDS Treatment Lingers in South Africa." *The New York Times*, 9 Mar. 2008, national edition, p. 8.

- Include the article "The" if it is part of the masthead title of the newspaper.
- If the article runs longer than one page (as with the first sample above), provide the first page number followed by a plus sign (+).
- The "B" in the first entry tells the reader the article can be found in section B of *The Wall Street Journal* published that day. Including "national edition" in the second example tells readers which version of *The New York Times* included the article you are citing.

Newspaper Article, No Author

"Children and AIDS." *The New York Times*, 22 Feb. 2005, national edition, p. 16.

- If the article is unsigned, begin the entry with the title. In your works cited list, alphabetize such entries by the first key word in the title (ignoring words like "the" or "a").

Book with One Author or Two Authors

Hinds, Maurene J. *Fighting the AIDS and HIV Epidemic: A Global Battle.* Enslow, 2008.

Douglas, Paul Harding, and Laura Pinsky. *The Essential AIDS Fact Book.* Pocket Books, 1991.

- If a book has one author, begin the entry with her or his name, last name first.
- If there are two authors, begin the entry with the name of author appearing first on the book's title page, again last name first. The second author's name goes in the normal order, and the two names are separated by a comma and the word "and."
- Note: only include the city of publication if you think it might help a reader locate the publisher, particularly one located outside North America.

Book with Three or More Authors

Wanjama, Leah Niambi, et al. *HIV and AIDS: The Pandemic.* Jomo Kenyatta Foundation, 2007.

- If a book has three or more authors, provide the name of the author appearing first on the title page, last name first, followed by a comma and "et al." ("and others").

Two or More Books by the Same Person

Squire, Connie. *AIDS Panic.* Routledge, 1997.

---. *HIV in South Africa: Talking about the Big Thing.* Routledge, 2007.

- When you have two or more books by the same author or authors, list them on your works cited list in alphabetical order by the first key word in the title.
- For the first work by the author, give his or her full name, last name first. For subsequent entries by the same author, instead of repeating the name, type three hyphens followed by a period. Then provide the title of the work and the other relevant information.

Book, Corporate Author

Anti-Gay Violence: Victimization and Defamation in 1986. National Gay and Lesbian Task Force, 1987.

Hastings Center. *AIDS: An Epidemic of Ethical Puzzles.* Dartmouth Publishing Company, 1991.

- If the book is written by the same organization that published it (as in the first example above), begin the entry with the title of the source. Otherwise, treat the corporate author just as you would an individual author, beginning the entry with that information (as in the second example).

Book, Later Edition

Fan, Hung Y., et al. *AIDS: Science and Society.* 5th ed., Jones and Bartlett, 2007.

- Indicate the edition of the book after the title.

Edited Book

Cohen, Ann, and Jack. M. Gorman, editors. *Comprehensive Textbook of AIDS Psychiatry.* Oxford UP, 2008.

Squire, Corrinne, editor. *Women and AIDS: Psychological Perspectives.* Sage, 1993.

- If the work has more than one editor, follow their names with "editors"; if there is only one, use "editor."

Book, No Author or Editor

Corporate Responses to HIV/AIDS: Case Studies from India. World Bank, 2007.

- When there is no author or editor, begin the entry with the title of the work.

Multivolume Book

Daintith, John, et al., editors. *A Biographical Encyclopedia of Scientists.* 2 vols. Facts on File, 1981.

- Indicate the number of volumes in a multivolume work after the title.

One Volume of a Multivolume Book

Dainith, John, et al., editors. *A Biographical Encyclopedia of Scientists.* Vol. 1, Facts on File, 1981.

- If you use only one volume of a multivolume work, indicate the volume number after the title.

English Translation of a Book

Jager, Hans, editor. *AIDS Phobia: Disease Pattern and Possibilities of Treatment.* Translated by Jacquie Welch, Halsted, 1988.

- Include the name of the translator introduced with "Translated by."

Article or Chapter from an Anthology

Patton, Cindy. "'With Champagne and Roses': Women at Risk from/in AIDS Discourse." *Women and AIDS,* edited by Corinne Squire, Sage, 1993, pp. 165–87.

- First, identify the author(s) of the article or chapter you cite in your work.
- Next, give the title of that article or chapter in quote marks. Note: if the title already includes quotations marks, the original quotation marks are shifted to single quotation marks in the citation.
- Provide the name of the work that contained the article or chapter, followed by the name of the editor(s) introduced with "edited by."
- Close with the publication information and the page numbers in the collection where the article or chapter can be found.

Article in a Reference Work

"Acquired Immune Deficiency Syndrome." *Encyclopedia Britannica: Micropeaedia,* 1990.

- If the author of the piece in the reference work is listed, start the entry with that. Otherwise, start with the title of the entry.
- Include the year the reference work was published.

Electronic Sources of Information

Many of the works cited entries for material found on the Internet closely resemble entries for the same material found in print but with some additional information. You will need to identify in your entries where you located the material, for example through a search of the Web, via email, or on YouTube. MLA encourages writers to include the URL of information they find on the Internet unless their teacher instructs them otherwise. Do not include "http://" or "https://" in the address. If in addition to a URL material also has a DOI (digital object identifier) number, use that rather than the URL

(DOI numbers never change for material even if the URL associated with it does change). If you think the information would be useful to your readers, also include the date you accessed information on the Internet; MLA does not require the date of access, however.

Entire Website

Aidsmap. NAM Publications, 2016, www.aidsmap.com/. Accessed 11 Jan. 2015.

AVERT. 1986–2016. www.avert.org/. Accessed 12 Jan. 2015.

- Begin your entry with the title of the website (which is italicized), then include its publisher, the year it was published, the website's URL, and, if appropriate, the date you accessed the information.
- If the title of the website and its publisher are essentially the same, you do not need to include the publisher in your citation (as in the second sample above).
- Use "Accessed" to introduce the date you visited the website as you researched your project and provide the date using day, month, and year (no commas).
- Note the period at the end of the URL and at the end of the citation.

Page on a Web Site

"Symptoms and Stages of HIV Infection." *AVERT*, 1 May 2015, www.avert. org/about-hiv-aids/symptoms-stages. Accessed 3 Apr. 2016.

- Include the author of the material (if one is listed), the title of the page in quotation marks, the title of the web site, the publisher (if different than the name of the website), the date the material was posted/last updated, the website's URL, and the date you accessed it.
- Pay attention to the punctuation employed to separate the various elements of the citation.
- Note: when typing your citations, you can break URLs at hyphens or backslashes.

Article in an Online Periodical

Ambinder, Marc. "Huck and AIDS." *The Atlantic*, 8 Dec. 2007, www. theatlantic.com/politics/archive/2007/12/huck-and-aids/51213/. Accessed 22 Mar. 2015.

- When you cite an article from the web version of a periodical, include the date the piece was posted online as well as the URL.

Article in an Online Scholarly Journal

Horner, Pilar, and Reza Nassir. "Social Cultural Stressors in Dominican Republic HIV/AIDS Prevention and Treatment." *Journal of AIDS and*

Clinical Research, vol. 4, no. 10, 6 Sept. 2013, doi: 10.4172/2155-6113.1000242. Accessed 24 Feb. 2015.

- When a scholarly journal only publishes online, still include the volume and issue numbers if they are provided, as well as the date it was posted. If the article has a DOI number, use it in your citation rather than a URL.

Article in an Online Scholarly Journal also Appearing in Print

Baliagh, Yehia, and Ian Frank. "Battling AIDS in America: An Evaluation of the National HIV/AIDS Strategy." *American Journal of Public Health*, vol. 101, no. 9, Sept 2011, pp. 4–8, doi: 10.2105/AJPH.2011.300259. Accessed 2 Jan. 2013.

Jacobson, Stephanie. "HIV/AIDS Interventions in an Aging Population." *Health Social Work*, vol. 36, no. 2, May 2011, pp. 149–56, nasw.publisher. ingentaconnect.com/content/nasw/hsw/2011/00000036/00000002/ art00008. Accessed 26 Sept. 2014.

- If you are citing the online version of a scholarly article that also appears in print, provide all the information you would normally include for the print version (including volume number and issue number as well as month and year of publication). If the article is published online in a stable format (for example, as a PDF rather than an HTML document) with the page numbers as they are in the print version, include the page numbers in your citation as well.
- If the article has a DOI number include it (as shown in the first example above); if not, include the URL (as shown in the second example above).

Article from an Online Database

Ruel, Erin, and Richard T. Campbell. "Homophobia and HIV/AIDS: Attitude Change in the Face of an Epidemic." *Social Forces*, vol. 84, no. 4, June 2006, pp. 2167–78. *JSTOR*, www.jstor.org/stable/3844494. Accessed 16 June 2014.

- If you cite information from an article in a journal that is included in its entirety in an online database, begin your citation with all the information you would normally include about the journal, ending with a period. Then include the name of the database in italics (as with "JSTOR" in the example above) and the database URL, followed by a period.

Newspaper on the Web

Holland, Jenny. "Delivering Hope by Another Route: H.I.V. Activists Collect Drugs for the Needy Outside the U.S." *The New York Times*,

15 Dec. 2011, www.nytimes.com/2001/12/15/nyregion/delivering-hope-another-route-hiv-activists-collect-drugs-for-needy-outside-us.html.

- The name of the newspaper is italicized. Include the article "The" if it is part of the masthead title of the newspaper.
- Include the date the article was published online and the URL.

An Image

Dillon, Tommy. "AIDS Quilt." Photograph. *The Huffington Post*, 13 Feb. 2012, www.huffingtonpost.com/2012/02/13/aids-memorial-quilt-san-francisco_n_1274035.html. Accessed 1 Apr. 2016.

- Start with the name of the person who created the image and the image title.
- Identify the images medium (in this case, "Photograph").
- Provide the publication information and the URL.

Book on the Web/Electronic Book

Fan, Hung Y, et al. *AIDS: Science and Society*. 6th ed., Jones and Bartlett, 2011. *Google Books*, books.google.com/books?isbn=0763773158.

- In addition to the publication information for the book—authors, title, edition number, publisher and date of publication, followed by a period, as in the example above—include the name of the website where you located the book (in italics) and its URL.

Video

"Famous People Who Died from Aids." *You Tube*, uploaded by SwoopsFilms, 10 May 2015, www.youtube.com/watch?v=v7F2ByOegYY. Accessed 1 Dec. 2015.

- Include the title of the video in quotation marks, the name of the website where it is located (in this case, YouTube), who uploaded it, the date it was uploaded, and the URL. Since YouTube is often an unstable source, this is an example where your date of access would be useful.

Email

Edwards, John. "Re: AIDS Resources." Received by Stephen Wilhoit, 31 July 2014.

- Begin with the name of the person who wrote the email and use the subject as the title. Close with the date you received it.

Blog Entry

Gordon, Noël. "New Senate Bill Would Help End HIV Discrimination." *HRC Blog*, Human Rights Campaign, 11 Dec. 2013, www.hrc.org/blog/new-senate-bill-would-end-hiv-discrimination. Accessed 1 May 2014.

- In addition to the author of the blog, provide its title, the name of the blog (in italics), the blog's owner, the date it was posted, and the URL. If available, include the time it was posted between the date and the URL (for example, "10:30 a.m.").

Online Reference Work

"AIDS." *Encyclopaedia Britannica Online*, 2 Mar. 2016, www.britannica.com/science/AIDS. Accessed 3 Mar. 2016.

- If the entry is signed, include the author's name; if not, begin with the entry's title.
- The title of the reference work is italicized.
- If the title of the site is essentially the same as its publisher, you do not need to include publication information.
- Include both the date the information was posted or last updated and the date you accessed it.

SAMPLE MLA-STYLE WORKS CITED LIST

Begin the works cited list on a separate sheet of paper at the end of your essay. Center "Works Cited" at the top of the page, then double-space before you begin listing your entries. Entries are alphabetized by the author's last name or by the first key word in the title if there is no author. The first line of each entry begins at the left margin, and all subsequent lines of each entry are indented one-half inch. The entire list is double-spaced.

Works Cited

Broadhead, Robert S., and Douglas D. Heckathorn. "AIDS Prevention Outreach among Injection Drug Users: Agency Problems and New Approaches." *Social Problems*, vol. 41, no. 3, Aug. 1994. pp. 473-95.

"Children and AIDS." *The New York Times*, 22 Feb. 2005, national edition, p. 16.

Cohen, Ann, and Jack. M. Gorman, editors. *Comprehensive Textbook of AIDS Psychiatry.* Oxford UP, 2008.

Fan, Hung Y, et al. *AIDS: Science and Society.* 6th ed., Jones and Bartlett, 2011. Google Books, books.google.com/books?isbn=0763773158.

Gordon, Noël. "New Senate Bill Would Help End HIV Discrimination." *HRC Blog*, Human Rights Campaign, 11 Dec. 2013, www.hrc.org/blog/new-senate-bill-would-end-hiv-discrimination.

Horner, Pilar, and Reza Nassir. "Social Cultural Stressors in Dominican Republic HIV/AIDS Prevention and Treatment." *Journal of AIDS and Clinical Research*, vol. 4, no. 10, 6 Sept. 2013, doi: 10.4172/2155-6113.1000242.

Kalichman, Seth, et al. "HIV Treatment Beliefs and Sexual Transmission Risk Behaviors among HIV Positive Men and Women." *Journal of Behavioral Medicine*, vol. 29, no. 5, Oct. 2006. pp. 401-10.

Minkel, J. R. "Dangling a Carrot for Vaccines." *Scientific American*, July 2006, pp. 39-40.

Squire, Connie. *AIDS Panic.* Routledge, 1997.

---. *HIV in South Africa: Talking about the Big Thing.* Routledge, 2007.

"Symptoms and Stages of HIV Infection." *AVERT*, 1 May 2015, www.avert.org/about-hiv-aids/symptoms-stages. Wanjama, Leah Niambi, et al. *HIV and AIDS: The Pandemic.* Jomo Kenyatta Foundation, 2007.

Appendix

....

PEER REVIEW GUIDELINES

In most cases, your instructor will provide you with a set of guidelines to follow when you review a peer's writing. If your teacher does not give you a set of guidelines to follow, you may want to employ the peer review procedures outlined below. To apply any set of guidelines effectively, though, you need to understand the purpose of peer review and commit yourself to improving your peer's writing. When peers review your work, remember that they are merely suggesting ways you might improve your writing. As the author of the piece, you are responsible for all final editing decisions.

PURPOSE

When you review a peer's writing, you can play three related roles, each serving a unique purpose: average reader, adviser, and editor. As an **average reader**, you offer your genuine response to the manuscript. You should let your peers know which aspects of their writing you find interesting, which parts you find boring, what is clear, what is confusing, what you would like to know more about, and what questions you have. As an **adviser**, along with offering your response to the manuscript, you also make specific suggestions to improve the piece. You can suggest changes in content, organization, format, or style. Finally, as an **editor**, you make specific suggestions for improving the piece and correct any problems you find in the writing.

Whatever role you play, your goal remains the same: to help your peer produce the most effective piece of writing possible. Peer review works best when it is truly reciprocal in nature: you do your best to improve your peer's writing because you know your peer is doing his or her best to improve your writing.

PROCEDURES TO FOLLOW

If you are asked to review a peer's writing, follow the guidelines your instructor distributes. If your teacher does not provide you specific guidelines to follow, employ the following procedures.

Step 1: **Read through the entire paper** carefully without marking anything.

Step 2: Consider whether the paper (or any part of it you are reviewing) **meets the needs of the assignment**. If it does not, tell your peer why you think it does not answer the assignment.

Step 3: Examine the paper's **content**. Point out which sections of the essay are clear, which need further development, which specifically address the assignment, and which seem to stray from it. Offer any suggestions you have for improving the paper's content.

Step 4: Examine the paper's **structure**. Note any problems with the paper's thesis statement or topic sentences. Comment on whether the writer provides clear and effective transitions between paragraphs or among sentences within the paragraphs. Note any passage where you lose track of the writer's train of thought. Finally, comment on the effectiveness of the opening and closing sections of the essay.

Step 5: Examine the paper's **style**. Note any awkward or confusing sentences (if you have a suggestion about how to improve the sentence, offer it). Look for consistency in voice, diction, and point of view, commenting on any problems you find. If you think that any passage is stylistically inappropriate given the assigned audience, let the writer know.

Step 6: **Proofread** for errors in spelling, punctuation, or typing. You can either circle errors you find and leave them for the author to correct or offer corrections of your own.

Step 7: Examine the paper's **documentation**. First, check to see that the author has documented every passage that needs to be documented, noting any questions you have. Second, note any errors you find in the documentation the author provides, such as problems with the documentation's placement, formatting, or punctuation. Finally, proofread the paper's works cited or reference list if there is one.

ACTING ON PEER REVIEWS

As an author, you have the final say concerning the changes you make to your essay. You can accept or reject your peer's suggestions, but whatever decision you make, base it on a careful consideration of your peer's comments.

Accepting every suggestion a peer reviewer offers is usually a bad idea, as is summarily rejecting every suggestion a reviewer makes. Consider each comment individually. Decide whether the peer reviewer's suggestion will improve your manuscript. If it will, make the change. If you think it will not, do not act on the suggestion. If you are unsure about making any change, talk it over with your instructor before you decide.

CREDITS

Selgelid, Michael. "A Moderate Approach to Enhancement" originally appeared in *Philosophy Now*, 91. © Michael Selgelid, 2012. Used with permission of Michael Selgelid.

Wechsler, Henry. "Getting Serious about Binge Drinking." Reprinted by permission from Henry Wechsler, *The Chronicle of Higher Education*. Copyright © 1998 by Henry Wechsler.

INDEX

Anthology of Readings

Anthology of Readings

VOCATION: HOW DO YOU KNOW WHAT TO DO WITH YOUR LIFE?

INTRODUCTION

What do you want to do with your life? What can you do to fill your life with meaning and significance? If you are like most students today, you are attending college primarily to prepare yourself for your future occupation, even if you are not sure, right now, what that occupation might be. The authors of readings in this chapter raise a number of important questions that will challenge you to consider the direction your life will take.

All of the authors discuss what it means to have a vocation or a calling in life and explore how we discover or discern what it will be. They believe that at some point in our lives, we all wrestle with the question of how we can lead a more fulfilling life by employing our talents, gifts, and time in the service of others. Some people may say that they have known their calling from childhood, that for as long as they can remember they have felt compelled to teach or practice medicine for example. For others, though, identifying and understanding their vocation comes later in life and attending college often plays a crucial role for them. College affords them the opportunity to identify their talents and interests and the time for introspection and exploration. As several of the authors point out, however, because vocational discernment is so highly personal and so frequently a spiritual quest, faculty are reluctant to discuss it in class or help their students in their journeys. In fact, the role faculty should play in helping students discover their vocations is a central question several of the authors explore.

As you read the essays in this chapter, consider how they speak to your own experiences and questions. What are you being called to do with *your* life?

On Freedom of Expression and Campus Speech Codes

The statement that follows was approved by the Association's Committee A on Academic Freedom and Tenure in June 1992 and adopted by the Association's Council in November 1994.

Freedom of thought and expression is essential to any institution of higher learning. Universities and colleges exist not only to transmit knowledge. Equally, they interpret, explore, and expand that knowledge by testing the old and proposing the new.

This mission guides learning outside the classroom quite as much as in class, and often inspires vigorous debate on those social, economic, and political issues that arouse the strongest passions. In the process, views will be expressed that may seem to many wrong, distasteful, or offensive. Such is the nature of freedom to sift and winnow ideas.

On a campus that is free and open, no idea can be banned or forbidden. No viewpoint or message may be deemed so hateful or disturbing that it may not be expressed.

Universities and colleges are also communities, often of a residential character. Most campuses have recently sought to become more diverse, and more reflective of the larger community, by attracting students, faculty, and staff from groups that were historically excluded or underrepresented. Such gains as they have made are recent, modest, and tenuous. The campus climate can profoundly affect an institution's continued diversity. Hostility or intolerance to persons who differ from the majority (especially if seemingly condoned by the institution) may undermine the confidence of new members of the community. Civility is always fragile and can easily be destroyed.

In response to verbal assaults and use of hateful language, some campuses have felt it necessary to forbid the expression of racist, sexist, homophobic, or ethnically demeaning speech, along with conduct or behavior that harasses.

Several reasons are offered in support of banning such expression. Individuals and groups that have been victims of such expression feel an understandable outrage. They claim that the academic progress of minority and majority alike may suffer if fears, tensions, and conflicts spawned by slurs and insults create an environment inimical to learning.

These arguments, grounded in the need to foster an atmosphere respectful of and welcoming to all persons, strike a deeply responsive chord in the academy. But, while we can acknowledge both the weight of these concerns and the thoughtfulness of those persuaded of the need for regulation, rules that ban or punish speech based upon its content cannot be justified. An institution of higher learning fails to fulfill its mission if it asserts the power to proscribe ideas—and racial or ethnic slurs, sexist epithets, or homophobic insults almost always express ideas, however repugnant. Indeed, by proscribing any ideas, a university sets an example that profoundly disserves its academic mission.

Some may seek to defend a distinction between the regulation of the content of speech and the regulation of the manner (or style) of speech. We find this distinction untenable in practice because offensive style or opprobrious phrases may in fact have been chosen precisely for their expressive power. As the United States Supreme Court has said in the course of rejecting criminal sanctions for offensive words:

> [W]ords are often chosen as much for their emotive as their cognitive force. We cannot sanction the view that the Constitution, while solicitous of the cognitive content of individual speech, has little or no regard for that emotive function which, practically speaking, may often be the more important element of the over-all message sought to be communicated.

The line between substance and style is thus too uncertain to sustain the pressure that will inevitably be brought to bear upon disciplinary rules that attempt to regulate speech.

Proponents of speech codes sometimes reply that the value of emotive language of this type is of such a low order that, on balance, suppression is justified by the harm suffered by those who are directly affected, and by the general damage done to the learning environment. Yet a college or university sets a perilous course if it seeks to differentiate between high-value and low-value speech, or to choose which groups are to be protected by curbing the speech of others. A speech code unavoidably implies an institutional competence to distinguish permissible expression of hateful thought from what is proscribed as thoughtless hate.

Institutions would also have to justify shielding some, but not other, targets of offensive language—proscribing uncomplimentary references to sexual but not to political preference, to religious but not to philosophical creed, or perhaps even to some but not to other religious affiliations. Starting down this path creates an even greater risk that groups not originally protected may later demand similar solicitude—demands the institution that began the process of banning some speech is ill equipped to resist.

Distinctions of this type are neither practicable nor principled; their very fragility underscores why institutions devoted to freedom of thought and expression ought not adopt an institutionalized coercion of silence.

Moreover, banning speech often avoids consideration of means more compatible with the mission of an academic institution by which to deal with incivility, intolerance, offensive speech, and harassing behavior:

1. Institutions should adopt and invoke a range of measures that penalize conduct and behavior, rather than speech—such as rules against defacing property, physical intimidation or harassment, or disruption of campus activities. All members of the campus community should be made aware of such rules, and administrators should be ready to use them in preference to speech-directed sanctions.

2. Colleges and universities should stress the means they use best—to educate—including the development of courses and other curricular and co-curricular experiences designed to increase student understanding and to deter offensive or intolerant speech or conduct. These institutions should, of course, be free (indeed encouraged) to condemn manifestations of intolerance and discrimination, whether physical or verbal.

3. The governing board and the administration have a special duty not only to set an outstanding example of tolerance, but also to challenge boldly and condemn immediately serious breaches of civility.

4. Members of the faculty, too, have a major role; their voices may be critical in condemning intolerance, and their actions may set examples for understanding, making clear to their students that civility and tolerance are hallmarks of educated men and women.

5. Student-personnel administrators have in some ways the most demanding role of all, for hate speech occurs most often in dormitories, locker rooms, cafeterias, and student centers. Persons who guide this part of campus life should set high standards of their own for tolerance and should make unmistakably clear the harm that uncivil or intolerant speech inflicts.

To some persons who support speech codes, measures like these—relying as they do on suasion rather than sanctions—may seem inadequate. But freedom of expression requires toleration of "ideas we hate," as Justice Holmes put it. The underlying principle does not change because the demand is to silence a hateful speaker, or because it comes from within the academy. Free speech is not simply an aspect of the educational enterprise to be weighed against other desirable ends. It is the very precondition of the academic enterprise itself.

May 25, 1994

Hate-Speech Codes That Will Pass Constitutional Muster

Lawrence White

Lawrence White is University Counsel at Georgetown University. This article is adapted from a presentation at the Stetson University College of Law's National Conference on Law and Higher Education.

It has been a trying few years for the drafters of hate-speech codes on college and university campuses. The University of Pennsylvania jettisoned its controversial speech code last fall after President Sheldon Hackney, during his confirmation hearing to be Chairman of the National Endowment for the Humanities, questioned whether such codes were the right approach to achieving civility on campus. This year, Central Michigan University became the latest institution to lose a court fight over its speech code. Continuing an unbroken line of victories by the American Civil Liberties Union, a federal judge held in January that Central Michigan had violated its basketball coach's right to free speech when he was disciplined under its "discriminatory harassment" code after he used a racial epithet during a closed-door team meeting. At Wesleyan University, the University of Michigan, and numerous other institutions, administrators have given up and repealed their codes.

Due largely to the court decisions, we now understand the arguments against campus speech codes. They use inherently vague terminology; they are overbroad, sweeping within their regulatory ambit not only pernicious language, but also language that enjoys constitutional protection. "It is technically impossible to write an anti-speech code that cannot be twisted against speech nobody means to bar," concluded Eleanor Holmes Norton, a former Georgetown University law professor who is now the District of Columbia's Delegate to Congress.

Despite the problems raised by speech codes, however, we must not forget that there are salutary purposes underlying the effort to draft codes banning derogatory and hurtful epithets. Such codes were intended to serve, and still serve, an important educational purpose: They are expressions of an institution's commitment to the victims of a pernicious and destructive form of behavior. Whenever anybody commits an act or utters a remark that is motivated by hatefulness, it causes harm to a real, flesh-and-blood victim. Hate-speech codes designed to protect victims are a noble endeavor. If institutions abandon the effort to draft policies against hateful speech, they are abandoning the victims the policies were meant to protect.

Campus administrators can learn important lessons from the court cases against the first generation of speech codes. In every instance, the codes that provoked court challenges were ambitiously, almost sweepingly, worded. Several of them, including those at the University of Michigan and the University of Wisconsin, were modeled on the Equal Employment Opportunity Commission's guidelines on sexual harassment. They used concepts and terminology—"intimidating environment for education," "express or implied threat to an individual's academic efforts"—awkwardly borrowed from employment law. They treated the university campus as a single, undifferentiated "workplace."

The language they used seemed almost deliberately provocative to civil libertarians—phrases such as "expressive behavior" (University of Wisconsin) and other wording that equated physical behavior with verbal behavior (Central Michigan University)—as though there were no distinction under the First Amendment.

What we have come to refer to as "hate speech" takes many forms on the nation's college campuses. The most prevalent involves remarks by students addressed to other students. For every high-profile case involving a campus speech by Khalid Abdul Muhammad of the Nation of Islam, there are literally dozens, maybe hundreds, of incidents that occur behind the closed doors of dormitory rooms, in dining halls, or in the corridors outside student pubs. We know, regrettably, that a strong correlation exists between hate speech and alcohol abuse.

Colleges and universities must now craft a second generation of codes that will serve the important institutional objective of protecting the victims of hateful acts and utterances without violating constitutional principles. These codes would:

*Differentiate between dormitories and classrooms. In an article that appeared in the *Duke Law Journal* in 1990, Nadine Strossen, president of the ACLU, observed that the right to free speech applies with different force in different parts of a college campus. That right, she wrote, "may not be applicable to—students' dormitory rooms. These rooms constitute the students' homes. Accordingly, under established free-speech tenets, students should have the right to avoid being exposed to others' expression by seeking refuge in their rooms." A policy that disciplined students for the hateful acts or utterances against other students in residence halls would probably bring three-quarters of all hate-speech episodes within the regulatory purview of college administrators without offending traditional free-speech precepts.

*Be tailored to the Supreme Court's decision in *R.A.V. v. St. Paul, Minn.* This 1992 decision suggests that anti-discrimination codes are on shaky ground constitutionally if they proscribe some hateful acts or utterances but not others. Any policy that prohibits categories of speech "because of" or "on the basis of" a specific factor—such as race, gender, or sexual orientation— runs the risk of violating the Court's stricture in *R.A.V.* that laws must not single out particular categories of hateful speech for penalties. As ironic as it sounds, the safest hate-speech code may be one that makes no mention of the very groups it is designed to protect.

*Use words emphasizing action and its effects, instead of speech. First Amendment jurisprudence recognizes an important distinction between speech and action and allows a greater degree of latitude when action is being regulated. The first generation of campus speech codes used vocabulary emphasizing speech, which virtually doomed them in advance—for example, they barred certain "comments" or "expressive behavior." By fostering the impression that these policies regulated pure speech, they made an easy target. The receptiveness of courts to arguments that the codes were overbroad— prohibiting speech that should be constitutionally protected along with utterances that deserve no protection (such as yelling "Fire!" in a crowded theater)—requires campuses to be more careful than they were in the past to draft constitutionally acceptable speech codes.

The second generation of codes should favor "action" vocabulary— prohibiting hostile conduct or behavior that might "incite immediate violence" (the latter being the exact phrasing used in the Supreme Court's half-century-old "fighting words" case, *Chaplinsky v. New Hampshire*). Instead of calling them "hate-speech codes," colleges and universities should refer to the new policies as "anti-hate" or "anti-discrimination" codes.

*Enhance the penalties for alcohol-related hate mongering. Most campus conduct codes allow the imposition of disciplinary sanctions for disorderly conduct or violations of drug and alcohol policies. It would be constitutionally defensible to treat hateful acts or utterances as an additional factor to be taken into account when meting out punishment for code violations. For example, a student found guilty of public drunkenness could be sentenced to attend a program designed to treat alcohol abuse, but the same inebriated student could be suspended or expelled for hurling racial epithets or threats at fellow students.

Drafting a new generation of campus codes to curb hate mongering, codes that zero in on areas of highest risk (dormitories, drunkenness) while avoiding the vagueness and overbreadth that doomed the first generation of codes, is an exercise worth undertaking. Colleges and universities began attempting to regulate hate speech a decade ago for an important reason—to communicate a message of support to the victims of hate. That reason is still compelling today. If institutions abandon the effort to implement constitutionally acceptable codes, they will be sending a message chillingly and accurately expressed by the Stanford Univeristy law professor Charles Lawrence in an article that accompanied Ms. Strossen's in the 1990 *Duke Law Journal:*

"I fear that by framing the debate as we have—as one in which the liberty of free speech is in conflict with the elimination of racism—we have advanced the cause of racial oppression and have placed the bigot on the moral high ground, fanning the rising flames of racism."

We all understand civil libertarians' concerns when universities approach the delicate task of regulating certain forms of expressive conduct. But civil libertarians in turn should appreciate the message that is communicated when the rights of insensitive, viciously motivated members of college and university communities are placed above victims' rights to an education untainted by bigoted animosity. By trimming their drafting sails to incorporate the lessons of the first round of court cases, college administrators can satisfy constitutional concerns and at the same time curb the most egregious forms of hate mongering on campus. Then they can send an appropriate message to perpetrator and victim alike: Hateful utterances and behavior are repugnant forms of conduct that colleges and universities will not tolerate.

Fairness To All: Free Speech and Civility in Conflict

"The harm of exercising certain constitutional rights in certain contexts is not a new concpt."
For Narrowly Tailored Limitations on Gender-Based Discriminatory Speech

Ann Browning Masters
St. John River Community College

Ann Browning Masters is a counselor on the St. Augustine campus of St. John River Community College.

A major issue on college campuses across the country is the extent to which institutions of higher learning may impose regulations or speech codes to ban sexually harassive speech that is believed to foster gender-based discrimination. This thorny problem, which sees to balance the competing interests of preserving free speech on campus while maintaining a learning environment that is free from harassive speech, goes to the heart of the nature of an institution of higher learning. Dr. Masters takes the position that narrowly crafted controls are necessary to make colleges and universities inviting to all. Dr. Dagley adopts the opposite perspective. He responds that even though speech codes may, so to speak, have their hearts in the right places by attempting to remove hateful speech from campuses, they are improper because they violate the First Amendment by undermining the purpose of institutions of higher learning as places where people can express their minds freely.

FOR NARROWLY TAILORED LIMITATIONS ON GENDER-BASED DISCRIMINATORY SPEECH

The following discussion is limited to the examination of issues pertaining to hostile environment harassment, where sexually harassive speech has been found actionable. This article illustrates how harm can be, and has been, perpetrated through speech that is sexually harassive and that the origin of certain case law used in prohibiting speech does not recognize the harm inflicted by the verbally or symbolically harassive hostile environment.

Current legal standards for limiting speech applied to slander and "fighting words" do not provide support for restricting the harassive speech of the hostile environment. When dealing with slander, the basis of harm is the loss from injury to "reputation, community standing, office, trade, business, or means of livelihood" (*Black's Law Dictionary*, 1990, p. 1244). This injury is akin to the harm of quid pro quo harassment, where tangible loss is suffered from not acquiescing to sexual demands. In hostile environment sexual harassment, however, noneconomic harm is experienced.

The fighting words standard of *Chaplinsky v. New Hampshire* (1942), which gives no protection for words which tend to incite an immediate breach of the peace, also provides difficulty in recognizing harm from sexually harassing words. This case law is reflective of a society that had evolved from one sanctioning duels as a method for resolving personal insult to viewing fisticuffs as a socially acceptable phenomenon for protesting unwelcome or demeaning words. Then, as now, it can be argued that physical violence as a method of conflict resolution was practiced mostly by men. Moreover, *Chaplinsky* recognized social acceptance of such physical violence by validating it as one natural response to insult, although it was not the most natural reply for women who felt themselves to be degraded by speech.[1] Because a "Thelma and Louise" standard of response to harassment has not entered social mores, it is unlikely that speech realistically could be abridged using this focus of *Chaplinsky.*

Case law that is de facto gender based, such as *Chaplinsky,* provides a standard for determining harm that will not be met by most of the population experiencing verbal hostile environment sexual harassment.[2] Case law of the nature also suggests that risking a charge of assault and battery is a viable method of indicating that sexual harassment is an egregious form of personal insult. Reasoning that ignores the fact that persons who wish to remain employed or in class often do not respond to verbal harassment in a physical manner is similar to reasoning that defines rape as occurring only after both arms and legs of the victim were broken during the commission of the crime.

Does the law that requires a tangible loss or imminent breach of peace in order to limit speech square with discrimination law that recognizes severe and pervasive discriminatory speech, even absent a tangible loss, as a violation of civil rights? An answer may be found in reviewing *Meritor Savings Bank v. Vinson* (1986), where the argument that harm occurs only from the tangible loss incurred by quid pro quo sexual harassment was not upheld. Instead, the Court recognized the Equal Employment Opportunities Commission's (EEOC) reliance on prior "judicial decisions and EEOC precedent holding that Title VII affords employees the right to work in an environment free from discriminatory intimidation, ridicule, and insult" (*Meritor*, p. 65). It reasoned that because this principle had been applied to harassment based on race, religion, and national origin, "a hostile environment based on discriminatory sexual harassment should not likewise be prohibited" (*Meritor*, p. 65) from being actionable. The egregiousness of the non-tangible harm of being forced to endure severe and pervasive discriminatory speech was, in effect, recognized in *Meritor.*

Research indicates that in addition to voluntarily dropping courses, changing majors, and changing graduate programs to avoid harassment, noneconomic harm from sexual harassment is reflected in negative changes in psychological and physical health and well-being.[3] Other categories of harm from a hostile environment include the time and effort costs of coping when considering or pursuing a case of hostile environment sexual harassment, negative differential social learning from the imposition of different gender standards for performance, punishment reflected in not allowing the person bringing a claim of hostile environment sexual harassment to continue in daily or planned routine, and altered or deflected educational or career goals due to coping with harassment (see Masters, Milford, & Curcio, 1993). Clearly, the harm from discriminatory speech has been well documented.

Given this review of harm, the antidote of counterspeech that is often suggested to counter offensive speech may be viewed as incomplete, ineffective, and sometimes inappropriate. Other research cites flaws in the "marketplace of ideas" metaphor concerning discriminatory speech (Strauss, 1990). This metaphor relies upon an opportunity for rational and open discussion, a chance for confrontation, and lack of retaliation that would preclude or inhibit discourse; in other words, a perfect marketplace. Because sexual harassment is an issue of power, it is hard to imagine a work or educational setting where subordinates would feel completely free to engage in confrontational dialogue with superiors who "rationally" find it acceptable to discriminate on the basis of gender.

Absent an opportunity for open and equal discussion and with concern for retaliation, to insist on counterspeech as a remedy for discriminatory speech almost guarantees that employees and students must also consider the consequences of quid pro quo discrimination if their superior chooses to view counterspeech as irrational, unprofessional, or insubordinate. This is an undue burden that superiors or other co-workers not subjected to discriminatory speech are not asked to bear.

Therefore, a narrowly tailored threshold for actionable discriminatory speech may be proposed on the basis of the effect of discriminatory speech and not the suppression of ideas. In *Harris v. Forklift Systems* (1993), the Supreme

Court has provided the framework for this threshold through its review of the intent of Title VII and clarification of actionable harm. Further support may be found in *Robinson v. Jacksonville Shipyards* (1991), where First Amendment concerns were addressed in relation to discriminatory speech.

Based on the above rulings, the following should be considered in determining whether speech is actionable sexual harassment:

1. Did the speech occur in an environment under the constraint of Title VII of the Civil Rights Act of 1964 or Title IX of the Education Amendments of 1972 (i.e., in a work or education setting?)
2. Was the speech unwelcome?
3. Was the speech pervasive or severe?
4. Does the complainant view the speech as discriminatory based on gender?
5. Would a reasonable person view the speech as discriminatory based on gender?
6. Was the complainant exposed to disadvantageous terms or conditions from the speech to which others of another gender were not exposed?
7. In reviewing all of the circumstances, does the environment appear hostile or abusive to a person or persons of one gender and not the other?
8. Does the educational institution or employer intend to express itself in the manner of the alleged discriminatory speech?
9. Is a discriminatory harm produced by the speech through disparate treatment or disparate impact based on gender?
10. Is the opportunity for the speech available in a different time, place, or manner?
11. Is the complainant a captive audience or part of a captive audience?
12. Does the speech have a discernible negative effect upon discipline, order, or morale in the environment?
13. Did the speech seem insulting or degrading based upon gender?
14. Would the speech have likely been addressed to a person of another gender?

With the exception of question 8, affirmative responses to the questions should indicate that the effect of the speech needs further examination. This framework for regulation of speech provides for the governmental interest of prohibiting discrimination by focusing on the differentiation by gender and ensuring content neutrality by focusing on the context and effect of the speech and not the suppression of the idea or its content.

A context—rather than content-based limitation differentiates between speech that discriminates and speech that promotes discrimination by focusing on effect and not message. This restriction has commonsense precedent concerning other constitutional rights. One may own a gun but may not be able to take or use it in certain settings such as a classroom. One may jokingly yell "Fire!" in the street, but not in the theater. The harm of exercising certain constitutional rights in certain contexts is not a new concept.

The difficulty in balancing compelling interests is certainly evident when considering freedom from discrimination and freedom of speech. However, the difficulty of the task does not justify its avoidance. The suggested context and effect-based approach provides a beginning that can be understood in relation to balancing other rights, affirms the right to work or become educated without the undue burden of discrimination, and recognizes the value of maintaining untrammeled avenues for expression.

NOTES

1. See the analysis of 1992 FBI Uniform Crime Reports by Steven Bennett Weisburd and Brian Levin (1994) concerning murder in the United States by sex of victim/offender where reported incidents of murder of female victim/male offender are significantly higher than incidents of male victim/female offender and female victim/female offender. The article also cited research on spousal murder indicating that men who murdered wives from whom they were separated viewed murder as a response to the "offense" of being left, obviously an extreme reaction of physical violence to behavior and speech that did not inflict physical harm and that occurs significantly less by women in the same situation.
2. See Truax (1989), Dozier (1990), and Fitzgerald (1993). Summaries of national reports indicate that 95% of sexual harassment is directed by men toward women and estimate that approximately 50% of women in work and education settings have experienced some form of sexual harassment.
3. These negative changes were found to include anxiety, depression, headaches, sleep disturbance, gastrointestinal disorders, weight loss/gain, nausea, sexual dysfunction, posttraumatic stress disorder, elevated fears of rape, and lowered self-esteem (Fitzgerald, 1993, pp. 1071–1072).

REFERENCES

Black's Law Dictionary. (1990). St. Paul, MN: West.

Chaplinsky v. New Hampshire, 315 U.S. 568, 572 (1942).

Dozier, J. (1990). Sexual harassment: It can happen here. *AGB Reports, 32,* 15–20.

Fitzgerald, L. (1993) Sexual Harassment: Violence against women in the workplace. *American Psychologist, 48,* 1070–1076.

Harris v. Forklift Systems, 106 S. Ct. 367 (1993).

Masters, A. B., Milford, A. C., & Curcio, J.L. (1993, June). *The cost of the hostile environment: An analysis of campus cases 1987–1992.* Paper presented at the annual meeting of the American Association of University Women Symposium on Gender Issues in the Classroom and on the Campus, Minneapolis, MN.

Meritor Savings Bank v. Vinson, 477 U.S. 57 (1986).

Robinson v. Jacksonville Shipyards, 760 F. Supp. 1486 (M.D. Fla. 1991).

Strauss, M. (1990). Sexist speech in the workplace. *Harvard Civil Rights-Civil Liberties Law Review, 25*(1).

Truax, A. (1989). Sexual harassment in higher education: What we've learned. *Thought and Action,* 5, 25–32.

Weisburd, B., & Levin, B. (1994) On the basis of sex: Recognizing gender-based bias crimes. *Stanford Law and Policy Review,* 5(2), 21–47.

December 1, 2006

Only Speech Codes Should Be Censored

Gary Pavela

Gary Pavela serves as director of judicial programs at the University of Maryland at College Park.

I often ask audience members at higher-education conferences how many of them come from campuses with "hate speech" codes. A substantial minority raise their hands, confirming research that about a third of the nation's colleges and universities continue to promulgate student disciplinary rules prohibiting expression that "subordinates" others or is "demeaning, offensive, or hateful."

Such continued adherence to speech codes is by now predictable, but remains puzzling. From a lawyer's perspective, the courts have spoken: Broadly written speech codes adopted by public institutions—and private institutions adhering to First Amendment standards—are unconstitutional. The legal parameters are becoming so well settled that enforcement of those codes may expose public-college administrators to personal liability for violating clearly established constitutional rights.

Understanding the speech-code phenomenon, however, requires looking beyond the law to the realities of campus politics. However sporadically enforced, speech codes serve the administrative purpose of broadcasting an easily identifiable institutional commitment to providing a safe and welcoming environment to a wide array of presumably vulnerable students. What's rarely considered, however, is the likely long-term impact on those very students whom administrators seek to protect.

We live in a disputatious society. Beyond a few narrowly defined exceptions to the First Amendment (such as "true threats," defamation, and "severe or pervasive sexual harassment"), our graduates won't be able to turn to a protective government to silence expression they don't like. How are we preparing them to participate in a contentious marketplace of ideas, other than training them to shout a reflexive "Shut up!"?

Court cases testing the limits of the First Amendment usually involve provocative expression. Provocative expression, in turn, tends to be associated with social, political, or ethnic minorities' striving to make themselves heard. Those minorities will be at greatest risk from speech-code enforcement, since majorities on college campuses and elsewhere are unlikely to censor themselves. A classic example in the higher-education setting is the 1973 U.S. Supreme Court decision in Papish v. Board of Curators of the University of Missouri. The petitioner in that case—a journalism graduate student with a prior history of circulating what the university regarded as "pornographic, indecent and obscene" literature from the Students for a Democratic Society—was expelled for selling an underground newspaper that featured a front-page cartoon depicting policemen raping the Statue of Liberty and the Goddess of Justice, and that contained an article with an expletive as a title.

The Supreme Court reversed the student's expulsion and stated that "the mere dissemination of ideas—no matter how offensive to good taste—on a state university campus may not be shut off in the name alone of 'conventions of decency.'" The court rejected the argument that the expression was "obscene" (i.e., appealed to prurient interests) and concluded that "precedents of this Court make it equally clear that neither the political cartoon nor the headline story involved in this case can be labeled as constitutionally obscene or otherwise unprotected."

There is nothing remarkable about the court's conclusion. It echoes Justice Hugo Black's classic dissenting opinion in Communist Party v. Control Board (1961) that the "freedoms of speech, press, petition and assembly guaranteed by the First Amendment must be accorded to the ideas we hate or sooner or later they will be denied to the ideas we cherish." And it can be found in more-recent decisions, like Rosenberger v. University of Virginia (1995), where the court saw student freedom of expression in a campus "marketplace of ideas" as the foundation of higher education itself:

"In ancient Athens, and, as Europe entered into a new period of intellectual awakening, in places like Bologna, Oxford, and Paris, universities began as voluntary and spontaneous assemblages or concourses for students to speak and to write and to learn. . . . For the University, by regulation, to cast disapproval on particular viewpoints of its students risks the suppression of free speech and creative inquiry in one of the vital centers for the nation's intellectual life, its college and university campuses."

What's striking, then, about the Papish case is not the majority opinion, but the dissents by Chief Justice Warren Burger and Justice William Rehnquist.

Chief Justice Burger summarized a core element of their argument when he wrote, "In theory, at least, a university is not merely an arena for the discussion of ideas by students and faculty; it is also an institution where individuals learn to express themselves in acceptable, civil terms." Burger's perspective—that student freedom of expression on college campuses could be circumscribed by pedagogical concerns both in and outside the classroom—would have provided a legal foundation for campus speech codes, had it ever attracted a majority on the court.

Yet out of many law-review articles promoting the campus speech-code movement in the 1980s, I found none that commended the Burger or Rehnquist dissents in Papish. That's a remarkable omission. Why not highlight a key dissent from the chief justice that advances your position? The only conceivable answer is that supporters of speech codes on the left were reluctant to concede that such codes were also attractive to the ideological right. In those heady, self-righteous days, no one wanted to acknowledge that giving universities broadly defined powers to censor uncivil speech might be used in ways most speech-code advocates wouldn't like.

Unfortunately, the fundamental agreement between the right and left on the need to promote campus civility was primarily a consensus about methodology. Both depended on punishment rather than education, suasion, and peer influence. The end result went beyond a series of failed speech codes at some of the nation's leading universities—all eventually struck down by the courts. It ultimately promoted a culture of silence on issues of race and constituted a lost opportunity to teach students how to confront "bad" expression with expression that was better reasoned and better expressed.

Perhaps the best post-mortem of a failed speech code involved the University of Wisconsin code, struck down by a federal court in 1991. In a 1993 Los Angeles Times Magazine article, the Pulitzer-Prize-winning writer Barry Siegel reported that Roger Howard—the associate dean of students at the Madison campus, an initial supporter of the code, and an administrator charged with its enforcement—eventually concluded that "it's better policy not to have a code. . . . The human instinct—or the American instinct—for censorship is just too strong." Howard was particularly concerned that the code promoted a "McCarthyesque venue. . . . I've heard of students saying 'Shhh—don't say anything about affirmative action, the university will punish you.' . . . I think there was a chilling effect."

Siegel's 1993 article on the demise of the UW code, however, also helps explain why speech codes continue to endure on other campuses more than a decade later: "Beyond the desired diversity of color and gender," he wrote, "surely there was also an enforced orthodoxy of thought and expression. . . . [A] mid all this talk of the code's value as symbol, it was a bit unclear just whom the symbol was meant to protect—minority students from harassment by racists or UW leadership from denunciation by minorities." Speech codes, in other words, may serve the primary purpose of diverting attention from more substantive issues of inclusion and civility, allowing administrators to focus on cosmetic approaches unlikely to produce any lasting change in campus cultures.

In 2003, following a lawsuit by a free-speech advocacy group, a federal judge issued an injunction against Shippensburg University that barred it from enforcing parts of its speech code. The university abandoned its code in 2004, even though the case's plaintiffs had not been punished for violating it. The court observed, "While we recognize that citing students under the suspect provisions has not been a common practice, in the hands of another administration these provisions could certainly be used to truncate debate and free expression by students." Indeed, one of the student plaintiffs in the case asserted that she "was reluctant to advance certain controversial theories or ideas regarding any number of political or social issues because . . . she feared that discussion of such theories might be sanctionable."

The Shippensburg case highlights that even dormant speech codes continue to depend upon explicit or implicit threats of punishment. The only beneficiaries of that approach have been a new cohort of campus conservative activists, who thrive on the excitement and attention of being portrayed as First Amendment martyrs.

College administrators simply haven't given sufficient thought to creative alternatives, even though recurring speech-code controversies have created opportunities to promote the holy grail of undergraduate education: enhanced skills in listening, reasoning, gathering and weighing evidence, considering the aims and feelings of others, and understanding core components of citizenship, like the responsibility to protect and promote constitutional freedoms.

Administrators looking for new approaches have several good examples to emulate, most arising out of an earlier era of speech-code development. The columnist Nat Hentoff described one possibility in a 1991 Washington Post article about the response of four black women at Arizona State University to a racially offensive flyer posted on a residence-hall door. Instead of seeking to invoke ASU's speech code, the women told the occupants why they objected to the flyer (which was promptly taken down). Then, with the support of ASU administrators, they helped organize a series of campus forums and discussions, as well as a residence-hall program on African-American history. Lively correspondence continued in the campus newspaper, culminating in a letter to the editor ("names withheld upon request") that read: "We would like to extend our sincerest and deepest apologies to anyone and everyone who was offended by the tasteless flyer that was displayed on our front door. . . . We did not realize the hurt that would come from this flyer. We now know that we caused great distress among many different people, and we would like again to apologize."

Similar outcomes elsewhere aren't guaranteed. Without proper leadership from college deans and presidents, intensely emotional issues can turn into shouting matches rather than thoughtful dialogue. At a minimum, however, offending students can be challenged to become First Amendment practitioners and active participants in a serious discussion, instead of First Amendment martyrs. And offended students can be encouraged and assisted in employing a broad range of strategies—holding open forums, conducting lawful demonstrations or vigils, or simply issuing invitations to public debates—that will help them acquire skills in challenging rather than censoring expression they don't like. Some schools have endorsed this approachprotecting "the right to think the unthinkable, discuss the unmentionable, and challenge the unchallengeable" in published guidelines, like the Yale University Policy on Freedom of Expression (written by the late C. Vann Woodward, one of America's most distinguished historians).

In his 1929 essay "The Aims of Education," Alfred North Whitehead wrote that: "the very intellectual revolution which has ever stirred humanity into greatness has been a passionate protest against inert ideas. Then, alas, with pathetic ignorance of human psychology, it has proceeded by some educational scheme to bind humanity afresh with inert ideas of its own fashioning." A better summary of the speech-code phenomenon would be hard to find. The ideals that gave life to the civil-rights movement arose out of an intense clash of ideologies and convictions. A whole new vocabulary of justice was created in the process. That vocabulary can't be frozen in amber. Each generation should be encouraged to develop the skills to contribute to it. Doing so requires an atmosphere of freedom—an atmosphere in which fundamental values are questioned, tested, reformulated, and revitalized, not turned into stale dogma.

The Real Impact of Virtual Worlds

By *Thomas A. Workman*

Thomas A. Workman *is an assistant professor of communications studies at the University of Houston-Downtown.*

HOW DIGITAL CULTURE SHAPES STUDENTS' MINDS

Colleges that try to set limits on students' use of the Internet often misread their motivations and the meaning of online life for them. Much of what we fear when we see kids spending hours online is filtered through our own generational lens. What looks like plagiarism, slander, copyright infringement, and embarrassing public behavior is for many students just creative and social entertainment.

Five key norms of the digital culture may explain how students think about technology and how we can help them manage it:

Digital Norm 1: Internet use as play. For the past five years, I've conducted focus groups for several research projects, resulting in conversations with more than 500 students from a wide variety of backgrounds. When I have asked how they used the Internet, their responses have usually suggested that online life is ultimately a recreational activity. YouTube's unbridled popularity among young adults, like many virtual communities, is because of its entertainment value, even in moments of political and social advocacy. A case in point: While Barack Obama and Ron Paul each worked tirelessly over weeks to build a Facebook group with one million members, Comedy Central's Stephen Colbert accomplished that in three days in his comic race for president.

As with the playground equipment in the schoolyard, however, what is intended for fun can still produce bruises and bleeding. It is the insults—along with the stalking, cyberbullying, photographs of illegal activity, and slanderous depictions of anyone who (at the moment) has lost favor with the student—that concern student-affairs professionals and campus lawyers. But being unsafe doesn't make Internet play any less exciting for students; it may actually add to the appeal. College students are particularly vulnerable to the sociological phenomenon of "edgework," where risk-taking increases the pleasure and excitement of recreational activities like cliff diving or parasailing. The notion of edgework explains why students engage in outrageous activities that become YouTube uploads and Facebook group photos, and why such posts and high-risk groups are so popular.

Indeed, thinking about virtual interaction as play helps us understand online student behavior as misdirected recreation rather than purposeful misconduct. That can enable us to develop more-effective learning opportunities and interventions. We can redirect the same creative energy that students use to post an elaborate video chronicle of a bar crawl—including violation of campus policies for pre-crawling in the alcohol-restricted residence hall or the provision of alcohol to underage friends—to an assignment where students work together online to solve a social problem.

Viewing the Internet as a playground also helps us understand the challenge of prohibition. When we attempt to limit students' Internet use, we find those who are most interested in high-risk recreation respond much the same way that they do to our alcohol-prohibition policies: with resistance, hiding, and strategic noncompliance. The result is a loss for student-affairs and other administrators who are trying to understand how students think. Although we may not like what we see, by being more open and accepting of students' online activity, we can gain valuable insights to help us design better learning environments and produce better policies and procedures.

Digital Norm 2: virtual identity as fictionalized personas. One of the more difficult concepts for those who were not raised to think digitally is the notion of virtual identity. The student leader who hosts a weekly Bible study may be a wild party animal online. The freshman wallflower, ignored in the real world, may become an international spy, corporate guru, or porn star.

Much like the suburban family that is deep in debt but still drives a Mercedes-Benz to appear affluent to the neighbors, the identities that students create in virtual worlds don't need to be accurate reflections of their daily lives. Rather, they must possess elements popular in whatever culture students seek membership. High-risk activity, sexuality, spirituality, even anti-authority rhetoric all serve the same purpose in declaring to the virtual world that "I personify these values and interests."

It is common, therefore, to see pictures, videos, and stories borrowed from other Web sites or staged for the digital camera. In studying online how students use alcohol, for example, I found that many students' profiles on Facebook and MySpace displayed photos of people with whom they had no direct relationship; the photos were simply lifted from other sites. Many of those photos appeared staged, with a lot of people simply posing in them.

Meanwhile, most students also think they can just commit "virtual suicide" and put an end to such fantasy identities with the push of the delete button. They often don't understand that, real or staged, the presence of a photo or comment will remain forever connected to them.

Given the fictional nature of many online identities, our response to inappropriate student postings may again need to be less punitive and more educational. Each posting offers an opportunity for a conversation about identity integration, an important aspect of emotional and moral development that doesn't always find its way into the college experience. At the very least, many colleges should take the opportunity to teach students the harsh realities of Internet memory, helping them realize that virtual identities may be harder to eliminate than they imagined—and can come back to haunt a student who has developmentally moved on.

Digital Norm 3: virtual socialization as a complement to live community. Ever since Internet social networks became popular, student-affairs professionals and sociologists have worried that the trend would lead to a population of students who were isolated and unable to develop healthy "offline" relationships. But as Nicole B. Ellison, Charles Steinfield, and Cliff Lampe, communications scholars at Michigan State University, noted in a 2007 study on students' use of Facebook and other online social-networking sites, "Online interactions do not necessarily remove people from their offline world but may indeed be used to support relationships and keep people in contact, even when life changes move them away from each other."

Howard Rheingold has argued in The Virtual Community: Homesteading on the Electronic Frontier (HarperPerennial, 1994) that virtual communities may actually be part of the remedy for the loss of live community. He contends that American community dissipated long before the Internet took hold, leading to a sense of isolation and a longing for connection across all generations—a thesis that Robert D. Putman supports in Bowling Alone (Simon and Schuster, 2000).

Institutions of higher education should begin thinking creatively about ways to use virtual community as an access point for students to have more live social interactions with one another, faculty members, and administrators. Abundant examples already exist: Facebook groups support live rallies and publicize local meetings, and YouTube videos of live events whet the appetite of students for more. Colleges should develop more-creative ways to build relationships with students by connecting Internet activities to well-designed, live social interactions. The University of Nebraska at Lincoln, for example, has used student Facebook groups—posted by student employees—to build interest and momentum for service-learning and other student events, making them feel less institutional.

Digital Norm 4: the global town square. A 2007 study on youth civic engagement by Kent E. Portney and Lisa O'Leary of Tufts University found that the majority of college students belong to at least four online political- or social-advocacy groups. With a global audience in place, millennials are moving from simple hijinks to what Neil Howe and the late William Strauss, authors of Millennials and the Pop Culture (Lifecourse Associates, 2006), have always contended they were capable of: postmodern civic engagement. College administrators are justifiably concerned about copyright infringement and other legal issues, especially given students' ability to simply copy documents about public issues and put them online. But rather than attempt to shut down student efforts, it would make more sense to harness that digital energy, protecting students from legal vulnerability by educating them about copyright law.

Digital Norm 5: online community as a response to barriers to live interactions. Particularly at large institutions, new students can become lost in a sea of faces, unable to build a sense of community despite the structure that surrounds them in residence halls or fraternities. Many institutions have worked hard to rectify that problem by instituting residential-learning communities and first-year-experience programs.

Yet, the heart of community involvement may not be structure, but personal satisfaction. In Communities in Cyberspace (Routledge, 1999), Marc A. Smith and Peter Kollock contend that virtual community provides three essential motivations for participation that may help us understand what's missing on our "offline" campuses:

Anticipated reciprocity: Instant messaging, cell texting, even YouTube uploads result in immediate gratification—a response. Someone will write back. A posting will be followed by comments. Many students feel entitled to some reciprocation and are unhappy when a professor or administrator speaks but won't listen, or demands high-quality work but won't give feedback. If live community is to compete with the virtual one, we'll need to take a lesson from the technology and create reciprocity in our offline interactions with this generation.

Increased recognition: Many millennials were raised to believe they are special, and providing them with the recognition that they crave has become complicated and problematic. Coeds flock to high-risk parties with the hope of being captured on "Girls Gone Wild," and young men seek notorious reputations as a way of not getting lost in the crowd. Even a judicial penalty for offensive or illegal uploads may lead to social recognition. But while colleges shouldn't condone that way to gain recognition, many have done little to replace it. Institutions should develop ways in which students can form healthy social identities in their offline lives.

Sense of efficacy: The Internet's greatest impact has been its ability to provide a voice for the many people who have no formal opportunity to speak in the real world. For students, the need for that empowerment is greater than many of us recognize. Virtual community provides an audience and a host of causes that make a significant difference, if only in the lives of their peers.

Students' virtual response to the Virginia Tech tragedy proves the point. Thus, colleges must find ways to help students meet their needs for self-efficacy offline as well as on.

There is no doubt that as technology continues to change, the generation of students will change alongside it. Our best preparation, then, is to train our own minds to think digitally, just like the students', so that we can best create policies, programs, and interactions that enable a student to connect the two worlds in ways that are productive, satisfying, and meaningful.

Generation Text:
The dark digital ages: 13 to 17

New Media – Mark Bauerlein

MARK BAUERLEIN is a professor of English at Emory University and author of The Dumbest Generation: How the Digital Age Stupefies Young Americans and Jeopardizes Our Future *(Tarcher/Penguin).*

Children between the ages of 13 and 17 who have a mobile phone average 1,742 text messages each month, according to a report by the Nielsen Company in September 2008. That comes to nearly 60 per day. They also make 231 voice calls each month, close to eight per day. They play games on the device as well, and browse the Web, take pictures and log hours of social networking.

No wonder so many of them consider the cellphone (for some it is a BlackBerry or an iPhone) an essential part of their lives. Half of all young people between the ages of 8 and 12 own one such device, according to a Harris Interactive poll conducted in July 2008. The rate rises to around four out of five for teenagers; that's a 36 percent increase over the previous three years, which means that these tools have swept into young people's lives with the dispatch and coerciveness of a youth fad (like Pokemon and Harry Potter). The devices are more than just consumer goods. They are signs and instruments of status.

The age-old force of peer pressure bears down hard. Indeed, 45 percent of the teens that sport one agree that "Having a cellphone is the key to my social life"—not just helpful or useful, but "the key." If you don't own a cellphone, if you can't text, game, network and chat, then you are out of the loop. It is like not being picked to play kickball back in the primitive days of neighborhood

317

sandlot gatherings. If a 16-year-old runs up 3,000 text messages in one month (and does not have a flat payment plan), mom and dad take the phone away. It's just a silly, expensive toy, they think. But the 16-year-old thinks, "You have destroyed my life!" And for them, this seems true. Digital tools are the primary means of social contact. When they lose them, kids feel excluded and unpopular, and nothing hits a 16-year-old harder than the disregard of other 16-year-olds. They do not care what 40-year-olds think, and they do not worry about what happened at Thermopylae or what Pope John Paul II said about the "splendor of truth." They care about what other students in biology class think, what happened last week at the party and what so-and-so said about them.

It is an impulse long preceding the advent of the microchip, but digital devices have empowered that impulse as never before. Think about the life stage of adolescence. Teenagers stand at a precarious threshold, no longer children and not yet adults, eager to be independent but lacking the equipment and composure. They have begun to leave the home and shed the influence of parents, but they don't know where they are headed, and most of them find meager materials beyond the home out of which to build their characters. So they look to one another, emulating dress and speech, forming groups of insiders and outsiders, finding comfort in boyfriends and girlfriends, and deflecting more or less tenuously the ever-present risk of embarrassment.

Everyone passes through this phase, but this generation's experience marks a crucial change in the process. In the past, social life proceeded intermittently, all day at school and for a few hours after school. Kids hung out for an afternoon over the weekend and enjoyed a movie or party on Friday or Saturday night. Other than that, social life pretty much ended. They went home for dinner and entered a private space with only a "landline" as a means of contact (which appears to young people today a restricted connection—show them a rotary phone and watch them scowl). Teenage social life and peer-to-peer contact had a limit.

Teenagers did not like it. I certainly didn't want to listen to my parents when I turned 16. But the limit was healthy and effectual. Adolescents needed then and need now a reprieve from the tribal customs and peer fixations of middle school and high school. Wounds from lunchroom gossip and bullying, as well as the blandishments of popularity and various niche-crowd memberships, disable the maturing process. These form a horizon of adolescent triumphs and set the knowledge of history, civics, religion, fine art and foreign affairs beyond the pale of useful and relevant acquisitions. If a sophomore sat down on a bus with the gang and said, "Hey, did you see the editorial on school funding in The Times this morning?" the rest would scrunch up their faces as if an alien being sat among them.

A Digital Defense

Not since 1972, when Richard Nixon ran against George McGovern, have so many 18- to 30-year-old Americans voted in a presidential election as they did last November. Young adults did more than vote in November 2008. Many of them campaigned for Barack Obama, harnessing the power of the Internet to cultivate new online communities and to disseminate the message of change that he espoused and many of the young embraced. Just before delivering his acceptance speech in Chicago's Grant Park, president-elect Obama sent bulk e-mail to his young-adult supporters, a fitting communiqué for this technologically advanced generation. "We just made history," he wrote, not just for helping to elect the first African-American president, but also for capturing the hearts and minds of young adults and mobilizing them for a larger cause.

Eboo Patel, director of the Interfaith Youth Corps and author of *Acts of Faith: The Story of an American Muslim, the Struggle for the Soul of a Generation,* is another person who believes in the potential of young adults and uses new media to reach them. Patel's organization brings together young people from many different faith traditions to do charitable work, build relationships and inspire peaceful dialogue among organized religions. But such programs can work only if the younger generation is open-minded. Modern information technologies help young people learn about the diversity of faith traditions and move away from the natural suspicion of the "other." The I.F.Y.C. Web site, for example, hosts an online community called Bridge Builders, a forum where young adult interfaith leaders can connect and share stories of success.

Technology does not make people smarter, but it can help them to connect and rally around a cause in which they believe. We who are age 35 and older cannot simply blame younger generations if they are not interested in the things we deem important. We need to share the blame for not giving them more of what Barack Obama and Eboo Patel have managed to offer them: a cause that transcends their individual needs and that is worth working, even suffering, for. Yes, video games, YouTube and Wikipedia can provide anesthetic brain candy, distractions and easy answers; but if used for a larger cause, technologies like these become tools that can encourage intellectual growth as well as personal, social and ethical development.

DAVID E. NANTAIS, *director of the Leadership Development Institute at the University of Detroit Mercy, has written for America about young adults.*

Youthful mores screen out such things, which is all the more reason for parents to offer an alternative. A home and leisure life separate from teen stuff exposes youths to heroes and villains that surpass the idols of the senior class, to places beyond the food court and Apple Store, to times well before the glorious day they got their driver's license. It acquaints them with adult duties, distant facts and values and truths they will not fully comprehend until much later. They don't like them and rarely find them meaningful, but in pre-digital times teens had nowhere else to go after they entered the front door. They had to sit at the dining table and listen to parents talk about grocery shopping, vacation plans, Nixon, gas prices and the news.

No longer. In 1980, when an angry parent commanded, "Go to your room—you're grounded!" the next few hours meant isolation for the teen. Today, the bedroom is not a private space. It's a social hub. For many kids, the bedroom at midnight provides a rich social life that makes daytime face-to-face conversations seem tame and slow. Amid the pillows with laptop or BlackBerry, they chat with buddies in 11th grade and in another state. Photos fly back and forth while classmates sleep, revelations spill forth in tweets ("OMG, Billy just called Betty his ——"), and Facebook pages gain flashier graphics.

In this dynamic 24/7 network, teen activity accrues more and more significance. The events of the day carry greater weight as they are recorded and circulated. The temptation for teens to be self-absorbed and self-project, to consider the details of their lives eminently memorable and share-able, grows and grows. As they give in online, teenagers' peer consciousness expands while their historical understanding, civic awareness and taste go dormant before they have even had much chance to develop.

This is the hallmark of what I have called the Dumbest Generation. These kids have just as much intelligence and ambition as any previous cohort, but they exercise them too much on one another. They are building youth culture into a ubiquitous universe, and as ever, youth culture is a drag on maturity. This time it has a whole new arsenal.

Viewpoint: Online Social Networks and Learning

Christine Greenhow

Christine Greenhow is an Assistant Professor of Learning Sciences and Technology in
the College of Education and the College of Information Studies (joint appointment) at the
University of Maryland, College Park, Maryland, USA. She studies literacies broadly within
online social network sites and the design of social networking applications for educational
purposes. Christine Greenhow can be contacted at: greenhow@umd.edu

ABSTRACT

Purpose—*This viewpoint essay seeks to argue that young people's online social
networking can serve as sites for and supports for student's learning in ways not
currently assessed.*

Design/methodology/approach—*The two themes presented are based on
a select review of the research literature as well as the author's explorations of
young people's online social networking practices within MySpace and Facebook,
two naturally occurring, youth-initiated sites, as well as in an online social
networking application designed for environmental science education and civic
action.*

Findings—*Two themes are presented: (1) social network sites can serve as direct
and indirect supports for learning, such as providing an emotional outlet for
school-related stress, validation of creative work, peer-alumni support for
school-life transitions, and help with school-related tasks: and (2) online social
networking can stimulate social and civic benefits, online and offline, which has
implications for education.*

Practical Implications—*Currently, social media are largely blocked in schools due to privacy, security, and copyright concerns. In the USA, the National Educational Technology Plan published in November 2010, and recent educational standards, both assume 24/7 access and use of newer web technologies for learning and advocate appropriation of technologies students already use, and prefer to use, for educational purposes. Consideration of how social media, such as social network sites, currently support informal learning may advance one's ability to construct effective social media-enabled environments for more formal learning purposes.*

Originality/value—*This paper presents concrete examples of how social network sites, typically seen as a distraction, might be re-envisioned as supports for revised student learning outcomes.*

Keywords *Learning, Social networking sites, Literacy, Social interaction*

Paper type *Viewpoint*

CHANGING EDUCATIONAL CONTEXTS

In the last decade, internet access, the nature of the web and contexts for learning have evolved, along with the emergence of desired competencies for learners, instructors, and administrators, and these changes impact constructs for learning, teaching, and paths for future research (Greenhow *et al.*, 2009a, b); young people now have more choices over what, how, and with whom they learn in a wide range of settings: classrooms, after school programs, home-school, formal online learning programs, and web-enabled spaces that dominate popular culture. Some of the most critical problems facing education today, as generally agreed upon by administrators, policy-makers, and researchers, are increasing young people's educational attainment, science and math learning, technological fluencies, communication skills, civic engagement and preparation for the twenty-first century workplace (Black and Lynch, 2003; Bureau of Labor Statistics, 2007; Collins and Halverson, 2009; Dohm and Shniper, 2007; National Center for Education Statistics, 2005; National Research Council, 2000; Putnam, 2000; Warschauer and Matuchniak, 2010).

ONLINE SOCIAL NETWORKING: CRISES OR COGNITIVE SURPLUS?

In this same context, adult educational discourses view with apprehension the internet-using practices and preferences of today's young people (Thurlow, 2006). Recent surveys report that use of social network sites, for instance, is the dominant out-of-school, leisure-time computer using activity among US adolescents of various ages, ethnicities, and income levels (Rideout *et al.*, 2010). A form of social media (Barnes, 2006), social network sites (SNS) are web-enabled services that "allow individuals to (1) construct a public or semi-public *profile* within a bounded system, (2) articulate a list of other *users* with whom they share a connection, and (3) view and traverse their *list of* connections and those made by others within the system" (Boyd and Ellison, 2007, p. 1). They feature prominent personal profiling, highlighting the connections between people and content (Cormode and Krishnamurthy, 2008), and allow people to visualize, interact with, and activate existing personal and professional networks, and to create connections with new ones unbounded by geographic distance. Yet, popular media accounts largely characterize young people's practices with social media like Facebook as deficient or harmful to academic achievement (Hamilton, 2009; Karpinski, 2009) as leading to declining standards of literacy (Bauerlein, 2009; Carr, 2008; Thurlow, 2006), and as a "threat to societal values" (Herring, 2007, p. 4).

On the other hand, outside education, a growing number of scholars and social commentators argue we are witnessing a *cognitive surplus* (Gladwell, 2005; Shirky, 2010) spurred by these very same forms of digital media and their attendant social practices—i.e. people volunteering their time, interest, and ingenuity online to participate in news, politics, business, fashion, government, etc.—and that this cognitive surplus can have societal benefits and can change our very notions of "knowledge" and the means of knowledge production (e.g. Wikipedia) (Giles, 2005).

For instance, observe the upstart teen bloggers, on the scene, in the campaign tent, or at the run-way show, pushing their reviews and images to the public while newspaper and magazine editors are still jockeying to feature those subjects in issues that will be published days or months later (Wilson, 2009). In the news industry, viewer participation in the form of online comments, independently produced videos, blog entries, and media-sharing options are being harnessed to enhance the accuracy, power and spread of centrally produced stories (e.g. CNN's documentary *Black in America*) (Nelson, 2008). In politics, potential voters don't just consume campaign propaganda, but help to shape and distribute it via blogs, home-grown videos, tweets and social network sites (Sheehy, 2008). Despite the economic downturn, businesses seeking to tap their employees "social connections, institutional memories and special skills—knowledge that large, geographically dispersed companies often have a difficult time obtaining" are investing in social networking software to connect the company's employees into a single web forum (Stone, 2007, p. C2). In fashion, once locked-down runway shows are now streamed live over the internet with some companies providing viewers with the option to signal their likes or dislikes via Facebook and immediately purchase items online, potentially disrupting traditional production cycles, magazine editors' influence, and industry definitions of fashion itself (Heyman, 2010). This Fall, within the US government, when the Department of Education (DOE) wanted "to identify and solve U.S. education's most pressing classroom problems" it turned to public educators as "creators of both educational processes and products, and as agents who must organize, manage, and assume risks in solving problems," as stated on its Challenge to Innovate website (see http://challenge.gov/ED/60-challenge-to-innovate-c2i). Using a social media space it accepted hundreds of problem submissions, and then invited public educators to review, vote for, and comment on the problems posted. Some of the problems identified were how can educators:

- Better incorporate students' voices in decision making?
- Facilitate parental involvement?
- Help students develop the literacy skills to succeed?

From the public's rankings of these problems, the US DOE will choose a select few to feature as it again turns to public educators to contribute their solutions.

Publishing in the *Stanford Social Innovation Review,* Scearce *et al,* (2010), in studying trends among non-profits, foundations and socially responsible businesses, argue that this facilitation of human relationships and connections via social media has the potential to garner significant organizational advantages, including:

- weaving community;
- encouraging greater openness and transparency;
- accelerating information-sharing;
- accessing more diverse perspectives;
- mobilizing people;
- stimulating collaborative knowledge-building; and ultimately
- reducing the cost of participation and coordination of resources and actions.

Disadvantages to facilitating relational practices via social media are that "half baked" ideas are made public, and those trying to manage work flows and processes must tackle concerns about brand and message control, privacy concerns, dealing with information overload, learning the range of technology options, and leveraging the right social media for one's purposes (Scearce *et al.*, 2010).

Two Themes: Social Network Sites and Learning

How should we think about these broader trends in relation to thinking about learning, teaching, and the incorporation of social media into education? To advance this conversation, I now synthesize what the educational research currently says about learning and social network sites, the aforementioned dominant form of social media used by US young people. My goal is to inform educational leaders, apprehensive or cautiously optimistic about young people's media-using practices, who are asking:

1. What are youth's purposes and practices with social network sites, and are they doing anything of educational value?
2. How might these understandings help us to design for wider civic participation, increasingly sophisticated interactions and accomplishments, and deal with potential dangers?
3. How can existing social networking technologies and attendant practices be appropriated and/or re-envisioned and re-worked to produce improvements in areas of educational priority such as educational attainment, the development of science, math and technology literacies, communication and twenty-first century skills, and preparation for future work lives?

Below I share two insights related to those questions, generated from a review of the educational literature (Greenhow *et al.*, 2009a), from explorations of young people's (ages 16–24) use of the social network sites MySpace and Facebook *in situ* (Greenhow and Robelia, 2009a, b; Greenhow and Burton, n.d.; Greenhow *et al.*, 2009), and an ongoing investigation of older adolescents' use of an open source social networking application, implemented within Facebook, and designed for informal science learning and civic action (Greenhow, n.d., 2010). Moreover, I suggest how each theme might inform the design of technology-mediated spaces for learning and questions we might ask in studying such spaces that would move us closer to understanding these questions above. The studies on which these insights are based included multiple sources of data gathered over the course of 2.5 years: surveys with high school students (n = 600) and college students (n = 346); content analysis of their MySpace and Facebook accounts; think-aloud protocols as students used their social network site; and focus groups and interviews with purposeful samples of high, medium, and low users.

SOCIAL NETWORK SITES CAN SERVE AS SUPPORTS FOR AND SITES OF LEARNING

Young people use social network sites for a wide-range of purposes; they piggyback on existing online socializing routines to co-opt SNSs as social learning resources in direct and indirect support of education-related tasks and values.

For example, the students we studied from low-income, urban families in the upper Midwestern part of the USA perceived their MySpace as providing social support, relational maintenance, and an outlet for self-expression and self-presentation (Greenhow and Robelia, 2009a, b). Social support has long been identified as an ecological construct that influences individual wellbeing (Schwarzer and Knoll, 2007) often as a buffer to stress, as moderator of stress's effects, or as direct emotional, psychological, cognitive or practical aid. Students believed their support networks were actually stronger after prolonged MySpace membership, citing various channels for communication and frequent personal profile updating as helping them feel closer to, and maintain an awareness of, their close and extended friends; they felt regular online social networking encouraged openness, sharing, and getting to know more "sides" of a person. The majority of students profiled demonstrated between 50 and 150 MySpace "friends" and possessed a nuanced understanding of "friend" that included both intimate friends and family as well as acquaintances, or new people they had just met.

Moreover, students used their online social network to fulfill social learning functions within and across informal and formal learning spheres of activity. The social learning functions included:

- obtaining validation and appreciation of creative work through feedback on their profile pages;
- peer/alumni support—that is, reaching out to former classmates to give or receive help in managing the ups and downs of high school or college life; and
- help with school-related tasks (Greenhow and Robelia, 2009a).

The latter took several forms: "chatting" online through MySpace to mitigate school-related stress, asking questions about instructions or deadlines, planning study groups, requesting educational resources from the network (e.g. "if they know a site that would help me with my project, they'll post it up and I can go see it"), gathering project materials, brainstorming ideas, sharing written work, and exchanging feedback. Interestingly, participants envisioned using a social network site as part of their college transition strategy and felt their regular use of their social network site was developing their creativity, communication skills, technology skills, and openness to divergent viewpoints (Greenhow and Robelia, 2009b). Additional focused research is needed to determine the accuracy of these perceptions across various groups of students.

Of course, it is not particularly surprising that young people would adapt the spaces they frequent for their educational-related purposes, as school-related activities and concerns dominate much of adolescent life. What is surprising is the presence of these behaviors and beliefs even among he majority of our low income high school students, a group understudied in the educational technology literature and presumably experiencing more barriers to (but potentially more to gain from) participating in social network sites where such social media are typically blocked in schools and public libraries (Greenhow *et al.*, 2009). Furthermore, where such informal sharing, peer validation and feedback, alumni support, and spontaneous help with school-related tasks has typically occurred offline, pre-dating the internet, these social processes, moved online into social network sites, can now be archived and tracked with social graphing software. In theory, we should be able to begin to identify what learning resources exactly are moving through the network, to and from whom, and with what impacts over time (e.g. How is learning contagious?) (Christakis and Fowler, 2009). If educational curricula have typically been consumed with learning *what* (learning science, math, social studies content) and with learning as *becoming* (learning to become a scientist or historian by applying the tools and practices of the discipline), we can now also focus deeper attention to understanding social learning: how people learn *with whom,* or learn to be contributors to local and global society with what degree of influence (Brown, 2008; Brown and Duguid, 2002). Moreover, educational designers might think about how some of the socio-technical features most utilized in naturally occurring, youth-initiated social network sites, like MySpace (e.g. multimedia identity-posting capabilities, frequent updating and sharing of microcontent, social search, linking users with content contributions, annotation, ranking, recommendation systems) could be incorporated into the personalized learning systems touted in the new US National Education Technology Plan (United States Department of Education, 2010).

ONLINE SOCIAL NETWORKING CAN STIMULATE SOCIAL AND CIVIC BENEFITS, ONLINE AND OFFLINE, WHICH CAN HAVE IMPLICATIONS FOR EDUCATION

For instance, "social capital" refers to resources or benefits available to people through their social interactions (Lin, 1999) and is valuable to feelings of trust, reciprocity and social cohesion (Putnam, 2000); it emphasizes the importance of developing a network, in that it comprises:

- resources embedded in the social structure;
- accessibility to such resources; and
- mobilization of such resources by individuals in purposeful actions (Lin, 1999, p. 35).

Thus, investment in social networks may benefit individuals through greater access to and use of information, influence, social credentials, and reinforcement of identity and recognition (Lin, 1999, p. 31). Research in education and human development has typically focused on two broad types of social capital among youth and families (rather than among peer networks):

1. *bridging capital,* derived from weak ties that afford us diverse perspectives and new information; and
2. *bonding capital,* derived from strong ties that come from close friends and family and afford us that shoulder to cry on (Putnam, 2000).

Most importantly, the presence of social capital in one's social networks has been linked to a number of educational outcomes, including educational achievement, educational attainment, and other academic and psychosocial outcomes (Dika and Singh, 2002). In other words, learners tend to do better and persist in educational settings when they feel a strong sense of social belonging and connectedness.

Interestingly, in studying predominantly white, middle-class, college students' use of Facebook ($n = 286$), Ellison *et al.* (2007) found that intensive use of Facebook was associated with higher levels of bridging capital, and to a lesser extent, bonding capital and maintained social capital, a concept the researchers developed to describe the ability to "mobilize resources from a previously inhabited network, such as ones high school" (Ellison *et al.,* 2007, p.; 25). They suggested that networking through these sites may help to crystallize relationships that might otherwise remain ephemeral, encouraging users to strengthen latent ties and maintain connections with former friends, thus allowing people to stay connected as they move from one offline community to another. They also found that college students with lower self-esteem gained more from their use of Facebook in terms of bridging social capital than the higher self-esteem respondents (Steinfield *et al.,* 2008). They concluded that Facebook affordances may help reduce barriers some college students experience in forming the kinds of large, diverse networks that are sources of bridging capital.

Replicating this study with high school students from low income families ($n = 607$), a group most at risk for lower levels of educational attainment, achievement, and dropping out, we have found positive associations between these students' use of the social network site, MySpace, and both bonding and bridging social capital. Moreover, qualitative data help to illuminate our survey findings and pinpoint the opportunities or barriers for forging and sustaining relationships through online social network sites. Interestingly, students we interviewed positively identified MySpace and Facebook as part of their learning and college transition strategy (Greenhow and Burton, n.d.; Greenhow and Robelia, 2009a, b). Although this particular exploration occurred only over the course of a spring semester, more longitudinal analysis and racking of learners as they move through high school and into college settings while continuing participation in their online social networks, may help us better understand these phenomena as supports for learning processes and educational outcomes we value.

Moreover, in our research on young people's use of an social networking application called "Hot Dish"—implemented within Facebook, the world's largest social network site—we found that through the design of the application we were able to tie users' online social activities to offline civic behavior (Greenhow, 2010; Greenhow, n.d.). For instance, Hot Dish is an open-source social networking application that facilitates information-sharing about environmental science issues, commentary and debate, and the completion of challenges designed to engage users in pro-environmental behavior around climate change. Located as a tab within one's existing Facebook profile, key features included the ability to post original story entries; share articles from online sources; browse or read articles deeply; curate, rank and comment on posted entries; craft a personal profile; showcase users' statistics and contributions; and participate in Action Team challenges, or activities both online and offline (e.g. writing a letter to the editor, signing an online petition, volunteering for an environmental organization, recycling, starting a local recycling program, engaging in green consumerism) which were showcased within the Hot Dish environment after members documented their completion of them. Similar to gaming environments, users earned points for completing offline challenges and these accumulating point totals were featured prominently in the online environment so that individuals got recognized for changes in offline behavior (environmental activism) and, as role models, stimulated others in the online environment to make changes. Could similar data-tracking and representational features be built into future educational context to foster preferred learning (and teaching) behaviors, role modeling, civic engagement and spread of practices we value not just in education but as members of a participatory democracy? This is just one interesting avenue for future research.

To further our understanding of the social and civic benefits briefly mentioned above, the field of education and information studies needs an accumulation of research and evaluation concerned with students' personal social networks and the interrelationships between online and offline, which have hitherto be under-explored in the social capital in education literature in its focus on parent-child, parent-teacher, or teacher-child face-to-face networks (Dika and Singh, 2002). Similar to studies of parents' personal social networks (Cochran and Walker, 2005) in family social science, we require additional research into learners' network formation and factors that influence social network membership across the learning ecology young people currently inhabit, not merely within the formal classroom. We also require further understanding of network engagement and the importance of personal initiatives (e.g. a student's personality, interest, a life event, developmental phase) that can operate independently on the degree to which students have helpful, collaborative, and satisfying network relationships (high engagement) (Walker and Greenhow, 2010). Finally, we need to better understand the social processes of network influence and the specific benefits available to learners or accruing in online social networks. For instance, how do offers of practical, just-in-time assistance, information, emotional or psychological aid, modeling, coaching, etc. influence learning over time?

Although popular media accounts have portrayed the internet—and its youth-initiated spaces such as social network sites—as distractions at best, and harmful at worst, these exploratory studies suggest alternative views; students' practices within these spaces, although not without potential negative consequences, may also have positive implications for learning, educational attainment, and youth development, helping young people develop social supports for school, caring and capital-enhancing social connections, and meaningful participation in civic life.

REFERENCES

Barnes, S.B. (2006), "A privacy paradox: social networking in the United States", *First Monday,* Vol. 11 No. 9, available at: http://firstmonday. org/issues/issue11_9/barnes (accessed November 5, 2010).

Bauerlein, M. (2009). *The Dumbest Generation: How the Digital Age Stupefies Young Americans and Jeopardizes Our Future (Or, Don't Trust Anyone under 30)*, Vol. 30, Tarcher, New York, NY.

Black, S.E. and Lynch, L.M. (2003), "What's driving the new economy? The benefits of workplace innovation", Center for Economic Studies, US Census Bureau, Washington, DC.

Boyd, D.M. and Ellison, N.B. (2007), "Social network sites: definition, history, and scholarship", *Journal of Computer-Mediated Communication*, Vol. 13 No. 1, available at: http://jcmc.indiana.edu/vol13/issue1/boyd.ellsion. html (accessed October 9, 2008).

Brown, J.S. (2008), "How to connect technology and content in the service of learning", *Chronicle of Higher Education*, Vol. 55 No. 8, available at: http://chronicle.com/free/v55/i08/08a12001.htm (accessed January 29, 2009).

Brown, J.S. and Duguid, P. (2002), *The Social Life of Information*, Harvard Business School Press, Cambridge, MA.

Bureau of Labor Statistics (2007), "The 30 fastest growing occupations covered in the 2008–2009 *Occupational Outlook Handbook*", available at www.bls.gov/news.release/ooh.t01.htm (accessed October 9, 2010).

Carr, N. (2008), "Is Google making us stupid? What the internet is doing to our brains", *The Atlantic Monthly*, July/August, available at: www.theatlantic.com/magazine/archive/2008/07/is-google-making-us-stupid/6868/ (accessed November 15, 2010).

Christakis, N. and Fowler, J. (2009), *Connected: The Surprising Power of Our Social Networks and How They Shape Our Lives*, Little, Brown & Co., New York, NY.

Cochran, M. and Walker, S. (2005), "Parenting and personal social networks", in Luster, T. and Ogakaki, L. (Eds), *Parenting: An Ecological Approach*, Lawrence Erlbaum Associates, Mahwah, NJ.

Collins, A. and Halverson, B. (2009), *Rethinking Education in the Age of Technology*, Teachers College Press, New York, NY.

Cormode, G. and Krishnamurthy, B. (2008), "Key differences between Web 1.0 and Web 2.0", *First Monday*, Vol. 13 No. 6, available at: www.uic.edu/htbin/cgiwrap/bin/ojs/index.php/fm/article/view/2125/1972 (accessed October 5, 2008).

Dika, S.L. and Singh, K. (2002). "Applications of social capital in educational literature: a critical synthesis", *Review of Educational Research*, Vol. 72 No. 1, pp. 31–60.

Dohm, A. and Shniper, L. (2007), "Occupational employment predictions to 2016", *Monthly Labor Review*, Vol. 86, US Bureau of Labor Statistics, Washington DC, available at www.bls.gov/opub/mlr/2007/11/art5full.pdf (accessed September 10, 2010).

Ellison, N.B., Steinfield, C. and Lampe, C. (2007), "The benefits of Facebook 'friends': social capital and college students' use of online social network sites", *Journal of Computer-mediated Communication,* Vol. 12 No. 4, available at: http://jcmc.indiana.edu/vol12/issue4/ellison.html

Giles, J. (2005). "Internet encyclopedias go head to head", *Nature,* Vol. 438 No. 7070, pp. 900–1.

Gladwell, M. (2005), "Brain candy: is pop culture dumbing us down or smartening us up?", *The New Yorker,* May 16, available at: www.newyorker. com/archive/2005/05/16/050516crbo_books (accessed October 10, 2010).

Greenhow, C. (n.d.), "The role of youth as cultural producers in a niche social network site", *New Directions in Youth Development: Theory, Research & Practice* (forthcoming).

Greenhow, C. (2010), "Literacies in a niche online social networking application", paper presented at the American Educational Research Association Annual Meeting, New Orleans, LA, April 8–11.

Greenhow, C. and Burton, L. (n.d.), "Help from my 'friends': social capital in the social network sites of low-income high school students", *Journal of Educational Computing Research* (forthcoming).

Greenhow, C. and Robelia, E. (2009a), "Old communication, new literacies: social network sites as social learning resources", *Journal of Computer-mediated Communication,* Vol. 14, pp. 1130–61.

Greenhow, C. and Robelia, E. (2009b), "Informal learning and identity formation in online social networks", *Learning, Media and Technology,* Vol. 34 No. 2, pp. 119–40.

Greenhow, C., Robelia, E. and Hughes, J. (2009a). "Web 2.0 and classroom research: what path should we take now?", *Educational Researcher,* Vol. 38 No. 4, pp. 246–59.

Greenhow, C., Robelia, E. and Hughes, J. (2009b). "Research on learning and teaching with Web 2.0: bridging conversations", *Educational Researcher,* Vol. 38 No. 4, pp. 280–3.

Greenhow, C., Walker, J.D. and Kim, S. (2009). "Millennial learners and net-savvy teens: examining internet use among low-income students", *Journal of Computing in Teacher Education,* Vol. 26 No. 2, pp. 63–9.

Hamilton, A. (2009), "What Facebook users share: lower grades", *Time Magazine,* April 14, available at: www.time.com/time/business/article/0,8599,1891111,00.html (accessed November 10, 2010).

Herring, S.C. (2007). "Questioning the generational divide: technological exoticism and adult construction of online youth identity", in Buckingham, D. (Ed.), *Youth, Identity, and Digital Media,* MIT Press, Cambridge, MA, pp. 71–94, available at: http://ella.slis.indiana.edu/~herring/macarthur.pdf (accessed January 30, 2009).

Heyman, S. (2010), "Technology gives everyone a great seat at shows", *The New York Times,* September 8, available at: http://tinyurl.com/2e2rcuc (accessed August 10, 2010).

Karpinski, A.C. (2009), "A description of Facebook use and academic performance among undergraduate and graduate students", paper presented at the Annual Meeting of the American Educational Research Association (AERA), San Diego, CA, May 5–10.

Lin, N. (1999), "Building a network theory of social capital", *Connections,* Vol. 22 No. 1, pp. 28–51.

National Center for Education Statistics (2005), *The Condition of Education in Brief,* NCES 2005095, National Center for Education Statistics, Washington, DC.

National Research Council (2000), *Inquiry and the National Science Education Standard,* National Academy, Washington, DC.

Nelson, M. (Executive Producer) (2008), "CNN presents: Black in America", television broadcast, July 23, Turner Broadcasting Service, New York, NY, available at: www.cnn.com/SPECIALS/2008/black.in.america/ (accessed March 23, 2010).

Putnam, R. (2000), *Bowling Alone: The Collapse and Revival of the American Community,* Simon & Schuster, New York, NY.

Rideout, V.J., Foehr, U.G. and Roberts, D.F. (2010), "Generation M2: media in the lives of 8- to 18-year-olds", Report No. 8010, January 20, Kaiser Family Foundation, Menlo Park, CA.

Scearce, D., Kasper, G. and Grant, H.M. (2010), "Working wikily", *Stanford Social Innovation Review,* available at: www.sdsireview.org/articles/entry/working_wikily/ (accessed September 9, 2010).

Schwarzer, R. and Knoll, N. (2007), "Functional roles of social support within the stress and coping process: a theoretical and empirical overview", *International Journal of Psychology,* Vol. 42 No. 4, pp. 243–52.

Sheehy, G. (2008), "Campaign Hillary: behind closed doors", *Vanity Fair,* August, pp. 79–86.

Shirky, C. (2010), *Cognitive Surplus: Creativity and Generosity in a Connected Age,* Penguin Press, New York, NY.

Steinfield, C., Ellison, N. and Lampe, C. (2008), "Social capital, self esteem, and use of online social network sites: a longitudinal analysis", *Journal of Applied Developmental Psychology,* Vol. 29, pp. 434–45.

Stone, B. (2007), "Social networking's next phase", *New York Times,* March 3, pp. C1–C2.

Thurlow, C. (2006), "From statistical panic to moral panic: the metadiscursive construction and popular exaggeration of new media language in the print media". *Journal of Computer-Mediated Communication,* Vol. 11 No. 3, available at: http://jcmc.indiana.edu/vol11/issue3/thurlow.html (accessed 15 November 2010).

United States Department of Education (2010), "Transforming American education: learning powered by technology", National Educational Technology Plan 2010, March 5, available at: www.ed.gov/sites/default/files/NEP-2010-final-report.pdf

Walker, S. and Greenhow, C. (2010), "The internet and human relationships: revisiting the personal social networks of parents", paper presented at the Council on Family Relations Annual Meeting, Minneapolis, MN, November 2–3.

Warschauer, M. and Matuchniak, T. (2010), "New technology and digital worlds: analyzing evidence of equity in access, use, and outcomes", *Review of Research in Education*, Vol. 34, pp. 179–225.

Wilson, E. (2009), "Bloggers crash fashion's front row", *The New York Times*, December 24, available at: www.nytimes.com/2009/12/27/fashion/27BLOGGERS.html# (accessed November 10, 2010).

Why Popular Culture in Education Matters

William M. Reynolds
Series editor, Cultural Studies Toward Transformative Curriculum and Pedagogy

Television, music, movies, the new technologies of enhanced video/computer games, and, of course, the ubiquitous Internet have transformed 'culture, especially popular culture, into the primary educational site in which youth learn about themselves and the larger world' (Giroux 2000: 108). Popular culture and critical media analysis enable youth to understand and participate in the representations that help to construct their identities. In the struggle over the symbolic order that characterizes our times, popular culture – developed by name brands and various forms of media, including the Hollywood film industry – is crucial in creating the identities and representations that our youth embrace. Compounded by an increasing number of corporate mergers, fewer companies are determining what this symbolic order will display: in fact, media conglomerates such as Time-Warner and Disney now have an overwhelming influence.

> What I would say to those who support only the study of 'highbrow' culture is, popular cultural artefacts are crucial to our understanding of the world that surrounds us.

In the wake of this symbolic order, what is represented to youth in classrooms – testable, discreet forms of pre-packaged information – has become increasingly insignificant to them: something to be suffered through, memorized, recalled and promptly forgotten in the quest for the real currency of postindustrial, military, carceral, global, corporate-order popular culture.

Popular culture is not only about media; it is about identity, commodities and their connection with education, curriculum, pedagogy and our notions of a just, democratic society. How do multiple interpretations of popular culture enhance our understandings of education and how can critical pedagogy – in the Freirean (2002) sense – be expanded to develop a student's critical consciousness (of issues of race, class, gender, and sexual preference)?

It becomes our responsibility, then, as educators, to prepare our students/ citizens, to learn how to use, consume, and to have personal power over the media. Empowerment comes when we are able to read media and make informed decisions about what we have read. Media have been, and may continue to become, the ultimate hegemonic WMD to a complacent or ignorant audience (Macedo and Steinberg 2007: xiv).

So, beyond the dismissive notions and comments of those who support only the study of the selective tradition of 'highbrow' culture – the canon – I would suggest that the critical analysis of popular cultural artefacts is crucial to understanding ourselves, our identities and the world that surrounds us. And, this is particularly important within the educational context. In fact, the study of popular culture assists youth, and all of us, in being less constructed, more constructing and allows us to see the obstacles in our path towards a more democratic and egalitarian society (see Reynolds 2011).

REFERENCES

Giroux, H. A. (2000), *Impure acts: The practical politics of cultural studies*, New York: Routledge. Macedo, D. and Steinberg, S. R. (2007), *Media literacy: A reader*, New York: Peter Lang.

Reynolds, W. M. (2012), 'Iron Man democracy: Militainment and democratic possibilities,' in A. Abdi and P. R. Carr (eds), *Educating for democratic consciousness: Counter-hegemonic possibilities*, New York: Peter Lang.

READ ON ...

William M. Reynolds | Georgia Southern University Series editor: Cultural Studies Toward Transformative Curriculum and Pedagogy, ISSN 2049-4025

What first attracted you to fashion and retail?

Like all young people I was attracted to the excitement of fashion and retail, but I think the major influence was MTV. I was a teenager and college student in the 1980s so my fashion influences were music videos and bands such as the Thompson Twins, Fun Boy Three, Bananarama and the Eurythmics. I tried to emulate Tom Bailey of the Thompson Twins by wearing big oversized T-shirts, baggy short pants and espadrilles. I even had long bobbed hair, which was dyed dark red, black, and blond...I am sure it was quite a sight.

Not to stereotype, but being a gay man fashion was one area where I felt at home. In high school I was pretty much a social outcast so I focused my energies into my studies and working part time at the local mall. I worked at The Gap and the other sales associates and managers were very encouraging and gave me positive reinforcement. I felt accepted there, and to this day I wonder what happened to that group of women because they really helped me to develop into a young man. I would love to thank them for all they did for me.

Why did you choose to make the switch from industry to academia and why do you think so many fashion, textiles and apparel scholars have a background in industry?

I made the switch from industry (management at The Gap and Banana Republic; branding strategist for The Limited Corporation; regional entertainment field merchant for Target Corporation) into academia in 2004 when my advisor from Ohio State University, Dr Patricia Cunningham, called to tell me about a position at Drexel University. In 2004, I became a tenure-track candidate in the department and in 2010 I was the first person to ever receive tenure at Drexel in design and merchandising. Drexel was a new experience for me because it is a private school and I had always been in public universities. The idea of private education has grown on me, however I still prefer the public model as it allows for more collegiality and fairness, as well as a balance in the education system for those who cannot afford the high tuition fees.

I disagree with your comment that so many fashion, textiles and apparel scholars have a background in industry: few really have extensive experience and most have worked just five years or less. It is rare to find someone with a wide background and who has worked for major corporations: someone who has both a Ph.D. and twenty-plus years of corporate fashion experience.

Do you think fashion scholarship has had an impact on the fashion business and clothing industry? And what do you think is the major tie between them?

I think that most fashion scholarship follows and examines the industry after the fact. But, I believe that fashion scholarship does influence industry professionals to re-examine what they have done in the past. But mostly the major tie between the two is that fashion companies look to academia for students – what we like to call 'fresh blood' – to work for them. They look to us to be the educators of future 'fashionistas'.

What is most important is that we professors examine where we send students to work. For example, if a department is constantly sending students to fashion companies that do not pay them during internships then they are doing a disservice to their students. Urban Outfitters was notorious for this for years, however they are now going to start paying students.

I think very few industry people even read fashion scholarship. If we think they do then we are kidding ourselves. I think the publishers need to do a better job of reaching out to the fashion companies to let them know they are there. Also, scholars need to do a better job of letting industry folks know we are here. We need to let industry 'see us' and know we want to work with them.

Do you think scholars working with popular culture have a responsibility to positively influence practitioners?

Yes I do. But more importantly, I think scholars need to let those who are working with popular culture know who they are influencing, as well as whether that influence is positive or negative. As you know, my research focuses on fashion branding and the companies using popular culture in their branding strategies are either positively reinforcing culture or sometimes having a negative effect.

For example, we are continually examining how sex influences fashion purchasing. This led me to examine the retailer Abercrombie & Fitch, who are constantly using sex in their ads in order to entice young people to buy their clothes. During 2007–2008, I did a case study of their flagship stores in New York, San Francisco and London. My goal was to focus on their male greeters, who are used at each one of these locations, in order to find out if this technique actually influences customers to shop. And it does! My research revealed that Abercrombie & Fitch is quite homoerotic and uses notions of hyper-masculinity to sell their products.

Do you have any advice for junior scholars working in the field who are looking to get their first position or get their first article or book published?

Yes I do: (1.) choose a good mentor, (2.) network – network – network, and (3.) do not be a narcissist.

Find a mentor who is involved in your discipline and enjoys helping others without any personal agenda. This is hard to do, but I found two (Dr Patricia Cunningham and Dr Gwendolyn Snead O'Neal) and they educated me on the importance of being both a good scholar and a 'people person'.

Go out and meet all kinds of scholars in various disciplines. Engage with them. Listen to what other people have to say. This will allow you to strategize your own research agenda and build your likelihood of getting published. For example, I received my first book contract simply by listening to others tell me that they wanted a textbook on branding. Then a publisher told me that he was looking for a story-like book about fashion branding. I informed him of my background and my interest in pursuing such a book and the rest was history.

Do not be a narcissist! The biggest thing that frustrates me at conferences is to see junior scholars (and senior scholars for that matter) who just give their papers and never attend the other conference sessions. This is very narcissistic behaviour: they do not believe that they need to listen. This will be their biggest downfall and I can guarantee that mentality will hold them back from being published and, more importantly, getting a job and tenure.

How do you define popular culture and do you see a distinction between what is high and low/popular culture? Do you believe popular culture will ever gain the respect of the Academy and be treated as an equal to science, medicine and technology, or even gain the respect that other more established areas within the humanities have attained?

Popular culture was formed because of the superior attitude of the academy, because of the idea that studying what everyday people did was not important, but as I hear many folks at the Popular Culture/American Culture Associations say, 'If it isn't popular it's not culture', and I firmly believe that. The postmodern period broke down these ideas. I think that contemporary scholars see this and I do believe that popular culture has gained respect across the disciplines. In almost all universities both the humanities and the arts have courses dedicated to the study of popular culture.

As to whether or not I think popular culture will be treated as equal to science, medicine and technology, I believe popular culture is the umbrella of these already. Look at how science, medicine and technology borrow from popular culture. Look at all the ads on television for pharmaceuticals and how they utilize mass trends to sell medications. Or how Apple created their 'Are you a Mac or PC?' campaign, which personified two archetypal individuals in order to sell technology. I do not think there is any discipline that does not use popular culture in some format when educating today's consumers.

You are an integral member of both the Popular Culture Association (PCA) and the International Textile and Apparel Association (ITAA). Can you tell us a bit about these associations and their respective missions?

I have been involved in both the ITAA and PCA/ACA since about 1996. I became involved because of my mentors: Dr Patricia Cunningham and Dr Gwendolyn Snead O'Neal.

At PCA I have served as the area chair for fashion, style, appearance, consumption and design, visual culture, and professional development. I have also been on the PCA/ACA board and am currently the vice-president for area chairs. I also serve on the editorial boards for the *Journal of Popular Culture* and the *Journal of American Culture*.

For the ITAA I have served as the chair for faculty and graduate student awards, was the conference chair for 2011, and will continue to serve the organization as the vendor and resource exhibitor chair for the 2012 conference in Hawaii.

I think PCA/ACA will continue to grow both domestically and internationally. We have regional organizations in the United States and now have branches of the organization in Australia, Asia and Europe. Last year all of our organizations combined had over 5,000 participants and that number keeps growing.

In your forthcoming book (edited with Vikki Karaminas), Fashion in Popular Culture, you are focusing on the relationship between fashion and popular culture. Can you provide us with some inside information about the project and why we should be excited about this particular book?

I am very excited because this is going to be an international book. We have scholars from across the globe doing various chapters. I am more excited because this book does not contain articles written by the 'usual suspects' and scholars of fashion, instead it includes new folks who have never published in our discipline. There is a wonderful chapter on homoeroticism and the leather jacket, which was written by Marvin Taylor, Director of the Fales Library at New York University. A new scholar, Alphonso McClendon, has written a piece on fashion, the jazz age and the notions of heroine chic, and I was so honoured to co-author a paper with up-and-coming scholar Alexandra Horner in which we deconstruct Lady Ga Ga and her use of gay iconic symbols in her clothing, ultimately suggesting that she is really 'Lady Gay Gay'.

How do you think fashion references/is influenced by popular culture and what is the relationship between fashion and popular culture?

There are two types of fashion: mass fashion and couture. While I believe that both are influenced by popular culture; mass fashion *really* reflects popular culture because it is what everyone wears. Fashion merchandisers are continuously analysing sales and looking at art, style, design, and people on the street in order to come up with what will be hot! Then they take these ideas to designers, who come up with the concepts for selling. Couture fashion tends to be viewed as an artistic endeavour and the 'fancy' of the designer . . . it is usually not worn. But fashion would be lost without popular culture.

How do you think popular culture affects branding and marketing within the fashion and retail industries?

For this question, everyone should run out and buy my book *Brand/Story: Ralph, Vera, Johnny, Billy and Other Adventures in Fashion Branding* (Fairchild Books)! My research has always focused on a multicultural perspective of fashion as it relates primarily to men's lifestyles. I think that branding experts borrow from popular culture in order to generate ads that consumers will understand. I also think that fashion designers derive the concepts for their designs by borrowing from popular culture. If we examine fashion from a historical perspective then we can see how popular culture has shaped mass fashion.

I edited a special issue of the *Journal of American Culture* in March 2009 dedicated to understanding this exact topic. My article, with Dr Dilia Lopez-Gydosh, examines African-American and Latino men and how they were – and are still – inspired through popular-music culture to dress in a specific way. Many fashionable looks have been created through music genres such as Daddy Yankee's style for his 'reggaeton' sounds.

Even cross-dressers are influenced by popular culture when they assemble a look. For example, the Style Network's Brini Maxwell, portrayed by Ben Sander, is a complete homage to retro 1950s–1960s dressing, and such women as *That Girl's* Marlo Thomas and *The Mary Tyler Moore Show's* Sue Ann Nivens, played by Betty White, in turn inspired him.

The high-end mass fashion designer Siki Im has been inspired by literature and film; William Golding's *Lord of the Flies* and then Bret Easton Ellis's *American Psycho* inspired his first collections, and even his most recent collection was designed around the film *La Haine* directed by Mathieu Kassovitz. Siki Im represents a new type of menswear designer who is not afraid to recognize that men want unique clothing and have individual style that is not traditional. His mix of eastern and western popular culture in menswear is what has made his brand a global success.

What do you perceive as the hot topics in fashion and popular culture, and what do you think will be important over the coming years?

I once had someone tell me that fashion branding was just a trend, but I think they are wrong. I believe branding is the link between fashion and popular culture because it is this business practice that allows popular culture to be infused into products and gives them 'life' so to speak. I think courses should be developed about this connection because it is through popular culture that brand images and stories are created. While marketing is just the process of advertising and displaying a fashion product in the public eye, it is branding that ensures everything – from the company's image, advertising, product, and even sales force – represents the brand in its entirety. Look at the consistency that Apple has across the world and how its entire package is coherent no matter what country you visit. A consumer can walk into an Apple store anywhere and know what they will experience.

What/who is your favourite brand/designer and why?

Hands down my favourite designer is Ralph Lauren. I like him because he has a solid brand image and his product lines are so diversified. He does not discriminate because he dresses a multitude of consumers; he has high-end lines such as his 'purple label' and 'double RL', as well as more mass lines such as 'chaps' at Kohl's and 'American living' at jcpenney. His customers are young, old, ethnic, Wasp, gay, straight – it simply does not matter. He proves this by being a wonderful philanthropist who gives to almost every charity. One year, he sponsored the Harvey Milk School for LGBT youth by selling 'I kiss boys' or 'I kiss girls' tote bags that he sold at his Rugby stores. And he was not afraid that this would hurt the Ivy League image of the store either.

He is a global brand that is timeless. I really like the fact that he is a self-made individual who started as a tie salesman at Brooks Brothers in the early 1960s. Ironically, I like the fact that he never graduated from college but has proven himself very successful. I hope I can meet him someday.

Read on . . .

Joseph H. Hancock
Drexel University
Co-editor: *Fashion in Popular
Culture: Literature, Media and Contemporary Studies, forthcoming 2013*

Small Change

Malcolm Gladwell

WHY THE REVOLUTION WILL NOT BE TWEETED

At four-thirty in the afternoon on Monday, February 1, 1960, four college students sat down at the lunch counter at the Woolworth's in downtown Greensboro, North Carolina. They were freshmen at North Carolina A. & T., a black college a mile or so away.

"I'd like a cup of coffee, please," one of the four, Ezell Blair, said to the waitress.

"We don't serve Negroes here," she replied.

The Woolworth's lunch counter was a long L-shaped bar that could seat sixty-six people, with a standup snack bar at one end. The seats were for whites. The snack bar was for blacks. Another employee, a black woman who worked at the steam table, approached the students and tried to warn them away. "You're acting stupid, ignorant!" she said. They didn't move. Around five-thirty, the front doors to the store were locked. The four still didn't move. Finally, they left by a side door. Outside, a small crowd had gathered, including a photographer from the Greensboro Record. "I'll be back tomorrow with A. & T. College," one of the students said.

By next morning, the protest had grown to twenty-seven men and four women, most from the same dormitory as the original four. The men were dressed in suits and ties. The students had brought their schoolwork, and studied as they sat at the counter. On Wednesday, students from Greensboro's "Negro" secondary school, Dudley High, joined in, and the number of protesters swelled to eighty. By Thursday, the protesters numbered three hundred, including three white women, from the Greensboro campus of the University of North Carolina. By Saturday, the sit-in had reached six hundred. People spilled out onto the street. White teen-agers waved Confederate flags. Someone threw a firecracker. At noon, the A. & T. football team arrived. "Here comes the wrecking crew," one of the white students shouted.

By the following Monday, sit-ins had spread to Winston-Salem, twenty-five miles away, and Durham, fifty miles away. The day after that, students at Fayetteville State Teachers College and at Johnson C. Smith College, in Charlotte, joined in, followed on Wednesday by students at St. Augustine's College and Shaw University, in Raleigh. On Thursday and Friday, the protest crossed state lines, surfacing in Hampton and Portsmouth, Virginia, in Rock Hill, South Carolina, and in Chattanooga, Tennessee. By the end of the month, there were sit-ins throughout the South, as far west as Texas. "I asked every student I met what the first day of the sitdowns had been like on his campus," the political theorist Michael Walzer wrote in Dissent. "The answer was always the same: 'It was like a fever. Everyone wanted to go.' " Some seventy thousand students eventually took part. Thousands were arrested and untold thousands more radicalized. These events in the early sixties became a civil-rights war that engulfed the South for the rest of the decade—and it happened without e-mail, texting, Facebook, or Twitter.

The world, we are told, is in the midst of a revolution. The new tools of social media have reinvented social activism. With Facebook and Twitter and the like, the traditional relationship between political authority and popular will has been upended, making it easier for the powerless to collaborate, coördinate, and give voice to their concerns. When ten thousand protesters took to the streets in Moldova in the spring of 2009 to protest against their country's Communist government, the action was dubbed the Twitter Revolution, because of the means by which the demonstrators had been brought together. A few months after that, when student protests rocked Tehran, the State Department took the unusual step of asking Twitter to suspend scheduled maintenance of its Web site, because the Administration didn't want such a critical organizing tool out of service at the height of the demonstrations. "Without Twitter the people of Iran would not have felt empowered and confident to stand up for freedom and democracy," Mark Pfeifle, a former national-security adviser, later wrote, calling for Twitter to be nominated for the Nobel Peace Prize. Where activists were once defined by their causes, they are now defined by their tools. Facebook warriors go online to push for change. "You are the best hope for us all," James K. Glassman, a former senior State Department official, told a crowd of cyber activists at a recent conference sponsored by Facebook, A. T. & T., Howcast, MTV, and Google. Sites like Facebook, Glassman said, "give the U.S. a significant competitive advantage over terrorists. Some time ago, I said that Al Qaeda was 'eating our lunch on the Internet.' That is no longer the case. Al Qaeda is stuck in Web 1.0. The Internet is now about interactivity and conversation."

These are strong, and puzzling, claims. Why does it matter who is eating whose lunch on the Internet? Are people who log on to their Facebook page really the best hope for us all? As for Moldova's so-called Twitter Revolution, Evgeny Morozov, a scholar at Stanford who has been the most persistent of digital evangelism's critics, points out that Twitter had scant internal significance in Moldova, a country where very few Twitter accounts exist. Nor does it seem to have been a revolution, not least because the protests—as Anne Applebaum suggested in the Washington Post—may well have been a bit of stagecraft cooked up by the government. (In a country paranoid about Romanian revanchism, the protesters flew a Romanian flag over the Parliament building.) In the Iranian case, meanwhile, the people tweeting about the demonstrations were almost all in the West. "It is time to get Twitter's role in the events in Iran right," Golnaz Esfandiari wrote, this past summer, in Foreign Policy. "Simply put: There was no Twitter Revolution inside Iran." The cadre of prominent bloggers, like Andrew Sullivan, who championed the role of social media in Iran, Esfandiari continued, misunderstood the situation. "Western journalists who couldn't reach—or didn't bother reaching?—people on the ground in Iran simply scrolled through the English-language tweets post with tag #iranelection," she wrote. "Through it all, no one seemed to wonder why people trying to coordinate protests in Iran would be writing in any language other than Farsi."

Some of this grandiosity is to be expected. Innovators tend to be solipsists. They often want to cram every stray fact and experience into their new model. As the historian Robert Darnton has written, "The marvels of communication technology in the present have produced a false consciousness about the past—even a sense that communication has no history, or had nothing of importance to consider before the days of television and the Internet." But there is something else at work here, in the outsized enthusiasm for social media. Fifty years after one of the most extraordinary episodes of social upheaval in American history, we seem to have forgotten what activism is.

Greensboro in the early nineteen-sixties was the kind of place where racial insubordination was routinely met with violence. The four students who first sat down at the lunch counter were terrified. "I suppose if anyone had come up behind me and yelled 'Boo,' I think I would have fallen off my seat," one of them said later. On the first day, the store manager notified the police chief, who immediately sent two officers to the store. On the third day, a gang of white toughs showed up at the lunch counter and stood ostentatiously behind the protesters, ominously muttering epithets such as "burr-head nigger." A local Ku Klux Klan leader made an appearance. On Saturday, as tensions grew, someone called in a bomb threat, and the entire store had to be evacuated.

The dangers were even clearer in the Mississippi Freedom Summer Project of 1964, another of the sentinel campaigns of the civil-rights movement. The Student Nonviolent Coordinating Committee recruited hundreds of Northern, largely white unpaid volunteers to run Freedom Schools, register black voters, and raise civil-rights awareness in the Deep South. "No one should go anywhere alone, but certainly not in an automobile and certainly not at night," they were instructed. Within days of arriving in Mississippi, three volunteers—Michael Schwerner, James Chaney, and Andrew Goodman—were kidnapped and killed, and, during the rest of the summer, thirty-seven black churches were set on fire and dozens of safe houses were bombed; volunteers were beaten, shot at, arrested, and trailed by pickup trucks full of armed men. A quarter of those in the program dropped out. Activism that challenges the status quo—that attacks deeply rooted problems—is not for the faint of heart.

What makes people capable of this kind of activism? The Stanford sociologist Doug McAdam compared the Freedom Summer dropouts with the participants who stayed, and discovered that the key difference wasn't, as might be expected, ideological fervor. " All of the applicants—participants and withdrawals alike—emerge as highly committed, articulate supporters of the goals and values of the summer program," he concluded. What mattered more was an applicant's degree of personal connection to the civil-rights movement. All the volunteers were required to provide a list of personal contacts—the people they wanted kept apprised of their activities—and participants were far more likely than dropouts to have close friends who were also going to Mississippi. High-risk activism, McAdam concluded, is a "strong-tie" phenomenon.

This pattern shows up again and again. One study of the Red Brigades, the Italian terrorist group of the nineteen-seventies, found that seventy per cent of recruits had at least one good friend already in the organization. The same is true of the men who joined the mujahideen in Afghanistan. Even revolutionary actions that look spontaneous, like the demonstrations in East Germany that led to the fall of the Berlin Wall, are, at core, strong-tie phenomena. The opposition movement in East Germany consisted of several hundred groups, each with roughly a dozen members. Each group was in limited contact with the others: at the time, only thirteen per cent of East Germans even had a phone. All they knew was that on Monday nights, outside St. Nicholas Church in downtown Leipzig, people gathered to voice their anger at the state. And the primary determinant of who showed up was "critical friends"—the more friends you had who were critical of the regime the more likely you were to join the protest.

So one crucial fact about the four freshmen at the Greensboro lunch counter—David Richmond, Franklin McCain, Ezell Blair, and Joseph McNeil—was their relationship with one another. McNeil was a roommate of Blair's in A. & T.'s Scott Hall dormitory. Richmond roomed with McCain one floor up, and Blair, Richmond, and McCain had all gone to Dudley High School. The four would smuggle beer into the dorm and talk late into the night in Blair and McNeil's room. They would all have remembered the murder of Emmett Till in 1955, the Montgomery bus boycott that same year, and the showdown in Little Rock in 1957. It was McNeil who brought up the idea of a sit-in at Woolworth's. They'd discussed it for nearly a month. Then McNeil came into the dorm room and asked the others if they were ready. There was a pause, and McCain said, in a way that works only with people who talk late into the night with one another, "Are you guys chicken or not?" Ezell Blair worked up the courage the next day to ask for a cup of coffee because he was flanked by his roommate and two good friends from high school.

The kind of activism associated with social media isn't like this at all. The platforms of social media are built around weak ties. Twitter is a way of following (or being followed by) people you may never have met. Facebook is a tool for efficiently managing your acquaintances, for keeping up with the people you would not otherwise be able to stay in touch with. That's why you can have a thousand "friends" on Facebook, as you never could in real life.

This is in many ways a wonderful thing. There is strength in weak ties, as the sociologist Mark Granovetter has observed. Our acquaintances—not our friends—are our greatest source of new ideas and information. The Internet lets us exploit the power of these kinds of distant connections with marvellous efficiency. It's terrific at the diffusion of innovation, interdisciplinary collaboration, seamlessly matching up buyers and sellers, and the logistical functions of the dating world. But weak ties seldom lead to high-risk activism.

In a new book called "The Dragonfly Effect: Quick, Effective, and Powerful Ways to Use Social Media to Drive Social Change," the business consultant Andy Smith and the Stanford Business School professor Jennifer Aaker tell the story of Sameer Bhatia, a young Silicon Valley entrepreneur who came down with acute myelogenous leukemia. It's a perfect illustration of social media's strengths. Bhatia needed a bone-marrow transplant, but he could not find a match among his relatives and friends. The odds were best with a donor of his ethnicity, and there were few South Asians in the national bone-marrow database. So Bhatia's business partner sent out an e-mail explaining Bhatia's plight to more than four hundred of their acquaintances, who forwarded the e-mail to their personal contacts; Facebook pages and YouTube videos were devoted to the Help Sameer campaign. Eventually, nearly twenty-five thousand new people were registered in the bone-marrow database, and Bhatia found a match.

But how did the campaign get so many people to sign up? By not asking too much of them. That's the only way you can get someone you don't really know to do something on your behalf. You can get thousands of people to sign up for a donor registry, because doing so is pretty easy. You have to send in a cheek swab and—in the highly unlikely event that your bone marrow is a good match for someone in need—spend a few hours at the hospital. Donating bone marrow isn't a trivial matter. But it doesn't involve financial or personal risk; it doesn't mean spending a summer being chased by armed men in pickup trucks. It doesn't require that you confront socially entrenched norms and practices. In fact, it's the kind of commitment that will bring only social acknowledgment and praise.

The evangelists of social media don't understand this distinction; they seem to believe that a Facebook friend is the same as a real friend and that signing up for a donor registry in Silicon Valley today is activism in the same sense as sitting at a segregated lunch counter in Greensboro in 1960. "Social networks are particularly effective at increasing motivation," Aaker and Smith write. But that's not true. Social networks are effective at increasing participation—by lessening the level of motivation that participation requires. The

Facebook page of the Save Darfur Coalition has 1,282,339 members, who have donated an average of nine cents apiece. The next biggest Darfur charity on Facebook has 22,073 members, who have donated an average of thirty-five cents. Help Save Darfur has 2,797 members, who have given, on average, fifteen cents. A spokesperson for the Save Darfur Coalition told Newsweek, "We wouldn't necessarily gauge someone's value to the advocacy movement based on what they've given. This is a powerful mechanism to engage this critical population. They inform their community, attend events, volunteer. It's not something you can measure by looking at a ledger." In other words, Facebook activism succeeds not by motivating people to make a real sacrifice but by motivating them to do the things that people do when they are not motivated enough to make a real sacrifice. We are a long way from the lunch counters of Greensboro.

The students who joined the sit-ins across the South during the winter of 1960 described the movement as a "fever." But the civil-rights movement was more like a military campaign than like a contagion. In the late nineteen-fifties, there had been sixteen sit-ins in various cities throughout the South, fifteen of which were formally organized by civil-rights organizations like the N.A.A.C.P. and CORE. Possible locations for activism were scouted. Plans were drawn up. Movement activists held training sessions and retreats for would-be protesters. The Greensboro Four were a product of this ground-work: all were members of the N.A.A.C.P. Youth Council. They had close ties with the head of the local N.A.A.C.P. chapter. They had been briefed on the earlier wave of sit-ins in Durham, and had been part of a series of movement meetings in activist churches. When the sit-in movement spread from Greensboro throughout the South, it did not spread indiscriminately. It spread to those cities which had preëxisting "movement centers"—a core of dedicated and trained activists ready to turn the "fever" into action.

The civil-rights movement was high-risk activism. It was also, crucially, strategic activism: a challenge to the establishment mounted with precision and discipline. The N.A.A.C.P. was a centralized organization, run from New York according to highly formalized operating procedures. At the Southern Christian Leadership Conference, Martin Luther King, Jr., was the unquestioned authority. At the center of the movement was the black church, which had, as Aldon D. Morris points out in his superb 1984 study, "The Origins of the Civil Rights Movement," a carefully demarcated division of labor, with various standing committees and disciplined groups. "Each group was task-oriented and coordinated its activities through authority structures," Morris writes. "Individuals were held accountable for their assigned duties, and important conflicts were resolved by the minister, who usually exercised ultimate authority over the congregation."

This is the second crucial distinction between traditional activism and its online variant: social media are not about this kind of hierarchical organization. Facebook and the like are tools for building networks, which are the opposite, in structure and character, of hierarchies. Unlike hierarchies, with their rules and procedures, networks aren't controlled by a single central authority. Decisions are made through consensus, and the ties that bind people to the group are loose.

This structure makes networks enormously resilient and adaptable in low-risk situations. Wikipedia is a perfect example. It doesn't have an editor, sitting in New York, who directs and corrects each entry. The effort of putting together each entry is self-organized. If every entry in Wikipedia were to be erased tomorrow, the content would swiftly be restored, because that's what happens when a network of thousands spontaneously devote their time to a task.

There are many things, though, that networks don't do well. Car companies sensibly use a network to organize their hundreds of suppliers, but not to design their cars. No one believes that the articulation of a coherent design philosophy is best handled by a sprawling, leaderless organizational system. Because networks don't have a centralized leadership structure and clear lines of authority, they have real difficulty reaching consensus and setting goals. They can't think strategically; they are chronically prone to conflict and error. How do you make difficult choices about tactics or strategy or philosophical direction when everyone has an equal say?

The Palestine Liberation Organization originated as a network, and the international-relations scholars Mette Eilstrup-Sangiovanni and Calvert Jones argue in a recent essay in International Security that this is why it ran into such trouble as it grew: "Structural features typical of networks—the absence of central authority, the unchecked autonomy of rival groups, and the inability to arbitrate quarrels through formal mechanisms—made the P.L.O. excessively vulnerable to outside manipulation and internal strife."

In Germany in the nineteen-seventies, they go on, "the far more unified and successful left-wing terrorists tended to organize hierarchically, with professional management and clear divisions of labor. They were concentrated geographically in universities, where they could establish central leadership, trust, and camaraderie through regular, face-to-face meetings." They seldom betrayed their comrades in arms during police interrogations. Their counterparts on the right were organized as decentralized networks, and had no such discipline. These groups were regularly infiltrated, and members, once arrested, easily gave up their comrades. Similarly, Al Qaeda was most dangerous when it was a unified hierarchy. Now that it has dissipated into a network, it has proved far less effective.

The drawbacks of networks scarcely matter if the network isn't interested in systemic change—if it just wants to frighten or humiliate or make a splash—or if it doesn't need to think strategically. But if you're taking on a powerful and organized establishment you have to be a hierarchy. The Montgomery bus boycott required the participation of tens of thousands of people who depended on public transit to get to and from work each day. It lasted a year. In order to persuade those people to stay true to the cause, the boycott's organizers tasked each local black church with maintaining morale, and put together a free alternative private carpool service, with forty-eight dispatchers and forty-two pickup stations. Even the White Citizens Council, King later said, conceded that the carpool system moved with "military precision." By the time King came to Birmingham, for the climactic showdown with Police Commissioner Eugene (Bull) Connor, he had a budget of a million dollars, and a hundred full-time staff members on the ground, divided into operational units. The operation itself was divided into steadily escalating phases, mapped out in advance. Support was maintained through consecutive mass meetings rotating from church to church around the city.

Boycotts and sit-ins and nonviolent confrontations—which were the weapons of choice for the civil-rights movement—are high-risk strategies. They leave little room for conflict and error. The moment even one protester deviates from the script and responds to provocation, the moral legitimacy of the entire protest is compromised. Enthusiasts for social media would no doubt have us believe that King's task in Birmingham would have been made infinitely easier had he been able to communicate with his followers through Facebook, and contented himself with tweets from a Birmingham jail. But networks are messy: think of the ceaseless pattern of correction and revision, amendment and debate, that characterizes Wikipedia. If Martin Luther King, Jr., had tried to do a wiki-boycott in Montgomery, he would have been steamrolled by the white power structure. And of what use would a digital communication tool be in a town where ninety-eight per cent of the black community could be reached every Sunday morning at church? The things that King needed in Birmingham—discipline and strategy—were things that online social media cannot provide.

The bible of the social-media movement is Clay Shirky's "Here Comes Everybody." Shirky, who teaches at New York University, sets out to demonstrate the organizing power of the Internet, and he begins with the story of Evan, who worked on Wall Street, and his friend Ivanna, after she left her smart phone, an expensive Sidekick, on the back seat of a New York City taxicab. The telephone company transferred the data on Ivanna's lost phone to a new phone, whereupon she and Evan discovered that the Sidekick was now in the hands of a teen-ager from Queens, who was using it to take photographs of herself and her friends.

When Evan e-mailed the teen-ager, Sasha, asking for the phone back, she replied that his "white ass" didn't deserve to have it back. Miffed, he set up a Web page with her picture and a description of what had happened. He forwarded the link to his friends, and they forwarded it to their friends. Someone found the MySpace page of Sasha's boyfriend, and a link to it found its way onto the site. Someone found her address online and took a video of her home while driving by; Evan posted the video on the site. The story was picked up by the news filter Digg. Evan was now up to ten e-mails a minute. He created a bulletin board for his readers to share their stories, but it crashed under the weight of responses. Evan and Ivanna went to the police, but the police filed the report under "lost," rather than "stolen," which essentially closed the case. "By this point millions of readers were watching," Shirky writes, "and dozens of mainstream news outlets had covered the story." Bowing to the pressure, the N.Y.P.D. reclassified the item as "stolen." Sasha was arrested, and Evan got his friend's Sidekick back.

Shirky's argument is that this is the kind of thing that could never have happened in the pre-Internet age—and he's right. Evan could never have tracked down Sasha. The story of the Sidekick would never have been publicized. An army of people could never have been assembled to wage this fight. The police wouldn't have bowed to the pressure of a lone person who had misplaced something as trivial as a cell phone. The story, to Shirky, illustrates "the ease and speed with which a group can be mobilized for the right kind of cause" in the Internet age.

Shirky considers this model of activism an upgrade. But it is simply a form of organizing which favors the weak-tie connections that give us access to information over the strong-tie connections that help us persevere in the face of danger. It shifts our energies from organizations that promote strategic and disciplined activity and toward those which promote resilience and adaptability. It makes it easier for activists to express themselves, and harder for that expression to have any impact. The instruments of social media are well suited to making the existing social order more efficient. They are not a natural enemy of the status quo. If you are of the opinion that all the world needs is a little buffing around the edges, this should not trouble you. But if you think that there are still lunch counters out there that need integrating it ought to give you pause.

Shirky ends the story of the lost Sidekick by asking, portentously, "What happens next?"—no doubt imagining future waves of digital protesters. But he has already answered the question. What happens next is more of the same. A networked, weak-tie world is good at things like helping Wall Streeters get phones back from teen-age girls. Viva la revolución.

By Malcolm Gladwell

Parenting and Popular Culture: Is This the Future of American Values?

Do children's values today scare you? They should.

Published on February 6, 2012 by Jim Taylor, Ph.D. in The Power of Prime

In researching my next parenting book, I came across several recent studies that I found truly disturbing. As you will see shortly, the results don't paint a pretty picture for the future of our children or our society as a whole. Even more damning is what it tells us about how parents are raising their children these days. Let's take a look a the findings.

One study analyzed the values expressed on the most popular television shows among so-called tweens (children ages 9–11) every decade from 1967 to 2007. Just so you can get a sense of how TV viewing has changed, here are the shows that were selected:1967: Andy Griffith, The Lucy Show; 1977: Laverne and Shirley, Happy Days; 1986: Growing Pains, Alf; 1997: Sabrina the Teenage Witch, Boy Meets World; 2007: American Idol, Hannah Montana.

The results revealed little change in values presented on the shows between 1967 and 1997, during which time, the five most expressed values were Community Feeling, Benevolence, Image, Tradition, and Popularity (three out of the five would generally be considered healthy). The five least expressed values were Fame, Physical Fitness, Hedonism, Spiritualism, and Financial Success (three out of five would generally be considered unhealthy).

Only during the most recent decade did a dramatic shift in values occur. The new top-five values were Fame, Achievement, Popularity, Image, and Financial Success (with Self-Centered and Power close behind). Related values that also became more prominent included Ambition, Comparison to Others, Attention Seeking, Conceitedness, Glamour, and Materialism. The latest bottom-five values were Spiritualism, Tradition, Security, Conformity, and

Benevolence (with Community Feeling to follow). I don't think the so-called values voters of today (or anyone else, for that matter) would have a hard time judging which would be considered healthy values and which wouldn't be.

An additional analysis of the data revealed a significant increase from 1997 to 2007 in the importance of fame to the main characters in the television shows. If you look at the popular tween shows today, for example, iCarly, they largely revolve around a young person pursuing fame and fortune, specifically through television, music, or fashion. I don't know about you, but just reading these findings makes me want to pack my wife and two young daughters in our car and live off the grid in northern Idaho.

Given that the values did not gradually shift during the decades studied, but rather changed abruptly in the last decade, the results can't be readily attributed to demographic patterns related to increased wealth or education. Instead, the most dramatic change, and the likely cause of these results in my view, is the rapid and all-encompassing emergence of new technology, which has given popular culture new and startling reach and influence on children.

Programming that expresses these value messages to your children are growing by the year. Since the data from this study were collected, more televisions shows aimed at the tween audience are being produced, including Glee, Big Time Rush, Victorious, and True Jackson. In fact, seven out of the top ten shows aimed at tweens are about teenagers who have achieved fame with careers in entertainment. Additionally, video games, such as Guitar Hero (in which everyone can be a rock star), and web sites, including Stardoll.com (the motto of which is "fame, fashion and friends"), help create media "supersystems" that envelop children in unhealthy values.

Of course, you could argue, as the creator of several of these tween TV shows does, that all children want to be stars and that the producers of these media are just giving tweens what they want. But that would be like saying that America was clamoring for American Idol or iPods before they were introduced (not true, of course). Admittedly, America is screaming for them now, but the causal direction of this relationship is clear.

You might also contend that your children aren't paying attention to popular culture's value messages, much less internalizing them. Unfortunately, preliminary research indicates that children are getting the messages from popular culture. According to a new focus-group study by the same researchers, fame is now the number-one aspirational value among children nine to eleven years old. Another survey of children under ten years of age found that, among their ten favorite things, being famous, attractive, and rich topped the list and being fat topped the list of worst things.

So, what does this say about the values our children are learning? Well, nothing good, that's for sure. These distorted values are definitely not going to prepare them for life in adulthood where, for most of us, narcissism and aspirations of wealth and fame don't usually play well with reality.

And who's to blame? We can't blame children because they're the victims here. It would be easy to point the finger at the "entertainment-industrial complex," but that would be like blaming sharks for killing their prey; it's simply what their DNA tells them to do. How about our government? Though some reasonable regulations of, for example, marketing to children on television, wouldn't seem unreasonable, even as someone with a decidedly left-leaning bent, I just don't believe it's the government's job to raise children. So, who's left? The parents, of course, who should be offering their children healthy values and perspectives that counterbalance the twisted values of popular culture.

Am I optimistic about future generations of our children (and for American society)? It all depends on whether parents are ready to step up and do what's best for their children. In other words, no, I'm not very optimistic.

Watching TV Makes You Smarter

By Steven Johnson

THE SLEEPER CURVE

SCIENTIST A: Has he asked for anything special?
SCIENTIST B: Yes, this morning for breakfast . . . he requested something
called "wheat germ, organic honey and tiger's milk."
SCIENTIST A: Oh, yes. Those were the charmed substances that some
years ago were felt to contain life-preserving properties.
SCIENTIST B: You mean there was no deep fat? No steak or cream pies
or . . . hot fudge?
SCIENTIST A: Those were thought to be unhealthy.

—*From Woody Allen's "Sleeper"*

On Jan. 24, the Fox network showed an episode of its hit drama "24," the real-time thriller known for its cliffhanger tension and often- gruesome violence. Over the preceding weeks, a number of public controversies had erupted around "24," mostly focused on its portrait of Muslim terrorists and its penchant for torture scenes. The episode that was shown on the 24th only fanned the flames higher: in one scene, a terrorist enlists a hit man to kill his child for not fully supporting the jihadist cause; in another scene, the secretary of defense authorizes the torture of his son to uncover evidence of a terrorist plot.

But the explicit violence and the post-9/11 terrorist anxiety are not the only elements of "24" that would have been unthinkable on prime-time network television 20 years ago. Alongside the notable change in content lies an equally notable change in form. During its 44 minutes – a real-time hour, minus 16 minutes for commercials – the episode connects the lives of 21 distinct characters, each with a clearly defined "story arc," as the Hollywood jargon has it: a defined personality with motivations and obstacles and specific relationships with other characters. Nine primary narrative threads wind their way through those 44 minutes, each drawing extensively upon events and information revealed in earlier episodes. Draw a map of all those intersecting plots and personalities, and you get structure that – where formal complexity is concerned – more closely resembles "Middlemarch" than a hit TV drama of years past like "Bonanza."

For decades, we've worked under the assumption that mass culture follows a path declining steadily toward lowest-common-denominator standards, presumably because the "masses" want dumb, simple pleasures and big media companies try to give the masses what they want. But as that "24" episode suggests, the exact opposite is happening: the culture is getting more cognitively demanding, not less. To make sense of an episode of "24," you have to integrate far more information than you would have a few decades ago watching a comparable show. Beneath the violence and the ethnic stereotypes, another trend appears: to keep up with entertainment like "24," you have to pay attention, make inferences, track shifting social relationships. This is what I call the Sleeper Curve: the most debased forms of mass diversion – video games and violent television dramas and juvenile sitcoms – turn out to be nutritional after all.

I believe that the Sleeper Curve is the single most important new force altering the mental development of young people today, and I believe it is largely a force for good: enhancing our cognitive faculties, not dumbing them down. And yet you almost never hear this story in popular accounts of today's media. Instead, you hear dire tales of addiction, violence, mindless escapism. It's assumed that shows that promote smoking or gratuitous violence are bad for us, while those that thunder against teen pregnancy or intolerance have a positive role in society. Judged by that morality-play standard, the story of popular culture over the past 50 years – if not 500 – is a story of decline: the morals of the stories have grown darker and more ambiguous, and the antiheroes have multiplied.

The usual counterargument here is that what media have lost in moral clarity, they have gained in realism. The real world doesn't come in nicely packaged public-service announcements, and we're better off with entertainment like "The Sopranos" that reflects our fallen state with all its ethical ambiguity. I happen to be sympathetic to that argument, but it's not the one I want to make here. I think there is another way to assess the social virtue of pop culture, one that looks at media as a kind of cognitive workout, not as a series of life lessons. There may indeed be more "negative messages" in the mediasphere today. But that's not the only way to evaluate whether our television shows or video games are having a positive impact. Just as important – if not more important – is the kind of thinking you have to do to make sense of a cultural experience. That is where the Sleeper Curve becomes visible.

TELEVISED INTELLIGENCE

Consider the cognitive demands that televised narratives place on their viewers. With many shows that we associate with "quality" entertainment – "The Mary Tyler Moore Show," "Murphy Brown," "Frasier" – the intelligence arrives fully formed in the words and actions of the characters on-screen. They say witty things to one another and avoid lapsing into tired sitcom cliches, and we smile along in our living rooms, enjoying the company of these smart people. But assuming we're bright enough to understand the sentences they're saying, there's no intellectual labor involved in enjoying the show as a viewer. You no more challenge your mind by watching these intelligent shows than you challenge your body watching "Monday Night Football." The intellectual work is happening on-screen, not off.

But another kind of televised intelligence is on the rise. Think of the cognitive benefits conventionally ascribed to reading: attention, patience, retention, the parsing of narrative threads. Over the last half-century, programming on TV has increased the demands it places on precisely these mental faculties. This growing complexity involves three primary elements: multiple threading, flashing arrows and social networks.

According to television lore, the age of multiple threads began with the arrival in 1981 of "Hill Street Blues," the Steven Bochco police drama invariably praised for its "gritty realism." Watch an episode of "Hill Street Blues" side by side with any major drama from the preceding decades – "Starsky and Hutch," for instance, or "Dragnet" – and the structural transformation will jump out at you. The earlier shows follow one or two lead characters, adhere to a single dominant plot and reach a decisive conclusion at the end of the episode. Draw an outline of the narrative threads in almost every "Dragnet" episode, and it will be a single line: from the initial crime scene, through the investigation, to the eventual cracking of the case. A typical "Starsky and Hutch" episode offers only the slightest variation on this linear formula: the introduction of a comic subplot that usually appears only at the tail ends of the episode. The vertical axis represents the number of individual threads, and the horizontal axis is time.

A "Hill Street Blues" episode complicates the picture in a number of profound ways. The narrative weaves together a collection of distinct strands – sometimes as many as 10, though at least half of the threads involve only a few quick scenes scattered through the episode. The number of primary characters – and not just bit parts – swells significantly. And the episode has fuzzy borders: picking up one or two threads from previous episodes at the outset and leaving one or two threads open at the end.

Critics generally cite "Hill Street Blues" as the beginning of "serious drama" native in the television medium – differentiating the series from the single-episode dramatic programs from the 50's, which were Broadway plays performed in front of a camera. But the "Hill Street" innovations weren't all that original; they'd long played a defining role in popular television, just not during the evening hours. The structure of a "Hill Street" episode – and indeed of all the critically acclaimed dramas that followed, from "thirtysomething" to "Six Feet Under" – is the structure of a soap opera. "Hill Street Blues" might have sparked a new golden age of television drama during its seven-year run, but it did so by using a few crucial tricks that "Guiding Light" and "General Hospital" mastered long before.

Bochco's genius with "Hill Street" was to marry complex narrative structure with complex subject matter. "Dallas" had already shown that the extended, interwoven threads of the soap-opera genre could survive the week-long interruptions of a prime-time show, but the actual content of "Dallas" was fluff. (The most probing issue it addressed was the question, now folk-loric, of who shot J.R.) "All in the Family" and "Rhoda" showed that you could tackle complex social issues, but they did their tackling in the comfort of the sitcom living room. "Hill Street" had richly drawn characters confronting difficult social issues and a narrative structure to match.

Since "Hill Street" appeared, the multi-threaded drama has become the most widespread fictional genre on prime time: "St. Elsewhere," "L.A. Law," "thirtysomething," "Twin Peaks," "N.Y.P.D. Blue," "E.R.," "The West Wing," "Alias," "Lost." (The only prominent holdouts in drama are shows like "Law and Order" that have essentially updated the venerable "Dragnet" format and thus remained anchored to a single narrative line.) Since the early 80's, however, there has been a noticeable increase in narrative complexity in these dramas. The most ambitious show on TV to date, "The Sopranos," routinely follows up to a dozen distinct threads over the course of an episode, with more than 20 recurring characters.

The total number of active threads equals the multiple plots of "Hill Street," but here each thread is more substantial. The show doesn't offer a clear distinction between dominant and minor plots; each story line carries its weight in the mix. The episode also displays a chordal mode of storytelling entirely absent from "Hill Street": a single scene in "The Sopranos" will often connect to three different threads at the same time, layering one plot atop another. And every single thread in this "Sopranos" episode builds on events from previous episodes and continues on through the rest of the season and beyond.

Put those charts together, and you have a portrait of the Sleeper Curve rising over the past 30 years of popular television. In a sense, this is as much a map of cognitive changes in the popular mind as it is a map of on-screen developments, as if the media titans decided to condition our brains to follow ever-larger numbers of simultaneous threads. Before "Hill Street," the conventional wisdom among television execs was that audiences wouldn't be comfortable following more than three plots in a single episode, and indeed, the "Hill Street" pilot, which was shown in January 1981, brought complaints from viewers that the show was too complicated. Fast-forward two decades, and shows like "The Sopranos" engage their audiences with narratives that make "Hill Street" look like "Three's Company." Audiences happily embrace that complexity because they've been trained by two decades of multi-threaded dramas.

Multi-threading is the most celebrated structural feature of the modern television drama, and it certainly deserves some of the honor that has been doled out to it. And yet multi-threading is only part of the story.

THE CASE FOR CONFUSION

Shortly after the arrival of the first-generation slasher movies – "Halloween," "Friday the 13th" – Paramount released a mock-slasher flick called "Student Bodies," parodying the genre just as the "Scream" series would do 15 years later. In one scene, the obligatory nubile teenage baby sitter hears a noise outside a suburban house; she opens the door to investigate, finds nothing and then goes back inside. As the door shuts behind her, the camera swoops in on the doorknob, and we see that she has left the door unlocked. The camera pulls back and then swoops down again for emphasis. And then a flashing arrow appears on the screen, with text that helpfully explains: "Unlocked!"

That flashing arrow is parody, of course, but it's merely an exaggerated version of a device popular stories use all the time. When a sci-fi script inserts into some advanced lab a nonscientist who keeps asking the science geeks to explain what they're doing with that particle accelerator, that's a flashing arrow that gives the audience precisely the information it needs in order to make sense of the ensuing plot. ("Whatever you do, don't spill water on it, or you'll set off a massive explosion!") These hints serve as a kind of narrative hand-holding. Implicitly, they say to the audience, "We realize you have no idea what a particle accelerator is, but here's the deal: all you need to know is that it's a big fancy thing that explodes when wet." They focus the mind on relevant details: "Don't worry about whether the baby sitter is going to break up with her boyfriend. Worry about that guy lurking in the bushes." They reduce the amount of analytic work you need to do to make sense of a story. All you have to do is follow the arrows.

By this standard, popular television has never been harder to follow. If narrative threads have experienced a population explosion over the past 20 years, flashing arrows have grown correspondingly scarce. Watching our pinnacle of early 80's TV drama, "Hill Street Blues," we find there's an informational wholeness to each scene that differs markedly from what you see on shows like "The West Wing" or "The Sopranos" or "Alias" or "E.R."

"Hill Street" has ambiguities about future events: will a convicted killer be executed? Will Furillo marry Joyce Davenport? Will Renko find it in himself to bust a favorite singer for cocaine possession? But the present-tense of each scene explains itself to the viewer with little ambiguity. There's an open question or a mystery driving each of these stories – how will it all turn out? – but there's no mystery about the immediate activity on the screen. A contemporary drama like "The West Wing," on the other hand, constantly embeds mysteries into the present-tense events: you see characters performing actions or discussing events about which crucial information has been deliberately withheld. Anyone who has watched more than a handful of "The West Wing" episodes closely will know the feeling: scene after scene refers to some clearly crucial but unexplained piece of information, and after the sixth reference, you'll find yourself wishing you could rewind the tape to figure out what they're talking about, assuming you've missed something. And then you realize that you're supposed to be confused. The open question posed by these sequences is not "How will this turn out in the end?" The question is "What's happening right now?"

The deliberate lack of hand-holding extends down to the microlevel of dialogue as well. Popular entertainment that addresses technical issues – whether they are the intricacies of passing legislation, or of performing a heart bypass, or of operating a particle accelerator – conventionally switches between two modes of information in dialogue: texture and substance. Texture is all the arcane verbiage provided to convince the viewer that they're watching Actual Doctors at Work; substance is the material planted amid the background texture that the viewer needs make sense of the plot.

Conventionally, narratives demarcate the line between texture and substance by inserting cues that flag or translate the important data. There's an unintentionally comical moment in the 2004 blockbuster "The Day After Tomorrow" in which the beleaguered climatologist (played by Dennis Quaid) announces his theory about the imminent arrival of a new ice age to a gathering of government officials. In his speech, he warns that "we have hit a critical desalinization point!" At this moment, the writer-director Roland Emmerich – a master of brazen arrow-flashing – has an official follow with the obliging remark: "It would explain what's driving this extreme weather." They might as well have had a flashing "Unlocked!" arrow on the screen.

The dialogue on shows like "The West Wing" and "E.R.," on the other hand, doesn't talk down to its audiences. It rushes by, the words accelerating in sync with the high-speed tracking shots that glide through the corridors and operating rooms. The characters talk faster in these shows, but the truly remarkable thing about the dialogue is not purely a matter of speed; it's the willingness to immerse the audience in information that most viewers won't understand. Here's a typical scene from "E.R.":

[WEAVER AND WRIGHT push a gurney containing a 16-year-old girl. Her parents, JANNA AND FRANK MIKAMI, follow close behind. CARTER AND LUCY fall in.]

WEAVER:	16-year-old, unconscious, history of biliary atresia.
CARTER:	Hepatic coma?
WEAVER:	Looks like it.
MR. MIKAMI:	She was doing fine until six months ago.
CARTER:	What medication is she on?
MRS. MIKAMI:	Ampicillin, tobramycin, vitamins a, d and k.

LUCY:	Skin's jaundiced.
WEAVER:	Same with the sclera. Breath smells sweet.
CARTER:	Fetor hepaticus?
WEAVER:	Yep.
LUCY:	What's that?
WEAVER:	Her liver's shut down. Let's dip a urine. [To CARTER] Guys, it's getting a little crowded in here, why don't you deal with the parents? Start lactulose, 30 cc's per NG.
CARTER:	We're giving medicine to clean her blood.
WEAVER:	Blood in the urine, two-plus.
CARTER:	The liver failure is causing her blood not to clot.
MRS. MIKAMI:	Oh, God. . . .
CARTER:	Is she on the transplant list?
MR. MIKAMI:	She's been Status 2a for six months, but they haven't been able to find her a match.
CARTER:	Why? What's her blood type?
MR. MIKAMI:	AB.

[This hits CARTER like a lightning bolt. LUCY gets it, too. They share a look.]

There are flashing arrows here, of course – "The liver failure is causing her blood not to clot" – but the ratio of medical jargon to layperson translation is remarkably high. From a purely narrative point of view, the decisive line arrives at the very end: "AB." The 16-year-old's blood type connects her to an earlier plot line, involving a cerebral-hemorrhage victim who – after being dramatically revived in one of the opening scenes – ends up brain-dead. Far earlier, before the liver-failure scene above, Carter briefly discusses harvesting the hemorrhage victim's organs for transplants, and another doctor makes a passing reference to his blood type being the rare AB (thus making him an unlikely donor). The twist here revolves around a statistically unlikely event happening at the E.R. – an otherwise perfect liver donor showing up just in time to donate his liver to a recipient with the same rare blood type. But the show reveals this twist with remarkable subtlety. To make sense of that last "AB" line – and the look of disbelief on Carter's and Lucy's faces – you have to recall a passing remark uttered earlier regarding a character who belongs to a completely different thread. Shows like "E.R." may have more blood and guts than popular TV had a generation ago, but when it comes to storytelling, they possess a quality that can only be described as subtlety and discretion.

EVEN BAD TV IS BETTER

Skeptics might argue that I have stacked the deck here by focusing on relatively highbrow titles like "The Sopranos" or "The West Wing," when in fact the most significant change in the last five years of narrative entertainment involves reality TV. Does the contemporary pop cultural landscape look quite as promising if the representative show is "Joe Millionaire" instead of "The West Wing"?

I think it does, but to answer that question properly, you have to avoid the tendency to sentimentalize the past. When people talk about the golden age of television in the early 70's – invoking shows like "The Mary Tyler Moore Show" and "All in the Family" – they forget to mention how awful most television programming was during much of that decade. If you're going to look at pop-culture trends, you have to compare apples to apples, or in this case, lemons to lemons. The relevant comparison is not between "Joe Millionaire" and "MASH"; it's between "Joe Millionaire" and "The Newlywed Game," or between "Survivor" and "The Love Boat."

What you see when you make these head-to-head comparisons is that a rising tide of complexity has been lifting programming at the bottom of the quality spectrum and at the top. "The Sopranos" is several times more demanding of its audiences than "Hill Street" was, and "Joe Millionaire" has made comparable advances over "Battle of the Network Stars." This is the ultimate test of the Sleeper Curve theory: even the junk has improved.

If early television took its cues from the stage, today's reality programming is reliably structured like a video game: a series of competitive tests, growing more challenging over time. Many reality shows borrow a subtler device from gaming culture as well: the rules aren't fully established at the outset. You learn as you play.

On a show like "Survivor" or "The Apprentice," the participants – and the audience – know the general objective of the series, but each episode involves new challenges that haven't been ordained in advance. The final round of the first season of "The Apprentice," for instance, threw a monkey wrench into the strategy that governed the play up to that point, when Trump announced that the two remaining apprentices would have to assemble and manage a team of subordinates who had already been fired in earlier episodes of the show. All of a sudden the overarching objective of the game – do anything to avoid being fired – presented a potential conflict to the remaining two contenders: the structure of the final round favored the survivor who had maintained the best relationships with his comrades. Suddenly, it wasn't enough just to have clawed your way to the top; you had to have made friends while clawing. The original "Joe Millionaire" went so far as to undermine the most fundamental convention of all – that the show's creators don't openly lie to the contestants about the prizes – by inducing a construction worker to pose as man of means while 20 women competed for his attention.

Reality programming borrowed another key ingredient from games: the intellectual labor of probing the system's rules for weak spots and opportunities. As each show discloses its conventions, and each participant reveals his or her personality traits and background, the intrigue in watching comes from figuring out how the participants should best navigate the environment that has been created for them. The pleasure in these shows comes not from watching other people being humiliated on national television; it comes from depositing other people in a complex, high-pressure environment where no established strategies exist and watching them find their bearings. That's why the water-cooler conversation about these shows invariably tracks in on the strategy displayed on the previous night's episode: why did Kwame pick Omarosa in that final round? What devious strategy is Richard Hatch concocting now?

When we watch these shows, the part of our brain that monitors the emotional lives of the people around us – the part that tracks subtle shifts in intonation and gesture and facial expression – scrutinizes the action on the screen, looking for clues. We trust certain characters implicitly and vote others off the island in a heartbeat. Traditional narrative shows also trigger emotional connections to the characters, but those connections don't have the same participatory effect, because traditional narratives aren't explicitly about strategy. The phrase "Monday-morning quarterbacking" describes the engaged feeling that spectators have in relation to games as opposed to stories. We absorb stories, but we second-guess games. Reality programming has brought that second-guessing to prime time, only the game in question revolves around social dexterity rather than the physical kind.

THE REWARDS OF SMART CULTURE

The quickest way to appreciate the Sleeper Curve's cognitive training is to sit down and watch a few hours of hit programming from the late 70's on Nick at Nite or the SOAPnet channel or on DVD. The modern viewer who watches a show like "Dallas" today will be bored by the content – not just because the show is less salacious than today's soap operas (which it is by a small margin) but also because the show contains far less information in each scene, despite the fact that its soap-opera structure made it one of the most complicated narratives on television in its prime. With "Dallas," the modern viewer doesn't have to think to make sense of what's going on, and not having to think is boring. Many recent hit shows – "24," "Survivor," "The Sopranos," "Alias," "Lost," "The Simpsons," "E.R." – take the opposite approach, layering each scene with a thick network of affiliations. You have to focus to follow the plot, and in focusing you're exercising the parts of your brain that map social networks, that fill in missing information, that connect multiple narrative threads.

Of course, the entertainment industry isn't increasing the cognitive complexity of its products for charitable reasons. The Sleeper Curve exists because there's money to be made by making culture smarter. The economics of television syndication and DVD sales mean that there's a tremendous financial pressure to make programs that can be watched multiple times, revealing new nuances and shadings on the third viewing. Meanwhile, the Web has created a forum for annotation and commentary that allows more complicated shows to prosper, thanks to the fan sites where each episode of shows like "Lost" or "Alias" is dissected with an intensity usually reserved for Talmud scholars. Finally, interactive games have trained a new generation of media consumers to probe complex environments and to think on their feet, and that gamer audience has now come to expect the same challenges from their television shows. In the end, the Sleeper Curve tells us something about the human mind. It may be drawn toward the sensational where content is concerned – sex does sell, after all. But the mind also likes to be challenged; there's real pleasure to be found in solving puzzles, detecting patterns or unpacking a complex narrative system.

In pointing out some of the ways that popular culture has improved our minds, I am not arguing that parents should stop paying attention to the way their children amuse themselves. What I am arguing for is a change in the criteria we use to determine what really is cognitive junk food and what is genuinely nourishing. Instead of a show's violent or tawdry content, instead of wardrobe malfunctions or the F-word, the true test should be whether a given show engages or sedates the mind. Is it a single thread strung together with predictable punch lines every 30 seconds? Or does it map a complex social network? Is your on-screen character running around shooting everything in sight, or is she trying to solve problems and manage resources? If your kids want to watch reality TV, encourage them to watch "Survivor" over "Fear Factor." If they want to watch a mystery show, encourage "24" over "Law and Order." If they want to play a violent game, encourage Grand Theft Auto over Quake. Indeed, it might be just as helpful to have a rating system that used mental labor and not obscenity and violence as its classification scheme for the world of mass culture.

Kids and grown-ups each can learn from their increasingly shared obsessions. Too often we imagine the blurring of kid and grown-up cultures as a series of violations: the 9-year-olds who have to have nipple broaches explained to them thanks to Janet Jackson; the middle-aged guy who can't wait to get home to his Xbox. But this demographic blur has a commendable side that we don't acknowledge enough. The kids are forced to think like grown-ups: analyzing complex social networks, managing resources, tracking subtle narrative intertwinings, recognizing long-term patterns. The grown-ups, in turn, get to learn from the kids: decoding each new technological wave, parsing the interfaces and discovering the intellectual rewards of play. Parents should see this as an opportunity, not a crisis. Smart culture is no longer something you force your kids to ingest, like green vegetables. It's something you share.

Steven Johnson is the author, most recently, of "Mind Wide Open." His book "Everything Bad Is Good for You: How Today's Popular Culture Is Actually Making Us Smarter," from which this article is adapted, will be published next month.

Celebrities Really Are More Narcissistic Than the Rest of Us

Dr. Drew Pinky

Particularly after the success of [my early career], I noticed my narcissism got dialed up. Suddenly, for a minute, I felt like everyone needed to take a knee and listen to what I had to say, because I fuckin' made it, and my way works, and all this stuff. Then [I'd] go home and I go, "Oh, my God, what's happening to me? I gotta get grounded here."

—Robert Downey, Jr.

I went from being a young senator to being considered for vice president, running for president . . . becoming a national public figure. All of which fed a self-focus, an egotism, a narcissism that leads you to believe you can do whatever you want, you're invincible and there will be no consequences."

—John Edwards, after his extramarital affair was revealed

Think about it. Just the thought of wanting to get into comedy—you have to think you are funny. You have to be narcissistic.

—Artie Lange, on The Howard Stern Show

I'd say it's the one quality that unites everybody in the film industry, whether you're an actor, a producer, a director, or a studio executive. You want people to look at you and love you and go, "Oh, you're wonderful." It's a nightmare. Narcissism is the part of my personality that I am the least proud of, and I certainly don't like to see it highlighted in everybody else I meet. It's like all things in life: You have these qualities in you that are awful, and the best you can do is to try to be aware of them and actively try to diminish them.

—Ben Affleck, Interview, December 1997

As we saw, everyone has narcissistic tendencies; narcissism can be a positive as well as a negative motivating force. When channeled productively, it can drive one's success and promote a healthy impulse to make one's mark in the world. There's no doubt in my mind that celebrities, as a rule, have high levels of narcissism. There's also no doubt in my mind that, whether through self-awareness, or intermittent or ongoing analysis and treatment, many celebrities are able to keep their narcissism under control, connect with their real selves, and engage in fully connected lives.

For instance, a star like Oprah Winfrey, who has admitted to childhood abuse and has struggled with sexual promiscuity and food issues, has seemingly learned to acknowledge, appreciate, and modulate any narcissistic tendencies she may have had. She is conscious of the effect her actions have on others, and has clearly benefited by channeling her strong motivational drive toward positive behaviors and incredible success, both for herself and for the countless others she now reaches out to help.

Many performers have talked openly about the narcissism they have seen in themselves or among others in their profession. Actor William Hurt, for example, has decried what he sees as the "pathological sickness" of our celebrity culture, describing celebrities and their fans as "narcissists on screen being consumed by narcissists off screen." Hurt recognizes the role of narcissism in any actor's psyche: "When you walk into a room, eyes are on you. . . . After enough years, you [develop] the confidence to stare back. But the mendacity of it is, you start to believe it – that somehow you are the center of the room, of the universe, somehow you are [better than] the people around you. . . . And then how do you work?"

Succeeding as an entertainer is extremely difficult. Those who try face constant rejection, even humiliation. Any entertainer can be a success one day and a complete failure the next. And few of those who become famous, or aspire to, are self-aware enough to acknowledge the psychological motivators that drove them. Strong narcissistic traits can propel certain people forward. While many may turn to substances along the way, it's their narcissism that ultimately drives them to get up and try again. Consider the former stars who continue to sign up for celebrity-based reality shows like *The Surreal Life, Celebrity Fit Club, I'm a Celebrity . . . Get Me Out of Here!*, or *Dancing with the Stars*: Nothing demonstrates a celebrity's basic drive for attention more powerfully than a willingness to check one's dignity at the door, week after week, in front of millions of viewers.

The more celebrities I met, the more apparent it was that these individuals possessed strongly pronounced narcissistic traits. The more I knew about the celebrities I met, the more obvious it was that these narcissistic traits were established long before the person became famous. I began to wonder if seeking to become famous was, in fact, a strategy for narcissists to manage – or even self-treat – their chronic feelings of emptiness. My experience and training told me that my theory was a highly plausible explanation for many of the celebrity behaviors I had observed.

But Mark, as a social scientist, was intent on scientifically studying this claim. There is a phenomenon called *self-selection* in which individuals with the same characteristics become a group that is defined by the characteristics that brought them together. If the world of celebrity was a self-selected group of narcissistic individuals, as I believed, Mark and I reasoned that it should be possible to demonstrate scientifically.

With that in mind, we launched what would be the first in-depth scientific study of celebrity personality.

To collect data for the study, we turned to a well-known psychological survey known as the Narcissistic Personality Inventory (NPI). Developed in the late 1970s, by psychological researchers Robert Raskin and Calvin S. Hall, the NPI has since been used in hundreds of narcissism studies. For our study, we used a refinement of the original survey published in 1988 by Raskin and Howard Terry.

The NPI alone cannot determine whether an individual suffers from narcissistic personality disorder. That kind of diagnosis must be performed in a clinical setting over an extended period of time. Rather, we used the NPI to identify and evaluate the levels of the seven component traits of narcissism we introduced earlier: authority, entitlement, exhibitionism, exploitativeness, self-sufficiency, superiority, and vanity. A true narcissistic personality manifests each of these characteristic traits to a varying degree.

To review those seven traits more closely:

Authority is related to superiority, and can be an asset under certain circumstances. A person needs authority to carry out responsibilities, sometimes without concern for others. An individual with a healthy sense of authority usually has the achievement and expertise to justify that authority, and is able to recognize the outcome of his actions on others. Unhealthy narcissists, on the other hand, are often highly authoritarian, even when such behavior undercuts their intentions. Moreover, highly narcissistic individuals often display unregulated aggression, and aggression can amplify authority in ways that can be quite unpleasant for others. Authoritarian narcissists generally feel justified in their actions and have little appreciation of the effect they have on others.

For narcissists with a high authority level, power and control are paramount. They are driven to regulate every aspect of their environment, including the actions of those around them, which is an unconscious compensation for feelings of childhood helplessness. Because narcissists have such a severely impaired ability to trust, they must present their opinions as unassailable. Paradoxically, the strident attitude of highly authoritarian narcissists often undercuts their chances of getting what they want from others. For instance, excessively authoritarian parents can make their children feel unheard, or, worse, convince them that their feelings don't matter. Rather than valuing their children as unique individuals with legitimate opinions of their own, they expect their children to step in line with their expectations, no questions asked.

It's no surprise that some celebrities seem to have an excessively high sense of their own authority; each new season, the competition-based reality shows turn up a handful of stars who eagerly seize the alpha-dog role (and usually succumb to their own hubris within a few episodes). This kind of behavior also marks those who use their fame to promote themselves as experts in areas unrelated to their profession, from politics to foreign policy to the efficacy of prescription drugs or psychiatry. Because their celebrity allows them to speak to millions, such figures can confuse the weight of their authority with that of international relations scholars, tenured economists, or experienced medical professionals.

Entitlement seems to be on the rise among narcissists today, and may be supported by a general tendency toward entitlement in our culture. The doctrine of "American exceptionalism" has long been a part of our national identity, and in a nation where "We're number one!" is the rallying cry, it's no surprise that many people feel they're entitled to have anything they want. What's more, if reality doesn't cooperate with their desires, they simply blame whoever gets in their way. Personal responsibility is the opposite of entitlement: To the highly entitled narcissist, to require any sacrifice is to trigger envy, resentment, and rage.

Entitlement is one of the narcissistic celebrity's most common coping mechanisms. Mark interviewed the owner of a business that runs the valet parking service at several Los Angeles celebrity hot spots. The owner reported that celebrities very often refuse, or "forget," to pay for the service of parking their cars. When confronted, they blame the staff for not telling them there was a charge, claim that they "never carry money," or simply try to leave without paying.

Some stars take things much further, demanding that businesses close their doors to regular customers so they can shop, sometimes without offering to pay for the merchandise they select. Concierge.com recently voted Mariah Carey one of the world's worst hotel guests for her diva behavior: According to hotel owners, she has demanded that her suites be equipped with gold faucets, new toilet seats, and mineral water for her to bathe in, and her dogs to drink. The Web site thesmokinggun.com has published scores of contract riders in which entertainers list their green room requirements, from the gratuitously inconvenient (hard-to-find foods, beverages served at specific temperatures, or a private flush toilet with a *new, unused* seat) to the outright ridiculous (freshly painting and decorating the dressing room to exacting instructions). And celebrities expect vendors at the gift suites at Hollywood events to provide them with extra goodie bags full of thousands of dollars' worth of free merchandise, from watches to jewelry to jeans.

Exhibitionism may be expressed as a desire to perform or speak before an audience, or it may decay to a primitive desire to be seen without clothing or even to act out in more dangerous ways. The stars of *Jackass*, Johnny Knox-ville and Steve-O, who attained celebrity by performing outrageous, arguably degrading stunts on themselves and others, serve as perfect examples of the latter breed of exhibitionism.

Some have speculated that such acting out may be deeply rooted in our genes, as a way to display genetic prowess and adaptability. In this theory, males (in particular) who survive dangerous stunts are displaying their biologi-cal capacity to survive in adversity. Such behavior obviously requires a narcis-sistic sense of invincibility. By the same token, it's been argued that both men and women who parade their sexuality openly are simply advertising their reproductive potential.

Exhibitionism can easily go off course when it becomes a compulsion or preoccupation. For evidence of Hollywood's penchant for exhibitionism, look no further than the parade of panty-free celebrities in recent years. But the Four Horsewomen aren't the only ones who have displayed their wares in a bid for public attention. At the age of twenty, Drew Barrymore leapt onto David Letterman's desk and flashed her breasts at him; she posed nude for *Playboy* the same year. Janet Jackson gave us the phrase "wardrobe mal-function" with her infamous Super Bowl appearance in 2004. Paparazzi rou-tinely scan beaches the world over with telephoto lenses, looking to catch Jennifer Aniston or the girls from *The Hills* sunbathing topless on the beach. Men aren't immune to the same behavior; just ask Matthew McConaughey or Mario Lopez, neither of whom can seem to find a shirt. Miley Cyrus may not have flashed much more than her midriff and bare back, but I can't help worrying that she's put herself on a slippery slope.

Yet nothing speaks to exhibitionism more than the explosion of celebrity sex tapes. In 1998, a home video of Pam Anderson and then-husband Tommy Lee having sex on a yacht was allegedly stolen from their home and distributed without their permission by the Internet Entertainment Group, although many now believe that Pam and Tommy played a behind-the-scenes role in the tape's release. In its initial distribution, the video generated $1.5 million in revenues and continues to sell well today. The Anderson-Lee video wasn't the first time we had seen famous people naked, of course; nude pictures of celebrities had circulated for years, and a surprising number of actresses and models had even agreed to pose in carefully retouched *Playboy* pictorials or to appear briefly nude in the occasional film. The closest thing to the Pam-and-Tommy tape was in 1988, when a blurry hotel-room tape nearly killed Rob Lowe's career.

But this was the first time one of the world's most desired women was seen onscreen having intimate relations, and much had changed in those ten years. By the mid-1990s, explicit sex of every kind was widely available online. But Pam Anderson was not a porn star, she was a mainstream actress. The moment that tape was released, it blurred the line between the private person and the performer. It gave anyone interested, whether casually or lasciviously, direct access to her sexuality, beyond even what the trained performers in porn films afford.

Twenty, even ten years earlier, Pam Anderson and Tommy Lee might have slinked off into exile, waiting for memories to fade. Instead, the incident only increased their Q rating. The old phenomenon of public shame was overridden by the temptations of narcissism. The tape spawned hundreds of copycats, and to this day new tapes surface constantly, particularly from minor celebrities hoping to reinvigorate their careers. The Internet gave rise to dozens of fakes, purporting to feature celebrities like Lindsay Lohan, Britney Spears, Jimi Hendrix, even Marilyn Monroe. But there were also plenty of authentic instances of celebrities playing amateur porn star:

- *Paris Hilton* and then-boyfriend Rick Salomon (2003). Their tape was ultimately approved by Paris and released under the title *1 Night in Paris* (2003).
- *Colin Farrell* and *Playboy* Playmate *Nicole Narain* (2004). Farrell successfully blocked distribution of the tape, only to see it surface on the Internet in 2006.
- *Gena Lee Nolan* of *Baywatch* and former husband Greg Fahlman (2004).
- *Pamela Anderson* and *Bret Michaels*, lead singer of Poison (2005).
- *Fred Durst* of Limp Bizkit and an unknown woman (2005).
- *Keeley Hazlett*, a model for British tabloid *The Sun*, and her ex-boyfriend (2007).
- *Amy Fisher*, the so-called Long Island Lolita who became famous for shooting her boyfriend's wife in 1992, and husband Lou Bellera (2008).
- *Verne Troyer* (Mini-Me from the Austin Powers movies) and his girlfriend, Ranae Shrider (2008).

When Dustin Diamond, who played the awkward adolescent Screech in the early '90s series *Saved by the Bell*, was widely mocked for his 2006 tape, it may have seemed like a death rattle for the sex-tape phenomenon. Then along came Kim Kardashian, a Hollywood club girl whose biggest claim to fame was being friends with Paris Hilton. When she appeared in a tape with rapper Ray J in 2007, it propelled her to instant fame, marking the first time a star was born purely because of a sex tape.

Exploitativeness is probably the most pernicious trait in the inventory. There is little positive usefulness to being exploitative, which requires a disregard for other people's priorities and feelings. Like any trait, it can appear in milder or stronger doses: It's only mildly exploitative, for example, to befriend someone who has an interesting career, wide intelligence, or even desirable possessions, in hopes of benefiting from the friendship. The true measure of the exploitation is in whether you get to know this new friend well, or simply use him for your own self-interest.

Individuals who are highly exploitative have trouble accurately appreciating other people's feelings. They are uncomfortable allowing themselves to be vulnerable or open in an interpersonal context, and prefer to keep their relationships utilitarian. They take advantage of situations to serve their own interests, whatever the cost to others. When former presidential candidate John Edwards admitted to having an affair with Rielle Hunter, a videographer he had hired to create Internet ads for his presidential campaign, he defended himself by exploiting a family tragedy, lamenting in a TV interview that he'd felt "slapped down to the ground when my son Wade died in April of 1996."

Arguably every stage mother is exploitative to some degree, but Dina Lohan, the mother of Lindsay Lohan, seems particularly willing to use her family's notoriety (thanks to Lindsay's exploits and to Dina's own particularly nasty divorce from her husband, Michael) to push her youngest daughter, Ali, into the spotlight. I can't imagine how Dina can believe that launching Ali onto the same show-business trajectory as Lindsay would result in a healthy lifestyle for her younger daughter. Yet, with Lindsay now out of her control, Dina, as mom and manager, has decided to build the reality show *Living Lohan* around Ali. Can eleven-year-old Cody be far behind?

In a similar vein, Britney and Jamie Lynne's mother, Lynne Spears, recently published a book about raising her daughters, a topic on which her authority is questionable at best. In *Through the Storm: A Real Story of Fame and Family in a Tabloid World*, she writes about "a dark period" in her Britney's life and discusses the challenges she faced in raising Britney and Jamie Lynn. Perhaps it would have been more revealing if Lynne Spears had waited a bit longer to write this book, as I believe that Britney literally owes her life to her mother and father's decision to step in and parent their adult daughter in the face of extremely challenging circumstances.

Self-sufficiency is one personality trait that doesn't sound like a liability. In clinical terms, self-sufficiency refers to a high degree of confidence in one's own ability or point of view. What could be wrong with that? The problem is that overly self-sufficient people can find it difficult to collaborate, or to register other people's points of view. Furthermore, when this trait strongly predominates, it can interfere with a person's ability to ask for help. For example, children who have survived trauma consistently hover close to their teacher until they hit their head or have some other tender need, at which point they hide in the corner and become unreachable. At just the moment when the child should be reaching out for help in dealing with an overwhelming feeling, he turns away from the person who can help, because prior experience has taught the child that his need will be either painfully ignored or purposely intensified.

In adulthood, this lesson can harden into a brittle self-sufficiency, locking the narcissist into his perceptions and experiences and closing off the potential for more flexible emotional regulation. Extreme self-sufficiency may even foster mild paranoia when the narcissist's worldview is challenged.

The celebrity world is full of people who put great stock in their own self-sufficiency. Donald Trump displays high levels of the trait, as does Gene Simmons, who prides himself on managing his career on his own, without agent or publicists. The rapper Snoop Dogg paraded his self-sufficiency in a conversation with MTV's Shaheem Reid last year: "Me and Pharrell [Williams] went into the studio last night, and we're gonna start on this album called *Ego Trippin'*. I'ma do the whole record. Me. By myself. I don't want no guest rappers, no singer, nothing. Just Snoop Dogg. I want you to feel me." But this brand of blustery narcissism isn't the only signifier of self-sufficiency: There are plenty of other examples, from working actors who claim they manage all their childcare themselves to the frequent tendency for celebrities to declare themselves experts in medical or health issues and, instead of asking for help from genuine professionals, turning to pseudo-professionals they declare to be "special" or "the best."

Superiority is closely related to authority and entitlement. It's a belief that one is better than others, and thus entitled to deference or special treatment. In moderation, this trait can help individuals to influence or lead others. However, when an individual with unhealthy feelings of superiority tries to assert his dominance over others, superiority can also devolve into threatening behavior. Studies show that rapists believe they are superior to women, and domestic violence commonly results from a compulsion to exert superiority over a partner one perceives as disobedient.

A person's feelings of superiority can be fed when he interacts regularly with a person or group he considers inferior. Hollywood lore is rife with stories of how celebrities torture their personal assistants, an image that's been a comic staple from *The Devil Wears Prada* to *Entourage*. The refrain "Don't you know who I am?" is the cry of the narcissist with high levels of superiority, who demands immediate recognition. The special treatment demanded by most celebrities sends a not-so-subtle signal that they consider themselves better than those around them.

Vanity, of course, has much to do with superiority and exhibitionism, but there are aspects of clinical vanity that go beyond a preoccupation with oneself and one's appearance. Vanity, which also involves an inflated sense of one's abilities, tends to fuel a narcissist's denial. We've all seen individuals who have some ability but clearly overestimate their talents or achievements. When forced to face reality, particularly after they have blatantly misrepresented their qualifications, narcissists are often able to carry on, clinging to their vain sense of self, often fueled by a sense of superiority and/or authority. (The defiant, deluded behavior of dismissed *American Idol* contestants comes to mind.)

It seems almost redundant to single out examples of vanity among genuine celebrities. Suffice to say, most of the entertainers I've met exhibit a strong sense of vanity, whatever their levels of attractiveness or talent. Think of the celebrities who appear in so-called candid photos every week, caught heading to the grocery store with their hair and makeup done and sporting four-inch heels. Or consider the celebrity who's caught in an unflattering photo, only to invite showers of praise a few months later for their remarkable weight loss or suddenly fresh-faced appearance. And, remember, vanity isn't always about appearance. When a book called *Trump Nation: The Art of Being the Donald* reported that Donald Trump's net worth was between $150 and $250 million, instead of the billions he claimed, Trump sued the author and publisher for $5 billion in damages, alleging that the claim hurt his "brand and reputation."

While not everyone with high levels of vanity will turn to the legal system to validate their narcissistic self-perceptions, the truth is that it's rare to find a narcissist who is not deeply preoccupied with how he appears to others. Lacking any deep sense of self, narcissists rely on their outward appearance for a sense of personal worth. When celebrities demand to be portrayed solely through idealized images, their vain projections become grist for a distorted measurement of beauty, success, and self-worth for the rest of us.

The Narcissistic Personality Inventory is what's called a *forced-choice* survey: Presented with two statements, the subject must choose the one he most agrees with, even if he doesn't completely agree with either. Individuals taking the NPI are given a booklet containing forty pairs of statements. In each case, one of the choices is the narcissistic choice; the other is the nonnarcissistic choice. The score is determined by adding up the number of narcissistic choices the subject makes out of a possible forty. (The full NPI and scoring key are provided in the appendix, along with information on how to determine your overall score, your component trait score, and what these scores may indicate regarding where you fall on the scale of narcissism.)

The forty pairs of questions are designed to measure the seven traits of narcissism just discussed. Some of the traits are more complex to assess than others, so more questions pertain to some traits than others. For instance, eight questions relate to authority, only three to vanity. Because each trait is a component of narcissism, an individual's answers will reveal which of the seven aspects of narcissism are most strongly reflected in his or her personality. This can be illuminating when observing and understanding particular behaviors.

Over a two-year period, we gave the survey to two groups of subjects: celebrities and MBA students. Mark and I gave the test to celebrities in person during their visits to the *Loveline* studio, a laid-back, nonthreatening environment away from fans and the paparazzi. The MBA students took the NPI online.

The celebrity group was comprised of two hundred people: 142 males and 58 females. For purpose of our study, we defined a celebrity as someone prominent enough to be invited to appear on *Loveline*. The show has been broadcast for more than 25 years, co-hosted most recently with "Stryker" (KROQ DJ, Ted Stryker), and engineered by Anderson Cowan. The show's producer, Ann Ingold, is careful to select only those celebrities she knows will draw an audience, but this includes a wide variety of people, from porn stars to Oscar winners, rappers to opera stars, A-list movie stars to D-list reality show contestants. Our sample group represented a broad cross section of the entertainment industry, including comedians, actors, reality TV personalities, and musicians, all of whom appear regularly on television, in the movies, in magazines, and in concerts. Our subjects had from one year to thirty-eight years of experience in the entertainment industry, with an average of twelve years.

When we first came up with the idea for the study, Mark was concerned that we might not find enough willing participants. However, once we began approaching the *Loveline* guests his fears were immediately allayed: Every single person we asked to complete the survey agreed to do so. Most of them were not only willing, but very curious and anxious to know the results. Though we told the participants the study was designed to assess aspects of their personalities, we did not reveal the precise nature of the test, lest we influence their answers. (A few guests were unable to complete the survey due to time constraints; their surveys were eliminated from the study.)

We were careful to follow well-established research procedures when administering the survey. We made it clear to each subject that their participation was voluntary and not a requirement of being on *Loveline* and that he or she could stop filling out the survey at any time. We also guaranteed everyone anonymity – although, as you'll see in the appendix, certain celebrities were willing to publicly share their scores.

In undertaking the study we hoped to demonstrate scientifically the popular assumption (and our own observation) that celebrities were not only narcissists, but more narcissistic than average people. Given the entertainment industry's focus on female attractiveness, we wondered whether narcissism in male and female celebrities would follow trends in the general population, where men have been shown to be more narcissistic than women. Our intuition told us that women who pursued celebrity were, in fact, more narcissistic than their male counterparts. If this was the case, we would be able to show another difference between the celebrity and general populations when it came to measuring levels of narcissistic traits. We were also very curious about whether certain types of celebrities would score higher than others on the test. Many people believe that actors are very narcissistic, for instance, but no one had ever looked at whether levels of certain narcissistic traits corresponded to particular types of work in the entertainment industry. Finally, it was clear that even experts were split on why celebrities were so narcissistic. Some thought the industry created narcissism, while we believed that narcissists were attracted to the industry.

Answering this chicken-and-egg question would offer important insights into the nature of celebrity.

With these four questions in mind, we analyzed the results of our data:

1. ARE CELEBRITIES MORE NARCISSISTIC THAN THE GENERAL POPULATION?

The celebrities we surveyed had an average score of 17.84 out of 40 on the Narcissistic Personality Inventory. But how does that measure up against the average American?

To answer this question, we compared our celebrity data to that gathered by psychologists Joshua Foster, Keith Campbell, and Jean Twenge, who administered the NPI to a very large cross section of people in the United States (2,546 participants). Their data, published in 2003, showed the average NPI score for all participants was 15.3, with the average American males scoring higher than females. Thus, on average, celebrities are 17 percent more narcissistic than the general public.

Next, we compared the celebrity results with those of the two hundred MBA students (144 males and 56 females) to whom Mark gave the test online. The students' average age was twenty-nine; they had an average of five years' work experience, and all were in the final year of their MBA program. Anyone who has watched *The Apprentice* has probably wondered about the levels of narcissism among America's aspiring business leaders, and we felt these MBA students would make a useful comparison to the celebrities. If the celebrities were more narcissistic than the general population that was one thing, but showing that they were more narcissistic than aspiring business leaders would be even more compelling.

And that's exactly what happened. The MBA students' average NPI score was 16.18, about 6 percent higher than the general population's, and about 10 percent lower than the celebrity average. Male MBAs were significantly more narcissistic than female MBAs, and scored higher than the female MBAs in entitlement and self-sufficiency.

2. WHO ARE MORE NARCISSISTIC: MALE OR FEMALE CELEBRITIES?

According to the *Diagnostic and Statistical Manual of Mental Disorders* (the DSM-IV-TR), the American Psychiatric Association's digest of all recognized mental health disorders, men are more narcissistic in general than females. As our study showed, male MBA students were more narcissistic than female MBAs. When it came to male versus female celebrities, however, the findings from our study were surprising.

Among celebrities, females were significantly more narcissistic than males. The average female score among our celebrities was 19.26; among males it was 17.27. That means that female celebrities are, on average, 26 percent more narcissistic than the general population.

To understand this result, we drilled deeper into the results, looking at how male and female celebrities scored on the various traits that comprise the NPI. In four of those categories – entitlement, authority, self-sufficiency, and exploitativeness – there were no significant differences between men and women celebrities. In three others, however – exhibitionism, superiority, and vanity – female celebrities scored significantly higher than their male counterparts. These results suggest that female celebrities have a greater preoccupation with their physical appearance, and a greater sense of superiority, compared to their male counterparts.

This trend may be more circumstantial than genetic. For a woman to believe she can get noticed in Hollywood – in a business that focuses on beauty, youth, and glamour – would be practically impossible without high levels of exhibitionism, superiority, and vanity. And those female celebrities who do manage to attain fame are all too aware that the shelf life of women in show business can be woefully short. Narcissism is what drives any celebrity to rationalize increasingly obvious rounds of plastic surgery, suggestive outfits, or nude photo shoots. To her, each is a necessary step to keeping her persona looking good and in the public eye.

3. WHICH GROUP OF CELEBRITIES IS MOST NARCISSISTIC ACTORS, MUSICIANS, REALITY TV PERSONALITIES, OR COMEDIANS?

Among those four groups, one clearly came out on top: According to our study, reality TV personalities are more narcissistic than any other group, with a very high average score of 19.45. Reality stars scored highest for authority, self-sufficiency, and vanity. Comedians came in second, at 18.89, actors third at 18.54, and musicians last at 16.67.

There are very concrete reasons that reality TV personalities are generally more narcissistic than even traditional celebrities. As discussed, reality-show producers have told us they consciously seek out contestants who are vain and controlling, because they make for more dramatic, watchable television. And research shows that narcissists tend to make a very good first impression, so it's no surprise that casting agents and producers would be drawn to hire them.

More obviously, the people who try out for reality shows have a strong desire to be seen. Many of them believe they deserve stardom simply because of who they are. Talent and achievement are not necessary prerequisites. In fact, despite the hundreds of reality shows that have come and gone in the last few years, only a handful of individuals have been able to garner any type of sustainable career from these opportunities, often by continuing to appear on reality shows.

Elisabeth Hasselbeck, a former shoe designer, parlayed a 2001 stint on *Survivor* (on which she finished fourth) into a gig as a judge at the Miss Teen

USA Pageant and a host on Style Network's *The Look for Less.* In 2003, she auditioned for a permanent spot joining three other hosts on *The View.* Known for her conservative point of view and tearful conflicts with her cohosts, Hasselbeck had the dubious distinction of being voted the "worst interviewer on TV" in a 2008 AOL poll.

Adrianne Curry, the winner of the first season of *America's Next Top Model,* didn't exactly choose a traditional modeling career after her appearance on the show catapulted her into the public eye. She did some runway and print, but it was her 2004 stint on a second reality TV series, *The Surreal Life,* that really launched her career as a celebrity. On that show she met Christopher Knight (a.k.a. Peter Brady), and they parlayed their rocky romance into a third reality show: *My Fair Brady.* With other film and radio work and an ongoing modeling career, including a cover and two *Playboy* pictorials, Curry is one of the few reality TV personalities who have successfully extended their fifteen minutes of fame.

The questions that make up the NPI also allow us to study each group's tendency to favor specific narcissistic traits, and these scores offer some interesting insights as well. Although musicians appear to be the least narcissistic celebrity group, they did register the second highest scores on entitlement and self-sufficiency. One explanation for this result may be that a career in music requires one to display an authentic talent, on stage in real time, night after night. Either you can sing or play well or you can't. You can't fake it, and you can't get by on looks alone. Yet that doesn't stop musically proficient narcissists from making outlandish requests for their entourage, or believing they don't need anyone else to help them succeed – classic expressions of entitlement and self-sufficiency.

Comedians had the second highest overall NPI scores, and they scored highest on four of the traits, including exhibitionism, superiority, entitlement, and exploitativeness. One reason for this may be that many comedians suffered traumatic or chaotic childhoods. Comedians don't generally trade on good looks, which jibes with their low scores on vanity, but they're usually intelligent and creative, and often aggressive; feelings of superiority and entitlement, and a willingness to exploit situations to their benefit, would serve any comedian well in a stand-up routine. For such personalities, comedy can offer a solution to their narcissistic impulses. As a kid, comedian Bob Saget remembers, he was "so insecure that I [was viewed as] either really popular, as I was so funny, or a total geek." He vividly remembers acting out, doing the kinds of "delinquent things [that] the guys in *Jackass* do, what Jamie Kennedy does, or Tom Green," in what he calls "a nine-year-old's cry for attention."

Finally, the group of working actors we surveyed was notable for scoring third on almost every trait measured by the survey. Many actors seem aware of the role their individual psychologies play in their profession. They often speak out to acknowledge their discomfort with attention from fans, and their understanding of the privileges that come with fame, sometimes even admitting that narcissism is both a professional given and a potential hazard.

Frankie Muniz, who played the title role in *Malcolm in the Middle*, has been acting on stage, film, and TV since the age of eight. He scored an extremely low 10 on the NPI, making him not only 44 percent less narcissistic than the average celebrity, but also 35 percent less narcissistic than the average individual. Not surprisingly, Muniz now considers himself retired from show business and is pursuing a career in professional auto racing. "I fell into acting by accident and stayed and I made a lot of money," he says. "I had no trouble leaving the celebrity lifestyle behind when I discovered my true passion for race-car driving."

Another working actor, Diora Baird (a former Guess Jeans model who has accumulated twenty-nine film and TV credits in the last three years), scored an 11 on the survey. Diora is an extremely attractive woman who initially built her reputation on her voluptuous physical assets, which are often featured in her film roles. Yet her scores in the traits of vanity and exhibitionism were extremely low. Her higher scores were in the area of exploitativeness and authority. Diora explained that she "never really wanted to show my body, as I am actually a very shy person. However, I knew it was a means to an end. So, I suppose I did exploit the situation initially." It's no surprise that as Diora's career continues to accelerate, she's been able to exercise her authority to take more control over the roles she takes, and is moving away from her sexually charged persona toward more serious roles as an actress.

There are doubtless plenty of working entertainers who fit this profile. You may not be able to name many immediately, but that's the point; these are working practitioners who stay out of the limelight and don't court publicity except to promote their projects.

We suspect that there are also many actors who, while likely to score high on a narcissistic scale, have cultivated degrees of self-awareness and empathy that assist them in recognizing and checking unhealthy displays of narcissism. For these actors, and any individual who is high on the narcissism scale, the key to their continued success is being able to express their narcissistic traits in positive ways and to avoid the narcissist's tendency to exploit others to achieve what they want.

4. DOES THE ENTERTAINMENT INDUSTRY CREATE NARCISSISTIC TENDENCIES AMONG CELEBRITIES, OR ARE THE CELEBRITIES NARCISSISTIC BEFORE ENTERING THE INDUSTRY?

To us, this was the key question. Most people probably assume that fame leads to narcissism, that a constant diet of attention and adulation will give anyone a swelled head. As we've seen, though, narcissism isn't about ego, it's more about self-loathing and emptiness. And its causes are easily misunderstood.

Even psychological professionals have differed over the origins of narcissism. In the last decade or so, Robert B. Millman, professor of psychiatry at Cornell Medical School and the medical adviser to Major League Baseball, has coined the term *acquired situational narcissism* to describe how the fawning behavior of the entertainment industry and the audience may lead to heightened narcissism in celebrities. Millman theorizes that the support system of sycophants surrounding athletes, actors, politicians, musicians, and others may lead these celebrities to develop unhealthy levels of narcissism.

There's no doubt that the coddling environment enjoyed by most celebrities can fuel an amplified expression of narcissistic traits. But Millman's theory doesn't jibe with the scientific consensus that the driving force behind narcissism is early childhood trauma. When we initiated our study, we believed that narcissism itself was the primary motivator for individuals seeking fame, rather than a byproduct of the fame itself. We also wanted to test that theory, so we asked all participants a very straightforward question: "How many years of experience do you have working in the entertainment industry since your first paycheck?" Among the two hundred celebrities we surveyed, the average number of years of experience was twelve. The newest celebrity had one year in the business, the most experienced had thirty-eight years.

The point of this experience question was to determine whether prolonged immersion in the celebrity lifestyle had a measurable effect on a person's level of narcissism. If the popular assumption (and Millman's theory) were true – that celebrity creates toxic levels of narcissism – we would expect the NPI scores of more experienced celebrities to be higher than those of younger or less seasoned stars. The data said otherwise. Our survey revealed no correlation between the length of a performer's career and his NPI score.

This is likely to ring true with anyone who works with celebrities in a clinical or professional setting. When I work with patients, it's apparent to me that the issues they're grappling with don't originate in the present day. What I uncover at the root of all unhealthy narcissistic personalities, without exception, is profound childhood trauma.

Of course, our study looked only at average scores, and it's possible that the NPI scores of some individuals may be influenced by their history in the industry; but testing individuals repeatedly throughout their careers to monitor their levels of narcissism would be highly impractical and, in truth, beside the point. All the most rigorous research on narcissism has demonstrated that, regardless of any situational triggers in adulthood, narcissism is a deep-seated and complex dysfunction. And every celebrity patient I have worked with has confirmed to me, through the stories they have shared, willingly or reluctantly, that their issues have their roots not in an excess of praise in adulthood, but through some much deeper, and more damaging, childhood experience.

The results of our study on celebrities and narcissism were published in the *Journal of Research in Personality* in October 2006. Our research had shown not only that celebrities were generally more narcissistic than average, but that there were significant differences between male and female entertainers, and that certain types of performers consistently ranked higher than others, exhibiting high levels of specific narcissistic traits. At the time of our study, the average score for a person taking the NPI was 15.3 out of 40. Among the two hundred celebrities taking part in our study, the average was 17.84. There was an inverse relationship between the levels of discernible skills and the levels of narcissistic traits: talented performers, like musicians, scored lower (16.67) than celebrities with no readily discernible skills, such as reality stars (19.45). Comedians had an average score of 18.89; working actors averaged 18.54.

The study struck a chord in the cultural zeitgeist and the media was quick to pick up on the fact that it centered on celebrities. *The New York Times Magazine* named it one of "The Top 70 Ideas of 2006," and it made international headlines: the *Los Angeles Times* ("Celeb Note to Self: You are Fabulous – A Scientific Study Shows that Stars Really are Narcissists First"); Norway's *Business Daily* ("Mirror, Mirror on the Wall – Stars Are Their Own Biggest Fans"); *China Daily* ("Celebrities Really are More Narcissistic"); the *New York Daily News* ("I Love Me – Mirror, Mirror on the Wall: We Pick NYC's Biggest Egos of Them All").

The media may have picked up the story, but they missed the message. Almost without exception, the interviews and articles echoed our friend (and my then-cohost of *Loveline*) Adam Carolla's initial reaction to the survey: "Is this groundbreaking – that celebrities are narcissistic? I mean, this is like you found out Liberace was gay." There were plenty of jokes about "celebrity narcissism" – but very little real, informative discussion about the study and what it might really be telling us about celebrities. In nearly every interview I tried to turn the conversation around – to help people understand what narcissism really was and the pain inherent in a narcissistic personality disorder. In interview after interview, Mark and I stressed how important it was to understand that narcissists weren't "in love with themselves," and that our societal preoccupation with celebrity was fraught with negative implications. From our perspective, the real headline here was that the celebrity behaviors so many people strive to emulate grow out of a genuine personality disorder – a discovery with troubling implications for all of society.

As you'll recall, celebrities – like all narcissists – aren't "in love with themselves." They rely on the world as a mirror, constantly gazing outward in search of gratification or affirmation, in order to stave off their unbearable feelings of internal emptiness. When the image in the looking glass disappoints them, or fails in some way, they turn to other solutions.

These other solutions – addiction, extreme vanity, sexual drama and dysfunctional relationships, exploitativeness, and outrageous entitlement – have come to dominate celebrity culture. And it is the celebrities and their outrageous behavior on one side, and our preoccupation with celebrity on the other, that gives rise to the notion of the Mirror Effect: the way that malignant forms of narcissism, as showcased by the media, can cause vulnerable everyday people to descend into dangerously narcissistic behaviors. And there is a third factor that significantly amplifies the Mirror Effect's potential influence on all of us: the twenty-first century media universe has become a potent delivery system with the power to spread those behaviors from celebrity circles to society at large.

Michigan Journal of Community Service Learning Fall 2008, pp.5–17

"A Double-Edged Sword": College Student Perceptions of Required High School Service-Learning

Susan R. Jones, Thomas C. Segar, and Anna L. Gasiorski

SUSAN R. JONES is an associate professor and program director in the College Student Personnel program at the University of Maryland-College Park. Much of her research focuses on service-learning in relation to requirements, resistance, student identity development, faculty motivations, and partnerships. She is a previous Ohio Campus Compact faculty fellow and has served on the boards of an AIDS service organization and after-school tutoring program.

THOMAS C. SEGAR is a doctoral student in the College Student Personnel program at the University of Maryland-College Park. He has held positions as a college administrator in residence life, multicultural student affairs, learning assistance, and disability support services for ten years prior to beginning doctoral studies. Tom earned his master's of science degree in counseling with a specialization in college student personnel from Shippensburg University of Pennsylvania, and his bachelor's of science degree in Psychology, with a certificate in African American studies, from the University of Maryland-College Park.

ANNA GASIORSKI currently works for the Ohio Learning Network as manager of quality data control. She is a doctoral candidate in the College Student Personnel program at the University of Maryland- College Park. She received her master's degree from the University of Michigan and her bachelor's degree from the College of William and Mary. Her research interests include service-learning and adult students, student resistance, and predictors of community service participation among college students.

This article presents the findings from a narrative inquiry exploring the perceived outcomes associated with a high school service-learning graduation requirement from a diverse group of college students. In particular, we were interested in participants' stories related to their experiences meeting the requirement, the meaning they made of the requirement, and the relationship between their high school experiences and college involvement. Results suggest a tenuous connection between the two because students focused primarily on completing their hours for the requirement and engaged in service primarily at their schools. Students perceived the requirement as a burden while in high school, but retrospectively understood the value of the requirement once they were in college, describing it as a "double-edged sword."

With increased national, university, and community attention focused on civic engagement and participation, service-learning is increasingly touted as an efficacious strategy to promote such goals (Eyler & Giles, 1999; Hart, Donnelly, Youniss, & Atkins, 2007; Metz & Youniss, 2003; Raskoff & Sundeen, 1999). Growing numbers of high school and college students are involved in community service and volunteering (Higher Education Research Institute, 2006; Spring, Dietz, & Grimm, 2006). Drawing upon data from the U.S. Census Bureau, the Corporation for National & Community Service (CNS) reports a 20% increase in the number of college students who volunteered from 2002 to 2005, attributing this in part to what they referred to as the "9/11 Generation." However, evidence exists to suggest that college students are involved in more "episodic," short-term volunteer activities which may not be directly related to the cultivation of patterns of participation needed for civic engagement (Dote, Cramer, Dietz, & Grimm, 2006; Marks & Jones, 2004) and that college student volunteer activity is on the decline (HERI, 2006). To promote a "culture of college service," the service-learning "pipeline" (Dote et al., p. 3) from high schools to college must be examined.

Community service and service-learning requirements are increasingly common among high schools and colleges, presumably as one strategy to promote continued community participation. Indeed, many school districts throughout the United States have established community service graduation requirements (Education Commission of the States, 2001). However, only Maryland has a statewide mandatory service-learning high school graduation requirement. Implemented in 1997, this mandate stipulates that all students who attend public high schools complete a minimum of 75 service-learning hours. Existing research on the link between required service and continued participation is mixed at best and does not match the certainty with which requirements are increasingly pursued in an effort to develop patterns of civic engagement and continued service (e.g., Deci & Ryan, 1987; Jennings &

Stoker, 2004; Jones & Hill, 2003; Marks & Jones, 2004; McLellan & Youniss, 2003; Metz & Youniss, 2003; Stukas, Clary, & Snyder, 1999). For example, CNS research reports that the state of Maryland is ranked 34th among all states in college student volunteering, with a 30.2% volunteering rate (Dote et al., 2006). This is surprising given that 46.2% of all Maryland public high school graduates become college students in the state's public and private colleges and universities (Maryland State Department of Education, 2006).

What is clear is that despite growing interest in service-learning in high schools and colleges, and investment of resources in promoting such activities, very little is known about the effectiveness of service-learning requirements in promoting civic engagement and continued community involvement (Niemi, Hepburn, & Chapman, 2000). No studies investigate how a statewide service-learning requirement influences students' future intentions to serve in college or beyond, or other outcomes associated with a requirement.

COMPETING RATIONALES FOR REQUIRED SERVICE

Early conceptual arguments associating education and service as a means of encouraging post secondary community involvement can be traced back over 100 years to educational pioneer John Dewey (Harkavy, 2004). More recent advocates such as Ernest Boyer (1983), former Federal Commissioner of Education, recommended mandatory high school service as a means of preparing students to assume responsibility for living as contributing members of their community and society during and after high school. Barber (1994) documented the historical trend of teaching citizenship through service noting that only in recent history has service been separated from education. This rationale positions service in primary and secondary education as a means of promoting continued service involvement in adulthood. Although these arguments may ring true for some, they are not grounded in or borne out in empirical research.

The number of college students who participated in service while in high school has steadily increased over the past two decades (Chronicle Almanac, 2007). According to the Cooperative Institutional Research Program about one-third of first-year college students graduated from high schools with some type of requirement for service (Vogelgesang, 2005). High school service requirements are more prevalent for students attending private and/or religious high schools (Raskoff & Sundeen, 1999). However, data on collegiate service involvement suggested the number of high school students continuing with service participation in college may be falling. Vogelgesang and Astin (2005) found that the number of high school seniors engaged in service has increased over the past decade, while participation in service during and after college has declined during the same time period.

RELATIONSHIP BETWEEN HIGH SCHOOL AND COLLEGE SERVICE

A review of empirical evidence suggests that the nature of the relationship between mandatory high school service and continued participation in college service is ambiguous. Although a number of studies (e.g., Astin & Sax, 1998; Berger & Milem, 2002; Eyler & Giles, 1999; Hart et al., 2007; Vogelgesang, 2005) have identified high school service as a predictor of college involvement, when the research has focused on required service the results are less clear. Further, the research that does exist examining the outcomes associated with required community service or service-learning suggests a disconnect between the espoused goals, objectives, and purposes of required service and what students actually experience. However, what is clear is that college students bring with them to higher education a whole range of characteristics, including the vestiges of their high school experiences (Cruce & Moore, 2007; McEwen, 2003).

For example, in two longitudinal studies of multiple student cohorts at one public high school in suburban Boston, Metz and Youniss (2003, 2005) found that the completion of a 40-hour service requirement was related to higher rates of high school volunteerism and also associated with an increase in students' intentions to volunteer in the future. However, consistent with HERI results, this study focused on intentions, rather than actual college service activity. In several studies that explored this relationship between high school and college participation, patterns emerge that suggest requirements do not necessarily result in continued service in college. Great variability exists in factors such as school structures to support the requirement and the nature of activities in which students engage to meet their requirement, which have been found to make a difference in outcomes associated with service (McLellan & Youniss, 2003). Further, Jennings and Stoker (2004), in a longitudinal quantitative study, found the effects of students' high school participation in community service may not immediately translate into college involvement.

Marks and Jones (2004) analyzed data from the National Educational Longitudinal Study (NELS) database which contains measures of several educational outcomes. They found that students who attended Catholic high schools and performed service as a requirement were more likely to discontinue serving in college. This trend held true for students who participated in community service as 10th graders or were mandated to perform community service as seniors. Students who were encouraged, but not required, to volunteer as 12th graders were more likely to continue volunteering in college.

Jones and Hill (2003) discovered that college students who participated in service in high school tended to continue in college if their motivation came from an internal commitment along with family and school encouragement. Those who participated more sporadically because of a requirement or to build up their resume were not likely to continue serving once they entered college.

Interviews with participants revealed two reasons against required service. First, if service is framed as a requirement, then it was no longer considered service. Second, students worked only toward completing the requirement and discontinued service once they met the conditions of the requirement. Service requirements can deter any lasting continued involvement in students as well as civic or social responsibility (Jones & Hill). Therefore, service becomes "just another homework assignment" (p. 524).

Finally, Stukas, Snyder, and Clary (1999), in a study of college students enrolled in a service-learning course, found that if students only perform service when required, they are less likely to freely volunteer in the future. This was affected by how much prior community service students had completed. Students with significant prior experience with service were less likely to be negatively influenced by required community service. However, if they had little to no prior experience, they were more likely to decide not to volunteer in the future. Researchers found that student choice regarding type of volunteering emerged as one way to counteract the negative impact of required service (Stukas, Snyder, & Clary).

The overall results from these studies suggest that students who participated in service in high school tended to continue in college if they made an internal commitment and received strong family and school encouragement. Further, those who participated more sporadically because of a requirement or to bolster their resume were not likely to continue serving once they entered college (Jones & Hill, 2003; Marks & Jones, 2004). To date, no studies provide compelling evidence to support the efficacy of required high school service-learning as an impetus for a sustained commitment to service during and after college. As a result, current evidence leaves few clues as to how college practitioners might counter the mediating deterrents to service that may be rooted in the high school experience.

The purpose of this research was to explore the perceived outcomes associated with a high school service-learning requirement from a diverse group of college students. In particular, we were interested in investigating the nature of the service-learning experiences participants had in meeting the requirement, the meaning they made of those experiences, and how these experiences influenced (or not) their college experiences. Specific research questions guiding the investigation included: (a)What meaning do college students make of their high school service-learning requirement? (b) What influence does a high school requirement have on college involvement, particularly continued community service? (c) What is the congruence between espoused goals of high schools and the actual learning as perceived by graduates? (d) What are student perceptions of the requirement? and (e) How do students understand their own service experiences?

METHOD

This study utilized a constructivist theoretical framework and a narrative methodological approach. Because we were interested in students' constructions of meaning of their high school service-learning experiences, a constructivist framework, which assumes knowledge is mutually constructed between researchers and participants (Denzin & Lincoln, 2000) and emphasizes the role of context (Flyvbjerg, 2001), was appropriate. A constructivist design situates the focus of the investigation on research participants' meaning making of their experiences and perceptions of outcomes related to the service requirement (Jones, Torres, & Arminio, 2006).

To access these experiences and perceptions, narrative inquiry was utilized as an approach that illuminates human experiences as lived and told as stories (Chase, 2005; Clandinin & Connelly, 2000; Creswell, 2007; Lieblich, Tuval-Mashiach, & Zilber, 1998). Chase identified five characteristics of narrative inquiry: (1) narrative researchers treat narrative as retrospective meaning making; (2) narratives represent verbal action in the constructing of an experience; (3) narratives are constrained and augmented by context and particulars of time and place; (4) narratives are shaped by the time and setting of the telling and thus, are variable; and (5) narrative researchers serve as narrators as they interpret the stories told (pp. 656-657). Narrative inquiry was particularly well-suited to research grounded in the nature of experiences, reflection on these experiences, and the stories that emerge (Clandinin & Connelly, 2000), such as uncovering narratives that make up the stories of students' experiences with service in high school.

Research Context

In 1997, Maryland became the first state to implement a mandatory service-learning high school graduation requirement stipulating that all students attending public high schools complete a minimum of 75 service-learning hours. More than 99% of graduating seniors complete the 75 hour service-learning requirement prior to graduating from high school (http://www.marylandpublicschools.org/MSDE/prog rams/service-learning/). Maryland residents make up 75.9% of the total undergraduate population at the University of Maryland; therefore the undergraduate population of the University of Maryland alone contributed more than one million hours of service during their high school career.

Procedures

Sampling. Expert nominators who served as informants and purposeful sampling were used to obtain information-rich cases (Patton, 2002). Twenty-three faculty and administrators whom we knew to have reputations for working closely with undergraduate students were sent letters describing the purpose of the study and asked to nominate Maryland undergraduate students from Maryland public high schools. Nominators represented a variety of functional areas within the university (e.g., residence life, campus programs, student judicial programs, academic honoraries and clubs, living learning programs, programs for underrepresented groups, student employment, faculty in scholars programs).We indicated to nominators that we were seeking a wide range of perspectives and experiences and that we were not only looking for undergraduate students who were involved on Maryland's campus, either in community service or other activities, but those less involved on campus or involved in their home communities. We also indicated that we were seeking participants from around the state of Maryland (e.g., rural, suburban, urban), various school sizes (e.g., small, medium, large), and representing diversity in social group membership (e.g., race, ethnicity, social class).

The invitation to nominate student participants resulted in 209 nominations, with 9 out of the 209 duplicate names. We then sent email invitations to each of these 200 students, letting them know they had been nominated for participation and inviting them to participate. This resulted in 54 affirmative responses. Of these 54, 10 were ineligible because they either attended a private Maryland high school or an out-of-state public high school. We then sent to the 44 eligible participants an interest form to complete which asked questions about their high school, how they met their service-learning requirement, when during high school they completed their hours, where their high school was located, college involvements and affiliations, as well as demographic questions related to racial-ethnic background, class year, religion, and age. Forty-three students returned interest forms and then, based on our sampling criteria (e.g., county of high school, racial-ethnic diversity, variety in college involvement), we selected 28 students to interview. Upon selecting these 28 students, we sent email messages to schedule interviews. Nineteen students responded to these requests to schedule interviews.

Participants. The sample included 9 men and 10 women; racial-ethnic background consisted of 5 Asian American (1 Pakistani, 1 Korean, 1 Vietnamese, 1 Filipino,1 Asian American), 2 Biracial, 4 African American/ Black, and 8 white; from 10 different counties in the state; and 4 first-year students, 1 sophomore, 9 juniors, and 5 seniors. High school enrollment ranged from 300 to 3000; three high schools were categorized as rural, four as urban, and 12 as suburban. Students' college involvement covered a wide range, from not involved at all to highly involved. Examples of involvement included student government, community service related living and learning programs, various advisory councils, honor societies, and curricular and co-curricular student organizations. All names used are pseudonyms chosen by each participant.

Data collection. Data were collected through two in-depth interviews with each participant. So as not to overwhelm participants with a team of three interviewers, we divided up participants so that each researcher individually interviewed a subset of participants. Two interviews were conducted with each participant, and each participant had the same interviewer for both interviews so that rapport could be developed and a relationship established. Consistent with narrative inquiry, interviews were semi-structured and open-ended to elicit stories about service-learning experiences and how each participant understood those experiences (Chase, 2005; Lieblich, Tuval-Mashiach, & Zilber, 1998). The protocol for the first interview was pilot tested with three students who met the study sampling criteria and was revised based upon their feedback and our experiences with the protocol. The same protocol was used for each participant. The first interview focused on students' experiences meeting the high school service-learning requirement, their perceptions of the requirement, and the meaning they made of these. Consistent with narrative inquiry, we asked participants questions such as "Tell me about your high school experience;" How did you fulfill your high school requirement?" and "Can you tell me a story that you remember from your high school service-learning experience that you still think about today?" The second interview was utilized as an initial member check with emerging themes and to focus on how the state of Maryland describes the service-learning experience. Each participant was shown a copy of "Maryland's Best Practices" and the statement that "all service-learning experiences should meet *all* [emphasis in original] of the Maryland's Best Practices for Service-Learning" (Maryland State Department of Education, 2005, p. 6) and asked to respond to these practices in light of their own experiences.

Data analysis. Data were analyzed using the constant comparative method (Charmaz, 2006, Strauss & Corbin, 1998), with attention to the content of the narratives, using a categorical content approach (Lieblich, Tuval-Mashiach, & Zilber, 1998) which enabled us both to study the individual stories of each participant, but also to look across the stories for themes. Each researcher independently read and coded every interview and generated themes. We then came together to compare our codes and themes and to generate the patterns within and across all the narratives. We were careful to maintain the "voices within each narrative" (Chase, 2005, p. 663) as well as to listen for the themes that emerged across the interviews. This process led to a continuous process of returning to the interviews themselves to refine the themes and to assure that the themes generated remained close to the words and meanings of all participants. The themes were further revised as we moved from more descriptive categories to analytical and interpretive themes generated to tell the story of these participants.

Trustworthiness

To assure that our interpretive narrative, or re-storying of participants' narrations, was recognizable to our participants, we conducted member checks (Lincoln & Guba, 1985) as a strategy to assure the trustworthiness of findings. We recognized that interpreting others' stories brings with it an ethical responsibility to stay close to participants' meanings (Abes & Jones, 2004; Jones, 2002). To this end we used the second interview as a member check with each participant, reviewing emerging themes with them. As our data analysis proceeded, we then sent each participant a narrative summary, a four-page interpretive re-telling of their stories, presented as one story, and asked them to review this to assure that it accurately captured their experiences and individual story. Out of the 19 participants, 13 responded to this essay and affirmed what they read by stating "this sounds like me." Trustworthiness was also enhanced by the presence of three researchers and our independent coding and analysis.

FINDINGS

The focus of this study was on the narratives of service associated with meeting a high school service-learning graduation requirement and particularly, the meaning college students made of their experiences. We found participants were very eager to discuss their perceptions of the requirement itself, their experiences meeting it, and their ideas about how their high school activities influenced their college experience. However, we were struck by the absence of a "transformative" (e.g., this changed my life) narrative so often found in the service-learning literature, largely due to the way in which the requirement was structured in the high schools. We found that to illuminate the perceived connection between the high school service-learning requirement and college involvement, the high school story needed to be told. We present here what our participants perceived to be "storyworthy" (Chase, 2005, p. 661) about their experiences in the form of three narratives: perceptions on the connection between high school and college (a (dis) serving narrative), their high school experiences (an acquiescent narrative), and a retrospective look back on the requirement (a tenuous narrative).

A(Dis) Serving Narrative: The Connection Between the High School Service-Learning Requirement and College Involvement

Few students expressed any connection between their high school requirement and their college experience, often because they did not learn much from their high school experience. Many either noted that they had not ever considered the possibility of a connection between their high school service-learning experience and college or they indicated that they needed to "take a break" from service. For example, Frank commented, "I don't think my high school service-learning requirement influenced my experiences in college. I never look at anything and say, 'oh, that's because of those 75 hours I did.'" Even those participants who were involved in college, including community service related activities, did not attribute their college participation to their high school experiences meeting the service-learning requirement. For example, Mackenzie commented that she didn't "think that my high school service-learning requirement has influenced my college experience at all. I didn't learn anything from the requirement." Upon reflection, L-B realized "I guess it would be more accurate to say is what I didn't learn is what's impacted me. It's made me want to learn more because I felt like I got cheated in high school in some ways." Others attributed their disinterest in college involvement, including community service-related activities, to the need to "move on" from high school service and "take a break from service," particularly given what they saw as an absence of available time in college.

The one area that many participants commented on in relation to a connection between high school and college was what they perceived as the development of job-related skills through their service-learning activities. These included learning time management, getting along with others, and dealing with difficult people. Karen noted, "I never really worked before and developed a good work ethic, even though I was not getting paid. It taught me how to be professional...how to deal with difficult people and work with a diverse group of peers." Most acknowledged their interpersonal gains came from working with people in their home town communities and indeed, for several participants, service became one vehicle for staying connected. For example, James described his service as "It kind of gives me a reason to go back home. I got from that [the requirement] the interest in still doing it [coaching middle school basketball] and staying rooted in the community where I'm from."

Whether a result of a mismatch between intended outcomes and the actual experience or not, participants' stories suggested the requirement itself had little to do with promoting continued service, civic engagement, or intrinsically driven community participation. To understand why this disconnect between high school and college exists, we turn to their high school experiences.

An Acquiescent Narrative: High School Experiences with the Requirement

Nearly all of our participants could recall how it is they learned of their high school service-learning requirement and went about meeting it. There was little enthusiasm in their voices as they relayed this information to us. Instead, they approached this requirement reluctantly and with little active protest, focusing on what they needed to do to "get it done." This narrative of acquiescence illuminates how participants became aware of the requirement and their perceptions of its purpose, how they met the requirement, and the high school's role in assisting.

"Look to your left and look to your right:" Becoming aware of the requirement. Participants conveyed a diversity of approaches used by their high schools in making them aware of the service-learning graduation requirement. However, all felt the burden of knowing that they would not graduate without meeting

the requirement. Keith described in great detail his freshmen year assembly, during which a senior administrator introduced the requirement by stating,

> 'Look to your left, look to your right, I guarantee one of you won't graduate because of the community service requirement . . . you can be a 4.0 student and get in to any college you want, but you won't graduate because of the community service requirement,' and I was like 'whoa.'

Perhaps because of the way the requirement was typically presented in the schools, many students perceived it as a burden, that was, as Veronikah noted, something administrators "hang over your head." Kyle lamented, "It's just what I have to do to graduate."

Stephanie recalled being told about the requirement in 9th grade and "that it was best to get it out of the way your freshmen year because you wouldn't get a diploma without it." Similarly, Frank was told in middle school "Get it done or you can't graduate." Whether meeting the requirement in middle school or high school, clearly the focus was on getting the requisite hours—this was a prevailing theme among all participants.

"It is all about the hours." Several participants noted awareness of the requirement as Nick stated:

> I guess when you were in the 9th grade they talked to you about it in English classes and said you had to have this many hours. It was not something that they pushed or that they announced or adver- tised very much. It was something that I guess you were expected to just do...I think most students could have gone through high school being totally unaware of it.

Amanda indicated that she was aware of the requirement but could not recall any of the details about how it is she came to know.

Despite knowledge of the graduation requirement, considered by some such as Bob as "common knowledge," there was quite a bit of ambiguity about what the requirement entailed (e.g., number of hours) and how to meet the requirement (what kind of service activity "counted"); and virtually no mention about why such a requirement existed in the first place. Instead, the focus of students' attention was on accumulating enough hours to meet the requirement. Although the Maryland State Department of Education Code of Regulations clearly specifies 75 hours of student service to meet the requirement, participants were less clear about what was expected. The range of responses to inquiries about their understanding of the requirement included several (3-5 participants) indicating a 60 hour commitment, several noting 36 hours, and several more only aware that they received 30 hours for graduating from middle school. For example, Eric reported, "It was automatic that whatever activities we took part in middle school, as soon as we graduated from the 8th grade, we would automatically get 30 community service hours. By high school I knew I only had to do 30 more hours." Mackenzie declared that her requirement was for "some random big number of hours." A few participants indicated that they were not sure how many hours they needed because it was unclear where their hours were coming from, but they kept appearing on their report cards. For example, several realized that participation in student honoraries and clubs, like National Honor Society (NHS) and the Gifted and Talented Program, brought automatic hours for them. Amelia, in commenting about her awareness of accruing hours, stated, "It was odd, because I kept on receiving credit, through my classes, and I didn't really know what I was receiving credit for. They kept just giving it for the AP classes, every year it would just keep on increasing and then you're done!"

What is it called?: "You can serve anything." The Maryland State Department of Education (2005) requirement is clearly identified as service-learning and is defined in their guidelines:

> Service-learning is a teaching method that combines meaningful service to the community with curriculum-based learning. Students improve their academic skills by applying what they learn in school to the real world; they then reflect on their experience to reinforce the link between their service and their learning. (p. 3)

Participants had very different definitions of service-learning and clearly, no common understanding. Much of how they defined service-learning was in relation to the requirement itself and for many, in opposition to the requirement. For instance, Karen captured the sentiment reflected in many of the participants stating that "service-learning" was "the official name" and "the way you meet the high school graduation requirement." Community service, however, was what you do when you are involved in the community and helping others.

B-E believed that "community service means you actually go out in to the community itself. Service-learning means to me you don't necessarily have to help the community, but it means that you are learning while you are serving something, but you can be serving anything."

James described the distinction in his view as "The difference is that in community service you can go into something once and pat yourself on the back when you leave the door. Community service is more personal service. Service-learning builds the perception that we are supposed to be learning and getting involved with what we are doing." For L-B, the distinction between service-learning and community service had to do with the bureaucratic steps associated with meeting the service-learning requirement, which were in place presumably to prompt learning. He stated, "I think the difference is that with service-learning there is something attached to it like a paper or an action statement. Community service you can learn nothing, you can just go out there and do something and not even think about it ten minutes later." Similarly to James, L-B reported earning his service-learning hours by participating in a car wash for the Bea Gaddy Foundation and by looking up Web sites related to cancer and writing them down for a teacher. Kelli's requirement was called "student service hours—or something like that. It was service-learning because we had to fill out the form."

Sara's requirement was called community service but she found

> it was more service-learning because I think that community service is interacting with people and bettering the community. Service-learning is like doing community service and learning from it, but we never really did community service. We were just learning about [emphasis added] the people we were supposed to be helping.

Sara's school organized "Homeless Days" for all students in a particular science class to meet the requirement. The focus of their service was to find the best way to insulate a cup for homeless people. Sara's reaction to this was the following:

> It was really weird...It was called community service, and we never really did anything besides make these insulated cups. Then there was this box outside and they were trying to tell us how people lived in boxes. I didn't see how this fulfilled the requirement, but it did... We had no interaction with anyone at all. We just insulated cups, and looked at boxes that they could live in.

Although these varying definitions reflect students trying to make sense of their experiences, all indicate confusion about service-learning and a mismatch between students' perceptions and the clear definition of service-learning provided by the Maryland State Department of Education.

What counts as service: How the requirement was met. Participants met their service-learning requirement in a great variety of ways. We generated a long list of activities through which participants garnered hours for service-learning credit in high school. A sampling of these activities included babysitting at participant's synagogue, teaching dance class at school, tutoring, recycling at the school, adopt-a-highway program, working for teachers, working in the attendance and guidance offices, Teen Court, through a number of student clubs and organizations, pie sales, planning a senior citizen prom, chorus, vacation bible school, working in soup kitchen at participant's church, donating blood, junior member of volunteer fire department, nursing home volunteer, park clean up, horse rescue farm, camp counselor, collecting eye glasses for the blind in Spain, and building houses for a week in Mexico. Although many of the students were quite proud of their involvement in these activities, it was striking how passively they were described to us and what little claim on them personally these activities seemed to make.

Many participants received hours for their participation in school sponsored or school-based activities such as Band, theatre stage crew, working in the guidance or attendance offices, picking up trash around the school, and assisting teachers with filing. In a nuanced interpretation, Crimson explained "there was some talk about service-learning. When I got hours for being in the band it was called community service, but when I got hours for working in the attendance office, it was service-learning. The two titles shifted depending on what you were doing." Both, apparently, qualified for meeting the service-learning requirement. In fact, much of their service was actually conducted in and around their schools and in the service of school improvement. For example, Bob explained, "So with service-learning, I could do things, not just volunteer work out in the community, but other things like being involved with school and doing stuff like that. It was all learning that revolved around service." Many of Bob's hours were accrued by helping the advisor ("typing things up for her") to a student organization at the school. Mackenzie noted "I was under the impression that service-learning was community hours that I had to do and I would have to go into the community and help. But it wasn't really like that." Most of Mackenzie's hours were met in English classes each year and included activities such as making books "for kids in underprivileged schools" or donating cans of food. However, it bothered Mackenzie that "I never found out what happened to the books we made and who they went to."

School as service brokerage: "They made it easy for us." Many participants expressed surprise and a bit of skepticism when describing how they received service hours for tasks that defied categorization. School personnel appeared to stretch the boundaries defining service beyond students' imagination. Participants shared example after example of earning their hours by completing tasks within the school, which they perceived as of primary benefit to the teachers and guidance counselors. Batika commented, "I also worked in the guidance office, helping out and answering the phones—it was fun and yeah, I got credit for that too." She went on to further illustrate "how helpful" the teachers were by sharing, "Some students even went up to teachers and said, 'Hey, I really need hours' and...teachers would just sign even if students didn't do anything." Bob relayed his experience, "There was assistance [for getting service hours], people would help out, a teacher would be like, 'ok well, why don't you stay after school a couple of days a week and like help me do this or that and then you can get some service hours.'" In the examples noted with regard to hours through band, the band director played an active role in facilitating the process for students involved, including waiving the reflection component. Crimson referred to this as "kind of unofficial under the table sort of thing. My band director would award people who were in the band... and just give you all of your hours."

Participants recognized this helpfulness as the schools' interest in assuring that students graduated, more so than necessarily advancing service-learning. As a result, they noted that often "real community service doesn't count" and observed the ways in which their peers "got around" the requirement. Participants were creative in their use of euphemisms to describe how students were able to meet their community service requirement. For example, Veronikah referred to the "things you could swing around to get hours" to describe activities that weren't clearly acceptable by the school's definition of what counted. According to her, students routinely exaggerated their hours because they "hated it and needed to get it done." As a result, Crimson mentioned that "you find a lot of stressed out seniors doing some oddball things just to get their hours." Mackenzie referred to this as "skating by without doing anything" and Frank discussed "fudging a few hours" and getting away with this, as did his peers. Several participants extended this "fudging" to describe what appeared to us as outright cheating to meet the requirement. This took the form of submitting hours for service that was never performed or getting credit for far more hours than the activity actually took. As Mackenzie explained, she received five service hours "for something that took 10 minutes to do."

A Tenuous Narrative of Required Service and Participation: A "Double-Edged Sword"

As college students looking back on their experiences meeting the service-learning graduation requirement, nearly all participants acknowledged the possibilities of such mandated service. They were able to see that benefits could be gained and recognized that they and their peers probably would not have been engaged in "service" through their schools had it not been for the requirement. However, the "forced" nature of service and the way in which they and their peers met the requirement rubbed them the wrong way. Several of them used the exact same phrase to capture this dilemma: "a double edged sword." Amelia conveyed this idea precisely:

> It is kind of like a doubled-edged sword, because it is positive, should help the student and the community as well; but the bad side, it is a requirement and reduces feelings of being altruistic, kind and loving, because it is seen just as a mandate that I'll just get done and it will be over with. This cuts down motivation to want to go out and help others and get excited about a great opportunity to go out and help. These benefits aren't highlighted.

Nearly every participant validated the benefits of serving others and the importance of making a contribution to the community, however, the mandated nature of their high school requirement left them cold. For example, L-B emphasized, "I'm very passionate about service in general. I don't know about it being forced upon you, especially in the way the high school does." Keith went further in suggesting, "It is a sense of duty, you can only give yourself, it can't be forced." They also recognized that the requirement, "lame" as it was and something "I hated along with everyone else because it was forced," brought about good activities, for which they were proud, and that without the requirement they would not have been involved in these ways. As Frank noted, "It [the requirement] may seem like a burden at first, but it is a good thing."

Related to this idea of the "double-edged sword," nearly all the participants had difficulty identifying the outcomes and benefits of the requirement to them as individuals. When prompted, they could articulate the larger goals and ideals they thought service-learning could accomplish, but this was not tied to their own experience. In fact, they were apologetic for this inability to come up with a compelling story related to their service. For example, when trying to identify personal outcomes associated with his service, L-B said, "Nothing overly meaningful, I'm sorry."

Several participants did share that their service experience helped them to feel good about themselves and more interested in "helping others." Others related their service to developing a work ethic, becoming more responsible, and learning to work with others. Karen, for example, noted, "I never really worked before. [You] learn so much about yourself as a worker." Others took pride in what they had accomplished through their service-learning experience and felt special and "more well-rounded" as a result; although this mostly had to do with exceeding the number of hours required and pride in giving back to their own communities (which included their high schools).

Despite their ambivalent impressions of the service-learning requirement based largely on their own experiences meeting it, nearly all participants could see the requirement doing more and communicated an interest in the possibilities. None would argue with the intended objectives of a service-learning requirement, but all thought the implementation could be improved upon greatly. In fact, when presented with the list of "Maryland's Best Practices for Service-Learning," several exclaimed "Wow, where did you get this? This is cool," and suggested that if their high schools had actually followed the guidelines, their experiences would have been much improved.

DISCUSSION AND IMPLICATIONS

We set out in this study to elicit the narratives of service associated with students meeting their high school graduation requirement for service-learning. We were also interested in how their high school experiences influenced their college involvement. In nearly all of our interviews with participants we were struck by what seemed to us an absence of the compelling narrative so often found in the service-learning literature. The rich description of their high school experiences acquiescing to the requirement, the narrow focus on completing their hours, and the diverse array of activities, mostly in-school, in which they engaged and counted to meet the requirement do provide a compelling story of a high school service-learning graduation requirement and what graduates are bringing with them to the college context. The results also suggest, consistent with several other studies, that the question is not simply about required versus voluntary service, but more so, how required service is structured in the school setting and the types of service in which students are involved (Jones & Hill, 2003; McLellan & Youniss, 2003).

Our participants were resisting what they perceived as the forced nature of the requirement, not the idea of service-learning or community service. However, their stories reveal that the resistance may have been less about the requirement per se and more so related to the ways in which it was structured in the schools and their ability to meet the requirement by engaging in activities that made very little claim on them psychologically, cognitively, or civically. Indeed, these activities were not congruent with definitions, including Maryland's own, of service-learning and focused more so on service to the schools and led to a tenuous connection between their high school requirement and continued service in college.

The results of this study contribute to what is often described as "mixed results" regarding the efficacy of required service in relation to both outcomes and promoting continued civic participation. Indeed, the very notion of the "double edged sword," as coined by several of our participants, captures the inability to lay claim to one position or the other. Although the goal of qualitative inquiry is not generalizability, the results of this study hold the potential to influence policy and practice. As both high schools and colleges continue to promote service-learning and students convey their interest in and intent to volunteer as members of the "9/11 generation" and the "Katrina generation," the results of this study provide several suggestions for closing the gap between what schools and colleges intend as outcomes and what students actually experience.

First, the array of activities in which students engaged to meet the requirement was dizzying. The majority of these activities took place in the school and with seemingly very little direction from school personnel. The integration of service into the curriculum as a pedagogical tool, consistent with many definitions of service-learning, was virtually absent. So too, was any mention of reflection. Only when prompted did students talk about reflection and always connected to the forms they needed to complete to get credit for their hours. This finding reinforces the importance of meaningful service and the quality of the placement, emphasized in definitions of service-learning and in the research on outcomes associated with service-learning (e.g., Eyler & Giles, 1999; Jacoby, 1996). Also, noted by McLellan and Youniss (2003), "It should not be surprising that these different types of service might produce variable effects" (p. 48). Further, as queried by Chapman (2002), "Does a student who learns that almost anything counts toward the service requirement—so long as he doesn't get paid—develop a keen sense of civil calling? Or does he hone his skill at gaming the system?" (p. 12). Unfortunately, our data suggest the latter may be the case. A more intentional effort to link intended outcomes and activities designed to produce those outcomes is sorely needed.

Second, and related, our results are consistent with those studies that reinforce the importance of structured service as high quality. Despite the occasional good teacher, or parents and churches, most of the participants in this study reported the need to figure out the service requirement on their own. Although not the focus of this study, we suspect that many schools are under-staffed and -resourced such that responding to this legislative mandate is challenging. Hence, they respond in ways to assure that students satisfy their graduation requirements by "making it easy" for students. Research does suggest however, that well designed service-learning makes a difference in producing desired outcomes (e.g., Eyler & Giles, 1999).

The Youth Volunteering and Engagement survey (Spring, Dietz, & Grimm, 2006) examined the benefits of "high quality" service-learning in K-12 education. High quality was defined by three elements: (1) students assist in the planning of the service activity, (2) students participate in regular service for a semester or longer, and (3) students reflect on their service experiences in class. Results found that 77% of all school-based service experiences had a least one of these elements, but only 10% had all three; and that students who participated in programs with all three elements were more than twice as likely as those with none of the quality elements to report that their service experience had a positive impact on them. In addition, as the research by McLellan and Youniss (2003) suggested, "when left to their own devices for fulfilling credit requirements...students tended to choose functionary work, which probably demanded little physical, cognitive, or emotional investment compared, say, with social service" (p. 56). Had students been engaged in high quality service-learning, the stories we heard may have sounded quite different.

In addition, this phenomenon of leaving the service choice and arrangements to the students led to a very narrow view of service-learning by students as only those activities connected to the requirement. In fact, a number of students were engaged in community service through their churches, families, or community organizations, but none of them talked about these activities as service-learning or in relation to the requirement. Tapping in to these familial, social, and community networks may help schools not only help students meet the service-learning requirement, but also, because service connected with these networks does tend to be more consistent with activities that require cognitive and emotional investment from students (McLellan & Youniss, 2003), to promote social responsibility and continued civic participation.

Finally, the relationship between the high school requirement and related service activities and college involvement was tenuous at best. This is consistent with the research that demonstrates that encouraged and high quality service, rather than required service, is more likely to contribute to continued service in college (Jones & Hill, 2003; Marks & Jones, 2004). Because of their emphasis on the required nature of service, several of our participants came to the university setting ready to "take a break" from service. This, and other experiences meeting the requirement, provides several cautions and implications for college educators interested in promoting service-learning and civic responsibility. First, students were not at all clear about what service-learning is and how it differs, if at all, from community service. College educators may need to help reframe students' misconceptions of service-learning and cannot presume that students will come to them with exposure to social issues through service or a commitment to civic engagement.

Because of these misconceptions, and their perspective that a service requirement is a "double-edged sword," engaging students who attended high schools with a service requirement may take extra effort and new strategies. Traditional recruitment methods (e.g., if I market it, they will come) may not work. These students may need to be approached more directly and by engaging them in meaningful service that draws them in. They also may not have the skills of reflection required for high quality service-learning, as reflection was not often a part of their high school experiences. Although absent from most of their high school experiences, research has shown that the most compelling service-learning, even when required, occurs when identity development is involved (Hart et al., 2007; Jones & Abes, 2004; Jones & Hill, 2003; McLellan & Youniss, 2003; Youniss & Yates, 1997). When service is connected to a student's evolving sense of self, then the motivation to engage in service becomes an internal one and a greater likelihood for continued involvement emerges because service becomes integral to identity construction.

Limitations

The results of this study must be considered in light of a few limitations. Although consistent with narrative inquiry, our sample of 19 is relatively small given that we invited 200 to participate and received 44 affirmative responses from those who met sampling criteria. We also included representation from a number of different counties across the state, but to provide a more comprehensive narrative, we did not analyze the data county by county. Because our focus was on students' stories, we are only able to comment on their perceptions and the nature of the service-learning requirement from their perspectives. We therefore, don't know much about the high school environments, except what the participants recalled. We can only speculate that if we interviewed high school teachers, for example, the story would shift. We also did not formerly assess students' general propensity for involvement in high school. Rounding out the picture is important and provides several areas for future research. Finally, as narrators of this story, we were very aware of our own stories as they intersected with the participants. As we noted, the absence of compelling stories from our participants caught our attention. Did this mean we missed the mark, or that our notion of what was "storyworthy" (Chase, 2005, p. 661) was not theirs? The presence of three researchers helped us to monitor our own subjectivity, but nonetheless we were aware of its presence.

Despite these limitations, this study provides compelling evidence about students' perceptions of and experiences with a high school service-learning graduation requirement. It is clear that the requirement alone does not automatically produce outcomes such as civic responsibility, commitment to one's community or social issues, or continued community service involvement. Students resisted the required nature of their community service; however, this was largely due to the way in which it was implemented in their schools. Had the schools been more actively involved in structuring the requirement and assuring meaningful service, it is reasonable to speculate that the outcomes for students would have looked quite different. None of them resisted service and giving back to the community; indeed, many of them were engaged in this kind of service outside of the requirement. The presence of the "double-edged sword" captures this dynamic and serves as an impetus for service-learning educators to sharpen the educational experience for students to produce intended outcomes. Indeed, as McLellan and Youniss (2003) urged, "service needs to be crafted as assiduously as science laboratories or writing seminars" (p. 56). Such a commitment will increase the likelihood that students experience more efficacious service-learning rather than simply "what I do to meet the requirement."

REFERENCES

Astin, A.W., & Sax, L.J. (1998). How undergraduates are affected by service participation. *Journal of College Student Development, 39,* 251-263.

Barber, B. (1994). *An aristocracy of everyone: The politics of education and the future of America.* New York: Ballantine Books.

Berger, J.B., & Milem, J.F. (2002). The impact of community service involvement on three measures of undergraduate self-concept. *NASPA Journal, 40,* 85-103.

Boyer, E. L. (1983). *High School: A report on secondary education in America.* New York: Harper and Row.

Charmaz, K. (2006). *Constructing grounded theory: A practical guide through qualitative analysis.* Thousand Oaks, CA: Sage.

Chapman, B. (2002). A bad idea whose time is past: The case against universal service. *Brookings Review, 20,* 10-13.

Chase, S.E. (2005). Narrative inquiry: Multiple lenses, approaches, voices. In N. K. Denzin & Y. S. Lincoln (Eds.), *Handbook of qualitative research 3rd ed.* (pp. 651-680). Thousand Oaks, CA: Sage.

Chronicle Almanac. (2007, August 31), 53. Retrieved on January 18, 2008, from: http://chronicle.com/weekly/almanac/2006/nation/nation.htm

Clandinin, D. J., & Connelly, F. M. (2000). *Narrative inquiry: Experience and story in qualitative research.* San Francisco: Jossey-Bass.

Creswell, J.W. (2007). *Qualitative inquiry and research design: Choosing among five traditions* (2nd ed.). Thousand Oaks, CA: Sage.

Cruce, T. M., & Moore, J. V. (2007). First-year students' plans to volunteer: An examination of the predictors of community service participation. *Journal of College Student Development, 48*, p. 655-673.

Deci, E. L., & Ryan, R. M. (1987). The support of autonomy and the control of behavior. *Journal of Personality and Social Psychology, 53*, 1024-1037.

Denzin, N. K., & Lincoln, Y. S. (2000). The discipline and practice of qualitative research. In N. K. Denzin & Y. S. Lincoln (Eds.), *Handbook of qualitative research* (pp. 105-117). Thousand Oaks, CA: Sage.

Dote, L., Cramer, K., Dietz, N., & Grimm, R. Jr. (2006). *College students helping America.* Washington, DC: Corporation for National and Community Service.

Education Commission of the States (2001). Institutionalized service-learning in the 50 states. Denver, CO.

Eyler, J., & Giles, D. E., Jr. (1999). *Where's the learning in service-learning?* San Francisco: Jossey-Bass.

Flyvbjerg, B. (2001) *Making social science matter: Why social inquiry fails and how it can succeed.* Cambridge: Cambridge University Press.

Harkavy, I. (2004). Service-learning and the development of democratic universities, democratic schools, and democratic good societies in the 21st century. In M.Welch & S. Billig (Eds.), *New perspectives on service-learning: Research to advance the field* (pp. 3-22). Greenwich, CT: Information Age Publishing.

Hart, D., Donnelly, T. M., Youniss, J., & Atkins, R. (2007). High school community service as a predictor of adult voting and volunteering. *American Educational Research Journal, 44*(1), 197-219.

Higher Education Research Institute. (2006). *The American freshman: National norms for fall 2006.* Los Angeles: University of California.

Jacoby, B., & Associates (1996). *Service-learning in higher education: Concepts and practices.* San Francisco: Jossey-Bass.

Jennings, K. M., & Stoker, L. (2004). Social trust and civic engagement across time and generations. *Acta Politica, 39*, 342-379.

Jones, S. R. (2002). (Re)Writing the word: Methodological strategies and issues in qualitative research. *Journal of College Student Development, 43*, 461-473.

Jones, S. R., & Abes, E. S. (2004). Enduring influences of service-learning on college students' identity development. *Journal of College Student Development, 45*, 149-166.

Jones, S. R., & Hill, K. E. (2003). Understanding patterns of commitment: Student motivation for community service involvement. *Journal of Higher Education, 74*, 516-539.

Jones, S.R., Torres,V., & Arminio, J. (2006).*Negotiating the complexities of qualitative research in higher education.* New York: Routledge.

Lieblich, A., Tuval-Mashiach, R., & Zilber, T. (1998). *Narrative research: Readings, analysis, interpretation.* Thousand Oaks, CA: Sage.

Lincoln, Y. S., & Guba, E. (1985). *Naturalistic inquiry.* Thousand Oaks, CA: Sage.

Marks, H. M. & Jones, S. R. (2004). Community service in the transition: Shifts and continuities in participation from high school to college. *Journal of Higher Education, 75,* 307-339.

Maryland State Department of Education. (2005). *Maryland student service-learning guidelines.* Baltimore, MD.

Maryland State Department of Education. (2006). *College performance of new Maryland high school graduates: Student outcome and achievement report.* Baltimore, MD: Author.

Maryland Student Service Alliance. (1995). *Maryland's best practices: An improvement guide for school-based service-learning.* Baltimore: Maryland State Department of Education.

McEwen, M. K. (2003) The nature and uses of theory. In S. R. Komives & D. B. Woodard (Eds.), *Student services: A handbook for the profession* (4th ed., (pp. 153-178). San Francisco: Jossey-Bass.

McLellan, J.A., & Youniss, J. (2003). Two systems of youth service: Determinants of voluntary and required youth community service. *Journal of Youth and Adolescence, 32*(1), 47-58.

Metz, E., & Youniss, J. (2003). A demonstration that school-based required service does not deter—but heightens— volunteerism. *PS Online,* 281-286.

Metz, E., & Youniss, J. (2005). Longitudinal gains in civic development through school-based required service. *Political Psychology, 26,* 413-437.

Moely, B. E., McFarland, M., Miron, D., Mercer, S., & Ilustre, V. (2002). Changes in college students' attitudes and intentions for civic involvement as a function of service-learning experience. *Michigan Journal of Community Service Learning, 9*(1), 18-26.

Niemi, R.G., Hepburn, M.A., & Chapman, C. (2000). Community service by high school students: A cure for civic ills? *Political Behavior, 22,* 46-69.

Patton, M. Q. (2002). *Qualitative evaluation and research methods* (3rd ed.). Newbury Park, CA: Sage.

Raskoff, S., & Sundeen, R. (1999). Community service programs in high schools. *Law and Contemporary Problems, 64*(4), 73-111.

Service-learning. (2003). Retrieved September 10, 2006, from http://www.marylandpublicschools.org/msde/programs/service-learning/service_learning.htm

Spring, K., Dietz, N., & Grimm, R. Jr. (2006). *Educating for active citizenship: Service-learning, school based service, and civic engagement.* Washington, DC: Corporation for National and Community Service.

Strauss, A., & Corbin, J. (1998). *Basics of qualitative research* (2nd ed.). Thousand Oaks, CA: Sage Publications.

Stukas, A. A., Snyder, M., & Clary, E. G. (1999). The effects of "mandatory volunteerism" on intentions to volunteer. *Psychological Science, 10*(1), 59-64.

Vogelgesang (2005). *Bridging from high school to college: Findings from the 2004 freshmen CIRP survey.* St. Paul, MN: National Youth Leadership Council.

Vogelgesang, L. J., & Astin, A. W. (2000). Comparing the effects of service-learning and community service. *Michigan Journal of Community Service Learning, 7,* 25-34.

Vogelgesang, L. J., & Astin, A.W. (2005). Post college civic engagement among graduates. *Higher Education Research Institute Research Report, 2,* 1-11.

Youniss, J., & Yates, M. (1997). *Community service and social responsibility in youth.* Chicago: University of Chicago Press.
Authors

Linking University and High School Students: Exploring the Academic Value of Service Learning

By Duncan MacLellan

Dr. Duncan MacLellan, Duncan MacLellan is an Assistant Professor in the Department of Politics and Public Administration at Ryerson University, and his teaching and research interests include educational politics and policy making at the local and provincial levels, state and teacher relations and local and urban governance issues. Duncan published an article on teacher unionism in the journal, Canadian and International Education and he is one of the authors of the book, Teachers' Unions in Canada.

Abstract: *While universities and colleges aim to become more inclusive and welcoming to students from a variety of backgrounds, major gaps remain in relation to particular high school students being admitted to postsecondary institutions. Located in Toronto, Canada's most culturally diverse city, Ryerson University is committed to both academic and applied learning. Building on that commitment, this paper focuses on one service learning project involving both university students enrolled in a senior level Ryerson course and high school students enrolled in a Grade 12 course located in downtown Toronto. This particular Toronto high school has not scored well in province-wide standardized tests and so few of its students apply to college or university. Bringing together these high school and university students in different activities over one semester will enable both groups to gain insights from each other. In addition, by using reflective assignments, Ryerson students can use course concepts to help ground their interactions with these high school students. Service learning has the potential to build linkages that help both university and high school students.*

Keywords: Service Learning, Urban Education, High School Students, University Students, Experiential Learning

INTRODUCTION

Service learning has been identified as an effective mechanism to engage university students in a variety of learning opportunities (Day, 2008; Webster, 2007). For this study, Ryerson University students, in a senior-level course, were linked with students enrolled in a Grade 12 course at Maple Heights High School.[1] This particular urban high school has not fared well in provincial standardized tests, and few of its students continue to pursue academic studies after high school. A number of scholars have pointed to the troubling fact that many urban high school students may be prone to disconnect from their academic studies, which could limit their future career options (Elson, Johns, and Petrie, 2007; Kenny, Simon, Kiley-Brabeck, and Lerner, 2002; Webster, 2007).[2]

Webster (2007) notes that a significant body of literature related to service learning focuses on white middle-class suburban schools. Only of late, has the focus begun to move toward demystifying university and college programs for youth from under-represented urban communities. Well-designed service learning projects in urban schools have the potential to provide university students with opportunities to link with high school students; therefore, enabling both groups to exchange ideas and views on a range of formal and informal topics (Brown, Heaton, and Wall, 2007; Webster, 2007).

The goal of this paper is to present a practice-based case study, which describes an innovative service learning project involving high school and university students. The research question is: Can service learning be a positive means for linking university and high school students?

REVIEW OF LITERATURE RELATED TO SERVICE LEARNING

Bringle and Hatcher's definition of service learning, referenced in Zlotkowski (2003), offers a useful lens to situate this study:

> We view service learning as a credit-bearing educational experience in which students participate in an organized service activity that meets identified community needs and reflects on the service activity to gain further understanding of the course content, a broader appreciation of the discipline, and an enhanced sense of civic responsibility. . . .(p. 64)

O'Quin (2003) refers to the *National and Community Trust Act*, which defines service learning '[a]s a method whereby students learn and develop through active participation in thoughtfully organized service that is conducted to meet the needs of communities' (2003, p. 3697). Some researchers relate service learning's pedagogy to John Dewey's scholarship, which views education as means for promoting democracy and engaging students in their communities (Ramsdell, 2004). More specifically, having a "good fit" between the course and the service learning experience, enables students, faculty, and community partners to see a project's value (Gupta, 2006; Hollander, Saltmarsh, and Zlotkowski, 2002).

Service learning can help students increase community awareness by applying their academic learning, knowledge, and skills to pre-identified local needs (Campus Contact, 2003; Frazer, Raasch, Pertzborn, and Bradley, 2007; Pearce, 2008). For service learning to be considered a viable pedagogic approach, it has to link with specific academic course content. The following quote fromEyler and Dwight, cited by Pearce (2008), responds to the question: Why service learning?

> I can honestly say that I've learned more in the last year (service learning) than I probably have learned in all four years of college. I have learned so much, maybe because I found something that I'm really passionate about, and it makes you care more to learn about it-and get involved and do more. You're not just studying to take a test and forget about it. You're learning and the experiences we have are staying with us. (p. 116)

In addition, as Pearce notes, "well designed, well-managed service learning can contribute to a student's learning and growth, while also helping to meet real community needs" (2008, p.119). The goal is to integrate service with the academic enterprise, so service reinforces and strengthens learning and learning reinforces and strengthens service. One primary goal of service learning is the use of reflection to help connect the broader context of service experience with course content (O'Quin, 2003).

CONNECTING AN URBAN UNIVERSITY TO SERVICE LEARNING

This project aimed to link university and high school students in a series of informal and formal activities that would help familiarize high school students to university. Given Ryerson's evolution, this current service learning project builds on a strong foundation of applied learning. Ryerson University began as a polytechnic school shortly after World War Two, and its mission remains to link academic studies with practical applications. In the mid-1990s, Ryerson was granted standing as a university but maintained its emphasis on career focused education. The 2008-2009 Ryerson University Calendar notes the following description:

> The special mission of Ryerson University is the advancement of applied knowledge and research to address societal need, and the provision of programs of study that provide a balance between theory and application and that prepare students for careers in professional and quasi-professional fields. As a leading centre of applied education, Ryerson is recognized as Canada's leader in career-focused education.... (Ryerson University, 2008, p. 14)

To help guide the organization of this service learning project, the instructor relied on the following definition provided by the Ryerson University Faculty of Arts Service Learning Office:

> Service Learning is a form of experiential learning that links classroom teaching and course readings with meaningful voluntary experiences and critical reflective practices. Students engage in projects and activities in the community in addition to their course work. Learning is facilitated through individual and collective critical reflection in course lectures and assignments that help students integrate 'real world' experiences with course concepts. Service Learning differs from volunteer work and internships/practica in that it focuses on both community priorities and student learning, rather than just on community need (volunteer work) or just on student learning....(Ryerson University, 2008a)

To provide context for this service learning project, a brief overview of significant demographic and socio-economic figures that relate to Toronto and Ryerson University will be helpful.

- During the past decade, close to 50% of Toronto's population of 2.5 million residents were born outside of Canada (City of Toronto, 2009).
- Approximately 25% of the 1 million immigrants that came to Canada from 2001-2006 settled in Toronto (City of Toronto, 2009).
- The 2006 national survey results indicate that 47% of Toronto's 2.5 million residents report themselves as being part of a visible minority (City of Toronto, 2009).
- The 2006 national survey also notes that Toronto's population is made up of residents who claim identity with one or more of the 200 distinct ethnic groups that reside in Toronto (City of Toronto, 2009).
- On Toronto's socio-economic front, during the past few decades, the proportion of middle-income neighborhoods has fallen from 50% to 32%. Yet the proportion of low and very-low income neighborhoods increased from 19% to 50% (MacLellan, 2008).

Ryerson's student population reflects Toronto's ethno cultural mosaic. In 2007, 42.6% of Ryerson's first-year student population came from the City of Toronto. The four suburban areas surrounding Toronto are referred to as the Greater Toronto Area (GTA), and with a combined population of 2.3 million residents, Ryerson drew another 40% of its first-year student population from the GTA. In 2007, close to 12% of Ryerson's first-year student population came from outside Toronto and the GTA but still within Ontario. Approximately 3.8% of Ryerson's first-year students came from a non-Ontario province or territory within Canada (Ryerson University, 2008b).

Maple Heights High School was selected as the site for this service learning project. To a certain degree, Maple Heights's student population is similar in composition to the City of Toronto and Ryerson University. In spring 2008, Maple Heights reported that close to 32% of its students have resided in Canada for less than five years (Toronto District School Board, 2009). Maple Heights's 2007-2008 school profile is presented in Table One.

Table 1: A Selected Profile of Maple Heights High School 2007-2008

	Province of Ontario	Maple Heights High School
Parentage of students who live in lower-income households	31%	16.5%
Percentage of students whose parents have some university education	21%	36.9%
Percentage of students who receive special education services	24%	12.5%
Percentage of students identified as gifted	0.1%	21.8%
Parentage of students whose first language is not English	56%	21.8%
Percentage of students who are new to Canada from non-English speaking country	21.3%	3.2%
Percentage of students who achieved provincial standard in academic math	19%	75%
Percentage of students who achieved provincial standard in applied math (2007-08)	15%	34%
Percentage of students in grade 10 who passed literacy test on their first attempt (2007-08)	42%	84%

These percentages are based on Ontario province-wide averages (Ontario Ministry of Education, 2008).

Methodology: Education Politics, Urban Schooling, and Social Capital

This qualitative study was prompted by a desire to utilize service learning as the vehicle to connect high school and senior university students. The instructor was contacted by a Ryerson University Faculty of Arts Service Learning staff member to inquire if there was interest in "twinning" his "Education Politics and Policy" course with a Grade 12 course at Maple Heights High School. The "Education Politics and Policy" course relies on cultural and social capital theories to help students understand the social context within which educational decisions are made. In particular, Pierre Bourdieu's work on cultural capital is utilized to explore the idea that schools draw unevenly on social and cultural resources of members of society. Often cultural experiences at home facilitate children's adjustment to both school and academic achievement. This in turn, converts cultural resources into what Bordieu refers to as cultural capital (Lareau, 1987).

Within this course, we discuss how social capital is utilized to enable certain people to gain access to powerful positions through direct and indirect employment of social connections (Oakes, 2005). Howard (2006) contends that social capital promotes linkages that are both formal (volunteering at your local school for a committee) and informal (inviting your neighbors to a barbeque). The benefits from these opportunities can result in personal as well as academic gains for parents and their children. Howard (2006) then asks the following research question: If schools included service learning programs, would these help to close the achievement gaps among different racial and ethnic groups? In his case study of a Seattle middle school, Howard's results, while limited, found that by engaging students in service learning activities, these students spent less time watching television. While Howard's sample size was small, it did offer the potential for service learning to assist academic learning (2006). In summary, both cultural and social capital theories were used to help structure a significant portion of the "Education Politics and Policy" course.

SERVICE LEARNING AT MAPLE HEIGHTS: RESEARCH DESIGN AND REFLECTIVE ASSIGNMENTS

In the lead up to organizing the research design for this service learning project, the instructor benefited from valuable insights offered by Ryerson's Service Learning Office and educators at Maple Heights. The core of this project relied on Ryerson students submitting three reflective assignments that enabled them to offer their thoughts and knowledge with regard to both informal and formal aspects of their placement at Maple Heights over five weeks. To present the observations that emerged from both the reflective assignments and informal conversations that the instructor had with Ryerson students regarding their placement at Maple Heights, it became important to organize these findings in an organized manner. After reviewing a number of scholarly works, the instructor chose to adopt Sterling's (2007) subheadings of Knowledge, Activities, and Reflections because of the appropriate fit provided for this service learning project.

Knowledge

For this paper, we can consider knowledge as concepts, facts, information, and prior experience in the context of experiential learning (Sterling, 2007;

Terry, 2005).More specifically, two aspects of knowledge can be considered. First, upon agreeing to participate in this service learning project, the instructor wanted to become informed about the principles of service learning. Second, the instructor was eager to gain "on the ground knowledge" related to Maple Heights High School. The course instructor and one of Ryerson's service learning liaison staff members met with Ms. Banks (pseudonym), the teacher responsible for Maple Heights's Grade 12 university-preparatory course, "Challenge and Change in Society" that was to be "twinned" with the "Education Politics and Policy" course. This meeting also offered Ms. Banks an opportunity to become familiar with the "Education Politics and Policy" course, and Ms. Banks provided the instructor with the following description of the "Challenge and Change in Society" course:

> This course examines theories and methodologies used in anthropology, psychology, and sociology to investigate and explain shifts in knowledge, attitudes, beliefs, and behavior, and their impact on society. Students will analyze cultural, social, and biological patterns in human societies, looking at the ways in which these patterns change over time. Students will also explore the ideas of classical and contemporary social theories, and will apply those ideas to the analysis of contemporary trends. (Ontario Ministry of Education, 2002, p. 1)

The instructor also attended a professional development workshop on evaluating reflective assignments. This workshop offered the instructor an opportunity to engage with other faculty in relation to constructive approaches to assessing reflective assignments. To create the three reflective assignments for the "Education Politics and Policy" course, attention was given to O'Quin's (2003) comment that one must consider course goals and objectives when designing reflective assignments that connect service learning with a course's academic content. Furthermore, there does not appear to be one "right" way for students to process and assimilate the learning that takes place through their service learning experiences. For this reason, faculty are best suited to select methods of assessment and reflection that meet course goals and learning objectives (Day, 2008; O'Quin, 2003).

As Young, Shinnar, Ackerman, Carruthers, and Young (2007) note, service learning must be more than community service, service-learning assignments must include two components: continuity and interaction. Continuity refers to connections between course materials and assignments—the application of skills and concepts learned in a course to real life situations. Interactions refer to the link between the objective nature of the assignment and the subjective experience—the impressions and thoughts of the student. The link is achieved through reflection. Reflection can come in the form of class discussions, journal writing, term papers, or other assignments that require students to critically reflect upon their experiences. Ramsdell (2004) contends that for service learning courses to be successful, the academic component must be equally as important as the service. The implications of this are that the volunteer work must be directly tied to the course curriculum.

The service learning component of the "Education Politics and Policy" course was voluntary. Nine of 29 students submitted applications for service learning at Maple Heights High School. Due to the fact that students would be working with young adults, the Toronto District School Board (TDSB) required each student who applied to complete a Police Reference Check (PRC). All nine students were accepted for the service learning project at Maple Heights. Shortly thereafter, Ryerson's Service Learning Office organized a half-day orientation session for Ryerson students involved in service learning at Maple Heights. A few days before the visit, an altercation occurred near Maple Heights School property that led the Principal to initiate a school lockdown. This item generated media attention, and a few Ryerson students emailed the instructor regarding the safety of Maple Heights. Ryerson's Service Learning Office sent an email to its Maple Heights service learning students, assuring them that all precautions would be taken to ensure their safety.

The visit remained as scheduled, and Ryerson university students gained a first-hand look at Maple Heights High School. Ryerson students were able to meet with Maple Heights's Principal and teaching staff involved with service learning. At this meeting, Ryerson students asked questions related to the school, and the Principal responded that many of the students attending Maple Heights are first-generation Canadians and a significant number are from low-income families. In addition, according to the Principal, some Maple Heights students are living on their own due to difficult family situations. The Principal also stated that the size of Maple Heights's English as a Second Language (ESL) Program reflects that many of its students are not fluent in English, in part, because of their recent entry into Canada. Geographically, the Principal noted that Maple Heights is located between two high achieving secondary schools; therefore, it has the stigma of being the school where students who cannot gain entry into the other two schools end up. Next Ryerson students met informally with the students they would be working with, this was followed by lunch in the school cafeteria, and then a student-led school tour.

Two weeks later, Maple Heights's service learning students were given a half-day orientation to Ryerson University. The aim of the visit was for these students to see the campus and to help demystify some aspects of higher education. The visit to Ryerson University involved meeting with Student Services personnel. Then Maple Height students met with a group of first-generation Ryerson students to chat informally about university life. A campus tour was organized and this was followed by a brief lecture from the instructor to enable Maple Height students to "experience" a university class.

Activities

Ryerson University students enrolled in service learning at Maple Heights were required to spend two hours per week over five weeks assisting Ms. Banks in a variety of formal and informal activities related to the "Challenge and Change in Society" course. After the first week of observing, Ryerson students were integrated more formally into "Challenge and Change in Society". To ease their transition into this course, Ryerson students were divided into two groups to coincide with the day of their weekly visits.

A Monday group member contacted the course instructor to inquire about using case studies from our "Education Politics and Policy" course as an activity at Maple Heights. The instructor agreed but on the condition that Ms. Banks approve, which she did after reviewing the four case studies. After dividing the class into four groups, with Ryerson students leading each group, Maple Heights students were asked to comment on the cases in relation to their "Challenge and Change in Society" course. Overall, as will be discussed in the reflections section, this activity was well-presented by the Monday group and well-received by Maple Heights students.

The Tuesday group's activity involved taking a cake, referred to as the "World Cake" to one of the "Challenge and Change in Society" classes. The cake was divided into the following geographic regions: North America, Latin America, Europe, Africa, and Asia-Pacific, and the size of each slice of cake represented the per capita gross income of each region. Students were then divided based on the five regions, and the region with the largest slice of cake was Asia and the smallest was Africa. Students representing "regions with small slices of cake" were encouraged to see if they could "trade" with "regions with large slices of cake", thereby increasing their "share" of cake. Immediately, students representing small-slice regions noticed large-slice regions were unwilling to share. To retaliate against this obstacle, one small-slice region "appropriated" a share of cake from a large-slice region to better balance regional incomes.

Reflections

FIRST REFLECTIVE ASSIGNMENT

This assignment involved Ryerson students describing their thoughts and observations related to their half-day orientation at Maple Heights. In particular, students were to compare their visit to Maple Heights to what they thought would be before them, and then to discuss Maple Heights in relation to their own high school experience. Some students found the Principal's responses to their questions a bit surprising because he was so forthright in describing the serious social and economic challenges before Maple Heights's students. Ryerson students commented that they did not realize the degree of poverty and disconnectedness within Maple Heights High School. In some of the first reflective assignments, Ryerson students were surprised at learning from the Principal, that financial difficulties prevent a number of Maple Heights's academically-eligible students from attending university or college. In addition, some Ryerson students were dismayed to learn, from the Principal, some Maple Heights students would like to attend university but had no one in their family to turn to for support, and also that some students felt pressure from their families to seek employment directly after high school. A Ryerson student, who had attended a neighboring high-achieving school, reflected on the perception that only students not bound for university enroll at Maple Heights.

SECOND REFLECTIVE ASSIGNMENT

Ryerson University students commented on how well their case studies and "world cake" activities were received by students in the "Challenge and Change in Society" course. Interestingly, Monday group members reported being pleased at the level of understanding these Maple Heights students demonstrated regarding the case studies, which focused on complex social issues such as: discrimination, racism, and sexual orientation in school and family settings. Tuesday group members were impressed by the degree of resourcefulness and insight Maple Heights students offered with respect to regional income distribution and social justice issues. Ms. Banks expressed gratitude for both the leadership and team-building skills evident in these Ryerson students and the high level of responsiveness from Maple Heights students. Ms. Banks indicated her interest in using the case studies in future offerings of "Challenge and Change in Society".

THIRD REFLECTIVE ASSIGNMENT

Ryerson service learning students were required to incorporate cultural and/ or social capital theories as the foundation through which to examine their experiences at Maple Heights. These Ryerson students offered detailed examples of how they came to realize the importance of schools as places that socialize citizens; furthermore, the degree to which one is socialized is dependent on both family and social circumstances. In discussing financial and family issues relating to attending college or university, some Ryerson students reflected that they too faced the same challenges as the Maple Heights students. The Maple Height students learned that what gave these current Ryerson students the drive to apply to university was family encouragement and financial support. In addition, Ryerson students noted that Maple Heights students found the Ryerson orientation session a rewarding and empowering experience. Furthermore, some Maple Height students commented positively to Ryerson students with regard to Ryerson's diverse student population. Ryerson students relayed to the Maple Heights students that many Ryerson students are also first-generation Canadians. As comfort levels grew, Ryerson students reflected that inquiries from Maple Heights students began to focus on university admission and financial requirements.

Ryerson students, in their third reflective assignment, commented that this service learning experience provided different ways to apply course theories hands on, and it gave them the opportunity to interact, learn, and become more familiar with the public school system. Ryerson students also found that service learning enhanced both their perspective on policy in action along with applying certain theories to practice. Students also offered that there was a connection between course content and service learning because the issues students dealt with at Maple Heights were portrayed in course readings and lectures. Ryerson students hoped that these Maple Heights students gained as much as they did from this service learning experience.

CONCLUSIONS

This service learning project was organized to enable Ryerson University students to volunteer their time at an urban high school, and to provide students in a Grade 12 course with an opportunity to interact with these students to help demystify university. The importance of establishing good rapport with the host organization at all stages of the service learning project is vital (Ramsdell, 2004). The initial site visit by the course instructor to Maple Heights was worthwhile, and the orientation sessions at Maple Heights and Ryerson University helped to strengthen this connection. As Ramsdell (2004) suggests, it is virtually impossible for the instructor to understand the organization's needs, and thus to prepare student volunteers, without being physically present to witness the surroundings in which the students will be working. During the site visit, the instructor was able to ascertain aspects of Maple Heights's student population and the setting within which Ryerson students would volunteer their time.

Ryerson students were required to write three reflective assignments that examined first, their perceptions of Maple Heights High School; second, an activity that their group had led at Maple Heights; and third, analyze their Maple Heights service learning experience, using theories discussed in our "Education Politics and Policy" course. Young et al. (2007) note, the benefits of service learning programs are that they may help to improve academic performance of both high school and university students in terms of boosting their sense of personal and social responsibility. Service-learning may also enhance other skills such as: critical thinking, communication, teamwork, problem solving, and time management. Ryerson students reflected that, in leading the case studies and world cake activities, their teamwork and communication skills were enhanced. A few students commented that they would like to enter the teaching profession, and that the Maple Heights service learning experience "opened their eyes" to the complexities of life in an urban high school. Jagla (2008) refers to this as enhancing the relevance of knowledge from service learning. By actively involving students in the process of constructing their own knowledge, they more readily see how it relates to the real world as opposed to just learning the theoretical concepts in isolation. As Catapano (2006) notes, placing people in real situations helps them to compare what they are learning in the course to what they are experiencing in their service learning project.

Ryerson students viewed their service learning experience as an effective way to connect high school and university students, and some hoped that this would motivate more high school students from underrepresented groups to attend university. In addition, service learning helped to break down some educational barriers because it offered university students a chance to get "real-life" experience in an urban school. Ryerson students were enthusiastic that service learning be incorporated in future offerings of "Education Politics and Policy". The instructor was hoping to include comments from Maple Heights students but was unable to due to tight time constraints related to when this service learning project ended. However, Ryerson students commented to the instructor that the verbal feedback they received from Maple Height students was very positive regarding this service learning project. The use of reflective assignments helped to ground this service learning project, both in relation to course expectations and interactions between Maple Heights and Ryerson students. Service learning has the potential to allow for "relevant and meaningful academic learning..." (Payne-Jackson, 2005, p. 60).

Yet, we must keep in mind that service learning is still in its infancy. Actual research in this field reflects the fact that service learning has been viewed quite broadly, so developing a theoretical body in this field has been challenging. Part of this problem stems from the absence of a clear theoretical base in terms of how service learning is to be considered; therefore, a number of theoretical perspective may apply. Furthermore, service learning would benefit from more robust studies based on qualitative, quantitative, or mixed methods. On a related note, service-learning researchers should be mindful not to overstate or over generalise their findings (Billig and Waterman, 2003).

With the above cautions in mind, some service learning projects have the potential to offer students a glimpse into real-world problems that may build on university or high school courses (Desrochers, 2006: Sterling, 2007). This service learning project enabled Ryerson students to widen their educational learning with practical experience, and it offered Maple Heights students the opportunity to help them demystify university. The instructor also became more aware, from visiting Maple Heights and reading Ryerson students' reflective assignments, of the widening social, cultural, and financial gaps that still disengage significant numbers of marginalize urban students from seeking educational training beyond high school. This study is limited in its ability to generalize results, and it is proposed that further research is needed to substantiate and advance the observations noted here.

REFERENCES

Billig, S., and Waterman, A. (2003). Studying service learning: Challenges and solutions. In S. Billing and A. Waterman, (Eds.), *Studying service-learning: Innovations in education research methodology* (pp. vii-xiv). Mahwah, NJ: Lawrence Erlbaum Associates, Publishers.

Brown, B., Heaton, P., & Wall, A. (2007). A service-learning elective to promote enhanced understanding in civic, cultural, and social issues and health disparitiesin pharmacy. *American Journal of Pharmaceutical Education*, 71(1), 1-7.

Campus Contact (2003). *Introduction to service learning toolkit. Readings and resources for faculty.* Providence, RI: Campus Compact.

Catapano, S. (2006). Teaching in urban schools: Mentoring pre-service teaches to apply advocacy strategies. *Mentoring & Tutoring: Partnership in Learning*, 14(1), 81-96.

City of Toronto (2009). *Toronto's racial diversity.* Retrieved 03 June 2009 from http://www.toronto.ca/toronto_facts/diverstiy.htm.

Day, D. (2008). Connecting student achievement and personal development: Service learning and academic personal development: Service learning and academic credit. *The International Journal of Learning*, 15(11), 41-50.

Desrochers, C. (2006). Educating preservice teaching for diversity: Perspectives on the possibilities and limitations of service learning. *Journal of Educational Thought*, 40(3), 263-280.

Elson, D., Johns, L., & Petrie, J. (2007). Jumpstart's service-learning initiative: Enhanced outcomes for at-risk children. In S. Gelmon & S. Billig, (Eds.), *Service learning: From passion to objectivity: International and cross-disciplinary perspectives on service-learning research* (pp. 65-88). Charlotte, NC: Information Age Publishing, Inc.

Frazer, L., Raasch, M., Pertzborn, D., & Bradley, F., (2007). The impact of community clients on student learning: The case of a university service-learning course *Journal of Experiential Education*, 29(3), 407-412.

Gupta, J. (2006). A model for interdisciplinary service-learning experience for social change. *Journal of Physical Therapy Education*, 20(3), 55-60.

Hollander, E., Saltmarsh, J., & Zlotkowski, E. (2002). Indicators of engagement. In M. Kenny, L. Simon, K. Kiley-Brabeck & R. Lerner (Eds.), *Learning to serve: Promoting civil society through service learning* (pp. 31-49). Norwell, MA: Kluwer Academic Publishers.

Howard, R. (2006). Bending toward justice: Service-learning and social capital as means to the tipping point. *Mentoring & Tutoring: Partnership in Learning*, 14(1), 5-15.

Jagla, V. (2008). Service – learning prepares teachers to meet the needs of diverse learners. *The International Journal of Learning*, 15(6), 1-7.

Kenny, M., Simon, L., Kiley-Brabeck, K., & Lerner, R. (2002). Promoting civil society through service learning: A view of the issues. In M. Kenny, L. Simon, K. Kiley-Brabeck, & R. Lerner, (Eds.), *Learning to serve:*

Promoting civil society through service learning (pp. 1-14). Norwell, MA: Kluwer Academic Publishers.

Lareau, A. (1987). Social class difference in family-school relationships: The importance of cultural capitalism. *Sociology of Education,* 60(2), 73-85.

MacLellan, D. (2008). Diversity and immigrant needs: Examining Toronto through a place-based approach. *Policy Matters.* No. 32, 1-13. Toronto, ON: Centre for Excellence in Research in Immigration and Settlement (CERIS).

Ontario Ministry of Education. (2002). *Course profile: Challenge and change in society. Grade 12 University/College Preparation.* Toronto, ON: Author.

Ontario Ministry of Education (2008). *Secondary school profiles.* Retrieved from http://www.edu.gov.on.ca on 09 June 2009.

Oakes, J. (2005). Keeping track: How schools structure inequality, (2nd ed.). New Haven, CT: Yale University Press.

O'Quin, J. (2003). Serve to learn and learn to serve. *The International Journal of Learning,* 10, 3697- 3704.

Payne-Jackson, A. (2005). A model of service learning. *The International Journal of Learning,* 12(10), 55-63.

Pearce, A. (2008). Finding your place in the world of service learning: Is the journey worth the effort? *The International Journal of Learning,* 15(10), 115-121.

Ramsdell, L. (2004). Reciprocity: The heart of service learning. *The International Journal of Learning,* 11, 523-527.

Ryerson University (2008). Ryerson University full-time undergraduate calendar 2008-2009. Toronto, ON: Author.

Ryerson University (2008a). *A toolkit for service learning course design.* Toronto, ON: Faculty of Arts, Ryerson University.

Ryerson University (2008b). *Progress indicators and related statistics for 2008.* Toronto: ON: Author.

Sterling, M. (2007). Service-learning and interior design: A case study. *Journal of Experiential Education,* 20(3), 331-343.

Terry, A. (2005). A K-12 development service-learning typology. *The International Journal of Learning,* 12(9), 321-330.

Toronto District School Board (2009). *Our school 2009-2010.* Toronto, ON: Author.

Webster, N. (2007). Enriching school connection and learning in African American urban youth: The impact of service-learning feasibility in inner-city Philadelphia. In S. Gelman & S. Billing (Eds.), *Service learning: From passion to objectivity: International and cross-disciplinary perspectives on service learning* (pp.159-176). Charlotte, NC: Information Age Publishing.

Young, C., Shinnar, R., Ackerman, R., Carruthers, C., & Young, D. (2007). Implementing and sustaining service-learning at the institutional level. *Journal of Experiential Education,* 29(3), 344-365.

Zlotkowski, E. (2003). Pedagogy and engagement. In Campus Compact (Ed.), *Introduction to service-learning toolkit: Readings and resources for faculty* (pp. 63-77). Providence, RI: Campus Compact Publishers.

FOOTNOTES

[1] Please note that Maple Heights is a pseudonym.

[2] The author would like to extend appreciation to Ryerson University's Service Learning Office, Ryerson's service learning students, and students and teaching staff at Maple Heights for their cooperation in this project.

Service Learning Promotes Positive Youth Development in High School

Both youths and communities benefit when students
engage in service learning in and out of school.

By Jonathan F. Zaff and
Richard M. Lerner

JONATHAN F. ZAFF is vice president of research and policy development, America's
Promise Alliance, Medford, Massachusetts, and RICHARD M. LERNER is director
of the Institute for Applied Research in Youth Development, Tufts University, Medford,
Massachusetts. The preparation of this article was supported in part by grants from the
National 4-H Council, the John Templeton Foundation, the Thrive Foundation for Youth, and
the National Science Foundation.

Nurturing young people's civic actions, motivations, and skills can have lasting benefits for both youth and society. This dynamic of mutual individual and societal benefit is a cornerstone of the Positive Youth Development perspective, which emphasizes young people's strengths and the potential for healthy growth (Lerner 2009). As an emerging theory of civic development and broader social contribution, Positive Youth Development asserts that internal assets (such as values and motivations) and the external assets in the lives of youths (such as civic and prosocial experiences in school and other arenas) work in concert to promote confidence, competence, connection, character, and caring—and to encourage young people's contributions to family, community, and civil society. These individual and social variables form the civic context in which youths develop (Zaff, Malanchuk, and Eccles 2008).

> Both required and voluntary school-based service results in increased rates of voting and volunteering in college and adulthood.

Service learning has become an important strategy for encouraging positive youth development and civic contribution by young people. Through service learning, young people experience valued civic participation in their communities and learn to identify community problems, prioritize solutions, and implement problem-solving strategies (Finn and Checkoway 1998). Service learning can help students develop civic motivation, skills, and commitment to continue contributing to civil society and democracy (Flanagan and Sherrod 1998).

For example, high school students who participated in Madison County Youth in Public Service demonstrated significant increases in civic efficacy, civic knowledge, social capital, and commitment to remain involved in the community (Kahne and Westheimer 2006). These students from a rural East Coast community spent a semester learning about government and then worked in small groups with government agencies to tackle real community issues. Projects included studying the feasibility of curbside recycling and developing a five-year plan for the fire and rescue department. Students who participated expressed strong satisfaction with their accomplishments and the commitment to remain engaged in civic affairs.

Youths Learning About Youth

What do out-of-school youths offer the workplace? If you ask the public or look at research statistics, it's easy to conclude: not much. Young people who don't complete high school are often disengaged not only from employment and education opportunities, but also their communities.

Eagle Rock School in Estes Park, Colorado, is an alternative high school for students who didn't thrive in mainstream settings. Its curriculum emphasizes experiential education and service learning. When the W.K. Kellogg Foundation decided to sponsor a national initiative called New Options for Youth, which explores various credentials as alternatives to high school diplomas, it did something unusual. Among the researchers the foundation engaged to collect data were service learning students from Eagle Rock.

Michael Soguero, a math teacher and director of professional development at Eagle Rock, said, "We were really thought of as partners in the project." Soguero's math class covered the use of statistics, and a research firm based in Atlanta, Georgia, offered the students training in the ethnographic skills of neutrality and objectivity in interviewing, surveying, and documentation. Through their carefully designed protocols, eight Eagle Rock students conducted surveys and qualitative interviews with more than 75 young men, predominantly black and Latino, from Baltimore, Maryland, and

Oakland, California, who hadn't succeeded in traditional school settings.

Because the Eagle Rock students had faced similar hurdles themselves, their base of empathy made the experience powerful. Interview subjects seemed more willing to disclose details about their thoughts and their lives with student-researchers. The project underscored the belief that young people are experts about a substantial number of things that adults are not.

Amanda Hansen, one of the young researchers, talked about what she found empowering about the project: "We were dealing with a real-life situation where we got to develop skills in finding a solution." Students explored aspirations and hurdles by asking their interview subjects such questions as, What do you want in life? What makes it hard for you to get it? "I love how I can relate to a lot of these out-of-school youths," said Hansen.

Over a four-month period, the students collected information from multiple perspectives and aggregated and analyzed their data. Students learned to look for patterns among the responses and correlations between the surveys and interviews. "They learned about navigating the real world," said Soguero.

At the end of their project, they flew to Michigan to present their findings to the Kellogg Foundation. Perhaps least surprising, they found that service learning was among the programs that help out-of-school youths take meaningful steps to employment.

Students also left the project feeling that the experience had a profound effect on their ability to make a difference and be involved in the issues affecting their communities.

— Caryn Pernu and Maddy Wegner

Evidence supports the role of service learning experiences in promoting positive youth development and civic contribution, although there are some important qualifications. Several studies have found that both required and voluntary school-based service results in increased rates of voting and volunteering in college and adulthood (Hart et al. 2007; Metz and Youniss 2005; Smith 1999). For example, Dávila and Mora (2007) found that young men were 29% more likely to graduate from college on time if they engaged in service to fulfill a class requirement during high school.

Many factors can affect young people's civic behavior. Parents, peers, and extracurricular activities that don't involve civic participation also appear to complement school-based civic experiences and those that occur outside school, leading to sustained civic participation (Zaff, Malanchuk, and Eccles 2008). The personal characteristics youths bring to civic experiences and the quality of their civic experiences all influence the effects of service learning programs. For these experiences to be successful, youths need to have a voice in identifying the community problem, planning the solution to the problem, and having time to reflect on their experiences (Morgan and Streb 2001).

In Youth in Public Service, changes in the student's civic context appear driven by the sense of satisfaction participants expressed about their accomplishments. For example, when youths felt community partners and other adults they worked with didn't take their views seriously, they had more frustrating experiences (Kahne and Westheimer 2006). In addition, if the service activity isn't relevant to them, youths' investment in the activity and any benefits for positive youth development may be diminished (Ginwright and James 2002). Because of this, teachers and other service learning practitioners should be aware that activities appealing to low-income, academically struggling youths in urban areas might be different from activities appealing to academically excelling, private school students living in suburbs.

VOLUNTARY VS. MANDATORY

Young people's values and motivations also predict participation in service activities (Zaff and Michelsen 2002), and youths disposed to civic participation before civic experiences might gain the most from the experiences (Zaff, Malanchuk, and Eccles 2008). Alternatively, service learning can motivate young people to engage in civic activity. Metz and Youniss (2005) found that high school students who were more inclined to perform voluntary service were not negatively affected by mandatory service. That is, being required to serve didn't have much effect on those already disposed to volunteer. However, among the group less inclined to service, students required to perform mandatory service showed a greater likelihood of civic interest and understanding, future voting, and conventional civic involvement after their experience.

THE BENEFITS OF SERVICE LEARNING PROGRAMS APPEAR TO OUTWEIGH THE LIABILITIES.

Nevertheless, mandatory service may not always be beneficial. Among 6th through 8th graders, Covitt (2002) found that girls had more positive attitudes about required service than boys, and that white students had more positive attitudes than black students. Interestingly, student attitudes about mandatory service requirements, but not the requirements themselves, had an effect on their intentions, caring, or sense of responsibility. Students who had more negative attitudes were less likely to feel responsible to serve and showed lowered intentions to serve. It may be, then, that mandatory community service would not have the long-term effects of increasing volunteerism that proponents expect, at least for youths who perceive themselves as least likely to volunteer freely.

Evidence shows that across the high school years, service learning experiences tend to help young people become more informed and engaged citizens, which supports the aspirations of families, educators, and policy makers. Service learning is linked to positive youth development and to the growth of positive civic characteristics and behaviors. The benefits of service learning programs appear to outweigh the liabilities.

Given the variation in the influences of these programs, more nuanced practice is needed, and the recent K-12 Service Learning Standards for Quality Practice should provide some guidance. Teachers and other practitioners should give young people opportunities to develop and implement service learning projects and should provide the time and direction to reflect on the learning and the service that students accomplish through their work. This process can have the added benefit of ensuring that youths are pursuing initiatives that interest and engage them. Furthermore, given that parents and the broader community are parts of the civic context and can complement young people's service learning experiences, educators interested in service learning can do more to encourage parents to talk with their children about the projects and to connect the projects to activities outside of school. K

REFERENCES

Covitt, Beth A. *Middle School Students' Attitudes Toward Required Chesapeake Bay Service Learning.* Washington, D.C.: Corporation for National and Community Service, 2002.

Dávila, Alberto, and Marie T. Mora. "Do Gender and Ethnicity Affect Civic Engagement and Academic Progress?" *CIRCLE Working Paper 53.* College Park, Md.: University of Maryland, 2007.

Finn, J.L., and Barry Checkoway. "Young People as Competent Community Builders: A Challenge to Social Work." *Social Work* 43, no. 4 (1998): 335-347.

Flanagan, Constance A., and Lonnie R. Sherrod. "Youth Political Development: An Introduction." *Journal of Social Issues* 54, no. 3 (1998): 447-456.

Ginwright, Shawn, and Taj James. "From Assets to Agents: Social Justice, Organizing, and Youth Development." *New Directions for Youth Development* 96 (2002): 27-46.

Hart, Daniel, Thomas M. Donnelly, James Youniss, and Robert Atkins. "High School Community Service as a Predictor of Adult Voting and Volunteering." *American Educational Research Journal* 44, no. 1 (2007): 197-219.

Kahne, Joe, and Joel Westheimer. "The Limits of Political Efficacy: Educating Citizens for a Democratic Society." *PS: Political Science and Politics* 39, no. 2 (2006): 289-296.

Lerner, Richard M. "The Positive Youth Development Perspective: Theoretical and Empirical Bases of a Strength-Based Approach to Adolescent Development." In *Oxford Handbook of Positive Psychology*, 2nd ed., ed. C.R. Snyder and S.J. Lopez. Oxford, U.K.: Oxford University Press, 2009.

Metz, Edward C., and James Youniss. "Longitudinal Gains in Civic Development Through School-Based Required Service." *Political Psychology* 26, no. 3 (2005): 413-437.

Morgan, William, and Matthew Streb. "Building Citizenship: How Student Voice in Service Learning Develops Civic Values." *Social Science Quarterly* 82, no. 1 (2001): 154-169.

Smith, Elizabeth S. "The Effects of Investment in the Social Capital of Youth on Political and Civic Behavior in Young Adulthood: A Longitudinal Analysis." *Political Psychology* 20, no. 3 (September 1999): 553-580.

Zaff, Jonathan F., and Erik Michelsen. "Encouraging Civic Engagement: How Teens Are (Or Are Not) Becoming Responsible Citizens." *Child Trends Research Brief*. Washington, D.C.: Child Trends, 2002.

Zaff, Jonathan F., Oksana Malanchuk, and Jacquelynne Eccles. "Predicting Positive Citizenship from Adolescence to Young Adulthood: The Effects of a Civic Context." *Applied Developmental Science* 12, no. 1 (2008): 38-53.

Free to Choose Service-Learning

By Michael P. Garber and Justin A. Heet

MICHAEL P. GARBER is a senior fellow and director of education policy at the Hudson Institute, Indianapolis, where **JUSTIN A. HEET** is a research analyst.

Service-learning, by its activist nature, can easily become politicized. Thus, in the view of Mr. Garber and Mr. Heet, it should exist only in schools that are freely chosen by the families of students who attend them.

Only Disciples of Ayn Rand could oppose the idea of service-learning. In the best situations, when service is part of a school's program, students are challenged to define themselves through a larger sense of their community and of their responsibility to it. They have the opportunity to apply their skills to problems that require judgment and leadership. Service-learning, if properly understood, can help re-create the functional communities that renowned University of Chicago sociologist James Coleman wrote about as being vital to increasing the amount of "social capital" generated by schools.

The problem is that service-learning, by its activist nature, can easily become politicized. Thus it should exist only in schools that are freely chosen by the families of students who attend them.

As beneficial as service-learning may be, it puts our public schools as they are now configured in an untenable position. The opponents of service-learning have often argued that "mandatory volunteerism" is an oxymoron. They're right. But that does not cover the full extent of the problem. In situations in which families are not free to choose the schools their children attend, the introduction of service-learning invariably leads to needless politicization of schools, in many cases weakens schools' ability to serve their primary mission of academic instruction, and attenuates the idea of service-learning itself.

Considerable political conflict already exists within the country's public schools. At school board meetings across the country, bitter arguments continue over the inclusion of various books in the curriculum, over whether or not evolution should be taught as a science, and even over whether Christopher Columbus was a hero or a villain. When implemented in schools that children are compelled to attend, service-learning adds considerable fuel to these fires.

Critics of the current state of service-learning rightly point out that most of its advocates lean strongly to the left side of the political spectrum. Moreover, most of the programs engaged in by students in the U.S. reflect a social-activist bent. We believe that it is the responsibility of schools (particularly those funded by taxpayers and run by government entities) to engage students in honest inquiry and an honest effort to understand the many perspectives on a given issue. It is not the role of the schools to engage in advocacy.

This criticism is equally valid from a "progressive" vantage point. What if students in the public schools in Greenville, South Carolina, teamed with Bob Jones University students to hold a protest outside an abortion clinic? Or what if students in Colorado participated in a signature-gathering campaign to put a referendum on the ballot banning special legal protection for homosexuals? What if students chose to volunteer their time at a drug-rehabilitation program run by a church, which required those receiving services to be members of the church and to accept religious instruction in order to get help?

A service-learning program in Maine highlights the slippery slope on which schools can find themselves. Seven freshmen at Sumner Memorial High School in Sullivan, Maine, recently lobbied the state legislature to prevent certain types of fishing in Taunton Bay. [1] The activities all took place with the oversight of the civics and service-learning instructor.

Many people may believe that Taunton Bay requires greater environmental protection. However, if increased regulation requires lobbying, it is clear that not everyone agrees with the idea. Perhaps the parents of students at the school make their living from the kind of fishing their children—or their children's classmates—seek to have banned. The issue is not who is right or wrong about fishing in Taunton Bay. The issue is that, like the communities of which they are a part, schools serve diverse constituencies. Some citizens will inevitably object when their tax dollars are used to advance causes with which they disagree.

It seems to us that schools with mandatory attendance areas (and no choice offered to parents) have two ways of dealing with the prospect of politicization, neither of which is desirable. First, in the tradition of Dewey, schools can welcome the fight. Many proponents feel that schools should support the social engineering that service-learning can engender. Joel Westheimer and

Joseph Kahne go so far as to criticize many service-learning programs for not being political *enough*. They claim that, in emphasizing personal responsibility or private charity, schools do not do enough to redefine students' conception of citizenship in terms of government action. They lament that few programs "ask students to assess corporate responsibility or the ways government policies improve or harm society. Few programs ask students to examine the history of social movements as levers for change." [2]

The second response schools might adopt is to attempt to avoid controversy by making service-learning as voluntary as possible. Many schools have already chosen this route. (Indeed, students in Bethlehem, Pennsylvania, and Chapel Hill, North Carolina, have sued their schools over "forced volunteerism.") Rather than ask all students in a class to work on the same project, schools can give students the right to design their own individual or small-group projects, thereby insulating their programs from some of the sting of forced volunteerism. At Harbor City Learning Center in Baltimore, Maryland—a school for at-risk youths that has received widespread attention for its service-learning program—the school's coordinator oversees students who are in "individual service placements." [3]

The problem with this individual-centered approach is that it diminishes the potential value of service-learning for students. Most service-learning advocates maintain that its promise is not simply the direct community benefit of the students' activities—e.g., cleaner streets, fewer children without toys on Christmas—but the indirect benefit of greater student awareness and sense of civic responsibility. Even the most optimistic proponents of service-learning acknowledge that these indirect benefits do not happen organically. They come about as a result of reflection, study, and guidance. The lasting lessons grow from working with one's peers to arrive at group solutions rather than from driving toward purely individual solutions. In other words, good service-learning requires what good learning always requires: interaction with other students and the mentoring of an innovative teacher who can help students bridge the gap between good intentions and good results.

Properly understood, service-learning holds tremendous potential for expanding and enriching a child's education. However, problems inevitably result when such programs are implemented in schools that are not freely chosen by the parents of students who attend them. When introduced in these schools, service-learning programs have enormous potential for polarizing, rather than fortifying, the greater school community. The answer is not to dispense with the educationally sound and commonsensical idea of service-learning. The answer is to allow parents to choose schools that are consistent with their priorities and beliefs.

Footnotes

1 Shawn O'Leary, "Students Lobby for Bill to Protect Bay," *Bangor Daily News,* 4 February 2000.

2 Joel Westheimer and Joseph Kahne, "Service-Learning Required: But What Exactly Do Students Learn?," *Education Week,* 26 January 2000, p. 32.

3 Suzanne Goldsmith, "The Community Is Their Textbook: Maryland's Experiment with Mandatory Service for Schools," *The American Prospect,* Summer 1995, p. 54.

Underage, Overweight: The Federal Government Needs to Halt the Marketing of Unhealthy Foods to Kids

Editors of Scientific American

The statistic is hard to swallow: in the U.S., nearly one in three children under the age of 18 is overweight or obese, making being overweight the most common childhood medical condition. These youngsters are likely to become heavy adults, putting them at increased risk of developing cardiovascular disease, type 2 diabetes and other chronic ailments. In February, First Lady Michelle Obama announced a campaign to fight childhood obesity. Helping parents and schools to instill healthier habits in kids is an important strategy in this battle. But the government must take further steps to solve the problem.

In an ideal world, adults would teach children how to eat healthily and would lead by example. But in reality, two thirds of U.S. adults are themselves overweight or obese. Moreover, the food and beverage industry markets sugar- and fat-laden goods to kids directly—through commercials on television, product placement in movies and video games, and other media. Its considerable efforts—nearly $1.7 billion worth in 2007—have met with sickening success: a recent study conducted by researchers at the University of California, Los Angeles, found that children who see more television ads tend to become fatter. You might expect that watching TV, being a sedentary activity, is responsible for obesity, but the study found that obesity is correlated not with television per se but with advertising. The more commercial programming children watched, the fatter they got compared with those who watched a comparable amount of public television or DVDs. The majority of products marketed during children's programming are foods.

As nutritionist Marion Nestle of New York University has written, society needs to "create a food environment that makes it easier for parents and everyone else to make better food choices." Protecting children from junk-food marketing would help create conditions conducive to achieving a healthy weight.

Unfortunately, like the tobacco industry before it, the food industry cannot be trusted to self-regulate in this regard. In a study published in the March *Pediatrics*, investigators looked at the prevalence of food and beverage brands in movies released between 1996 and 2005. They noted, for instance, that although Coca-Cola and PepsiCo have pledged to not advertise during children's television programming, their products routinely appear in movies aimed at kids.

Likewise, in the March *Public Health Nutrition*, researchers reported a 78 percent increase from 2006 to 2008 in the use of cartoon characters, toys and other child-oriented cross promotions on food packaging—much of it for nutritionally bereft foods. A whopping 65 percent of these cross promotions came from food manufacturers that have opted into the Children's Food and Beverage Advertising Initiative, sponsored by the Council of Better Business Bureaus, which promises to limit advertising to kids but allows participants to decide for themselves whether to restrict in-store marketing. Such examples of ineffectual commitments on the part of the food industry abound.

In December a group of U.S. agencies—the Federal Trade Commission, the Centers for Disease Control and Prevention, the Food and Drug Administration, and the Department of Agriculture—proposed standards for foods and beverages that are marketed to children between the ages of two and 17. The agencies sensibly recommended that such foods must provide a meaningful contribution to a healthy diet by meeting specified requirements; that the amounts of saturated fat, trans fat, sugar and salt in these foods must not exceed limits set by the group; and that certain clearly healthy foods—such as those that are 100 percent fruits, vegetables or whole grains—may be marketed to kids without meeting the other two standards.

The interagency working group is due to submit a report containing its final recommendations to Congress by July 15. The standards are worthy but have one problem: as they stand, they would be voluntary. They should be mandatory, not optional, and the FDA should implement and enforce them.

The estimated cost of treating obesity-related ailments in adults was $147 billion for 2009. With the health care system already faltering, allowing companies to decide for themselves whether to peddle junk food to kids is a fox-and-henhouse policy this country simply cannot afford any longer.

The Kids Question

How can commerce and responsibility be balanced when marketing food to children?
We ask a food marketer, a business philosopher and a politician

Martin Glenn, Craig Smith and Debra Shipley

Martin Glenn President, PepsiCo UK

The premise here is that consumer goods companies would have any desire to communicate in an irresponsible way, and for my part, I would disagree with such a suggestion. No smart company would want to communicate irresponsibly to parents or their children, because it goes against their best interests.

A company's biggest assets are its brands, and consumer trust in brands is fundamental to its existence. One-and-a-half million consumers make a decision to buy Walkers crisps every day—if they believed we were misleading them, they would very quickly stop buying our brand.

Let's take a step back and look at the role played by advertising. Advertising helps to raise awareness in a commercially competitive environment and encourages brand choice. But while it may encourage consumers to try something once, if the product or service is not good quality or doesn't deliver a consumer need, consumers will not come back for more. In short, advertising cannot make consumers do things they don't want to do; it needs to work with consumer interest and desire.

Why do we believe companies such as ours advertise responsibly? First, because the majority of us are responsible companies and we want to be considered as such by the consumers we serve. Second, because there are very stringent advertising codes of practice in place—particularly with regard to children—that ensure we advertise our products or services responsibly. In the case of snack products, the code ensures our advertising does not encourage children to over-consume or replace main meals with snacks.

And third, because we seek not only to adhere to the letter of the codes, but to practise the spirit of them too. In the case of Walkers, we provide relevant nutritional information on our packs that allows consumers to make an informed choice about the products they eat. We also carry healthy lunchbox suggestions on the back of our multi-packs that clearly define the role of our products in the diet—in other words, as a treat.

We also know that advertising features way down the ranking of influences on children's habits. Research shows that it lies in ninth position, far behind the more significant influences of family and friends.

So why is advertising to children such a hot topic at the moment? Because it's currently seen by some as a major cause of the rise in obesity. But we know that this is simply not true. Advertising is only a very minor driver, if a driver at all, in the obesity issue.

What we need to do, if we are to move this debate forward, is to focus our efforts on addressing the real causes of obesity; too much energy consumed and not enough being expended through activity and exercise.

The right approach to tackling the obesity issue is a holistic one from all stakeholders—in other words, the food industry, the government, schools and parents—which addresses both sides of the equation: calories in and out.

The food industry must continue to provide ever-greater choice to the consumer, through development of healthier products. There is also an opportunity to provide more consistent information to consumers about the nutritional content of food across all sectors of the industry. At the same time, schools and parents must help to educate their children about the importance of a balanced lifestyle and a balanced diet. The government must provide them with the appropriate resources to enable them to do that.

PepsiCo would welcome the opportunity to play its part in helping address the issue of obesity. Companies such as ours should be included, not excluded from being a key part of the solution—not least because as owners of brands that consumers trust, and champions in consumer communication, we have much to offer.

However, companies such as PepsiCo cannot unilaterally take initiatives in this area without the context being right, and it is up to the government to help set the right tone and clarify the process—for example, which government ministry should lead the way—in order to get constructive engagement.

Craig Smith–Associate Professor of Marketing and Ethics and Associate Dean of the Full-time MBA Programme, London Business School

Let's assume there is clear evidence that the advertising of food to children is a major factor in unhealthy diets and, given insufficient physical activity, that this leads to increased obesity. We might well conclude that the advertising is unethical. Indeed, according to the American Marketing Association, marketers should be guided by 'the basic rule of professional ethics: not knowingly to do harm'.

Moral philosophy might also support a judgment of unethical conduct. Utilitarianism, in its simplest form, requires that we consider the consequences for all affected parties and assess whether the act results in the greatest overall welfare, relative to other acts. So, while we need to consider the effects of food advertising on children's diets, we should also allow for other effects, such as better-quality children's programming—which benefits from ad revenues—the sensory pleasures of food, and the entertainment value of ads.

Our analysis might also extend to the healthcare costs of obesity (£3.6bn by 2010) and reduced revenues for food producers and commercial TV. We may conclude welfare is not maximized by advertising to children. But this analysis is problematic given the difficulty of knowing all consequences and weighing up better health versus sensory pleasures.

Because of the challenges in applying moral theories to marketing ethics, I developed the Consumer Sovereignty Test (CST). It ca be used to evaluate ethical issues within the marketer-consumer relationship. It suggests marketers have an obligation to ensure consumers are capable of informed choice. More specifically, the CST requires an assessment of capability (are consumers vulnerable?), information (is it adequate and available?), and choice (are consumers free to choose?). With food advertising to children, the test suggests consumer sovereignty is compromised because of the subjects' vulnerability. The practice is also ethically problematic if children, rather than parents, are the consumer decision-makers.

According to the CST, advertising unhealthy foods to adults is not ethically problematic. They are free to choose from a variety of food, are considered capable of making dietary decisions, understand the persuasive intent of ads and, arguably, have sufficient access to information about a healthy diet. In contrast, all marketing to children under eight is ethically suspect. Advertisers may claim children are simply young consumers—but children lack the conceptual abilities required to make consumer decisions.

The issue of obesity demands policy intervention. But to what extent should measures be directed against advertising to children? The options under consideration by the Food Standards Agency (FSA) range from industry self-regulation to legislation on TV advertising and labeling. With uncertainty about the contribution of marketing to the unhealthy shift in children's diets relative to other influences—parents, peers, school—it is difficult to assert conclusively that advertising restrictions would reverse the trend.

Restrictions may generally be considered contrary to consumer interest, but arguably not in the context of advertising to children, given the inappropriateness of targeting under-eights. And as a review by the FSA shows, there is a balance of evidence suggesting ads do have some effect on children's diets.

Decisions on such a policy must balance the cost of government intervention against the possible benefit of dietary improvements. Such measures must also be part of a broader programme that includes the promotion of exercise and healthier diets.

From an industry perspective, the responsible approach would be to accept the likely effect of advertising and adopt FSA suggestions. Some have acted already: Coca-Cola announced it would no longer advertise to under-12s. This approach has pragmatic appeal. The evidence suggests regulatory intervention is warranted. It is perhaps inevitable if industry fails to act.

Debra Shipley–MP for Stourbridge and a Member of the Culture, Media and Sport Committee

In November last year, I introduced a Bill into the House of Commons to ban the advertising of food and drink high in sugar, salt and fat from children's TV. The Bill ran out of parliamentary time, but the response from the public, professionals and politicians was overwhelming.

As the scale of the childhood obesity and diabetes problem in the UK has become more widely known, the demand for action has become louder and more determined. Almost 100 national organisations back the campaign, ranging from health charities such as the British Heart Foundation to respected groups such as the Women's Institute. The tide has now turned against those who pretend there is no problem, as more people realise that banning children's TV advertisements for certain foods is moderate, reasonable and worthwhile.

The evidence that childhood obesity is a serious problem is overwhelming. The Chief Medical Officer for England has called it 'a health time bomb' and we are warned that today's youngsters may be the first generation that will live shorter lives than their parents.

At age six, one in five children in England are overweight, and a further one in ten are obese. By age 15, these figures have risen to 31% and 17% respectively. Even worse, the first obesity-related cases of Type Two diabetes in Caucasian adolescents have now been reported in the UK.

Is advertising the only cause? No. More must be done to encourage physical activity and improve labeling and food education. But advertising is a significant contributory factor.

The recent Food Standards Agency review examined 119 pieces of research on the topic and concluded that there was a clear impact at the level of both brand and type of food consumed. The University of Liverpool later found that all children over-consume after exposure to food ads, and obese children are particularly susceptible.

Some—usually those with vested interests within the food, drink and advertising industries—will deny the link, but in one hour of children's viewing on Five, kids may see 11 advertisements for foods high in fat, salt or sugar. I doubt that food manufacturers have so little faith in the advertising profession that they honestly believe this does not have a cumulative impact on children's eating patterns.

Jingles are designed specifically to appeal to children and to be catchy and memorable. They are accompanied by images of happy children being made happier by eating and drinking these products. The underlying message to parents viewing with their children is to make their children happy by providing these products.

The question is, where do we draw the line between commercial freedom and protecting public health? I believe that any government action should ultimately place the health of our children as a higher priority than the budget of children's television programmes or the financial concerns of a multinational, multi-billion-pound food and drink industry.

When culture, media and sport secretary Tessa Jowell comes to make her decision on whether or not to stop the ruthless and cynical targeting of small children with food and drink products high in fat, sugar and salt, she should ignore the rich and powerful industry lobby. Instead, she should do what only she has the power to do; ban food and drink advertising high in fat, sugar and salt from children's television.

Policy Statement—Children, Adolescents, Obesity, and the Media

Keywords: media, obesity, overweight, screen time, junk food, television

ABSTRACT

Obesity has become a worldwide public health problem. Considerable research has shown that the media contribute to the development of child and adolescent obesity, although the exact mechanism remains unclear. Screen time may displace more active pursuits, advertising of junk food and fast food increases children's requests for those particular foods and products, snacking increases while watching TV or movies, and late-night screen time may interfere with getting adequate amounts of sleep, which is a known risk factor for obesity. Sufficient evidence exists to warrant a ban on junk-food or fast-food advertising in children's TV programming. Pediatricians need to ask 2 questions about media use at every well-child or well-adolescent visit: (1) How much screen time is being spent per day? and (2) Is there a TV set or Internet connection in the child's bedroom? *Pediatrics* 2011;128:201–208

INTRODUCTION

Obesity represents a clear and present danger to the health of children and adolescents. Its prevalence among American youth has doubled in the past 3 decades,[1] and there are now more overweight and obese adults in the United States than adults of normal weight.[2] However, obesity is also a worldwide problem; rates are increasing in nearly every country.[3,4] It is increasingly clear that the media, particularly TV, play an important role in the etiology of obesity.[5] As a result, many countries are now establishing new regulations for advertising to children on TV, and many government health agencies are now issuing recommendations for parents regarding the amount of time children spend watching TV.[6] Unfortunately, there are currently no data relating other media to obesity.

MEDIA AND OBESITY

There are a number of ways that watching TV could be contributing to obesity: (1) increased sedentary activity and displacement of more physical pursuits; (2) unhealthy eating practices learned from both the programming and the advertisements for unhealthy foods; (3) increased snacking behavior while viewing; and (4) interference with normal sleep patterns. However, most researchers now agree that the evidence linking excessive TV-viewing and obesity is persuasive.[7-9] There have been dozens of longitudinal and correlational studies documenting a connection.[9] An increasing number of these studies hold ethnicity and socioeconomic status—known to be key factors in obesity— constant and still reveal that TV-viewing is a significant contributor to obesity.[7,10] Results of the longitudinal studies are particularly convincing. For example, a remarkable 30-year study in the United Kingdom found that a higher mean of daily hours of TV viewed on weekends predicted a higher BMI at the age of 30. For each additional hour of TV watched on weekends at age 5, the risk of adult obesity increased by 7%.[11] A group of researchers in Dunedin, New Zealand, followed 1000 subjects from birth to 26 years of age and found that average weeknight TV-viewing between the ages of 5 and 15 years was strongly predictive of adult BMI.[12] In a study of 8000 Scottish children, viewing more than 8 hours of TV per week at age 3 was associated with an increased risk of obesity at age 7.[13] Also, in 8000 Japanese children, more TV-viewing at age 3 resulted in a higher risk of being overweight at age 6.[14] Numerous American studies have had similar findings.[15-23]

The presence of a TV set in a child's bedroom seems to exacerbate the impact of TV-viewing on children's weight status.[24-28] A study of 2343 children aged 9 to 12 years revealed that having a bedroom TV set was a significant risk factor for obesity, independent of physical activity.[24] A cross-sectional study of 2761 parents with young children in New York found that 40% of the 1- to 5-year-olds had a bedroom TV, and those who did were more likely to be overweight or obese.[25] Teenagers with a bedroom TV spent more time watching TV, less time being physically active, ate fewer family meals, had greater consumption of sweetened beverages, and ate fewer vegetables than did teenagers without a bedroom TV.[26]

Recent correlational studies have also found a strong association between time spent watching TV and blood glucose level control in young people with diabetes,[29] type 2 diabetes mellitus,[30] insulin resistance,[31] metabolic syndrome,[32] hypertension,[33,34] and high cholesterol levels.[35-37] Furthermore, when TV time is diminished, so are measures of adiposity.[38,39]

MECHANISMS

How might time spent with media result in obesity? Contrary to popular opinion, overweight and obesity probably result from small, incremental increases in caloric intake (or increases in sedentary activities).[40] An excess intake of 50 kcal/day (eg, an extra pat of butter) produces a weight gain of 5 lb/year. Drinking a can of soda per day produces a weight gain of 15 lb/year.[41] Nearly 40% of children's caloric intake now comes from solid fat and added sugars, and soda or fruit drinks provide nearly 10% of total calories.[42] Because obesity is caused by an imbalance between energy intake and energy expenditure, screen time may contribute in several different ways.

DISPLACEMENT OF MORE ACTIVE PURSUITS

Children spend more time with media than in any other activity except for sleeping—an average of more than 7 hours/day.[43] Many studies have found that physical activity decreases as screen time increases,[44-46] but many other studies have not.[47-49] Children and teenagers who use a lot of media may tend to be more sedentary in general,[7,50] or researchers' measures of physical activity may be too imprecise.[9] Nevertheless, increasing physical activity, decreasing media time, and improving nutritional practices have been shown to prevent the onset of obesity, if not decrease existing obesity as well.[51-55] Some of the newer interactive video games may be useful in this way.[56,57] For example, a study of preteens playing *Dance Revolution* and Nintendo's *Wii Sports* found that energy expenditure was equivalent to moderate-intensity walking.[58]

UNHEALTHY EATING HABITS AND EFFECTS OF ADVERTISING

Children and teenagers who watch more TV tend to consume more calories or eat higher-fat diets,[59-64] drink more sodas,[65] and eat fewer fruits and vegetables.[66] Some researchers have argued that the viewing of TV while eating suppresses cues of satiety, which leads to overeating.[60] Others believe that viewers are primed to choose unhealthy foods as a consequence of viewing advertisements for foods high in fat, salt, and/or sugar and low in nutritional content ("junk food").[61] On any given day, 30% of American youngsters are eating fast food and consuming an additional 187 kcal (equaling 6 lb/year).[67,68] Fast food is big business: Americans spend more than $110 billion annually on it, which is more than that spent on higher education, computers, or cars.[69] A December 2010 study examined 3039 possible meal combinations at a dozen restaurant chains and found only 12 meals that met nutrition criteria for preschoolers. The same study found that 84% of parents had purchased fast food for their children in the previous week.[70] More than 80% of all advertisements in children's programming are for fast foods or snacks,[71-73] and for every hour that children watch TV, they see an estimated 11 food advertisements.[74]

Although exposure to food ads has decreased in the past few years for young children,[73] it has increased for adolescents.[75]

In 2009, the fast-food industry alone spent $4.2 billion on advertising in all media.[70] A study of 50,000 ads from 2003–2004 on 170 top-rated shows found that 98% of food ads seen by children aged 2 to 11 years and nearly 90% of food ads seen by teenagers are for products that are high in fat, sugar, and/or sodium and low in nutritional content (junk food).[76] A newer study of 1638 hours of TV and nearly 9000 food ads found that young people see an average of 12 to 21 food ads per day, for a total of 4400 to 7600 ads per year, yet they see fewer than 165 ads that promote fitness or good nutrition.[77] In 1 study, black children viewed 37% more ads than other youth.[78] New technology is enabling advertisers to reach young children and teenagers with a variety of online interactive techniques.[79–82] A study of the top 5 brands in 8 different food and beverage categories found that all of them had Internet Web sites: 63% had advergames (games used to advertise the product), 50% had cartoon characters, and 58% had a designated children's area.[79] Half of the Web sites urged children to ask their parents to buy the products, yet only 17% contained any nutritional information.[79] Teenagers' cell phones can be targeted by fast-food companies that can offer teenagers a discount on fast food as they walk by a particular restaurant.[81]

Available research results clearly indicate that advertising is effective in getting younger children to request more high-fat/low-nutrition food (junk food) and to attempt to influence their parents.[5,9,83–85] For example, a 2006 study of 827 third-grade children followed for 20 months found that total TV time and total screen media time predicted future requests for advertised foods and drinks.[86] Even brief exposures to TV food ads can influence children as young as preschool age in their food choices.[87] In 1 recent experiment, children consumed 45% more snacks when exposed to food advertising while watching cartoons than advertising for other products.[64] Similarly, children who played an online advergame that marketed healthy foods were more likely to eat healthy snacks than those who played an online advergame that advertised junk food.[82] Perhaps the most convincing study about the impact of advertising involved 63 children who tasted 5 pairs of identical foods (eg, French fries) and beverages (eg, milk) from unbranded packaging versus branded packaging. The results of the experiment revealed that the children strongly preferred the branded food and drinks to the unbranded foods.[88]

To illustrate the power of marketing, compare the commitment of the Robert Wood Johnson Foundation to spend $100 million per year to try to decrease childhood obesity with the fact that the food industry spends more than that every month marketing primarily junk food and fast food to young people.[84,89] Food is also unhealthily portrayed in most TV programming and movies.[9,84,90,91] A study of the 30 highest-rated programs among 2- to 5-year-olds found that an average child would see more than 500 food references per week, half of which were to empty-calorie or high-fat/sugar/salt foods

(D. L. G. Borzekowski, EdD, "Watching What They Eat: A Content Analysis of Televised Food References Reaching Preschool Children," unpublished manuscript, 2001). In an analysis of 100 films from 1991 through 2000, fats and sweets were the most common foods depicted.[91] Hollywood product placements are also being used to influence the food preferences and purchasing patterns of children and adolescents.[92,93] In the 200 movies examined from 1996 to 2005, a total of 1180 brand placements were identified. Candy (26%) and salty snacks (21%) were the most prevalent food brands, sugar-sweetened beverages (76%) were the most prevalent beverage brands, and fast food composed two-thirds of the food retail establishment brand placements.[93]

EFFECT OF MEDIA ON SLEEP HABITS

TV and other media are known to displace or disturb young people's sleep patterns.[5,94,95] A longitudinal study of adolescents in New York found that viewing 3 or more hours/day of TV doubled the risk of difficulty falling asleep compared with adolescents who watch less than 1 hour/day.[96] There is also now evidence that later bedtimes and less sleep may be associated with a greater risk of obesity.[97–101] The mechanism may be that sleep loss leads to increased snacking and consumption of less healthy foods to maintain energy,[102,103] that sleep deprivation leads to fatigue and therefore greater sedentary behavior,[104] or that children who do not get enough sleep have metabolic changes as well.[105]

Stress may also play a role, although there are only a handful of studies that have studied this subject so far. For example, a Scottish study of nearly 1500 4- to 12-year-olds found that heavier TV use produced greater psychological stress in children and that this effect was independent of, but exacerbated by, decreases in exercise.[106]

CONCLUSIONS

Media clearly play an important role in the current epidemic of childhood and adolescent obesity. The sheer number of advertisements that children and adolescents see for junk food and fast food have an effect. So, too, does the shift away from good nutritional practices that increased media screen time seems to create. Any success in dealing with the current epidemic will require a major change in society's recognition of media exposure as a major risk factor for obesity and in young people's media habits and the advertisements to which they are exposed.[107,108]

RECOMMENDATIONS

1. Pediatricians should ask parents and patients 2 key questions about media use: (1) How much time per day does the child or teenager spend with

screen media? and (2) Is there a TV set or unrestricted, unmonitored Internet connection throughout the house, including in the child's bedroom?[109] This recommendation should be incorporated into every well-child visit, as outlined in *Bright Futures.*[110]

2. Pediatricians should encourage parents to discuss food advertising with their children as they monitor children's TV-viewing and teach their children about appropriate nutrition.[111-113]

3. Pediatricians should continue to counsel parents to limit total noneducational screen time to no more than 2 hours/day, to avoid putting TV sets and Internet connections in children's bedrooms, to coview with their children, to limit nighttime screen media use to improve children's sleep, and to try strongly to avoid screen exposure for infants under the age of 2 years. In a recent study of 709 7- to 12-year-olds, children who did not adhere to the American Academy of Pediatrics guidelines of less than 2 hours/day of screen time[114] and 11,000 to 13,000 pedometer steps per day were 3 to 4 times more likely to be overweight.[115] Conversely, preschool-aged children who ate dinner with their parents, got adequate sleep, and had limited screen-time hours had a 40% lower prevalence of obesity than those exposed to none of these routines.[116]

4. Pediatricians should work with community groups and schools to implement media education programs in child care centers, schools, and community-based programs such as the YMCA. Such programs that teach children how to understand and interpret advertisements may have the potential to immunize young people against harmful media effects.[117] In addition, programs that educate parents about limiting media use in general have already been shown to be highly effective.[8,38,39,118,119]

5. Pediatricians should work with their state chapters, the AAP, parent and public health groups, and the White House[120] to do the following:

- Ask Congress, the Federal Trade Commission, and the Federal Communications Commission to implement a ban on junk-food advertising during programming that is viewed predominantly by young children.[84,121,122] Currently, several European countries restrict food advertising aimed at young children.[123] Several food manufacturers have already indicated a willingness to implement such a ban voluntarily,[124,125] but it remains to be seen whether they will follow through.[126-128] For example, children's cereals remain considerably unhealthier than adult cereals; they contain 85% more sugar, 65% less fiber, and 60% more sodium.[129] One-quarter of all food and beverage advertising originates from companies that do not participate in the initiative, and two-thirds of all advertising by companies that do participate is still for food and beverages of low nutritional value.[85] In addition, the food and beverage industry remains steadfastly opposed to any regulation. For example, in 2007, 1 soft drink company spent more than $1.7 million to lobby against marketing restrictions and school nutrition legislation.[130] Two recent studies showed that a ban on fast-food ads would reduce the number of overweight children and adolescents in the United States by an estimated 14% to 18%.[131,132] Just eliminating federal tax deductions for fast-food ads that target children would reduce childhood obesity by 5% to 7%.[131] On the other hand, advertisements and public service announcements for health foods and healthy nutritional practices should be encouraged. One recent experiment showed that children exposed to attractive advertisements for healthy foods develop significantly more positive attitudes than children shown junk-food ads.[133]

- Ask Congress and the Federal Communications Commission to prohibit interactive advertising involving junk food or fast food to children via digital TV, cell phones, and other media[79–81,121] and to ban payments for product placement in movies. Restoring power to the Federal Trade Commission to more tightly regulate children's advertising could be another way of accomplishing this goal.[84,134,135]
- Ask Congress to fund media research (eg, the Children Media Research and Advancement Act [CAMRA]). More research is specifically needed to determine (1) how heavy media use in children reflects or contributes to psychosocial elements of the child's life, such as stress in the home, (2) how new media technologies may be playing a role in exacerbating exposure to ads or encouraging more sedentary behavior, and (3) which of the above-mentioned mechanisms is most responsible for contributing to obesity and how such mechanisms can be ameliorated.[83,134]
- Encourage the production of more counteradvertising and more prosocial video games[136,137] and Web sites that encourage children to choose healthy foods.[82]

6. Pediatricians should be aware that children with high levels of screen time have higher levels of childhood stress, which puts them at risk not only for obesity but also for a number of stress-associated morbidities (eg, mood disorders, substance abuse, diabetes, cardiovascular disease, asthma).[138] Consequently, displacing screen time with more prosocial or resilience-building activities (eg, exercise, imaginative or social play) is an important approach to addressing a wide array of societal ills including obesity.[139]

LEAD AUTHOR

Victor C. Strasburger, MD

COUNCIL ON COMMUNICATIONS AND MEDIA, 2010–2011

Deborah Ann Mulligan, MD, Chairperson
Tanya Remer Altmann, MD
Ari Brown, MD
Dimitri A. Christakis, MD
Kathleen Clarke-Pearson, MD
Holly Lee Falik, MD
David L. Hill, MD
Marjorie J. Hogan, MD
Alanna Estin Levine, MD
Kathleen G. Nelson, MD
Gwenn S. O'Keeffe, MD

FORMER EXECUTIVE COMMITTEE MEMBERS

Gilbert L. Fuld, MD, Immediate Past Chairperson
Benard P. Dreyer, MD
Regina M. Milteer, MD
Donald L. Shifrin, MD
Victor C. Strasburger, MD

CONTRIBUTOR

Amy Jordan, PhD

LIAISONS

Michael Brody, MD—American Academy of Child and Adolescent Psychiatry
Brian Wilcox, PhD—American Psychological Association

STAFF

Gina Ley Steiner
Veronica Laude Noland

REFERENCES

1. Skelton JA, Cook SR, Aunger P, Klein JD, Barlow SE. Prevalence and trends of severe obesity among US children and adolescents. *Acad Pediatr.* 2009;9(5):322–329

2. Ogden CL, Carroll MD, McDowell MA, Flegal KM. Obesity among adults in the United States: no statistically significant chance since 2003–2004. *NCHS Data Brief.* 2007;(1):1–8

3. Preidt R. Overweight now a global problem. Available at: http://abcnews.go.com/ print?id 4509129. Accessed April 29, 2010

4. Guthold R, Cowan MJ, Autenrieth CS, Kahn L, Riley LM. Physical activity and sedentary behavior among schoolchildren: a 34-country comparison. *J Pediatr.* 2010;157(1):43–49

5. Jordan AB, Strasburger VC, Kramer-Golinkoff EK, Strasburger VC. Does adolescent media use cause obesity and eating disorders? *Adolesc Med State Art Rev.* 2008;19(3):431–449

6. Kelly B, Halford JC, Boyland EJ, et al. Television food advertising to children: a global perspective. *Am J Public Health.* 2010;100(9):1730–1736

7. Jordan AB. Heavy television viewing and childhood obesity. *J Child Media.* 2007;1(9):45–54

8. Dennison BA, Edmunds LS. The role of television in childhood obesity. *Progr Pediatr Cardiol.* 2008;25(2):191–197

9. Strasburger VC, Wilson BJ, Jordan AB. *Children, Adolescents, and the Media.* 2nd ed. Thousand Oaks, CA: Sage; 2009

10. Singh GK, Kogan MD, Van Dyck PC, Siahpush M. Racial/ethnic, socioeconomic, and behavioral determinants of childhood and adolescent obesity in the United States: analyzing independent and joint associations. *Ann Epidemiol.* 2008;18(9):682–695

11. Viner RM, Cole TJ. Television viewing in early childhood predicts adult body mass index. *J Pediatr.* 2005;147(4):429–435

12. Hancox RJ, Milne BJ, Poulton R. Association between child and adolescent television viewing and adult health: a longitudinal birth cohort study. *Lancet.* 2004;364(9430):257–262

13. Reilly JJ, Armstrong J, Dorosty AR, et al; Avon Longitudinal Study of Parents and Children Study Team. Early life risk factors for obesity in childhood: cohort study. *BMJ.* 2005;330(7504):1357

14. Sugimori H, Yoshida K, Izuno T, et al. Analysis of factors that influence body mass index from ages 3 to 6 years: a study based on the Toyama cohort study. *Pediatr Int.* 2004;46(3):302–310

15. Proctor MH, Moore LL, Gao D, et al. Television viewing and change in body fat from preschool to early adolescence: the Framingham Children's Study. *Int J Obes Relat Metab Disord.* 2003;27(7):827–833

16. Kaur H, Choi WS, Mayo MS, Harris KJ. Duration of television watching is associated with increased body mass index. *J Pediatr.* 2003;143(4):506–511

17. Lumeng JC, Rahnama S, Appugliese D, Kaciroti N, Bradley RH. Television exposure and overweight risk in preschoolers. *Arch Pediatr Adolesc Med.* 2006;160(4):417–422

18. O'Brien M, Nader PR, Houts RM, et al. The ecology of childhood overweight: a 12-year longitudinal analysis. *Int J Obes (Lond).* 2007;31(9):1469–1478

19. Henderson VR. Longitudinal associations between television viewing and body mass index among white and black girls. *J Adolesc Health.* 2007;41(6):544–550

20. Boone JE, Gordon-Larsen P, Adair LS, Popkin BM. Screen time and physical activity during adolescence: longitudinal effects on obesity in young adulthood. *Int J Behav Nutr Phys Act.* 2007;4:26. Available at: www.ijbnpa.org/content/4/1/26. Accessed June 19, 2009

21. Davison BA, Marshall SJ, Birch LL. Crosssectional and longitudinal associations between TV viewing and girls' body mass index, overweight status, and percentage of body fat. *J Pediatr.* 2006;149(1):32–37

22. Danner FW. A national longitudinal study of the association between hours of TV viewing and the trajectory of BMI growth among US children. *J Pediatr Psychol.* 2008;33(10):1100–1107

23. Meyer AM, Evenson KR, Couper DJ, Stevens J, Pereira MA, Heiss G. Television, physical activity, diet, and body weight status: the ARIC cohort. *Int J Behav Nutr Phys Act.* 2008;5(1):68. Available at: www.ijbnpa.org/content/5/1/68. Accessed June 19, 2009

24. Adachi-Mejia AM, Longacre MR, Gibson JJ, Beach ML, Titus-Ernstoff LT, Dalton MA. Children with a TV set in their bedroom at higher risk for being overweight. *Int J Obes (Lond).* 2007;31(4):644–651

25. Dennison BA, Erb TA, Jenkins PL. Television viewing and television in bedroom associated with overweight risk among low-income preschool children. *Pediatrics.* 2002;109(6):1028–1035

26. Barr-Anderson DJ, van den Berg P, Neumark-Sztainer D, Story M. Characteristics associated with older adolescents who have a television in their bedrooms. *Pediatrics.* 2008;121(4):718–724

27. Delmas C, Platat C, Schweitzer B, Wagner A, Oujaa M, Simon C. Association between television in bedroom and adiposity throughout adolescence. *Obesity.* 2007;15(10):2495–2503

28. Sisson SB, Broyles ST, Newton RL Jr, Baker BL, Chernausek SD. TVs in the bedrooms of children: does it impact health and behavior? *Prev Med.* 2011;52(2):104–108

29. Margeirsdottir HD, Larsen JR, Brunborg C, Sandvik L, Dahl-Jørgensen K; Norwegian Study Group for Childhood Diabetes. Strong association between time watching television and blood glucose control in children

and adolescents with type I diabetes. *Diabetes Care.* 2007;30(6):1567–1570

30. Hu FB, Li TY, Colditz GA, Willett WC, Manson JE. Television watching and other sedentary behaviors in relation to risk of obesity and type 2 diabetes mellitus in women. *JAMA.* 2003;289(14):1785–1791

31. Hardy LL, Denney-Wilson E, Thrift AP, Okely AD, Baur LA. Screen time and metabolic risk factors among adolescents. *Arch Pediatr Adolesc Med.* 2010;164(7):643–649

32. Mark AE, Janssen I. Relationship between screen time and metabolic syndrome in adolescents. *J Public Health (Oxf).* 2008;30(2):153–160

33. Pardee PE, Norman GJ, Lustig RH, Preud'homme D, Schwimmer JB. Television viewing and hypertension in obese children. *Am J Prev Med.* 2007;33(6):439–443

34. Martinez-Gomez D, Tucker J, Heelan KA, Welk GJ, Eisenmann JC. Associations between sedentary behavior and blood pressure in children. *Arch Pediatr Adolesc Med.* 2009;163(8):724–730

35. Fung TT, Rimm EB, Spiegelman D, et al. Association between dietary patterns and plasma biomarkers of obesity and cardiovascular disease risk. *Am J Clin Nutr.* 2001;73(1):61–67

36. Martinez-Gomez D, Rey-López JP, Chillón P, et al; AVENA Study Group. Excessive TV viewing and cardiovascular disease risk factors in adolescents. The AVENA crosssectional study. *BMC Public Health.* 2010;10:274

37. Stamatakis E, Hamer M, Dunstan DW. Screen-based entertainment time, allcause mortality, and cardiovascular events: population-based study with ongoing mortality and hospital events followup. *J Am Coll Cardiol.* 2011;57(3):292–299

38. Robinson TN. Reducing children's television viewing to prevent obesity: a randomized controlled trial. *JAMA.* 1999;282(16):1561–1567

39. Epstein LH, Roemmich JN, Robinson JL, et al. A randomized trial of the effects of reducing television viewing and computer use on body mass index in young children. *Arch Pediatr Adolesc Med.* 2008;162(3):239–245

40. Dietz WH Jr. Television, obesity, and eating disorders. *Adolesc Med.* 1993;4(3):543–549

41. Apovian CM. Sugar-sweetened soft drinks, obesity, and type 2 diabetes. *JAMA.* 2004; 292(8):978–979

42. Reedy J, Krebs-Smith SM. Dietary sources of energy, solid fats, and added sugars among children and adolescents in the United States. *J Am Diet Assoc.* 2010;110(10):1477–1484

43. Rideout V. Generation M2: *Media in the Lives of 8- to 18-Year-Olds.* Menlo Park, CA: Kaiser Family Foundation; 2010

44. Nelson MC, Neumark-Sztainer D, Hannan PJ, Sirard JR, Story M. Longitudinal and secular trends in physical activity and sedentary behavior

during adolescence. Pediatrics. 2006;118(6). Available at: www.pediatrics.org/cgi/content/full/118/6/e1627

45. Hardy LL, Bass SL, Booth ML. Changes in sedentary behavior among adolescent girls: a 2.5-year prospective cohort study. *J Adolesc Health*. 2007;40(2):158–165

46. Sisson SB, Broyles ST, Baker BL, Katzmarzyk PT. Screen time, physical activity, and overweight in U.S. youth: National Survey of Children's Health 2003. *J Adolesc Health*. 2010;47(3):309–311

47. Burdette HL, Whitaker RC. A national study of neighborhood safety, outdoor play, television viewing, and obesity in preschool children. *Pediatrics*. 2005;116(3):657–662

48. Taveras EM, Field AE, Berkey CS, et al. Longitudinal relationship between television viewing and leisure-time physical activity during adolescence. *Pediatrics*. 2007;119(2). Available at: www.pediatrics.org/cgi/content/full/119/2/e314

49. Melkevik O, Torsheim T, Iannotti RJ, Wold B. Is spending time in screen-based sedentary behaviors associated with less physical activity: a cross national investigation. *Int J Behav Nutr Phys Act*. 2010;7:46

50. Vandewater E, Shim M, Caplovitz A. Linking obesity and activity level with children's television and video game use. *J Adolesc*. 2004;27(1):71–85

51. Epstein LH, Paluch RA, Consalvi A, Riordan K, Scholl T. Effects of manipulating sedentary behavior on physical activity and food intake. *J Pediatr*. 2002;140(3):334–339

52. Washington R. One way to decrease an obesogenic environment. *J Pediatr*. 2005;147(4):417–418

53. Dietz WH. What constitutes successful weight management in adolescents? *Ann Intern Med*. 2006;145(2):145–146

54. Goldfield GS, Mallory R, Parker T, et al. Effects of open-loop feedback on physical activity and television viewing in overweight and obese children: a randomized, controlled trial. *Pediatrics*. 2006;118(1). Available at: www.pediatrics.org/cgi/content/full/118/1/e157

55. Haerens L, Deforche B, Maes L, Stevens V, Cardon G, De Bourdeaudhuij. Body mass effects of a physical activity and healthy food intervention in middle schools. *Obesity*. 2006;14(5):847–854

56. Mellecker RR, McManus AM. Energy expenditure and cardiovascular responses to seated and active gaming in children. *Arch Pediatr Adolesc Med*. 2008;162(9):886–891

57. Pate RR. Physically active video gaming: an effective strategy for obesity prevention? *Arch Pediatr Adolesc Med*. 2008;162(9):895–896

58. Graf DL, Pratt LV, Hester CN, Short KR. Playing active video games increases energy expenditure in children. *Pediatrics*. 2009;124(2):534–540

59. Robinson TN, Killen JD. Ethnic and gender differences in the relationships between television viewing and obesity, physical activity and dietary fat intake. *J Health Educ.* 1995;26(2 suppl):S91–S98

60. Blass EM, Anderson DR, Kirkorian HL, Pempek TA, Price I, Koleini MF. On the road to obesity: television viewing increases intake of high-density foods. *Physiol Behav.* 2006;88(4–5):597–604

61. Zimmerman FJ, Bell JF. Associations of television content type and obesity in children. *Am J Public Health.* 2010;100(2):334–340

62. Wiecha JL, Peterson KE, Ludwig DS, Kim J, Sobol A, Gortmaker SL. When children eat what they watch: impact of television viewing on dietary intake in youth. *Arch Pediatr Adolesc Med.* 2006;160(4):436–442

63. Barr-Anderson DJ, Larson NI, Nelson MC, Neumark-Sztainer D, Story M. Does television viewing predict dietary intake five years later in high school students and young adults? *Int J Behav Nutr Phys Activity.* 2009;6:7. Available at: www.ijbnpa.org/content/6/1/7. Accessed March 25, 2011

64. Harris JL, Bargh JA, Brownell KD. Priming effects of television food advertising on eating behavior. *Health Psychol.* 2009;28(4):404–413

65. Giammattei J, Blix G, Marshak HH, Wollitzer AO, Pettitt DJ. Television watching and soft drink consumption: associations with obesity in 11- to 13-year old schoolchildren. *Arch Pediatr Adolesc Med.* 2003;157(9):882–886

66. Krebs-Smith S, Cook A, Subar A, Cleveland L, Friday J, Kahle LL. Fruit and vegetable intakes of children and adolescents in the United States. *Arch Pediatr Adolesc Med.* 1996;150(1):81–86

67. Bowman SA, Gortmaker SL, Ebbeling CB, Pereira MA, Ludwig DS. Effects of fast-food consumption on energy intake and diet quality among children in a national household survey. *Pediatrics.* 2004;113(1 pt 1):112–118

68. Brownell KD. Fast food and obesity in children. *Pediatrics.* 2004;113(1 pt 1):132

69. Schlosser E. *Fast Food Nation.* Boston, MA: Houghton Mifflin; 2001

70. Harris JL, Schwartz MB, Brownell KD, et al. *Evaluating Fast Food Nutrition and Marketing to Youth.* New Haven, CT: Yale Rudd Center for Food Policy & Obesity; 2010

71. Harrison K, Marske AL. Nutritional content of foods advertised during the television programs children watch most. *Am J Public Health.* 2005;95(9):1568–1574

72. Powell LM, Szczypka G, Chaloupka FJ, Braunschweig CL. Nutritional content of television food advertisements seen by children and adolescents in the United States. *Pediatrics.* 2007;120(3):576–583

73. Kunkel D, McKinley C, Stitt C. *Food Advertising During Children's Programming: A Two-Year Comparison.* Tucson, AZ: University of Arizona; 2010

74. Stitt C, Kunkel D. Food advertising during children's television programming on broadcast and cable channels. *Health Commun.* 2008;23(6):573–584

75. Powell LM, Szczypka G, Chaloupka FJ. Trends in exposure to television food advertisements among children and adolescents in the United States. *Arch Pediatr Adolesc Med.* 2010;164(9):794–802

76. Powell LM, Szczypka G, Chaloupka FJ. Exposure to food advertising on television among US children. *Arch Pediatr Adolesc Med.* 2007;161(6):553–560

77. Gantz W, Schwartz N, Angelini JR, Rideout V. *Food for Thought: Television Food Advertising to Children in the United States.* Menlo Park, CA: Kaiser Family Foundation; 2007

78. Harris JL, Weinberg ME, Schwartz MB, Ross C, Ostroff J, Brownell KD. *Trends in Television Food Advertising.* New Haven, CT: Yale Rudd Center for Food Policy & Obesity; 2010

79. Weber K, Story M, Harnack L. Internet food marketing strategies aimed at children and adolescents: a content analysis of food and beverage brand Web sites. *J Am Diet Assoc.* 2006;106(9):1463–1466

80. Moore ES. *It's Child's Play: Advergaming and the Online Marketing of Food to Children.* Menlo Park, CA: Kaiser Family Foundation; 2006

81. Montgomery KC, Chester J. Interactive food and beverage marketing: targeting adolescents in the digital age. *J Adolesc Health.* 2009;45(3 suppl):S18–S29

82. Pempek TA, Calvert SL. Tipping the balance: use of advergames to promote consumption of nutritious foods and beverages by low-income African American children. *Arch Pediatr Adolesc Med.* 2009;163(7):633–637

83. Institute of Medicine. *Preventing Childhood Obesity: Health in the Balance.* Washington, DC: National Academies Press; 2005

84. Harris JL, Pomeranz JL, Lobstein T, Brownell KD. A crisis in the marketplace: how food marketing contributes to childhood obesity and what can be done. *Annu Rev Public Health.* 2009;30:211–225

85. Kunkel D, McKinley C, Wright P. *The Impact of Industry Self-regulation on the Nutritional Quality of Foods Advertised on Television to Children.* Oakland, CA: Children Now; 2009

86. Chamberlain LJ, Wang Y, Robinson TN. Does children's screen time predict requests for advertised products? *Arch Pediatr Adolesc Med.* 2006;160(4):363–368

87. Borzekowski DLG, Robinson TN. The 30-second effect: an experiment revealing the impact of television commercials on food preferences of preschoolers. *J Am Diet Assoc.* 2001;101(1):42–46

88. Robinson TN, Borzekowski DLG, Matheson DM, Kraemer HC. Effects of fast food branding on young children's taste preferences. *Arch Pediatr Adolesc Med.* 2007;161(8):792–292

89. Robert Wood Johnson Foundation. *F as in Fat 2009: How Obesity Policies Are Failing in America.* Princeton, NJ: Robert Wood Johnson Foundation; 2009. Available at: http://healthyamericans.org/reports/obesity2009. Accessed April 29, 2010

90. Greenberg BS, Rosaen SF, Worrell TR, Salmon CT, Volkman JE. A portrait of food and drink in commercial TV series. *Health Commun.* 2009;24(4):295–303

91. Bell R, Berger C, Townsend M. *Portrayals of Nutritional Practices and Exercise Behavior in Popular American Films, 1991–2000.* Davis, CA: Center for Advanced Studies of Nutrition and Social Marketing, University of California-Davis; 2003

92. Eisenberg D. It's an ad, ad, ad world. *Time Magazine.* August 26, 2002:38–42. Available at: www.time.com/time/magazine/article/0,9171,1101020902-344045,00.html. Accessed April 29, 2010

93. Sutherland LS, MacKenzie T, Purvis LA, Dalton M. Prevalence of food and beverage brands in movies, 1996–2005. *Pediatrics.* 2010;125(3):468–474

94. Zimmerman FJ. *Children's Media Use and Sleep Problems: Issues and Unanswered Questions.* Menlo Park, CA: Kaiser Family Foundation; 2008

95. Landhuis CE, Poulton R, Welch D, Hancox RJ. Childhood sleep time and long-term risk for obesity: a 32-year prospective birth cohort study. *Pediatrics.* 2008;122(5):955–960

96. Johnson JG, Cohen P, Kasen S, First MB, Brook JS. Association between television and sleep problems during adolescence and early adulthood. *Arch Pediatr Adolesc Med.* 2004;158(6):562–568

97. Sekine M, Yamagami T, Handa K, et al. A dose-response relationship between short sleeping hours and childhood obesity: results of the Toyama Birth Cohort Study. *Child Care Health Dev.* 2002;28(2):163–170

98. Agras W, Hammer L, McNicholas F, Kraemer H. Risk factors for child overweight: a prospective study from birth to 9.5 years. *J Pediatr.* 2004;145(1):20–25

99. Taheri S. The link between short sleep duration and obesity: we should recommend more sleep to prevent obesity. *Arch Dis Child.* 2006;91(11):881–884

100. Bell JF, Zimmerman FJ. Shortened nighttime sleep duration in early life and subsequent childhood obesity. *Arch Pediatr Adolesc Med.* 2010;164(9):840–845

101. Lytle LA, Pasch K, Farbaksh K. Is sleep related to obesity in young adolescents [abstract]? Presented at: Pediatric Academic Societies meeting; May 4, 2010; Vancouver, British Columbia, Canada

102. Wells TT, Cruess DG. Effects of partial sleep deprivation on food consumption and food choice. *Psychol Health.* 2006;21(1):79–86

103. Oliver G, Wardle J. Perceived effects of stress on food choice. *Physiol Behav.* 1999;66(3):511–515

104. Nelson MC, Gordon-Larsen P. Physical activity and sedentary behavior patterns are associated with selected adolescent health risk behaviors. *Pediatrics.* 2006;117(4):1281–1290

105. Van Cauter E, Holmback U, Knutson K, et al. Impact of sleep and sleep loss on neuroendocrine and metabolic function. *Horm Res.* 2007;67(suppl 1):2–9

106. Hamer M, Stamatakis E, Mishra G. Psychological distress, television viewing and physical activity in children aged 4 to 12 years. *Pediatrics.* 2009;123(5):1263–1268

107. Jordan AB, Robinson TN. Children, television viewing, and weight status: summary and recommendations from an expert panel meeting. *Ann Am Acad Polit Soc Sci.* 2008;615(1):119–132

108. Brownell KD, Schwartz MB, Puhl RM, Henderson KE, Harris JL. The need for bold action to prevent adolescent obesity. *J Adolesc Health.* 2009;45(3 suppl):S8–S17

109. Strasburger VC. First do no harm: why have parents and pediatricians missed the boat on children and media? *J Pediatr.* 2007;151(4):334–336

110. Hagan JF Jr, Shaw JS, Duncan PM, eds. *Bright Futures: Guidelines for Health Supervision of Infants, Children, and Adolescents.* Elk Grove Village, IL: American Academy of Pediatrics; 2008

111. Harris JL, Bargh JA. Television viewing and unhealthy diet: implications for children and media interventions. *Health Commun.* 2009;24(7):660–673

112. He M, Piche L, Beynon C, Harris S. Screen-related sedentary behaviors: children's and parents' attitudes, motivations, and practices. *J Nutr Educ Behav.* 2010;42(1):17–25

113. Carlson SA, Fulton JE, Lee SM, Foley JT, Heitzler C, Huhman M. Influence of limit-setting and participation in physical activity on youth screen time. *Pediatrics.* 2010; 126(1). Available at: www.pediatrics.org/cgi/content/full/126/1/e89

114. American Academy of Pediatrics, Committee on Public Education. Media education. *Pediatrics.* 1999;104(2 pt 1):341–343

115. Laurson KR, Eisenmann JC, Welk G, Wickel EE, Gentile DA, Walsh DA. Combined influence of physical activity and screen time recommendations on childhood overweight. *J Pediatr.* 2008;153(2):209–214

116. Anderson SE, Whitaker RC. Household routines and obesity in US preschool-aged children. *Pediatrics.* 2010;125(3):420–428

117. McCannon R. Media literacy/media education. In: Strasburger VC, Wilson BJ, Jordan AJ, eds. *Children, Adolescents, and the Media.* 2nd ed. Thousand Oaks, CA: Sage; 2009:519–569

118. Gortmaker SL. Innovations to reduce television and computer time and obesity in childhood. *Arch Pediatr Adolesc Med.* 2008;162(3):283–284

119. Escobar-Chaves SL, Markham CM, Addy RC, Greisinger A, Murray NG, Brehm B. The Fun Families Study: intervention to reduce children's TV viewing. *Obesity (Silver Spring).* 2010;18(suppl 1):S99–S101

120. White House Task Force on Childhood Obesity. *Solving the Problem of Childhood Obesity Within a Generation: Report to the President.* Washington, DC: Executive Office of the President of the United States; 2010. Available at: www.letsmove.gov/sites/letsmove.gov/files/TaskForce_on_Childhood_Obesity_May2010_FullReport.pdf. Accessed January 12, 2011

121. American Academy of Pediatrics, Committee on Communications. Children, adolescents, and advertising [published correction appears in *Pediatrics.* 2007;119(2):424]. *Pediatrics.* 2006;118(6):2563–2569

122. Pomeranz JL. Television food marketing to children revisited: the Federal Trade Commission has the constitutional and statutory authority to regulate. *J Law Med Ethics.* 2010;38(1):98–116

123. Strasburger VC. Adolescents and the media. In: Rosenfeld W, Fisher M, Alderman E, eds. *Textbook of Adolescent Medicine.* Elk Grove Village, IL: American Academy of Pediatrics; 2011;359–373

124. Gold J. Snickers maker will aim higher. *Albuquerque Journal.* February 7, 2007:B4

125. Union of European Beverages Associations. *International Council of Beverages Associations Adopts Groundbreaking Guidelines on Marketing to Children* [press release]. Brussels, Belgium: Union of European Beverages Associations; May 20, 2008

126. Wilde P. Self-regulation and the response to concerns about food and beverage marketing to children in the United States. *Nutr Rev.* 2009;67(3):155–166

127. Schwartz MB, Ross C, Harris JL, et al. Breakfast cereal industry pledges to self-regulate advertising to youth: will they improve the marketing landscape? *J Public Health Policy.* 2010;31(1):59–73

128. Noah T. Toy story: why self-regulation of children's advertising is a joke. *Slate Magazine.* Available at: www.slate.com/id/2278241. Accessed January 12, 2011

129. Harris JL, Schwartz MB, Brownell KD, et al. *Cereal FACTS: Evaluating the Nutrition Quality and Marketing of Children's Cereals.* New Haven, CT: Rudd Center for Food Policy and Obesity; 2009

130. Associated Press. Coca-cola spent more than $1.7M to lobby. February 21, 2007

131. Chou SY, Rashad I, Grossman M. Fast-food restaurant advertising on television and its influence on childhood obesity. *J Law Econ.* 2008;51(4):599–618

132. Veerman JL, Van Beeck EF, Barendregt JJ, Mackenbach JP. By how much would limiting TV food advertising reduce childhood obesity? *Eur J Public Health.* 2009;19(4):365–369

133. Dixon HG, Scully ML, Wakefield MA, White VM, Crawford DA. The effects of television advertisements for junk food versus nutritious food on children's food attitudes and preferences. *Soc Sci Med.* 2007;65(7):1311–1323

134. Larson N, Story M. *Food and Beverage Marketing to Children and Adolescents: What Changes Are Needed to Promote Healthy Eating Habits?* Princeton, NJ: Robert Wood Johnson Foundation; 2008

135. Pertschuk M. The little agency that could. *The Nation.* June 29, 2009:21–22

136. Durant NH. Not just fun and games: harnessing technology to address childhood obesity. *Child Obes.* 2010;6(5):283–284

137. Biddiss E, Irwin J. Active video games to promote physical activity in children and youth: a systematic review. *Arch Pediatr Adolesc Med.* 2010;164(7):664–672

138. Strasburger VC, Jordan AB, Donnerstein E. Health effects of media on children and adolescents. *Pediatrics.* 2010;125(4):756–767

139. Ginsburg KR; American Academy of Pediatrics, Committee on Communications and Committee on Psychosocial Aspects of Child and Family Health. The importance of play in promoting healthy child development and maintaining strong parent-child bonds. *Pediatrics.* 2007;119(1):182–191

www.pediatrics.org/cgi/doi/10.1542/peds.2011–1066

doi:10.1542/peds.2011–1066

PEDIATRICS (ISSN Numbers: Print, 0031–4005; Online, 1098–4275).

Women in America: Indicators of Social and Economic Well-Being

White House Council on Women and Girls

III. EMPLOYMENT

Over the past several decades, women have dramatically reshaped their role in the nation's labor force. They have become much more likely to work or seek work outside the home. They are also employed in more varied occupations and are more likely to work year-round. In addition, women have attained higher levels of education. Reflecting their greater work activity and education, women's earnings as a proportion of men's earnings have grown over time and women are contributing increasingly important shares of family incomes, but the earnings gap between men and women remains. As more women have entered the labor force, interest has risen in how they divide their time between their jobs and other activities.

LABOR FORCE PARTICIPATION

The labor force participation rate for women—the percentage of all adult women who are working or looking for work—rose steadily during the latter half of the 20th century.[1] This rate increased from about 33 percent in 1950 to 61 percent in 1999. During the first decade of this century, it has held steady at around 61 percent. In contrast, men's labor force participation rate has declined steadily since the 1950s.

Despite the trends of recent decades, women remain less active in the labor market than men. The labor force participation rate of adult women (age 20 and older) was still significantly lower than that of adult men, 61 percent versus 75 percent in 2009. Moreover, on average, women at every educational level and at every age spend fewer weeks in the labor force than do men. The differences between men and women in labor force attachment are much smaller among those with a college degree or more education.[2]

As part of the overall growth of women's presence in the labor force, the participation rate of mothers also increased. From 1975 to 2000, the labor force participation rate of mothers with children under age 18 rose from 47 percent to a peak of 73 percent. This rate receded to about 71 percent in 2004, where it has remained through 2009. Unmarried mothers had a higher labor force participation rate than their married counterparts, 76 percent compared to 70 percent in 2009.

OCCUPATIONS

The jobs working women perform also have changed as their market activity has increased. A larger share of women now works in management, professional, and related occupations.[3] In 2009, women accounted for 51 percent of all persons employed in these occupations, somewhat more than their share of total employment (47 percent).

One reason for the shift in occupations is women's greater educational attainment. Among women age 25–64 in the labor force, 36 percent held college degrees in 2009, compared to 11 percent in 1970. Over the same period, the proportion of women workers with less than a high school diploma fell from 34 percent to 7 percent. Individuals with higher levels of education generally have better access to higher paying jobs than do individuals with less education. The earnings of both women and men age 25 and older without a high school diploma were less than half of those with a college degree, respectively.

EARNINGS AND CONTRIBUTIONS

The earnings gap between women and men has narrowed over time, but it remains. Among full-time wage and salary workers, women's weekly earnings as a percent of men's have increased from 62 percent in 1979 to 80 percent in 2009.[4,5] This comparison of earnings is on a broad level and does not control for many factors that can be significant in explaining or further highlighting earnings differences.

As women's earnings have risen, working wives' contributions to their family incomes also have risen. In 2008, working wives contributed 29 percent of their families' incomes, up by 5 percentage points from 1988, when wives' earnings accounted for 24 percent of their families' total incomes. The proportion of wives earning more than their husbands also has grown. In 1988, 18 percent of working wives whose husbands also worked earned more than their spouses; in 2008, the proportion was 27 percent.[6] Dual-earner couples made up 57 percent of all married-couple families in 2008, compared to 46 percent in 1970.[7]

Working women spend their days somewhat differently than do working men. In 2009, on the days that they worked, employed married women age 25–54 spent less time in labor market work and work-related activities than did employed married men in the same age group—7 hours and 40 minutes, compared to about 8 hours and 50 minutes. However, these employed wives spent about 40 minutes more time than did their male counterparts doing household activities such as cooking, housework, and household management.

1. **After decades of significant increases, the labor force participation rate for women has held steady in recent years.**

   - The labor force participation rate for women (age 20 and older) nearly doubled between 1948 (32 percent) and 1997 (61 percent). Since 1997, it has held steady (61 percent in 2009). The labor force participation rate for men (age 20 and older) has fallen from about 89 percent in 1948 to 75 percent in 2009. (See chart.)

   - At all levels of educational attainment, the labor force participation rate of men was higher than that of their female counterparts. In 2009, the participation rate of women with less than a high school diploma was only 34 percent, compared to 59 percent for men. Among those with college degrees or higher, the participation rate of women was 73 percent, compared to 82 percent for men.

   - Between 2005 and 2009, the labor force participation rate increased for White women (59.7 percent to 60.4 percent) and Hispanic women (57.4 percent to 59.2 percent). By comparison, the rate for Black women, who have the highest labor force participation among women, has edged down (64.4 percent to 63.4 percent). For men, labor force participation continued to fall across all racial and ethnic groups.

   - Among mothers age 16 and over, those with older children (age 6 to 17 only) were more likely to be in the labor force (77 percent) in 2009 than those with children age 5 or younger (64 percent).

   - The labor force participation rate of persons age 55 and older began to rise in 1996 for both women and men, but the pace of the increase has slowed in recent years.

Labor Force Participation
(Percent of Persons Age 20 and Older, 1948–2009)

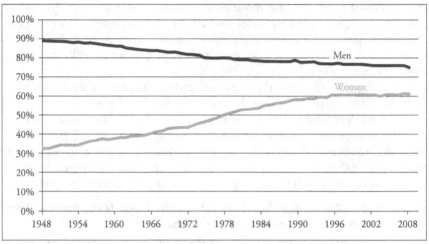

Source: Bureau of Labor Statistics

2. **Unemployment rates for women have risen less than for men in recent recessions.**

- During the past four recessions, the unemployment rate among women rose less than the rate for men. During the most recent recession, the unemployment rate among women (age 20 and older) rose from 4.4 percent to 7.7 percent; by comparison, the rate for men (age 20 and older) more than doubled, from 4.4 percent to 9.9 percent. (See chart.)

- Prior to the 1980s, the unemployment rate for women tended to be higher than the rate for men. Since the early 1980s, the jobless rates for both men and women have tracked one another quite closely during economic expansions. (See chart.)

- During the past four recessions, the relatively large increases in the jobless rates among men can be attributed to their concentration in more cyclically sensitive occupations, such as manufacturing production and construction.

- In contrast, women are more concentrated in less cyclically sensitive and more rapidly growing occupations, such as health care, which has dampened the impact of recent recessions on their unemployment rates.

Unemployment Rates

(Percent of Persons Age 20 and Older in the Labor Force, Seasonally Adjusted,
January 1948– December 2010)

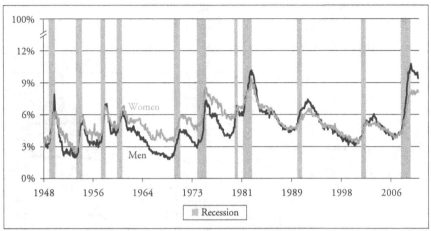

Source: Bureau of Labor Statistics

3. **More women than men work part time, and women and men have roughly equal access to flexible work schedules.**

- Historically, women have been more likely than men to work part time (less than 35 hours per week). In 2009, 24 percent of employed women (age 20 and older) worked part time, compared to 11 percent of men. (See chart.)

- Women are considerably more likely to work year round than they were in past decades. In 2009, 75 percent of women worked year round, up from 51 percent in 1968. The proportion of men who worked year round changed little over this same time period (from 74 percent to 76 percent).

- In May 2004, about 30 percent of wage and salary workers reported having flexible schedules that allowed them to vary their work hours to some degree. Between 1985 and 2004, the proportions of employed men and women able to vary their work hours were about equal; the same was true of both mothers and fathers who work.

Part Time Work

(Percent of Employed Persons Age 20 and Older, Seasonally Adjusted,
January 1968–December 2010)

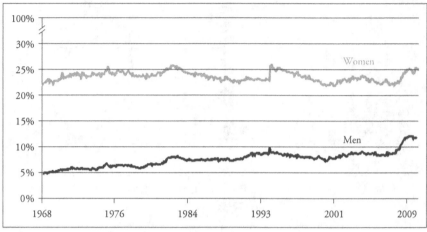

Source: Bureau of Labor Statistics

- Due to the nature of the work required for each particular job, the prevalence of flexible schedules varies by occupation. In May 2004, the proportion of White and Asian workers in occupations in which they could vary their schedules exceeded that of other groups. About 30 percent of employed Whites and Asians could vary their work hours, while the proportion was closer to 21 percent among Black workers and those of Hispanic ethnicity.

4. **Education pays for both women and men, but the pay gap persists.**
   - Earnings for both women and men typically increase with higher levels of education. However, the male-female pay gap persists at all levels of education for full-time workers (35 or more hours per week). (See chart.)
   - Earnings of full-time female workers have risen by 31 percent since 1979, compared to a 2 percent rise in male earnings. In addition, earnings for women with college degrees rose by 33 percent since 1979 while those of their male counterparts rose by 22 percent.
   - At all levels of education, women earned about 75 percent as much as their male counterparts in 2009. Although both women and men with less than a high school diploma have experienced declines in earnings since 1979, the drop for women (9 percent) was significantly less than that for men (28 percent).
   - The earnings gap between women and men narrowed for most age groups from 1979 to 2009. The women's-to-men's earnings ratio

Earnings by Educational Attainment
(Median Weekly Earnings of Full-Time Workers Age 25 and Older, Annual Averages, 2009)

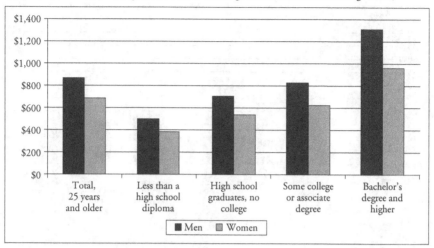

Source: Bureau of Labor Statistics

among 25- to 34-year-olds, rose from 68 percent in 1979 to 89 percent in 2009, and the ratio for 45- to 54-year-olds increased from 57 percent to 74 percent.

- Compared to the earnings of all men (of all race and ethnic groups), Black women earned 71 percent and Hispanic women earned 62 percent as much in 2009. White and Asian women earned 82 percent and 95 percent as much as all men, respectively.

- Compared to their direct male counterparts, however, White women earned 79 percent as much as White men in 2009, while Asian women earned 82 percent as much as Asian men. For Blacks and Hispanics, the figures were 94 percent and 90 percent, respectively.

5. **Women and men continue to work in different occupations.**
   - While women are three times more likely to work in administrative support jobs than men, relatively few women have construction, production, or transportation jobs. (See chart.)

   - While women are more likely than men to work in professional and related occupations, they are more highly represented in the lower-paying jobs within this category. For example, in 2009, professional women were more likely (nearly 70 percent) to work in the relatively low-paying education (with $887 median weekly earnings) and health care ($970 median weekly earnings) occupations, compared to 32 percent of male professionals.

Employment by Occupation

(Percent of Employed Persons Age 16 and Older in Major Occupation Groups, 2009)

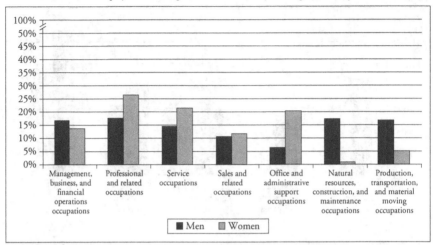

Source: Bureau of Labor Statistics

- In 2009, only 7 percent of female professionals were employed in the relatively high paying computer ($1,253 median weekly earnings) and engineering fields ($1,266 median weekly earnings), compared to 38 percent of male professionals.

- The proportion of women working in management, business, and finance jobs has increased from 9 percent to 14 percent since 1983.

- Women continue to be concentrated in a small number of traditionally female occupations. In 2009, nearly one-fifth of all women were employed in just five occupations: secretaries, registered nurses, elementary school teachers, cashiers, and nursing aides.

6. **Female-headed families have the lowest family earnings among all family types.**

   - Family earnings levels among female-headed families were the lowest among all family types in both 1988 and 2008, despite increasing by 27 percent over this timeframe. (See chart.) A family is a group of two or more people living together and related by birth, marriage, or adoption.

   - In 2008, female-headed families with children earned 30 percent less than their counterparts without children, although their earnings grew faster (43 percent) than the other family types between 1988 and 2008.

   - Over the past two decades, women's earnings have constituted a growing share of family income in all family types.

   - Married couples had the highest family incomes. Incomes for married-couple families with children increased by 28 percent from 1988 to

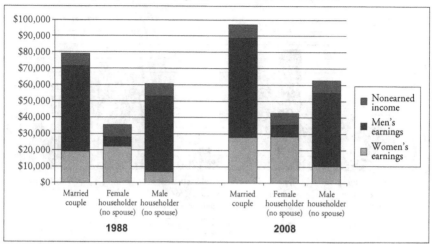

Family Income by Family Type

(Family Heads Under Age 65, in 2008 Dollars, 1988 and 2008)

Source: Census Bureau

2008, while incomes for married couple families without children increased by 16 percent over the same period.

- In female-headed families with children, nonearned income as a share of total family income has declined sharply, from 24 percent in 1988 to 16 percent in 2008. About 63 percent of nonearned income for female-headed families with children in poverty is government cash transfer income.

7. **In families where both husband and wife are employed, employed wives spend more time in household activities than do employed husbands.**

- On an average workday in 2009, employed married women spent 1.6 hours in household activities and an additional hour caring for household members. In contrast, employed married men spent nearly one hour in household activities and about 40 minutes caring for household members. (See chart.)

- On average in 2009, employed husbands spent about 3.2 hours engaged in leisure and sports activities on workdays, and employed wives spent about 2.7 hours. (See chart.) For both employed husbands and wives, watching television accounted for just over half of this time (1.8 hours and 1.4 hours, respectively).

- Employed married men spent more time in labor market work and related activities (including commuting) on an average workday in 2009 than did employed married women—8.8 hours and 7.6 hours, respectively. (See chart.)

Time Spent on Workdays

(Average Hours in Selected Activities on a Workday by Employed,
Married Persons Age 25–54, 2009)

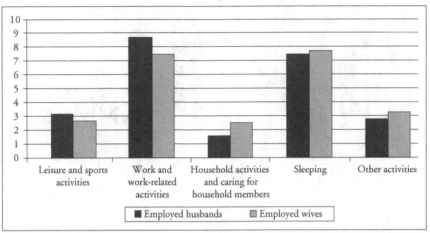

Source: Bureau of Labor Statistics

- On days that they worked, 87 percent of married women also engaged in household activities in 2009, compared to 65 percent of married men. Wives were more likely to do housework and prepare food, while husbands were more likely to care for the lawn and do home maintenance.

- On an average workday in 2009, employed single mothers spent 37 minutes more in labor market work and related activities than did employed married mothers.

8. **Women are more likely than men to do volunteer work.**

- In 2009, 30 percent of women volunteered, compared to 23 percent of men. Women most frequently volunteered with religious organizations (34 percent of all female volunteers), followed by educational or youth service related organizations (28 percent). (See chart.)

- Female volunteers were most likely to fundraise (13 percent); collect, prepare, distribute, or serve food (12 percent); or tutor or teach (11

Volunteer Work

(Percent of Persons Age 16 and Older Doing Unpaid Volunteer Activities Through or for a Main Organization, by Type of Organization, 2009)

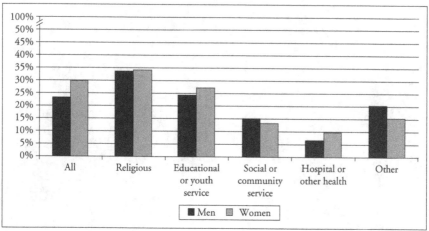

Source: Bureau of Labor Statistics

percent). Male volunteers were most likely to engage in general labor (12 percent); coach, referee, or supervise sports teams (9 percent); provide professional or management assistance (9 percent); or fundraise (9 percent).

Senate Joint Economic Committee Committee Hearing: Equal Pay for Equal Work? New Evidence on the Persistence of the Gender Pay Gap

*Testimony by **Randy Albelda**, Professor of Economics, University of Massachusetts-Boston*

Madam Chairwomen and members of the committee: Thank you for this opportunity to testify about the persistent wage gap between men and women. My name is Randy Albelda and I am a professor of economics and senior research associate at the Center for Social Policy at the University of Massachusetts Boston. I am a labor economist and my expertise is on women's economic status.

While there has been progress in reducing the pay gap between men and women over the last several decades, it is still the case that women, on average, make less than men.

While there are some differences in what men and women "bring" to the workplace that influence levels of pay, these differences account for only a small part of the gender wage gap—the difference in men's and women's pay. Further, the differences in skill levels and experience have been narrowing over the last three decades and doing so at a faster pace than the wage gap is narrowing. There are three enduring and intersecting reasons why women's pay is less than men's: workplace discrimination; occupational sorting; and family responsibilities.

473

The Wage Gap:

In the mid-1970s, the National Organization for Women issued "59" buttons, calling attention to the fact that year-round, full-time women workers earned 59 cents to every man's dollar. Today we could replace those with "78" buttons. [n1]

This graph on the following page comes from the most recent US Census Bureau's Income, Poverty, and Health Insurance Coverage in the United States report. It provides a nice illustration of the median annual earnings of year-round, full-time men and women workers from 1960 through 2007, adjusted for inflation. The most substantial gains were made in the 1980s, with the wage ratio of women's earnings to men's earnings narrowing from .60 in 1980 to .72 in 1990. In the 1990s, there was very little change in this ratio—moving from .72 in 1990 to .74 in 2000. [n2]

Different work, different pay? No. The gender pay gap persists even after taking into account hours worked, skill levels and occupations.

As noted above, looking only at full-time year-round workers, women's annual median earnings are 78 percent of men's. Similarly, the median weekly earnings of full-time wage and salary women workers was 80 percent of men's in 2007. [n3]

Women have somewhat less work time experience than men, which would explain some of the pay gap. However, it explains less and less of that gap over time and several studies have found that each year of men's experience pays off at a higher rate than an additional year of women's work experience.[n4]

Women workers bring higher educational levels to the workplace than do men [n5], which is one reason why "human capital" endowments explain less of the pay gap now than they did in the 1980s.[n6] Still, female college graduates working full-time earned 80 percent less than male college graduates just one year out of school in 2001. [n7]

Women tend to work in different types of jobs than do men. But, even when men and women work in the same fields or even the same occupations, women typically earn less than men.

- The starting salaries for women college graduates were $1,443 less than they were for men in the same fields. [n8]
- Across the occupational landscape, women make less than men. The table below depicts the wage gap (using median usual weekly earnings of full-time wage and salary workers) for some detailed occupations. Of the over 100 detailed occupations with median earnings listed, there are only six in which women's earnings are higher than those of men. [n9]

The Gender Wage Gap in Selected Detailed Occupations, 2006
Managerial Occupations:
Chief executives .72
Human resource specialists .81
Professional Occupations Lawyers .70
Elementary and middle school teachers .90
Service Occupations Security guards .84
Home health care aides .89
Sales and Office Occupations Retail salesperson .68
Secretaries/administrative asst. 1.04
Construction occupations .86
Production and transportation Occupations Electronic assemblers .76
Bus drivers .80
Source: Table 18 of U.S. Department of Labor, U.S. Bureau of Labor Statistics, Women in the Labor Force: A Databook (2008 Edition).

Francine Blau and Lawrence Kahn show that in 2004 after controlling for education, experience, occupation and industry, women earned 83.5 percent of what men did, compared to 81.6 percent without any of those adjustments. That means these factors explain less than 2 percentage points (10 percent) of the entire wage gap between men and women, leaving most of it unexplained by measurable differences between men's and women's attributes. [n10]

Economists have explored the gender pay gap for many decades and produced hundreds (if not 1000s) of articles and reports to explain the reasons for the gender pay gap. No matter how sophisticated and complex their models, they always find that some portion of the wage gap is unexplained by the sets of variables for which they can measure differences between men's and women's education levels, work experiences, ages, occupation or industry in which they work, or region of the country they reside. Because the wage differences cannot be explained by any of the differences in workers' traits, this unexplained portion of the wage gap is attributed to gender discrimination.

- A recent meta-regression analysis that compiled the results of 49 econometric studies of the gender wage gap over the last decade found that on average, there was still a substantial gap—women earned 70 percent of what men did, after adjusting for all the various factors that help explain wage difference. [n11]
- In a forthcoming study of college professors in one specific college of a large public university, researchers controlled for years experience, mobility, teaching and research productivity, and department and found that even in the identical job in the same institution women made three percent less than men. [n12]

Progress toward pay equity has stalled over the last decade.

- The unexplained portion of gender gap (the part attributable to discrimination) got considerably smaller in the 1980s and hardly fell at all in the 1990s. [n13]

There are three intersecting reasons why women's pay is less than men's: workplace discrimination; occupational sorting; and family responsibilities.

- Lilly Ledbetter's experience reminds us that workplace discrimination still exists. Routinely women are not hired at all, hired at lower wages and not promoted over equally qualified men. This shows up in economists' studies as the part of the earnings gaps that can't be attributed to anything else. In addition, using experimental approaches, economists find considerable evidence of hiring discrimination as well. [n14]
- Women are in different occupations than men. Men are much more likely to be in construction and manufacturing jobs which pay more than female dominated jobs with comparable skill levels such as administrative assistants and retail salespersons.[n15] While about one-third of all women are in professional and managerial jobs, these too are often sex segregated, with women predominating in teaching, nursing and social work jobs and men predominating in architecture, engineering and computer occupations. Finally, women predominate in both high and low paying jobs in the "care sector"—the industries which educate our children, provide us with health services, and take care of young children, disabled adults and the elderly. There is a care work wage penalty. Careful research has shown that care workers, in part because they compete with unpaid workers at home, are not rewarded commensurately with their skills and experience.[n16] This sector is large.

About 20 percent of all workers work in the care sector and women comprise 75 percent of all workers.[17]

- Family responsibilities squeeze women's work time and preclude them from taking and keeping jobs that make few or no accommodations for these responsibilities. Jobs that require long hours, often pay well and provide a strong set of employer benefits, but employers also usually assume the workers in those jobs are unencumbered by household and family responsibilities. This "ideal" worker can (and often does) work overtime or just about any time an employer wants.[18] Workers with family responsibilities do not have that flexibility. Regardless of their skill levels, these workers often must work fewer hours or trade off wages for more time flexibility. Research clearly demonstrates a mothers' wage penalty. Mothers earn less than women with the same sets of skills and are rewarded less for experience than are men or women who are not mothers. Some of this is a result of time demands and less job flexibility, but some is attributable to discrimination against workers with family responsibilities.[19]

The recession makes addressing this issue especially important because women's earnings are a vital, if not main component, of family well-being.

- One third of all households are headed by women. Of these households, one-quarter are families with children.[20] Women are almost always the only support of these households.
- One half of households have married couples.[21] In these households, 64 percent of wives are employed, compared to 48 percent in 1970. Further, wives' earnings comprise 35 percent of family income, up from 27 percent in 1970.[22]
- In this recession, more men have lost jobs than women have, since men—so far—are disproportionately found in the hardest hit sectors.[23] As a result, even more households are more dependent on women's earnings. Unequal pay hurts these households.
- The stimulus package will help both men and women, but differently.
- Increased funds for physical infrastructure, improved medical record keeping, and green energy investments will likely create many more jobs for men than women. Assuring access to these jobs and trade apprenticeship programs would be useful for women's employment in these male-dominated and often well-paying jobs.
- Increased funding to the states, especially for health care and education, will help reduce the number of layoffs for more women, since they are more heavily employed in these sectors than are men. However, state budget deficits are deep and even with stimulus funds there will be large cuts to the care sector, which will increase women's unemployment. The cuts will also put more pressure on women's unpaid work time, as their families lose needed care.

REDUCING THE PAY GAP

There are several things that would boost women's wages and reduce the pay gap.

Addressing Workplace Discrimination
- Ensure that our current anti-discrimination laws are enforced.
- Pass the Paycheck Fairness Act. This will strengthen penalties for discrimination and prohibit employer retaliation for workers who inquire about wage practices.
- Pass the Employee Free Choice Act. Unions boost women's wages and improve the likelihood they will have health insurance at work. [n24] Unions also provide workers structured mechanisms to pursue employer discrimination claims.

Addressing Occupational Sorting
- Increase the minimum wage since women predominate in low-wage jobs.
- Support improved wages for care workers. Care work is heavily supported by federal, state and local government funds. This is because care work has many positive spillover effects, making it a vital public good. Government funds for child care and elder care can assure that workers in these fields are compensated appropriately and have opportunities for professional development.
- Target stimulus money to assure that women are included in physical infrastructure projects.

Addressing Family Responsibility Discrimination
- Make sure that current laws that protect workers with caregiving responsibilities, such as the Family and Medical Leave Act, are enforced.
- Extend the Family and Medical Leave Act to cover more workers.
- Support the Family Leave Insurance Act of 2009 which would provide workers with 12 weeks of paid family and medical leave.
- Develop legislation that encourages employers to negotiate with employees over flexible work arrangements.

[n1] In 2007, year-round, full-time women earners made $35,102 while men earned $45,113. Carmen DeNavas-Walt, Bernadette D. Proctor, and Jessica C. Smith, U.S. Census Bureau, Current Population Reports, P60-235, Income, Poverty, and Health Insurance Coverage in the United States: 2007, U.S. Government Printing Office, Washington, DC, 2008; Table 1.

[n2] Ibid, Table A-2.

[n3] U.S. Department of Labor, U.S. Bureau of Labor Statistics, Highlights of Women's Earnings in 2007, Report 1008, October 2008, Chart 1 (accessed 4-23-09 at http://www.bls.gov/cps/cpswom2007.pdf).

[n4] Lalith Munasinghe, Tania Reif and Alice Henriques, "Gender gap in wage returns to job tenure and experience. Labour Economics, 2008: 1296–1916.

This study looked at US men's and women job experience in the early part of their careers with longitudinal data (National Longitudinal Survey of Youth) for the years 1979–1994 (ages 14–22 in 1979 (making the sample between 29–37 years old in 1994). They found men with high school degrees or less worked an average of 6.7 years compared to women's 5.9 years. For those with more than a high school degree, the average amount of work experience was 7.8 years for men and 7.3 years for women. Men worked, on average, about 6 more hours per week than did women. Men accrued 15 percent higher wage growth from an additional year of experience than women. Similar results can be found in Audrey Light and Manuelita Ureta, "Early-Career Work Experience and Gender Wage Differentials" Journal of Labor Economics 1995,13 (1) and Pamela Loprest, "Gender Differences in Wage Growth and Job Mobility" American Economic Review 1992, 82 (5).

[n5] In 2007, 35 percent of all women ages 25–64 in the labor force had a college degree compared to 33 percent of men. Conversely, 42 percent of men ages 25–64 in the labor force had a high school diploma or less education compared to 35 percent of women. Calculated by author from data provided in U.S. Department of Labor, U.S. Bureau of Labor Statistics, Women in the Labor Force: A Databook (2008 Edition) Table 8, (accessed 4-23-09 at http://www.bls.gov/cps/wlf-table8-2008.pdf).

[n6] Francine Blau and Lawrence Kahn, "The US Gender Pay Gap in the 1990s: Slowing Convergence," Industrial and Labor Relations Review, 2006, 60(1):45–66.

[n7] Judy Goldberg Dey and Catherine Hill, Behind the Pay Gap, Washington DC: American Association of University Women Educational Foundation, 2007.

[n8] Judith McDonald and Robert Thornton, "Do New Male and Female College Graduates Receive Unequal Pay?" Journal of Human Resources, 2007, 52(1): 32–48.

[n9] U.S. Department of Labor, U.S. Bureau of Labor Statistics, Women in the Labor Force: A Databook (2008 Edition) Table 18, (accessed 4-23-09 at http://www.bls.gov/cps/wlf-table8-2008.pdf).

[n10] The authors use Current Population Survey data and look at average hourly wages for full-time workers. Francine Blau and Lawrence Kahn, "The Gender Pay Gap" The Economists' Voice, Berkeley Electronic Press, 2007: 1–6.

[n11] Stephen Stanley and T.D. Jarrell, "Declining Bias and Gender Wage Discrimination? A Meta-Regression Analysis. Journal of Human Resources, 2004, 36(3): 828–838.

[n12] Melissa Binder et al. "Gender Pay Differences for the Same Work: Evidence from a United States Public University" forthcoming, Feminist Economics.

[n13] Francine Blau and Lawrence Kahn, "The US Gender Pay Gap in the 1990s: Slowing Convergence," Industrial and Labor Relations Review, 2006, 60(1):45–66.

[n14] David Neumark, using equally experienced male and female "pseudo" applicants, found high-priced restaurants were much more likely to both interview or offer jobs to men ("Sex Discrimination in Restaurant Hiring: An Audit Study," Quarterly Journal of Economics, 1996, 111(3):915–41). Claudia Golden and Cecilia Rouse found that the probability that women would advance and be hired by symphony orchestras was higher when auditions were "blind" (i.e. the gender of the applicant auditioning was unknown) than when they were not ("Orchestrating Impartiality: The Impact of 'Blind' Auditions on Female Musicians," American Economic Review, 2000, 90(4): 715–41).

[n15] In 2007, the median weekly salary of someone in construction occupations was $619 but as a secretary was $583; for a production occupations the week median salary was $559 compared to $494 for a retail salesperson. U.S. Department of Labor, U.S. Bureau of Labor Statistics, Women in the Labor Force: A Databook (2008 Edition) Table 18 (accessed 4-23-09 at http://www.bls.gov/cps/wlf-table8-2008.pdf).

[n16] Paula England, Michelle Budig and Nancy Folbre, "Wages of Virtue: The Relative Pay of Care Work" Social Problems 2002;49(4):455–474; and Nancy Folbre, The Invisible Heart: Economics and Family Values, New York: New Press, 2001.

[n17] Randy Albelda, Mignon Duffy and Nancy Folbre, "Taking Care: The Costs and Contributions of Care Work in Massachusetts" University of Massachusetts, forthcoming.

[n18] See Randy Albelda, Robert Drago and Steven Shulman, Unlevel Playing Fields: Understanding Wage Inequality and Discrimination, Boston, MA: Economics Affairs Bureau 2004, Chapter 7; Joan Williams, Unbending Gender: Why Family and Work Conflict and What to Do About It. New York: Oxford University Press, 2001; Robert Drago, Striking a Balance: Work, Family, Life, Boston, MA: Dollars and Sense, 2007.

[n19] Wendy Single-Rushton and Jane Waldfogel, "Motherhood and Women's Earnings in Anglo-American, Continental European, and Nordic Countries" Feminist Economics 2007,13(2):55–91; Joni Hersh and Leslie Stratton., "Housework and Wages" Journal of Human Resources 2002, 37(1):217–229; and Deboarah Anderson, Melissa Binder and Kate Krause, "Experience, Heterogeneity, Work Effort and Work-Schedule Flexibility" Industrial and Labor Relations Review, 2003, 56(2): 273–294; and Michelle Budig and Paula England, "The Wage Penalty for Motherhood" American Sociological Review, 2001,66(2), 204–225

[n20] U.S. Census Bureau, America's Families and Living Arrangements: 2007, Tables F1 and FM-1, (accessed 2-13-09 from http://www.census.gov/

population/socdemo/hh-fam/cps2007/tabF1-all.xls and http://www.census.gov/population/socdemo/hh-fam/fm1.xls.

[n21] Ibid.

[n22] U.S. Department of Labor, U.S. Bureau of Labor Statistics, Women in the Labor Force: A Databook (2008 Edition),Tables 23 and 24 (accessed 4-23-09 at http://www.bls.gov/cps/wlf-table8-2008.pdf).

[n23] Heather Boushey, Equal Pay for Breadwinners, Washington, DC: Center for American Progress, 2009.

[n24] John Schmitt Unions and Upward Mobility for Women Workers, Washington DC: Center for Economic and Policy Research, 2008.

"Families Can't Afford the Gender Wage Gap"

Heather Boushey,
Jessica Arons, Lauren Smith

Heather Boushey is Senior Economist, **Jessica Arons** is Director of the Women's Health and Rights Program, and **Lauren Smith** is a Research Assistant at the Center for American Progress.

It's no longer breaking news this Equal Pay Day that women are a crucial part of today's workforce. Women edged up to just 50 percent of workers on U.S. payrolls for the first time in October 2009, and two-thirds of American families with children now rely on a woman's earnings for a significant portion of their family's income. *The Shriver Report: A Woman's Nation Changes Everything,* which we released last fall, identified areas where American institutions have and haven't caught up with the realities of today's workforce. Chief among the shortcomings is the fact that a gender pay gap persists almost 50 years after the passage of the Equal Pay Act.

The gender pay gap has taken on added importance as men have been more likely than women to lose jobs during the Great Recession. This loss of a man's paycheck means that millions of families now rely on a woman's job to make ends meet. The persistent gender pay gap is adding insult to injury for families already hit hard by unemployment.

Our newly analyzed state-by-state data demonstrate that mothers in every state and the District of Columbia are financially supporting their families—and many are their family's primary breadwinner. Women's earnings are critical to their families' financial stability. Yet they continue to face a career wage gap that sets them back hundreds of thousands of dollars throughout their lives. Women face this gap regardless of their education, occupation, or where they live.

Congress took an important step in the fight for equal pay last year by passing the Lilly Ledbetter Fair Pay Act, but it has sidelined two pieces of legislation that also directly address the underlying causes of the gender pay gap. The Paycheck Fairness Act would amend portions of the Equal Pay Act to provide stronger enforcement of prohibitions against wage discrimination. The Fair Pay Act would require employers to provide equal pay for jobs that are comparable in skill, effort, responsibility, and working conditions.

It's time for government and businesses to make good on their commitments to American families by taking concrete steps to eliminate the gender wage gap.

FAMILIES RELY ON WOMEN'S EARNINGS

More than 12 million families with children rely primarily on women's earnings. More than a third of mothers in working families in every state but Wyoming and Utah are the family's primary breadwinner—these women provide at least half of a couple's earnings or are single working mothers. The District of Columbia has the highest share of breadwinner mothers, with 63.8 percent of mothers in working families bringing home at least half of their family's earnings.

More than 19 million families with children have a mother that is a breadwinner or co-breadwinner bringing home at least a quarter of the family's earnings. More than half of mothers in almost every state play this role. Utah is the only exception, with 46 percent of mothers as breadwinners or co-breadwinners. But this still means that 4 in 10 working families with children in Utah rely on a mother's earnings.

More than 6 in 10 families with children in 42 states rely on a woman to serve as breadwinner or co-breadwinner. These states are mostly in the eastern half of the country. The District of Columbia again leads the pack with 77.9 percent of mothers acting as their family's breadwinner or co-breadwinner.

A CAREER WAGE GAP

Even though women are significant contributors to their family's economic well-being, they continue to earn less than their male colleagues. Full-time, full-year working women still earn only 77 cents for every dollar that men earn. This wage gap is even larger for women of color. African-American women earn 61 cents and Latinas earn 52 cents for every dollar a white non-Hispanic man earns.

And this inequity accumulates over a lifetime into a shockingly high career wage gap. The career gap lowers women's earnings over a lifetime and reduces their long-term assets and that of their families. The typical woman loses $431,000 in pay over a 40-year career. But the gap is higher in some states than others. The career wage gap is at least $300,000 in 12 states, $400,000 in 23 states, $500,000 in 10 states, and exceeds $600,000 for women living in Wyoming and Alaska.

Education is clearly a route to higher earnings, but getting a degree does not necessarily lead to fair pay over a lifetime of work. The career gap for women with less than a high school education is about $300,000 and more than double that at $723,000 for women with a bachelor's degree or higher. In the 42 states where data is available, the career wage gap for women with at least a bachelor's degree was more than $500,000 in six states, more than $600,000 in 17 states and the District of Columbia, at least $700,000 in 13 states, and exceeds $800,000 in two states. The highest career wage gap for college-educated women is for those who live in Virginia, who lose more than $1 million over a 40-year career.

The career wage gaps are largest for women working in management and finance, sales, and professional occupations. Women working in Connecticut in management and finance jobs face $969,000 in lost earnings throughout their career. And Virginia is home to two of the highest career wage gaps for women in specific job categories—$774,000 for women in sales and $999,000 for women in professional occupations. The smallest career wage gap is for women working as office support staff in California, who lose $134,000 over a career, women in service jobs in Nevada who lose $216,000, and women in production in Tennessee who lose $358,000.

NEXT STEPS FOR EQUAL PAY

The House passed the Paycheck Fairness Act last year, but no action occurred in the Senate until a March 2010 hearing before the Senate Committee on Health, Education, Labor, and Pensions. Nearly all of the committee's senators attended the hearing, which suggests it could become a priority in the months ahead. President Obama was a co-sponsor of the Paycheck Fairness Act when he was in the Senate, and we now need his leadership to push for progress on this vital issue for working families, especially since so many families have been hard hit by the economic downturn.

Congress should move forward with the Paycheck Fairness Act and the Fair Pay Act, and businesses should review their compensation schemes to ensure pay equity for every one of their employees. America's working families cannot afford to wait any longer for a fair day's pay.

DATA AND METHODOLOGY

Wage data in this column comes from the American Community Survey, using the Integrated Public Use Microdata Series from the Minnesota Population Center and analyzed by Jeff Chapman.

The data for analysis of the career wage gap is limited to women and men between the ages of 25 and 64 who worked 50 to 52 weeks during 2008 and typically worked 35 or more hours per week. Workers are divided into 5- and 10-year age groups: 25- to 29-year-olds, 30- to 34-year-olds, and so on. Median wages are calculated separately for women and men within each age group. The wage gap is calculated by subtracting the male median wage from the female median wage. We sum the gap across age groups to illustrate the lifetime wage gap given today's wage difference. Data are not presented where insufficient samples sizes do not allow for meaningful calculation of medians. The wage gap presented here is not necessarily representative of a typical woman's experience, but it is an illustration of the scope of the problem.

Occupational categories follow the Standard Occupation Classification—which the Bureau of Labor Statistics and the Census Bureau use to classify occupations—and are then combined into broad groups. An occupation is classified by the type of work performed and many occupations are found in multiple industries. More information on the classification can be found at http://www.bls.gov/soc/.

Breadwinner mothers include single mothers who work and married mothers who earn as much or more than their husbands. Co-breadwinners include all breadwinners as well as wives who bring home at least 25 percent of the couple's earnings, but less than half. This analysis only includes families with at least one worker and with children under age 18 living in the home.

Interactive Map: The Persistent Career Wage Gap
Interactive Map: Women Provide for Their Families
Download memo with additional data (pdf)

Why The Gender Gap
Won't Go Away. Ever.

Kay S. Hymowitz

Kay S. Hymowitz *is the William E. Simon Fellow at the Manhattan Institute.*

Early this past spring, the White House Council on Women and Girls released a much-anticipated report called *Women in America*. One of its conclusions struck a familiar note: today, as President Obama said in describing the document, "women still earn on average only about 75 cents for every dollar a man earns. That's a huge discrepancy."

It *is* a huge discrepancy. It's also an exquisite example of what journalist Charles Seife has dubbed "proofiness." Proofiness is the use of misleading statistics to confirm what you already believe. Indeed, the 75-cent meme depends on a panoply of apple-to-orange comparisons that support a variety of feminist policy initiatives, from the Paycheck Fairness Act to universal child care, while telling us next to nothing about the well-being of women.

This isn't to say that all is gender-equal in the labor market. It is not. It also isn't to imply that discrimination against women doesn't exist or that employers shouldn't get more creative in adapting to the large number of mothers in the workplace. It does and they should. But by severely overstating and sensationalizing what is a universal predicament (I'm looking at you, Sweden and Iceland!), proofers encourage resentment-fueled demands that no government anywhere has ever fulfilled—and that no government ever will.

Let's begin by unpacking that 75-cent statistic, which actually varies from 75 to about 81, depending on the year and the study. The figure is based on the average earnings of full-time, year-round (FTYR) workers, usually defined as those who work 35 hours a week or more.

But consider the mischief contained in that "or more." It makes the full-time category embrace everyone from a clerk who arrives at her desk at 9 AM and leaves promptly at 4 PM to a trial lawyer who eats dinner four nights a week—and lunch on weekends—at his desk. I assume, in this case, that the clerk is a woman and the lawyer a man for the simple reason that—and here is an average that proofers rarely mention—full-time men work more hours than full-time women do. In 2007, according to the Bureau of Labor Statistics, 27 percent of male full-time workers had workweeks of 41 or more hours, compared with 15 percent of female full-time workers; meanwhile, just 4 percent of full-time men worked 35 to 39 hours a week, while 12 percent of women did. Since FTYR men work more than FTYR women do, it shouldn't be surprising that the men, on average, earn more.

The way proofers finesse "full-time" can be a wonder to behold. Take a recent article in the *Washington Post* by Mariko Chang, author of a forthcoming book on the wealth gap between women and men. Chang cites a wage difference between "full-time" male and female pharmacists to show how "even when they work in the same occupation, men earn more." A moment's Googling led me to a 2001 study in the *Journal of the American Pharmacists Association* concluding that male pharmacists worked 44.1 hours a week, on average, while females worked 37.2 hours. That study is a bit dated, but it's a good guess that things haven't changed much in the last decade. According to a 2009 article in the *American Journal of Pharmaceutical Education*, female pharmacists' preference for reduced work hours is enough to lead to an industry labor shortage.

The other arena of mischief contained in the 75-cent statistic lies in the seemingly harmless term "occupation." Everyone knows that a CEO makes more than a secretary and that a computer scientist makes more than a nurse. And most people wouldn't be shocked to hear that secretaries and nurses are likely to be women, while CEOs and computer scientists are likely to be men. That obviously explains much of the wage gap.

But proofers often make the claim that women earn less than men *doing the exact same job*. They can't possibly know that. The Labor Department's occupational categories can be so large that a woman could drive a truck through them. Among "physicians and surgeons," for example, women make only 64.2 percent of what men make. Outrageous, right? Not if you consider that there are dozens of specialties in medicine: some, like cardiac surgery, require years of extra training, grueling hours, and life-and-death procedures; others, like pediatrics, are less demanding and consequently less highly rewarded. Only 16 percent of surgeons, but a full 50 percent of pediatricians, are women. So the statement that female doctors make only 64.2 percent of what men make is really on the order of a tautology, much like saying that a surgeon working 50 hours a week makes significantly more than a pediatrician working 37.

A good example of how proofers get away with using the rogue term "occupation" is *Behind the Pay Gap*, a widely quoted 2007 study from the American Association of University Women whose executive summary informs us in its second paragraph that "one year out of college, women working full time earn only 80 percent as much as their male colleagues earn." The report divides the labor force into 11 extremely broad occupations determined by the Department of Education. So ten years after graduation, we learn, women who go into "business" earn considerably less than their male counterparts do. But the businessman could be an associate at Morgan Stanley who majored in econ, while the businesswoman could be a human-relations manager at Foot Locker who took a lot of psych courses. You don't read until the end of the summary—a point at which many readers will have already Tweeted their indignation—that when you control for such factors as education and hours worked, there's actually just a 5 percent pay gap. But the AAUW isn't going to begin a report with the statement that women earn 95 percent of what their male counterparts earn, is it?

Now, while a 5 percent gap will never lead to a million-woman march on Washington, it's not peanuts. Over a year, it can add up to real money, and over decades in the labor force, it can mean the difference between retirement in a Boca Raton co-op and a studio apartment in the inner suburbs. Many studies have examined the subject, and a consensus has emerged that when you control for what researchers call "observable" differences—not just hours worked and occupation, but also marital and parental status, experience, college major, and industry—there is still a small unexplained wage gap between men and women. Two Cornell economists, Francine Blau and Lawrence Kahn, place the number at about 9 cents per dollar. In 2009, the CONSAD Research Corporation, under the auspices of the Labor Department, located the gap a little lower, at 4.8 to 7.1 percent.

So what do we make of what, for simplicity's sake, we'll call the 7 percent gap? You can't rule out discrimination, whether deliberate or unconscious. Many women say that male bosses are more comfortable dealing with male workers, especially when the job involves late-night meetings and business conferences in Hawaii. This should become a smaller problem over time, as younger men used to coed dorms and female roommates become managers and, of course, as women themselves move into higher management positions. It's also possible that male managers fear that a female candidate for promotion, however capable, will be more distracted by family matters than a male would be. They might assume that women are less able to handle competition and pressure. It's even possible that female managers think such things, too.

No, you can't rule out discrimination. Neither can you rule out other, equally plausible explanations for the 7 percent gap. The data available to researchers may not be precise; for instance, it's extremely difficult to find accurate measures of work experience. There's also a popular theory that women are less aggressive than men when it comes to negotiating salaries.

The point is that we don't know the reason—or, more likely, reasons—for the 7 percent gap. What we do know is that making discrimination the default explanation for a wage gap, as proofers want us to do, leads us down some weird rabbit holes. Asian men and women earn more than white men and women do, says the Bureau of Labor Statistics. Does that mean that whites are discriminated against in favor of Asians? Female cafeteria attendants earn more than male ones do. Are men discriminated against in that field? Women who work in construction earn almost exactly what men in the field do, while women in education earn considerably less. The logic of default discrimination would lead us to conclude that construction workers are more open to having female colleagues than educators are. With all due respect to the construction workers, that seems unlikely.

MEN WORK MORE HOURS THAN WOMEN DO.
Number of American Full-Time Workers, 2007

35–39 HOURS PER WEEK   40 HOURS PER WEEK   41+ HOURS PER WEEK

2,419,000   5,347,000   39,091,000   32,937,000   15,319,000   6,497,000

Source: Bureau of Labor Statistics   GRAPH BY ROBERT PIZZO

So why do women work fewer hours, choose less demanding jobs, and then earn less than men do? The answer is obvious: kids. A number of researchers have found that if you consider only childless women, the wage gap disappears. June O'Neill, an economist who has probably studied wage gaps as much as anyone alive, has found that single, childless women make about 8 percent more than single, childless men do (though the advantage vanishes when you factor in education). Using Census Bureau data of pay levels in 147 of the nation's 150 largest cities, the research firm Reach Advisors recently showed that single, childless working women under 30 earned 8 percent more than their male counterparts did.

That's likely to change as soon as the children arrive. Mothers, particularly those with young children, take more time off from work; even when they are working, they're on the job less. *Behind the Pay Gap* found that "among women who graduated from college in 1992–93, more than one-fifth (23 percent) of mothers were out of the work force in 2003, and another 17 percent were working part time," compared with under 2 percent of fathers in each case. Other studies show consistently that the first child significantly reduces a woman's earnings and that the second child cuts them even further.

The most compelling research into the impact of children on women's careers and earnings—one that also casts light on why women are a rarity at the highest levels of the corporate and financial world—comes from a 2010 article in the *American Economic Journal* by Marianne Bertrand of the University of Chicago and Claudia Goldin and Lawrence Katz of Harvard. The authors selected nearly 2,500 MBAs who graduated between 1990 and 2006 from the University of Chicago's Booth School of Business and followed them as they made their way through the early stages of their careers. If there were discrimination to be found here, Goldin would be your woman. She is coauthor of a renowned 2000 study showing that blind auditions significantly increased the likelihood that an orchestra would hire female musicians.

Here's what the authors found: right after graduation, men and women had nearly identical earnings and working hours. Over the next ten years, however, women fell way behind. Survey questions revealed three reasons for this. First and least important, men had taken more finance courses and received better grades in those courses, while women had taken more marketing classes. Second, women had more career interruptions. Third and most important, mothers worked fewer hours. "The careers of MBA mothers slow down substantially within a few years of first birth," the authors wrote. Though 90 percent of women were employed full-time and year-round immediately following graduation, that was the case with only 80 percent five years out, 70 percent nine years out, and 62 percent ten or more years out—and only about half of women with children were working full-time ten years after graduation. By contrast, almost all the male grads were working full-time and year-round. Furthermore, MBA mothers, especially those with higher-earning spouses, "actively chose" family-friendly workplaces that would allow them to avoid long hours, even if it meant lowering their chances to climb the greasy pole.

In other words, these female MBAs bought tickets for what is commonly called the "mommy track." A little over 20 years ago, the *Harvard Business Review* published an article by Felice Schwartz proposing that businesses make room for the many, though not all, women who would want to trade some ambition and earnings for more flexibility and time with their children. Dismissed as the "mommy track," the idea was reviled by those who worried that it gave employers permission to discriminate and that it encouraged women to downsize their aspirations.

But as Virginia Postrel noted in a recent *Wall Street Journal* article, Schwartz had it right. When working mothers can, they tend to spend less time at work. That explains all those female pharmacists looking for reduced hours. It explains why female lawyers are twice as likely as men to go into public-interest law, in which hours are less brutal than in the partner track at Sullivan & Cromwell. Female medical students tell researchers that they're choosing not to become surgeons because of "lifestyle issues," which seems to be a euphemism for wanting more time with the kids. Thirty-three percent of female pediatricians are part-timers—and that's not because they want more time to play golf.

In the literature on the pay gap and in the media more generally, this state of affairs typically leads to cries of injustice. The presumption is that women pursue reduced or flexible hours because men refuse to take equal responsibility for the children and because the United States does not have "family-friendly policies." Child care is frequently described as a burden to women, a patriarchal imposition on their ambitions, and a source of profound inequity. But is this attitude accurate? Do women *want* to be working more, if only the kids—and their useless husbands—would let them? And do we know that more government support would enable them to do so and close the wage gap?

Actually, there is no evidence for either of these propositions. If women work fewer hours than men do, it appears to be because they want it that way. About two-thirds of the part-time workforce in the United States is female. According to a 2007 Pew Research survey, only 21 percent of working mothers with minor children want to be in the office full-time. Sixty percent say that they would prefer to work part-time, and 19 percent would like to give up their jobs altogether. For working fathers, the numbers are reversed: 72 percent want to work full-time and 12 percent part-time.

In fact, women choose fewer hours—despite the resulting gap in earnings—all over the world. That includes countries with generous family leave and child-care policies. Look at Iceland, recently crowned the world's most egalitarian nation by the World Economic Forum. The country boasts a female prime minister, a law requiring that the boards of midsize and larger businesses be at least 40 percent female, excellent public child care, and a family leave policy that would make NOW members swoon. Yet despite successful efforts to get men to take paternity leave, Icelandic women still take considerably more time off than men do. They also are far more likely to work part-time. According to the Organisation for Economic Co-operation and Development (OECD), this queen of women-friendly countries has a bigger wage gap—women make 62 percent of what men do—than the United States does.

Sweden, in many people's minds the world's gender utopia, also has a de facto mommy track. Sweden has one of the highest proportions of working women in the world and a commitment to gender parity that's close to a national religion. In addition to child care, the country offers paid parental leave that includes two months specifically reserved for fathers. Yet moms still take four times as much leave as dads do. (Women are also more likely to be in lower-paid public-sector jobs; according to sociologist Linda Haas, Sweden has "one of the most sex-segregated labor markets in the world.") Far more women than men work part-time; almost *half* of all mothers are on the job 30 hours a week or less. The gender wage gap among full-time workers in Sweden is 15 percent. That's lower than in the United States, at least according to the flawed data we have, but it's hardly the feminist Promised Land.

The list goes on. In the Netherlands, over 70 percent of women work part-time and say that they want it that way. According to the Netherlands Institute for Social Research, surveys found that only 4 percent of female part-timers wish that they had full-time jobs. In the United Kingdom, half of female GPs work part-time, and the National Health Service is scrambling to cope with a dearth of doctor hours. Interestingly enough, countries with higher GDPs tend to have the highest percentage of women in part-time work. In fact, the OECD reports that in many of its richest countries, including Denmark, Sweden, Iceland, Germany, the U.K., and the U.S., the percentage of the female workforce in part-time positions has gone *up* over the last decade.

So it makes no sense to think of either the mommy track or the resulting wage differential as an injustice to women. Less time at work, whether in the form of part-time jobs or fewer full-time hours, is what many women want and what those who can afford it tend to choose. Feminists can object till the Singularity arrives that women are "socialized" to think that they have to be the primary parent. But after decades of feminism and Nordic engineering, the continuing female tropism toward shorter work hours suggests that that view is either false or irrelevant. Even the determined Swedes haven't been able to get women to stick around the office.

That doesn't mean that the mommy track doesn't present a problem, particularly in a culture in which close to half of all marriages break down. A woman can have a baby, decide to reduce her hours and her pay, forgo a pension, and then, ten years later, watch her husband run off with the Pilates instructor. The problem isn't what it used to be when women had fewer degrees and less work experience during their childless years; women today are in better shape to jump-start their careers if need be. The risk remains, however.

It's not at all clear how to solve this problem or even if there is a solution, especially during these fiscally challenged days. But one thing is clear: the wage-gap debate ought to begin with the mommy track, not with proofy statistics.

Getting Inked:
Tattoos And College Students

Lauren Manuel and Eugene P. Sheehan

GETTING INKED: TATTOOS AND COLLEGE STUDENTS: By **Manuel, Laura, Sheehan, Eugene P.**, College Student Journal, 01463934, Dec2007 Part B, Vol. 41, Issue 4

This study explores whether college students with tattoos or piercings demonstrate extreme personalities and behaviors. Participants were 46 men and 164 women (mean=20.0 years). Questions assessed participants' attitudes toward tattooing, presence of a tattoo, and participation in risk taking behaviors. Participants completed the Personality Research Form (PRF) Form E (Jackson, 1984). Those with tattoos scored higher in autonomy (mean=9.96) than those without tattoos (mean=5.55). Women with tattoos scored higher on impulsivity (p=.04). Men with piercings were significantly higher on exhibitionism (p=.02) and sentience (p=.04), and significantly lower on harm avoidance (p=.05). Women with piercings were significantly higher on social recognition (p=.04). Those with and without tattoos reported similar attitudes toward tattoos and levels of risk taking behavior.

Tattooing had a long history even prior to the discovery of a tattooed man embedded in ice, a find that suggested the practice occurred circa 3300 B.C. (Rademackers & Schoenthal, 1992). Prior to that discovery, it was thought that tattooing was primarily an ancient Egyptian practice dating from circa 2000 B.C. (Nadler, 1983). Tattooing was brought to the New World in 1769 by sailors returning from voyages to the South Pacific (Post, 1968; Sanders, 1991). Although the association with sailors has never completely dissipated (Armstrong, Murphy, Sallee & Watson, 2000; Mallon & Russell, 1999; Sanders, 1991; Yamamoto, Seeman, & Boyd, 1963), the practice of tattooing became more widespread and occasionally socially acceptable in the Western world after that time (Sanders, 1991). Tattooing enjoyed a brief period of popularity in the late 19th Century in England, and in the United States in the 1920s (Sanders, 1991). It later began to be relegated to the socially marginal (Armstrong, 1991; Fox, 1976; Post, 1968; Sanders, 1991).

Piercing has almost as long a history as tattooing, having been practiced by Egyptian pharaohs, Mayans, and Roman centurions (Armstrong, 1996). Body piercing is sometimes studied along with tattooing, partly because people with tattoos often have piercings (Buhrich, 1983; Frederick & Bradley, 2000). Piercing, particularly in adolescents, is usually done in tattoo parlors (Armstrong, 1996) or is self-inflicted (Martin, 1997). For women, ear piercing has come to be viewed as a mainstream practice but piercing eyebrows, nose, cheeks, or other areas appears to symbolize one's disaffection from society, much like tattooing (Sanders, 1988). Body piercing other than the earlobe has been associated with the gay subculture (Buhrich, 1983). Researchers in one recent study found that the younger individuals begin piercing the more likely they are to exhibit antisocial tendencies (Frederick & Bradley, 2000). However, piercing is generally regarded as less extreme than tattooing because removing the body jewelry will ordinarily cause the pierced hole to heal (Armstrong, 1996). This may explain why this practice of body alteration has been only briefly mentioned in the literature and rarely studied in its own right.

Tattoos have been empirically associated with a several deviant behaviors (Braithwaite, Stephens, Bowman, Milton, & Braithwaite, 1998; Buhrich, 1983; Ceniceros, 1998; Drews, Allison, & Probst, 2000; Raspa & Cusack, 1990; Verberne, 1969) and criminality (Fox, 1976; Mallon & Russell, 1999; Post, 1968; Taylor, 1970; Yakamoto et al, 1963). Research on tattoos has documented a strong relationship between people with tattoos and antisocial personalities (Post, 1968; Raspa & Cusack, 1990; Taylor, 1968) or actual criminal conduct (Fox, 1976; Measey, 1972; Roc, Howell, & Payne, 1974; Taylor, 1968; Taylor, 1970). For example, studies have documented that more heavily tattooed Naval detainees were more likely to have a previous naval or civilian offense (Measey, 1972). Taylor (1968) found that among delinquent girls incarcerated in juvenile facilities, the more heavily tattooed were more aggressive, uncooperative, and unstable in addition to being more criminal in their attitude and behavior. Female prison inmates with tattoos were more likely to have been in all four types of institutions—juvenile halls, reformatories, jails, and prisons (Fox, 1976).

In a later study, Taylor (1970) attempted to obtain a control group to match his incarcerated girls, 55% of whom were tattooed, but failed because "there was only 1 tattooed woman non-offender available of any age" (p.88). Tattooed women prisoners had more violent and aggressive offenses in addition to more prior convictions (Taylor, 1970). While in prison, women with tattoos were more frequently charged with violation of prison rules, with fighting, and with insubordination (Fox, 1976). In research involving college student respondents, males with tattoos were more likely to report having been arrested and females with tattoos were more likely to report shoplifting (Drews et al., 2000). Tattooed people have been found to be more likely to engage in substance abuse (Braithwaite et al., 1998; Ceniceros, 1998; Drews et al., 2000; Dhossche, Snell, & Larder, 1999; Raspa and Cusack, 1990) and risk taking behaviors (Armstrong, 1991; Ceniceros, 1998; Grief, Hewitt, & Armstrong, 1999). In a study of people who played Russian roulette, there was a strong correlation between this form of risk taking and the kind and quantity of the person's tattoos and body piercings (Ceniceros, 1998). As the severity of the tattoos and piercings increased, all forms of violent behavior increased (Ceniceros, 1998).

Prior studies have reported strong associations between tattoos and homosexual orientation for both males (Buhrich, 1983), and females (Fox, 1976; Taylor, 1970). However, Grief et al. (1999) reported that 87% of their tattooed college student respondents claimed a heterosexual orientation; less than 1% reported a homosexual preference. Grief et al.'s study consisted of college students from 18 universities, 69% of the participants were 18-22 years old. In that study, 24% of the respondents with tattoos reported having 6 to 10 sexual partners and 26% reported having more than 11 partners. In the National Health and Social Life Survey (NHSLS) 15% of the participants 18-24 had 5-10 sex partners and 11% had more than 10 since age 18 (Michael, Gagnon, Laumann, & Kolata, 1994). Although the two studies are obviously not directly comparable, it would appear that tattooed respondents in the Grief study were above national averages for the number of sexual partners.

A less stable heterosexual adjustment has also been found in several studies (Taylor, 1968; Yamamoto et al., 1963). Grief et al. (1999) found that 12% of college respondents reported engaging in bisexual activity. Buhrich (1983) also found a strong association between tattooing and sexual sadomachism, bondage, or fetishism. However, in a recent study of young adults who were mostly college students, only 3% of tattooers or piercers reported engaging in sadomasochistic activities (Frederick & Bradley, 2000).

The association of tattoos with mental illness has been frequently investigated. Tattooing has been empirically associated with personality disorders (Armstrong, 1991; Caplan, Komaroni, & Rhodes, 1996; Ceniceros, 1998; Measey, 1972; Post, 1968) and psychopathic personality (McKerracher & Watson, 1969; Yakamoto, et al., 1963). In Measey's (1972) study of Royal Navy detainees, the correlation with personality disorder increased in significance with the number of tattoos possessed; 48% of those with no tattoos had a personality disorder whereas the percentage increased to 58% for those with 1 to 4 tattoos and up to 82% for those with more than 16 tattoos. Raspa and Cusack (1990) found the association between personality disorders and tattoos so clear that they state "finding a tattoo on physical examination should alert the physician to the possibility of an underlying psychiatric condition" (p. 1481).

One recent study linked the practice of tattooing and suicide (Dhossche, et al., 1999). Suicides and accidental deaths were matched in a 3-year case-control study and it was found that 57% of the young suicides were tattooed compared to 29% of the accidental deaths. The researchers concluded that tattoos may be possible markers for lethality from both suicide and accidental death due to the correlations with substance abuse and personality dysfunction (Dhossche, et al., 1999).

Sanders (1988) has described tattoos as "marks of dissaffliation" with society which become "voluntary stigma" for the bearers, marking their owners as being apart from the mainstream culture. People obtaining tattoos are usually aware of this attribute of tattoos and often state that they obtained the tattoo in order to feel unique (Armstrong, 1991; Sanders, 1988; DeMello, 1995; Phelan & Hunt, 1998), mark their independence (Armstrong, 1991; Sanders, 1991), or as a sign of special affiliation (Armstrong et al., 2000; Measey, 1972; Phelan & Hunt, 1998).

Although tattoos remain negatively regarded by the public (Armstrong, 1991; Armstrong et al., 2000; Hawkins & Popplestone, 1964) and are proscribed by most mainstream religions (Post, 1968; Raspa & Cusack, 1990; Taylor, 1968), it is clear that the popularity of obtaining a tattoo, known as 'getting inked' (Mason, 1991), is rising again (Houghton et al., 1995; Inch & Huws, 1993; Mallon & Russell, 1999; Mason, 1991). The city council of New York was recently persuaded to lift a 37-year ban on tattoo parlors within the city (Kennedy, 1997). Tattoo parlors are the fifth largest growth business in the United States (Armsrong & Fell, 2000; Vail, 1999). It was estimated that there were about 300 tattoo parlors in the United States in the early 1970s compared to about 4,000 in 1991 (Mason, 1991).

The practice remains common among servicemen (Armstrong et al., 2000; Mallon & Russell, 1999), so common, in fact, that the Marine Corp was forced to codify rules on what tattoos recruits may have ("Taboo Tattoos" 1996). Tattooing is also clearly more popular among certain groups, such as the National Basketball Association. Thirty-five percent of the members have tattoos (Ewey, 1998; Mallon & Russell, 1999). Additionally, it is generally agreed that the practice of tattooing is more widespread among prison populations (Fox, 1976, DiFrancesco, 1990; Houghton, Durkin, Parry, Turbett, Odgers, 1996; Mallon & Russell, 1999; Taylor, 1968) and people in mental health institutions (Raspa & Cusak, 1990).

Perhaps the population with the most dramatic increase in tattooing is that of women (Armstrong, 1991; DeMello, 1995; Inch & Huws, 1993; Nadler, 1983; Sanders, 1991). In the past 20 years, the number of women getting tattooed has quadrupled (Nadler, 1983). It is estimated that 40-50% of the clients in tattoo parlors are women (Armstrong, 1991; Sanders, 1991).

Estimates for the prevalence of tattooing itself have varied from a low of 3% in a random national survey conducted in 1990 (Armstrong & Fell, 2000) to 25% of people 15-25 years old (Armstrong et al., 2000). The Alliance of Professional Tattooists estimates that 15-20% of teenagers are tattooed (Braithwaite et al., 1998). Nationwide estimates vary from 7 million people to 20 million people with tattoos (Grief, et al., 1999; Martin et al., 1995).

Some researchers argue that the trend in tattooing and piercing indicates a shift in fashion and a break with body art's exclusive association with lower class people and deviant activities (DeMello, 1995; Ewey, 1998; Martin, 1997). In this argument, the concept that tattoos or piercings are a form of self-mutilation or a way of expressing a negative attitude is rejected (Frederick & Bradley, 2000; Martin, 1997). However, little evidence has been presented to demonstrate that the association between tattooing and various negative behaviors or personality disorders was unjustified in the past or has changed in the current culture.

In this study, we asked two research questions. Research question #1: Are college students who have tattoos more extreme in their personalities and behavior?

Research question #2: Are college students with piercings more extreme in their personalities and behaviors?

METHOD

Participants

Participants in the present study were 210 men and women ranging in age from 17 to 37 with a mean age of 20.0 years. Within the total group, there were 46 men and 164 women participants. Participants were all recruited from psychology classes at a western university.

MEASURES

A set of 12 questions was created to assess the participants' attitudes toward tattooing. An additional 16 questions were asked of those who reported having a tattoo to determine their attitudes toward their own tattoos, the kind of tattoo they had, where it was located on the body, and how old they were when they obtained the tattoo. Participants were also asked to report on body piercings, specifically where they were pierced and how old they were when they modified their body. Seven questions were asked about various behaviors such as driving above the speed limit, smoking marijuana, drinking too much alcohol, engaging in unprotected sex, and shoplifting. Participants were also asked to provide background information about their age, sex, academic major, career plans, race/ethnicity, marital status, and the population size of their hometown.

Participants were then asked to fill in the Personality Research Form (PRF)-Form E (Jackson, 1984). This personality inventory has 352 true-false items. The PRF-E has a reading level of 6th grade (Schinka & Borum, 1994) and was not challenging for any of the student participants. The norms for PRF-E were obtained from college samples and therefore this instrument was considered appropriate for this particular sample (Jackson, 1987). The PRF-E measures the following personality traits: abasement, achievement, affiliation, aggression, autonomy, change, cognitive structure, defendence, dominance, endurance, exhibition, harmavoidance, impulsivity, nurturance, order, play, sentience, social recognition, succorance, understanding, and desirability. The instrument also has a scale for infrequency to detect implausible responses.

PROCEDURE

Surveys were administered to the students in all levels of psychology courses at a Western university. The participants were given course credit for their participation. Participants were given a debriefing sheet when they turned in their completed forms to the primary researcher.

RESULTS

Of the total sample of 210 people, 67 participants had tattoos (32%) and 135 (64%) had piercings. Of the 46 men in the study, 30% reported having obtained a tattoo. Of the 164 women in the study, 53 (32%) reported having tattoos. Most of the women (75%) reported some piercing, primarily ear piercing. Only twelve men reported piercing.

Men and women with tattoos were both higher in autonomy on the PRF-E with a mean score of 6.96 (SD=3.44) compared to their non-tattooed peers' mean score of 5.55 (SD=2.93). When the sexes were viewed separately, the correlation remained for both sexes (men r=.38, p=.008; women r=.17; p=.03). Women with tattoos also scored higher on the PRF-E on impulsivity (r=.16, p=.04).

Men who had pierced their bodies were significantly higher on exhibitionism (r=.34, p=.02) and sentience (r=.31, p=.04). They were significantly lower on harm avoidance (r=-.30, p=.05). Women with piercings, however, were significantly higher on social recognition (r=.16, p=.04).

Both tattooed and non-tattooed students reported similar attitudes toward tattoos, agreeing that they are mainstream and that lots of people have tattoos these days. In addition, there were no differences between the groups on any of the seven behavioral questions (e.g. "I drink too much", "I engage in unprotected sex").

DISCUSSION

A high scorer on autonomy on the PRF-E is defined as a person who "tries to break away from restraints, confinement, or restrictions of any kind...may be rebellious when faced with restraints" (Jackson, 1984, p. 6). The defining trait adjectives also describe the person as "unmanageable, free, self-reliant, independent, autonomous, rebellious, unconstrained, individualistic, ungovernable, self-determined, non-conforming, uncompliant, undominated, resistant, lone-wolf" (Jackson, 1984, p.6). The findings in this study would seem to concur with previous studies that found people with tattoos willing to be regarded as outside mainstream society (e.g., Sanders, 1988, 1991) and therefore are not surprising.

Previous studies have also noted the correlation between impulsivity and tattooing so this finding also supports prior research. Two additional questions related to impulsivity were asked of people who had obtained tattoos: whether they intended to obtain another tattoo and whether they regretted the one(s) they already had. The mean for the former question was 2.5, indicating the midpoint between agreeing and disagreeing. For most people, one tattooing experience may be enough.

In this study, people with tattoos averaged 3.5 on the question about regret (between disagree 3 and strongly disagree 4) indicating they do not yet regret getting a tattoo. Regret is a frequent experience among older people with tattoos (Martin, et al., 1995). It is possible that the reason that these participants do not regret their decision to tattoo is partly due to the fact that people in this study obtained their first tattoo at an average age of 18.2 years and were an average age of 19.8 at the time of the study. It may be a few years yet before any "tattoers' remorse" becomes evident.

Given that there are 21 personality scales on the PRF-E and only two personality variables with significant differences between those with and without tattoos, these results support the recent finding that in some populations, tattooing may be more normal than abnormal (Frederick & Bradley, 2000). There were few differences in the groups.

In addition it seems reasonable that reasons for piercing may be very different by gender. Women may pierce their ears or other body parts in order to be normative, although this may be considered attention-seeking behavior in men. Female participants scored high on social recognition that is described as "approval seeking, proper, and well-behaved" (Jackson, 1984, p. 7). This finding would be in keeping with someone who goes along with normative behavior, which ear piercing clearly is for females. On the other hand, male piercers scored high in exhibitionism, described as being "dramatic, ostentatious, and showy", and sentience, described as being "aesthetic, sensitive, and open to experience" (Jackson, 1984, p. 7). In addition, male piercers scored lower on harmavoidance, described as someone who is not pain avoidant, does not avoid risks, and is not self-protecting.

As with previous studies, this study also found that women tended to place their tattoos on 'private skin'. Fully 48% of the women with tattoos chose the lower back as the first location for a tattoo. In their initial tattooing, only six chose the relatively public area of the upper arm and seven selected the ankle (25%).

Of the 17 women reporting a second tattoo, eight (47%) of them also reported tattoos in relatively private areas (upper or lower back, chest, torso). Only five women reported obtaining a third tattoo (80% on private skin) and only one woman obtained a fourth (on private skin).

For men, upper arms (4) or upper backs (5) were the most popular locations for a first tattoo. Only 5 men reported having second tattoos and these were again located in the upper arm or upper back. Two men had a third tattoo choosing the upper arm and chest for those tattoos. No men reported having a fourth tattoo.

In conclusion, the results of this study concur with most studies in finding that people choosing to tattoo are different on some personality variables. However, in this college population the differences were not as extreme as they have been in previous studies involving less normative people (e.g. incarcerated people, suicides, and mental health facilities).

AUTHOR NOTE

Correspondence concerning this paper should be addressed to the second author: Dr. Eugene P. Sheehan, College of Education, Box 106, University of Northern Colorado, Greeley, CO 80639.

REFERENCES

Armstrong, M. (1991). Career oriented women with tattoos. Image-The Journal of Nursing Scholarship, 23(4), 215-220.

Armstrong, M. (1995). Adolescent tattooing: Educating vs. pontificating. Pediatric Nursing, 21,(6), 561.

Armstrong, M. (1996). You pierced your what? Pediatric Nursing, 22(3), 236-238.

Armstrong, M., & Fell, P. (2000). Body art: Regulatory issues and the NEHA body art model code. Journal Of Environmental Health, 62(19), 25.

Armstrong, M. L., Murphy, K. P., Sallee, A., & Watson, M. (2000). Tattooed army soldiers: Examining the incidence, behavior, risk. Military Medicine, 165(2), pp. 135-141.

Armstrong, M., Murphy, K. P., Sallee, A., & Watson, A. (2000). Tattooed army soliders: examining the incidence, behavior, risk. Military Medicine, 165(2), 135-141.

Braithwaite, R., Stephens, T., Bowman, N., Milton, M., and Braithwaite, K. (1998). Tattooing and body piercing. Corrections Today, 60(2), 120-121, 178.

Buhrich, N. (1983). The association of erotic piercing with homosexuality, sadistic bondage, fetishism, and tattoos. Archives of Sexual Behavior, 12(2), 167-171.

Caplan, R., Komaromi, J., & Rhodes, M. (1996). Obessive-compulsive disorder and tattooing and bizarre sexual practice. British Journal of Psychiatry, 168(3), 379-380.

Ceniceros, S. (1998). Tattooing, body piercing, and Russian roulette. Journal of Nervous and Mental Disease, 186(8), 503-504.

DeMello, M. (1995). Not just for bikers anymore: Popular representation of American tattooing. Journal of Popular Culture, 29(3), 37-52.

Dhossche, D., Snell, K. S., & Larder, S. (2000). A case-control study of tattoos in young suicide victims as a possible marker of risk. Journal of Affective Disorders, 59(2), 165-168.

DiFrancesco, C. (1990). "Dermal body language" among prison inmates: The multiple unprofessional tattoo. Unpublished Doctoral Dissertation, University of Mississippi.

Drews, D., Allison, C., & Probst, J. (2000). Behavior and self concept differences in tattooed and nontattooed college students. Psychological Reports, 86, 475-481.

Ewey, M. (1998, July 1). Who has a tattoo and where? Ebony, 76.

Fox, J. (1976). Self-imposed stigmata: A study among female inmates. Unpublished Doctoral Dissertation, State University of New York at Albany.

Frederick, C. M., & Bradley, K. A. (2000). A different kind of normal? Psychological and motivational characteristics of young adult tattooers and body piercers. North American Journal of Psychology, 2(2), 379-392.

Greif, J., Hewitt, W., & Armstrong, M. (1999). Tattooing and body piercing. Clinical Nursing Research, 8(4), 368-385.

Hawkins, R., & Popplestone, J. (1964). The tattoo as exoskeletal defense. Perceptual and Motor Skills, 19, 500.

Houghton, S., Durkin, K., & Carroll, A. (1995). Children's and adolescents awareness of the physical and mental health risks associated with tattooing: A focus group study. Adolescence, 30(120), 971-988.

Houghton, S., Durkin, K., Parry, E., Turbett, Y., & Odgers, P. (1996). Amateur tattooing practices and beliefs among high school adolescents. Journal of Adolescent Health, 19, 420-425.

Inch, H. & Huws, R. (1993). Tattooed female psychiatric patients. British Journal of Psychiatry, 162, 128.

Jackson, D. (1984). Personality Research Form Manual. Port Huron, Mi. Research Psychologists Press, Inc.

Kennedy, R. (1997, February 26). City council gives tattooing its mark of approval. The New York Times, pp. B1, B5.

McKerracher, D. W. & Watson, R. A. (1969). Tattoo marks and behavior disorder. British Journal of Criminology, 9, 167-171.

Mallon, W. K. & Russell, M. (1999). Clinical and forensic significance of tattoos. Topics in Emergency Medicine, 21, 21-29.

Martin, A. (1997). On teenagers and tattoos. Journal of American Academy of Child Psychiatry, 36(6), 860-861.

Martin, R., Dogen, H., Colin, M., Annin, P., Gegax, T. T. (1995, Feb.6). Turning in the badges of rebellion: Tattooing hits the morning after. Newsweek, 46.

Mason, M. (1991, Jan. 7). Every picture tells a story from sailor to sales representative: Tattoos go mainstream. Newsweek, 117.

Measey, L.G. (1972). The psychiatric and social relevance of tattoos in Royal Navy detainees. British Journal of Criminology, 19(2), 182186.

Micheal, R. T., Gagnon, J. H., Laumann, E. O. & Kolata, G. (1994). Sex in America: A definitive survey. Boston: Little, Brown & Co.

Nadler, S. (1983). Why more women are being tattooed. Glamour, 196-198.

Phelan, M. P. & Hunt, Scott (1998). Prison gang members' tattoos as identity work: The visual communication of moral careers. Symbolic Interaction, 21(3), 277-298.

Post, R. S. (1968). The relationship of tattoos to personality disorders. Journal of Criminal Law, Criminology, and Police Science, 59(4), 516-524.

Rademaekers, W. & Schoenthal, R. (1992, Oct. 26). The Iceman's secrets. Time, 140(17), 62-67.

Raspa, R. F. & Cusack, J. (1990). Psychiatric implications of tattoos. American Family Physician, 41, 1481-1486.

Roc, A., Howell, R. & Payne, J. R. (1974). Comparison of prison inmates with and without juvenile records. Psychological Reports, 34, 1315-1319.

Sanders, C. (1988). Becoming and being tattooed. Journal of Contemporary Ethnography, 16(4), 395-432.

Sanders, C. (1991). Memorial decoration: Women, tattooing, and the meanings of body alteration. Michigan Quarterly Review, 30, 146-157.

Schinka, J. & Borum, R. (1994) Readability of normal personality inventories. Journal of Personnel Assessment, 6(1), 95-101.

"Taboo Tattoos" (1996, April 8). Time, 18.

Taylor, A. J. W. (1968). A search among Borstal girls for the psychological and social significance of their tattoos. British Journal of Criminology, 8, 171-185.

Taylor, A. J. W. ((1970). Tattooing among male and female offenders of different ages in different types of institutions. Genetic Psychology Monographs, 81, 81-119.

Vail, D. A. (1999). Tattoos are like potato chips...you can't have just one: The process of becoming and being a collector. Deviant Behavior 20, 253-273.

Verberne, J. P. (1969). The personality traits of tattooed adolescent offenders. British Journal of Criminology, 9, 172-175.

Yamamoto, J., Seeman, W., & Boyd, L. (1963). The tattooed man. Journal of Nervous and Mental Disease, 136, 365.

Tattooing: Mind, Body and Spirit. The Inner Essence of the Art

Frankie J. Johnson

University of Pittsburgh at Bradford

Editor's Note: **Ms. Johnson** *was the grand prize winner of the undergraduate student paper competition held at the 56th annual conference.*

ABSTRACT

This research began to understand why people choose to get tattoos. The reason was to find out if getting a tattoo was a novelty or if there was more to it than just what we can see inked on their skin. The interest of this research lies in the feeling, emotion, human awareness of expression, and the deeper meaning on the inside that coincides with what is seen only as skin deep on the outside.

Open-ended interviews were conducted, over a period of six months, with four tattoo artists and thirteen people that have tattoos. Time was spent in a local tattoo studio talking with people who were getting a tattoo or who had already been tattooed.

The reasons and the meaning behind getting a tattoo were found to vary as much as the number of people getting tattoos. The similar thread running through the reasons for getting a tattoo, however, was that tattooing is a form of self-expression.

INTRODUCTION

The subject of tattooing has been of interest to this researcher for many years, toying with the idea of getting one on every milestone year that was celebrated. However, enough nerve was never conjured up to go through with it. Then, a few years ago, a talented young artist, who does tattooing for a living, entered the scene. Several of her paintings, done in different media, promoted a certain energy in their presence that was magnetic. It was not known, to the researcher, that she was also a tattoo artist. The researcher's ingrained image of a tattoo artist was extremely the opposite of what was found in her. Her talent, her almost shy, meditative energy, and her knowledge gave a reason to question an unfounded opinion of the art of tattooing. Beginning to relate to it with a new awareness, the desire to acquire a tattoo rose to a new level. One no longer wanted just a cute little ladybug on the foot. The tattoo had to have meaning, to resonate with the spirit within, and portray the intent from which one lives their life.

The research of symbols, sayings, meanings of colors, and different types of tattoos, began while thinking of the places on ones body that one would comfortably wear a tattoo. This led me to wonder why other people got tattooed and what their tattoo meant to them, if anything. How does one arrive at the decision to make a permanent statement on their body? In this paper, the desire is to gain a wider knowledge of the art of tattooing and the people involved in it.

WHO GETS TATTOOS

For purposes of this research, the concentration is on tattooing in Western societies. According to researcher Shannon Bell (1999), there is a differentiation between people who have tattoos and tattooed people. The people who have tattoos only have one or two; usually personal images strategically placed so as not to be seen. Tattooed people have many tattoos, usually larger and more colorful and placed so they can be seen. She states that they have "crossed the point of no return" (Bell 1999: 56) and have chosen to socialize in the subculture of tattooists and others as heavily tattooed as they are. This action allows them to avoid the reactions of the general population and "fully embrace marginalization" (Bell 1999: 56).

Studies over the last ten years show that people from all types of occupations, ages, and social classes are getting tattoos at an increasing rate (Armstrong 1991). According to a study done by Armstrong and Pace-Murphy (1997); 10% of high school adolescents have tattoos. Studies done between 2000 and 2002 found that 16-23% of college students surveyed have tattoos and thirty seven percent of military recruits in basic training have tattoos, with 64% of them entering the military with them, having had them done between the ages of 15 and 21 years old (Armstrong, Pace-Murphy, Sallee, and Watson 2000).

An article in *Newsweek* dated January of 1991 by M. Mason states "from sailor to sales rep: tattoos go mainstream. . . . It's (tattooing) moved up the cultural system. The clients are more and more commonly people in managerial and professional positions." (p. 60)

However, several articles show that those getting tattoos come from all walks of life.

An article in *MacLean's* dated September of 1991 by N. Underwood tells of a 39-year-old mother, who is a bartender, and her 18-year-old daughter getting matching tattoos. One mother, at age 42, decided to get a tattoo after her daughter did, according to the *National Catholic Reporter* (Vineyard 1999). In 2005, *Herizons* magazine had an article by Alexis Keinlen that told of a 46-year-old mother getting a tattoo to memorialize the death of her 20-year-old son.

An article in *Spirituality and Health* dated February of 2006 by Mandi Caruso features a middle age post mastectomy woman who had both breasts removed because of cancer. She has a tattoo across her chest depicting her love of the water and surfing.

Another group that gets tattoos is the convicts. There is a difference between an inmate and a convict. The convict is more covered with tattoos, portraying the acceptance of the lifestyle and marginalization for life (Bell 1999).

Before the 1960s rock stars, popular athletes, and other youth icons were the people that displayed their tattoos. In the late 1980s tattooing was described as "trendy" and "no longer restricted to socially marginal groups" (Forbes 2001: 775). A significant number of well-educated middle-class people began to come on the tattoo scene (Forbes 2001).

The research indicates that there is no one group, no one age or gender, no one personality, and no particular level of social status that get tattoos. Just as diverse as who gets a tattoo are the reasons why people get their tattoos.

WHY PEOPLE GET TATTOOS

According to Bell (1999), American tattooing is unique. Tattoos are images and literal interpretations of things, not surprising because America is a consumer society. Bell states that the meaning of the act of tattooing is "inextricably linked" (p. 54) to the chosen image itself. Any permanent mark on the body signifies a person's separation from the mainstream of culture, and a tattoo can separate someone from society at large. Separation from society is a large factor in her theory about tattoos and why people get them. She states, "tattooing is a struggle for individualization in a society that is increasingly impersonal" (p. 54). They are a sign of resistance to the impermanent and conservative world of today. She quotes Vaclav Havel as saying that being tattooed is synonymous with "living the truth" (p. 54); your own personal truth.

Christensen (2000) found many reasons for getting tattoos including "expressing individuality, communicating rebellion, defining group membership, conveying spiritual meaning, or marking milestones such as life or death" (Christensen 2000: 432, as cited in Armstrong, Owen, Roberts, and Koch 2002). Tattooed career women said that the tattoo "helped them feel good, unique, and special" (Armstrong 1991: 219, as cited in Armstrong, Owen, Roberts, and Koch 2002). Among adolescents and college students, the purpose for their tattoo was "expressing myself" and the reason for doing it with a tattoo was "I just wanted one" (Armstrong and McConnell 1994; Armstrong and Pace-Murphy 1997; Greif et al., 1999: 368, as cited in Armstrong, Owen, Roberts, and Koch 2002). Forbes (2001) found college students "just liked the looks of it"(p. 778) and they offered the tattoo as a form of self-expression. Military recruits' reasons were to "be myself, I don't need to impress people anymore" and because they just wanted one (Armstrong et al. 2000: 137, as cited in Armstrong, Owen, Roberts, and Koch 2002).

Bell also refers to Paul Willis's theory on symbolic creativity, which states that even though the lives of young people are not involved in the arts, they are full of expressions, signs, and symbols to establish the young persons presence, identity and meaning. Being tattooed is an act of this creativity. Forming an identity is important to young and old, and for some, tattoos can be a symbolic part of this identity. Tattoos can honor their family or lover, display their religious beliefs or patriotism, or their association with a certain group (Bell 1999).

Bell writes that women choose softer, more personal images for tattoos and place them where they can be hidden. Men choose macho imagery and place them where they can be seen. Tattoos have long been associated with men because of the stereotype of the tattooed person and the pain associated with it, so when a woman gets tattoos, it is regarded as a resistance to female beauty as society commonly sees it. She writes; "it takes a strong will and sense of self (identity) to withstand the blatant and piercing stares" (p. 56) because of the stigma still attached that differs in every culture and city. As stated earlier, it creates a separation from mainstream society (Bell, 1999).

Prison tattoos are "identity claimers" (p. 55), according to Bell, that are associated with gang or group membership. Prison tattoos are done with single needles and with no color, so they appear very different than tattoos done professionally in a tattoo studio. This difference in imagery and the way it is done creates a class marker between prison and professional tattoos for all of society to see (Bell 1999). Some prison inmates bring their own equipment; a sharpened guitar string for a needle and a melted down checker piece for the ink, according to an article by Ronald Day in *Body Positive* magazine (2005).

An article in *Jet* magazine dated July 2001 writes that athletes get tattoos for several reasons. One athlete has tattoos that portray his attitude in life, such as "Only the Strong Survive" (p. 46), and some that are dedicated to his family and friends. Another uses them to express himself through meaningful symbols. Yet another says his tattoos "revolve around my life. I think tattoos are something that tell who you are and how you feel" (p. 46).

There are myths that people get tattoos for personal advertisement and that every tattoo means something explicit. Some people do get a tattoo with the intention of others seeing and interpreting it, yet others have a tattoo in places that cannot be seen by the general public because it is a symbol for their self and those that they are intimate with. The more tattoos a person has, the less meaning the actual tattoo has. The meaning is in the act of getting the tattoo. It becomes less about it meaning something to them down the road, and more about it being aesthetically pleasing (Bell 1999). "Meanings change, beauty and truth are eternal" (Bell 1999: 57).

Bell writes that tattooing goes beyond the lack of depth of the visually based American consumer society that is superficial in nature. She says that American tattooing is a "product of this surface-oriented society" (Bell 1999: 57) and quotes Marshal Blonsky:

[Surface] is a characteristic of our fast-flowing time, where everything has to communicate fast and move on. . . . Depth is a category that pretends to penetrate surface. . . . First impressions are decisive [and] surface is individuated by apparel. . . . The search for interiority merely creates more surface. (Blonsky: 17)

There is no other form of adornment or decoration that is permanent. Fashions allow change of mind, tattooing does not. The most common concern about tattoos is their permanence (Bell 1999). This fear of permanence says a lot about society and "its unwillingness to commit to identity and accept the consequences. To do something permanent is to be unable to take it back—it is to live in truth for eternity" (Bell 1999:57).

An article in *Print* dated Jan/Feb 1995 written by Akiko Busch writes of the decoration factor of tattoos. A couple got tattoos together when they decided to get married because they thought it to be more expressive of commitment than jewelry. Another person chose their tattoo because they could imagine being "accompanied through life by such an emblem" (Busch 1995: 112). Tattoos are about intimacy, image and identity (Busch 1995). A young 15-year-old girl got a tattoo, with her mother's permission, as an attempt to reclaim her body with a protective talisman on herself because of being a victim of a crime (Vineyard 1999).

A lot of women get tattoos to reclaim their bodies or to mark incidents in their lives. A mother, father, and several friends of a student that died got tattoos to mark the loss. It is a constant reminder of him and a symbol of the relationship and closeness he had with each one. The pain of getting it done was welcomed as a pain that could be controlled amongst all of the emotional pain that could not be controlled. Another woman got her whole arm tattooed to represent a reclaiming of her childhood. Women tend to get tattoos to mark a change in the way they see themselves, not to change the way society sees them (Keinlen, 2005).

In Cultural Anthropology journal, 1997, Daniel Rosenblatt writes about the "modem primitive", meaning the tattooed person of today in the Western world. Linking modern day tattooing with the ancient world brings in a long history and thus exemplifies it as a human practice. Identifying with tattooing in other cultures allows people to feel like they're connecting with the history of humanity (Rosenblatt 1997). It allows us to see tattooing as a spiritual activity because it is ancient and widespread and "is seen as an expression of a basic human need for rituals that give life meaning" (p. 303) and connects the tattooed person to the rest of humanity (Hardy, as cited in Rosenblatt 1997). The modern tattooed person is seeking other truths and other ways of knowing the world. The tattoo can connect the person wearing it to knowledge of powers in "nature" that the "primitive" people knew in intimacy (Zuluata, as cited in Rosenblatt 1997). The growing popularity of tattooing in the Western world may be interpreted as a sign of a bigger change in society (Rosenblatt 1997). Maybe we are no longer the "monolithic engine of rationality"(p. 304) that we are imagined to be (Rosenblatt 1997).

Judeo-Christian and Jewish tradition look down on tattooing. This is another factor in linking tattoos to identification with non-Western or alternative ways of thought. The outdated social stigma attached to tattooing is melting away. Tattooing is beginning to be seen as more of a meaningful art than a "brand". Tattoos seem to be about representing or expressing an aspect of the self, both in public and privately. It reflects the duality in our notion of the self, and is an attempt to bring these two aspects together (Rosenblatt 1997).

Some people get tattoos to express the aspects of them that go against the stereotyping of society. It can be a process of self-exploration, affirmation of self, and/or a mask. It opens the person up to the world by expressing beliefs or feelings in a visible manner, yet it can create a barrier against the world (Handel, as cited in Rosenblatt 1997).

In Rosenblatt's piece, he quotes Fakir Musafar; "The purpose of the tattoo is to do something for the person, to help them realize the individual magic latent within them [Vale and Juno 1989:11]". The tattoo can be a way to get in touch with the private, intuitive self and can be an act of reclaiming the self. There is a relationship between controlling your body and realizing yourself as an individual. This is why tattoos are popular in prison—no one can take away your skin. They are an expression of freedom (Hardy, as cited in Rosenblatt 1997).

The issue of power and control is also prevalent in the youth who get tattoos according to Georg Simmel in his 1950 essay, "The Metropolis and Mental Life". In this essay he writes of conformity and mistrust in modern life producing an uneasiness that leads people to look for ways to express individuation and find self-fulfillment. He states that deviance is an outlet for this (Koch, Roberts, Cannon, Armstrong, and Owen 2004).

Lyman and Scott (1970) take this idea further by discussing four sites in which the individuation may occur: public territories, home territories, interactional territories, and body territories. Body territories are the most private and sacred of the territories. Even though body territories are sometimes regulated socially, the person can also claim it as a place of self-expression. The body is a viable way to express oneself symbolically, especially if the person has limited access to the other territorial forms. Irwin (2001) and Velliquette and Murray (2002) agree and add that tattoos "represent both a moral passage of sorts and also an attempt to individuate oneself from the larger society" (Koch, Roberts, Cannon, Armstrong, and Owen 2004: p. 83). It is a public display of self-concept and is important in developing the social self for some people (Koch et al. 2004).

For some people, getting a tattoo means that they have done something real about their relationship to the world because of its permanence and its connection to their inner self. The tattoo can express and take away their unhappiness with the roles society offers them, and it can bring them a refuge from societal conditioning. The ancient background of tattoos makes them a human and permanent commitment rather than a fad of society, therefore, tattoos become a culturally recognized way to express self. The body is a way of expressing and altering the relationship between self and society. It uses the skin, sexuality, the body and the "primitive" connection as key symbolic domains to recover and express the self. Primitive cultures encourage development of intuition and magic and allow for more expression of individuality than we do in Western culture. So, a tattoo in Western culture makes the person look different, and also gives their difference a greater meaning. It brings some part of the personal inner self out and makes it part of the social self, and frees the person from society to become human instead of Western. In having control over their body, the person has control over their self, which becomes a powerful emotional experience (Rosenblatt 1997).

Memorial tattoos are popular, especially among the military. Many Marines in Iraq get tattoos as "a way to give ink-and-skin permanence to friends taken young. It's like death—it's forever" (Phillips 2006: A8). "It's also never forget the cost of war, to get people to understand what they're asking for when they support war" (Phillips 2006: A8). For some, the pain of the needle eased the guilt of having survived and the sorrow of the loss. Some said that feeling the pain made it okay that the others got killed and they didn't. It became a way to remember their brothers (Phillips 2006).

Mary Kosut brings another theory of motivation forth in her 2005 article in Deviant Behavior journal where she contributes that some motivations for getting a tattoo are characterized as negative (Kosut 2005). The desire to be tattooed "may be the result of deficiency or because of low levels of cortical arousal and a need for constant stimulation" (Copes and Forsyth 1993; Favazza 1996, as cited in Kosut 2005: 82). Her article also provides that tattoo artists have been associated with "non-normative behavior" (p. 83).

This train of thought has been redefined and reinterpreted throughout the nineteenth and twentieth centuries because of the amount of trained artists in the field of tattooing (Kosut 2005).

METHODS OF RESEARCH

Data were collected through interviews with thirteen people that have tattoos, a sample consisting of seven women and six men ranging in age from 20–65 years old. Four tattoo artists, two men and two women were interviewed. One evening was spent "hanging out" in a tattoo studio observing and interacting with the patrons that visited. Several conversations were had, which did not constitute an interview as such, with students on campus and other people that happened to come in contact with the researcher elsewhere. The researcher designed and had her own tattoo done.

Five of the people were interviewed in person; the other seven were interviewed online by computer. Face-to-face interviews consisting of both closed and open-ended questions were tape recorded and conducted in tattoo studios. The researcher's interest in the subject and her desire to get a tattoo seemed to make for a deep connection with those that she interviewed.

WHO GETS TATTOOS ACCORDING TO THE TATTOO ARTISTS

Tattoo artists claimed that a wide range of people get tattoos. The two male tattoo artists said "everybody" and then went on to elaborate. Mike, a 61-year-old tattoo artist, has been tattooing for 35 or 36 years. He says he has tattooed people from all walks of life; doctors, nurses, lawyers, and surgeons. His clients are mainly a younger crowd ranging from ages 18-40 years, although he said that he gets a considerable amount of people from the 40-70's age group too.

There are also many women in their 60's that he has tattooed. He told a story of five women that all worked in the same office together coming in for tattoos. They all had different reasons, but all got them done.

Rick is a "30-something" tattoo artist that has been tattooing since he graduated from art school. He said that people who get tattoos are anywhere from 18-70 years old, and can range from cops to criminals. He tattooed a 70-year-old funeral director.

The two women tattoo artists that I interviewed went into a little more detail when asked who got tattoos. Lori, who is in her late 30's, is also an art school graduate and started tattooing to support her family when her children were young. She says that people that have been hurt as a child, recovering addicts that don't spend their money on drinking or drugs anymore, bike club members, and just "normal, ordinary" people came in for tattoos. The ages range from 18 years to the oldest at 77 years old.

Janice is 33 years old and no longer does tattooing. She has artistic talent and expressed it through tattooing others. When asked who gets tattoos, she stated:

"The stereotypical 20-year-old guy with a bit of a chip on his shoulder-the James Dean type. Obviously though, women are a larger audience than ever before...and we would see many older men getting touch ups and cover-ups. A lot of college aged people. A sprinkling of retirees . . . she was 77. So, there are all types...but the stats are correct, college age kids, mostly male are the biggest audience. . ."

WHY PEOPLE GET TATTOOS ACCORDING TO THE TATTOO ARTISTS

The reasons and meaning behind the tattoo were as numerous as the people who get them. The artists who do the tattoos were an excellent source of information on this topic. Mike, the tattoo artist, says that people see a lot of it on television and on stars, athletes, and people in public exposure. He did a tattoo on a 78-year-old male who had wanted a tattoo all of his life, but his wife wouldn't let him get one. She passed on, so he got it done. Mike said that younger women wear tattoos like jewelry; it was to beautify. A girl and her brothers got praying hands with a rosary as a memorial to their father when he passed. There was a gentleman that came into his studio undecided about what he wanted. He looked at wolves howling at the moon, bats, and the grim reaper and wanted to work up a scene with them in it. When asked what he did for a living, he said he was a gravedigger. For him, the tattoos were an expression of himself and what he does in life. Mike has also been working on a fellow since 1991 or 1992 who has about 90-98% of his body covered in tattoos. Mike didn't know the reason for it, other than the fellow just likes them. He said, "they have their own reasons and I don't question them". According to Mike, most of it is an expression of themselves. It makes them feel different about themselves, "like a new outfit", it just feels new.

Rick also said it is a form of self-expression. With young kids it is sometimes because a popular person has it. He had a family come in for tattoos when their little girl was hit by a car and killed. He did her portrait on three of the family members. He tattoos the workers at the county jail as well as the inmates. He said that the tattoos are a source of commonality among the prisoners and the workers, something that they can talk about. He found it rare that anyone does it for the pain or because they are addicted to any part of getting a tattoo. He said that "everybody has an instinct to express themselves" whether it be for a rite of passage or for a keepsake.

Lori told of many reasons for people getting a tattoo. Some want to prove their love to a particular person. Some men want their newborn's name and footprint copied from the birth certificate "to attempt to prove their happiness or eternal bond" and comment that the mother will be happy to see it (the tattoo). Some just do it for themselves because they are happy that they just had a baby. People that have been hurt get a tattoo to claim themselves..."it's their skin, this is a decision I'm making...a large number of them say they do not feel any pain at all. Some do it to see if they can feel pain that way". There are people that say, "they love the feel, they really don't care what the image is, and they simply want to feel that sensation". If a "biker" has just purchased a motorcycle, part of the package is to get the bike emblem. They said, "their skin is still soft and supple and hasn't been exposed to the wind yet."

She has had countless people tattoo animal's names and/or portraits, and they would cry from the loss while getting it done. Others get a tattoo to memorialize a loved one. She said, "a family actually believed if they all were together in the shop getting a tattoo for the same person, that person's spirit would be aware of what was happening and they could feel his presence".

She tattoos as many women as she does men. She tattooed a 77-year-old woman that had been in the hospital. The woman thought that she was dying, so when she was released from the hospital, she did the things that she regretted not doing in her lifetime. "A tattoo of a rose was at the top of her list". A 72-year-old man came in to her shop and had two large tattoos of naked women covered. The tattoos had bothered him for years and he was ashamed of them.

Lori did see a lot of influence from television and movies in where people want their tattoos placed on their body. They thought it would make them more like the image on the screen; not physically but through an emotional connection to the character portrayed.

Janice found that most of her clients wanted a tattoo because they are "cool" or they "have always wanted one". She says another reason is for a tribute to someone or some event in his or her life.

Overall, the tattoo artists interviewed could not state a typical reason for getting a tattoo or a typical person that gets a tattoo. They see a very diversified clientele who each have their own unique reason for getting a tattoo. The only commonality, that the artists experienced, is that their clientele do it as a means of self-expression.

WHY GET A TATTOO ACCORDING TO THE CLIENTS

The interviews with those who actually wear tattoos opened up a whole new world to me. The reasons for getting one come from many different levels of themselves. It was thought that one would find a main theme or reason for having ink engraved into your body permanently. Aside from tattoos being some type of an expression, all other reasons are too diversified to compartmentalize into specific categories.

One reason for getting a tattoo is to remember something (whether it was a fleeting moment or a deep happening) such as, a person, an animal, an event, something sad or something happy. A tattoo is a permanent way to remember, an expression of life or a means to assert ones independence or individuality.

There are many other reasons, including women getting tattoos for the beauty, the aesthetic value of having beautiful art on their body. New beginnings, such as adulthood, divorce, marriage, death, birth, etc. warrant a tattoo for some people.

Some people actually appreciate the pain saying that it is temporary pain for a permanent effect. "If it was easy everyone would do it", one interviewee said, so the pain sets them apart from the rest of society.

One of my online interviews said that usually the reason "isn't as emotional or meaningful as many might hope or think". This person got tattoos to remember the city she lived in or to mark happy or sad times in her life. Therefore, many of her tattoos did not have a great meaning.

Another said her tattoos are symbolic of various things, mainly belief structures. She said she gets tattoos "to remind myself of various things, that period of my life, my mind set at the time, or just that I shouldn't take shit from people". Someone else said that they get tattoos to be different from most people, not because they wanted to be noticed, but "because they are a window to your personality". They also remind them of their past, which they thought of as a good thing.

A female interviewed online said that hers is a very personal design. She looked for six years to find the right one, and then altered it to fit her. She is working on designs for three more tattoos that are also very meaningful to her. One will be a ladybug because her mother used to call her "her little ladybug". She is going through some rough times with her family and getting this tattoo will remind her that she and her mom still love each other even through all of this. She thinks of tattoos "as accentuating an already beautiful form—the human body". She felt the "art was already in me; it's a mark on my eternal soul that I wanted to share with those around me. It's not adding or subtracting from me, it's simply bringing an element of myself to the surface". Tattoos are an expression of life for her.

Another online interview of a female found that she got her first tattoo at age 16 as a birthday present for herself. She was "instantly addicted" and got her second one two days later. Her reason was because she loved the way tattoos look. She now has some that memorialize those that she has lost. She finds tattoos "a lot like fashion" and that people get them to feel good about themselves. She is a sailor by trade but had to live on land for a few years, so she got her arm tattoo because she "wanted the ocean with me no matter how far the water was!" and because she worked in male dominant positions and "wanted to be perceived as tougher than your average, high maintenance girl". She stated that she has grown "older and wiser" since then and no longer wants to carry that perception. However, the tattoo still remains as a memory of that time in her life.

Memorial tattoos are quite popular. An online interview with another female was about her memorial tattoo. She had always wanted a tattoo and the passing of her father was her excuse to get one. Her father was an avid gardener so she got a small rose with the stem bending around to "cradle the words 'Daddy's girl'". It is a yellow rose because her power color is yellow. This tattoo also represents a reclaiming of her independence after a divorce from a man who would not let her get a tattoo.

A gentleman wrote online that he "was actually pleased by the adrenaline rush" that made him woozy while sitting seven hours being tattooed.

There were those that compared it to art in other forms. One online interviewee said that she got her tattoo "because I wanted to wear my art, not just hang it on the wall". Another stated:

> For many of us, asking why we like tattoos, or even asking why we like a certain design, is like asking someone why they like a certain Mozart piece, or a certain Van Gogh painting, etc. Tattoos are one of many forms of art—and personally, I think about the coolest medium (i.e. living skin) that I can imagine.

Jolene had always talked about getting a tattoo and just never did until going through a "messy, ugly divorce". At that time she was learning about herself and who she wanted to be, and she was depressed and worried so she began exploring spirituality. She is Native American so tattoos came as a "natural way for me to explore and ultimately express these issues."

Her first tattoo was to cover scars on her stomach. She was ashamed of them, so the tattoo enabled her to cover the scar and to "honor my body and forgive it for being less than perfect." Now, instead of being ashamed of her body, she could be proud of it because of the meaning the tattoo holds for her. She chose to have a tribal sun tattooed encircling her navel.

She states:

> I chose a tribal sun for my stomach piece...it encircles my navel and for me, the sun is the source of life... and my stomach/womb has been a source of life as well, despite its visible imperfections. My next piece was an ankle wrap which is very colorful and has the word "Justice" written in runes. Justice is the Latin meaning of my name, and also a significant source of strength in my life...to me it means karma...it goes around my ankle and has no beginning or end...like karma it keeps coming around. My next two pieces were a ring with my children's birthstones in it, and a crescent moon on my left breast. Moons being the symbol of the goddess, and the left side of our bodies being associated with our feminine energies, and my breasts being the source of food for babies...plus, I was in a car wreck and almost lost that breast...so I honor that breast and thank it for performing miracles, feeding babies despite its flaws and the damage that has been done to it. My fifth piece is a full back mural. It incorporates a stained glass panel of the sun and the phases of the moon, depicts a goddess pouring water (emotion) from a pitcher into a pool of water, a hummingbird (my Native American animal guide and a symbol of the element of air) a tiger lily (which reminds me of creative energies and the element of fire) growing out of a field (element of earth) and the runes which spell out "I am Woman, I am Life." My final piece is my engagement ring from my second marriage.

She has more than one tattoo because she felt she "needed more than one story to help tell about the me who is on the inside". She felt that she had taken back control of her body. She had been taking it for granted and had forgotten that it is connected to her soul. She believes her body should reflect who she is on the inside.

A 21-year-old male college student said that he got his first tattoo at age 18. In the beginning he wanted to get it because his dad did not want him to, but when he got to the tattoo studio and saw the beauty of the artist's work, he had more of an urge to get one. He now has the Chinese symbol for "gates to heaven" in the middle of his back because "if the gates to heaven are behind me then that means I'm already in heaven and the tribal wings I have around that is my wings for when I'm in heaven". He has a tribal shield around his left nipple, over his heart, to protect him from people that may try to hurt him, "mainly females". "TRIP" tattooed on his lower left arm is his nickname for all to see who he is without him having to tell them. The tattoo on his lower back has his zodiac sign incorporated into it. He also admitted to getting more than one tattoo, not only because he liked the way they look, but because of the pain.

During the researcher's evening observing at the tattoo studio she interviewed a gentleman and his wife. He was getting his first tattoos; she already has three. The researcher watched as he got his done and he allowed her to interview him during the process. He is a 28-year-old construction worker and father of two children, one boy and one girl. He was getting a portrait of his daughter on his left forearm and his son on his right forearm. He said he promised his daughter he would have her tattooed on him because then he "always got her on me". His children would be "on me forever". He wants everyone to see them.

His wife is 25 years old and got her first tattoo when she was 18. Her father drew it and she had just had her son, so she put her son's name into what her father drew. She will have it forever to remember her father and her son. Her other tattoos consist of one on her chest that is a butterfly with "Mimi" on it (what her nephews call her), and one around her right wrist that is made up of her niece's, nephew's, and son's initials. She said the bracelet effect is feminine and "no one knows what it really is". She likes that hers can be hidden from others, but that she can see them.

My interview with Tony, a 21-year-old employee of the tattoo studio, is the final entry. He is studying to be a body piercer and also works with the mentally handicapped at the Resource Center in his town. He got his first tattoo just before he turned 21. His friend was leaving for college and they both wanted something that represented their friendship, so they got a broken heart tattooed on both wrists. He said that he has always wanted something on his wrist so he can see it. He also has a lion, his zodiac sign, tattooed on his left forearm. The tattoos make him feel stronger. He stated:

> It is a constant reminder of not only relationships that I have, but also things
> that people loose in life, things that can mean to me just open and endless pos-
> sibilities. I put things on my body that reminds me of myself, who I am, where I

came from, plus the things that I want to do in life—learn and the things that I go through. It's almost like an empowerment. The world of body mods is a very beautiful thing. It was around before civilized culture was. You have the tribes in Africa and the Indians here in the Americas that... all their art is very beautiful to me. We as human beings are almost reclaiming that—it's just a more technological society (today).

As for the researcher's own experience of entering into the world of the tattooed, she too has an outward expression of her inner self for all to see. Like most of the people that she read about or interviewed, the meaning of what she has inked on her body is much deeper than the visual image that can be seen. It is not there to be pretty, but is a reminder to her, every time she looks at it, of her beliefs and the intentions she strives to live. Her tattoo is a chameleon to remind her that the only thing in life that is constant is change. The colors that she chose each have a symbolic meaning and representation. The infinity symbol on its back represents that there is no beginning and there is no end, and that life holds endless possibilities. The OM symbol signifies God, Creation and the Oneness of all Creation. It represents the unmanifest and the manifest aspects of God. The eyes of the chameleon are a symbol that means "spirit of all creation" honoring all that is, seen and unseen. The spider has been her animal totem since her vision quest four years ago. Its symbolic meaning is far too lengthy to delve into here. The tattoo is on her foot to remind her of being grounded and staying true to Mother Earth. It also reminds her that life is all about the journey that one walks and not about the destination.

The pain that she experienced getting the tattoo reminded her of what one sometimes needs to go through in life to be true to one's beliefs and oneself It may feel painful for a while, at times almost unbearable, but if one trusts and has faith that all will turn out exactly as it needs to be for the highest and best for all involved, one can live in love without fear.

DISCUSSION

Since ancient times, people worldwide have gotten tattoos. Why would that be? Possibly because of the changes previously discussed, the depressing times, and the crisis that the world is in now. People have the perception that so much is out of their control. Making their mark on the only thing that we have some control of (our body) is a way of easing our anxiety about the world situation, a way of having some control over something. Also, in times of crisis people tend to look for spiritual meaning in life, a meaning that they can hold on to forever, something larger and more powerful than the material world.

According to my data, tattoos are a form of self-expression, a way to touch the depths of one's feelings and bring those feelings out for one's own observation or for the observation of others. Tattoos are a way of expressing thoughts, beliefs, triumphs and trials, and a way of memorializing a loved one, possibly to the extent of feeling control over death by immortalizing their memory forever on one's body to carry with one throughout one's life.

Respondents say tattoos are a way of connecting to that inner self that gets lost in the sea of the material world. Tattoos are a reminder of one's roots, one's ancestors, and the time when everything meant something or had a purpose. There is so much in today's society that is without purpose and without a connection to give meaning to life and the way it is lived. Interviewees said that tattoos can connect the spiritual inner self to the material world that one lives in, or they can separate one from the material world and take one to a place within oneself that longs to be experienced and expressed.

In this fast paced, technological society where everybody is becoming a number, being tattooed is a way of remaining a person, something capable of feeling and expression. It is possibly another coping mechanism that helps an individual get along in the world as it is today. A person's tattoo may look exactly like someone else's, but the feeling and meaning of what it represents to each one of them is entirely different. No one or no thing can take that away from them, not even the worldly powers that control everything else in society.

Tattoos can represent or express anything the person wearing it wants it to without getting "permission" from society to do so. It is a freedom from the many societal restrictions. In the world of crisis today that is commanded by fear, one's body is the only space that is sacred. The only true haven and refuge that one has is one's inner self, one's inner reality, and one's inner essence. Tattooing is a way to bridge the gap between one's inner reality and the outer reality of the world one must live in.

In conclusion, the reasons for getting a tattoo and the meaning behind what is visibly seen are as varied as the people involved. Whether a person gets a tattoo "just because he likes how it looks" or because it symbolizes something for them, the tattoo is a form of self-expression. The purpose of wearing this art on one's body rather than hanging it on a wall signifies a total commitment to what it stands for. It is the most permanent form of self-expression, with no escape from it. It is everywhere they go, they carry it with them, and it is a part of them. It is connected to one's mind and one's body for their time spent here on earth, and connected to their spirit, their inner essence forever.

REFERENCES

Armstrong, Myrna L. 1991 ."Career-oriented women with tattoos." *Image: Journal of Nursing Scholarship* 23 (4): 215-20.
Armstrong, M.L.,Owen, D.C., Roberts, A.E., and Koch, J.R. 2002. "College students and tattoos: The influence of image, identity, friends, and family." *Journal of Psychosocial Nursing* 40(10): 1-8.

Armstrong, M.L., Owen, D.C., Roberts, A.E., and Koch, J.R. 2002. "College tattoos: More than skin deep." *Dermatology Nursing* 14 (5): 317-323.

Armstrong, M.L., and Pace-Murphy, K. 1997. "Tattooing: Another risk-behavior in adolescents warranting national health teaching." *Applied Nursing Research* 10(4): 181-189.

Armstrong, M.L., Pace-Murphy, K., Sallee, A.S., and Watson, M.G. 2000. "Tattooed army soldiers: Examining the incidence, behavior, and risk." *Military Medicine* 165, 37-40.

Bell, Shannon. 1999. "Tattooed: A participant observer's exploration of meaning." *Journal of American Culture* 22 (2): 53-58.

Blonsky,Marshall. 1992. *American Mythologies,* New York: Oxford UP.

Busch, Akiko. 1995. "My decorated self." *Print,* January/February 95, 49 (1): 112.

Caruso, Mandi. 2006. "Alive with passion." *Spirituality and Health,* February 06, 9(1): 38-43.

Christensen, M.H. 2000. "Photo essay: Tattoos." *Public Health Reports* 115 (5):430-435.

Copes, J. and C. Forsyth. 1993. "The tattoo: A social psychological explanation." *International Review of Modern Sociology* 23: 83-89.

Day, Ronald F. 2005. "Tattooing in prison: An innocuous practice or a conduit for Hep C?" *Body Positive,* June 05, 18 (1).

Favazza, A. 1996. Bodies under siege: *Self-mutilation and body modification in culture and Psychiatry.* Baltimore and London: Johns Hopkins University Press.

Forbes, G.B. 2001. "College students with tattoos and piercings: Motives, family experiences, personality factors, and perception by others." *Psychological Reports* 89: 774-786.

Greif, J., Hewitt, W., and Armstrong, M.L. 1999. "Tattooing and body piercing: Body art practices among college students." *Clinical Nursing Research* 8 (4): 368-385.

Irwin, Katherine. 2001. "Legitimating the first tattoo: Moral passage through informal interaction." *Symbolic Interaction* 24 (1): 49-73.

Jet Magazine. 2001. "Athletes Tell the Meaning Behind Their Tattoos." July 9, 2001. 100(14):46.

Keinlen, Alexis. 2005. "Skin deep: Tatttoos mark the body's surface. But their inspiration draws from a deeper source." *Herizons,* Fall 2005, 19 (2): 24-28.

Koch, Jerome R., Roberts, Alden E., Cannon, Julie Harms, Armstrong, M.L., and Owen, Donna C. 2004. "College students, tattooing, and the health belief model: Extending social psychological perspectives on youth culture and deviance." *Sociological Spectrum* 25: 79-102.

Kosut, Mary. 2006. "Mad artists and tattooed perverts: Deviant discourse and the social construction of cultural categories." *Deviant Behavior* 27: 73-95.

Lyman, S.M. & Scott, M.B. 1970. *A Sociology of the Absurd*. New York: Meredith.

Mason, M. 1991. "Every picture tells a story." January 7, 1991, *Newsweek* 117 (1):2-4.

Phillips, Michael M. 2006. "Politics & Economics: Tattoos honor marines killed in Iraq and help the survivors." *The Wall Street Journal* February. 15, 2006, pg. A8.

Rosenblatt, Daniel. 1997. "The antisocial skin: Structure, resistance, and "modern primitive" adornment in the United States." *Cultural Anthropology* 12(3): 287-334.

Underwood, N. 1991. "Designs on the body." *Maclean's*, September 9, 1991, 104(36): 42.

Vale, V. & Juno, A. 1989. *Modern primitives. An investigation of contemporary adornment and ritual*. San Francisco: Re/Search Publications.

Velliquette, Ann M., and Jeff B. Murray. 2002. "The New Tattoo Subculture." Pp. 68-80 in *Mapping the Social Landscape: Readings in Sociology*, edited by Susan J. Ferguson. Mountain View, CA: Mayfield Publishing Company.

Vineyard, Mary. 1999. "Tattoo made its mark on this mother." *National Catholic Reporter*, February 19, 1991, 35 (16): 23.

Designer Babies: Eugenics Repackaged or Consumer Options?

By Stephen L. Baird

Stephen L. Baird is a technology education teacher at Bayside Middle School, Virginia Beach, Virginia and adjunct faculty member at Old Dominion University.

The forces pushing humanity towards attempts at self-modification, through biological and technological advances, are powerful, seductive ones that we will be hard-pressed to resist.

Almost three decades ago, on July 25, 1978, Louise Brown, the first "test-tube baby" was born. The world's first "test-tube" baby arrived amid a storm of protest and hand-wringing about science gone amok, human-animal hybrids, and the rebirth of eugenics. But the voices of those opposed to the procedure were silenced when Brown was born. She was a happy, healthy infant, and her parents were thrilled. The doctors who helped to create her, Patrick Steptoe and Robert Edwards, could not have been more pleased. She was the first person ever created outside a woman's body and was as natural a baby as had ever entered the world. Today in vitro *fertilization* (IVF) is often the unremarkable choice of tens of thousands of infertile couples whose only complaint is that the procedure is too difficult, uncertain, and expensive. What was once so deeply disturbing now seems to many people just another part of the modern world. Will the same be said one day of children with genetically enhanced intelligence, endurance, and other traits? Or will such attempts—if they occur at all—lead to extraordinary problems that are looked back upon as the ultimate in twenty-first century hubris? (Stock, 2006.)

Soon we may be altering the genes of our children to engineer key aspects of their character and physiology. The ethical and social consequences will be profound. We are standing at the threshold of an extraordinary, yet troubling, scientific dawn that has the potential to alter the very fabric of our lives, challenging what it means to be human, and perhaps redesigning our very selves. We are fast approaching the most consequential technological threshold in all of human history: the ability to alter the genes we pass to our children. Genetic engineering is already being carried out successfully on nonhuman animals. The gene that makes jellyfish fluorescent has been inserted into mice embryos, resulting in glow-in-the-dark rodents. Other mice have had their muscle mass increased, or have been made to be more faithful to their partners, through the insertion of a gene into their normal genetic make-up. But this method of genetic engineering is thus far inefficient. In order to produce one fluorescent mouse, several go wrong and are born deformed. If human babies are ever to be engineered, the process would have to become far more efficient, as no technique involving the birth of severely defective human beings to create a "genetically enhanced being" will hopefully ever be tolerated by our society (Designing, 2005). Once humans begin genetically engineering their children for desired traits, we will have crossed a threshold of no return. The communities of the world are just beginning to understand the full implications of the new human genetic technologies. There are few civil society institutions, and there are no social or political movements, critically addressing the immense social, cultural, and psychological challenges these technologies pose.

Until recently, the time scale for measuring change in the biological world has been tens of thousands, if not millions of years, but today it is hard to imagine what humans may be like in a few hundred years. The forces pushing humanity toward attempts at self-modification, through biological and technological advances, are powerful, seductive ones that we will be hard-pressed to resist. Some will curse these new technologies, sounding the death knell for humanity, envisioning the social, cultural, and moral collapse of our society and perhaps our civilization. Others see the same technologies as the ability to take charge of our own evolution, to transcend human limitations, and to improve ourselves as a species. As the human species moves out of its childhood, it is time to acknowledge our technological capabilities and to take responsibility for them. We have little choice, as the reweaving of the fabric of our genetic makeup has already begun.

THE BASIC SCIENCE

Biological entities are comprised of millions of cells. Each cell has a nucleus, and inside every nucleus are strings of deoxyribonucleic acid (DNA). DNA carries the complete information regarding the function and structure of organisms ranging from plants and animals to bacterium. Genes, which are sequences of DNA, determine an organism's growth, size, and other charac-teristics. Genes are the vehicle by which species transfer inheritable characteris-tics to successive generations. Genetic engineering is the process of artificially manipulating these inheritable characteristics.

Genetic engineering in its broadest sense has been around for thousands of years, since people first recognized that they could mate animals with specific characteristics to produce offspring with desirable traits and use agricultural seed selectively. In 1863, Mendel, in his study of peas, discovered that traits were transmitted from parents to progeny by discrete, independent units, later called genes. His observations laid the groundwork for the field of genetics (Genetic, 2006).

Modern human genetic engineering entered the scientific realm in the nineteenth century with the introduction of Eugenics. Although not yet technically considered "genetic engineering," it represented society's first attempt to scientifically alter the human evolutionary process. The practice of human genetic engineering is considered by some to have had its beginnings with in vitro fertilization (IVF) in 1978. IVF paved the way for preimplantation genetic diagnosis (PGD), also referred to as preimplantation genetic selection (PGS). PGD is the process by which an embryo is microscopically examined for signs of genetic disorders. Several genetically based diseases can now be identified, such as Downs Syndrome, Tay-Sachs Disease, Sickle Cell Anemia, Cystic Fibrosis, and Huntington's disease. There are many others that can be tested for, and both medical and scientific institutes are constantly searching for and developing new tests. For these tests, no real genetic engineering is taking place; rather, single cells are removed from embryos using the same process as used during in vitro fertilization. These cells are then examined to identify which are carrying the genetic disorder and which are not. The embryos that have the genetic disorder are discarded, those that are free of the disorder are implanted into the woman's uterus in the hope that a baby will be born without the genetic disorder. This procedure is fairly uncontroversial except with those critics who argue that human life starts at conception and therefore the embryo is sacrosanct and should not be tampered with. Another use for this technique is gender selection, which is where the issue becomes slightly more controversial. Some disorders or diseases are gender-specific, so instead of testing for the disease or disorder, the gender of the embryo is determined and whichever gender is "undesirable" is discarded. This brings up ethical issues of gender selection and the consequences for the gender balance of the human species.

A more recent development is the testing of the embryos for tissue matching. The embryos are tested for a tissue match with a sibling that has already developed, or is in danger of developing, a genetic disease or disorder. The purpose is to produce a baby who can be a tissue donor. This type of procedure was successfully used to cure a six-year-old-boy of a rare blood disorder after transplanting cells from his baby brother, who was created to save him. Doctors say the technique could be used to help many other children with blood and metabolic disorders, but critics say creating a baby in order to treat a sick sibling raises ethical questions (Genetic, 2006).

The child, Charlie Whitaker, from Derbyshire, England, was born with Diamond Blackfan Anemia, a condition that prevented him from creating his own red blood cells. He needed transfusions every three weeks and drug infusions nearly every night. His condition was cured by a transplant of cells from the umbilical cord of his baby brother Jamie, who was genetically selected to be a donor after his parents' embryos were screened to find one with a perfect tissue match. Three months after his transplant, Charlie's doctors said that he was cured of Diamond Blackfan Anemia, and the prognosis is that Charlie can now look forward to a normal quality of life (Walsh, 2004). Is this the beginning of a slippery slope toward "designer" or "spare parts" babies, or is the result that there are now two healthy, happy children instead of one very sick child a justification to pursue and continue procedures such as this one? Policymakers and ethicists are just beginning to pay serious attention. A recent working paper by the President's Council on Bioethics noted that "as genomic knowledge increases and more genes are identified that correlate with diseases, the applications for PGD will likely increase greatly," including diagnosing and treating medical conditions such as cancer, mental illness, or asthma, and nonmedical traits such as temperament or height. "While currently a small practice," the Council's working paper declares, "PGD is a momentous development. It represents the first fusion of genomics and assisted reproduction—effectively opening the door to the genetic shaping of offspring" (Rosen, 2003).

In one sense PGD poses no new eugenic dangers. Genetic screening using amniocentesis has allowed parents to test the fitness of potential offspring for years. But PGD is poised to increase this power significantly: It will allow parents to choose the child they want, not simply reject the ones they do not want. It will change the overriding purpose of IVF, from a treatment for fertility to being able to pick and choose embryos like consumer goods—producing many, discarding most, and desiring only the chosen few.

The next step in disease elimination is to attempt to refine a process known as "human germline engineering" or "human germline modification." Whereas preimplantation genetic diagnosis (PGD) affects only the immediate offspring, germline engineering seeks to affect the genes that are carried in the ova and sperm, thus eliminating the disease or disorder from all future generations, making it no longer inheritable. The possibilities for germline engineering go beyond the elimination of disease and open the door for modifications to human longevity, increased intelligence, increased muscle mass, and many other types of genetic enhancements. This application is by far the more consequential, because it opens the door to the alteration of the human species. The modified genes would appear not only in any children that resulted from such procedures, but in all succeeding generations.

The term germline refers to the germ or germinal cells, i.e., the eggs and sperm. Genes are strings of chemicals that help create the proteins that make up the body. They are found in long coiled chains called chromosomes located in the nuclei of the cells of the body. Genetic modification occurs by inserting genes into living cells. The desired gene is attached to a viral vector, which has the ability to carry the gene across the cell membrane. Proposals for inheritable genetic modification in humans combine techniques involving in vitro fertilization, gene transfer, stem cells, and cloning. Germline modification would begin by using IVF to create a single-cell embryo or zygote. This embryo would develop for about five days to the blastocyst stage (very early embryo consisting of approximately 150 cells. It contains the inner cell mass, from which embryonic stem cells are derived, and an outer layer of cells called the trophoblast that forms the placenta. (It is approximately 1/10 the size of the head of a pin.) At this point embryonic stem cells would be removed. These stem cells would be altered by adding genes using viral vectors. Colonies of altered stem cells would be grown and tested for successful incorporation of the new genes. Cloning techniques would be used to transfer a successfully modified stem cell nucleus into an enucleated egg cell. This "constructed embryo" would then be implanted into a woman's uterus and brought to term. The child born would be a genetically modified human (Inheritable, 2003).

Proponents of germline manipulation assume that once a gene implicated in a particular condition is identified, it might be appropriate and relatively easy to replace, change, supplement, or otherwise modify that gene. However, biological characteristics or traits usually depend on interactions among many genes and, more importantly, the activity of genes is affected by various processes that occur both inside the organism and in its surroundings. This means that scientists cannot predict the full effect that any gene modification will have on the traits of people or other organisms.

There is no universally accepted ideal of biological perfection. To make intentional changes in the genes that people will pass on to their descendants would require that we, as a society, agree on how to classify "good" and "bad" genes. We do not have the necessary criteria, nor are there mechanisms for establishing such measures. Any formulation of such criteria would inevitably reflect particular current social biases. The definition of the standards and the technological means for implementing them would largely be determined by economically and socially privileged groups (Human, 2004).

Summary

"Designer babies" is a term used by journalists and commentators—not by scientists—to describe several different reproductive technologies. These technologies have one thing in common: they give parents more control over what their offspring will be like. Designer babies are made possible by progress in three fields:

1. Advanced Reproductive Technologies. In the decades since the first "test tube baby" was born, reproductive medicine has helped countless women conceive and bear children. Today there are hundreds of thousands of humans who were conceived thanks to in vitro fertilization. Other advanced reproductive technologies include frozen embryos, egg and sperm donations, surrogate motherhood, pregnancies by older women, and the direct injection of a sperm cell into an egg.

2. Cell and Chromosome Manipulation. The past decade has seen astonishing breakthroughs in our knowledge of cell structure. Our ability to transfer chromosomes (the long threads of DNA in each cell) has led to major developments in cloning. Our knowledge of stem cells will make many new therapies possible. As we learn more about how reproduction works at the cellular level, we will gain more control over the earliest stages of a baby's development.

3. Genetics and Genomics. With the mapping of the human genome, our understanding of how DNA affects human development is only just beginning. Someday we might be able to switch bits of DNA on or off as we wish, or replace sections of DNA at will; research in that direction is already well underway.

Human reproduction is a complex process. There are many factors involved in the reproduction process: the genetic constitution of the parents, the condition of the parents' egg and sperm, and the health and behavior of the impregnated mother. When you consider the enormous complexity of the human genome, with its billions of DNA pairs, it becomes clear that reproduction will always have an element of unpredictability. To a certain extent we have always controlled our children's characteristics through the selection of mates. New technologies will give us more power to influence our children's "design"—but our control will be far from total (Designer, 2002).

Since the term "designer babies" is so imprecise, it is difficult to untangle its various meanings so as to make judgments about which techniques are acceptable. Several different techniques have been discussed, such as screening embryos for high-risk diseases, selecting the sex of a baby, picking an embryo for specific traits, genetic manipulation for therapeutic reasons, and genetic manipulation for cosmetic reasons. Although, to date, none of these techniques are feasible, recent scientific breakthroughs and continued work by the scientific community will eventually make each a possibility in the selection process for the best possible embryo for implantation.

ARGUMENTS FOR DESIGNER BABIES

1. Using whatever techniques are available to help prevent certain genetic diseases will protect children from suffering debilitating diseases and deformities and reduce the financial and emotional strain on the parents. If we want the best for our children, why shouldn't we use the technology?
2. The majority of techniques available today can only be used by parents who need the help of fertility clinics to have children; since they are investing so much time and money in their effort to have a baby, shouldn't they be entitled to a healthy one?
3. A great many naturally conceived embryos are rejected from the womb for defects; by screening embryos, we are doing what nature would normally do for us.
4. Imagine the reaction nowadays if organ transplantation were to be prohibited because it is "unnatural"—even though that is what some people called for when transplantation was a medical novelty. It is hard to see how the replacement of a defective gene is any less "natural" than the replacement of a defective organ. The major difference is the entirely beneficial one that medical intervention need occur only once around the time of conception, and the benefits would be inherited by the child and its descendants.

ARGUMENTS AGAINST DESIGNER BABIES

1. We could get carried away "correcting" perfectly healthy babies. Once we start down the slippery slope of eliminating embryos because they are diseased, what is to stop us from picking babies for their physical or psychological traits?
2. There is always the looming shadow of eugenics. This was the motivation for some government policies in Europe and the United States in the first half of the twentieth century that included forced sterilizations, selective breeding, and "racial hygiene." Techniques that could be used for designing babies will give us dangerous new powers to express our genetic preferences.
3. There are major social concerns—such as: Will we breed a race of super humans who look down on those without genetic enhancements? Will these new technologies only be available to the wealthy—resulting in a lower class that will still suffer from inherited diseases and disabilities? Will discrimination against people already born with disabilities increase if they are perceived as genetically inferior?
4. Tampering with the human genetic structure might actually have unintended and unpredictable consequences that could damage the gene pool.

5. Many of the procedures related to designing babies involve terminating embryos; many disapprove of this on moral and religious grounds.

As our technical abilities progress, citizens will have to cope with the ethical implications of designer babies, and governments will have to define a regulatory course. We will have to answer some fundamental questions: How much power should parents and doctors have over the design of their children? How much power should governments have over parents and doctors? These decisions should be made based on facts and on our social beliefs.

REFERENCES

Designer Babies. (2002). The Center for the Study of Technology and Society. Retrieved September 14, 2006 from www.tecsoc.org/biotech/focusbabies.htm

Designing Babies: The Future of Genetics. (2005). BBC News. Retrieved September 22, 2006 from http://news.bbc.co.uk/1/hi/health/590919.stm

Genetic Engineering and the Future of Human Evolution. (2006). Future Human Evolution Organization. Retrieved September 19, 2006 from www.human-evolution.org/geneticbasics.php

Human Germline Manipulation. (2004). Council for Responsible Genetics. Retrieved October 18, 2006 from www.gene-watch.org/programs/cloning/germlineposition.html

Inheritable Genetic Modification. (2003). Center for Genetics and Society. Retrieved October 05, 2006 from www.gene-watch.org/programs/cloning/germlineposition.html

Rosen, C. (2003). The New Atlantis. A Journal of Technology and Society. Retrieved October 14, 2006 from www.thenewatlantis.com/archive/2/rosen.htm

Stock, G. (2005). Best Hope, Worst Fear. Human Germline Engineering. Retrieved October 05, 2006 from http://research.arc2.ucla.edu/pmts/germline/bhwf.htm

Walsh, F. (2004). Brother's Tissue "Cures" Sick Boy. BBC News. Retrieved September 27, 2006 from http://news.bbc.co.uk/1/hi/health/3756556.stm

Designer Babies: Choosing Our Children's Genes

Bonnie Steinbock

Bonnie Steinbock teaches philosophy at the State University of New York, Albany

The phrase "designer babies" refers to genetic interventions into pre-implantation embryos in the attempt to influence the traits the resulting children will have. At present, this is not possible, but many people are horrified by the mere thought that parents might want to choose their children's genes, especially for non-disease traits. I want to argue that the objections are usually not well articulated, and that even when they are, it's far from obvious that such interventions would be wrong.

What precisely is the objection? Of course, there are safety objections, especially ones arising from unforeseen and harmful side-effects. For example, in mice, researchers have shown that the addition of a certain gene made them better at running mazes, but also made them hyper-sensitive to pain. Such a possibility would rule out most, if not all, genetic enhancement. However, safety objections are raised by all new technologies, and do not usually instigate calls for blanket prohibition. The interesting question is, assuming genetic enhancement of the embryo is safe and effective, may such techniques ethically be used by parents?

Do the critics base their opposition on a general objection to the attempt to influence children's traits? Surely not. That is exactly what parents are supposed to do. To get our children to be healthy, well mannered, intellectually curious, and well behaved we control what they eat, have them vaccinated, teach them manners, read to them, and discipline them when they misbehave. It would be absurd for a parent to say, "I never attempt to influence my children's development. I just love them for who they are." Thus, it is not influencing our children's traits that is objectionable, but rather the means to accomplish this, that is, choosing their genes. But even this has to be further refined, since just the choice of a partner—surely not morally objectionable in itself—is a way of choosing our children's genes. As Steven Pinker has put it, "Anyone who has been turned down for a date has been a victim of the human drive to exert control over half the genes of one's future children."

Perhaps the objection is not to exerting control over traits, but rather to completely determining in advance what traits one's children will or will not have. Genetic interventions, it may be thought, enable more control over what our children will be like than other modes of shaping children. If this is the objection, it embodies the "fallacy of genetic determinism", the view that our genes determine who we are and what we are like. Of course genes play a role in the traits we have, but what we are actually like is the result of multiple genes interacting with each other, and all of them interacting with the environment. In fact, even if you could choose the entire genome of a child (for example, by cloning), you would not have complete control over the child's traits. As Princeton microbiologist Lee Silver has put it, "all that anyone will ever get from the use of cloning, or any other reproductive technology, is an unpredictable son or daughter, who won't listen to his parents any more than my children will listen to me".

Thus, the very term "designer babies" is a misnomer. No one will ever be able to design a child, that is, determine in advance what talents, skills, abilities, virtues, and vices the child will have. Perhaps the objection is to the fact that the child's genes were chosen for him by his parents, thus forcing the child to have certain talents and not others. For example, it might be thought that if the child's parents picked genes associated with musical ability, their child would be forced to be a musician, when maybe he or she would rather have been an athlete. But this makes no sense. Consider a child of musicians who inherits musical ability naturally. That child may become a musician, but he or she certainly isn't forced to do so because of his genetic inheritance. Far from it; if the child doesn't practice, he won't become a musician, no matter what his genetic make-up.

Admittedly, when parents choose their children's genes, they do so without the child's knowledge and consent. However, this is true of all of us, not just those who are genetically modified. None of us chooses our own genes. What is the moral significance in the fact that our genes were imposed on us due to someone's choice as opposed to just chance? Some people believe that genetically modified people would have personalities, thoughts, and feelings that would be less real, less authentic than the personalities of non-modified people. But this too makes no sense, as an example will reveal. In 2003, Avshalom Caspi and colleagues reported in *Science* that a functional polymorphism in the promoter region of the serotonin transporter (5-HTT) gene may be associated with a predisposition towards depression.

Individuals with one or two copies of the short allele of the 5-HTT promoter polymorphism become depressed more often after stressful events than individuals homozygous for the long allele. So if you're lucky enough to have inherited two long alleles of 5-HTT, you may be more likely to be a cheerful, resilient sort of person than someone who inherited two short alleles. What if it were possible to genetically modify embryos to replace the short alleles with long ones? Would the resulting people not really be as cheerful or resilient as those who naturally inherited the long alleles? Of course not. A more serious objection stems from the idea that people who want to choose, in advance, the traits their child will have, and are willing to spend so much money to get a child with certain traits, demonstrate a kind of desire for perfectionism that seems incompatible with being a good parent. An insistence on having a child of a certain sort, whether a musician or an athlete or a politician, amounts to parental tyranny. As Thomas Murray has put the point, "When parents attempt to shape their children's characteristics to match their preferences and expectations, such an exercise of free choice on the parents' part may constrain their child's prospects for flourishing."

An argument related to parental tyranny has been made by a member of the US President's Council on Bioethics, Michael Sandel. Sandel suggests that genetic engineering threatens what he calls the "ethic of giftedness". He argues that "To appreciate our children as gifts is to accept them as they come, not as objects of our design or products of our will or instruments of our ambition."

This notion of giftedness resonates with many people, because it represents an ideal of parenting that most of us embrace. Sandel contrasts the ethic of giftedness with a style of parenting he calls "hyper-parenting", which ignores the child's own talents and abilities, and instead forces the child to do what will satisfy parental dreams and aspirations. A hyper-parent might insist that a child play sports, when he or she would rather be in the drama club, or that all the child's free time be spent in pursuit of getting into a prestigious university. We can all agree that hyperparents are obnoxious, but is there a necessary connection between hyper-parenting and interest in genetic modification of the embryo? No doubt many hyperparents would be interested in genetically modifying their embryos, but it doesn't follow that everyone who would opt for genetic modification would be hyper-parents. That depends, I think, on the traits chosen, and the reasons for choosing them. If the traits sought were ones that could reasonably be thought to benefit the child, whatever path the child might choose, traits that would help a person flourish, traits that good parents would want to instill in their children anyway, such as kindness, generosity, compassion, or creativity, it is hard to see why choosing such traits, by genetic or conventional means, would be hyper-parenting.

A final objection to "designer children" is that this would exacerbate social differences and the gap between rich and poor. I seriously doubt that genetic interventions would have more of an influence than existing causes of inequality, such as rotten neighbourhoods and lousy schools. In any event, prebirth genetic enhancement could be used to combat social inequality, by giving children from disadvantaged backgrounds a leg up.

Genetic enhancement of embryos is, for the present, science fiction. Its opponents think that we need to ban it now, before it ever becomes a reality. What they have not provided are clear reasons to agree. Their real opposition is not to a particular means of shaping children, but rather to a certain style of parenting. Rather than fetishising the technology, the discussion should focus on which parental attitudes and modes of parenting help children to flourish. It may be that giving children "genetic edges" of certain kinds would not constrain their lives and choices, but actually make them better. That possibility should not be dismissed out of hand.

Designer Babies: What are the Ethical and Moral Issues?

TK McGhie

Correspondence: **Ms TK McGhie**, (Final Year Medical Student, C/o Dean's Office, Faculty of Medical Sciences, The University of the West Indies, Kingston 7, Jamaica, West Indies. E-mail: tkmcghie@yahoo.com This essay won the Medical Protection Society Essay Competition 2001.

The twentieth century can easily be dubbed the biotechnology century, with particularly huge leaps and bounds in the area of reproductive technology. The first milestone and hallmark achievement of this came in 1978 with the birth of Louise Brown, the first test tube baby. From then, *in vitro* fertilization (IVF) has revolutionized medical treatment of infertility, accounting for over 200,000 successful births worldwide (1). The next milestone came with the controversial 1996 birth of the icon for biotechnology, Dolly, the Scottish cloned sheep. Dolly became the first large animal to be cloned from genetic material taken from an adult egg. The potential of human ingenuity in the biological sciences has grown tremendously. Just two years after the birth of Dolly, two research teams from the United States of America (USA) opened another area of biotechnology with the isolation of stem cells. Subsequent to this, there has been the successful completion of the controversial human genome project, an international scientific collaboration that mapped the "blueprint of life", the genetic material of the human deoxyribonucleic acid (DNA) molecule in 2000. Then emerged the advent of genetic manipulation with such feats as mice being engineered to be smarter with greater memory capacity and a genetically modified monkey (2).

With the mapping of the human genome, researchers have access to a wealth of information of thousands of inherited disorders, with the ability to screen for disease even before conception. In fact, even before the completion of the project, there was pre-implantation genetic diagnosis (PGD) in which doctors do limited analysis of an embryo's genes in the laboratory, screening out those that may have defects. The genetic information provided by the human genome may be used by prospective parents to find out a range of traits of an embryo such as eye colour, height and intelligence. That may mean making complex choices about which embryos to implant in the mother. Already doctors can now increase the number of babies born of a particular gender. As the ability to predict traits expands, it will change the very nature of reproduction and it raises perhaps the most topical issue in biotechnology today: the prospect of "designer babies".

The tag, "designer baby", has been bestowed by those with concerns that the reach of reproductive technology could be expanded to eventually facilitate the screening of healthy embryos in advance of implantation for positive subjective characteristics such as physical appearance. Under some debate is a broader ascription of the term "designer baby" to include any circumstance where there is genetic manipulation of the reproductive process such that a desired outcome is attained with respect to the characteristics of the embryo. Thus, a cloned embryo may be considered a "designer baby", having been engineered to have a pre-determined genetic make-up. Also labelled as "designer babies" are those who are selected specifically so that they may have genes that allow them to be disease free and suitable donors of stem cells to matched recipients.

By this definition, "designer babies" are already a reality. On February 14, 2002, the world's second baby to be born with desired genetic characteristics known in advance was born in Britain. This infant was created, in effect, for his five year-old leukaemic sibling who may require a bone marrow transplant if he should relapse in the next few years. The need to create a sibling arose because there was no suitable matched family member or registered donor (3).

The ruling that paved the way for British couples to select an IVF baby to provide a cure for another of their children came from the Human Fertilization and Embryology Authority (HFEA) which said that, in some cases, it might be acceptable for embryos to be checked to see if they were a match for an existing child. This would enable blood from the new baby's umbilical cord to be used in bone marrow transplants. This had enabled the first couple from the USA to give birth to a son who would provide a match for their daughter with Fanconi's anaemia (4). There are similar hopes for a couple in Leeds,

England, whose son has thalassaemia. With no match, either within his family or on international bone marrow registers, this child's only hope is the creation of a matched sibling, a "designer baby". The HFEA, which regulated the use of IVF embryos in the United Kingdom (UK), has given the green light in the case from Leeds, ruling that only those embryos already being tested for genetic flaws (PGD) could be tissue typed. Effectively, the body ruled that where PGD is already being undertaken the use of tissue typing to save the life of a sibling could be justified, but only in those circumstances and under strict controls. Even where the creation of a designer baby is seen to be of life saving importance, the ethical questions still arise.

Gender selection is another possibility in the creation of "designer babies". The technology for doing this has existed for quite some time with a Maryland genetics and *in vitro* fertilization clinic boasting a 92.9% success rate in determining the gender of a child (5). However, it has been used almost exclusively for couples with legitimate fears of having babies with certain genetic diseases. For example, male embryos might be rejected because there is a great likelihood that they may be carriers of haemophilia.

As with all technologies, the danger arises where its application steps beyond the realms for which it was originally designed, especially where the question of exploration comes in; this is the genesis of the concerns in designer babies. Is this indeed the beginning of being able to choose the right colour of the eyes, the right intelligence, athletic prowess or artistic skills? Will it be like buying a new car, where you decide which package of accessories you want?

Unfortunately, ethics and moral development tend to lag behind technological advancements. This is particularly so with human genetic manipulation. With the prospects of designer babies, the ethical and moral issues need to be addressed as a matter of urgency. The ethical issues are mainly related to the context and the process by which they are derived, particularly the creation and ultimate destruction of embryos and the implication on human health. The moral issues are multifocal, ranging from concerns regarding traditional family values, to the question of eugenics and the creation of a master race.

ETHICAL CONSIDERATIONS

Some of the first ethical issues to be considered arose from the use of PGD to select potential donors of stem cells. The ruling by HFEA, though helpful to couples in a very limited and restricted number of cases, has raised many ethical questions about the welfare of the child created for a specific purpose. Whereas the stem cell harvesting is harmless, a bone marrow transplant is not without risk and is an extremely uncomfortable procedure. Where is the line going to be drawn? Even where the approved procedure is not going to put the child through any pain and distress, is it in the best interest of the child to be created as a tissue match for someone else? The child has effectively been brought into the world because it is a medical commodity. There is the concern that the child would be obliged to give other stem cells to a sibling later in life. Being a perfect match for their sibling and having been created essentially as donors, does this child lose the right to choose? If a kidney or any other donation is needed by the sibling, must the designer child be obligated to provide it?

Perhaps the most urgent issue arises in the context and process that may lead to the birth of the early designer babies. As pointed out by scholars, early experiments involving cloning are likely to result in a number of clinical failures and lead to miscarriage, necessitating numerous abortions or births of massively deformed offspring. Early animal experiments, involving cloning, have shown poor outcomes for primates with abnormally high prenatal and antenatal death rates. Since cloning technology itself may be used to create designer babies, examination of the findings in experiments thus far warrants close scrutiny as regards safety. Animal cloning has been shown to be very unsuccessful with an average success rate of 1.4 to 2%. Even the most recent cloning endeavours have been riddled with failure. The first successful cloning of a household pet, a cat called *cc* (copy cat) achieved in December of 2001 and reported to the world in February of 2002, saw the creation of 82 embryos which were implanted into seven surrogate mothers from which only a single fetal clone was derived. This clone which was created by the fusion of harvested cells from the mouth of an adult cat and cat-donor eggs emptied of its genetic material, later died in utero. Researchers then turned to cumulus cells from the ovaries of a female cat creating five cloned embryos that were implanted once again, this time yielding the cloned cat (6). Many critics view *cc* as an ethical dry run for human cloning and they are troubled by how the rehearsal is going. Surely, it cannot be ethical to subject humans to trial and error of this sort, especially, when the psychological trauma of disappointment in failed attempts is considered with respect to hopeful mothers?

Even with successful genetic manipulation, there is the possibility of unforeseen defects manifesting themselves later in life. Recent studies of cloning experiments suggest that a number of defects, often created in the reprogramming of the egg, do not manifest themselves until later in the life of the clones, with some undergoing spectacular unforeseen deaths. Cloning experiments with mice, pigs, sheep and cattle have reported that even apparently normal animals develop disorders at variable times later. Extreme obesity was one such problem in many cloned animals including Dolly who, incidentally, has been reported to also suffer from arthritis. Even in the most recent cloning of cats, some of the animals were being plagued by fatal heart and lung defects in infancy (7). From these results obtained, many scientists theorize that in cloned humans the gene expression flaws could affect personality, intelligence and other human attributes.

Given the limits of our knowledge of important questions about the functioning of genes, there is a general limit to what would be ethically acceptable. Remembering the consequences of using new drugs, like thalidomide, without adequate knowledge of their effects, the risk of unforeseen harm as it relates to modifying germ cells represents a most serious and unacceptable danger in that it may not only harm babies that are the immediate result of the change but could afflict, indefinitely, many subsequent generations. On this basis, human genetic manipulation may be deemed unethical, especially when its reversal is not guaranteed.

Genetic enhancement assumes the right to create and destroy embryos not because of genetic disease, but because of other features not to one's desire. This is an ethical dilemma depending on the status that is accorded an embryo. Defining an embryo ethically has always been surrounded by much debate, giving rise to a spectrum where at one end it is seen as a ball of cells and nothing more, unable to survive outside the womb and devoid of feelings and consciousness. At this end of the spectrum, reproductive and stem cell uses are equally permissible. At the other end of the spectrum, an embryo must be accorded the status of humanity from conception onwards and any technology creating dispensable embryos is forbidden. The present UK act finds middle ground in the spectrum, decreeing that human embryo command a special respect "that is due to human life at all stages of its development" (Code of practice; 1998. Human Fertilization and Embryology Authority). By this, embryos should be used only under certain circumstances and selection of gender or enhanced intelligence is thus deemed a trivial means of throwing away an embryo.

Indeed, the issue of gender selection raises the question of whether parents should be able to select the gender of their child. Would it be ethical for people with fertility problems to choose which fertilized embryos get implanted and have the rest discarded as being the 'wrong' gender? According to the American Society for Reproductive Medicine, a group that establishes ethical guidelines for fertility clinics, the answer is "Yes", reporting in the process that many requests have been made over the years. Despite the fact that this approval of gender selection carries with it situation-specific actions, such as cases where a couple who already have a child of one gender may be allowed to ethically choose the implantation of embryos which would make sure their next child was of the opposite gender, there are still many ethical issues that arise. With this comes the potential for inherent gender discrimination and reinforcement of gender bias in society as a whole, inappropriate control over nonessential characteristics of children, unnecessary medical burdens and costs for parents, and inappropriate and potentially unfair use of limited medical resources. If physicians are using their skills for non-medical reasons, then those resources become less accessible. In 1997, the Parliamentary Assembly of the Council of Europe, comprising members of parliaments (MPs) from 41 countries, passed the European Convention on Human Rights and Biomedicine. It lays down that genetic testing can only be done for health purposes and gender selection must not be permitted except to avoid a serious hereditary sex-linked disease. This draws the line between a serious medical condition and consumer preference. To allow commonplace gender selection is to cross that ethical line. Once crossed, there would be no logical reason not to allow any form of preference in babies—blond hair, intelligence or musical ability.

Arguments for application of the technology in its various forms, as it relates to reproduction, have been put forward mainly on the grounds of procreative autonomy; a couple's right to control their own role in procreation unless the state has a compelling reason for denying them that control. Can this right outweigh the issues raised thus far?

One great supporter of "designer babies", James Watson, who with Francis and Crick shared a Nobel Prize for the discovery of the DNA double helix in 1953, suggests that this right could supersede the concerns that prevail; stating that "the fears over the creation of "designer babies" is misplaced and that the potential benefits of controlling the ultimate engine of human evolution far outweighs the risks" (8). The general consensus, however, seems to be that parents do not 'own' their children and the consequences of their actions will only be suffered by their offspring and not themselves. Thus they should not be entitled to engineer their children solely for their own purposes.

With inventive technologies comes the issue of patenting. Many of the new processes associated with genetic manipulation have been developed in the private sector, and this leads to concerns that proprietary rights to these technologies might mean that many developing countries will be unable to access them should they become safe and socially acceptable. Will there be patenting of genes or transgenic creations? And is the ownership rights of genes and other living matter as intellectual property acceptable? Furthermore, the patenting of gene sequences and biotechnology techniques with broad applications, as is usually the case when a new technology begins, means that developing countries, in particular, may be excluded from affordable access to technologies that they may urgently need. Yet another ethical question is, what would the technology be used for?

Next comes the question of cost. If deemed socially acceptable and safe, will it be available only to a few rich patients, effectively putting profit before human needs? The private company that backed the successful cloning of the cat, "Genetic Savings and Clone", issued a statement forewarning potential cloners that it will cost them "five figures" in $US until the procedure becomes "streamlined" (6). How much will it cost to clone a human being?

MORAL CONSIDERATIONS

Most of the thoughts put forward from a moral perspective stand in opposition to the very notion of "designer babies". With regard to the issue of creating life to save that of another, the moral questions raised are difficult: why should persons die if there is a possibility for them to live? But then, is it right to create a human being for a certain purpose? The creation of a human being exclusively for the benefit of another is a violation of the moral requirement not to use others only as a means. Should wrong be done if good comes of it? All children should be born for their own sake, not as a purpose for someone else's benefit.

There is a great distinction between remedying genetic defects that significantly impact on morbidity, quality and length of life, and pursuing enhancement of human qualities; the first being more acceptable than the latter, which invokes the idea of a division between superior and inferior beings. With the effort to remove genetic defects and the recognition and selection of particular traits through genetic engineering, comes the implied devaluation of persons possessing the defects of lacking the preferred attributes.

Genetic enhancement may represent a new phase of the eugenics movement, that in the early decades of the twentieth century was literally an effort to breed better human beings by encouraging the reproduction of people with "good" genes and discouraging those with "bad" genes in an effort to improve humanity. Eugenicists effectively lobbied for social legislation to keep racial and ethnic groups separate and to sterilize people considered "genetically unfit". Elements of the American eugenics movement were models for the Nazis, whose adaptation of eugenics culminated in the Holocaust. Could the creation of "designer babies" pursue the Nazi ideology of racial purification or worse still, seek to produce a master race that could engineer an underclass of slaves to serve it? This apparent practice of eugenics would be gravely immoral since it fails to show unconditional respect for all human life without exception. Would it amount to a form of human hubris where, in attempting to play God, we find ourselves confronted with an uncontrollable monster of our own making?

Proponents of genetic enhancement may argue that if parents choose to spend their money to give children advantages they should be allowed to, that after all they are already able to do that environmentally by sending their children to private schools or providing better healthcare. However, it is arguable that the advantages of genetic enhancement far surpass those that can be provided by environmental input, such as better education, and as such confer an unfair edge to "designer babies".

Another unfortunate implication is that when parents choose personality traits of their offspring, abortions will become commonplace when they discover, in advance, that the child has traits not desired by them. Should abortions be legitimized for this reason? The lack of subjective traits within a viable offspring should not become an indication for abortions.

With regard to cloning as a potential source of "designer babies", certain questions must be resolved before it can be considered permissible as a remedy for human infertility: Is cloning unnatural self-engineering? Will failures such as deformed offspring be acceptable? Who is socially responsible for cloned humans? Do clones have rights and legal protection? The most formidable challenge is how to define a clone in terms of traditional institutions of family and parenting. Will clones have autonomy? Worse yet, will they be forced to be like their genetic twin? Many legal scholars argue that cloning will violate a child's right to an open future; a child born as the genetic copy of another may feel undue pressure to become like or different from its progenitor.

One opposing perspective put forward, that may not have much weight, comes from some moralists who, having swung from denial that genes have an important effect on behaviour, say that a cloned individual's behaviour will be ultimately determined by the individual's genetic make-up. Indeed, like identical twins, clones will be similar but not the same because of socialization and the influence of the environment on the womb.

To try to reproduce may be a basic human right but as soon as one specifies what sort of child one must have, it becomes a matter of human preference and not human rights. What right has anyone to programme a genetic advantage for their children just because they happen to be rich enough to afford it? Is consumer choice becoming a moral absolute? Moral codes stress that a child is not a right but a gift. We are losing the concept that life is given to us by a higher force and it is not ours to demand or to manipulate.

Whether it is genetic enhancement or cloning, there is a general repugnance for styles of reproduction with such profound potential for vanity that it threatens the freedom of children and the nature of family. This also represents the potential breaching of a natural barrier that is moral in character, taking humans into a realm of self-engineering that truly exceeds any prior experimentation with reproductive technology.

In most areas of science, it matters little to the public whether a particular theory is right or wrong, but in some cases of human genetics, it matters a great deal. The very term 'genetic engineering' conjures up the image of Frankenstein and his maker, Mary Shelley, the unintentional fairy godmother of human genetics. The social obligation that scientists have, as distinct from those responsibilities they share with all citizens, comes from their having access to specialized knowledge of how the world works, not easily accessible to others. Their obligation is both to make public any social implications of their work and its technological applications, and to give some assessment of its reliability and potential harm.

Should the creation of "designer babies" become the new milestone in reproductive biotechnology, all of the processes and the context within which they are applied must be strictly regulated by ethical bodies truly representing the interests of the wider society. Counselling should be mandatory where parents opt for genetic selection. They should be fully informed of all the risks of the procedures and given counselling regarding unrealistic expectations of the outcome that may be largely unpredictable, especially as time passes in the life of the child.

CONCLUSION

Despite the myriad of concerns about "designer babies", the reproductive technology has profound potential benefit for the relief of suffering by eliminating genes encoding disease and for advancing the understanding of human evolution. But without intense review and regard for the ethical and moral issues surrounding it, its potential may be thwarted. Most ethical issues in medicine are best resolved by consideration of the rights of the people involved to determine their own future. Are individuals capable of making the correct decisions in relation to science and its application? Thomas Jefferson's advice is commendable: "I know no safe depository of the ultimate powers of the society but the people themselves, and if we think them not enlightened enough to exercise that control with wholesome discretion, the remedy is not to take it from them but to inform their direction" (9). Unfortunately, the moral issues are not that easily addressed.

REFERENCES

1. The fertility race, twenty years of test-tube babies. *news.mpr.org: 1997*
2. BBC News/SCI/TECH.GM monkey first. *news.bbc.co.uk; 2001.*
3. BBC ON LINE. Baby with selected gene born in Britain. *Bbc.com; 2001*
4. gkt Scientific Editorial. Embryonic selection.
5. BBC ON LINE. Gender selection: the debate. *Bbc.com; 2002.*
6. Kluger J. Here Kitty kitty. Time: February 25, 2002
7. Associated Press. Study raises human cloning doubts. *Wired.com; 2002.*
8. TWJ Headline News. DNA pioneer wants to rid society of genetic defects. *Watchmanjournal.org; 2001.*
9. Wolpert L. Learning to love the grey. *Ring.org.uk; 2000.*

Confronting Inequality

Paul Krugman

Paul Krugman teaches economics at Princeton and writes an op-ed column in the *New York Times*. He was awarded the Nobel Prize in Economics in 2008. Krugman is the author of many books, among them *The Age of Diminished Expectations* (1989) and *The Great Unraveling: Losing Our Way in the New Century* (2003). "Confronting Inequality" is a chapter from his 2007 book, *The Conscience of a Liberal*.

The America I grew up in was a relatively equal middle class society. Over the past generation, however, the country has returned to Gilded Age levels of inequality. In this chapter I'll outline policies that can help reverse these changes. I'll begin with the question of values. Why should we care about high and rising inequality?

One reason to care about inequality is the straightforward matter of living standards. The lion's share of economic growth in America over the past thirty years has gone to a small, wealthy minority, to such an extent that it's unclear whether the typical family has benefited at all from technological progress and the rising productivity it brings. The lack of clear economic progress for lower- and middle-income families is in itself an important reason to seek a more equal distribution of income.

Beyond that, however, is the damage extreme inequality does to our society and our democracy. Ever since America's founding, our idea of ourselves has been that of a nation without sharp class distinctions—not a leveled society of perfect equality, but one in which the gap between the economic elite and the typical citizen isn't an unbridgeable chasm. That's why Thomas Jefferson wrote, "The small landholders are the most precious part of a state."[1] Translated into modern terms as an assertion that a broad middle class is the most precious part of a state, Jefferson's statement remains as true as ever. High inequality, which has turned us into a nation with a much-weakened middle class, has a corrosive effect on social relations and politics, one that has become ever more apparent as America has moved deeper into a new Gilded Age.

THE COSTS OF INEQUALITY

One of the best arguments I've ever seen for the social costs of inequality came from a movement conservative trying to argue the opposite. In 1997 Irving Kristol, one of the original neoconservative intellectuals, published an article in the *Wall Street Journal* called "Income Inequality Without Class Conflict." Kristol argued that we shouldn't worry about income inequality, because whatever the numbers may say, class distinctions are, in reality, all but gone. Today, he asserted,

> income inequality tends to be swamped by even greater social equality. . . . In all of our major cities, there is not a single restaurant where a CEO can lunch or dine with the absolute assurance that he will not run into his secretary. If you fly first class, who will be your traveling companions? You never know. If you go to Paris, you will be lost in a crowd of young people flashing their credit cards.[2]

By claiming that income inequality doesn't matter because we have social equality, Kristol was in effect admitting that income inequality *would* be a problem if it led to social inequality. And here's the thing: It does. Kristol's fantasy of a world in which the rich live just like you and me, and nobody feels socially inferior, bears no resemblance to the real America we live in.

Lifestyles of the rich and famous are arguably the least important part of the story, yet it's worth pointing out that Kristol's vision of CEOs rubbing shoulders with the middle class is totally contradicted by the reporting of Robert Frank of the *Wall Street Journal,* whose assigned beat is covering the lives of the wealthy. In his book *Richistan* Frank describes what he learned:

> Today's rich had formed their own virtual country. . . . [T]hey had built a self-contained world unto themselves, complete with their own health-care system (concierge doctors), travel network (Net Jets, destination clubs), separate economy. . . . The rich weren't just getting richer; they were becoming financial foreigners, creating their own country within a country, their own society within a society, and their economy within an economy.[3]

The fact is that vast income inequality inevitably brings vast social inequality in its train. And this social inequality isn't just a matter of envy and insults. It has real, negative consequences for the way people live in this country. It may not matter much that the great majority of Americans can't afford to stay in the eleven-thousand-dollar-a-night hotel suites popping up in luxury hotels around the world.[4] It matters a great deal that millions of middle-class families buy houses they can't really afford, taking on more mortgage debt than they can safely handle, because they're desperate to send their children to a good school—and intensifying inequality means that the desirable school districts are growing fewer in number, and more expensive to live in.

Elizabeth Warren, a Harvard Law School expert in bankruptcy, and Amelia Warren Tyagi, a business consultant, have studied the rise of bankruptcy in the United States. By 2005, just before a new law making it much harder for individuals to declare bankruptcy took effect, the number of families filing for bankruptcy each year was five times its level in the early 1980s. The proximate reason for this surge in bankruptcies was that families were taking on more debt—and this led to moralistic pronouncements about people spending too much on luxuries they can't afford. What Warren and Tyagi found, however, was that middle-class families were actually spending *less* on luxuries than they had in the 1970s. Instead the rise in debt mainly reflected increased spending on housing, largely driven by competition to get into good school districts. Middle-class Americans have been caught up in a rat race, not because they're greedy or foolish but because they're trying to give their children a chance in an increasingly unequal society.[5] And they're right to be worried: A bad start can ruin a child's chances for life.

Americans still tend to say, when asked, that individuals can make their own place in society. According to one survey 61 percent of Americans agree with the statement that "people get rewarded for their effort," compared with 49 percent in Canada and only 23 percent in France.[6] In reality, however, America has vast inequality of opportunity as well as results. We may believe that anyone can succeed through hard work and determination, but the facts say otherwise.

There are many pieces of evidence showing that Horatio Alger stories are very rare in real life. One of the most striking comes from a study published by the National Center for Education Statistics, which tracked the educational experience of Americans who were eighth graders in 1988. Those eighth graders were sorted both by apparent talent, as measured by a mathematics test, and by the socioeconomic status of their parents, as measured by occupations, incomes, and education.

The key result is shown in Table 1. Not surprisingly, both getting a high test score and having high-status parents increased a student's chance of finishing college. But family status mattered more. Students who scored in the

TABLE 1. PERCENTAGE OF 1988 EIGHTH GRADERS FINISHING COLLEGE

	SCORE IN BOTTOM QUARTILE	SCORE IN TOP QUARTILE
Parents in Bottom Quartile	3	29
Parents in Top Quartile	30	74

Source: National Center for Education Statistics, *The Condition of Education 2003*, 47.

bottom fourth on the exam, but came from families whose status put them in the top fourth—what we used to call RDKs, for "rich dumb kids," when I was a teenager—were more likely to finish college than students who scored in the top fourth but whose parents were in the bottom fourth. What this tells us is that the idea that we have anything close to equality of opportunity is clearly a fantasy. It would be closer to the truth, though not the whole truth, to say that in modern America, class—inherited class—usually trumps talent.

Isn't that true everywhere? Not to the same extent. International comparisons of "intergenerational mobility," the extent to which people can achieve higher status than their parents, are tricky because countries don't collect perfectly comparable data. Nonetheless it's clear that Horatio Alger has moved to someplace in Europe: Mobility is highest in the Scandinavian countries, and most results suggest that mobility is lower in the United States than it is in France, Canada, and maybe even Britain. Not only don't Americans have equal opportunity, opportunity is less equal here than elsewhere in the West.

It's not hard to understand why. Our unique lack of universal health care, all by itself, puts Americans who are unlucky in their parents at a disadvantage: Because American children from low-income families are often uninsured, they're more likely to have health problems that derail their life chances. Poor nutrition, thanks to low income and a lack of social support, can have the same effect. Life disruptions that affect a child's parents can also make upward mobility hard—and the weakness of the U.S. social safety net makes such disruptions more likely and worse if they happen. Then there's the highly uneven quality of U.S. basic education, and so on. What it all comes down to is that although the principle of "equality of opportunity, not equality of results" sounds fine, it's a largely fictitious distinction. A society with highly unequal results is, more or less inevitably, a society with highly unequal opportunity, too. If you truly believe that all Americans are entitled to an equal chance at the starting line, that's an argument for doing something to reduce inequality.

America's high inequality, then, imposes serious costs on our society that go beyond the way it holds down the purchasing power of most families. And there's another way in which inequality damages us: It corrupts our politics. "If there are men in this country big enough to own the government of the United States," said Woodrow Wilson in 1913, in words that would be almost inconceivable from a modern president, "they are going to own it."[7] Well, now there are, and they do. Not completely, of course, but hardly a week goes by without the disclosure of a case in which the influence of money has grotesquely distorted U.S. government policy.

As this book went to press, there was a spectacular example: The way even some Democrats rallied to the support of hedge fund managers, who receive an unconscionable tax break. Through a quirk in the way the tax laws have been interpreted, these managers—some of whom make more than a billion dollars a year—get to have most of their earnings taxed at the capital gains rate, which is only 15 percent, even as other high earners pay a 35 percent rate.

The hedge fund tax loophole costs the government more than $6 billion a year in lost revenue, roughly the cost of providing health care to three million children.[8] Almost $2 billion of the total goes to just twenty-five individuals. Even conservative economists believe that the tax break is unjustified, and should be eliminated.[9]

Yet the tax break has powerful political support—and not just from Republicans. In July 2007 Senator Charles Schumer of New York, the head of the Democratic Senatorial Campaign Committee, let it be known that he would favor eliminating the hedge fund loophole only if other, deeply entrenched tax breaks were eliminated at the same time. As everyone understood, this was a "poison pill," a way of blocking reform without explicitly saying no. And although Schumer denied it, everyone also suspected that his position was driven by the large sums hedge funds contribute to Democratic political campaigns.[10]

The hedge fund loophole is a classic example of how the concentration of income in a few hands corrupts politics. Beyond that is the bigger story of how income inequality has reinforced the rise of movement conservatism, a fundamentally undemocratic force. Rising inequality has to an important extent been caused by the rightward shift of our politics, but the causation also runs the other way. The new wealth of the rich has increased their influence, sustaining the institutions of movement conservatism and pulling the Republican Party even further into the movement's orbit. The ugliness of our politics is in large part a reflection of the inequality of our income distribution.

More broadly still, high levels of inequality strain the bonds that hold us together as a society. There has been a long-term downward trend in the extent to which Americans trust either the government or one another. In the sixties, most Americans agreed with the proposition that "most people can be trusted"; today most disagree.[11] In the sixties, most Americans believed that the government is run "for the benefit of all"; today, most believe that it's run for "a few big interests."[12] And there's convincing evidence that growing inequality is behind our growing cynicism, which is making the United States seem increasingly like a Latin American country. As the political scientists Eric Uslaner and Mitchell Brown point out (and support with extensive 'data), "In a world of haves and have-nots, those at either end of the economic spectrum have little reason to believe that 'most people can be trusted' . . . social trust rests on a foundation of economic equality."[13]

THE ARITHMETIC OF EQUALIZATION

Suppose we agree that the United States should become more like other advanced countries, whose tax and benefit systems do much more than ours to reduce inequality. The next question is what that decision might involve.

In part it would involve undoing many of the tax cuts for the wealthy that movement conservatives have pushed through since 1980. Table 2 shows what has happened to three tax rates that strongly affect the top 1 percent of the U.S. population, while having little effect on anyone else. Between 1979 and 2006 the top tax rate on earned income was cut in half; the tax rate on capital gains was cut almost as much; the tax rate on corporate profits fell by more than a quarter. High incomes in America are much less taxed than they used to be. Thus raising taxes on the rich back toward historical levels can pay for part, though only part, of a stronger safety net that limits inequality.

The first step toward restoring progressivity to the tax system is to let the Bush tax cuts for the very well off expire at the end of 2010, as they are now scheduled to. That alone would raise a significant amount of revenue. The nonpartisan Urban-Brookings Joint Tax Policy Center estimates that letting the Bush tax cuts expire for people with incomes over two hundred thousand dollars would be worth about $140 billion a year starting in 2012. That's enough to pay for the subsidies needed to implement universal health care. A tax-cut rollback of this kind, used to finance health care reform, would significantly reduce inequality. It would do so partly by modestly reducing incomes at the top: The Tax Policy Center estimates that allowing the Bush tax cuts to expire for Americans making more than two hundred thousand dollars a year would reduce the aftertax incomes of the richest 1 percent of Americans by about 4.5 percent compared with what they would be if the Bush tax cuts were made permanent. Meanwhile middle- and lower-income Americans would be assured of health care—one of the key aspects of being truly middle class.[14]

Another relatively easy move from a political point of view would be closing some of the obvious loopholes in the U.S. system. These include the rule described earlier that allows financial wheeler-dealers, such as hedge fund managers, to classify their earnings as capital gains, taxed at a 15 percent rate rather than 35 percent. The major tax loopholes also include rules that let corporations, drug companies in particular, shift recorded profits to low-tax jurisdictions overseas, costing billions more; one recent study estimates that tax avoidance by multinationals costs about $50 billion a year.[15]

TABLE 2. THREE TOP RATES (PERCENTAGE)

	TOP TAX ON EARNED INCOME	TOP TAX ON LONG-TERM. CAPITAL GAINS	TOP TAX ON CORPORATE PROFITS
1979	70	28	48
2006	35	15	35

Source: Urban-Brookings Tax Policy Center <http://taxpolicycenter.org/taxfacts/tfdb/tftemplate.cfm>.

Going beyond rolling back the Bush cuts and closing obvious loopholes would be a more difficult political undertaking. Yet there can be rapid shifts in what seems politically realistic. At the end of 2004 it seemed all too possible that Social Security, the centerpiece of the New Deal, would be privatized and effectively phased out. Today Social Security appears safe, and universal health care seems within reach. If universal health care can be achieved, and the New Deal idea that government can be a force for good is reinvigorated, things that now seem off the table might not look so far out.

Both historical and international evidence show that there is room for tax increases at the top that go beyond merely rolling back the Bush cuts. Even before the Bush tax cuts, top tax rates in the United States were low by historical standards—the tax rate on the top bracket was only 39.6 percent during the Clinton years, compared with 70 percent in the seventies and 50 percent even *after* Reagan's 1981 tax cut. Top U.S. tax rates are also low compared with those in European countries. For example, in Britain, the top income tax rate is 40 percent, seemingly equivalent to the top rate of the Clinton years. However, in Britain employers also pay a social insurance tax—the equivalent of the employer share of. FICA[*] here—that applies to all earned income. (Most of the U.S. equivalent is levied only on income up to a maximum of $97,500.) As a result very highly paid British employees face an effective tax rate of almost 48 percent. In France effective top rates are even higher. Also, in Britain capital gains are taxed as ordinary income, so that the effective tax rate on capital gains for people with high income is 40 percent, compared with 15 percent in the United States.[16] Taxing capital gains as ordinary income in the United States would yield significantly more revenue, and also limit the range of tax abuses like the hedge fund loophole.

Also, from the New Deal until the 1970s it was considered normal and appropriate to have "super" tax rates on very-high-income individuals. Only a few people were subject to the 70 percent top bracket in the 70s, let alone the 90 percent-plus top rates of the Eisenhower years. It used to be argued that a surtax on very high incomes serves no real purpose other than punishing the rich because it wouldn't raise much money, but that's no longer true. Today the top 0.1 percent of Americans, a class with a minimum income of about $1.3 million and an average income of about $3.5 million, receives more than 7 percent of all income—up from just 2.2 percent in 1979.[17] A surtax on that income would yield a significant amount of revenue, which could be used to help a lot of people. All in all, then, the next step after rolling back the Bush tax cuts and implementing universal health care should be a broader effort to restore the progressivity of U.S. taxes, and use the revenue to pay for more benefits that help lower- and middle-income families.

---

[*] FICA Federal Insurance Contributions Act, an employment tax that helps fund Social Security and Medicare.

Realistically, however, this would not be enough to pay for social expenditures comparable to those in other advanced countries, not even the relatively modest Canadian level. In addition to imposing higher taxes on the rich, other advanced countries also impose higher taxes on the middle class, through both higher social insurance payments and value-added taxes—in effect, national sales taxes. Social insurance taxes and VATs are not, in themselves, progressive. Their effect in reducing inequality is indirect but large: They pay for benefits, and these benefits are worth more as a percentage of income to people with lower incomes.

As a political matter, persuading the public that middle-income families would be better off paying somewhat higher taxes in return for a stronger social safety net will be a hard sell after decades of antitax, antigovernment propaganda. Much as I would like to see the United States devote another 2 or 3 percent of GDP* to social expenditure beyond health care, it's probably an endeavor that has to wait until liberals have established a strong track record of successfully using the government to make peoples' lives better and more secure. This is one reason health care reform, which is tremendously important in itself, would have further benefits: It would blaze the trail for a wider progressive agenda. This is also the reason movement conservatives are fiercely determined not to let health care reform succeed.

REDUCING MARKET INEQUALITY

Aftermarket policies can do a great deal to reduce inequality. But that should not be our whole focus. The Great Compression† also involved a sharp reduction in the inequality of market income. This was accomplished in part through wage controls during World War II, an experience we hope won't be repeated. Still, there are several steps we can take.

The first step has already been taken: In 2007 Congress passed the first increase in the minimum wage within a decade. In the 1950s and 1960s the minimum wage averaged about half of the average wage. By 2006, however, the purchasing power of the minimum wage had been so eroded by inflation that in real terms it was at its lowest point since 1955, and was only 31 percent of the average wage. Thanks to the new Democratic majority in Congress, the minimum is scheduled to rise from its current $5.15 an hour to $7.25 by 2009. This won't restore all the erosion, but it's an important first step.

There are two common but somewhat contradictory objections often heard to increasing the minimum wage. On one hand, it's argued that raising the minimum wage will reduce employment and increase unemployment. On

---

* GDP Gross domestic product. One measure of income and output for a country's economy.

† See paragraph 40.

the other it's argued that raising the minimum will have little or no effect in raising wages. The evidence, however, suggests that a minimum wage increase will in fact have modest positive effects.

On the employment side, a classic study by David Card of Berkeley and Alan Krueger of Princeton, two of America's best labor economists, found no evidence that minimum wage increases in the range the United States has experienced led to job losses.[18] Their work has been furiously attacked both because it seems to contradict Econ 101 and because it was ideologically disturbing to many. Yet it has stood up very well to repeated challenges, and new cases confirming its results keep coming in. For example, the state of Washington has a minimum wage almost three dollars an hour higher than its neighbor Idaho; business experiences near the state line seem to indicate that, if anything, Washington has gained jobs at Idaho's expense. "Small-business owners in Washington," reported the *New York Times*, "say they have prospered far beyond their expectation. . . . Idaho teenagers cross the state line to work in fast-food restaurants in Washington."

All the empirical evidence suggests that minimum wage increases *in the range that is likely to take place* do not lead to significant job losses. True, an increase in the minimum wage to, say, fifteen dollars an hour would probably cause job losses, because it would dramatically raise the cost of employment in some industries. But that's not what's on—or even near—the table.

Meanwhile minimum wage increases can have fairly significant effects on wages at the bottom end of the scale. The Economic Policy Institute estimates that the worst-paid 10 percent of the U.S. labor force, 13 million workers, will gain from the just-enacted minimum wage increase. Of these, 5.6 million are currently being paid less than the new minimum wage, and would see a direct benefit. The rest are workers earning more than the new minimum wage, who would benefit from ripple effects of the higher minimum.

The minimum wage, however, matters mainly to low-paid workers. Any broader effort to reduce market inequality will have to do something about incomes further up the scale. The most important tool in that respect is likely to be an end to the thirty-year tilt of government policy against unions.

The drastic decline in the U.S. union movement was not, as is often claimed, an inevitable result of globalization and increased competition. International comparisons show that the U.S. union decline is unique, even though other countries faced the same global pressures. Again, in 1960 Canada and the United States had essentially equal rates of unionization, 32 and 30 percent of wage and salary workers, respectively. By 1999 U.S. unionization was down to 13 percent, but Canadian unionization was unchanged. The sources of union decline in America lie not in market forces but in the political climate created by movement conservatism, which allowed employers to engage in union-busting activities and punish workers for supporting union organizers. Without that changed political climate, much of the service economy—especially giant retailers like Wal-Mart—would probably be unionized today.

A new political climate could revitalize the union movement—and revitalizing unions should be a key progressive goal. Specific legislation, such as the Employee Free Choice Act, which would reduce the ability of employers to intimidate workers into rejecting a union, is only part of what's needed. It's also crucial to enforce labor laws already on the books. Much if not most of the antiunion activity that led to the sharp decline in American unionization was illegal even under existing law. But employers judged, correctly, that they could get away with it.

The hard-to-answer question is the extent to which a newly empowered U.S. union movement would reduce inequality. International comparisons suggest that it might make quite a lot of difference. The sharpest increases in wage inequality in the Western world have taken place in the United States and in Britain, both of which experienced sharp declines in union membership. (Britain is still far more unionized than America, but it used to have more than 50 percent unionization.) Canada, although its economy is closely linked to that of the United States, appears to have had substantially less increase in wage inequality—and it's likely that the persistence of a strong union movement is an important reason why. Unions raise the wages of their members, who tend to be in the middle of the wage distribution; they also tend to equalize wages among members. Perhaps most important, they act as a countervailing force to management, enforcing social norms that limit very high and very low pay even among people who aren't union members. They also mobilize their members to vote for progressive policies. Would getting the United States back to historical levels of unionization undo a large part of the, Great Divergence? We don't know—but it might, and encouraging a union resurgence should be a major goal of progressive policy.

A reinvigorated union movement isn't the only change that could reduce extreme inequalities in pay. A number of other factors discouraged very high paychecks for a generation after World War II. One was a change in the political climate: Very high executive pay used to provoke public scrutiny, congressional hearings, and even presidential intervention. But that all ended in the Reagan years.

Historical experience still suggests that a new progressive majority should not be shy about questioning private-sector pay when it seems outrageous. Moral suasion was effective in the past, and could be so again.

ANOTHER GREAT COMPRESSION?

The Great Compression, the abrupt reduction in economic inequality that took place in the United States in the 1930s and 1940s, took place at a time of crisis. Today America's state is troubled, but we're not in the midst of a great depression or a world war. Correspondingly, we shouldn't expect changes as drastic or sudden as those that took place seventy years ago. The process of reducing inequality now is likely to be more of a Great Moderation than a Great Compression.

Yet it is possible, both as an economic matter and in terms of practical politics, to reduce inequality and make America a middle-class nation again. And now is the time to get started.

NOTES

1. Thomas Jefferson, letter to James Madison, 28 Oct. 1785 <http://press-pubs.uchicago.edu/founders/documents/v1ch15s32.html>.
2. Irving Kristol, "Income Inequality Without Class Conflict," *Wall Street Journal* 18 Dec. 1997: A22.
3. Robert Frank, *Richistan: A Journey Through the American Wealth Boom and the Lives of the New Rich* (Crown, 2007) 3–4.
4. "Suites for the Sweet," Newsweek International July 2–9 <http://www.msnbc.msn.com/id/19388720/site/newsweek>, part of a special report on "Secret Habits of the Super Rich."
5. Elizabeth Warren and Amelia Warren Tyagi, "What's Hurting the Middle Class," *Boston Review* (Sept./Oct. 2005) <http://bostonreview.net/BR30.5/warrentyagi.html>.
6. Tom Hertz, *Understanding Mobility in America* (Center for American Progress, 2006) <http://www.americanprogress.org/issues/2006/04/b157998I.html>.
7. Woodrow Wilson, *The New Freedom* (Doubleday, 1913), Project Gutenberg <http://www.gutenberg.org/files/14811/14811-h/14811-h.htm>.
8. "Tax Breaks for Billionaires," Economic Policy Institute Policy Memorandum no. 120 <http://www.epi.org/content.cfm/pm120>.
9. See, for example, Jessica Holzer, "Conservatives Break with GOP Leaders on a Tax Bill," *The Hill* 18 July 2007 <http://thehill.com/leading-the-news/conservatives-break-with-gop-leaders-on-a-tax-bill-2007-07-18.html>.
10. "In Opposing Tax Plan, Schumer Supports Wall Street Over Party," *New York Times* 30 July 2007: A1.
11. Eric M. Uslaner and Mitchell Brown, "Inequality, Trust, and Civic Engagement," *American Politics Research* 33.6 (2005): 868–94.
12. *The ANES Guide to Public Opinion and Electoral Behavior*, table 5A.2 <http://electionstudies.org/nesguide/toptable/tab5a_2.htm>.
13. Uslaner and Brown, "Inequality, Trust, and Civic Engagement."
14. Tax Policy Center, "Options to Extend the 2001–2006 Tax Cuts, Static Impact on Individual Income and Estate Tax Liability and Revenue ($ billions), 2008–17," Table T07-0126 <http://taxpolicycenter.org/TaxModel/tmdb/Content/PDF/T07-0126.pdf>.
15. Kimberly A. Clausing, "Multinational Firm Tax Avoidance and U.S. Government Revenue" (working paper, Wellesley College, Wellesley, MA, 2007).

16. OECD Tax Database <http://www.oecd.org/ctp/taxdatabase>.

17. Piketty and Saez, 2005 preliminary estimates <http://elsa.berkeley.edu/~saez/TabFig2005prel.xls>.

18. David Card and Alan B. Krueger, "Minimum Wages and Employment: A Case Study of the Fast-Food Industry in New Jersey and Pennsylvania," *American Economic Review* 84.4 (1994): 772–93.

JOINING THE CONVERSATION

1. Krugman begins by asking the "so what?" question in paragraph 1: "Why should we care about high and rising inequality?" How does he answer this question?

2. What evidence does Krugman provide for the prevalence of economic inequality in U.S. society? How convincing is this evidence to you?

3. Notice how many direct quotations Krugman includes. Why do you think he includes so many? What, if anything, do the quotations contribute that a summary or paraphrase would not?

4. In paragraph 4 Krugman quotes someone whose views he does not agree with, but then uses those views to support his own argument. How do you know he is quoting a view that he disagrees with?

5. Write an essay responding to Krugman, agreeing with him on some points and disagreeing with him on others. Start by summarizing his arguments before moving on to give your own views.

The American Dream: Dead, Alive, or on Hold?

Brandon King

University of Cincinnati

What is the true state of the so-called "American Dream" today? Is it still around, waiting to be achieved by those who work hard enough, or is it effectively dead, killed off by the Great Recession and the economic hardships that many Americans have come to face? Statistics reveal alarming facts, including trillions of dollars lost in the stock market (Paradis, 2009). While these losses, combined with admittedly high unemployment in the past few years, have contributed to seemingly dismal prospects for prosperity in the United States, I believe that the ideals and values of the American Dream are still very much alive. In fact, the original term "American Dream" was coined during the Great Depression by James Truslow Adams, who wrote that the American dream "is that dream of a land in which life should be better and richer and fuller for everyone, with opportunity for each according to ability and achievement, regardless of social class or circumstances of birth" (1931). I would redefine the American Dream today as the potential to work for an honest, secure way of life and save for the future. Many liberal economists and activists say that the American Dream is dead, but I say that it's more alive and important than ever—and that it is the key to climbing out of the Great Recession, overcoming inequality, and achieving true prosperity.

Despite the harshness of the Great Recession, a 2009 *New York Times* survey found that 72 percent of Americans still believed it was possible to start poor, work hard, and become rich in America (Seelye, 2009). In the same survey, Americans were also asked questions about what they believed constituted being "successful," with the majority naming things such as a steady job, financial security for the future, being able to retire without struggling, and having a secure place of residence. Less common were responses about owning a home or car and being able to buy other expensive goods, implying a subtle shift from the American Dream of the past to a more modest one today. In many ways, the American Dream of today is a trimmed down version of its former self. The real sign of success in our society used to be owning expensive items, namely cars and homes, and acquiring more material wealth. Living the American Dream meant going from dirt poor to filthy rich and becoming more than you could have ever imagined. Today, most people do not strive for a rags-to-riches transition, and instead prefer a stable, middle-class lifestyle, one in which they can focus on saving money for the future and having secure employment. For example, more and more people now rent their homes instead of buying; a recent study showed a decrease in home ownership from 69% in 2005 to about 66.5% in 2010, and an increase in renter households of 1.1 million (Hoak, 2011). Americans are scrutinizing their spending habits more intensely, as shown in a survey completed in 2009 showing that approximately two-thirds of Americans have permanently changed their spending habits as a result of the Great Recession and that one-fourth hope to save more money for the future (Frietchen, 2009).

Looking at the fragile economy today, it is tempting to focus on the unevenness of the recovery: the stock market has made impressive rebounds in recent months, but the unemployment rate remains high. Thanks to bailouts for large corporations and stimulus measures intended to generate growth, economic activity seems to be on its way towards pre-recession levels, but the economy remains fragile. Weak national real estate markets, sluggish job growth, and the slow recovery of liquid assets lost during the recession are obstacles to a full recovery.

To many, the most worrisome problem is inequality: that wealth is concentrated into the hands of a rich minority. One economist, Robert Reich, even says that "As long as income and wealth keep concentrating at the top, and the great divide between America's have-mores and have-lesses continues to widen, the Great Recession won't end, at least not in the real economy" (Reich, 2009). The essence of Reich's argument is that Wall Street will effectively deter any meaningful recovery on Main Street. Another economist, Paul Krugman, holds a similar position, writing that "The lion's share of economic growth in America over the past thirty years has gone to a small, wealthy minority," and that "the lack of clear economic progress for lower and middle income families is in itself an important reason to seek a more equal distribution of income" (2007). Krugman believes that the American Dream is no longer possible for most Americans, and that the government should enact policies to close the income gap.

We may have genuine inequality issues and a sizable divide between the rich and poor, and we might have an economy that is recovering too slowly for public interest. The American Dream, however, is based on perception, on the way someone *imagines* how to be successful. How can anyone claim that because there are more poor people than rich, or more power and wealth concentrated at the top, that the entire premise of the American Dream is dead? In fact, the safeguards of the welfare system, including the minimum wage and unemployment benefits, were long ago put in place to protect the poorest Americans. During the Great Recession, the federal government decided that raising the minimum wage would stimulate worker productivity and help close the income gap. In reality, however, it has done little to make the poor richer. In fact, raising the minimum wage, which makes labor more expensive, could force companies to cut back and hire fewer workers.

With a different approach to fixing the economy, some economists and politicians argue that supporting the richest sectors of the American economy will bring economic stability and a full recovery. They claim that a sizable income gap does not necessarily prevent individuals in the lower and middle classes from achieving the American Dream. I agree: government funding for Wall Street and struggling businesses makes the economy healthier. I believe that we should keep in mind the ways in which large businesses and financial institutions enable many others to attain economic stability and security. For example, providing money to businesses may encourage them to hire more people, thereby increasing job opportunities. Just last year, President Obama presented a proposal, later passed by Congress, establishing a $33 billion tax credit to provide incentives for businesses to hire more workers and increase existing wages (Gomstyn, 2010). Increased support for Wall Street could in this way make the overall economy healthier so that everyone has increased opportunities.

Some, however, argue that raising taxes on the rich and on America's wealthy businesses is an effective means of closing the income gap. For *New York Times* columnist Bob Herbert, our economic problems are the result of bad policy decisions that have led to the rapid migration of American jobs overseas, the degradation of the American education system, and continuous costly wars. His primary point in a recent *New York Times* column was that America "does not have the common sense to raise taxes," his solution to solving inequality issues and achieving greater economic security (2010). Robert Reich and Paul Krugman concur with Herbert's analysis and recommend raising taxes (Krugman, 2007). My question for Herbert is, "Given the Great Recession and the tough economic climate that we continue to live in, would raising taxes still be the prudent thing to do?" Maybe Herbert believes that higher taxes for the rich would help solve the issue of inequality, but in reality, it would not help people achieve the American Dream at all. According to writer Dana Golden (2009), the more wealth the rich accumulate, the more they will spend it, thereby stimulating the economy. She also points out that the creation of wealth and its subsequent use is one way jobs are created, even in difficult economic times. Taxing the rich only decreases their spending potential and thus their ability to stimulate the economy.

In contrast to Herbert's bleak view, economist Cal Thomas responds to arguments about inequality issues by arguing that "The rules for achieving the American Dream may no longer be taught and supported by culture, but that doesn't mean that they don't work" (2010). Indeed, the media inundate us with countless images and stories of struggling workers and the growing ranks of the poor while suggesting that the American Dream is simply beyond the grasp of the vast majority of Americans. Thomas's response is that only because of "unrestrained liberalism" are the true means of realizing the American Dream being more and more eroded in our society. Despite the recent recession, Thomas and others like him have faith that as long as people believe they have a chance of becoming better off than they are today, then the American Dream is intact. Instead of trying to interfere with the enterprise that creates jobs and growth, we should rely on the values of the American Dream: that anybody can climb out of hardship and achieve success. Only then will the American Dream remain alive for future generations.

Just last year, a newspaper editor in Atlanta stated that, "the Great Recession didn't kill the American Dream. But the promise of a good life in exchange for hard, honest work has been bruised and frayed for millions of middle class Americans" (Chapman, 2010). The idea of the American Dream has in fact suffered in recent years, although it is my belief that this is not new. As a nation, we have dealt with economic downturns in the past, and the American Dream has faced trials and tests before. The economic panics of the late 1970s and after the 9/11 terrorist attacks are both prime examples. Even since the height of the Great Recession, however, we have adapted the values contained within the American Dream to meet new challenges. Of course, some will be quick to say that these changes have only come about as a result of the greed and corruption of the rich and powerful. Like laissez-faire economists and Wall Street supporters, however, I believe that it is necessary and imperative to continue supporting the business mechanisms that sustain our economy. The American Dream will continue to exist as part of the American psyche, not artificially stimulated by government regulations to change income distribution. If the Great Recession has taught us anything, it is that planning for the future by saving more and enacting policies that sustain economic growth are what will keep the American Dream alive.

REFERENCES

Adams, J. T. (1931). *Epic of America*. Boston: Little, Brown.

Chapman, D. (2010, December 10). American dream deferred, not dead. *Atlanta Journal-Constitution*. Retrieved from http://www.ajc.com/

Frietchen, C. (2009, October 24). Imagining yourself post-recession: Survey shows spending-habit changes [Web log post]. *Productopia: A World Without Buyer's Remorse*. Retrieved from http://www.consumersearch.com/blog/imagining-yourself-post-recession-survey-shows-spending habit-changes#

Golden, D. (2009, January 10). The economy, credit and trickle down economics (the ripple effect). *EzineArticles*. Retrieved from http://ezinearticles

.com/?The-Economy,-Credit-and-Trickle-Down-Economics-(The-Ripple-Effect)&id=1865774

Gomstyn, A. (2010, January 29). Obama announces $33B hiring tax credit. *ABC News*. Retrieved from http://abcnews.go.com/

Herbert, B. (2010). Hiding from reality. *The New York Times*. Retrieved from http://www.nytimes.com/

Hoak, A. (2011, February 8). More people choosing to rent, not buy, their home. *MarketWatch*. Retrieved from http://www.marketwatch.com/

Krugman, P. (2007). *The conscience of a liberal*. New York, NY: Norton.

Paradis, T. (2009, October 10). The statistics of the great recession. *Huffington Post*. Retrieved from http://www.huffingtonpost.com/

Reich, R. (2009, December 27). 2009: The year Wall Street bounced back and Main Street got shafted. *Huffington Post*. Retrieved from http://www.huffingtonpost.com/

Seelye, K. (2009, May 7). What happens to the American Dream in a recession? *The New York Times*. Retrieved from http://www.nytimes.com/

Thomas, C. (2010, November 23). Is the American Dream over? *Townhall*. Retrieved from http://townhall.com/columnists/CalThomas/2010/11/23/is_the_american_dream_over

The Myth of the American Dream

By Steve Hargreaves

The American Dream is supposed to mean that through hard work and per-severance, even the poorest people can make it to middle class or above. But it's actually harder to move up in America than it is in most other advanced nations.

It's easier to rise above the class you're born into in countries like Japan, Germany, Australia, and the Scandinavian nations, according to research from University of Ottawa economist and current Russell Sage Foundation Fellow Miles Corak.

Among the major developed countries, only in Italy and the United King-dom is there less economic mobility, according to Corak.

The research measures "intergenerational earnings elasticity"–a type of economic mobility that measures the correlation between what your parents make and what you make one generation later – in a number of different coun-tries around the world.

MOST AMERICANS BORN INTO THE LOWER CLASS STAY IN THE LOWER CLASS

Economists aren't certain exactly why some countries have a greater degree of mobility than others, but they do point to certain similarities.

Greater current inequality: The more unequal a society is currently, the greater the chance that the children will be stuck in the same sphere. This is because wealthy families are able to provide things like tutors and extracurricular activities – and the time to pursue them – that **poorer families** often cannot.

Also, education matters a lot more now than it did 100 years ago in terms of getting a good job.

"The rich can pump a lot more money into their kids' future," said Corak.

This helps explain why countries like China, India and many South American nations also exhibit relatively little economic mobility.

Families: Having a stable home life is also associated with the ability to climb the economic ladder, said Corak. The United States tends to have higher rates of divorce, single-parent homes, and teenage pregnancy than many other industrialized countries.

Social policies: Countries that redistribute wealth – through, say, higher taxes on the rich and more spending on the poor – tend to have greater social mobility, said Francisco Ferreira, an economist at the World Bank.

This is especially true when it comes to education spending. Critics have long contended that the U.S. system for funding education – where school funding is largely based on property taxes – perpetuates inequality far more so than a system that taxes the whole country for schools, then redistributes that money to the districts that are most needy.

RELATED: WHY THE HIGHEST PAID PEOPLE MAKE SO MUCH MONEY

If why Americans have a harder time making it into the middle class is a bit of a mystery to economists, why Americans cling to the belief that it's still easy to do is even more baffling.

It could be because, during the late 1800s and early 1900, the United States was a much more mobile country than Britain, said Jason Long, an economist at Wheaton College in Illinois.

"It's clear that Americans still believe that America has exceptional mobility, and that's not true," said Long. He calling it "vexing" that "lots of people could be systematically mistaken about verifiable, factual information."

But no society has total mobility. Class is always going to be somewhat correlated to one's upbringing, Corak noted.

First Published: December 9, 2013: 7:00 AM ET

Social Class and the Hidden Curriculum of Work

Jean Anyon
(From: Journal of Education, Vol. 162, no. 1, Fall 1980.)

It's no surprise that schools in wealthy communities are better than those in poor communities, or that they better prepare their students for desirable jobs. It may be shocking, however, to learn how vast the differences in schools are – not so much in resources as in teaching methods and philosophies of education. Jean Anyon observed five elementary schools over the course of a full school year and concluded that fifth-graders of different economic backgrounds are already being prepared to occupy particular rungs on the social ladder. In a sense, some whole schools are on the vocational education track, while others are geared to produce future doctors, lawyers, and business leaders. Anyon's main audience is professional educators, so you may find her style and vocabulary challenging, but, once you've read her descriptions of specific classroom activities, the more analytic parts of the essay should prove easier to understand. Anyon is chairperson of the Department of Education at Rutgers University, Newark; This essay first appeared in Journal of Education, *volume 162, no. 1, in the Fall 1980 edition.*

Scholars in political economy and the sociology of knowledge have recently argued that public schools in complex industrial societies like our own make available different types of educational experience and curriculum knowledge to students in different social classes. Bowles and Gintis[1] for example, have argued that students in different social-class backgrounds are rewarded for classroom behaviors that correspond to personality traits allegedly rewarded in the different occupational strata – the working classes for docility and obedience, the managerial classes for initiative and personal assertiveness. Basil Bernstein, Pierre Bourdieu, and Michael W. Apple focusing on school knowledge, have argued that knowledge and skills leading to social power and regard (medical, legal, managerial) are made available to the advantaged social groups but are withheld from the working classes to whom a more "practical" curriculum is offered (manual skills, clerical knowledge). While there has been considerable argumentation of these points regarding education in England, France, and North America, there has been little or no attempt to investigate these ideas empirically in elementary or secondary schools and classrooms in this country.[3]

This article offers tentative empirical support (and qualification) of the above arguments by providing illustrative examples of differences in student *work* in classrooms in contrasting social class communities. The examples were gathered *as* part of an ethnographical[4] study of curricular, pedagogical, and pupil evaluation practices in five elementary schools. The article attempts a theoretical contribution as well and assesses student work in the light of a theoretical approach to social-class analysis . . . It will be suggested that there is a "hidden curriculum" in schoolwork that has profound implications for the theory – and consequence – of everyday activity in education. . . .

THE SAMPLE OF SCHOOLS

The social-class designation of each of the five schools will be identified, and the income, occupation, and other relevant available social characteristics of the students and their parents will be described. The first three schools are in a medium-sized city district in northern New Jersey, and the other two are in a nearby New Jersey suburb.

The first two schools I will call *working class schools*. Most of the parents have blue-collar jobs. Less than a third of the fathers are skilled, while the majority are in unskilled or semiskilled jobs. During the period of the study (1978–1979), approximately 15 percent of the fathers were unemployed. The large majority (85 percent) of the families are white. The following occupations are typical: platform, storeroom, and stockroom workers; foundry-men, pipe welders, and boilermakers; semiskilled and unskilled assembly-line operatives; gas station attendants, auto mechanics, maintenance workers, and security guards. Less than 30 percent of the women work, some part-time and some full-time, on assembly lines, in storerooms and stockrooms, as waitresses, barmaids, or sales clerks. Of the fifth-grade parents, none of the wives of the skilled workers had jobs. Approximately 15 percent of the families in each school are at or below the federal "poverty" level;[5] most of the rest of the family incomes are at or below $12,000, except some of the skilled workers whose incomes are higher. The incomes of the majority of the families in these two schools (at or below $12,000) are typical of 38.6 percent of the families in the United States.[6]

The third school is called the *middle-class school*, although because of 5 neighborhood residence patterns, the population is a mixture of several social classes. The parents' occupations can he divided into three groups: a small group of blue-collar "rich," who are skilled, well-paid workers such as printers, carpenters, plumbers, and construction workers. The second group is composed of parents in working-class and middle-class white-collar jobs: women in office jobs, technicians, supervisors in industry, and parents employed by the city (such as firemen, policemen, and several of the school's teachers). The third group is composed of occupations such as personnel directors in local firms, accountants, "middle management," and a few small capitalists (owners of shops in the area). The children of several local doctors attend this school. Most family incomes are between $13,000 and $25,000, with a few higher. This income range is typical of 38.9 percent of the families in the United States.[7]

The fourth school has a parent population that is at the upper income level of the upper middle class and is predominantly professional. This school will be called the *affluent professional school.* Typical jobs are: cardiologist, interior designer, corporate lawyer or engineer, executive in advertising or television. There are some families who are not as affluent as the majority (the family of the superintendent of the district's schools, and the one or two families in which the fathers are skilled workers). In addition, a few of the families are more affluent than the majority and can be classified in the capitalist class (a partner in a prestigious Wall Street stock brokerage firm). Approximately 90 percent of the children in this school are white. Most family incomes are between $40,000 and $80,000. This income span represents approximately 7 percent of the families in the United States.[8]

In the fifth school the majority of the families belong to the capitalist class. This school will be called the *executive elite school* because most of the fathers are top executives (for example, presidents and vice-presidents) in major United States-based multinational corporations – for example, AT&T, RCA, Citibank, American Express, U.S. Steel. A sizable group of fathers are top executives in financial firms in Wall Street. There are also a number of fathers who list their occupations as "general counsel" to a particular corporation, and these corporations are also among the large multi-nationals. Many of the mothers do volunteer work in the Junior League, Junior Fortnightly, or other service groups; some are intricately involved in town politics; and some are themselves in well-paid occupations. There are no minority children in the school. Almost all the family incomes are over $100,000 with some in the $500,000 range. The incomes in this school represent less than 1 percent of the families in the United States.[9]

Since each of the five schools is only one instance of elementary education in a particular social class context, I will not generalize beyond the sample. However, the examples of schoolwork which follow will suggest characteristics of education in each social setting that appear to have theoretical and social significance and to be worth investigation in a larger number of schools.

THE WORKING CLASS SCHOOLS

In the two working-class schools, work is following the steps of a procedure. The procedure is usually mechanical, involving rote behavior and very little decision making or choice. The teachers rarely explain why the work is being assigned, how it might connect to other assignments, or what the idea is that lies behind the procedure or gives it coherence and perhaps meaning or significance. Available textbooks are not always used, and the teachers often prepare their own dittos or put work examples on the board. Most of the rules regarding work are designations of what the children are to do; the rules are steps to follow. These steps are told to the children by the teachers and are often written on the board. The children are usually told to copy the steps as notes. These notes are to be studied. Work is often evaluated not according to whether it is right or wrong but according to whether the children followed the right steps.

The following examples illustrate these points. In math, when two-digit division was introduced, the teacher in one school gave a four-minute lecture on what the terms are called (which number is the divisor, dividend, quotient, and remainder). The children were told to copy these names in their notebooks. Then the teacher told them the steps to follow to do the problems, saying, "This is how you do them." The teacher listed the steps on the board, and they appeared several days later as a chart hung in the middle of the front wall: "Divide, Multiply, Subtract, Bring Down." The children often did examples of two-digit division. When the teacher went over the examples with them, he told them what the procedure was for each problem, rarely asking them to conceptualize or explain it themselves: "Three into twenty-two is seven; do your subtraction and one is left over." During the week that two-digit division was introduced (or at any other time), the investigator did not observe any discussion of the idea of grouping involved in division, any use of manipulables, or any attempt to relate two-digit division to any other mathematical process. Nor was there any attempt to relate the steps to an actual or possible thought process of the children. The observer did not hear the terms *dividend, quotient,* and so on, used again. The math teacher in the other working-class school followed similar procedures regarding two-digit division and at one point her class seemed confused. She said, "You're confusing yourselves. You're tensing up. Remember, when you do this, it's the same steps over and over again—and that's the way division always is." Several weeks later, after a test, a group of her children "still didn't get it," and she made no attempt to explain the concept of dividing things into groups or to give them manipulables for their own investigation. Rather, she went over the steps with them again and told them that they "needed more practice."

In other areas of math, work is also carrying out often unexplained fragmented procedures. For example, one of the teachers led the children through a series of steps to make a 1-inch grid on their paper *without* telling them that they were making a 1-inch grid or that it would be used to study scale. She said, "Take your ruler. Put it across the top. Make a mark at every number. Then move your ruler down to the bottom. No, put it across the bottom. Now make a mark on top of every number. Now draw a line from . . ." At this point a girl said that she had a faster way to do it and the teacher said, "No, you don't; you don't even know what I'm making yet. Do it this way or it's wrong." After they had made the lines up and down and across, the teacher told them she wanted them to make a figure by connecting some dots and to measure that, using the scale of 1 inch equals 1 mile. Then they were to cut it out. She said, "Don't cut it until I check it."

In both working-class schools, work in language arts is mechanics of punctuation (commas, periods, question marks, exclamation points), capitalization, and the four kinds of sentences. One teacher explained to me, "Simple punctuation is all they'll ever use." Regarding punctuation, either a teacher or a ditto stated the rules for where, for example, to put commas. The investigator heard no classroom discussion of the aural context of punctuation (which, of course, is what gives each mark its meaning). Nor did the investigator hear any statement or inference that placing a punctuation mark could be a decision-making process, depending, for example, on one's intended meaning. Rather, the children were told to follow the rules. Language arts did not involve creative writing. There were several writing assignments throughout the year but in each instance the children were given a ditto, and they wrote answers to questions on the sheet. For example, they wrote their "autobiography" by answering such questions as "Where were you born?" "What is your favorite animal?" on a sheet entitled "All About Me."

In one of the working-class schools, the class had a science period several times a week. On the three occasions observed, the children were not called upon to set up experiments or to give explanations for facts or concepts. Rather, on each occasion the teacher told them in his own words what the book said. The children copied the teacher's sentences from the board. Each day that preceded the day they were to do a science experiment, the teacher told them to copy the directions from the book for the procedure they would carry out the next day and to study the list at home that night. The day after each experiment, the teacher went over what they had "found" (they did the experiments as a class, and each was actually a class demonstration led by the teacher). Then the teacher wrote what they "found" on the board, and the children copied that in their notebooks. Once or twice a year there are science projects. The project is chosen and assigned by the teacher from a box of 3-by-5-inch cards. On the card the teacher has written the question to he answered, the books to use, and how much to write. Explaining the cards to the observer, the teacher said, "It tells them exactly what to do, or they couldn't do it."

Social studies in the working-class schools is also largely mechanical, rote work that was given little explanation or connection to larger contexts. In one school, for example, although there was a book available, social studies work was to copy the teacher's notes from the board. Several times a week for a period of several months the children copied these notes. The fifth grades in the district were to study United States history. The teacher used a booklet she had purchased called "The Fabulous Fifty States." Each day she put information from the booklet in outline form on the board and the children copied it. The type of information did not vary: the name of the state, its abbreviation, state capital, nickname of the state, its main products, main business, and a "Fabulous Fact" ("Idaho grew twenty-seven billion potatoes in one year. That's enough pota- toes for each man, woman, and . . .") As the children finished copying the sen- tences, the teacher erased them and wrote more. Children would occasionally go to the front to pull down the wall map in order to locate the states they were copying, and the teacher did not dissuade them. But the observer never saw her refer to the map; nor did the observer ever hear her make other than perfunctory remarks concerning the information the children were copying. Occasionally the children colored in a ditto and cut it out to make a stand-up figure (representing, for example, a man roping a cow in the Southwest). These were referred to by the teacher as their social studies "projects."

Rote behavior was often called for in classroom work. When going over 15 math and language art skills sheets, for example, as the teacher asked for the answer to each problem, he fired the questions rapidly, staccato, and the scene reminded the observer of a sergeant drilling recruits: above all, the questions demanded that you stay at attention: "The next one? What do I put here? . . . Here? Give us the next." Or "How many commas in this sentence? Where do I put them . . . The next one?"

The four fifth grade teachers observed in the working-class schools attempted to control classroom time and space by making decisions without consulting the children and without explaining the basis for their decisions. The teacher's control thus often seemed capricious. Teachers, for instance, very often ignored the bells to switch classes – deciding among themselves to keep the children after the period was officially over to continue with the work or for disciplinary reasons or so they (the teachers) could stand in the hall and talk. There were no clocks in the rooms in either school, and the children often asked, "What period is this?" "When do we go to gym?" The children had no access to materials. These were handed out by teachers and closely guarded. Things in the room "belonged" to the teacher: "Bob, bring me my garbage can." The teachers continually gave the children orders. Only three times did the investigator hear a teacher in either working-class school preface a directive with an unsarcastic "please," or "let's" or "would you." Instead, the teachers said, "Shut up," "Shut your mouth," "Open your books," "Throw your gum away-if you want to rot your teeth, do it on your own time." Teach- ers made every effort to control the movement of the children, and often shouted, ' "Why are you out of your seat??!!" If the children got permission to leave the room, they had to take a written pass with the date and time. . . .

MIDDLE-CLASS SCHOOL

In the middle-class school, work is getting the right answer. If one accumu- lates enough right answers, one gets a good grade. One must follow the direc- tions in order to get the right answers, but the directions often call for some figuring, some choice, some decision making. For example, the children must often figure out by themselves what the directions ask them to do and how to get the answer: what do you do first, second, and perhaps third? Answers are usually found in books or by listening to the teacher. Answers are usually words, sentences, numbers, or facts and dates; one writes them on paper, and one should be neat. Answers must be given in the right order, and one cannot make them up.

The following activities are illustrative. Math involves some choice: one may do two-digit division the long way or the short way, and there are some math problems that can be done "in your head." When the teacher explains how to do two-digit division, there is recognition that a cognitive process is involved; she gives you several ways and says, "I want to make sure you understand what you're doing-so you get it right"; and, when they go over the homework, she asks the *children* to tell how they did the problem and what answer they got.

In social studies the daily work is to read the assigned pages in the textbook and to answer the teacher's questions. The questions are almost always designed to check on whether the students have read the assignment and understood it: who did so-and-so; what happened after that; when did it happen, where, and sometimes, why did it happen? The answers are in the book and in one's understanding of the book; the teacher's hints when one doesn't know the answers are to "read it again" or to look at the picture or at the rest of the paragraph. One is to search for the answer in the "context," in what is given.

Language arts is "simple grammar, what they need for everyday life." The language arts teacher says, "They should learn to speak properly, to write business letters and thank-you letters, and to understand what nouns and verbs and simple subjects are." Here, as well, actual work is to choose the right answers, to understand what is given. The teacher often says, "Please read the next sentence and then I'll question you about it." One teacher said in some exasperation to a boy who was fooling around in class, "If you don't know the answers to the questions I ask, then you can't stay in this *class!* [pause] You *never* know the answers to the questions I ask, and it's not fair to me-and certainly not to you!"

Most lessons are based on the textbook. This does not involve a critical perspective on what is given there. For example, a critical perspective in social studies is perceived as dangerous by these teachers because it may lead to controversial topics; the parents might complain. The children, however, are often curious especially in social studies. Their questions are tolerated and usually answered perfunctorily. But after a few minutes the teacher will say, "All right, we're not going any farther. Please open your social studies workbook." While the teachers spend a lot of time explaining and expanding on what the textbooks say, there is little attempt to analyze how or why things happen, or to give thought to how pieces of a culture, or, say, a system of numbers or elements of a language fit together or can be analyzed. What has happened in the past and what exists now may not be equitable or fair, but (shrug) that is the way things are and one does not confront such matters in school. For example, in social studies after a child is called on to read a passage about the pilgrims, the teacher summarizes the paragraph and then says, "So you can see how strict they were about everything." A child asks, "Why?" "Well, because they felt that if you weren't busy you'd get into trouble." Another child asks, "Is it true that they burned women at the stake?" The teacher says, "Yes, if a woman did anything strange, they hanged them. [*sic*] What would a woman do, do you think, to make them burn them? [*sic*] See if you can come up with better answers than my other [social studies] class." Several children offer suggestions, to which the teacher nods but does not comment. Then she says, "Okay, good," and calls on the next child to read.

Work tasks do not usually request creativity. Serious attention is rarely given in school work on *how* the children develop or express their own feelings and ideas, either linguistically or in graphic form. On the occasions when creativity or self-expression is requested, it is peripheral to the main activity or it is "enriched" or "for fun." During a lesson on what similes are, for example, the teacher explains what they are, puts several on the board, gives some other examples herself, and then asks the children if they can "make some up." She calls on three children who give similes, two of which are actually in the book they have open before them. The teacher does not comment on this and then asks several others to choose similes from the list of phrases in the book. Several do so correctly, and she says, "Oh good! You're picking them out! See how good we are?" Their homework is to pick out the rest of the similes from the list.

Creativity is not often requested in social studies and science projects, either. Social studies projects, for example, are given with directions to "find information on your topic" and write it up. The children are not supposed to copy but to "put it in your own words." Although a number of the projects subsequently went beyond the teacher's direction to find information and had quite expressive covers and inside illustrations, the teacher's evaluative comments had to do with the amount of information, whether they had "copied," and if their work was neat.

The style of control of the three fifth-grade teachers observed in this school varied from somewhat easygoing to strict, but in contrast to the working-class schools, the teachers' decisions were usually based on external rules and regulations—for example, on criteria that were known or available to the children. Thus, the teachers always honor the bells for changing classes, and they usually evaluate children's work by what is in the textbooks and answer booklets.

There is little excitement in schoolwork for the children, and the assignments are perceived as having little to do with their interests and feelings. As one child said, what you do is "store facts up in your head like cold storage – until you need it later for a test or your job." Thus, doing well is important because there are thought to be *other* likely rewards: a good job or college.[10]

AFFLUENT PROFESSIONAL SCHOOL

In the affluent professional school, work is creative activity carried out independently. The students are continually asked to express and apply ideas and concepts. Work involves individual thought and expressiveness, expansion and illustration of ideas, and choice of appropriate method and material. (The class is not considered an open classroom, and the principal explained that because of the large number of discipline problems in the fifth grade this year they did not departmentalize. The teacher who agreed to take part in the study said she is "more structured this year than she usually is.) The products of work in this class are often written stories, editorials and essays, or representations of ideas in mural, graph, or craft form. The products of work should not be like anybody else's and should show individuality. They should exhibit good design, and (this is important) they must also fit empirical reality. The relatively few rules to be followed regarding work are usually criteria for, or limits on, individual activity. One's product is usually evaluated for the quality of its expression and for the appropriateness of its conception to the task. In many cases, one's own satisfaction with the product is an important criterion for its evaluation. When right answers are called for, as in commercial materials like SRA (Science Research Associates) and math, it is important that the children decide on an answer as a result of thinking about the idea involved in what they're being asked to do. Teacher's hints are to "think about it some more."

The following activities are illustrative. The class takes home a sheet requesting each child's parents to fill in the number of cars they have, the number of television sets, refrigerators, games, or rooms in the house, and so on. Each child is to figure the average number of a type of possession owned by the fifth grade. Each child must compile the "data" from all the sheets. A calculator is available in the classroom to do the mechanics of finding the average. Some children decide to send sheets to the fourth-grade families for comparison. Their work should be "verified" by a classmate before it is handed in.

Each child and his or her family has made a geoboard. The teacher asks the class to get their geoboards from the side cabinet, to take a handful of rubber bands, and then to listen to what she would like them to do. She says, "I would like you to design a figure and then find the perimeter and area. When you have it, check with your neighbor. After you've done that, please transfer it to graph paper and tomorrow I'll ask you to make up a question about it for someone. When you hand it in, please let me know whose it is and who verified it. Then I have something else for you to do that's really fun. [pause] Find the average number of chocolate chips in three cookies. I'll give you three cookies, and you'll have to *eat* your way through, I'm afraid!" Then she goes around the room and gives help, suggestions, praise, and admonitions that they are getting noisy. They work sitting, or standing up at their desks, at benches in the back, or on the floor. A child hands the teacher his paper and she comments, "I'm not accepting this paper. Do a better design." To another child she says, "That's fantastic! But you'll never find the area. Why don't you draw a figure inside [the big one] and subtract to get the area?"

The school district requires the fifth grade to study ancient civilization (in particular, Egypt, Athens, and Sumer). In this classroom, the emphasis is on illustrating and re-creating the culture of the people of ancient times. The following are typical activities: the children made an 8mm film on Egypt, which one of the parents edited. A girl in the class wrote the script, and the class acted it out. They put the sound on themselves. They read stories of those days. They wrote essays and stories depicting the lives of the people and the societal and occupational divisions. They chose from a list of projects, all of which involved graphical presentations of ideas: for example. "Make a mural depicting the division of labor in Egyptian society."

Each wrote and exchanged a letter in hieroglyphics with a fifth grader in another class, and they also exchanged stories they wrote in cuneiform. They made a scroll and singed the edges so it looked authentic. They each chose an occupation and made an Egyptian plaque representing that occupation, simulating the appropriate Egyptian design. They carved their design on a cylinder of wax, pressed the wax into clay, and then baked the clay. Although one girl did not choose an occupation but carved instead a series of gods and slaves, the teacher said, "That's all right, Amber, it's beautiful." As they were working the teacher said, "Don't cut into your clay until you're satisfied with your design."

Social studies also involves almost daily presentation by the children of some event from the news. The teacher's questions ask the children to expand what they say, to give more details, and to be more specific. Occasionally she adds some remarks to help them see connections between events.

The emphasis on expressing and illustrating ideas in social studies is accompanied in language arts by an emphasis on creative writing. Each child wrote a rebus story for a first grader whom they had interviewed to see what kind of story the child liked best. They wrote editorials on pending decisions by the school board and radio plays, some of which were read over the school intercom from the office and one of which was performed in the auditorium. There is no language arts textbook because, the teacher said, "The principal wants us to be creative." There is not much grammar, but there is punctuation. One morning when the observer arrived, the class was doing a punctuation ditto. The teacher later apologized for using the ditto. "It's just for review," she said. "I don't teach punctuation that way. We use their language." The ditto had three unambiguous rules for where to put commas in a sentence. As the teacher was going around to help the children with the ditto, she repeated several times, "where you put commas depends on how you say the sentence; it depends on the situation and what you want to say. Several weeks later the observer saw another punctuation activity. The teacher had printed a five-paragraph story on an oak tag and then cut it into phrases. She read the whole story to the class from the book, then passed out the phrases. The group had to decide how the phrases could best be put together again. (They arranged the phrases on the floor.) The point was not to replicate the story, although that was not irrelevant, but to "decide what you think the best way is." Punctuation marks on cardboard pieces were then handed out, and the children discussed and then decided what mark was best at each place they thought one was needed. At the end of each paragraph the teacher asked, "Are you satisfied with the way the paragraphs are now? Read it to yourself and see how it sounds." Then she read the original story again, and they compared the two.

Describing her goals in science to the investigator, the teacher said, "We use ESS (Elementary Science Study). It's very good because it gives a hands-on experience—so they can make *sense* out of it. It doesn't matter whether it [what they find] is right or wrong. I bring them together and there's value in discussing their ideas."

The products of work in this class are often highly valued by the children and the teacher. In fact, this was the only school in which the investigator was not allowed to take original pieces of the children's work for her files. If the work was small enough, however, and was on paper, the investigator could duplicate it on the copying machine in the office.

The teacher's attempt to control the class involves constant negotiation. She does not give direct orders unless she is angry because the children have been too noisy. Normally, she tries to get them to foresee the consequences of their actions and to decide accordingly. For example, lining them up to go see a play written by the sixth graders, she says, "I presume you're lined up by someone with whom you want to sit. I hope you're lined up by someone you won't get in trouble with." . . .

One of the few rules governing the children's movement is that no more than three children may be out of the room at once. There is a school rule that anyone can go to the library at any time to get a book. In the fifth grade I observed, they sign their name on the chalkboard and leave. There are no passes. Finally, the children have a fair amount of officially sanctioned say over what happens in the class. For example, they often negotiate what work is to be done. If the teacher wants to move on to the next subject, but the children say they are not ready, they want to work on their present projects some *more*, she very often lets them do it.

EXECUTIVE ELITE SCHOOL

In the executive elite school, work is developing one's analytical intellectual powers. Children are continually asked to reason through a problem, to produce intellectual products that are both logically sound and of top academic quality. A primary goal of thought is to conceptualize rules by which elements may fit together in systems and then to apply these rules in solving a problem. Schoolwork helps one to achieve, to excel, to prepare for life.

The following are illustrative. The math teacher teaches area and perimeter by having the children derive formulas for each. First she helps them, through discussion at the board, to arrive at A=WXL as a formula (not *the* formula) for area. After discussing several, she says, "Can anyone make up a formula for perimeter? Can you figure that out yourselves? [pause] Knowing what we know, can we think of a formula?" She works out three children's suggestions at the board, saying to two, "Yes, that's a good one," and then asks the class if they can think of any more. No one volunteers. To prod them, she says, "If you use rules and good reasoning, you get many ways. Chris, can you think up a formula?"

She discusses two-digit division with the children as a decision-making process. Presenting a new type of problem to them, she asks, "What's the *first* decision you'd make if presented with this kind of example? What is the first thing you'd *think*? Craig?" Craig says, "To find my first partial quotient." She responds, "Yes, that would be your first decision. How would you do that?" Craig explains, and then the teacher says, "OK, we'll see how that works for you." The class tries his way. Subsequently, she comments on the merits and shortcomings of several other children's decisions. Later, she tells the investigator that her goals in math are to develop their reasoning and mathematical thinking and that, unfortunately, "there's no time for manipulables."

While right answers are important in math, they are not "given" by the book or by the teacher but may be challenged by the children. Going over some problems in late September the teacher says, "Raise your hand if you do not agree." A child says, "I don't agree with sixty-four." The teacher responds, "OK, there's a question about sixty-four. [to class] Please check it. Owen, they're disagreeing with you. Kristen, they're checking yours." The teacher emphasized this repeatedly during September and October with statements like "Don't be afraid to say you disagree. In the last [math] class, somebody disagreed, and they were right. Before you disagree, check yours, and if you still think we're wrong, then we'll check it out." By Thanksgiving, the children did not often speak in terms of right and wrong math problems but of whether they agreed with the answer that had been given.

There are complicated math mimeos with many word problems. Whenever they go over the examples, they discuss how each child has set up the problem. The children must explain it precisely. On one occasion the teacher said, "I'm more—just as interested in *how* you set up the problem as in what answer you find. If you set up a problem in a good way, the answer is *easy* to find.

Social studies work is most often reading and discussion of concepts and independent research. There are only occasional artistic, expressive, or illustrative projects. Ancient Athens and Sumer are, rather, societies to analyze. The following questions are typical of those that guide the children's independent research. "What mistakes did Pericles make after the war?" "What mistakes did the citizens of Athens make?" "What are the elements of a civilization?" "How did Greece build an economic empire?" "Compare the way Athens chose its leaders with the way we choose ours." Occasionally the children are asked to make up sample questions for their social studies tests. On an occasion when the investigator was present, the social studies teacher rejected a child's question by saying, "That's just fact. If I asked you that question on a test, you'd complain it was just memory! Good questions ask for concepts."

In social studies—but also in reading, science, and health—the teachers initiate classroom discussions of current social issues and problems. These discussions occurred on every one of the investigator's visits, and a teacher told me, "These children's opinions are important – it's important that they learn to reason things through." The classroom discussions always struck the observer as quite realistic and analytical, dealing with concrete social issues like the following: "Why do workers strike?" "Is that right or wrong?" "Why do we have inflation, and what can be done to stop it?" "Why do companies put chemicals in food when the natural ingredients are available?" and so on. Usually the children did not have to be prodded to give their opinions. In fact, their statements and the interchanges between them struck the observer as quite sophisticated conceptually and verbally, and well-informed. Occasionally the teachers would prod with statements such as, "Even if you don't know [the answers], if you think logically about it, you can figure it out." And "I'm asking you [these] questions to help you think this through."

Language arts emphasizes language as a complex system, one that should be mastered. The children are asked to diagram sentences of complex grammatical construction, to memorize irregular verb conjugations (he lay, he has lain, and so on . . .), and to use the proper participles, conjunctions, and interjections in their speech. The teacher (the same one who teaches social studies) told them, "It is not enough to get these right on tests; you must use what you learn [in grammar classes] in your written and oral work. I will grade you on that."

Most writing assignments are either research reports and essays for social studies or experiment analyses and write-ups for science. There is only an occasional story or other "creative writing" assignment. On the occasion observed by the investigator (the writing of a Halloween story), the points the teacher stressed in preparing the children to write involved the structural aspects of a story rather than the expression of feelings or other ideas. The teacher showed them a filmstrip, "The Seven Parts of a Story," and lectured them on plot development, mood setting, character development, consistency, and the use of a logical or appropriate ending. The stories they subsequently wrote were, in fact, well-structured, but many were also personal and expressive. The teacher's evaluative comments, however, did not refer to the expressiveness or artistry but were all directed toward whether they had "developed" the story well.

Language arts work also involved a large amount of practice in presentation of the self and in managing situations where the child was expected to be in charge. For example, there was a series of assignments in which each child had to be a "student teacher." The child had to plan a lesson in grammar, outlining, punctuation, or other language arts topic and explain the concept to the class. Each child was to prepare a worksheet or game and a homework assignment as well. After each presentation, the teacher and other children gave a critical appraisal of the "student teacher's" performance. Their criteria were: whether the student spoke clearly, whether the lesson was interesting, whether the student made any mistakes, and whether he or she kept control of the class. On an occasion when a child did not maintain control, the teacher said, "When you're up there, you have authority and you have to use it. I'll back you up."

The executive elite school is the only school where bells do not demarcate the periods of time. The two fifth-grade teachers were very strict about changing classes on schedule, however, as specific plans for each session had been made. The teachers attempted to keep tight control over the children during lessons, and the children were sometimes flippant, boisterous, and occasionally rude. However, the children may be brought into line by reminding them that "It is up to you." "You must control yourself," "you are responsible for your work," you must "set your own priorities." One teacher told a child, "You are the only driver of your car-and only you can regulate your speed." A new teacher complained to the observer that she had thought "these children" would have more control.

While strict attention to the lesson at hand is required, the teachers make relatively little attempt to regulate the movement of the children at other times. For example, except for the kindergartners the children in this school do not have to wait for the bell to ring in the morning; they may go to their classroom when they arrive at school. Fifth graders often came early to read, to finish work, or to catch up. After the first two months of school, the fifth-grade teachers did not line the children up to change classes or to go to gym, and so on, but, when the children were ready and quiet, they were told they could go—sometimes without the teachers.

In the classroom, the children could get materials when they needed them and took what they needed from closets and from the teacher's desk. They were in charge of the office at lunchtime. During class they did not have to sign out or ask permission to leave the room; they just got up and left. Because of the pressure to get work done, however, they did not leave the room very often. The teachers were very polite to the children, and the investigator heard no sarcasm, no nasty remarks, and few direct orders. The teachers never called the children "honey" or "dear" but always called them by name. The teachers were expected to be available before school, after school, and for part of their lunchtime to provide extra help if needed.

The foregoing analysis of differences in schoolwork in contrasting social class contexts suggests the following conclusion: the "hidden curriculum" of schoolwork is tacit preparation for relating to the process of production in a particular way. Differing curricular, pedagogical, and pupil evaluation practices emphasize different cognitive and behavioral skills in each social setting and thus contribute to the development in the children of certain potential relationships to physical and symbolic capital,[11] to authority, and to the process of work. School experience, in the sample of schools discussed here, differed qualitatively by social class. These differences may not only contribute to the development in the children in each social class of certain types of economically significant relationships and not others but would thereby help to reproduce this system of relations in society. In the contribution to the reproduction of unequal social relations lies a theoretical meaning and social consequence of classroom practice.

The identification of different emphases in classrooms in a sample of contrasting social class contexts implies that further research should be conducted in a large number of schools to investigate the types of work tasks and interactions in each to see if they differ in the ways discussed here and to see if similar potential relationships are uncovered. Such research could have as a product the further elucidation of complex but not readily apparent connections between everyday activity in schools and classrooms and the unequal structure of economic relationships in which we work and live.

NOTES

1. S. Bowles and H. Gintes, *Schooling in Capitalist America: Educational Reform and the Contradictions of Economic Life* (New York: Basic Books, 1976). [Author's note]
2. B. Bernstein, *Class, Codes and Control, Vol. 3. Towards a Theory of Educational Transmission*, 2d ed. (London: Routledge & Kegan Paul, 1977); P. Bourdieu and J. Passeron, *Reproduction in Education, Society and Culture* (Beverly Hills, Calif.: Sage, 1977); M.W. Apple, *Ideology and Curriculum* (Boston: Routledge Kegan Paul, 1979). [Author's note]
3. But see, in a related vein, M.W. Apple and N. King, "What Do Schools Teach?" *Curriculum Inquiry* 6 (1977); 341–58; R.C. Rist, *The Urban School: A Factory for Failure* (Cambridge, Mass.: MIT Press, 1973). [Author's note]
4. *ethnographical:* Based on an anthropological study of cultures or subcultures-the "cultures" in this case being the five schools being observed.
5. The U.S. Bureau of the Census defines *poverty* for a nonfarm family of four as a yearly income of $6,191 a year or less. U.S. Bureau of the Census, *Statistical Abstract of the United States: 1978* (Washington, D.C.: U.S. Government Printing Office, 1978), p. 465, table 754. [Author's note]
6. U.S. Bureau of the Census, "Money Income in 1977 of Families and Persons in the United States," *Current Population Reports* Series P-60, no. 118 (Washington, D.C.: U.S. Government Printing Office, 1978), p. 2, table A. [Author's note]

7. Ibid. [Author's note]

8. This figure is an estimate. According to the Bureau of the Census, only 2.6 percent of families in the United States have money income of $50,000 or over. U.S. Bureau of the Census, *Current Population Reports* Series P-60. For figures on income at these higher levels, see J.D. Smith and S. Franklin, "The Concentration of Personal Wealth, 1922-1969," *American Economic Review* 64 (1974): 162–67. [Author's note]

9. Smith and Franklin, "The Concentration of Personal Wealth." [Author's note]

10. A dominant feeling expressed directly and indirectly by teachers in this school, was boredom with their work. They did, however, in contrast to the working-class schools, almost always carry out lessons during class times. [Author's note]

11. *physical and symbolic capital:* Elsewhere Anyon defines *capital* as "property that is used to produce profit, interest, or rent": she defines *symbolic capital* as the knowledge and skills that "may yield social and cultural power."

The Puzzling Puzzles of Harry Harlow and Edward Deci

Daniel H. Pink

In the middle of the last century, two young scientists conducted experiments that should have changed the world—but did not.

Harry F. Harlow was a professor of psychology at the University of Wisconsin who, in the 1940s, established one of the world's first laboratories for studying primate behavior. One day in 1949, Harlow and two colleagues gathered eight rhesus monkeys for a two-week experiment on learning. The researchers devised a simple mechanical puzzle like the one pictured on the next page. Solving it required three steps: pull out the vertical pin, undo the hook, and lift the hinged cover. Pretty easy for you and me, far more challenging for a thirteen-pound lab monkey.

The experimenters placed the puzzles in the monkeys' cages to observe how they reacted—and to prepare them for tests of their problem-solving prowess at the end of the two weeks. But almost immediately, something strange happened. Unbidden by any outside urging and unprompted by the experimenters, the monkeys began playing with the puzzles with focus, determination, and what looked like enjoyment. And in short order, they began figuring out how the contraptions worked. By the time Harlow tested the monkeys on days 13 and 14 of the experiment, the primates had become quite adept. They solved the puzzles frequently and quickly; two-thirds of the time they cracked the code in less than sixty seconds.

Now, this was a bit odd. Nobody had taught the monkeys how to remove the pin, slide the hook, and open the cover. Nobody had rewarded them with food, affection, or even quiet applause when they succeeded. And that ran counter to the accepted notions of how primates—including the bigger-brained, less hairy primates known as human beings—behaved.

Scientists then knew that two main drives powered behavior. The first was the biological drive. Humans and other animals are to sate their hunger, drank to quench their thirst, and copulated to satisfy their carnal urges. But that wasn't happening here. "Solution did not lead to food, water, or sex gratification," Harlow reported.[1]

But the only other known drive also failed to explain the monkeys' peculiar behavior. If biological motivations came from within, this second drive came from without—the rewards and punishments the environment delivered for behaving in certain ways. This was certainly true for humans, who responded exquisitely to such external forces. If you promised to raise our pay, we'd work harder. If you held out the prospect of getting an A on the test, we'd study longer. If you threatened to dock us for showing up late or for incorrectly completing a form, we'd arrive on time and tick every box. But that didn't account for the monkeys' actions either. As Harlow wrote, and you can almost hear him scratching his head, "The behavior obtained in this investigation poses some interesting questions for motivation theory, since significant learning was attained and efficient performance maintained without resort to special or extrinsic incentives."

What else could it be?

To answer the question, Harlow offered a novel theory—what amounted to a *third* drive: "The performance of the task," he said, "provided intrinsic reward." The monkeys solved the puzzles simply because they found it gratifying to solve puzzles. They enjoyed it. The joy of the task was its own reward.

If this notion was radical, what happened next only deepened the confusion and controversy. Perhaps this newly discovered drive—Harlow eventually called it "intrinsic motivation"—was real. But surely it was subordinate to the other two drives. If the monkeys were rewarded—with raisins!—for solving the puzzles, they'd no doubt perform even better. Yet when Harlow tested that approach, the monkeys actually made *more* errors and solved the puzzles *less* frequently. "Introduction of food in the present experiment," Harlow wrote, "served to disrupt performance, a phenomenon not reported in the literature."

Now, this was *really* odd. In scientific terms, it was akin to rolling a steel ball down an inclined plane to measure its velocity—only to watch the ball float into the air instead. It suggested that our understanding of the gravitational pulls on our behavior was inadequate—that what we thought were fixed laws had plenty of loopholes. Harlow emphasized the "strength and persistence" of the monkeys' drive to complete the puzzles. Then he noted:

> It would appear that this drive . . . may be as basic and strong as the [other] drives. Furthermore, there is some reason to believe that [it] can be as efficient in facilitating learning.[2]

At the time, however, the prevailing two drives held a tight grip on scientific thinking. So Harlow sounded the alarm. He urged scientists to "close down large sections of our theoretical junkyard" and offer fresher, more accurate accounts of human behavior.[3] He warned that our explanation of why we did what we did was incomplete. He said that to truly understand the human condition, we had to take account of this third drive.

Then he pretty much dropped the whole idea.

Rather than battle the establishment and begin offering a more complete view of motivation, Harlow abandoned this contentious line of research and later became famous for studies on the science of affection.[4] His notion of this third drive bounced around the psychological literature, but it remained on the periphery—of behavioral science and of our understanding of ourselves. It would be two decades before another scientist picked up the thread that Harlow had so provocatively left on that Wisconsin laboratory table.

In the summer of 1969, Edward Deci was a Carnegie Mellon University psychology graduate student in search of a dissertation topic. Deci, who had already earned an MBA from Wharton, was intrigued by motivation but suspected that scholars and businesspeople had misunderstood it. So, tearing a page from the Harlow playbook, he set out to study the topic with the help of a puzzle.

Deci chose the Soma puzzle cube, a then popular Parker Brothers offering that, thanks to YouTube, retains something of a cult following today. The puzzle, shown below, consists of seven plastic pieces—six comprising four one-inch cubes, one comprising three one-inch cubes. Players can assemble the seven pieces into a few million possible combinations—from abstract shapes to recognizable objects.

For the study, Deci divided participants, male and female university students, into an experimental group (what I'll call Group A) and a control group (what I'll call Group B). Each participated in three one-hour sessions held on consecutive days.

Here's how the sessions worked: Each participant entered a room and sat at a table on top of which were the seven Soma puzzle pieces, drawings of three puzzle configurations, and copies of *Time*, *The New Yorker*, and *Playboy*. (Hey, it was 1969.) Deci sat on the opposite end of the table to explain the instructions and to time performance with a stopwatch.

In the first session, members of both groups had to assemble the Soma pieces to replicate the configurations before them. In the second session, they did the same thing with different drawings—only this time Deci told Group A that they'd be paid $1 (the equivalent of nearly $6 today) for every configuration they successfully reproduced. Group B, meanwhile, got new drawings but no pay. Finally, in the third session, both groups received new drawings and had to reproduce them for no compensation, just as in session one. (See the table below.)

HOW THE TWO GROUPS WERE TREATED

	Day 1	Day 2	Day 3
Group A	*No reward*	*Reward*	*No reward*
Group B	*No reward*	*No reward*	*No reward*

The twist came midway through each session. After a participant had assembled the Soma puzzle pieces to match two of the three drawings, Deci halted the proceedings. He said that he was going to give them a fourth drawing—but to choose the right one, he needed to feed their completion times into a computer. And—this being the late 1960s, when room-straddling mainframes were the norm and desktop PCs were still a decade away—that meant he had to leave for a little while.

On the way out, he said, "I shall be gone only a few minutes, you may do whatever you like while I'm gone." But Deci wasn't really plugging numbers into an ancient teletype. Instead, he walked to an adjoining room connected to the experiment room by a one-way window. Then, for exactly eight minutes, he watched what people did when left alone. Did they continue fiddling with the puzzle, perhaps attempting to reproduce the third drawing? Or did they do something else—page through the magazines, check out the centerfold, stare into space, catch a quick nap?

In the first session, not surprisingly, there wasn't much difference between what the Group A and Group B participants did during that secretly watched eight-minute free-choice period. Both continued playing with the puzzle, on average, for between three and a half and four minutes, suggesting they found it at least somewhat interesting.

On the second day, during which Group A participants were paid for each successful configuration and Group B participants were not, the unpaid group behaved mostly as they had during the first free-choice period. But the paid group suddenly got *really* interested in Soma puzzles. On average, the people in Group A spent more than five minutes messing with the puzzle, perhaps getting a head start on that third challenge or gearing up for the chance to earn some beer money when Deci returned. This makes intuitive sense, right? It's consistent with what we believe about motivation: Reward me and I'll work harder.

Yet what happened on the third day confirmed Deci's own suspicions about the peculiar workings of motivation—and gently called into question a guiding premise of modern life. This time, Deci told the participants in Group A that there was only enough money to pay them for one day and that this third session would therefore be unpaid. Then things unfolded just as before—two puzzles, followed by Deci's interruption.

During the ensuing eight-minute free-choice period, the subjects in the never-been-paid Group B actually played with the puzzle for a little longer than they had in previous sessions. Maybe they were becoming ever more engaged; maybe it was just a statistical quirk. But the subjects in Group A, who previously had been paid, responded differently. They now spent significantly *less* time playing with the puzzle—not only about two minutes less than during their paid session, but about a full minute less than in the first session when they initially encountered, and obviously enjoyed, the puzzles.

In an echo of what Harlow discovered two decades earlier, Deci revealed that human motivation seemed to operate by laws that ran counter to what most scientists and citizens believed. From the office to the playing field, we knew what got people going. Rewards—especially cold, hard cash—intensified interest and enhanced performance. What Deci found, and then confirmed in two additional studies he conducted shortly thereafter, was almost the opposite. "When money is used as an external reward for some activity, the subjects lose intrinsic interest for the activity," he wrote.[5] Rewards can deliver a short-term boost—just as a jolt of caffeine can keep you cranking for a few more hours. But the effect wears off—and, worse, can reduce a person's longer-term motivation to continue the project.

Human beings, Deci said, have an "inherent tendency to seek out novelty and challenges, to extend and exercise their capacities, to explore, and to learn." But this third drive was more fragile than the other two; it needed the right environment to survive. "One who is interested in developing and enhancing intrinsic motivation in children, employees, students, etc., should not concentrate on external-control systems such as monetary rewards," he wrote in a follow-up paper.[6] Thus began what for Deci became a lifelong quest to rethink why we do what we do—a pursuit that sometimes put him at odds with fellow psychologists, got him fired from a business school, and challenged the operating assumptions of organizations everywhere.

"It was controversial," Deci told me one spring morning forty years after the Soma experiments. "Nobody was expecting rewards would have a negative effect."

This is a book about motivation. I will show that much of what we believe about the subject just isn't so—and that the insights that Harlow and Deci began uncovering a few decades ago come much closer to the truth. The problem is that most businesses haven't caught up to this new understanding of what motivates us. Too many organizations—not just companies, but governments and nonprofits as well—still operate from assumptions about human potential and individual performance that are outdated, unexamined, and rooted more in folklore than in science. They continue to pursue practices such as short-term incentive plans and pay-for-performance schemes in the face of mounting evidence that such measures usually don't work and often do harm. Worse, these practices have infiltrated our schools, where we ply our future workforce with iPods, cash, and pizza coupons to "incentivize" them to learn. Something has gone wrong.

The good news is that the solution stands before us—in the work of a band of behavioral scientists who have carried on the pioneering efforts of Harlow and Deci and whose quiet work over she last half-century offers us a more dynamic view of human motivation. For too long, there's been a mismatch between what science knows and what business does. The goal of this book is to repair that breach.

Drive has three parts. Part One will look at the flaws in our reward-and-punishment system and propose a new way to think about motivation. How the prevailing view of motivation is becoming incompatible with many aspects of contemporary business and life. The seven reasons why carrot-and-stick extrinsic motivators often produce the opposite of what they set out to achieve. (Following that is a short addendum, that shows the special circumstances when carrots and sticks actually can be effective.) What I call "Type I" behavior, a way of thinking and an approach to business grounded in the real science of human motivation and powered by our third drive—our innate need to direct our own lives, to learn and create new things, and to do better by ourselves and our world.

Part Two will examine the three elements of Type I behavior and show how individuals and organizations are using them to improve performance and deepen satisfaction.

Part Three, the Type I Toolkit, is a comprehensive set of resources to help you create settings in which Type I behavior can flourish. Here you'll find everything from dozens of exercises to awaken motivation in yourself and others, to discussion questions for your book club, to a supershort summary of *Drive* that will help you fake your way through a cocktail party. And while this book is mostly about business, in this section I'll offer some thoughts about how to apply these concepts to education and to our lives outside of work.

But before we get down to all that, let's begin with a thought experiment, one that requires going back in time—to the days when John Major was Britain's prime minister, Barack Obama was a skinny young law professor, Internet connections were dial-up, and a blackberry was still just a fruit.

The Rise and Fall of Motivation 2.0

Imagine it's 1996. You sit down with an economist—an accomplished business school professor with a Ph.D. in economics. You say to her: "I've got a crystal ball here that can peer fifteen years into the future. I'd like to test your forecasting powers."

She's skeptical, but she decides to humor you.

"I'm going to describe two new encyclopedias—one just out, the other to be launched in a few years. You have to predict which will be more successful in 2011."

"Bring it," she says.

"The first encyclopedia comes from Microsoft. As you know, Microsoft is already a large and profitable company. And with last year's introduction of Windows 95, it is becoming an era-defining colossus. Microsoft will fund this encyclopedia. It will pay professional writers and editors to craft articles on thousands of topics. Well-compensated managers will oversee the project to ensure it's completed on budget and on time. Then Microsoft will sell the encyclopedia on CD-ROMs and later online.

"The second encyclopedia won't come from a company. It will be created by tens of thousands of people who write and edit articles for fun. These hobbyists won't need any special qualifications to participate. And nobody will be paid a dollar or a euro or a yen to write or edit articles. Participants will have to contribute their labor—sometimes twenty and thirty hours per week—for free. The encyclopedia itself, which will exist online, will also be free—no charge for anyone who wants to use it.

"Now," you say to the economist, "think forward fifteen years. According to my crystal ball, in 2011, one of these encyclopedias will be the largest and most popular in the world and the other will be defunct. Which is which?"

In 1996, I doubt you could have found a single sober economist anywhere on planet Earth who would not have picked that first model as the success. Any other conclusion would have been laughable—contrary to nearly every business principle she taught her students. It would have been like asking a zoologist who would win a 200-meter footrace between a cheetah and your brother-in-law. Not even close.

Sure, that ragtag band of volunteers might produce something. But there was no way its product could compete with an offering from a powerful profit-driven company. The incentives were all wrong. Microsoft stood to gain from the success of its product; everyone involved in the other project knew from the outset that success would earn them nothing. Most important, Microsoft's writers, editors, and managers were paid. The other project's contributors were not. In fact, it probably *cost* them money each time they performed free work instead of remunerative labor. The question was such a no-brainer that our economist wouldn't even have considered putting it on an exam for her MBA class. It was too easy.

But you know how things turned out.

On October 31, 2009, Microsoft pulled the plug on *MSN Encarta*, its disc and online encyclopedia, which had been on the market for sixteen years. Meanwhile, Wikipedia—that second model—ended up becoming the largest and most popular encyclopedia in the world. Just nine years after its inception, Wikipedia had more than 17 million articles in some 270 languages, including 3.5 million in English alone.[1]

What happened? The conventional view of human motivation has a very hard time explaining this result.

THE TRIUMPH OF CARROTS AND STICKS

Computers—whether the giant mainframes in Deci's experiments, the iMac on which I'm writing this sentence, or the mobile phone chirping in your pocket—all have operating systems. Beneath the surface of the hardware you touch and the programs you manipulate is a complex layer of software that contains the instructions, protocols, and suppositions that enable everything to function smoothly. Most of us don't think much about operating systems. We notice them only when they start failing—when the hardware and software they're supposed to manage grow too large and complicated for the current operating system to handle. Then our computer starts crashing. We complain. And smart software developers, who've always been tinkering with pieces of the program, sit down to write a fundamentally better one—an upgrade.

Societies also have operating systems. The laws, social customs, and economic arrangements that we encounter each day sit atop a layer of instructions, protocols, and suppositions about how the world works. And much of our societal operating system consists of a set of assumptions about human behavior.

In our very early days—I mean *very* early days, say, fifty thousand years ago—the underlying assumption about human behavior was simple and true.

We were trying to survive. From roaming the savannah to gather food to scrambling for the bushes when a saber-toothed tiger approached, that drive guided most of our behavior. Call this early operating system Motivation 1.0. It wasn't especially elegant, nor was it much different from those of rhesus monkeys, giant apes, or many other animals. But it served us nicely. It worked well. Until it didn't.

As humans formed more complex societies, bumping up against strangers and needing to cooperate in order to get things done, an operating system based purely on the biological drive was inadequate. In fact, sometimes we needed ways to *restrain* this drive—to prevent me from swiping your dinner and you from stealing my spouse. And so in a feat of remarkable cultural engineering, we slowly replaced the existing version with one more compatible with how we'd now begun working and living.

At the core of this new and improved operating system was a revised and more accurate assumption: Humans are more than the sum of our biological urges. That first drive still mattered—no doubt about that—but it didn't fully account for who we are. We also had a second drive—to seek reward and avoid punishment more broadly. And it was from this insight that a new operating system—call it Motivation 2.0—arose. (Of course, other animals also respond to rewards and punishments, but only humans have proved able to channel this drive to develop everything from contract law to convenience stores.)

Harnessing this second drive has been essential to economic progress around the world, especially during the last two centuries. Consider the Industrial Revolution. Technological developments—steam engines, railroads, widespread electricity—played a crucial role in fostering the growth of industry. But so did less tangible innovations—in particular, the work of an American engineer named Frederick Winslow Taylor. In the early 1900s, Taylor, who believed businesses were being run in an inefficient, haphazard way, developed what he called "scientific management." His invention was a form of "software" expertly crafted to run atop the Motivation 2.0 platform. And it was widely and quickly adopted.

Workers, this approach held, were like parts in a complicated machine. If they did the right work in the right way at the right time, the machine would function smoothly. And to ensure that happened, you simply rewarded the behavior you sought and punished the behavior you discouraged. People would respond rationally to these external forces—these extrinsic motivators—and both they and the system itself would flourish. We tend to think that coal and oil have powered economic development. But in some sense, the engine of commerce has been fueled equally by carrots and sticks.

The Motivation 2.0 operating system has endured for a very long time. Indeed, it is so deeply embedded in our lives that most of us scarcely recognize that it exists. For as long as any of us can remember, we've configured our organizations and constructed our lives around its bedrock assumption: The way to improve performance, increase productivity, and encourage excellence is to reward the good and punish the bad.

Despite its greater sophistication and higher aspirations, Motivation 2.0 still wasn't exactly ennobling. It suggested that, in the end, human beings aren't much different from livestock—that the way to get us moving in the right direction is by dangling a crunchier carrot or wielding a sharper stick. But what this operating system lacked in enlightenment, it made up for in effectiveness. It worked well—extremely well. Until it didn't.

As the twentieth century progressed, as economies grew still more complex, and as the people in them had to deploy new, more sophisticated skills, the Motivation 2.0 approach encountered some resistance. In the 1950s, Abraham Maslow, a former student of Harry Harlow's at the University of Wisconsin, developed the field of humanistic psychology, which questioned the belief that human behavior was purely the ratlike seeking of positive stimuli and avoidance of negative stimuli. In 1960, MIT management professor Douglas McGregor imported some of Maslow's ideas to the business world. McGregor challenged the presumption that humans are fundamentally inert—that absent external rewards and punishments, we wouldn't do much. People have other, higher drives, he said. And these drives could benefit businesses if managers and business leaders respected them.

In the same era, and in a similar spirit, Frederick Herzberg, a psychologist-turned-management professor, proposed that two key factors determined how people fared on the job. The first were "hygiene" factors—extrinsic rewards such as pay, working conditions, and job security. Their absence created dissatisfaction, but their presence didn't lead to job satisfaction. The second were "motivators"—things like enjoyment of the work itself, genuine achievement, and personal growth. These internal desires were what really boosted both satisfaction and performance and were where managers ought to focus their attention. Meanwhile, W. Edwards Deming, whose work was embraced in Japan with the same ferocity with which it was ignored in the U.S., argued that the route to quality and continual improvement was intrinsic motivation rather than extrinsic motivators like bonuses, incentive plans, and forced rankings. Thanks in part to McGregor, Herzberg, and Deming, companies evolved a bit. Dress codes relaxed, schedules became more flexible. Many organizations looked for ways to grant employees greater autonomy and to help them grow. These refinements repaired some weaknesses, but they amounted to a modest improvement rather than a thorough upgrade—Motivation 2.1.

And so this general approach remained intact—because it was, after all, easy to understand, simple to monitor, and straightforward to enforce. But in the first ten years of this century—a period of truly staggering underachievement in business, technology, and social progress—we've discovered that this sturdy, old operating system doesn't work nearly as well. It crashes—often and unpredictably. It forces people to devise workarounds to bypass its flaws. Most of all, it is proving incompatible with many aspects of contemporary business. And if we examine those incompatibility problems closely, we'll realize that modest updates—a patch here or there—will not solve the problem. What we need is a full-scale upgrade.

THREE INCOMPATIBILITY PROBLEMS

Motivation 2.0 still serves some purposes well. It's just deeply unreliable. Sometimes it works; many times it doesn't. And understanding its defects will help determine which parts to keep and which to discard as we fashion an upgrade. The glitches fall into three broad categories. Our current operating system has become far less compatible with, and at times downright antagonistic to: how we *organize* what we do; how we *think about* what we do; and how we *do* what we do.

HOW WE ORGANIZE WHAT WE DO

Go back to that encyclopedic showdown between Microsoft and Wikipedia. The assumptions at the heart of Motivation 2.0 suggest that such a result shouldn't even be possible. Wikipedia's triumph seems to defy the laws of behavioral physics.

Now, if this all-volunteer, all-amateur encyclopedia were the only instance of its kind, we might dismiss it as an aberration, an exception that proves the rule. But it's not. Instead, Wikipedia represents the most powerful new business model of the twenty-first century: open source.

Fire up your home computer, for example. When you visit the Web to check the weather forecast or order some sneakers, you might be using Firefox, a free open-source Web browser created almost exclusively by volunteers around the world. Unpaid laborers who give away their product? That couldn't be sustainable. The incentives are all wrong. Yet Firefox now has more than 350 million users.

Or walk into the IT department of a large company anywhere in the world and ask for a tour. That company's corporate computer servers could well run on Linux, software devised by an army of unpaid programmers and available for free. Linux now powers one in four corporate servers. Then ask an employee to explain how the company's website works. Humming beneath the site is probably Apache, free open-source Web server software created and maintained by a far-flung global group of volunteers. Apache's share of the corporate Web server market: 52 percent. In other words, companies that typically rely on external rewards to manage their employees run some of their most important systems with products created by nonemployees who don't seem to need such rewards.

And it's not just the tens of thousands of software projects across the globe. Today you can find: open-source cookbooks; open-source textbooks; open-source car design; open-source medical research; open-source legal briefs; open-source stock photography; open-source prosthetics; open-source credit unions; open-source cola; and for those for whom soft drinks won't suffice, open-source beer.

This new way of organizing what we do doesn't banish extrinsic rewards. People in the open-source movement haven't taken vows of poverty. For many, participation in these projects can burnish their reputations and sharpen their skills, which can enhance their earning power. Entrepreneurs have launched new, and sometimes lucrative, companies to help organizations implement and maintain open-source software applications.

But ultimately, open source depends on intrinsic motivation with the same ferocity that older business models rely on extrinsic motivation, as several scholars have shown. MIT management professor Karim Lakhani and Boston Consulting Group consultant Bob Wolf surveyed 684 open-source developers, mostly in North America and Europe, about why they participated in these projects. Lakhani and Wolf uncovered a range of motives, but they found "that enjoyment-based intrinsic motivation, namely how creative a person feels when working on the project, is the strongest and most pervasive driver."[2] A large majority of programmers, the researchers discovered, reported that they frequently reached the state of optimal challenge called "flow." Likewise, three German economists who studied open-source projects around the world found that what drives participants is "a set of predominantly intrinsic motives"—in particular, "the fun . . . of mastering the challenge of a given software problem" and the "desire to give a gift to the programmer community."[3] Motivation 2.0 has little room for these sorts of impulses.

What's more, open source is only one way people are restructuring what they do along new organizational lines and atop different motivational ground. Let's move from software code to the legal code. The laws in most developed countries permit essentially two types of business organizations—profit and nonprofit. One makes money, the other does good. And the most prominent member of that first category is the publicly held corporation—owned by shareholders and run by managers who are overseen by a board of directors. The managers and directors bear one overriding responsibility: to maximize shareholder gain. Other types of business organizations steer by the same rules of the road. In the United States, for instance, partnerships, S corporations, C corporations, limited liability companies, and other business configurations all aim toward a common end. The objective of those who run them—practically, legally, in some ways morally—is to maximize profit.

Let me give a rousing, heartfelt, and grateful cheer for these business forms and the farsighted countries that enable their citizens to create them. Without them, our lives would be infinitely less prosperous, less healthy, and less happy. But in the last few years, several people around the world have been changing the recipe and cooking up new varieties of business organizations.

For example, in April 2008, Vermont became the first U.S. state to allow a new type of business called the "low-profit limited liability company." Dubbed an L3C, this entity is a corporation—but not as we typically think of it. As one report explained, an L3C "operate[s] like a for-profit business generating at least modest profits, but its primary aim [is] to offer significant social benefits." Three other U.S. states have followed Vermont's lead.[4] An L3C in North Carolina, for instance, is buying abandoned furniture factories in the state, updating them with green technology, and leasing them back to beleaguered furniture manufacturers at a low rate. The venture hopes to make money, but its real purpose is to help revitalize a struggling region.

Meanwhile, Nobel Peace Prize winner Muhammad Yunus has begun creating what he calls "social businesses." These are companies that raise capital, develop products, and sell them in an open market but do so in the service of a larger social mission—or as he puts it, "with the profit-maximization principle replaced by the social-benefit principle." The Fourth Sector Network in the United States and Denmark is promoting "the for-benefit organization"— a hybrid that it says represents a new category of organization that is both economically self-sustaining and animated by a public purpose. One example: Mozilla, the entity that gave us Firefox, is organized as a "for-benefit" organization. And three U.S. entrepreneurs have invented the "B Corporation," a designation that requires companies to amend their bylaws so that the incentives favor long-term value and social impact instead of short-term economic gain.[5]

Neither open-source production nor previously unimagined "not only for profit" businesses are yet the norm, of course. And they won't consign the public corporation to the trash heap. But their emergence tells us something important about where we're heading. "There's a big movement out there that is not yet recognized as a movement," a lawyer who specializes in for-benefit organizations told *The New York Times*.[6] One reason could be that traditional businesses are profit maximizers, which square perfectly with Motivation 2.0. These new entities are *purpose maximizers*—which are unsuited to this older operating system because they flout its very principles.

HOW WE THINK ABOUT WHAT WE DO

When I took my first economics course back in the early 1980s, our professor—a brilliant lecturer with a Patton-like stage presence—offered an important clarification before she'd chalked her first indifference curve on the blackboard. Economics, she explained, wasn't the study of money. It was the study of behavior. In the course of a day, each of us was constantly figuring the cost and benefits of our actions and then deciding how to act. Economists studied what people did, rather than what we said, because we did what was best for us. We were rational calculators of our economic self-interest.

When I studied law a few years later, a similar idea reappeared. The newly ascendant field of "law and economics" held that precisely because we were such awesome self-interest calculators, laws and regulations often impeded, rather than permitted, sensible and just outcomes. I survived law school in no small part because I discovered the talismanic phrase and offered it on exams: "In a world of perfect information and low transaction costs, the parties will bargain to a wealth-maximizing result."

Then, about a decade later, came a curious turn of events that made me question much of what I'd worked hard, and taken on enormous debt, to learn. In 2002, the Nobel Foundation awarded its prize in economics to a guy who wasn't even an economist. And they gave him the field's highest honor largely for revealing that we *weren't* always rational calculators of our economic self-interest and that the parties often *didn't* bargain to a wealth-maximizing result. Daniel Kahneman, an American psychologist who won the Nobel Prize in economics that year for work he'd done with Israeli Amos Tversky, helped force a change in how we think about what we do. And one of the implications of this new way of thinking is that it calls into question many of the assumptions of Motivation 2.0.

Kahneman and others in the field of behavioral economics agreed with my professor that economics was the study of human economic behavior. They just believed that we'd placed too much emphasis on the *economic* and not enough on the *human*. That hyperrational calculator-brained person wasn't real. He was a convenient fiction.

Play a game with me and I'll try to illustrate the point. Suppose somebody gives me ten dollars and tells me to share it—some, all, or none—with you. If you accept my offer, we both get to keep the money. If you reject it, neither of us gets anything. If I offered you six dollars (keeping four for myself), would you take it? Almost certainly. If I offered you five, you'd probably take that, too. But what if I offered you two dollars? Would you take it? In an experiment replicated around the world, most people rejected offers of two dollars and below.[7] That makes no sense in terms of wealth maximization. If you take my offer of two dollars, you're two dollars richer. If you reject it, you get nothing. Your cognitive calculator knows two is greater than zero—but because you're a human being, your notions of fair play or your desire for revenge or your simple irritation overrides it.

In real life our behavior is far more complex than the textbook allows and often confounds the idea that we're purely rational. We don't save enough for retirement even though it's to our clear economic advantage to do so. We hang on to bad investments longer than we should, because we feel far sharper pain from losing money than we do from gaining the exact same amount. Give us a choice of two television sets, we'll pick one; toss in an irrelevant third choice, and we'll pick the other. In short, we are irrational—and predictably so, says economist Dan Ariely, author of *Predictably Irrational*, a book that offers an entertaining and engaging overview of behavioral economics.

The trouble for our purposes is that Motivation 2.0 assumes we're the same robotic wealth-maximizers I was taught we were a couple of decades ago. Indeed, the very premise of extrinsic incentives is that we'll always respond rationally to them. But even most economists don't believe that anymore. Sometimes these motivators work. Often they don't. And many times, they inflict collateral damage. In short, the new way economists think about what we do is hard to reconcile with Motivation 2.0.

What's more, if people do things for lunk-headed, backward-looking reasons, why wouldn't we also do things for significance-seeking, self-actualizing reasons? If we're predictably irrational—and we clearly are—why couldn't we also be predictably transcendent?

If that seems far-fetched, consider some of our other bizarre behaviors. We leave lucrative jobs to take low-paying ones that provide a clearer sense of purpose. We work to master the clarinet on weekends although we have little hope of making a dime (Motivation 2.0) or acquiring a mate (Motivation 1.0) from doing so. We play with puzzles even when we don't get a few raisins or dollars for solving them.

Some scholars are already widening the reach of behavioral economics to encompass these ideas. The most prominent is Bruno Frey, an economist at the University of Zurich. Like the behavioral economists, he has argued that we need to move beyond the idea of *Homo Oeconomicus* (Economic Man, that fictional wealth-maximizing android). But his extension goes in a slightly different direction—to what he calls *Homo Oeconomicus Maturus* (or Mature Economic Man). This figure, he says, "is more 'mature' in the sense that he is endowed with a more refined motivational structure." In other words, to fully understand human economic behavior, we have to come to terms with an idea at odds with Motivation 2.0. As Frey writes, "Intrinsic motivation is of *great importance* for all economic activities. It is inconceivable that people are motivated solely or even mainly by external incentives."[8]

HOW WE DO WHAT WE DO

If you manage other people, take a quick glance over your shoulder. There's a ghost hovering there. His name is Frederick Winslow Taylor—remember him from earlier in the chapter?—and he's whispering in your ear. "Work," Taylor is murmuring, "consists mainly of simple, not particularly interesting, tasks. The only way to get people to do them is to incentivize them properly and monitor them carefully." In the early 1900s, Taylor had a point. Today, in much of the world, that's less true. Yes, for some people work remains routine, unchallenging, and directed by others. But for a surprisingly large number of people, jobs have become more complex, more interesting, and more self-directed. And that type of work presents a direct challenge to the assumptions of Motivation 2.0.

Begin with complexity. Behavioral scientists often divide what we do on the job or learn in school into two categories: "algorithmic" and "heuristic." An algorithmic task is one in which you follow a set of established instructions down a single pathway to one conclusion. That is, there's an algorithm for solving it. A heuristic task is the opposite. Precisely because no algorithm exists for it, you have to experiment with possibilities and devise a novel solution. Working as a grocery checkout clerk is mostly algorithmic. You do pretty much the same thing over and over in a certain way. Creating an ad campaign is mostly heuristic. You have to come up with something new.

During the twentieth century, most work was algorithmic—and not just jobs where you turned the same screw the same way all day long. Even when we traded blue collars for white, the tasks we carried out were often routine. That is, we could reduce much of what we did—in accounting, law, computer programming, and other fields—to a script, a spec sheet, a formula, or a series of steps that produced a right answer. But today, in much of North America, Western Europe, Japan, South Korea, and Australia, routine white-collar work is disappearing. It's racing offshore to wherever it can be done the cheapest. In India, Bulgaria, the Philippines, and other countries, lower-paid workers essentially run the algorithm, figure out the correct answer, and deliver it instantaneously from their computer to someone six thousand miles away.

But offshoring is just one pressure on rule-based, left-brain work. Just as oxen and then forklifts replaced simple physical labor, computers are replacing simple intellectual labor. So while outsourcing is just beginning to pick up speed, software can already perform many rule-based, professional functions better, more quickly, and more cheaply than we can. That means that your cousin the CPA, if he's doing mostly routine work, faces competition not just from five-hundred-dollar-a-month accountants in Manila, but from tax preparation programs anyone can download for thirty dollars. The consulting firm McKinsey & Co. estimates that in the United States, only 30 percent of job growth now comes from algorithmic work, while 70 percent comes from heuristic work.[9] A key reason: Routine work can be outsourced or automated; artistic, empathic, nonroutine work generally cannot.[10]

The implications for motivation are vast. Researchers such as Harvard Business School's Teresa Amabile have found that external rewards and punishments—both carrots and sticks—can work nicely for algorithmic tasks. But they can be devastating for heuristic ones. Those sorts of challenges—solving novel problems or creating something the world didn't know it was missing—depend heavily on Harlow's third drive. Amabile calls it the intrinsic motivation principle of creativity, which holds, in part: "Intrinsic motivation is conducive to creativity; controlling extrinsic motivation is detrimental to creativity."[11] In other words, the central tenets of Motivation 2.0 may actually *impair* performance of the heuristic, right-brain work on which modern economies depend.

Partly because work has become more creative and less routine, it has also become more enjoyable. That, too, scrambles Motivation 2.0's assumptions. This operating system rests on the belief that work is *not* inherently enjoyable—which is precisely why we must coax people with external rewards and threaten them with outside punishment. One unexpected finding of the psychologist Mihaly Csikszentmihalyi, is that people are much more likely to report having "optimal experiences" on the job than during leisure. But if work is inherently enjoyable for more and more people, then the external inducements at the heart of Motivation 2.0 become less necessary. Worse, as Deci began discovering forty years ago, adding certain kinds of extrinsic rewards on top of inherently interesting tasks can often dampen motivation and diminish performance.

Once again, certain bedrock notions suddenly seem less sturdy. Take the curious example of Vocation Vacations. This is a business in which people pay their hard-earned money . . . to work at another job. They use their vacation time to test-drive being a chef, running a bike shop, or operating an animal shelter. The emergence of this and similar ventures suggests that work, which economists have always considered a "disutility" (something we'd avoid unless we received a payment in return), can often be a "utility" (something we'd pursue even in the absence of a tangible return).

Finally, because work is supposed to be dreary, Motivation 2.0 holds that people need to be carefully monitored so they don't shirk. This idea, too, is becoming less relevant and, in many ways, less possible. Consider, for instance, that America alone now has more than 18 million of what the U.S. Census Bureau calls "non-employer businesses"—businesses without any paid employees. Since people in these businesses don't have any underlings, they don't have anybody to manage or motivate. But since they don't have bosses themselves, there's nobody to manage or motivate them. They have to be self-directed.

So do people who aren't technically working for themselves. In the United States, 33.7 million people telecommute at least one day a month, and 14.7 million do so every day—placing a substantial portion of the workforce beyond the gaze of a manager, forcing them to direct their own work.[12] And even if many organizations haven't opted for measures like these, they're generally becoming leaner and less hierarchical. In an effort to reduce costs, they trim the fatty middle. That means managers oversee larger numbers of people and therefore scrutinize each one less closely.

As organizations flatten, companies need people who are self-motivated. That forces many organizations to become more like open source projects. Nobody "manages" the open source contributors. Nobody sits around trying to figure out how to "motivate" them. That's why Linux and Wikipedia and Firefox work. Routine, not-so-interesting jobs require direction; nonroutine, more interesting work depends on self-direction. One business leader, who didn't want to be identified, said it plainly. When he conducts job interviews, he tells prospective employees: "If you need me to motivate you, I probably don't want to hire you."

To recap, Motivation 2.0 suffers from three compatibility problems. It doesn't mesh with the way many new business models are organizing what we do—because we're intrinsically motivated purpose maximizers, not only extrinsically motivated profit maximizers. It doesn't comport with the way that twenty-first-century economics thinks about what we do—because econo-mists are finally realizing that we're full-fledged human beings, not single-minded economic robots. And perhaps most important, it's hard to reconcile with much of what we actually do at work—because for growing numbers of people, work is often creative, interesting, and self-directed rather than unrelentingly routine, boring, and other-directed. Taken together, these com-patibility problems warn us that something's gone awry in our motivational operating system.

But in order to figure out exactly what, and as an essential step in fashion-ing a new one, we need to take a look at the bugs themselves.

Seven Reasons Carrots and Sticks (Often) Don't Work ...

An object in motion will stay in motion, and an object at rest will stay at rest, unless acted on by an outside force.

That's Newton's first law of motion. Like Newton's other laws, this one is elegant and simple—which is part of its power. Even people like me, who bumbled though high school physics, can understand it and can use it to interpret the world.

Motivation 2.0 is similar. At its heart are two elegant and simple ideas:

> *Rewarding an activity will get you more of it. Punishing an activity will get you less of it.*

And just as Newton's principles can help us explain our physical environment or chart the path of a thrown ball, Motivation 2.0's principles can help us comprehend our social surroundings and predict the trajectory of human behavior.

But Newtonian physics runs into problems at the subatomic level. Down there—in the land of hadrons, quarks, and Schrödinger's cat—things get freaky. The cool rationality of Isaac Newton gives way to the bizarre unpredictability of Lewis Carroll. Motivation 2.0 is similar in this regard, too. When rewards and punishments encounter our third drive, something akin to behavioral quantum mechanics seems to take over and strange things begin to happen.

Of course, the starting point for any discussion of motivation in the workplace is a simple fact of life: People have to earn a living. Salary, contract payments, some benefits, a few perks are what I call "baseline rewards." If someone's baseline rewards aren't adequate or equitable, her focus will be on the unfairness of her situation and the anxiety of her circumstance. You'll get neither the predictability of extrinsic motivation nor the weirdness of intrinsic motivation. You'll get very little motivation at all. The best use of money as a motivator is to pay people enough to take the issue of money off the table.

But once we've cleared the table, carrots and sticks can achieve precisely the *opposite* of their intended aims. Mechanisms designed to increase motivation can dampen it. Tactics aimed at boosting creativity can reduce it. Programs to promote good deeds can make them disappear. Meanwhile, instead of restraining negative behavior, rewards and punishments can often set it loose—and give rise to cheating, addiction, and dangerously myopic thinking.

This is weird. And it doesn't hold in all circumstances (about which more after this chapter). But as Edward Deci's Soma puzzle experiment demonstrates, many practices whose effectiveness we take for granted produce counterintuitive results: They can give us less of what we want—and more of what we don't want. These are the bugs in Motivation 2.0. And they rise to the surface whether we're promising rupees in India, charging shekels in Israel, drawing blood in Sweden, or painting portraits in Chicago.

LESS OF WHAT WE WANT

One of the most enduring scenes in American literature offers an important lesson in human motivation. In Mark Twain's *The Adventures of Tom Sawyer*, Tom faces the dreary task of whitewashing Aunt Polly's 810-square-foot fence. He's not exactly thrilled with the assignment. "Life to him seemed hollow, and existence but a burden," Twain writes.

But just when Tom has nearly lost hope, "nothing less than a great, magnificent inspiration" bursts upon him. When his friend Ben ambles by and mocks Tom for his sorry lot, Tom acts confused. Slapping paint on a fence isn't a grim chore, he says. It's a fantastic privilege—a source of, ahem, intrinsic motivation. The job is so captivating that when Ben asks to try a few brushstrokes himself, Tom refuses. He doesn't relent until Ben gives up his apple in exchange for the opportunity.

Soon more boys arrive, all of whom tumble into Tom's trap and end up whitewashing the fence—several times over—on his behalf. From this episode, Twain extracts a key motivational principle, namely "that Work consists of whatever a body is OBLIGED to do, and that Play consists of whatever a body is not obliged to do." He goes on to write:

> There are wealthy gentlemen in England who drive four-horse passenger-coaches twenty or thirty miles on a daily line, in the summer, because the privilege costs them considerable money; but

if they were offered wages for the service, that would turn it into work and then they would resign.[1]

In other words, rewards can perform a weird sort of behavioral alchemy: They can transform an interesting task into a drudge. They can turn play into work. And by diminishing intrinsic motivation, they can send performance, creativity, and even upstanding behavior toppling like dominoes. Let's call this the Sawyer Effect.[*] A sampling of intriguing experiments around the world reveals the four realms where this effect kicks in.

INTRINSIC MOTIVATION

Behavioral scientists like Deci began discovering the Sawyer Effect nearly forty years ago, although they didn't use that term. Instead, they referred to the counterintuitive consequences of extrinsic incentives as "the hidden costs of rewards." That, in fact, was the title of the first book on the subject—a 1978 research volume that was edited by psychologists Mark Lepper and David Greene.

One of Lepper and Greene's early studies (which they carried out with a third colleague, Robert Nisbett) has become a classic in the field and among the most cited articles in the motivation literature. The three researchers watched a classroom of preschoolers for several days and identified the children who chose to spend their "free play" time drawing. Then they fashioned an experiment to test the effect of rewarding an activity these children clearly enjoyed.

The researchers divided the children into three groups. The first was the "expected-award" group. They showed each of these children a "Good Player" certificate—adorned with a blue ribbon and featuring the child's name—and asked if the child wanted to draw in order to receive the award. The second group was the "unexpected-award" group. Researchers asked these children simply if they wanted to draw. If they decided to, when the session ended, the researchers handed each child one of the "Good Player" certificates. The third group was the "no-award" group. Researchers asked these children if they wanted to draw, but neither promised them a certificate at the beginning nor gave them one at the end.

Two weeks later, back in the classroom, teachers set out paper and markers during the preschool's free play period while the researchers secretly observed the students. Children previously in the "unexpected-award" and "no-award" groups drew just as much, and with the same relish, as they had before the experiment. But children in the first group—the ones who'd expected and then received an award—showed much less interest and spent

---

[*] Here's the two-sided definition of the Sawyer Effect: practices that can either turn play into work or turn work into play.

much less time drawing.[2] The Sawyer Effect had taken hold. Even two weeks later, those alluring prizes—so common in classrooms and cubicles—had turned play into work.

To be clear, it wasn't necessarily the rewards themselves that dampened the children's interest. Remember: When children didn't expect a reward, receiving one had little impact on their intrinsic motivation. Only *contingent* rewards—if you do this, then you'll get that—had the negative effect. Why? "If-then" rewards require people to forfeit some of their autonomy. Like the gentlemen driving carriages for money instead of fun, they're no longer fully controlling their lives. And that can spring a hole in the bottom of their motivational bucket, draining an activity of its enjoyment.

Lepper and Greene replicated these results in several subsequent experiments with children. As time went on, other researchers found similar results with adults. Over and over again, they discovered that extrinsic rewards—in particular, contingent, expected, "if-then" rewards—snuffed out the third drive.

These insights proved so controversial—after all, they called into question a standard practice of most companies and schools—that in 1999 Deci and two colleagues reanalyzed nearly three decades of studies on the subject to confirm the findings. "Careful consideration of reward effects reported in 128 experiments lead to the conclusion that tangible rewards tend to have a substantially negative effect on intrinsic motivation," they determined. "When institutions—families, schools, businesses, and athletic teams, for example—focus on the short-term and opt for controlling people's behavior," they do considerable long-term damage.[3]

Try to encourage a kid to learn math by paying her for each workbook page she completes—and she'll almost certainly become more diligent in the short term and lose interest in math in the long term. Take an industrial designer who loves his work and try to get him to do better by making his pay contingent on a hit product—and he'll almost certainly work like a maniac in the short term, but become less interested in his job in the long term. As one leading behavioral science textbook puts it, "People use rewards expecting to gain the benefit of increasing another person's motivation and behavior, but in so doing, they often incur the unintentional and hidden cost of undermining that person's intrinsic motivation toward the activity."[4]

This is one of the most robust findings in social science—and also one of the most ignored. Despite the work of a few skilled and passionate popularizers—in particular, Alfie Kohn, whose prescient 1993 book, *Punished by Rewards*, lays out a devastating indictment of extrinsic incentives—we persist in trying to motivate people this way. Perhaps we're scared to let go of Motivation 2.0, despite its obvious downsides. Perhaps we can't get our minds around the peculiar quantum mechanics of intrinsic motivation.

Or perhaps there's a better reason. Even if those controlling "if-then" rewards activate the Sawyer Effect and suffocate the third drive, maybe they actually get people to perform better. If that's the case, perhaps they're not so bad.

So let's ask: Do extrinsic rewards boost performance? Four economists went to India to find out.

HIGH PERFORMANCE

One of the difficulties of laboratory experiments that test the impact of extrinsic motivators like cash is the cost. If you're going to pay people to perform, you have to pay them a meaningful amount. And in the United States or Europe, where standards of living are high, an individually meaningful amount multiplied by dozens of participants can rack up unsustainably large bills for behavioral scientists.

In part to circumvent this problem, a quartet of economists—including Dan Ariely, whom I mentioned—set up shop in Madurai, India, to gauge the effects of extrinsic incentives on performance. Because the cost of living in rural India is much lower than in North America, the researchers could offer large rewards without breaking their own banks.

They recruited eighty-seven participants and asked them to play several games—for example, tossing tennis balls at a target, unscrambling anagrams, recalling a string of digits—that required motor skills, creativity, or concentration. To test the power of incentives, the experimenters offered three types of rewards for reaching certain performance levels.

One-third of the participants could earn a small reward—4 rupees (at the time equal to about a day's pay in Madurai) for reaching their performance targets. One-third could earn a medium reward—40 rupees (about two weeks' pay). And one-third could earn a very large reward—400 rupees (nearly five months' pay).

What happened? Did the size of the reward predict the quality of the performance?

Yes. But not in the way you might expect. As it turned out, the people offered the medium-sized bonus didn't perform any better than those offered the small one. And those in the 400-rupee super-incentivized group? They fared worst of all. By nearly every measure, they lagged behind both the low-reward and medium-reward participants. Reporting the results for the Federal Reserve Bank of Boston, the researchers wrote, "In eight of the nine tasks we examined across the three experiments, higher incentives led to *worse* performance."[5]

Let's circle back to this conclusion for a moment. Four economists—two from MIT, one from Carnegie Mellon, and one from the University of Chicago—undertake research for the Federal Reserve System, one of the most powerful economic actors in the world. But instead of affirming a simple business principle—higher rewards lead to higher performance—they seem to refute it. And it's not just American researchers reaching these counterintuitive conclusions. In 2009, scholars at the London School of Economics—alma mater of eleven Nobel laureates in economics—analyzed fifty-one studies of corporate pay-for-performance plans. These economists' conclusion: "We find that financial incentives . . . can result in a negative impact on overall performance."[6] On both sides of the Atlantic, the gap between what science is learning and what business is doing is wide.

"Many existing institutions provide very large incentives for exactly the type of tasks we used here," Ariely and his colleagues wrote. "Our results challenge [that] assumption. Our experiment suggests . . . that one cannot assume that introducing or raising incentives always improves performance." Indeed, in many instances, contingent incentives—that cornerstone of how businesses attempt to motivate employees—may be "a losing proposition."

Of course, procrastinating writers notwithstanding, few of us spend our working hours flinging tennis balls or doing anagrams. How about the more creative tasks that are more akin to what we actually do on the job?

CREATIVITY

For a quick test of problem-solving prowess, few exercises are more useful than the "candle problem." Devised by psychologist Karl Duncker in the 1930s, the candle problem is used in a wide variety of experiments in behavioral science. Follow along and see how you do.

You sit at a table next to a wooden wall and the experimenter gives you the materials shown below: a candle, some tacks, and a book of matches.

Your job is to fix the candle to the wall so that the wax doesn't drip on the table. Think for a moment about how you'd solve the problem. Many people begin by trying to tack the candle to the wall. But that doesn't work. Some light a match, melt the side of the candle, and try to adhere it to the wall. That doesn't work either. But after five or ten minutes, most people stumble onto the solution, which you can see below.

The key is to overcome what's called "functional fixedness." You look at the box and see only one function—as a container for the tacks. But by thinking afresh, you eventually see that the box can have another function—as a platform for the candle. To reprise language, the solution isn't algorithmic (following a set path) but heuristic (breaking from the path to discover a novel strategy).

What happens when you give people a conceptual challenge like this and offer them rewards for speedy solutions? Sam Glucksberg, a psychologist now at Princeton University, tested this in the early 1960s by timing how quickly two groups of participants solved the candle problem. He told the first group that he was timing their work merely to establish norms for how long it typically took someone to complete this sort of puzzle. To the second group he offered incentives. If a participant's time was among the fastest 25 percent of all the people being tested, that participant would receive $5. If the participant's time was the fastest of all, the reward would be $20. Adjusted for inflation, those are decent sums of money for a few minutes of effort—a nice motivator.

How much faster did the incentivized group come up with a solution? On average, it took them nearly three and a half minutes *longer*.[7] Yes, three and a half minutes longer. (Whenever I've relayed these results to a group of businesspeople, the reaction is almost always a loud, pained, involuntary gasp.) In direct contravention to the core tenets of Motivation 2.0, an incentive designed to clarify thinking and sharpen creativity ended up clouding thinking and dulling creativity. Why? Rewards, by their very nature, narrow our focus. That's helpful when there's a clear path to a solution. They help us stare ahead and race faster. But "if-then" motivators are terrible for challenges like the candle problem. As this experiment shows, the rewards narrowed people's focus and blinkered the wide view that might have allowed them to see new uses for old objects.

Something similar seems to occur for challenges that aren't so much about cracking an existing problem but about iterating something new. Teresa Amabile, the Harvard Business School professor and one of the world's leading researchers on creativity, has frequently tested the effects of contingent rewards on the creative process. In one study, she and two colleagues recruited twenty-three professional artists from the United States who had produced both commissioned and noncommissioned artwork. They asked the artists to randomly select ten commissioned works and ten noncommissioned works. Then Amabile and her team gave the works to a panel of accomplished artists and curators, who knew nothing about the study, and asked the experts to rate the pieces on creativity and technical skill.

"Our results were quite startling," the researchers wrote. "The commissioned works were rated as significantly less creative than the noncommissioned works, yet they were not rated as different in technical quality. Moreover, the artists reported feeling significantly more constrained when doing commissioned works than when doing non-commissioned works." One artist whom they interviewed describes the Sawyer Effect in action:

> Not always, but a lot of the time, when you are doing a piece for someone else it becomes more "work" than joy. When I work for myself there is the pure joy of creating and I can work through the night and not even know it. On a commissioned piece you have to check yourself—be careful to do what the client wants.[8]

Another study of artists over a longer period shows that a concern for outside rewards might actually hinder eventual success. In the early 1960s, researchers surveyed sophomores and juniors at the School of the Art Institute of Chicago about their attitudes toward work and whether they were more intrinsically or extrinsically motivated. Using these data as a benchmark, another researcher followed up with these students in the early 1980s to see how their careers were progressing. Among the starkest findings, especially for men: "The less evidence of extrinsic motivation during art school, the more success in professional art both several years after graduation and nearly twenty years later." Painters and sculptors who were intrinsically motivated, those for whom the joy of discovery and the challenge of creation were their own rewards, were able to weather the tough times—and the lack of remuneration and recognition—that inevitably accompany artistic careers. And that led to yet another paradox in the Alice in Wonderland world of the third drive. "Those artists who pursued their painting and sculpture more for the pleasure of the activity itself than for extrinsic rewards have produced art that has been socially recognized as superior," the study said. "It is those who are least motivated to pursue extrinsic rewards who eventually receive them."[9]

The principle holds for scientists as well. In one 2009 study, MIT's Pierre Azoulay and his colleagues compared two different ways to incentivize creativity in the sciences. They examined scientists who received grants from the U.S. National Institutes of Health (NIH), which emphasizes external controls such as "short review cycles, pre-defined deliverables, and renewal policies unforgiving of failure." Then they looked at scientists at the Howard Hughes Medical Institute (HHMI), whose funding process "tolerates early failure, rewards long-term success, and gives its appointees great freedom to experiment." The result? HHMI investigators produced high-impact papers at a much higher rate than their similarly accomplished NIH counterparts.

Amabile and others have found that extrinsic rewards can be effective for algorithmic tasks—those that depend on following an existing formula to its logical conclusion. But for more right-brain undertakings—those that demand flexible problem-solving, inventiveness, or conceptual understanding—contingent rewards can be dangerous. Rewarded subjects often have a harder time seeing the periphery and crafting original solutions. This, too, is one of the sturdiest findings in social science—especially as Amabile and others have refined it over the years.[10] For artists, scientists, inventors, schoolchildren, and the rest of us, intrinsic motivation—the drive to do something because it is interesting, challenging, and absorbing—is essential for high levels of creativity. But the "if-then" motivators that are the staple of most businesses often stifle, rather than stir, creative thinking. As the economy moves toward more right-brain, conceptual work—as more of us deal with our own versions of the candle problem—this might be the most alarming gap between what science knows and what business does.

Good Behavior

Philosophers and medical professionals have long debated whether blood donors should be paid. Some claim that blood, like human tissue or organs, is special—that we shouldn't be able to buy and sell it like a barrel of crude oil or a crate of ball bearings. Others argue that we should shelve our squeamishness, because paying for this substance will ensure an ample supply.

But in 1970, British sociologist Richard Titmuss, who had studied blood donation in the United Kingdom, offered a bolder speculation. Paying for blood wasn't just immoral, he said. It was also inefficient. If Britain decided to pay citizens to donate, that would actually *reduce* the country's blood supply. It was an oddball notion, to be sure. Economists snickered. And Titmuss never tested the idea; it was merely a philosophical hunch.[11]

But a quarter-century later, two Swedish economists decided to see if Titmuss was right. In an intriguing field experiment, they visited a regional blood center in Gothenburg and found 153 women who were interested in giving blood. Then—as seems to be the custom among motivation researchers—they divided the women into three groups.[12] Experimenters told those in the first group that blood donation was voluntary. These participants could give blood, but they wouldn't receive a payment. The experimenters offered the second group a different arrangement. If these participants gave blood, they'd each receive 50 Swedish kronor (about $7). The third group received a variation on that second offer: a 50-kronor payment with an immediate option to donate the amount to a children's cancer charity.

Of the first group, 52 percent of the women decided to go ahead and donate blood. They were altruistic citizens apparently, willing to do a good deed for their fellow Swedes even in the absence of compensation.

And the second group? Motivation 2.0 would suggest that this group might be a bit more motivated to donate. They'd shown up, which indicated intrinsic motivation. Getting a few kronor on top might give that impulse a boost. But—as you might have guessed by now—that's not what happened. In this group, only 30 percent of the women decided to give blood. Instead of increasing the number of blood donors, offering to pay people *decreased* the number by nearly half.

Meanwhile, the third group—which had the option of donating the fee directly to charity—responded much the same as the first group. Fifty-three percent became blood donors.[*]

Titmuss's hunch might have been right, after all. Adding a monetary incentive didn't lead to more of the desired behavior. It led to less. The reason: It tainted an altruistic act and "crowded out" the intrinsic desire to do something good.[13] Doing good is what blood donation is all about. It provides what the American Red Cross brochures say is "a feeling that money can't buy." That's why voluntary blood donations invariably increase during natural disasters and other calamities.[14] But if governments were to pay people to help their neighbors during these crises, donations might decline.

That said, in the Swedish example, the reward itself wasn't inherently destructive. The immediate option to donate the 50-kronor payment rather than pocket it seemed to negate the effect. This, too, is extremely important. It's not that all rewards at all times are bad. For instance, when the Italian government gave blood donors paid time off work, donations increased.[15]

---

[*] The results for the 119 men in the experiment were somewhat different. The payment had no statistically significant effect, positive or negative, on the decision to give blood.

The law removed an obstacle to altruism. So while a few advocates would have you believe in the basic evil of extrinsic incentives, that's just not empirically true. What is true is that mixing rewards with inherently interesting, creative, or noble tasks—deploying them without understanding the peculiar science of motivation—is a very dangerous game. When used in these situations, "if-then" rewards usually do more harm than good. By neglecting the ingredients of genuine motivation—autonomy, mastery, and purpose—they limit what each of us can achieve.

MORE OF WHAT WE DON'T WANT

In the upside-down universe of the third drive, rewards can often produce less of the very things they're trying to encourage. But that's not the end of the story. When used improperly, extrinsic motivators can have another unintended collateral consequence: They can give us more of what we *don't* want. Here, again, what business does hasn't caught up with what science knows. And what science is revealing is that carrots and sticks can promote bad behavior, create addiction, and encourage short-term thinking at the expense of the long view.

UNETHICAL BEHAVIOR

What could be more valuable than having a goal? From our earliest days, teachers, coaches, and parents advise us to set goals and to work mightily to achieve them—and with good reason. Goals work. The academic literature shows that by helping us tune out distractions, goals can get us to try harder, work longer, and achieve more.

But recently a group of scholars from the Harvard Business School, Northwestern University's Kellogg School of Management, the University of Arizona's Eller College of Management, and the University of Pennsylvania's Wharton School questioned the efficacy of this broad prescription. "Rather than being offered as an 'over-the-counter' salve for boosting performance, goal setting should be prescribed selectively, presented with a warning label, and closely monitored," they wrote.[16] Goals that people set for themselves and that are devoted to attaining mastery are usually healthy. But goals imposed by others—sales targets, quarterly returns, standardized test scores, and so on—can sometimes have dangerous side effects.

Like all extrinsic motivators, goals narrow our focus. That's one reason they can be effective; they concentrate the mind. But as we've seen, a narrowed focus exacts a cost. For complex or conceptual tasks, offering a reward can blinker the wide-ranging thinking necessary to come up with an innovative solution. Likewise, when an extrinsic goal is paramount—particularly a short-term, measurable one whose achievement delivers a big payoff—its presence can restrict our view of the broader dimensions of our behavior. As the cadre of business school professors write, "Substantial evidence demonstrates that in addition to motivating constructive effort, goal setting can induce unethical behavior."

The examples are legion, the researchers note. Sears imposes a sales quota on its auto repair staff—and workers respond by over-charging customers and completing unnecessary repairs. Enron sets lofty revenue goals—and the race to meet them by any means possible catalyzes the company's collapse. Ford is so intent on producing a certain car at a certain weight at a certain price by a certain date that it omits safety checks and unleashes the dangerous Ford Pinto.

The problem with making an extrinsic reward the only destination that matters is that some people will choose the quickest route there, even if it means taking the low road.

Indeed, most of the scandals and misbehavior that have seemed endemic to modern life involve shortcuts. Executives game their quarterly earnings so they can snag a performance bonus. Secondary school counselors doctor student transcripts so their seniors can get into college.[17] Athletes inject themselves with steroids to post better numbers and trigger lucrative performance bonuses.

Contrast that approach with behavior sparked by intrinsic motivation. When the reward is the activity itself—deepening learning, delighting customers, doing one's best—there are no shortcuts. The only route to the destination is the high road. In some sense, it's impossible to act unethically because the person who's disadvantaged isn't a competitor but yourself.

Of course, all goals are not created equal. And—let me emphasize this point—goals and extrinsic rewards aren't inherently corrupting. But goals are more toxic than Motivation 2.0 recognizes. In fact, the business school professors suggest they should come with their own warning label: *"Goals may cause systematic problems for organizations due to narrowed focus, unethical behavior, increased risk taking, decreased cooperation, and decreased intrinsic motivation. Use care when applying goals in your organization."*

If carrots-as-goals sometimes encourage unworthy behavior, then sticks-as-punishment should be able to halt it, right? Not so fast. The third drive is less mechanistic and more surprising than that, as two Israeli economists discovered at some day care centers.

In 2000, economists Uri Gneezy and Aldo Rustichini studied a group of child care facilities in Haifa, Israel, for twenty weeks.[18] The centers opened at 7:30 A.M. and closed at 4:00 P.M. Parents had to retrieve their children by the closing time or a teacher would have to stay late.

During the first four weeks of the experiment, the economists recorded how many parents arrived late each week. Then, before the fifth week, with the permission of the day care centers, they posted the following sign:

ANNOUNCEMENT:
Fine for Coming Late

As you all know, the official closing time of the day care center is 1600 every day. Since some parents have been coming late, we (with the approval of the Authority for Private Day-Care Centers in Israel) have decided to impose a fine on parents who come late to pick up their children.

As of next Sunday a fine of NS 10* will be charged every time a child is collected after 1610. This fine will be calculated monthly, it is to be paid together with the regular monthly payment.

Sincerely,

The manager of the day-care center

The theory underlying the fine, said Gneezy and Rustichini, was straightforward: "When negative consequences are imposed on a behavior, they will produce a reduction of that particular response." In other words, thwack the parents with a fine, and they'll stop showing up late.

But that's not what happened. "After the introduction of the fine we observed a steady *increase* in the number of parents coming late," the economists wrote. "The rate finally settled, at a level that was higher, and *almost twice as large* as the initial one."[19] And in language reminiscent of Harry Harlow's head scratching, they write that the existing literature didn't account for such a result. Indeed, the "possibility of an increase in the behavior being punished was not even considered."

Up pops another bug in Motivation 2.0. One reason most parents showed up on time is that they had a relationship with the teachers—who, after all, were caring for their precious sons and daughters—and wanted to treat them fairly. Parents had an intrinsic desire to be scrupulous about punctuality. But the threat of a fine—like the promise of the kronor in the blood experiment—edged aside that third drive. The fine shifted the parents' decision from a partly moral obligation (be fair to my kids' teachers) to a pure transaction (I can buy extra time). There wasn't room for both. The punishment didn't promote good behavior; it crowded it out.

ADDICTION

If some scientists believe that "if-then" motivators and other extrinsic rewards resemble prescription drugs that carry potentially dangerous side effects, others believe they're more like illegal drugs that foster a deeper and more pernicious dependency. According to these scholars, cash rewards and shiny trophies can provide a delicious jolt of pleasure at first, but the feeling soon

---

* The fine was per child, so a parent with two children would have to pay twenty Israeli shekels (NS 20) for each instance of tardiness. When the experiment was conducted, ten Israeli shekels was equivalent to about three U.S. dollars.

dissipates—and to keep it alive, the recipient requires ever larger and more frequent doses.

The Russian economist Anton Suvorov has constructed an elaborate econometric model to demonstrate this effect, configured around what's called "principal-agent theory." Think of the principal as the motivat*or*—the employer, the teacher, the parent. Think of the agent as the motivat*ee*—the employee, the student, the child. A principal essentially tries to get the agent to do what the principal wants, while the agent balances his own interests with whatever the principal is offering. Using a blizzard of complicated equations that test a variety of scenarios between principal and agent, Suvorov has reached conclusions that make intuitive sense to any parent who's tried to get her kids to empty the garbage.

By offering a reward, a principal signals to the agent that the task is undesirable. (If the task were desirable, the agent wouldn't need a prod.) But that initial signal, and the reward that goes with it, forces the principal onto a path that's difficult to leave. Offer too small a reward and the agent won't comply. But offer a reward that's enticing enough to get the agent to act the first time, and the principal "is doomed to give it again in the second." There's no going back. Pay your son to take out the trash—and you've pretty much guaranteed the kid will never do it again for free. What's more, once the initial money buzz tapers off, you'll likely have to increase the payment to continue compliance.

As Suvorov explains, "Rewards are addictive in that once offered, a contingent reward makes an agent expect it whenever a similar task is faced, which in turn compels the principal to use rewards over and over again." And before long, the existing reward may no longer suffice. It will quickly feel less like a bonus and more like the status quo—which then forces the principal to offer larger rewards to achieve the same effect.[20]

This addictive pattern is not merely blackboard theory. Brian Knutson, then a neuroscientist at the National Institute on Alcohol Abuse and Alcoholism, demonstrated as much in an experiment using the brain scanning technique known as functional magnetic resonance imaging (fMRI). He placed healthy volunteers into a giant scanner to watch how their brains responded during a game that involved the prospect of either winning or losing money. When participants knew they had a chance to win cash, activation occurred in the part of the brain called the nucleus accumbens. That is, when the participants anticipated getting a reward (but not when they anticipated losing one), a burst of the brain chemical dopamine surged to this part of the brain. Knutson, who is now at Stanford University, has found similar results in subsequent studies where people anticipated rewards. What makes this response interesting for our purposes is that the same basic physiological process—this particular brain chemical surging to this particular part of the brain—is what happens in addiction. The mechanism of most addictive drugs is to send a fusillade of dopamine to the nucleus accumbens. The feeling delights, then dissipates, then demands another dose. In other words, if we watch how people's brains respond, promising them monetary rewards and giving them cocaine, nicotine, or amphetamines look disturbingly similar.[21] This could be one reason that paying people to stop smoking often works in the short run. It replaces one (dangerous) addiction with another (more benign) one.

Rewards' addictive qualities can also distort decision-making. Knutson has found that activation in the nucleus accumbens seems to predict "both risky choices and risk-seeking mistakes." Get people fired up with the prospect of rewards, and instead of making better decisions, as Motivation 2.0 hopes, they can actually make worse ones. As Knutson writes, "This may explain why casinos surround their guests with reward cues (e.g., inexpensive food, free liquor, surprise gifts, potential jackpot prizes)—anticipation of rewards activates the [nucleus accumbens], which may lead to an increase in the likelihood of individuals switching from risk-averse to risk-seeking behavior."[22]

In short, while that dangled carrot isn't all bad in all circumstances, in some instances it operates similar to a rock of crack cocaine and can induce behavior similar to that found around the craps table or roulette wheel—not exactly what we hope to achieve when we "motivate" our teammates and coworkers.

SHORT-TERM THINKING

Think back to the candle problem again. The incentivized participants performed worse than their counterparts because they were so focused on the prize that they failed to glimpse a novel solution on the periphery. Rewards, we've seen, can limit the *breadth* of our thinking. But extrinsic motivators—especially tangible, "if-then" ones—can also reduce the *depth* of our thinking. They can focus our sights on only what's immediately before us rather than what's off in the distance.

Many times a concentrated focus makes sense. If your office building is on fire, you want to find an exit immediately rather than ponder how to rewrite the zoning regulations. But in less dramatic circumstances, fixating on an immediate reward can damage performance over time. Indeed, what our earlier examples—unethical actions and addictive behavior—have in common, perhaps more than anything else, is that they're entirely short-term. Addicts want the quick fix regardless of the eventual harm. Cheaters want the quick win—regardless of the lasting consequences.

Yet even when the behavior doesn't devolve into shortcuts or addiction, the near-term allure of rewards can be harmful in the long run. Consider publicly held companies. Many such companies have existed for decades and hope to exist for decades more. But much of what their executives and middle managers do each day is aimed single-mindedly at the corporation's performance over the next three months. At these companies, quarterly earnings are an obsession. Executives devote substantial resources to making sure the earnings come out just right. And they spend considerable time and brain-power offering guidance to stock analysts so that the market knows what to expect and therefore responds favorably. This laser focus on a narrow, near-term slice of corporate performance is understandable. It's a rational response to stock markets that reward or punish tiny blips in those numbers, which, in turn, affect executives' compensation.

But companies pay a steep price for not extending their gaze beyond the next quarter. Several researchers have found that companies that spend the most time offering guidance on quarterly earnings deliver significantly *lower* long-term growth rates than companies that offer guidance less frequently. (One reason: The earnings-obsessed companies typically invest less in research and development.)[23] They successfully achieve their short-term goals, but threaten the health of the company two or three years hence. As the scholars who warned about goals gone wild put it, "The very presence of goals may lead employees to focus myopically on short-term gains and to lose sight of the potential devastating long-term effects on the organization."[24]

Perhaps nowhere is this clearer than in the economic calamity that gripped the world economy in 2008 and 2009. Each player in the system focused only on the short-term reward—the buyer who wanted a house, the mort-gage broker who wanted a commission, the Wall Street trader who wanted new securities to sell, the politician who wanted a buoyant economy during reelection—and ignored the long-term effects of their actions on themselves or others. When the music stopped, the entire system nearly collapsed. This is the nature of economic bubbles: What seems to be irrational exuberance is ultimately a bad case of extrinsically motivated myopia.

By contrast, the elements of genuine motivation that we'll explore later, by their very nature, defy a short-term view. Take mastery. The objective itself is inherently long-term because complete mastery, in a sense, is unattainable. Even Roger Federer, for instance, will never fully "master" the game of tennis. But introducing an "if-then" reward to help develop mastery usually backfires. That's why school-children who are paid to solve problems typically choose easier problems and therefore learn less.[25] The short-term prize crowds out the long-term learning.

In environments where extrinsic rewards are most salient, many people work only to the point that triggers the reward—and no further. So if students get a prize for reading three books, many won't pick up a fourth, let alone embark on a lifetime of reading—just as executives who hit their quarterly numbers often won't boost earnings a penny more, let alone contemplate the long-term health of their company. Likewise, several studies show that paying people to exercise, stop smoking, or take their medicines produces terrific results at first—but the healthy behavior disappears once the incen-tives are removed. However, when contingent rewards aren't involved, or when incentives are used with the proper deftness, performance improves and understanding deepens. Greatness and nearsightedness are incompatible.

Meaningful achievement depends on lifting one's sights and pushing toward the horizon.

CARROTS AND STICKS: *THE SEVEN DEADLY FLAWS*

1. They can extinguish intrinsic motivation.
2. They can diminish performance.
3. They can crush creativity.
4. They can crowd out good behavior.
5. They can encourage cheating, shortcuts, and unethical behavior.
6. They can become addictive.
7. They can foster short-term thinking.

...and the Special Circumstances
When They Do

Carrots and sticks aren't all bad. If they were, Motivation 2.0 would never have flourished so long or accomplished so much. While an operating system centered around rewards and punishments has outlived its usefulness and badly needs an upgrade, that doesn't mean we should scrap its every piece. Indeed, doing so would run counter to the science. The scholars exploring human motivation have revealed not only the many glitches in the traditional approach, but also the narrow band of circumstances in which carrots and sticks do their jobs reasonably well.

The starting point, of course, is to ensure that the baseline rewards—wages, salaries, benefits, and so on—are adequate and fair. Without a healthy baseline, motivation of any sort is difficult and often impossible.

But once that's established, there are circumstances where it's okay to fall back on extrinsic motivators. To understand what those circumstances are, let's return to the candle problem. In his study, Sam Glucksberg found that the participants who were offered a cash prize took longer to solve the problem than those working in a reward-free environment. The reason, you'll recall, is that the prospect of a prize narrowed participants' focus and limited their ability to see an inventive, nonobvious solution.

In the same experiment, Glucksberg presented a separate set of participants with a slightly different version of the problem. Once again, he told half of them he was timing their performance to collect data—and the other half that those who posted the fastest times could win cash. But he altered things just a bit. Instead of giving participants a box full of tacks, he emptied the tacks onto the desk as shown below.

Can you guess what happened?

This time, the participants vying for the reward solved the problem *faster* than their counterparts. Why? By removing the tacks and displaying the empty box, Glucksberg eliminated the functional fixedness obstacle and essentially revealed the solution. He transformed a challenging right-brain task into a routine left-brain one. Since participants simply had to race down an obvious path, the carrot waiting for them at the finish line encouraged them to gallop faster.

Glucksberg's experiment provides the first question you should ask when contemplating external motivators: *Is the task at hand routine?* That is, does accomplishing it require following a prescribed set of rules to a specified end?

For routine tasks, which aren't very interesting and don't demand much creative thinking, rewards can provide a small motivational booster shot without the harmful side effects. In some ways, that's just common sense. As Edward Deci, Richard Ryan, and Richard Koestner explain, "Rewards do not undermine people's intrinsic motivation for dull tasks because there is little or no intrinsic motivation to be undermined."[1] Likewise, when Dan Ariely and his colleagues conducted their Madurai, India, performance study with a group of MIT students, they found that when the task called for "even rudimentary cognitive skill," a larger reward "led to poorer performance." But "as long as the task involved only mechanical skill, bonuses worked as they would be expected: the higher the pay, the better the performance."[2]

This is extremely important. Although advanced economies now revolve less around those algorithmic, rule-based functions, some of what we do each day—especially on the job—still isn't all that interesting. We have TPS reports to fill out and boring e-mail to answer and all manner of drudge work that doesn't necessarily fire our soul. What's more, for some people, much of what they do *all day* consists of these routine, not terribly captivating, tasks. In these situations, it's best to try to unleash the positive side of the Sawyer Effect by attempting to turn work into play—to increase the task's variety, to make it more like a game, or to use it to help master other skills. Alas, that's not always possible. And this means that sometimes, even "if-then" rewards are an option.

Let's put this insight about rewards and routines into practice. Suppose you're a manager at a small nonprofit organization. Your design team created a terrific poster promoting your group's next big event. And now you need to send the poster to twenty thousand members of your organization. Since the costs of outsourcing the job to a professional mailing firm are too steep for your budget, you decide to do the work in-house. Trouble is, the posters came back from the printer much later than you expected and they need to get in the mail this weekend.

What's the best way to enlist your staff of ten, and maybe a few others, in a massive weekend poster mailing session? The task is the very definition of routine: The people participating must roll up the posters, slide them into the mailing tubes, cap those tubes, and apply a mailing label and the proper postage. Four steps—none of them notably interesting.

One managerial option is coercion. If you're the boss, you could force people to spend their Saturday and Sunday on this mind-numbing project. They might comply, but the damage to their morale and long-term commitment could be substantial. Another option is to ask for volunteers. But face it: Most people can think of far better ways to spend a weekend.

So in this case, an "if-then" reward might be effective. For instance, you could promise a big office-wide party if everybody pitches in on the project. You could offer a gift certificate to everyone who participates. Or you could go further and pay people a small sum for every poster they insert, enclose, and send—in the hope that the piecework fee will boost their productivity.

While such tangible, contingent rewards can often undermine intrinsic motivation and creativity, those drawbacks matter less here. The assignment neither inspires deep passion nor requires deep thinking. Carrots, in this case, won't hurt and might help. And you'll increase your chances of success by supplementing the poster-packing rewards with three important practices:

- **Offer a rationale for why the task is necessary.** A job that's not inherently interesting can become more meaningful, and therefore more engaging, if it's part of a larger purpose. Explain why this poster is so important and why sending it out now is critical to your organization's mission.
- **Acknowledge that the task is boring.** This is an act of empathy, of course. And the acknowledgment will help people understand why this is the rare instance when "if-then" rewards are part of how your organization operates.
- **Allow people to complete the task their own way.** Think autonomy, not control. State the outcome you need. But instead of specifying precisely the way to reach it—how each poster must be rolled and how each mailing label must be affixed—give them freedom over how they do the job.

That's the approach for routine tasks. What about for other sorts of undertakings?

For work that requires more than just climbing, rung by rung, up a ladder of instructions, rewards are more perilous. The best way to avoid the seven deadly flaws of extrinsic motivators is to avoid them altogether or to downplay them significantly and instead emphasize the elements of deeper motivation—autonomy, mastery, and purpose—that we'll explore later in the book. But in the workplace, a rigid adherence to this approach bumps up against a fact of life: Even people who do groovy, creative, right-brain work still want to be paid. And here Teresa Amabile has shed some light on how to use rewards in a way that reckons with life's realities but reduces extrinsic motivators' hidden costs.

Go back to the study in which Amabile and two colleagues compared the quality of commissioned and noncommissioned paintings from a group of artists. A panel of experts, blind to what the investigators were exploring, consistently rated the noncommissioned artwork as more creative. One reason is that several artists said their commissions were "constraining"—that they found themselves working toward a goal they didn't endorse in a manner they didn't control. However, in the same study, Amabile also discovered that when the artists considered their commissions "enabling"—that is, "the commission enabled the artist to do something interesting or exciting"[3]—the creativity ranking of what they produced shot back up. The same was true for commissions the artists felt provided them with useful information and feedback about their ability.

This is a crucial research insight. The science shows that it is possible—though tricky—to incorporate rewards into nonroutine, more creative settings without causing a cascade of damage.

So suppose we're back at your nonprofit nine months later. The mailing went out flawlessly. The poster was a hit. The event was a smash. You're planning another for later this year. You've settled on the date and found your venue. Now you need an inspiring poster to captivate imaginations and draw a crowd.

What should you do?

Here's what you *shouldn't* do: Offer an "if-then" reward to the design staff. Do not stride into their offices and announce: "If you come up with a poster that rocks my world or that boosts attendance over last year, then you'll get a ten-percent bonus." Although that motivational approach is common in organizations all over the world, it's a recipe for reduced performance. You'll likely get activity—but not much creativity. Creating a poster isn't routine. It requires conceptual, breakthrough, artistic thinking. And as we've learned, "if-then" rewards are an ideal way to squash this sort of thinking.

Your best approach is to have already established the conditions of a genuinely motivating environment. The baseline rewards must be sufficient. That is, the team's basic compensation must be adequate and fair—particularly compared with people doing similar work for similar organizations. Your nonprofit must be a congenial place to work. And the people on your team must have autonomy, they must have ample opportunity to pursue mastery, and their daily duties must relate to a larger purpose. If these elements are in place, the best strategy is to provide a sense of urgency and significance—and then get out of the talent's way.

But you may still be able to boost performance a bit—more for future tasks than for this one—through the delicate use of rewards. Just be careful. Your efforts will backfire unless the rewards you offer meet one essential requirement. And you'll be on firmer motivational footing if you follow two additional principles.

The essential requirement: *Any extrinsic reward should be unexpected and offered only after the task is complete.*

Holding out a prize at the beginning of a project—and offering it as a contingency—will inevitably focus people's attention on obtaining the reward rather than on attacking the problem. But introducing the subject of rewards after the job is done is less risky.

In other words, where "if-then" rewards are a mistake, shift to "now that" rewards—as in "Now that you've finished the poster and it turned out so well, I'd like to celebrate by taking you out to lunch."

As Deci and his colleagues explain, "If tangible rewards are given unexpectedly to people after they have finished a task, the rewards are less likely to be experienced as the reason for doing the task and are thus less likely to be detrimental to intrinsic motivation."[4]

Likewise, Amabile has found in some studies "that the highest levels of creativity were produced by subjects who received a reward as a kind of a bonus."[5] So when the poster turns out great, you could buy the design team a case of beer or even hand them a cash bonus without snuffing their creativity. The team didn't expect any extras and getting them didn't hinge on a particular outcome. You're simply offering your appreciation for their stellar work. But keep in mind one ginormous caveat: Repeated "now that" bonuses can quickly become expected "if-then" entitlements—which can ultimately crater effective performance.

At this point, by limiting rewards for nonroutine, creative work to the unexpected, "now that" variety, you're in less dangerous waters. But you'll do even better if you follow two more guidelines.

First, *consider nontangible rewards.* Praise and positive feedback are much less corrosive than cash and trophies. In fact, in Deci's original experiments, and in his subsequent analysis of other studies, he found that "positive feedback can have an enhancing effect on intrinsic motivation."[6] So if the folks on the design team turn out a show-stopping poster, maybe just walk into their offices and say, "Wow. You really did an amazing job on that poster. It's going to have a huge impact on getting people to come to this event. Thank you." It sounds small and simple, but it can have an enormous effect.

Second, *provide useful information.* Amabile has found that while controlling extrinsic motivators' can clobber creativity, "informational or enabling motivators can be conducive" to it.[7] In the workplace, people are thirsting to learn about how they're doing, but only if the information isn't a tacit effort to manipulate their behavior. So don't tell the design team: "That poster was perfect. You did it exactly the way I asked." Instead, give people meaningful information about their work. The more feedback focuses on specifics ("great use of color")—and the more the praise is about effort and strategy rather than about achieving a particular outcome—the more effective it can be.

In brief, for creative, right-brain, heuristic tasks, you're on shaky ground offering "if-then" rewards. You're better off using "now that" rewards. And you're best off if your "now that" rewards provide praise, feedback, and useful information.

The Mindsets

Carol Dweck

When I was a young researcher, just starting out, something happened that changed my life. I was obsessed with understanding how people cope with failures, and I decided to study it by watching how students grapple with hard problems. So I brought children one at a time to a room in their school, made them comfortable, and then gave them a series of puzzles to solve. The first ones were fairly easy, but the next ones were hard. As the students grunted, perspired, and toiled, I watched their strategies and probed what they were thinking and feeling. I expected differences among children in how they coped with the difficulty, but I saw something I never expected.

Confronted with the hard puzzles, one ten-year-old boy pulled up his chair, rubbed his hands together, smacked his lips, and cried out, "I love a challenge!" Another, sweating away on these puzzles, looked up with a pleased expression and said with authority, "You know, I was *hoping* this would be informative!"

What's wrong with them? I wondered. I always thought you coped with failure or you didn't cope with failure. I never thought anyone *loved* failure. Were these alien children or were they on to something?

Everyone has a role model, someone who pointed the way at a critical moment in their lives. These children were my role models. They obviously knew something I didn't and I was determined to figure it out—to understand the kind of mindset that could turn a failure into a gift.

What did they know? They knew that human qualities, such as intellectual skills, could be cultivated through effort. And that's what they were doing—getting smarter. Not only weren't they discouraged by failure, they didn't even think they were failing. They thought they were learning.

I, on the other hand, thought human qualities were carved in stone. You were smart or you weren't, and failure meant you weren't. It was that simple. If you could arrange successes and avoid failures (at all costs), you could stay smart. Struggles, mistakes, perseverance were just not part of this picture.

Whether human qualities are things that can be cultivated or things that are carved in stone is an old issue. What these beliefs mean for you is a new one: What are the consequences of thinking that your intelligence or personality is something you can develop, as opposed to something that is a fixed, deep-seated trait? Let's first look in on the age-old, fiercely waged debate about human nature and then return to the question of what these beliefs mean for you.

WHY DO PEOPLE DIFFER?

Since the dawn of time, people have thought differently, acted differently, and fared differently from each other. It was guaranteed that someone would ask the question of why people differed—why some people are smarter or more moral—and whether there was something that made them permanently different. Experts lined up on both sides. Some claimed that there was a strong physical basis for these differences, making them unavoidable and unalterable. Through the ages, these alleged physical differences have included bumps on the skull (phrenology), the size and shape of the skull (craniology), and, today, genes.

Others pointed to the strong differences in people's backgrounds, experiences, training, or ways of learning. It may surprise you to know that a big champion of this view was Alfred Binet, the inventor of the IQ test. Wasn't the IQ test meant to summarize children's unchangeable intelligence? In fact, no. Binet, a Frenchman working in Paris in the early twentieth century, designed this test to identify children who were not profiting from the Paris public schools, *so that new educational programs could be designed to get them back on track*. Without denying individual differences in children's intellects, he believed that education and practice could bring about fundamental changes in intelligence. Here is a quote from one of his major books, *Modern Ideas About Children*, in which he summarizes his work with hundreds of children with learning difficulties:

> A few modern philosophers . . . assert that an individual's intelligence is a fixed quantity, a quantity which cannot be increased. We must protest and react against this brutal pessimism. . . . With practice, training, and above all, method, we manage to increase our attention, our memory, our judgment and literally to become more intelligent than we were before.

Who's right? Today most experts agree that it's not either – or. It's not nature *or* nurture, genes *or* environment. From conception on, there's a constant give and take between the two. In fact, as Gilbert Gottlieb, an eminent neuroscientist, put it, not only do genes and environment cooperate as we develop, but genes *require* input from the environment to work properly.

At the same time, scientists are learning that people have more capacity for lifelong learning and brain development than they ever thought. Of course, each person has a unique genetic endowment. People may start with different temperaments and different aptitudes, but it is clear that experience, training, and personal effort take them the rest of the way. Robert Sternberg, the present-day guru of intelligence, writes that the major factor in whether people achieve expertise "is not some fixed prior ability, but purposeful engagement." Or, as his forerunner Binet recognized, it's not always the people who start out the smartest who end up the smartest.

WHAT DOES ALL THIS MEAN FOR YOU? THE TWO MINDSETS

It's one thing to have pundits spouting their opinions about scientific issues. It's another thing to understand how these views apply to you. For twenty years, my research has shown that *the view you adopt for yourself* profoundly affects the way you lead your life. It can determine whether you become the person you want to be and whether you accomplish the things you value. How does this happen? How can a simple belief have the power to transform your psychology and, as a result, your life?

Believing that your qualities are carved in stone—the *fixed mindset*—creates an urgency to prove yourself over and over. If you have only a certain amount of intelligence, a certain personality, and a certain moral character—well, then you'd better prove that you have a healthy dose of them. It simply wouldn't do to look or feel deficient in these most basic characteristics.

Some of us are trained in this mindset from an early age. Even as a child, I was focused on being smart, but the fixed mindset was really stamped in by Mrs. Wilson, my sixth-grade teacher. Unlike Alfred Binet, she believed that people's IQ scores told the whole story of who they were. We were seated around the room in IQ order, and only the highest-IQ students could be trusted to carry the flag, clap the erasers, or take a note to the principal. Aside from the daily stomachaches she provoked with her judgmental stance, she was creating a mindset in which everyone in the class had one consuming goal—look smart, don't look dumb. Who cared about or enjoyed learning when our whole being was at stake every time she gave us a test or called on us in class?

I've seen so many people with this one consuming goal of proving themselves—in the classroom, in their careers, and in their relationships. Every situation calls for a confirmation of their intelligence, personality, or character. Every situation is evaluated: *Will I succeed or fail? Will I look smart or dumb? Will I be accepted or rejected? Will I feel like a winner or a loser?*

But doesn't our society value intelligence, personality, and character? Isn't it normal to want these traits? Yes, but . . .

There's another mindset in which these traits are not simply a hand you're dealt and have to live with, always trying to convince yourself and others that you have a royal flush when you're secretly worried it's a pair of tens. In this mindset, the hand you're dealt is just the starting point for development. This *growth mindset* is based on the belief that your basic qualities are things you can cultivate through your efforts. Although people may differ in every which way—in their initial talents and aptitudes, interests, or temperaments—everyone can change and grow through application and experience.

Do people with this mindset believe that anyone can be anything, that anyone with proper motivation or education can become Einstein or Beethoven? No, but they believe that a person's true potential is unknown (and unknowable); that it's impossible to foresee what can be accomplished with years of passion, toil, and training.

Did you know that Darwin and Tolstoy were considered ordinary children? That Ben Hogan, one of the greatest golfers of all time, was completely uncoordinated and graceless as a child? That the photographer Cindy Sherman, who has been on virtually every list of the most important artists of the twentieth century, *failed* her first photography course? That Geraldine Page, one of our greatest actresses, was advised to give it up for lack of talent?

You can see how the belief that cherished qualities can be developed creates a passion for learning. Why waste time proving over and over how great you are, when you could be getting better? Why hide deficiencies instead of overcoming them? Why look for friends or partners who will just shore up your self-esteem instead of ones who will also challenge you to grow? And why seek out the tried and true, instead of experiences that will stretch you? The passion for stretching yourself and sticking to it, even (or especially) when it's not going well, is the hallmark of the growth mindset. This is the mindset that allows people to thrive during some of the most challenging times in their lives.

A VIEW FROM THE TWO MINDSETS

To give you a better sense of how the two mindsets work, imagine—as vividly as you can—that you are a young adult having a really bad day:

> One day, you go to a class that is really important to you and that you like a lot. The professor returns the midterm papers to the class. You got a C+. You're very disappointed. That evening on the way back to your home, you find that you've gotten a parking ticket. Being really frustrated, you call your best friend to share your experience but are sort of brushed off.

What would you think? What would you feel? What would you do?

When I asked people with the fixed mindset, this is what they said: "I'd feel like a reject." "I'm a total failure." "I'm an idiot." "I'm a loser." "I'd feel worthless and dumb—everyone's better than me." "I'm slime." In other words, they'd see what happened as a direct measure of their competence and worth.

This is what they'd think about their lives: "My life is pitiful." "I have no life." "Somebody upstairs doesn't like me." "The world is out to get me." "Someone is out to destroy me." "Nobody loves me, everybody hates me." "Life is unfair and all efforts are useless." "Life stinks. I'm stupid. Nothing good ever happens to me." "I'm the most unlucky person on this earth."

Excuse me, was there death and destruction, or just a grade, a ticket, and a bad phone call?

Are these just people with low self-esteem? Or card-carrying pessimists? No. When they aren't coping with failure, they feel just as worthy and optimistic—and bright and attractive—as people with the growth mindset.

So how would they cope? "I wouldn't bother to put so much time and effort into doing well in anything." (In other words, don't let anyone measure you again.) "Do nothing." "Stay in bed." "Get drunk." "Eat." "Yell at someone if I get a chance to." "Eat chocolate." "Listen to music and pout." "Go into my closet and sit there." "Pick a fight with somebody." "Cry." "Break something." "What is there to do?"

What is there to do! You know, when I wrote the vignette, I intentionally made the grade a C+, not an F. It was a midterm rather than a final. It was a parking ticket, not a car wreck. They were "sort of brushed off," not rejected outright. Nothing catastrophic or irreversible happened. Yet from this raw material the fixed mindset created the feeling of utter failure and paralysis.

When I gave people with the growth mindset the same vignette, here's what they said. They'd think:

"I need to try harder in class, be more careful when parking the car, and wonder if my friend had a bad day."

"The C+ would tell me that I'd have to work a lot harder in the class, but I have the rest of the semester to pull up my grade."

There were many, many more like this, but I think you get the idea. Now, how would they cope? Directly.

"I'd start thinking about studying harder (or studying in a different way) for my next test in that class, I'd pay the ticket, and I'd work things out with my best friend the next time we speak."

"I'd look at what was wrong on my exam, resolve to do better, pay my parking ticket, and call my friend to tell her I was upset the day before."

"Work hard on my next paper, speak to the teacher, be more careful where I park or contest the ticket, and find out what's wrong with my friend."

You don't have to have one mindset or the other to be upset. Who wouldn't be? Things like a poor grade or a rebuff from a friend or loved one—these are not fun events. No one was smacking their lips with relish. Yet those people with the growth mindset were not labeling themselves and throwing up their hands. Even though they felt distressed, they were ready to take the risks, confront the challenges, and keep working at them.

SO, WHAT'S NEW?

Is this such a novel idea? We have lots of sayings that stress the importance of risk and the power of persistence, such as "Nothing ventured, nothing gained" and "If at first you don't succeed, try, try again" or "Rome wasn't built in a day." (By the way, I was delighted to learn that the Italians have the same expression.) What is truly amazing is that people with the fixed mindset would not agree. For them, it's "Nothing ventured, nothing lost." "If at first you don't succeed, you probably don't have the ability." "If Rome wasn't built in a day, maybe it wasn't meant to be." In other words, risk and effort are two things that might reveal your inadequacies and show that you were not up to the task. In fact, it's startling to see the degree to which people with the fixed mindset do not believe in effort.

What's also new is that people's ideas about risk and effort grow out of their more basic mindset. It's not just that some people happen to recognize the value of challenging themselves and the importance of effort. Our research has shown that this *comes directly* from the growth mindset. When we teach people the growth mindset, with its focus on development, these ideas about challenge and effort follow. Similarly, it's not just that some people happen to dislike challenge and effort. When we (temporarily) put people in a fixed mindset, with its focus on permanent traits, they quickly fear challenge and devalue effort.

We often see books with titles like *The Ten Secrets of the World's Most Successful People* crowding the shelves of bookstores, and these books may give many useful tips. But they're usually a list of unconnected pointers, like "Take more risks!" or "Believe in yourself!" While you're left admiring people who can do that, it's never clear how these things fit together or how you could ever become that way. So you're inspired for a few days, but basically the world's most successful people still have their secrets.

Instead, as you begin to understand the fixed and growth mindsets, you will see exactly how one thing leads to another—how a belief that your qualities are carved in stone leads to a host of thoughts and actions, and how a belief that your qualities can be cultivated leads to a host of different thoughts and actions, taking you down an entirely different road. It's what we psychologists call an *Aha!* experience. Not only have I seen this in my research when we teach people a new mindset, but I get letters all the time from people who have read my work.

They recognize themselves: "As I read your article I literally found myself saying over and over again, 'This is me, this is me!' " They see the connections: "Your article completely blew me away. I felt I had discovered the secret of the universe!" They feel their mindsets reorienting: "I can certainly report a kind of personal revolution happening in my own thinking, and this is an exciting feeling." And they can put this new thinking into practice for themselves *and* others: "Your work has allowed me to transform my work with children and see education through a different lens," or "I just wanted to let you know what an impact—on a personal and practical level—your outstanding research has had for hundreds of students."

SELF-INSIGHT: WHO HAS ACCURATE VIEWS OF THEIR ASSETS AND LIMITATIONS?

Well, maybe the people with the growth mindset don't think they're Einstein or Beethoven, but aren't they more likely to have inflated views of their abilities and try for things they're not capable of? In fact, studies show that people are terrible at estimating their abilities. Recently, we set out to see who is most likely to do this. Sure, we found that people greatly misestimated their performance and their ability. *But it was those with the fixed mindset who accounted for almost all the inaccuracy.* The people with the growth mindset were amazingly accurate.

When you think about it, this makes sense. If, like those with the growth mindset, you believe you can develop yourself, then you're open to accurate information about your current abilities, even if it's unflattering. What's more, if you're oriented toward learning, as they are, you *need* accurate information about your current abilities in order to learn effectively. However, if everything is either good news or bad news about your precious traits—as it is with fixed-mindset people—distortion almost inevitably enters the picture. Some outcomes are magnified, others are explained away, and before you know it you don't know yourself at all.

Howard Gardner, in his book *Extraordinary Minds*, concluded that exceptional individuals have "a special talent for identifying their own strengths and weaknesses." It's interesting that those with the growth mindset seem to have that talent.

WHAT'S IN STORE

The other thing exceptional people seem to have is a special talent for converting life's setbacks into future successes. Creativity researchers concur. In a poll of 143 creativity researchers, there was wide agreement about the number one ingredient in creative achievement. And it was exactly the kind of perseverance and resilience produced by the growth mindset.

You may be asking again, *How can one belief lead to all this—the love of challenge, belief in effort, resilience in the face of setbacks, and greater (more creative!) success?* You'll see exactly how this happens: how the mindsets change what people strive for and what they see as success. How they change the definition, significance, and impact of failure. And how they change the deepest meaning of effort. You'll see how these mindsets play out in school, in sports, in the workplace, and in relationships. You'll see where they come from and how they can be changed.

GROW YOUR MINDSET

Which mindset do you have? Answer these questions about intelligence. Read each statement and decide whether you mostly agree with it or disagree with it.

1. Your intelligence is something very basic about you that you can't change very much.
2. You can learn new things, but you can't really change how intelligent you are.
3. No matter how much intelligence you have, you can always change it quite a bit.
4. You can always substantially change how intelligent you are.

Questions 1 and 2 are the fixed-mindset questions. Questions 3 and 4 reflect the growth mindset. Which mindset did you agree with more? You can be a mixture, but most people lean toward one or the other.

You also have beliefs about other abilities. You could substitute "artistic talent," "sports ability," or "business skill" for "intelligence." Try it.

It's not only your abilities; it's your personal qualities too. Look at these statements about personality and character and decide whether you mostly agree or mostly disagree with each one.

1. You are a certain kind of person, and there is not much that can be done to really change that.
2. No matter what kind of person you are, you can always change substantially.
3. You can do things differently, but the important parts of who you are can't really be changed.
4. You can always change basic things about the kind of person you are.

Here, questions 1 and 3 are the fixed-mindset questions and questions 2 and 4 reflect the growth mindset. Which did you agree with more?

Did it differ from your intelligence mindset? It can. Your "intelligence mindset" comes into play when situations involve mental ability.

Your "personality mindset" comes into play in situations that involve your personal qualities—for example, how dependable, cooperative, caring, or socially skilled you are. The fixed mindset makes you concerned with how you'll be judged; the growth mindset makes you concerned with improving.

Here are some more ways to think about mindsets:

- Think about someone you know who is steeped in the fixed mindset. Think about how they're always trying to prove themselves and how they're supersensitive about being wrong or making mistakes. Did you ever wonder why they were this way? (Are you this way?) Now you can begin to understand why.
- Think about someone you know who is skilled in the growth mindset— someone who understands that important qualities can be cultivated. Think about the ways they confront obstacles. Think about the things

they do to stretch themselves. What are some ways you might like to change or stretch yourself?

- Okay, now imagine you've decided to learn a new language and you've signed up for a class. A few sessions into the course, the instructor calls you to the front of the room and starts throwing questions at you one after another.

Put yourself in a fixed mindset. Your ability is on the line. Can you feel everyone's eyes on you? Can you see the instructor's face evaluating you? Feel the tension, feel your ego bristle and waver. What else are you thinking and feeling?

Now put yourself in a growth mindset. You're a novice—that's why you're here. You're here to learn. The teacher is a resource for learning. Feel the tension leave you; feel your mind open up.

The message is: You can change your mindset.

The Truth About Ability and Accomplishment

Try to picture Thomas Edison as vividly as you can. Think about where he is and what he's doing. Is he alone? I asked people, and they always said things like this:

"He's in his workshop surrounded by equipment. He's working on the phonograph, trying things. He succeeds! [Is he alone?] Yes, he's doing this stuff alone because he's the only one who knows what he's after."

"He's in New Jersey. He's standing in a white coat in a lab-type room. He's leaning over a lightbulb. Suddenly, it works! [Is he alone?] Yes. He's kind of a reclusive guy who likes to tinker on his own."

In truth, the record shows quite a different fellow, working in quite a different way.

Edison was not a loner. For the invention of the lightbulb, he had thirty assistants, including well-trained scientists, often working around the clock in a corporate-funded state-of-the-art laboratory!

It did not happen suddenly. The lightbulb has become the symbol for that single moment when the brilliant solution strikes, but there was no single moment of invention. In fact, the lightbulb was not one invention, but a whole network of time-consuming inventions each requiring one or more chemists, mathematicians, physicists, engineers, and glassblowers.

Edison was no naïve tinkerer or unworldly egghead. The "Wizard of Menlo Park" was a savvy entrepreneur, fully aware of the commercial potential of his inventions. He also knew how to cozy up to the press—sometimes beating others out as *the* inventor of something because he knew how to publicize himself.

Yes, he was a genius. But he was not always one. His biographer, Paul Israel, sifting through all the available information, thinks he was more or less a regular boy of his time and place. Young Tom was taken with experiments and mechanical things (perhaps more avidly than most), but machines and technology were part of the ordinary midwestern boy's experience.

What eventually set him apart was his mindset and drive. He never stopped being the curious, tinkering boy looking for new challenges. Long after other young men had taken up their roles in society, he rode the rails from city to city learning everything he could about telegraphy, and working his way up the ladder of telegraphers through nonstop self-education and invention. And later, much to the disappointment of his wives, his consuming love remained self-improvement and invention, but only in his field.

There are many myths about ability and achievement, especially about the lone, brilliant person suddenly producing amazing things.

Yet Darwin's masterwork, *The Origin of Species*, took years of teamwork in the field, hundreds of discussions with colleagues and mentors, several preliminary drafts, and half a lifetime of dedication before it reached fruition.

Mozart labored for more than ten years until he produced any work that we admire today. Before then, his compositions were not that original or interesting. Actually, they were often patched-together chunks taken from other composers.

This chapter is about the real ingredients in achievement. It's about why some people achieve less than expected and why some people achieve more.

MINDSET AND SCHOOL ACHIEVEMENT

Let's step down from the celestial realm of Mozart and Darwin and come back to earth to see how mindsets create achievement in real life. It's funny, but seeing one student blossom under the growth mindset has a greater impact on me than all the stories about Mozarts and Darwins. Maybe because it's more about you and me—about what's happened to us and why we are where we are now. And about children and their potential.

Back on earth, we measured students' mindsets as they made the transition to junior high school: Did they believe their intelligence was a fixed trait or something they could develop? Then we followed them for the next two years.

The transition to junior high is a time of great challenge for many students. The work gets much harder, the grading policies toughen up, the teaching becomes less personalized. And all this happens while students are coping with their new adolescent bodies and roles. Grades suffer, but not everyone's grades suffer equally.

No. In our study, only the students with the fixed mindset showed the decline. They showed an immediate drop-off in grades, and slowly but surely did worse and worse over the two years. The students with the growth mindset showed an *increase* in their grades over the two years.

When the two groups had entered junior high, their past records were indistinguishable. In the more benign environment of grade school, they'd earned the same grades and achievement test scores. Only when they hit the challenge of junior high did they begin to pull apart.

Here's how students with the fixed mindset explained their poor grades. Many maligned their abilities: "I am the stupidest" or "I suck in math." And many covered these feelings by blaming someone else: "[The math teacher] is a fat male slut . . . and [the English teacher] is a slob with a pink ass." "Because the teacher is on crack." These interesting analyses of the problem hardly provide a road map to future success.

With the threat of failure looming, students with the growth mindset instead mobilized their resources for learning. They told us that they, too, sometimes felt overwhelmed, but their response was to dig in and do what it takes. They were like George Dantzig. Who?

George Dantzig was a graduate student in math at Berkeley. One day, as usual, he rushed in late to his math class and quickly copied the two homework problems from the blackboard. When he later went to do them, he found them very difficult, and it took him several days of hard work to crack them open and solve them. They turned out not to be homework problems at all. They were two famous math problems that had never been solved.

THE LOW-EFFORT SYNDROME

Our students with the fixed mindset who were facing the hard transition saw it as a threat. It threatened to unmask their flaws and turn them from winners into losers. In fact, in the fixed mindset, adolescence is one big test. *Am I smart or dumb? Am I good-looking or ugly? Am I cool or nerdy? Am I a winner or a loser?* And in the fixed mindset, a loser is forever.

It's no wonder that many adolescents mobilize their resources, not for learning, but to protect their egos. And one of the main ways they do this (aside from providing vivid portraits of their teachers) is by not trying. This is when some of the brightest students, just like Nadja Salerno-Sonnenberg, simply stop working. In fact, students with the fixed mindset tell us that their main goal in school—aside from looking smart—is to exert as little effort as possible. They heartily agree with statements like this:

"In school my main goal is to do things as easily as possible so I don't have to work very hard."

This low-effort syndrome is often seen as a way that adolescents assert their independence from adults, but it is also a way that students with the fixed mindset protect themselves. They view the adults as saying, "Now we will measure you and see what you've got." And they are answering, "No you won't."

John Holt, the great educator, says that these are the games all human beings play when others are sitting in judgment of them. "The worst student we had, the worst I have ever encountered, was in his life outside the classroom as mature, intelligent, and interesting a person as anyone at the school. What went wrong? . . . Somewhere along the line, his intelligence became disconnected from his schooling."

For students with the growth mindset, it doesn't make sense to stop trying. For them, adolescence is a time of opportunity: a time to learn new subjects, a time to find out what they like and what they want to become in the future.

Later, I'll describe the project in which we taught junior high students the growth mindset. What I want to tell you now is how teaching them this mindset unleashed their effort. One day, we were introducing the growth mindset to a new group of students. All at once Jimmy—the most hard-core turned-off low-effort kid in the group—looked up with tears in his eyes and said, "You mean I don't have to be dumb?" From that day on, he worked. He started staying up late to do his homework, which he never used to bother with at all. He started handing in assignments early so he could get feedback and revise them. He now believed that working hard was not something that made you vulnerable, but something that made you smarter.

FINDING YOUR BRAIN

A close friend of mine recently handed me something he'd written, a poem-story that reminded me of Jimmy and his unleashed effort. My friend's second-grade teacher, Mrs. Beer, had had each student draw and cut out a paper horse. She then lined up all the horses above the blackboard and delivered her growth-mindset message: "Your horse is only as fast as your brain. Every time you learn something, your horse will move ahead."

My friend wasn't so sure about the "brain" thing. His father had always told him, "You have too much mouth and too little brains for your own good." Plus, his horse seemed to just sit at the starting gate while "everyone else's brain joined the learning chase," especially the brains of Hank and Billy, the class geniuses, whose horses jumped way ahead of everyone else's. But my friend kept at it. To improve his skills, he kept reading the comics with his mother and he kept adding up the points when he played gin rummy with his grandmother.

> And soon my sleek stallion
> bolted forward like Whirlaway,
> and there was no one
> who was going to stop him.
> Over the weeks and months
> he flew forward overtaking
> the others one by one.
> In the late spring homestretch
> Hank's and Billy's mounts were ahead
> by just a few subtraction exercises, and
> when the last bell of school rang,

my horse won—"By a nose!"
Then I knew I had a brain:
I had the horse to prove it.
          —Paul Wortman

Of course, learning shouldn't really be a race. But this race helped my friend discover his brain and connect it up to his schooling.

THE COLLEGE TRANSITION

Another transition, another crisis. College is when all the students who were the brains in high school are thrown together. Like our graduate students, yesterday they were king of the hill, but today who are they?

Nowhere is the anxiety of being dethroned more palpable than in premed classes. I mentioned our study of tense but hopeful undergraduates taking their first college chemistry course. This is the course that would give them—or deny them—entrée to the premed curriculum, and it's well known that students will go to almost any lengths to do well in this course.

At the beginning of the semester, we measured students' mindsets, and then we followed them through the course, watching their grades and asking about their study strategies. Once again we found that the students with the growth mindset earned better grades in the course. Even when they did poorly on a particular test, they bounced back on the next ones. When students with the fixed mindset did poorly, they often didn't make a comeback.

In this course, everybody studied. But there are different ways to study. Many students study like this: They read the textbook and their class notes. If the material is really hard, they read them again. Or they might try to memorize everything they can, like a vacuum cleaner. That's how the students with the fixed mindset studied. If they did poorly on the test, they concluded that chemistry was not their subject. After all, "I did everything possible, didn't I?"

Far from it. They would be shocked to find out what students with the growth mindset do. Even I find it remarkable.

The students with growth mindset completely took charge of their learning and motivation. Instead of plunging into unthinking memorization of the course material, they said: "I looked for themes and underlying principles across lectures," and "I went over mistakes until I was certain I understood them." They were studying to learn, not just to ace the test. And, actually, this was why they got higher grades—not because they were smarter or had a better background in science.

Instead of losing their motivation when the course got dry or difficult, they said: "I maintained my interest in the material." "I stayed positive about taking chemistry." "I kept myself motivated to study." Even if they thought the textbook was boring or the instructor was a stiff, they didn't let their motivation evaporate. That just made it all the more important to motivate themselves.

I got an e-mail from one of my undergraduate students shortly after I had taught her the growth mindset. Here's how she used to study before: "When faced with really tough material I tend[ed] to read the material over and over." After learning the growth mindset, she started using better strategies—that worked:

> Professor Dweck:
>
> When Heidi [the teaching assistant] told me my exam results today I didn't know whether to cry or just sit down. Heidi will tell you, I looked like I won the lottery (and I feel that way, too)! I can't believe I did SO WELL. I expected to "scrape" by. The encouragement you have given me will serve me well in life. . . .
>
> I feel that I've earned a noble grade, but I didn't earn it alone. Prof. Dweck, you not only teach [your] theory, you SHOW it. Thank you for the lesson. It is a valuable one, perhaps the most valuable I've learned at Columbia. And yeah, I'll be doing THAT [using these strategies] before EVERY exam!
>
> Thank you very, very much (and you TOO Heidi)!
>
> No longer helpless,
> June

Because they think in terms of learning, people with the growth mindset are clued in to all the different ways to create learning. It's odd. Our pre-med students with the fixed mindset would do almost anything for a good grade—except take charge of the process to make sure it happens.

CREATED EQUAL?

Does this mean that anyone with the right mindset can do well? Are all children created equal? Let's take the second question first. No, some children are different. In her book *Gifted Children*, Ellen Winner offers incredible descriptions of prodigies. These are children who seem to be born with heightened abilities and obsessive interests, and who, through relentless pursuit of these interests, become amazingly accomplished.

Michael was one of the most precocious. He constantly played games involving letters and numbers, made his parents answer endless questions about letters and numbers, and spoke, read, and did math at an unbelievably early age. Michael's mother reports that at four months old, he said, "Mom, Dad, what's for dinner?" At ten months, he astounded people in the supermarket by reading words from the signs. Everyone assumed his mother was doing some kind of ventriloquism thing. His father reports that at three, he was not only doing algebra, but discovering and proving algebraic rules. Each day, when his father got home from work, Michael would pull him toward math books and say, "Dad, let's go do work."

Michael must have started with a special ability, but, for me, the most outstanding feature is his extreme love of learning and challenge. His parents could not tear him away from his demanding activities. The same is true for every prodigy Winner describes. Most often people believe that the "gift" is the ability itself. Yet what feeds it is that constant, endless curiosity and challenge seeking.

Is it ability or mindset? Was it Mozart's musical ability or the fact that he worked till his hands were deformed? Was it Darwin's scientific ability or the fact that he collected specimens nonstop from early childhood?

Prodigies or not, we all have interests that can blossom into abilities. As a child, I was fascinated by people, especially adults. I wondered: *What makes them tick?* In fact, a few years back, one of my cousins reminded me of an episode that took place when we were five years old. We were at my grandmother's house, and he'd had a big fight with his mother over when he could eat his candy. Later, we were sitting outside on the front steps and I said to him: "Don't be so stupid. Adults like to think they're in charge. Just say yes, and then eat your candy when you want to."

Were those the words of a budding psychologist? All I know is that my cousin told me this advice served him well. (Interestingly, he became a dentist.)

CAN EVERYONE DO WELL?

Now back to the first question. Is everyone capable of great things with the right mindset? Could you march into the worst high school in your state and teach the students college calculus? If you could, then one thing would be clear: With the right mindset and the right teaching, people are capable of a lot more than we think.

Garfield High School was one of the worst schools in Los Angeles. To say that the students were turned off and the teachers burned out is an understatement. But without thinking twice, Jaime Escalante (of *Stand and Deliver* fame) taught these inner-city Hispanic students college-level calculus. With his growth mindset, he asked "*How* can I teach them?" not "*Can* I teach them?" and "*How* will they learn best?" not "*Can* they learn?"

But not only did he teach them calculus, he (and his colleague, Benjamin Jimenez) took them to the top of the national charts in math. In 1987, only three other public schools in the country had more students taking the Advanced Placement Calculus test. Those three included Stuyvesant High School and the Bronx High School of Science, both elite math-and-science-oriented schools in New York.

What's more, most of the Garfield students earned test grades that were high enough to gain them college credits. In the whole country that year, only a few hundred Mexican American students passed the test at this level. This means there's a lot of intelligence out there being wasted by underestimating students' potential to develop.

MARVA COLLINS

Most often when kids are behind—say, when they're repeating a grade—they're given dumbed-down material on the assumption that they can't handle more. That idea comes from the fixed mindset: These students are dim-witted, so they need the same simple things drummed into them over and over. Well, the results are depressing. Students repeat the whole grade *without learning any more than they knew before.*

Instead, Marva Collins took inner-city Chicago kids who had failed in the public schools and treated them like geniuses. Many of them had been labeled "learning disabled," "retarded," or "emotionally disturbed." Virtually all of them were apathetic. No light in the eyes, no hope in the face.

Collins's second-grade public school class started out with the lowest-level reader there was. By June, they reached the middle of the fifth-grade reader, studying Aristotle, Aesop, Tolstoy, Shakespeare, Poe, Frost, and Dickinson along the way.

Later when she started her own school, *Chicago Sun-Times* columnist Zay Smith dropped in. He saw four-year-olds writing sentences like "See the physician" and "Aesop wrote fables," and talking about "diphthongs" and "diacritical marks." He observed second graders reciting passages from Shakespeare, Longfellow, and Kipling. Shortly before, he had visited a rich suburban high school where many students had never heard of Shakespeare. "Shoot," said one of Collins's students, "you mean those rich high school kids don't know Shakespeare was born in 1564 and died in 1616?"

Students read huge amounts, even over the summer. One student, who had entered as a "retarded" six-year-old, now four years later had read twenty-three books over the summer, including *A Tale of Two Cities* and *Jane Eyre.* The students read deeply and thoughtfully. As the three-and four-year-olds were reading about Daedalus and Icarus, one four-year-old exclaimed, "Mrs. Collins, if we do not learn and work hard, we will take an Icarian flight to nowhere." Heated discussions of *Macbeth* were common.

Alfred Binet believed you could change the quality of someone's mind. Clearly you can. Whether you measure these children by the breadth of their knowledge or by their performance on standardized tests, their minds had been transformed.

Benjamin Bloom, an eminent educational researcher, studied 120 outstanding achievers. They were concert pianists, sculptors, Olympic swimmers, world-class tennis players, mathematicians, and research neurologists. Most were not that remarkable as children and didn't show clear talent before their training began in earnest. Even by early adolescence, you usually couldn't predict their future accomplishment from their current ability. Only their continued motivation and commitment, along with their network of support, took them to the top.

Bloom concludes, "After forty years of intensive research on school learning in the United States as well as abroad, my major conclusion is: What any person in the world can learn, *almost* all persons can learn, *if* provided with the appropriate prior and current conditions of learning." He's not counting the 2 to 3 percent of children who have severe impairments, and he's not counting the top 1 to 2 percent of children at the other extreme that include children like Michael. He *is* counting everybody else.

ABILITY LEVELS AND TRACKING

But aren't students sorted into different ability levels for a reason? Haven't their test scores and past achievement shown what their ability is? Remember, test scores and measures of achievement tell you where a student is, but they don't tell you where a student could end up.

Falko Rheinberg, a researcher in Germany, studied schoolteachers with different mindsets. Some of the teachers had the fixed mindset. They believed that students entering their class with different achievement levels were deeply and permanently different:

"According to my experience students' achievement mostly remains constant in the course of a year."

"If I know students' intelligence I can predict their school career quite well."

"As a teacher I have no influence on students; intellectual ability."

Like my sixth-grade teacher, Mrs. Wilson, these teachers preached and practiced the fixed mindset. In their classrooms, the students who started the year in the high-ability group ended the year there, and those who started the year in the low-ability group ended the year there.

But some teachers preached and practiced a growth mindset. They focused on the idea that all children could develop their skills, and in their classrooms a weird thing happened. It didn't matter whether students started the year in the high- or the low-ability group. Both groups ended the year way up high. It's a powerful experience to see these findings. The group differences had simply disappeared under the guidance of teachers who taught for improvement, for these teachers had found a way to reach their "low-ability" students.

How teachers put a growth mindset into practice is the topic of a later chapter, but here's a preview of how Marva Collins, the renowned teacher, did it. On the first day of class, she approached Freddie, a left-back second grader, who wanted no part of school. "Come on, peach," she said to him, cupping his face in her hands, "we have work to do. You can't just sit in a seat and grow smart. . . . I promise, you are going to *do*, and you are going to *produce*. I am not going to let you fail."

SUMMARY

The fixed mindset limits achievement. It fills people's minds with interfering thoughts, it makes effort disagreeable, and it leads to inferior learning strategies. What's more, it makes other people into judges instead of allies.

Whether we're talking about Darwin or college students, important achievements require a clear focus, all-out effort, and a bottomless trunk full of strategies. Plus allies in learning. This is what the growth mindset gives people, and that's why it helps their abilities grow and bear fruit.

IS ARTISTIC ABILITY A GIFT?

Despite the widespread belief that intelligence is born, not made, when we really think about it, it's not so hard to imagine that people can develop their intellectual abilities. The intellect is so multifaceted. You can develop verbal skills or mathematical-scientific skills or logical thinking skills, and so on. But when it comes to artistic ability, it seems more like a God-given gift. For example, people seem to naturally draw well or poorly.

Even I believed this. While some of my friends seemed to draw beautifully with no effort and no training, my drawing ability was arrested in early grade school. Try as I might, my attempts were primitive and disappointing. I was artistic in other ways. I can design, I'm great with colors, I have a subtle sense of composition. Plus I have really good eye – hand coordination. Why couldn't I draw? I must not have the gift.

I have to admit that it didn't bother me all that much. After all, when do you really *have* to draw? I found out one evening as the dinner guest of a fascinating man. He was an older man, a psychiatrist, who had escaped from the Holocaust. As a ten-year-old child in Czechoslovakia, he and his younger brother came home from school one day to find their parents gone. They had been taken. Knowing there was an uncle in England, the two boys walked to London and found him.

A few years later, lying about his age, my host joined the Royal Air Force and fought for Britain in the war. When he was wounded, he married his nurse, went to medical school, and established a thriving practice in America.

Over the years, he developed a great interest in owls. He thought of them as embodying characteristics he admired, and he liked to think of himself as owlish. Besides the many owl statuettes that adorned his house, he had an owl-related guest book. It turned out that whenever he took a shine to someone, he asked them to draw an owl and write something to him in this book. As he extended this book to me and explained its significance, I felt both honored and horrified. Mostly horrified. All the more because my creation was not to be buried somewhere in the middle of the book, but was to adorn its very last page.

I won't dwell on the intensity of my discomfort or the poor quality of my artwork, although both were painfully clear. I tell this story as a prelude to the astonishment and joy I felt when I read *Drawing on the Right Side of the Brain*. On the opposite page are the before-and-after self-portraits of people who took a short course in drawing from the author, Betty Edwards. That is, they are the self-portraits drawn by the students when they entered her course and *five days later* when they had completed it.

Aren't they amazing? At the beginning, these people didn't look as though they had much artistic ability. Most of their pictures reminded me of my owl. But only a few days later, everybody could really draw! And Edwards swears that this is a typical group. It seems impossible.

Edwards agrees that most people view drawing as a magical ability that only a select few possess, and that only a select few will ever possess. But this is because people don't understand the components—the *learnable* components—of drawing. Actually, she informs us, they are not drawing skills at all, but *seeing* skills. They are the ability to perceive edges, spaces, relationships, lights and shadows, and the whole. Drawing requires us to learn each component skill and then combine them into one process. Some people simply pick up these skills in the natural course of their lives, whereas others have to work to learn them and put them together. But as we can see from the "after" self-portraits, everyone can do it.

Here's what this means: *Just because some people can do something with little or no training, it doesn't mean that others can't do it (and sometimes do it even better) with training.* This is so important, because many, many people with the fixed mindset think that someone's early performance tells you all you need to know about their talent and their future.

JACKSON POLLOCK

It would have been a real shame if people discouraged Jackson Pollock for that reason. Experts agree that Pollock had little native talent for art, and when you look at his early products, it showed. They also agree that he became one of the greatest American painters of the twentieth century and that he revolutionized modern art. How did he go from point A to point B?

Twyla Tharp, the world-famous choreographer and dancer, wrote a book called *The Creative Habit*. As you can guess from the title, she argues that creativity is not a magical act of inspiration. It's the result of hard work and dedication. *Even for Mozart*. Remember the movie *Amadeus*? Remember how it showed Mozart easily churning out one masterpiece after another while Salieri, his rival, is dying of envy? Well, Tharp worked on that movie and she says: Hogwash! Nonsense! "There are no 'natural' geniuses."

Dedication is how Jackson Pollock got from point A to point B. Pollock was wildly in love with the idea of being an artist. He thought about art all the time, and he did it all the time. Because he was so gung-ho, he got others to take him seriously and mentor him until he mastered all there was to master and began to produce startlingly original works. His "poured" paintings, each completely unique, allowed him to draw from his unconscious mind and convey a huge range of feeling. Several years ago, I was privileged to see a show of these paintings at the Museum of Modern Art in New York. I was stunned by the power and beauty of each work.

Can anyone do *anything*? I don't really know. However, I think we can now agree that people can do a lot more than first meets the eye.

THE DANGER OF PRAISE AND POSITIVE LABELS

If people have such potential to achieve, how can they gain faith in their potential? How can we give them the confidence they need to go for it? How about praising their ability in order to convey that they have what it takes? In fact, more than 80 percent of parents told us it was necessary to praise children's ability so as to foster their confidence and achievement. You know, it makes a lot of sense.

But then we began to worry. We thought about how people with the fixed mindset already focus too much on their ability: "Is it high enough?" "Will it look good?" Wouldn't praising people's ability focus them on it even more? Wouldn't it be telling them that that's what we value and, even worse, that we can read their deep, underlying ability from their performance? Isn't that teaching them the fixed mindset?

Adam Guettel has been called the crown prince and savior of musical theater. He is the grandson of Richard Rodgers, the man who wrote the music to such classics as *Oklahoma!* and *Carousel*. Guettel's mother gushes about her son's genius. So does everyone else. "The talent is there and it's major," raved a review in *The New York Times*. The question is whether this kind of praise encourages people.

What's great about research is that you can ask these kinds of questions and then go get the answers. So we conducted studies with hundreds of students, mostly early adolescents. We first gave each student a set of ten fairly difficult problems from a nonverbal IQ test. They mostly did pretty well on these, and when they finished we praised them.

We praised some of the students for their ability. They were told: "Wow, you got [say] eight right. That's a really good score. You must be smart at this." They were in the Adam Guettel *you're-so-talented* position.

We praised other students for their effort: "Wow, you got [say] eight right. That's a really good score. You must have worked really hard." They were not made to feel that they had some special gift; they were praised for doing what it takes to succeed.

Both groups were exactly equal to begin with. But right after the praise, they began to differ. As we feared, the ability praise pushed students right into the fixed mindset, and they showed all the signs of it, too: When we gave them a choice, they rejected a challenging new task that they could learn from. They didn't want to do anything that could expose their flaws and call into question their talent.

When Guettel was thirteen, he was all set to star in a Metropolitan Opera broadcast and TV movie of *Amahl and the Night Visitors*. He bowed out, saying that his voice had broken. "I kind of faked that my voice was changing. . . . I didn't want to handle the pressure."

In contrast, when students were praised for effort, 90 percent of them wanted the challenging new task that they could learn from.

Then we gave students some hard new problems, which they didn't do so well on. The ability kids now thought they were not smart after all. If success had meant they were intelligent, then less-than-success meant they were deficient.

Guettel echoes this. "In my family, to be good is to fail. To be *very* good is to fail. . . . The only thing *not* a failure is to be great."

The effort kids simply thought the difficulty meant "Apply more effort." They didn't see it as a failure, and they didn't think it reflected on their intellect.

What about the students' enjoyment of the problems? After the success, everyone loved the problems, but after the difficult problems, the ability students said it wasn't fun anymore. It can't be fun when your claim to fame, your special talent, is in jeopardy.

Here's Adam Guettel: "I wish I could just have fun and relax and not have the responsibility of that potential to be some kind of *great man*." As with the kids in our study, the burden of talent was killing his enjoyment.

The effort-praised students still loved the problems, and many of them said that the hard problems were the most fun.

We then looked at the students' performance. After the experience with difficulty, the performance of the ability-praised students plummeted, even when we gave them some more of the easier problems. Losing faith in their ability, they were doing worse than when they started. The effort kids showed better and better performance. They had used the hard problems to sharpen their skills, so that when they returned to the easier ones, they were way ahead.

Since this was a kind of IQ test, you might say that praising ability lowered the students' IQs. And that praising their effort raised them.

Guettel was not thriving. He was riddled with obsessive-compulsive tics and bitten, bleeding fingers. "Spend a minute with him—it takes only one— and a picture of the terror behind the tics starts to emerge," says an interviewer. Guettel has also fought serious, recurrent drug problems. Rather than empowering him, the "gift" has filled him with fear and doubt. Rather than fulfilling his talent, this brilliant composer has spent most of his life running from it.

One thing is hopeful—his recognition that he has his own life course to follow that is not dictated by other people and their view of his talent. One night he had a dream about his grandfather. "I was walking him to an elevator. I asked him if I was any good. He said, rather kindly, 'You have your own voice.' "

Is that voice finally emerging? For the score of *The Light in the Piazza*, an intensely romantic musical, Guettel won the 2005 Tony Award. Will he take it as praise for talent or praise for effort? I hope it's the latter.

There was one more finding in our study that was striking and depressing at the same time. We said to each student: "You know, we're going to go to other schools, and I bet the kids in those schools would like to know about the problems." So we gave students a page to write out their thoughts, but we also left a space for them to write the scores they had received on the problems.

Would you believe that almost 40 percent of the ability-praised students *lied* about their scores? And always in one direction. In the fixed mind-set, imperfections are shameful—especially if you're talented—so they lied them away.

What's so alarming is that we took ordinary children and made them into liars, simply by telling them they were smart.

Right after I wrote these paragraphs, I met with a young man who tutors students for their College Board exams. He had come to consult with me about one of his students. This student takes practice tests and then lies to him about her score. He is supposed to tutor her on what she doesn't know, but she can't tell him the truth about what she doesn't know! And she is paying money for this.

So telling children they're smart, in the end, made them feel dumber and act dumber, but claim they were smarter. I don't think this is what we're aiming for when we put positive labels—"gifted," "talented," "brilliant"—on people. We don't mean to rob them of their zest for challenge and their recipes for success. But that's the danger.

Here is a letter from a man who'd read some of my work:

Dear Dr. Dweck,

It was painful to read your chapter . . . as I recognized myself therein.

As a child I was a member of The Gifted Child Society and continually praised for my intelligence. Now, after a lifetime of not living up to my potential (I'm 49), I'm learning to apply myself to a task. And also to see failure not as a sign of stupidity but as lack of experience and skill. Your chapter helped see myself in a new light.

Seth Abrams

This is the danger of positive labels. There are alternatives, and I will return to them later in the chapter on parents, teachers, and coaches.

NEGATIVE LABELS AND HOW THEY WORK

I was once a math whiz. In high school, I got a 99 in algebra, a 99 in geometry, and a 99 in trigonometry, and I was on the math team. I scored up there with the boys on the air force test of visual-spatial ability, which is why I got recruiting brochures from the air force for many years to come.

Then I got a Mr. Hellman, a teacher who didn't believe girls could do math. My grades declined, and I never took math again.

I actually agreed with Mr. Hellman, but I didn't think it applied to *me*. *Other* girls couldn't do math. Mr. Hellman thought it applied to me, too, and I succumbed.

Everyone knows negative labels are bad, so you'd think this would be a short section. But it isn't a short section, because psychologists are learning *how* negative labels harm achievement.

No one knows about negative ability labels like members of stereotyped groups. For example, African Americans know about being stereotyped as lower in intelligence. And women know about being stereotyped as bad at math and science. But I'm not sure even they know how creepy these stereotypes are.

Research by Claude Steele and Joshua Aronson shows that even checking a box to indicate your race or sex can trigger the stereotype in your mind and lower your test score. Almost anything that reminds you that you're black or female before taking a test in the subject you're supposed to be bad at will lower your test score—a lot. In many of their studies, blacks are equal to whites in their performance, and females are equal to males, when no stereotype is evoked. But just put more males in the room with a female before a math test, and down goes the female's score.

This is why. When stereotypes are evoked, they fill people's minds with distracting thoughts—with secret worries about confirming the stereotype. People usually aren't even aware of it, but they don't have enough mental power left to do their best on the test.

This doesn't happen to everybody, however. It mainly happens to people who are in a fixed mindset. It's when people are thinking in terms of fixed traits that the stereotypes get to them. Negative stereotypes say: "You and your group are permanently inferior." Only people in the fixed mindset resonate to this message.

So in the fixed mindset, both positive and negative labels can mess with your mind. When you're given a positive label, you're afraid of losing it, and when you're hit with a negative label, you're afraid of deserving it.

When people are in a growth mindset, the stereotype doesn't disrupt their performance. The growth mindset takes the teeth out of the stereotype and makes people better able to fight back. They don't believe in permanent inferiority. And if they *are* behind—well, then they'll work harder and try to catch up.

The growth mindset also makes people able to take what they can and what they need even from a threatening environment. We asked African American students to write an essay for a competition. They were told that when they finished, their essays would be evaluated by Edward Caldwell III, a distinguished professor with an Ivy League pedigree. That is, a representative of the white establishment.

Edward Caldwell III's feedback was quite critical, but also helpful—and students' reactions varied greatly. Those with a fixed mindset viewed it as a threat, an insult, or an attack. They rejected Caldwell and his feedback.

Here's what one student with the fixed mindset thought: "He's mean, he doesn't grade right, or he's obviously biased. He doesn't like me."

Said another: "He is a pompous asshole. . . . It appears that he was searching for anything to discredit the work."

And another, deflecting the feedback with blame: "He doesn't understand the conciseness of my points. He thought it was vague because he was impatient when he read it. He dislikes creativity."

None of them will learn anything from Edward Caldwell's feedback.

The students with the growth mindset may also have viewed him as a dinosaur, but he was a dinosaur who could teach them something.

"Before the evaluation, he came across as arrogant and overdemanding. [After the evaluation?] 'Fair' seems to be the first word that comes to mind. . . . It seems like a new challenge."

"He sounded like an arrogant, intimidating, and condescending man. [What are your feeling about the evaluation?] The evaluation was seemingly honest and specific. In this sense, the evaluation could be a stimulus . . . to produce better work."

"He seems to be proud to the point of arrogance. [The evaluation?] He was intensely critical. . . . His comments were helpful and clear, however. I feel I will learn much from him."

The growth mindset allowed African American students to recruit Edward Caldwell III for their own goals. They were in college to get an education and, pompous asshole or not, they were going to get it.

Do I Belong Here?

Aside from hijacking people's abilities, stereotypes also do damage by making people feel they don't belong. Many minorities drop out of college and many women drop out of math and science because they just don't feel they fit in.

To find out how this happens, we followed college women through their calculus course. This is often when students decide whether math, or careers involving math, are right for them. Over the semester, we asked the women to report their feelings about math and their sense of belonging in math. For example, when they thought about math, did they feel like a full-fledged member of the math community or did they feel like an outsider; did they feel comfortable or did they feel anxious; did they feel good or bad about their math skills?

The women with the growth mindset—those who thought math ability could be improved—felt a fairly strong and stable sense of belonging. And they were able to maintain this even when they thought there was a lot of negative stereotyping going around. One student described it this way: "In a math class, [female] students were told they were wrong when they were not (they were in fact doing things in novel ways). It was absurd, and reflected poorly on the instructor not to 'see' the students' good reasoning. It was alright because we were working in groups and we were able to give & receive support among us students. . . . We discussed our interesting ideas among ourselves."

The stereotyping was disturbing to them (as it should be), but they could still feel comfortable with themselves and confident about themselves in a math setting. They could fight back.

But women with the fixed mindset, as the semester wore on, felt a shrinking sense of belonging. And the more they felt the presence of stereotyping in their class, the more their comfort with math withered. One student said that her sense of belonging fell because "I was disrespected by the professor with his comment, 'that was a good guess,' whenever I made a correct answer in class."

The stereotype of low ability was able to invade them—to define them—and take away their comfort and confidence. I'm not saying it's their fault by any means. Prejudice is a deeply ingrained societal problem, and I do not want to blame the victims of it. I am simply saying that a growth mindset helps people to see prejudice for what it is—*someone else's* view of them—and to confront it with their confidence and abilities intact.

TRUSTING PEOPLE'S OPINIONS

Many females have a problem not only with stereotypes, but with other people's opinions of them in general. They trust them too much.

One day, I went into a drugstore in Hawaii to buy dental floss and deodorant, and, after fetching my items, I went to wait in line. There were two women together in front of me waiting to pay. Since I am an incurable time stuffer, at some point I decided to get my money ready for when my turn came. So I walked up, put the items way on the side of the counter, and started to gather up the bills that were strewn throughout my purse. The two women went berserk. I explained that in no way was I trying to cut in front of them. I was just preparing for when my turn came. I thought the matter was resolved, but when I left the store, they were waiting for me. They got in my face and yelled, "*You're a bad-mannered person!*"

My husband, who had seen the whole thing from beginning to end, thought they were nuts. But they had a strange and disturbing effect on me, and I had a hard time shaking off their verdict.

This vulnerability afflicts many of the most able, high-achieving females. Why should this be? When they're little, these girls are often so perfect, and they delight in everyone's telling them so. They're so well behaved, they're so cute, they're so helpful, and they're so precocious. Girls learn to trust people's estimates of them. "Gee, everyone's so nice to me; if they criticize me, it must be true." Even females at the top universities in the country say that other people's opinions are a good way to know their abilities.

Boys are constantly being scolded and punished. When we observed in grade school classrooms, we saw that boys got *eight* times more criticism than girls for their conduct. Boys are also constantly calling each other slobs and morons. The evaluations lose a lot of their power.

A male friend once called me a slob. He was over to dinner at my house and, while we were eating, I dripped some food on my blouse. "That's because you're such a slob," he said. I was shocked. It was then that I realized no one had ever said anything like that to me. Males say it to each other all the time. It may not be a kind thing to say, even in jest, but it certainly makes them think twice before buying into other people's evaluations.

Even when women reach the pinnacle of success, other people's attitudes can get them. Frances Conley is one of the most eminent neurosurgeons in the world. In fact, she was the first woman ever given tenure in neurosurgery at an American medical school. Yet careless comments from male colleagues—even assistants—could fill her with self-doubt. One day during surgery, a man condescendingly called her "honey." Instead of returning the compliment, she questioned herself. "Is a honey," she wondered, "especially *this* honey, good enough and talented enough to be doing this operation?"

The fixed mindset, plus stereotyping, plus women's trust in people's assessments: I think we can begin to understand why there's a gender gap in math and science.

That gap is painfully evident in the world of high tech. Julie Lynch, a budding techie, was already writing computer code when she was in junior high school. Her father and two brothers worked in technology, and she loved it, too. Then her computer programming teacher criticized her. She had written a computer program and the program ran just fine, but he didn't like a shortcut she had taken. Her interest evaporated. Instead, she went on to study recreation and public relations.

Math and science need to be made more hospitable places for women. And women need all the growth mindset they can get to take their rightful places in these fields.

WHEN THINGS GO RIGHT

But let's look at the times the process goes right.

The Polgar family has produced three of the most successful female chess players ever. How? Says Susan, one of the three, "My father believes that innate talent is nothing, that [success] is 99 percent hard work. I agree with him." The youngest daughter, Judit, is now considered the best woman chess player of all time. She was not the one with the most talent. Susan reports, "Judit was a slow starter, but very hardworking."

A colleague of mind has two daughters who are math whizzes. One is a graduate student in math at a top university. The other was the first girl to rank number one in the country on an elite math test, won a nationwide math contest, and is now a neuroscience major at a top university. What's their secret? Is it passed down in the genes? I believe it's passed down in the mindset. It's the most growth-mindset family I've ever seen.

In fact, their father applied the growth mindset to *everything*. I'll never forget a conversation we had some years ago. I was single at the time, and he asked me what my plan was for finding a partner. He was aghast when I said I didn't have a plan. "You wouldn't expect your *work* to get done by itself," he said. "Why is this any different?" It was inconceivable to him that you could have a goal and not take steps to make it happen.

In short, the growth mindset lets people—even those who are targets of negative labels—use and develop their minds fully. Their heads are not filled with limiting thoughts, a fragile sense of belonging, and a belief that other people can define them.

GROW YOUR MINDSET

- Think about your hero. Do you think of this person as someone with extraordinary abilities who achieved with little effort? Now go find out the truth. Find out the tremendous effort that went into their accomplishment—and admire them *more*.

- Think of times other people outdid you and you just assumed they were smarter or more talented. Now consider the idea that they just used better strategies, taught themselves more, practiced harder, and worked their way through obstacles. You can do that, too, if you want to.

- Are there situations where you get stupid—where you disengage your intelligence? Next time you're in one of those situations, get yourself into a growth mindset—think about learning and improvement, not judgment—and hook it back up.

- Do you label your kids? *This one is the artist and that one is the scientist.* Next time, remember that you're not helping them—even though you may be praising them. Remember our study where praising kids' ability lowered their IQ scores. Find a growth-mindset way to compliment them.

- More than half of our society belongs to a negatively stereotyped group. First you have all the women, and then you have all the other groups who are not supposed to be good at something or other. Give them the gift of the growth mindset. Create an environment that teaches the growth mindset to the adults and children in your life, especially the ones who are targets of negative stereotypes. Even when the negative label comes along, they'll remain in charge of their learning.

The Student Fear Factor

Rebecca D. Cox

I would not have expected Eva to panic during her first composition class. Eva's reports of her high school preparation for college, her prior experiences in English classes, and her attitude toward writing in general all suggested that she would feel optimistic about Comp 1A. Furthermore, she spoke of her family's strong support for postsecondary education as well as her own commitment to a career that requires a college degree (that of schoolteacher). Eva asserted that although her parents had not put *a lot* of pressure on her (or on her younger sister), they did "make sure we know it's good to come to college." In fact, her parents continually reiterated the school-career connection: "You're working now, but you've got to go to school, because you've got to get a career." Eva's mother served as a role model in this regard: she had recently begun a postsecondary degree program to advance her own career goals. Despite the many reasons for Eva to feel at least relatively confident about her ability to succeed, she felt a sense of alarm when she was introduced to the objectives and structure of her first-semester English class: "That first day, when the professor said that it's going to be an essay after an essay, I was scared. I was like, 'Oh, my God, I'm not going to be able to make it.' . . . Just the fact that she said, 'Oh, you get an essay after an essay after an essay'—that's what scared me."

Eva's case is by no means unique. Regardless of age, ethnicity, academic background, educational goals, or the path to college, students reveal tremendous anxiety about their educational trajectories and ability to succeed in college. This chapter focuses on the "total fear factor," as one student aptly described it—a dimension of the student experience that has emerged in every study I have conducted, across community colleges in different regions of the country and with a highly diverse range of students. The recurrence of this fear factor in such varied contexts attests to its profound effect in shaping students' college experiences. This Chapter explores the phenomenon, the nature and ource of students' anxiety, and the strategies for managing those fears that students employ.

STUDENT ANXIETY

Regardless of the path that had led each student to college, enrolling in college courses proved to be an immensely stressful transition. For recent high school graduates as well as those outside the "traditional" age range, entering college marked a high-risk and anxiety-provoking transition in their adult lives.

Students fresh from high school, for instance, indicated that the transition into college represented a crucial threshold to adulthood. Melanie, a recent high school graduate and a first-semester college student at Lake Shore Community College in the Southwest, described her initiation to college as follows:

> Here, I've had to really break out of the comfort zone of high school, and I've had to be very much more independent. In high school, if you didn't do homework, you were able to copy off a kid, one of your friends, or you were able to find out information from one of your friends if you skipped a day or whatever. But here, it's pretty much, if I skip, it's my fault. If I don't turn it in, it's my fault. And it's all dependent upon me, and it's made me a lot more independent. It's really pushed me into an area that I don't want to go, but I have to. I mean, it's not, college isn't so much an academic life, but it's also a very social and emotional part of who you are, too.
>
> In high school, everyone tells you what to do, they tell you what classes to take, they direct you in certain ways, they put you in categories, and they put you in smart classes or dumb classes. And here in college, nobody does that for you. You have to figure it out on your own. I think college makes you a lot more serious.

Early in her first semester, Melanie had indeed taken a serious approach to college. She had developed both specific long-term career plans and a detailed strategy for realizing them. She would complete two years of college coursework at Lake Shore Community College. At the same time, she would complete some core requirements through the state university's online program. The next step consisted of transferring to the university, where she would earn a B.A. in psychology, then a Ph.D. She knew that an internship would be required for her to become a psychologist, and she had estimated the time it would take for her to become a practicing psychologist. All these steps, she noted, were crucial if she was not to "waste any time," and she described the effort she put into developing a logical plan. "I've had to figure out degree plans, courses at LSCC that can transfer to——University, the online courses at State that can transfer to the university; and as much as the counselors have helped me—I mean, they are really good at what they do—but a lot of this is set on you. And I think that really helps you grow as a person, because in the real world, nobody helps you besides your family. Nobody's going to help you. So, yeah, I think I have gotten a little more serious."

In many ways, Melanie fit the profile of a successful college student. She had formulated a clear and seemingly realistic educational plan, she was attending school full-time, she could draw financial and emotional support from her family while pursuing her goals, and she evaded the disadvantages that first-generation college goers face. In addition, she spoke positively about her academic preparation for college; for example, Melanie noted how fortunate she had been to attend a high school where "they didn't pressure us to make great grades, but you were more socially accepted within the school if you were a smart kid." And although Melanie had not necessarily earned the highest grades there—she mentioned "doing a lot better, gradewise" at the community college than she had during high school—she had enjoyed the opportunity to take "higher-level" classes, such as Advanced Placement English Literature. During her final semester in high school, she had taken one class at the community college, which made her feel more prepared for her first semester as a full-time student at the college.

Despite these advantages, Melanie spoke vividly of the fears she confronted on matriculating. Recalling the anxiety she had felt on the first day of the fall semester, she told me, "When I came on my first day here, as I was walking up through that parking lot—I had to park all the way over there at the other end, because it was, like, crazy packed here, on the first day. I remember walking up, thinking, 'I'm all by myself now.' Not literally, but the decisions that I make from today on, I'm going to have to make on my own. My family can advise me, but when it comes down to the nitty-gritty, the decision that I make is going to be my fault, or it's going to be my achievement. You know what I mean? And I think that was just a lot."

This realization, Melanie confided, was too much to handle: "My body just said, 'This is too much stress, this is too much'"—so much that she rushed from the parking lot to the closest women's room, feeling sick to her stomach.

MELANIE

> Melanie took four classes her first semester in college: composition, math, psychology, and French. Taking all four at once was challenging, but she felt that she was a serious student, committed to doing well. Throughout our conversation about her classes, Melanie contrasted her college coursework with her high school experience, and in doing so, consistently highlighted the increased academic pressure of college. For example, she described the fast pace of her French class, as compared with the Spanish classes she took in high school: "I never realized how fast college would be—comparing

one year of high school with one semester of college. It's really fast pacing. Like, I'm taking French right now, and that has really kicked me in the bum. Because in high school, you have two weeks to learn one section. And here it's like one day you learn a section, the next day you learn another section, it's just so fast paced, but I'm doing pretty good. . . . I think it's just because I've eliminated, like, my close, close friends, and all that kind of stupid high school drama that you go through, because in high school it's not really about academics."

Young adults such as Melanie were not the only ones to view the first semester of college as scary, unfamiliar, or life-changing. Individuals well outside the "traditional" college age range also spoke of the stress of assuming the responsibilities of college. Colleen, who had dropped out of high school at the age of fifteen, decided to return to school when her own children reached school age. At that point, she told herself, "Well, this is the right time for me, and the right time in my life, and I'm mature enough to handle it." Still, she admitted, "it was still really scary. Oh, my God, it was a life-altering change."

Because nearly every student viewed a college degree as essential to her future, they were all embarking on high-stakes ventures. Many lacked the kind of "college knowledge" typical of middle-class students and remained uncertain about how to approach the degree track and their coursework.[1] As a consequence, even as the vast majority of students were convinced that their future success hinged on their obtaining a college degree, they also revealed tremendous anxiety about the educational and occupational paths they were embarking on. A significant component of students' stress was directly linked to their doubts about succeeding in college and realizing their career goals.[2]

For some students, this fear—a natural part of any life transition—was heightened by their past experiences with failure in academic contexts. The frequent mentions of failure in student interviews included tales of having made bad decisions, performed poorly at various levels of elementary and secondary school, failed at specific assignments in high school courses, and failed or dropped classes at the postsecondary level. In addition, many students had fallen down on one or more of the entry-level assessments, whether in reading, writing, or math. In the case of math, the majority of the students I met had failed the test and had been required to enroll in at least one remedial math class before taking courses to fulfill the college math requirement. Thus, for many students, past failure provided objective evidence of their academic inadequacy.

Even students who did not explicitly discuss past failures revealed an underlying lack of confidence, and gnawing doubts about their capacity to succeed in college. For many, their very presence at a community college—the least selective and lowest tier of colleges—offered proof of their minimal academic competence. In other words, whereas admission to a selective college—

or even one that is less selective—offers some indication that a student has the capacity to succeed at that school, even this tenuous assurance is not available to students who enter a college with an open-admissions policy.

THE FEAR FACTOR

By enrolling in college courses, committing to a degree plan, and envisioning long-term objectives that depended on success at the community college, each student had stepped into the role of college student. The many students who seriously doubted their ability to succeed, however, were anxiously waiting for their shortcomings to be exposed, at which point they would be stopped from pursuing their goals. Fragile and fearful, these students expressed their concern in several ways: in reference to college professors, particular courses or subject matter, and the entire notion of college itself—whether at the two- or the four-year level. At the core of different expressions of fear, however, were the same feelings of dread and the apprehension that success in college would prove to be an unrealizable dream.[3]

Students admitted to feeling intimidated by professors' academic knowledge and by teachers' power to assess students and assign grades. Essentially, students were afraid that the professor would irrevocably confirm their academic inadequacy. When students described their stereotypical image of the university professor, a coherent picture emerged. Associating this ideal professor type with prestigious universities, students portrayed professors as "looking down on" students. One student, for example, spoke of his preconceived image of college professors as "all high and mighty," and Colleen spoke of the "pompous-ass professor" type. She associated this type with the elite universities, noting, "When you think of Yale, you're thinking pompous-ass professors."

From Colleen's perspective, her philosophy instructor tended "to act like he's teaching at Yale or something." During her interview with me, she addressed him in absentia, with this request: "Come down to our level a little bit. I know you have a lot of stuff to teach us, but don't be so high on that pedestal that we can't reach you." Her belief in the philosophy professor's clear superiority shaped Colleen's approach to the course. She explained,

> It got to where I did not feel comfortable approaching him about anything, because I felt like he was this so-smart guy that I'm going to look really stupid in his eyes if I ask him any questions at all. And so I don't feel comfortable asking him anything. I just go to class, and I sit in the back of the classroom now, whereas I started at the front of the classroom. I sit in the back, behind whoever else I can find, so he doesn't even have to look at me. So I'm just kind of hiding in the back, thinking, "Yes, I'm going to pass this class, somehow."

Colleen's philosophy teacher was not at all typical. Except for Colleen, when students alluded to the "so-smart" or "high and mighty professors," they noted that their community college professors did not fall into that category. Melanie, for instance, insisted that her community college instructors did not match her preconceptions about college professors. "When I was a high school student, I very much got the idea that college was very anonymous, that all you were, really, was a name on a page. You know, you really weren't a person." The difference between the stereotypical professor and students' actual professors did not mean, however, that students were unafraid of or unintimidated by their community college instructors.

Both Serena and Ryan provided examples of professors who were not "all high and mighty," but rather "kind of friendly." Yet their interactions with these professors still reflected an intimidating distance between professor and student. In describing his history professor, for instance, Ryan noted, "There's kind of something about him that, I don't know, makes me kind of hesitant to say something to him. He's kind of friendly, but it's just, I don't really know, something about him is just . . ." (his voice trailed off). Serena offered a similar description of her hesitancy about meeting professors during their office hours. "Like, some professors will be like, 'Oh, I'll be in my office,' but you're real hesitant to go to them, because of the way they are."

In fact, Colleen's avoidance strategy in her philosophy course represented a frequent student behavior. In this case, her approach was particularly interesting because she had demonstrated a high level of assertiveness in other situations—both on her own behalf and for other students. She had confronted the tutors at the writing center, for example, and had advised several younger students in her classes to consult with their instructors when problems arose. That Colleen would resort to hiding from her philosophy teacher suggests that other younger or less assertive students would be even more likely to react that way to stressful classroom encounters.

A wide range of courses, subject matter, and assignments caused students to worry. Math and composition, however, evoked by far the greatest anxiety for the vast majority of students. Students' fear of the composition course was particularly intense.[4] As the portal to more exclusive classes, composition plays a crucial role in selection of students. Those who successfully complete the course are judged proficient in the general writing skills deemed necessary for further academic study. Thus, the outcome for each student in composition holds important consequences for his or her educational trajectory and ability to succeed as a college student. Not by coincidence, among community college offerings this high-stakes course has some of the highest dropout rates—second only to those in math courses.

Kyra, who put off taking the course until her very last semester, noted, "I just had a fear of English, like this total fear factor." Likewise, Linda, who enrolled in and then dropped the course multiple times before finally completing it, explained, "The only reason why I waited is because I hate writing. I was always afraid of it—I think I've always had that problem."

Students' explanations for their anxiety often highlighted inadequate instruction in the past. "Oh, high school teachers [sigh]. I wrote two papers, I think, and that was it. And we never had to edit or anything. Yeah, I knew I was going to have a very hard time" (Suzanne).

Significantly, however, students who feared composition class did not necessarily perceive their high school preparation as inadequate. Anxiety and low self-confidence also plagued students who spoke favorably of their former English teachers or commented on the rigor of their high school English curriculum.[5]

This was certainly true for Eva, the student we met at the beginning of this chapter whose first day of class caused her to think, "I'm not going to make it." Jenn—another student who had earned As in her high school English classes—offered a more vivid description of her first day of college, at which point she, too, questioned whether she could handle the work required in composition. "I just saw all the work, and my heart was beating, and I'm just thinking, 'This is not real. There's no way college can be this hard.' It was just like they were throwing information at you, and just expecting you to be okay with it."

Although male students were much less likely than female students to offer unsolicited accounts of feeling anxious or unprepared, they too admitted that particular courses had generated nervousness. Diego, for example, expressed a sense of amazement at his success in composition class, particularly in light of his dislike of writing. As he explained, "I like reading, but I don't like writing. So I was surprised at my accomplishments in this class."

Becky: So it kind of sounds like you were very nervous about how well you would do.

Diego: Yes, yes, yes. I did come in like that. This is my worst, my—actually, I'm passing this class—but this was the one I was most afraid of.

Similarly, Carlos was worried about submitting essays in composition class "because of the fear and because I didn't know exactly what [the teacher] wanted."

Looking back, Carlos explained how his fears had initially paralyzed him, making his coursework more difficult: "It was like I thought I wouldn't make it, like I wasn't going to be able to make it. And I made it hard and it wasn't that hard." When I asked how he made his coursework harder, he elaborated, "It was the negative touch. It wasn't that I couldn't make it or I didn't do this right or I did this wrong. It was just that I was afraid. . . . Maybe it was the fear of college, too. . . . I think that's one of the things that makes a lot of people fail."

When asked, near the end of the semester, about their experiences at the start of the semester, some students admitted nonchalantly that they had anticipated that their courses would be more difficult. Claudia for instance commented, "I just expected more work. Like I'd never have time for anything else." Such students did not explicitly mention any anxiety around their original expectations, but it is possible that they, too, had experienced some nervousness at the start of their community college experience.

Students who expressed confidence in their ability to succeed at the community college level were not necessarily as certain about the four-year level. Several students noted that taking classes at the community college had made them change their minds about transferring to a four-year college. Taking courses had convinced Nereida, for example, that she wasn't really "college material." She planned to continue at the two-year college but had decided not to transfer. Similarly, Susan did not want to transfer to the nearby university, she explained, "'cause I don't think I can hang." In reference to his own plan to transfer to a four-year college in California, Sebastian mused: "I just wonder how I would do at a four-year college, like at a Cal State or a UC. I'm sure things are turned up a notch over there."

His experience at Hillcrest Community College (HCC) had led Sebastian to conclude that you can "use HCC to mold your education; then, if you're really serious, you can go on to a four-year college." Describing himself as not yet motivated "all the way," Sebastian contended that once he reached that point, he would "probably really cut back on work and just focus on school and try to give a good push for a year or two, get something accomplished." His fear revolved around the four-year experience in store for him once he did get really serious. "I'm just hoping that these classes that I'm taking aren't these totally, like—I don't know the word—more like a waste of time; like doing all this easy stuff, when really I'm not aware of all the higher classes that I should be trying to take and get into." Nikki also confessed to her past and present fears of college. While discussing her transfer goals, she concluded: "So, we shall see. It's scary—very scary. . . . I'm so unsure of what to expect at the next level. It was scary to come here— I wasn't sure what to expect, but it was okay. It turned out okay, I guess."

SEBASTIAN

This was Sebastian's second semester at the college, and he was taking three classes while working part-time at a video store. The previous semester, he had worked full-time and started with four courses, but he found that he "started to fall behind." Since he had changed his work schedule, Sebastian wasn't particularly worried about his courses. "Like English: so far it's good, it's pretty easy, not really bad at all, compared to high school—I hated English." In part he attributed it to his own maturity as a student: "Now that I'm in college, I'm a little more mature and . . . I can get something out of it now."

Sebastian hadn't yet enrolled in any college-level classes, however; that semester, he was taking three basic skills classes, one for math, one for reading, and one for writing. In all the classes, but especially the English courses, he felt confident about his ability to do well. "I feel prepared; I feel comfortable doing all the work. It's all easy for me." Sebastian's anxiety was reserved for the future courses; he admitted, "But, um, I'm going to see how English 1A goes, because that's like freshman English."

FEAR MANAGEMENT

Fear of failing as college students drove some to employ preventive strategies. Choosing such actions (or inaction), however, could easily divert students from accomplishing their original goals. This risk was what puzzled me about students like Eva. When I interviewed her, she and her classmates in Composition 1A were nearly all assured of passing the course. Yet even she, a competent and conscientious student who "always knew [she] would attend college," had considered quitting on day one of the course. Nor was she the only one to respond in that way. Jenn's anxieties on her first day almost led her to drop out of college altogether. Jenn prefaced her account by saying, "I really wasn't ready to come, at all. I wasn't ready for it altogether, just wasn't ready for another year of school. I was in a new town, at a new school. And I just didn't know what to expect."

The first day of school was a Tuesday, a day when all her courses were scheduled to meet. Before going to the first class of the day, Jenn spoke to her mother.

I called her up, and I said, "I'm on my way to school." She says, "Okay, I'll talk to you later on," and I said "okay." I went to my first class, had like a four-and-a-half-hour break, and then went to my other three, went home, and I thought, "I quit."

Then I called my mom up, and I tell her, "I quit. Yeah, I quit here." She asks, "How do you plan on living?" and I say, "I don't know. I don't know how I plan on living. I don't care." She says, "Jenn, it can't be that bad," and I say, "You want to hear what the hell I have to do?" And I went syllabus by syllabus, day by day. And she was just like, "Well, just take it one day at a time. Don't get overwhelmed." And I'm just thinking, "Don't get overwhelmed? It's a little late for that!"

So I sat there and bawled with Mama for three hours. Then I talked to my sister, and my sister tells me, "I'll help you out." So eventually, after like four hours of talking with my mom, and an hour and a half talking with my sister, they convinced me that I could do this, that I've been through tougher stuff than this, and that it'd be no big deal.

Clearly, quitting is the ultimate fear management strategy, because it offers a means of eliminating the source of anxiety; however, students did not necessarily opt out of school altogether. Other strategies offered students ways of continuing their studies, while warding off the worst forms of personal failure.

JENN

> Although Jenn had received all As in high school, she described her-
> self as "absolutely not" prepared for college. When I asked her to
> explain, she told me that her older sister, who had taken Advanced
> Placement (AP) courses in high school, had reported being totally
> unprepared for college. In fact, her sister was constantly challeng-
> ing Jenn, telling her, " 'You need to take harder classes—these are
> just simple classes.'" Her sister also told Jenn, "'You're making all
> As. There is a problem here.' And she's like, 'You don't study. You
> barely do your homework.' She said, 'You know, you wait until the
> last minute to do your homework.' And she's like, 'I just don't see
> how you're making all As, when you're really not doing anything.'"
> Jenn was so nervous about college that for the entire summer after
> high school graduation she tried to avoid thinking about registering
> for classes at the community college she planned to attend. If her
> mother hadn't been "getting on her" about it, she might not have
> followed through. Describing how the pressure affected her, Jenn
> provided an example from the summer: "So my mom was just on
> me. 'We need to get your scheduling done, dah, dah, dah,' and it
> was like, 'I'm overwhelmed. Don't bother me, don't talk to me.' I
> didn't talk to her for like three weeks."

One such strategy consisted of scaling back. Several students had been admitted to nearby four-year colleges, but had chosen instead to start their college careers in a less stressful environment. Adriana told me, that she had made a good decision, stating, "I think it's a good way to start because I'm afraid if I would have gone straight to [Research University], I would have been stressed out, because it would have been such a bigger thing."

Similarly, Ashley told me, "I'm just kind of getting my feet wet in the whole college experience thing. I'm new to the city, so I'm new to the area and everything, and I got accepted to Western State, but I got—I don't want to say I got scared, but I just wanted to save my own money, not be a burden on my parents. So I'm doing that and going to school here, and it is [pause]—it's smaller classes, and you get to [pause]—it's better. I'm gradually getting up there. And then I'll go, I'm going to go to Western State probably next fall, or the fall after—I'm not sure." When I asked her if she could break it down and assign percentages to her different reasons, Ashley came up with an estimate of 20 percent for saving money. "I really don't want to be a burden, and I'm probably going to get like financial aid and stuff. But, yeah, it's not that big. . . . I don't know, maybe like 20 percent." As far as the time to "gradually get up there" and be ready for the four-year college, "probably over 50 percent. Yeah, that's probably the biggest reason, is just really wanting to be ready."

For Ashley, the underlying fear involved being exposed—in front of the teacher and her peers—as too stupid for college classes. "I don't want to be the stupid kid in class, where everyone else is raising their hand, and I'm the only one not. And I know it's not going to be like that, but it's one of my biggest fears."

In both instances, highly capable students with excellent records of performance in high school took themselves out of high-risk situations by scaling down and starting at LSCC.

Students with more marginal academic backgrounds were similarly driven by their fears to scale back their educational goals. Nereida and Susan were taking themselves off the baccalaureate track. Others spoke of newly formulated career plans, born of a desire to do "less school." Examples of students who spoke of such scaled-back plans included Suzanne, who was considering cosmetology, and Mariella, who spoke of earning a certificate instead of an associate's degree. For still others, scaling back would result in their withdrawing from school altogether.

A second fear management strategy was to redefine success and failure. Some students, who described the advantages that sprang from specific experiences of failure, exhibited remarkable resilience in the face of disappointments and derailed plans. This ability to reframe disappointments and failures as fortuitous twists of fate was expressed most eloquently by a Latino student named Carlos. Midway through his first semester of college, Carlos's composition instructor, Michelle, recommended that he withdraw from the course, to avoid receiving an F.[6] When I asked Carlos how disappointed he was that he would have to repeat the course, he responded with the phrase "No hay malque por bien no venga" (There is no bad thing that can't turn out for the good) and explained, "It's okay, because now I'm going to focus more on the other classes. And right now, music is really hard stuff right now, so I'm going to focus on music and my other classes. It won't affect me on my financial aid because I had fifteen hours, so now I have twelve."

Other students seemed to be formulating protective rationalizations for imminent failure. For instance, near the end of the semester, Yolanda disclosed that she had many outstanding composition assignments. She had attended every class session, and noted that she had learned a lot of grammar (especially pronouns) by taking the class. In the same conversation, she offered a range of definitions of success in Comp 1A:

> Success for one person can be, "I've actually conquered it by making the A I wanted to make." "I went to all the classes," can be a success. "I flunked the classes, but yet I understand what a pronoun is," can be a success. . . .
>
> And so you win some, you lose some. I may lose three hundred dollars and flunk in this class, but when I take the class again,

> I guarantee you that I'll come back with a little bit more fire under me and say, "Okay, I know what you want done. So I know what I need, and I'm going to get it done."

With this revised definition of success, Yolanda could finish the semester without completing the assignments and therefore fail the course, yet still retain a sense of efficacy that would enable her to return to LSCC the following semester to retake Comp 1A. In fact, Yolanda did not pass Comp 1A that semester. During the interview, she had expressed confidence that she was able to do the required coursework, and yet, two-thirds of the way through the semester, she had not yet submitted any of the essay assignments to her instructor. Yolanda was not unique in this regard. Across six sections of composition at LSCC, I observed students who attended class through the end of the semester, completed the assigned readings, and participated in the in-class activities—yet failed to submit written work for their instructors to grade. Still other students had disappeared altogether, silently withdrawing from the course and joining the 40 percent who did not complete Comp 1A.

A third fear management strategy consisted simply of avoiding any formal assessment. Every assessment-related activity posed the risk of exposing to others (both professors and peers) what students already suspected: their overall unfitness for college. Thus, not participating in classroom discussions, avoiding conversations with the professor—whether inside or outside the classroom—or choosing not to attend class sessions offered fear-driven students another reprieve from exposure. Students have admitted that silence during class—whether in whole-group or small-group configurations—results from anxiety, not from laziness or lack of caring. Some students deal with test-taking anxiety by avoiding particular tests; others end up taking the test, only to stop attending class before they find out the results. The greatest risk, of course, lies in graded assessments of student performance. In the absence of evidence from assessments, students can still cling—however tenuously—to their identity as college students.

Jenn, who had reported feeling overwhelmed on day one by the course-work outlined on various syllabi, decided not to quit immediately, but she came to that decision only after hours of discussion with her family. When I asked Jenn how often, after that first day at LSCC, she reconsidered dropping out, she replied, "I would think that, probably, with every first test that there was." In other words, the prospect of submitting the first graded assignment for each course was the most terrifying part of the semester. Barbara told about her first English class, during which the instructor administered an in-class writing assignment. With a sense of hopelessness, Barbara attempted to draft some sort of response; and at the end of the class, Barbara recalled, "I walked up to [the professor's] desk. I handed her my paper and I said, 'I don't know what you want written down. I have no idea what an essay is.' . . . She looked at me and I told her, 'I'm not coming back.'" This particular example highlights the irony of such avoidance strategies, that students' efforts to manage their fear of failure can easily lead to failure.

Elisa's experience with the research paper assignment illustrates the extent to which her fear of failure drove her to the brink of actual failure. On the day the research paper was due in Julie's class, I had a conversation with Elisa and Charmaine, neither of whom was ready to submit a draft of the assignment. Whereas Charmaine expressed confidence that she would submit one soon, Elisa spoke of her loathing for the research paper assignment. In fact, she told us, she had withdrawn from Comp 1A during the spring semester after getting stuck on this very assignment. At this point in the fall course, with Julie as her instructor, Elisa had chosen a topic (the influence of media images on women) and begun brainstorming about possible theses; however, she voiced concern about finding more sources and demonstrated hesitance regarding the appropriateness of the topic for the research paper assignment. When I asked whether she had talked to her instructor, Julie, about those concerns, she replied, "But I feel so bad—I'm so far behind and I don't want her to know." Instead, Elisa thought that she would probably withdraw from the course and try again next semester.

Upon urging from Charmaine and me, Elisa did meet with Julie to discuss the research paper. Julie later reported to me that Elisa had successfully completed the assignment. "Her research paper she finally submitted to me was A work. I mean, I chuckled. I wrote a comment back to her: 'LOL—I'm laughing out loud because your paper is awesome, and you were worried sick about submitting this paper to me, and this is your best paper.' "

When it came to learning, Elisa's strategy of avoidance was clearly counterproductive. Such an approach to the assignment made sense only in light of her conviction that she was not a competent college student. From this perspective, error—whether past or potential, real or imagined—plays a destructive role, by chipping away at each student's self-conception as a competent college student. Not surprisingly, students exhibited very low tolerance for feeling confused or making mistakes, phenomena they could easily attribute to their own inadequacy rather than to the process of learning new skills or information.[7]

This was certainly true of Natalie, a second-semester student at a California college. During her interview, Natalie assessed herself as entirely "unready" for college, attributing it to a personal character flaw—a form of fear-induced lack of effort.

> I'm scared of hard stuff. I'm intimidated by hard stuff, so that's probably holding me back. I need more courage. . . . I'm a scaredy-cat; I say, "That class is too hard," instead of trying it out and applying myself. That's what's wrong with me.
>
> I turned in my first paper and I got an X. I mean, you're supposed to get like, a B over X, or a C over X, so that you can have a chance to fix what you made a mistake in and then get that C. And

I didn't get anything over that X—I just got an X. . . . See, that's why I don't turn anything in. . . . That's why I don't like turning anything in, because every time I do, I get a bad grade.

Natalie had carefully examined the syllabus for some clue about the mysterious X she'd received but still did not understand what it meant. Her friend, also in the class, chimed in, "That just means you got to rewrite the whole thing." Natalie disagreed, however. According to the written policies, "He said no rewriting. He said, Don't rewrite the papers, just correct them."

It is difficult to understand why Natalie did not complete any assignments after her initial X grades. Not only did she demonstrate familiarity with the syllabus and various course documents, in noting the correct instructions for students who receive an "over X" grade, but her understanding of the regulations also reflected careful reading of these relatively complicated texts. Yet her confusion about the X stymied her, instead of propelling her to investigate further. She continued to attend class, she participated in the small-group exercises, and she prepared for in-class quizzes. She did nothing about the incomplete essay, however. Nor did she submit any other essays. Instead, she avoided the problem. While her instructor waited fruitlessly for Natalie to seek his help, he assumed that she did not care about the course. In the end, both teacher and student interpreted her performance as the result of individual deficits.

IMPLICATIONS FOR STUDENT SUCCESS

Using the example of his first math test of the semester, Carlos discussed his realization that the best plan was to work through the fear. On the day of the math test, he related, "I got panicked. And then I thought, 'Well, I'm going to try it,' and then I started writing and it was okay. That was it. I just got two problems wrong. And actually I got the first- or the second-highest grade in the class."

Carlos thus pinpointed the conundrum facing fearful students: fear drives them to the point of quitting, yet making the effort in the face of that fear may provide the evidence that they can succeed.

Of huge significance regarding this phenomenon is the fact that I generally interviewed students at the end of the semester. By that point, many others had already quietly disappeared from the class. A few of the students who attended the last few weeks of class might have ended up failing the course, but for the most part, I interviewed the most successful students. At the same time, I do not believe that I would have gained the same insights about student fear had I interviewed students who did not persist. Nor do I believe that the students I interviewed at the end of the semester would have admitted their prior fears had they not believed that they were going to complete their courses successfully. In other words, students who acknowledged their fears did so in the past tense; they had felt that way at the start of the semester but had progressed over the course of it toward feeling less afraid and more confident. I suspect that had they still harbored those shameful feelings of inadequacy, the instinct to avoid being evaluated would have prevented them from admitting their fears, perhaps even to themselves.

The depth of fear among the most successful and resilient students—students who had persisted in their courses until the end of the semester—suggests that at least some students who had withdrawn from the course or failed to complete the graded coursework were pushed over the brink by their fears, into failure. For individuals who started the semester feeling unequal to "college student" demands, it was easy to perceive every dimension of college and college coursework as overly confusing and too difficult. Such students avoided the forms of active engagement that would have improved their chances of succeeding, while simultaneously diverting instructors' attention from the core reason for their counterproductive behavior. In other words, such defenses against fear seriously undermined their chances of passing the course. In light of the large number of students who fail or withdraw from Comp 1A at community colleges, it is very likely that many employed the counterproductive strategies described by the students I have spoken with. Students like Jenn and Eva felt like quitting at the start of the semester, but other students actually did so at various points throughout the semester.

With a few exceptions, the composition students I interviewed had mustered enough courage to submit written work throughout the semester and ultimately completed the course successfully. Judged by the end-of-semester outcomes, the depth of fear that the interview respondents had experienced at the start of the semester was unwarranted. Once students overcame the biggest obstacle—once they submitted the most fear-inducing assignment—their performance far exceeded their initial pessimistic predictions. They had been able to overcome their fears without resorting to passive strategies of disengagement or dropping out.

For those who did pass the course, one of the most important lessons was that when they submitted the writing assignments, their deepest fears were disproved. For Kyra, who spoke to me of her "total fear factor" in Comp 1A, doing well in the class provided evidence of her writing competence. As she put it, "So that kind of in itself indicates that I'm not as bad as I thought I was. And my fear is maybe just in my head, rather than actual fact." Similarly, Linda concluded at the end of the semester, "I hated writing, but now I feel that I know that I can. I feel better now. I'm not afraid like I was before."

Similarly, Jenn, who had left the first class session ready to quit school, described how her attitude changed after she had submitted the first graded assignment. "But once I got my first paper accepted for English, I was so excited. It made me want to go and write some more. Yeah, it made me want to go and write some more, and after my second paper, my mom just told me, 'I don't think anybody's given you the chance to write. I don't think anybody's given you what you needed, to learn.' "

Individuals who are familiar with what is required and who are relatively confident from the start of their success as college students are most likely to achieve success. Conversely, those who are least conversant with the norms of higher education are at a distinct disadvantage; they are more likely to feel like outsiders and to doubt their ability to fit in. Indeed, for fearful students, every interaction in the classroom and with their professors outside class holds the potential to confirm their feelings of inadequacy. Yet the same strategies that relieve their fear can prove counterproductive for completing college course-work. In particular, avoiding assessment precludes the chance of proving their academic merit. Thus the fear of failure—rather than actual failure or evidence of unsuitability—prevents full commitment and engagement. How such fears and counterproductive strategies might be countered is therefore an impor-tant consideration in promoting student success. How individual professors have addressed the issue—indeed, *that* professors need to address the issue—lies at the heart.

"How is That Helping Us?"

Rebekah Nathan, in her account of the year she spent living like a first-year college student, describes a critical revelation. She explains that as a college professor she had an incomplete understanding of students that often led her to address classroom problems in ways that were bound to fail. Only after her "freshman year" investigating students' behavior and intentions more closely did she finally recognize this truth. "I could see why my former 'solutions' had not changed [students'] behavior. Like many of my teaching and administrative colleagues, I often design solutions to student problems that do not address the actual source of the problem. The miscalculations come from faulty assumptions concerning what good students do and how they organize their academic lives." So too have my own studies of college students clarified how professors' best intentions can go awry, and underscored the need to probe beneath the surface of students' performance. The earlier chapters illustrate how students' preconceptions and expectations inevitably complicate the dynamics of teaching and learning in college classrooms. Professors may craft solutions that miss the mark; just as easily, students may not understand the "solution" as it is intended.

Given students' pragmatic approach to education as a means to achieve their career goals and their efforts to avoid wasting time or money, it would be easy to imagine that these students cared about earning the credential but were not much concerned with learning. A superficial look at their approach to coursework suggests that students were attempting to "succeed at school without really learning," as the education historian David Labaree put it.[2] A more thorough examination of students' orientation to college, however, reveals that students sincerely hoped to learn something important and meaningful in college. At the same time, their understanding of important and meaningful information was tightly linked to practical goals, and it reflected rather narrowly defined conceptions of knowledge and learning. More than once I have spoken to students who questioned their professors' typical instructional strategy. They ask, "How is that supposed to help me?" As we have seen, when students determine that their learning goals are not being realized, they tend to rethink their postsecondary plans altogether or to just want to "get it over."

MAKING THE GRADE

Regardless of a student's academic background, career aspirations, or level of interest in the subject matter, the grading procedures in each class exert a huge influence on everyone's approach to the coursework. Typically, students' highest priority is to satisfy the instructor's criteria for passing the course. As Mariella put it, "I have to pass the class, in order to have a good grade point average, in case I do ever want to transfer. Not necessarily a good GPA—but I have to do what [the professor] tells us to do, so I can pass the class, so I can get somewhere."

Even the most self-confident and academically accomplished students mentioned the centrality of grades in the learning process. Luis, a self-described "serious" and highly motivated student, was one of the few who identified himself as both well prepared for college and knowledgeable about it. When Luis explained how his high school experience had prepared him for college, he stated, "I was very prepared, because my junior and senior years I had a lot of AP courses. And so we had college-level work to do, and most of the time my teachers actually acted like college professors. They didn't really care about your grade, they just let you go—and if you failed a test, that's too bad. So I didn't feel like nervous about college. I was actually excited." In framing the relationship between professor and students, Luis contended that professors don't really care about students' grades or whether students fail. From this perspective, the task of objectively evaluating college students' performances both supersedes concern with outcomes and places the full responsibility for passing the course on students. This aspect of the college experience, Luis suggests, is the one that elicits the most anxiety from students. A student named Clay expressed this point more explicitly: "I think some people are intimidated by their professors, because they control their grades. And they don't want to look like a fool, because they don't understand a subject, or maybe they have asked before, they didn't really get an explanation, and they don't want to come back and ask the same question."

Clay, who had initially started college at the state's flagship university, did not consider himself a typical community college student. He thought of himself as savvier, more capable of meeting high academic standards than many of his peers at the community college. This attitude came through when he talked about how much other students fear writing. In speaking about those who feel intimidated, he describes what he sees as typical community college students but does not include himself in that category.

The grading system for each course directs students to focus their attention on the material they deem essential to completing graded assignments. Passing each course, and remaining a college student, are dependent on the student's understanding what the instructor plans to assess and the exact assessment procedures. In every classroom, this need leads to demands for nitty-gritty logistical and procedural details about the course assessments.[3] When students do not believe that they have enough information about the grading criteria or about the instructor's guidelines for a particular assignment, I have seen them ask—and ask and ask—what often appear to be petty questions about minutiae. The sociologist Howard Becker has called this approach "making the grade."[4]

Indeed, students at every level of education are faced with grading systems that reward a grade-focused approach to their courses: figuring out what each instructor expects when it comes to graded performance, and how to meet the expectations most efficiently. Howard Becker and his coauthors have termed this the GPA perspective. They contend that it derives from students' acceptance of the rules handed down to them by administrators and faculty. "The student emphasis on grades arises, then, in response to an academic environment that also emphasizes grades. In a relationship of subjection in which the higher echelon dictates what will be institutionalized as valuable, making and enforcing rules to implement that choice, members of the lower echelon must, if they are to act effectively and remain members of the organization, accept that judgment and shape their own actions accordingly."[5]

Thus, the strategies that students adopt to make the grade, such as allocating most of their effort to graded assignments, seeking information about the grading criteria, and trying to negotiate over instructors' grading decisions, are common responses to a fundamental condition of schooling.

Becker, Geer, and Hughes first explored this perspective in great detail in their study of medical school students at the University of Kansas. Throughout the study, they document how the assessment system at the medical school penalized students who targeted their study efforts at the information they thought would be most relevant to their future practice as doctors. Students needed to study selectively, because the volume of material to learn was entirely unmanageable. Hence, selecting the correct material to study was vital to academic success. But in the end the students who earned the best grades employed a different criterion for directing their study efforts—they relied on the instructor to define what would be tested. In that context, the success of medical students was predicated on their determining the instructor's expectations for each graded assignment.[6]

The bottom line for students everywhere is to save time and find the "clearest and most authoritative source of knowledge," even though it means losing patience with information that is "not both easily grasped and concrete."[7] Students therefore depend on instructors to explain which information will count in graded assessments and to clearly delineate the grading criteria for those assessments.

Ultimately, students' primary objective in each course—to do what the instructor tells them to do in order to get the grade—shapes their conceptions of useful knowledge and the best strategies for gaining that knowledge. The course material that students across different colleges deemed significant tended to take the form of factual, testable knowledge—the kind of knowledge that Colleen referred to as "informative information." Speaking of the assistance she had received at the writing lab, she described the two most helpful tutors by saying, "They're fresh, they have lots of ideas, they have informative information for you." Colleen's phrasing reflected a view shared by her peers: some course material is not informative, some course material is informative, and students must identify and learn the informative kind.

Students' desire to absorb the "informative information" in an efficient manner led to several common critiques of instruction. Some criticisms focused on the volume of information provided in class. These resulted from two kinds of experiences: feeling bombarded with details without knowing how to distinguish the essential facts (what would be tested), or perceiving the instruction as failing to provide enough factual information. In either case, the underlying assumption of students' critiques was that instruction should be both efficient and "informative."

James's take on bad instruction, for instance, centered on his instructor's inefficiency in presenting relevant information. "My psychology teacher, sometimes he gives an example of what we are saying with his own experience of what happened outside, so he uses outside information to address the question you have . . . ; so sometimes, what he says doesn't matter to what we are saying in class. And sometimes he repeats something over and over, so I'm like, 'Okay, we had that before, so you don't have to repeat it again.' "

For James, useful knowledge comprised the facts that would appear on the test. From this perspective, inefficient and useless instruction included anything additional, whether that information went beyond the essential facts, represented "outside," experiential knowledge, or simply appeared to James to exist beyond the scope of the textbook. To judge from his own account, James seems to have successfully distinguished which information really "mattered" for the course, and as a result he was easily passing it. He therefore viewed certain instructional strategies—explaining concepts through real-life examples or highlighting critical information through repetition—as both unnecessary and inefficient.

Other students who were enrolled in psychology courses but not getting the grades they wanted reported being utterly confused by "outside information." Unlike James, these students were not successfully identifying what would be tested, or how it would be tested. Mariella, for example, interpreted much of the activity during class sessions as the sharing of opinions and personal stories.

> The professor just kind of gives us objectives and she doesn't really discuss the book. I'm not asking for her to do that. But at least talk about something that the class has to do.
>
> Then on tests, she tests us about stuff that's in the book, but then she comes up with her own stuff. For example, she gives an example of a person, and asks, 'Would a behavioral psychologist treat this?' So she kind of comes out with brand-new things. And a lot of people are lost in that class, too.
>
> It goes back to how they give their own opinions, or they teach us what they think is right. . . . and it's not really a class. Do you know what I mean? I came in here thinking I was going to learn something.
>
> The only classes I feel that I learned something is in math and in criminal justice. Because, for example, my criminal justice teacher, he just kind of gives us notes up there and that's our test. Right. And then I understand it.

Mariella's perspective on textbooks was more flexible than other students' ("I'm not asking her to [discuss the book]"). Nevertheless, she articulated the widespread notion that the important course material is information that it is factual and concrete. She cited two courses, math and criminal justice, in which the tested information consisted largely of rules and other concrete data that can be memorized. Moreover, clear instruction was given in the criminal justice course, where the instructor wrote notes on the board, then tested the students on that information. This instructional approach is good, according to Mariella: as she explained, "Then I understand it." In her psychology class, however, Mariella's instructor solicited discussion of personal stories and opinions—none of which constituted important knowledge in Mariella's eyes. Moreover, she thought, the instructor constructed confusing tests, in asking for responses that went far beyond the concrete facts. By offering a profile of an individual and asking students, "Would a behavioral psychologist treat this person?" the instructor was asking students to apply their knowledge of psychology, but Mariella viewed this kind of question as requiring "brand-new" information.

Mariella appreciated her math course and her criminal justice course because she viewed the information as objectively true, applicable to other classes in the same field, and transferable to practical situations. For her, the rules of algebra and the law functioned as unchanging facts, as opposed to the professor's "opinion" (as she saw the material presented in psychology or English). Ultimately, for Mariella and her peers, the most valuable material she could learn consisted of the facts: those recorded in textbooks, in PowerPoint presentations, or on the blackboard. Because these facts, they assumed, would be assessed on tests, students understood the primary goal of most classes as transcribing those facts for later memorization.

Ryan's description of his government course offers another typical example of this perspective. He identified it as his favorite course and added, "I don't know about enjoying it, but it's—he's a good teacher." When pressed to explain the good aspects of the government instructor's approach, Ryan said, "His lectures correlate a lot with the test, which is kind of rare in some of these classes. He just teaches the material good. I mean, he's organized. He has his notes on PowerPoint, and you can go on his website and print them out before class, and those are the notes that he goes over in class, so you can just follow along with him. You're kind of preexposed to them, so it's a lot easier. [The notes] usually have everything that you need on them, but . . . if it's not on there, you just write it in." In Ryan's mind, the three features of good instruction were clear and organized presentation of information, distribution of PowerPoint handouts matching the lecture slides, and the straightforward assessments by the instructor of students' knowledge ("His lectures correlate a lot with the test"). Although Ryan couldn't say that he actually enjoyed the class, he viewed the course as one that provided the necessary facts in an efficient (organized) manner.

JENN

Throughout the semester that I sat in on Jenn's English class, I observed the classroom activities from my usual seat at the back of the classroom. From the first week of class, Jenn sat in the seat at the end of the second row, against the wall. At the desk immediately in front of her sat Matt, and every class session I observed Matt and Jenn engage in whispered conversations, on what seemed like an ongoing basis. Throughout the semester, I wondered about them. Had they struck up a friendship based on being in the same class together? Were they conferring about course-related matters, or were they just shooting the breeze? Either way, were they paying attention to the class?

I had my chance to find out near the end of the semester, when I interviewed Jenn. I asked her what she and her friend Matt talked about in class. Jenn's answer was a total surprise. Matt was far from being a friend; he always initiated the conversation, and she didn't want to talk to him at all. "He likes to talk. He's like, 'I'll sit there and talk to you.'" She didn't really even respond to Matt, she asserted, he just kept talking to her. And it continued, she told me, because she just "didn't have it in" her to tell him to stop talking to her. With this explanation, Jenn was transformed immediately from a student bold enough to whisper through an entire class session into an entirely different person: an intensely shy woman, too timid to ask her classmate to stop bothering her, in part because "he likes to talk."

From my interview with Jenn, I learned that she was far from disengaged from her English course. English was her favorite class that semester, and since she didn't really respond to Matt's whispered comments, she didn't think he distracted her attention from learning how to write. Indeed, she was supremely pleased with how much she had learned, noting, "That's probably the only English class I've ever enjoyed in my whole entire life, and I've learned a heil of a lot more than I have in my whole years of school. . . . Oh yeah, I definitely learned how to do a lot of things I didn't know how to do before."

"GETTING IT OVER"

All students wanted to make the grade efficiently. The grade each student aimed for, however, varied from course to course, depending on the subject matter, the value the student placed on the objectives of the course, and its relevance to the student's career goals. In the end, if a student concluded that the coursework offered no "useful" knowledge, then "getting it over with"—doing only the minimal work required for a passing grade—proved paramount. In other words, students all hoped to "get the grade"; the decision to exert minimal effort meant doing only enough work to "*just* get the grade."

Students usually began new courses with some sense of the potential for learning. When students viewed an area of study as pertinent to their chosen occupation, their initial approach to the coursework was hopeful: they were hopeful of learning important and usable information. The desire to learn something relevant may exist at the heart of any students' efforts: "Why do we have to learn this?" might be one of the most familiar questions middle school and high school teachers hear.

At times, however, students are certain that particular courses will offer them nothing of use. In such instances, students adopt the "get it over" strategy from the outset of the course. This is often the case, certainly, for students pursuing specialized technical fields, such as computer networking or engineering, who enroll in general education courses. Indeed, some students have a pretty narrow interpretation of "useful." Liz, for example, the student who aspired to a career in radio production (and was working part-time at a local radio station), insisted that her math and English courses were a complete waste of time. She already knew enough math to get along in life—she could balance her checkbook without difficulty—and she certainly had no plans to write essays as part of her career. The only course she described as worthwhile was Mass Communications, which she viewed as immediately practical. As for the other courses, however, her attitude, as we saw, "What's the point? There's a lot of stuff you don't use, so what's the point of learning it?"

Ryan's description of the college's general education requirements (the basic classes) reflected the same definition of worthwhile subject matter.

"I think right now, everybody—like, during their freshman, sophomore year of college—they take a bunch of basic classes, and so there's a bunch of those that you're not really interested in. And then, once you get later on, like maybe junior or senior year, you get more specific classes to your major, and then you enjoy those more."

In composition courses, which were structured around the premise that the revision process would improve students' writing skills, the "get it over" strategy seriously undermined that learning opportunity. For instance, Linda's approach to revising her essays consisted of carefully making every change that her teacher recommended, completing each assignment as quickly as possible, and eventually passing the course with a C. When Linda admitted in her interview that she tried to incorporate changes into her papers even when she didn't understand them, I asked whether she ever asked her teacher to explain those comments. "I never [pause] no" was Linda's answer. "I just correct them and I just get it over and get it accepted—'Accept my paper and let's go,'—that's it. That's the class. I don't care, as long as I pass it." After all, she added, "I don't plan to be an English major."

Kevin adopted a slightly different strategy in composition. Instead of making every change suggested by his instructor, Kevin operated by asking himself, "What is the *least* amount of change I need to make to get the revised paper accepted?" For instance, on Kevin's first draft of his research paper, his instructor had recommended a series of revisions, including rewriting the introduction, tightening up the thesis statement, removing some irrelevant quotes, eliminating a section with irrelevant citations, and adding topic sentences to each paragraph. Kevin expressed dismay at the feedback, asserting that he did not want to do very much work on the revision. He resisted the idea of eliminating sections, for example, because he feared that his paper would no longer meet the minimum word requirement. Even the idea of moving sentences around struck him as being too much effort, and he reiterated several times, "I just want to get it accepted."

Not every student shared this narrow perspective on the value of English composition. Eliana believed that what she learned in composition could enhance her writing and thinking skills both in and out of school. In addition, she spoke of her engagement with the ideas she encountered in composition class, and how much she appreciated the opportunity to examine issues as matters for debate. There were other students like Eliana, but they were a minority. In general, the vast majority of college students I encountered expressed the "get it over" attitude toward at least one of their courses. The attitude manifests itself in minimal effort, disengagement, and, most likely, minimal learning.

The most unfortunate aspect of this widespread approach is that so many students adopted it after enrolling in particular courses; many of the students who spoke of frustration or disenchantment with their coursework indicated that they had made the decision to work merely for a passing grade only after the course failed to meet their expectations.

Students' initial orientations—and their judgments about whether particular courses would offer something worth learning—were subject to change over the span of each semester. In instances when a student entered a course with a pessimistic attitude about its value, a positive experience could change his mind. Sam was one such student—in his case, he experienced a marked turnaround in his view of college altogether. "Now that I've come here, I've changed my opinion, because I see that they actually teach things in college, whereas they really didn't in high school." During high school Sam felt he was "being pressured to go to a place that is just basically there to waste your time." In contrast, he was not "being pressured to go" to college, and it was turning out to be "a place where you're going to learn something." As he put it, "Not having to go, but then going and seeing that there's education there—it's like an extra thing, . . . it's like two plusses."

Unfortunately, the reverse was far more typical: students entered particular courses with hopeful attitudes—eager, or at least interested in learning something of use during the semester. I found myself surprised at the extent of disappointment that students expressed, and the frequency with which students moved from initial optimism to disillusionment. Ryan, for instance, commented on his psychology teacher, whose lectures contained material that seemed to conflict with information he had learned the preceding year in his AP psychology class. When I asked Ryan whether he had ever asked his instructor about the discrepancies, he replied, "I've thought about saying something that would kind of disprove him, but I just keep quiet, do the work and—yeah, just get the grade."

In the end, some students who worked to get college over with had relinquished any hope of learning. As Paul put it, "I'm not learning anything about history. I just go to class, and I sit there, and I do the assignments. I study when you've got to study for the exam, and that's it." But this was not necessarily true of everyone. Sebastian reflected, "I'm not taking it all in—I know that. . . . I'm just doing the homework to get a grade, it seems like, and I'm getting my grade back. . . . But I guess I'll learn some of that stuff later on."

SEBASTIAN

Sebastian viewed his English courses as eminently useful. This may have been, in part, because they were required, and Sebastian needed to pass them before he would be allowed to take certain college-level courses. For Sebastian, the desire to learn was directly related to being "motivated." He characterized himself as "pretty motivated," though he noted that his level of commitment during high school had been very low. "Because I got this lack of motivation in me. It's getting better. It was really bad in high school; I wouldn't care about anything. . . . Like, I never really read a book before. In high school, I just read the Cliff

Notes, or whatever; I never read the books. And when I did, they were so boring."

Sebastian felt engaged by and interested in his current courses. In contrast to his high school experience. In addition, he described both his English classes as requiring commitment if students were to do well. For him, that meant reading the books in his basic reading skills course, keeping up with the homework in his writing skills course, and in general, wanting more than to just get a grade. In the case of his writing course, he would recommend the course and the professor to those who shared his commitment: "I'd recommend Mr. Burke to someone else; I'd recommend him to someone who's motivated about school, and they wanted to learn—then I'd say, 'Take this guy, because he can help you out.' Someone who just wanted a grade, wanted to get by: I wouldn't take that class at all." In his own case, Sebastian had stuck with the course because he didn't want just to "get by."

On the surface, the two most common approaches, getting the grade and getting it over (or "*just* getting the grade") seem to illustrate a disheartening pattern of student disengagement and lack of interest in real learning. Indeed, they could easily be attributed to students' lack of motivation and jaded response to schooling or interpreted as the inevitable consequence of grading systems that provide incentives for students to expend as little thought and energy as possible in fulfilling the requirements.[8]

Yet in fact these approaches emerged from students' best and most sincere efforts to learn something in college. Although students approached courses with the single-minded goal of getting an acceptable grade, they didn't necessarily view efforts to "make the grade" as distinct from learning the subject matter. On the contrary, students exhibited idealism about the connection between learning and earning grades. At times, students seemed to depend on the grading system to promote learning. Felicia, for example, spoke disparagingly of the pass-fail writing assignments in her composition course. She criticized the incentive structure of pass-fail grading.[9] "I don't like it because you write the essay, but if you do better than C [pass], you still just get the pass. . . . It doesn't really make you think, 'I've got to try my best.' Like, on most essays you try your best, write the best you can, but this one, it's like you can try your best, but you're only going to get a pass." Instead of encouraging students to meet minimum standards, Felicia argued, tests and essays should challenge students to learn at a higher level.

In fact, as Becker, Geer, and Hughes have contended, working to "get the grade" offers the most efficient strategy for studying. Because the grading system indicates what the instructor thinks is the most important material to learn, detailed instructions about each assignment (and the grading criteria) help students distinguish between essential and secondary material and eliminate the guesswork about how to study. Furthermore, attending to activities and assignments that do not "count" in the final grade may very well be a waste of time. With no certain reward, students may wonder, why risk it?

Talisha experienced her history class as a waste. Reporting the disappointment she felt with the learning afforded by the class, she explained, "It's so annoying. I found out like two, three weeks ago—no, I found out like a month ago—that his lecture didn't count, and I kept coming in hopes that something would be revealed to me, some spit of knowledge would be imparted into my soul. But every time he opens the book, give me about thirty minutes, then I'm asleep without fail, because I'm just bored. I'm already tired."

Talisha's efforts to go above and beyond what was required were not rewarded with enhanced learning or greater knowledge. Her perception served to reaffirm for her the widely held notion that learning results primarily from energy expended on graded assignments and activities.

In light of students' fears and their desire to succeed in school and "get somewhere" in life, students are pressured to figure out exactly what they need to do to pass each graded assignment. For students who go into college without much notion of the standards and expectations for college-level work, receiving specific guidelines for each assignment becomes even more critical. This need is heightened when students perceive each professor as promoting different standards. Mariella identified the problem when she described professor as all having different teaching styles—each one seemingly teaching what he or she "thinks is right." Mariella appeared especially concerned because of past experiences in school: teachers didn't really teach anything ("except for elementary, because teachers really teach you there"). From her perspective, she had "been cheated from education" in her previous encounters with school.

In the case of composition, she explained how "different styles" might cause problems.

> What is really right for a good paper? Everybody has their standards. So if Mr. Dobbs is teaching me, and he thinks this is a good paper, then what if I do what he told me to do, and I take it to another professor and maybe that's not his standards? And if my teacher says, 'Well, it's not a good paper,' what am I supposed to do?
>
> So what is right? So that's very vague; there's no curriculum—I mean, is that what all the teachers think is a good paper? Or is that just his opinion? Do you know?

If Mariella does not gain absolute, concrete knowledge from her coursework, then what has she learned, and how will she succeed in the next class?

Her complaint is directly related to the typical undergraduate student's experience, which Gerald Graff describes as being tossed around in a disconnected, incoherent curriculum. For many students, he contends,

> the curriculum represents not a coherent intellectual world with conventions and practices anyone can internalize and apply to the specific challenges of each discipline, but an endless series of instructors' pref-

erences that you psych out, if you can, and then conform to, virtually starting over from scratch in each new course. Some instructors want you to recall and give back information without interpretation or judgment, whereas others want you to express your own ideas. Some instructors think there are clear-cut answers to questions, whereas others (often in the same discipline) think there are no right answers and that those who think so are naïve or authoritarian.[10]

Consequently, the most effective strategy for "psyching out" an instructor's preferences is to ask questions about how grades will be assigned and to focus on the graded assignments.

Students' dismissive attitudes toward particular activities arise from their certainty that the activities will not help them with the graded assignments. But it is not necessarily just about the grade. Sarah's complaint centered on one of her classmates in composition, who consistently extended the time spent discussing the assigned readings. "And I understand she wants to sit there, but don't waste my time for forty-five minutes, talking about the same story that we were talking about the moment we walked in the door. I want to learn something. I don't care about the story that we read yesterday. I want to learn something today. So that just irritated me." Sarah's criticism suggests that time spent on activities not tied to graded work is wasted, because it detracts from learning.

Underlying the frustration Sarah expressed was her assumption that learning does not result from engaging in discussion with her peers or listening to such discussion. Sarah conceded that her classmate had the right to talk about the readings—but only for a limited amount of time. In part, this view reflects Sarah's conception of learning as something that happens when the instructor presents the course material. With respect to what counts as useful information, Sarah's complaint highlights a view that every other student also expressed: Course content that appears in the form of instructors' opinions, fellow students' input, or other unverifiable statements is not particularly "informative."

In sum, disengagement on the part of students resulted less from their not wanting to learn anything than from their convictions about what activities might enable learning. In Mariella's case, she very much wanted to learn how to write a good paper, and she thought that she would do so in composition. Once she determined that she wasn't really learning anything, however, she adopted the "get it over" attitude. "I'm not very concerned, since—this class doesn't make me very happy. So I kind of just go through it, and I don't take a lot of time—my time—for this class. I just write what he told me to write, just to get over it."

By the end of the semester, she had decided, "As long as I pass the class, I don't care. [pause] I shouldn't be having that attitude, but . . ." Mariella attributed what she termed her bad attitude to her frustration with the content and instruction for the composition course. "I care [about doing better than just passing], but I get frustrated to a point that I just don't care anymore."

MELANIE

> Even though she wasn't necessarily "the best" student in high school, Melanie enjoyed taking "upper-level" classes, including an Advanced Placement English class during her senior year. She noted, "I just really enjoyed that class so much, because when you're in high-level classes, it's a very relaxed atmosphere, because the teacher already knows that in order to be here, you have to be studious, you have to have determination, and work hard and things like that. And so a lot of the times we would just have discussions on the books that we read over the night, or we would take quizzes and things like that, but I really, really love that kind of upper-level kind of atmosphere." By contrast, though, she explained that she did not apply the same level of determination to all her courses or assignments. When she regarded assignments as stupid or a waste of her time, she didn't bother to try hard. In the case of writing assignments, for example, "I find that if I really believe in something, if I love it enough, then I can write pretty extraordinary, for me, within my confines. But if it's something stupid, like 'What did you do over the summer?' I kind of give it a half-ass effort. I mean, that's just the way I am."

The most significant aspect of students' disappointment was not simply the failure to see the relevance of courses—but the way students conceived of knowledge or meaningful information. From the perspective of college faculty members, some of these students appear to be entirely clueless. A highly regarded English professor at a California community college put it most bluntly: "Of course you get a group of kids who have no conception of what college is all about."

The frequent incidents of student frustration and disillusionment indicate students' desire to learn. Students' understanding of what is worth learning—as well as how one goes about learning—is the source of much of the difficulty. These conceptions of college are often incompatible with faculty members' expectations of college students.

What is most problematic about this mismatch of expectations is that students are not generally equipped with the "skills" or knowledge to determine what their professors expect or how to meet the expectations. Many community college students have immense difficulty figuring out how to learn effectively in specific situations or why they are having trouble with a subject.

Yolanda offers an instructive example. In explaining her criticism of her history professor, who required students to purchase an expensive text, Yolanda's key complaint hinged on the lack of assigned readings from the text: "But he doesn't use the book. And I expressed that to the counselors, and they're like, 'Well, you know, he should. And maybe next time, keep the book and see if another teacher is going to use the book, and call the teacher before you sign up for the class.' That's not my job. My job is to take the class. His job is to teach. And if he suggests a book, he needs to let me know before if he's not going to use it." Yolanda did not conceptualize teaching and learning as an integrated process or as an ongoing interaction between professor and students. Instead, her remarks presupposed a clear separation between professor and students. From her perspective, once the professor has fulfilled his responsibility of explaining and informing, the responsibility moves to the students.

The distinction between the responsibilities of the teacher and the responsibilities of the students also emerged in Mara's interview comments. Trying to explain the source of her difficulty in a prior history class, Mara mused, "Yeah, I don't know. It wasn't like, 'This isn't in the book.' It wasn't like, 'We didn't talk about this in class.' And it wasn't like his lectures weren't really informative. And I really enjoyed his class. I wasn't very good at taking his tests, which is the grade, unfortunately."

In her efforts to determine why the course was difficult for her, Mara ran through a standard list of student grievances, dismissing each possibility in turn. This list revealed her premises about what constitutes bad (and in turn, good) instruction. In other words, the instructor was good, in the sense that (a) his lectures were "really informative," and (b) he didn't introduce questions on the test that were unrelated to the textbook or the lectures. Despite these positive pedagogical features, Mara did not do well in the course, and in the end, she chalked it up to her difficulty with taking the tests. And yet she was unable to explain how or why she had trouble with them. The reasons for her failure remained a mystery, and a better understanding of how to take the tests (and by implication, how to learn) remained beyond her grasp. Mara may have felt responsible for something she did not know how to achieve, but her conception of learning—as something that she alone must accomplish—decreased the likelihood that she would seek the necessary assistance from her instructors.

I do not want to suggest that students share no responsibility for their learning. The way that students like Mara and Yolanda understood the division of responsibility between instructor and student, however, focused their attention on what to learn but not how to learn it. Even more important, their ideas about what to learn were not necessarily congruent with their instructors' assumptions. The following exchange I had with Mariella reinforces this point:

> *Mariella:* Mr. Dobbs does put stuff on the board, and I appreciate that. That's like my enlightenment, when I see that stuff on the board and I write everything down.
> *Becky:* Okay. So what would the comp class be like if you were going to learn something from it?

> *Mariella:* Well, just maybe like actually have him going on the board and teaching us sometime, not just . . . Like, for example, I don't agree with him the way he gives us out random essays that he finds and other stuff. . . . I would just rather him show us: if it's a Comp 1 class, he's supposed to teach us how to write a good essay.

In contrast to Mariella, I did not view the handouts as "random essays." Rather, the essays provided models of different rhetorical strategies and allowed Mr. Dobbs to illustrate his discussion with specific examples. In addition, some of his selections presented arguments about the value of writing and the power of words. Analyzing the arguments offered students the opportunity to discuss aspects of "argument literacy," as Gerald Graff describes it, while examining a diverse range of opinions on why and how academic literacy affects individuals' lives. In fact, by deconstructing models of good writing, examining the building blocks, and discussing strategies for constructing and combining those building blocks, Mr. Dobbs made a consistent effort to "show" students how to write a good essay. This is not the way Mariella understood the activity, however.

Mariella had hoped to learn something useful from composition—that she was not doing so led her to question the value of the class, as well as the value of earning an associate's degree. By the end of the semester, she complained that she had been advised poorly; she was enrolled in courses that she did not want to take; and a certificate would be a better goal than a degree.

At times, the understanding students have of meaningful, relevant knowledge and how to acquire it leads them to approach course curricula in ways that conflict with instructors' objectives. In some instances—perhaps many— preconceptions lead students to understand the course content and objectives very differently than their professors anticipate. Even when students try to determine instructors' criteria for graded assignments, students' own assumptions about information and relevant knowledge shape the way they interpret (and misinterpret) professors' intentions. The end result is that students' approaches to their coursework frequently differ from what faculty members expect or hope for in class.

In an effective learning environment, part of the instructor's responsibility involves understanding how students perceive the curriculum and the learning objectives and, when necessary, helping students revise their perceptions in a way that supports the instructor's vision of learning. Only then can a teacher close the enormous gap between her expectations and the students' approach to their coursework.

From *Opening Skinner's Box* by Lauren Slater. New York: Norton, 2004.

Opening Skinner's Box

Lauren Slater

B. F. Skinner, America's leading neo-behaviorist, was born in 1904 and died in 1990. He is known in the field of psychology for his famous animal experiments in which he demonstrated the power of rewards and reinforcements to shape behavior. Using food, levers, and other environmental cues, Skinner demonstrated that what appear to be autonomous responses are really cued, and in doing so he threw into question the long-cherished notion of free will. Skinner spent much of his scientific career studying and honing what he came to call operant conditioning, the means by which humans can train humans and other animals to perform a whole range of tasks and skills through positive reinforcement.

Skinner claimed that the mind, or what was then called mentalism, was irrelevant, even nonexistent, and that psychology should only focus on concrete measurable behaviors. His vision was to build a worldwide community where the government would consist of behavioral psychologists who could condition, or train, its citizens into phalanxes of benevolent robots. Of all the twentieth century's psychologists, his experiments and the conclusions he drew about the mechanistic nature of men and women may be the most reviled, yet continuously relevant to our increasingly technological age.

So this, perhaps, is the story. There's a man called Skinner, which is an ugly name by any account, a name with a knife in it, an image of a skinned fish flopping on a dock, its heart barely visible in its mantle of muscle, ka-boom. Say the name Skinner to twenty college-educated people and most will respond with an adjective like "evil." This I know to be true, as I've done it as an experiment. And yet in 1971, *Time Magazine* named him the most influential living psychologist. And a 1975 survey identified him as the best-known scientist in the United States. Still today, everywhere, his experiments are held in the highest esteem.

So why this infamy? Here's why. In the 1960s, Skinner gave an interview to biographer Richard I. Evans in which he openly admitted that his efforts at social engineering had implications for fascism and might be used for totalitarian ends. The story goes that Skinner desired nothing more than to shape—and shape is the operative word here—the behavior of people subjected to gears and boxes and buttons, whatever humanity he touched turning to bone. The legend says he built a baby box in which he kept his daughter Deborah for two full years in order to train her, tracking her progress on a grid. The legend also says that when she was thirty-one she sued him for abuse in a genuine court of law, lost the case, and shot herself in a bowling alley in Billings, Montana. None of this is true, and yet the myths persist. Why? What is it about Skinner that so scares us?

Type "B. F. Skinner" into your search engine and you will get thousands of hits, among them the Web site of an outraged father who damned the man for murdering an innocent child; a Web site with a skull, and Ayn Rand writing, "Skinner is so obsessed with the hatred of man's mind and virtue, so intense and consuming a hatred that it consumes itself and in the end what we have are only gray ashes and a few stinking coals"; a memorial of sorts for Deborah, who had supposedly died in the 1980s: "Deborah, our hearts go out to you." And then a tiny red link that reads, "for Deborah Skinner herself, click here." I did. A picture of a brown-haired, middle-aged woman scrolled down. The caption said that here was Deborah Skinner herself, that her suicide was a myth, that she was alive and well.

Myths. Legends. Stories. Tall tales. What is Skinner's true legacy? Perhaps the challenge of understanding Skinner's experiments will be primarily discriminatory, separating content from controversy, a sifting through. Writes psychologist and historian John A. Mills, "[Skinner] was a mystery wrapped in a riddle wrapped in an enigma."

I decide to wade in, slowly.

He was born in 1904. This much is for sure. Beyond that, though, what I find is a tangle of contradictions. He was one of America's premier behaviorists, a man of real rigidity who slept in a bright yellow cubicle from Japan called a *bed-doe*, but at the same time he could not work unless his desk was cluttered, and he said of his own course, "It is amazing the number of trivial accidents which have made a difference. . . . I don't believe my life was planned at any point." But then he often wrote he felt like god and "a sort of savior to humanity."

When Skinner was a fellow at Harvard, he met and fell in love with a woman named Yvonne, who would later become his wife. I see them on

Friday nights, driving to Monhegan's Gull Pond with the black convertible top folded back and some kind of moody jazz playing on the radio. Once at the pond, they take off their clothes and skinny-dip, the brackish waters on their bodies, the cool night air, the moon a snipped hole in the sky. I read in a dusty text in the basement of a library that after training sessions, he used to take his caged pigeons out and hold them in his huge hand, stroking their downy heads with his first finger.

I was very surprised to learn that before he went to Harvard to study psychology in 1928, Skinner's aspiration was to be a novelist, and he had spent eighteen prior months holed up in his mother's attic writing lyric prose. How he went from lyric prose to timed rates of reinforcement is not all clear to me—how a man can make such a sharp swerve. He writes that when he was around twenty-three, he came across an article by H. G. Wells in the *New York Times Magazine* in which Wells stated that given the chance between saving the life of Ivan Pavlov or George Bernard Shaw, Wells would choose Pavlov, because science is more redemptive than art.

And indeed, the world needed redemption. The Great War had ended one decade ago. Shell-shocked soldiers suffered from flashbacks and depressions; asylums were packed; there was an urgent need for some kind of treatment scheme. When Skinner went to Harvard, in 1928, as a graduate student, the scheme was largely psychoanalytic. Everyone everywhere was lying down on leather couches and fishing ephemeral tidbits from their pasts. Freud ruled, along with the venerable William James, who had written *The Varieties of Religious Experience*, a text about introspective soul states, with not one equation in it. That, in fact, was the state of psychology when Skinner entered; it was a numberless field sharing more with philosophy than physiology. A typical leading question in the field might be, "What is it within us that sees, feels and thinks every moment when we are awake, vanishes temporarily when we sleep and disappears permanently or instantly when we die?"

Introspection. Mentalism. These were the tropes into which Skinner stepped, a lean young man with a stiff helmet of hair flipped up at the top in greased pompadour. His eyes were fierce blue, like chips of a china plate. He wanted, he writes, to make a real difference, to feel things palpable in his hands and in his heart. Poised between the first world war and a future one soon to come, Skinner may have sensed—although he would reject such a flimsy word—the need for action, for interventions and results that could be bronzed, each one, like bullets.

He therefore avoided anything "soft." He started off in Hudson Hoagland's physiology course studying frog reflexes. He pricked the taut skin of a frog's thigh and measured the animal's jerk, and then its jump. His hands smelled swampy, and he was full of vigor.

One day, early in his Harvard career, Skinner came across the Harvard Psychology Workshop in Emerson Hall. Skinner saw an array of instruments, pieces of red tin, chisels, nails, and nuts in Salisbury cigarette tins. I imagine his hands itched then. He wanted to do something great, and he had always been dexterous, wielding scissors and saws with precision. So there, in that tiny shop, Skinner started to build his famous boxes out of cast-off wires and rusty nails and blackened bits he found.

Did he know what he was building, and the huge effects it would have on American psychology? Was he pursuing a prepackaged vision, or just following the lyric push and pull of a tin-and-wire poem, so in the end what he saw surprised even him: a box operated by compressed air, a silent releasing mechanism, all gadgets and gears, the box an ordinary object that, like ladders and mirrors and black cats, immediately acquired a kind of dense glow.

Of this time Skinner writes, "[I] began to become unbearably excited. Everything I touched suggested new and promising things to do."

Late at night now, in his rented rooms, Skinner was reading Pavlov, to whom he owes an enormous debt, and Watson, to whom he owes a lesser but still significant debt. Pavlov, the great Russian scientist, had practically lived in his lab, such was his dedication. He had spent years studying the salivary glands of his beloved canines. Pavlov discovered that the salivary gland could be conditioned to leak at the sound of a bell. Skinner liked that idea, but he wanted to go beyond a small mucous membrane, he wanted the whole entire organism; where was the poetry in saliva?

Pavlov discovered what is called classical conditioning. This simply means that a person can take a preexisting animal reflex, like blinking or being startled or salivating, and condition it so it occurs in response to a new stimulus. Thus, the famous bell—a stimulus—that Pavlov's dogs learned to associate with food and salivated at the sound of. Now, this might not seem like a great discovery to you or me, but back then this was huge. This was as hot as the spliced atom or the singular position of the sun. Never, ever before in all of human history had people understood how *physiological* were our supposed mental associations. Never before had people understood the sheer malleability of the immutable animal form. Pavlov's dogs drooled and the world tipped over twice.

Skinner wondered. He was up there in his rooms, and he had made some of his not-yet-famous, or infamous, boxes, which were still empty, and there were always squirrels just below in Harvard Yard. He watched the squirrels and wondered if it would be possible to, say, condition the whole shebang, not just a simple silly gland. In other words, could a person shape a behavior— what Skinner came to call an operant—that was not a reflex? Conditioned or not, salivation is and was and always will be a reflex, a fully formed action that occurs on its own in addition to being brought on by a bell. However, when you jump in the air, or sing "Howdy Doodie," or press a lever in the hopes of finding food, you are not acting reflexively. You are just behaving. You are operating on your environment. If one can condition cartwheels, or other supposedly free-form movements? Would it be possible to take a completely random movement, like turning one's head to the right, and reward it consistently, so pretty soon the person keeps looking to the right, the operant inscribed? And if this was possible, how far could it go? What sorts of hoops might we learn to jump through, and with what sort of awful ease? Skinner wondered. He moved, I imagine, his hands this way and that. He leaned way out on the window ledge and smelled squirrel, a musky odor of night and scat, of fur and flowers.

In June of that year, Skinner was given rats by a departing graduate student. He brought the animals to a box. Then he started. After a long, long time, years in fact, he discovered that these rats, who have brains no bigger than a boiled bean, could quickly learn how to press a lever if they were rewarded with food. Thus, while Pavlov focused on an animal's behavior in response to a *prior stimulus*—the bell—Skinner focused on an animal's behavior in response to an after-the-fact *consequence*—the food. It was a subtle and not terribly exciting nuance to Pavlov's earlier work, and a frank extension of Thorndike's studies, which had already demonstrated that cats in slatted boxes that were rewarded for accidentally stepping on a treadle could learn to do so purposefully. But Skinner went further than these two men. After he demonstrated that his rodents could, by accident, step on the lever and release a pellet, and then turn the accident into intention based on prior reward, he played with removing or altering the rate at which the rewards occurred and by doing so, Skinner discovered replicable and universal laws of behavior that still hold true today.

For instance, after Skinner consistently rewarded the lever-pressing rat with food, he tried what he called a fixed-ratio schedule. In this scenario, if the animal pressed the lever three times, he'd get his goodie. Or five times. Or twenty times. Picture yourself as a rat. First, whenever you press a lever, you get food. Then, you press the lever once and you don't get food; you do it again, still no food. You do it again and down the silver spout comes a pellet. You eat the pellet and walk away. You come back for more. This time, you don't bother pressing once with your pink padded foot. You press three times. The reinforcement contingencies change the way in which the animal responds.

Skinner also played around with what he termed fixed-interval schedules and extinction. In the extinction version of the experiment Skinner removed the reinforcer all together. He discovered that if he ceased rewarding the rats with food, they would eventually cease pressing the lever even when they heard the pellets' raining sound. Using a cumulative recorder attached to his box, Skinner could pictorially plot just how long it takes to learn a response when it is regularly rewarded and how long it takes to extinguish a response when it is abruptly discontinued. His ability to precisely measure these rates under differing circumstances yielded quantifiable data on how organisms learn and on how we can predict and control the learning outcome. With the achievement of predictability and control, a true science of behavior was born, with bell curves and bar graphs and plot points and math, and Skinner was the first one to do it to such a nuanced and multileveled extent.

But Skinner didn't stop there. He then proceeded to what he called variable schedules of reinforcement, and it was here that he made his most significant discoveries. He tried intermittently rewarding the animals with food when they pressed the lever, so that most times the animals came away empty, but every once in a while, after, say, the fortieth bar press, or the sixtieth, they'd get a treat. Intuition tells us that random and far-flung rewards would lead to hopelessness and extinction of behavior; they didn't. Skinner discovered that by intermittently rewarding the rats with food, they would continue to press that lever like some sort of saw-toothed junkie, regardless of the outcome. He experimented with what happens when intermittent rewards are given at regular intervals (say, every fourth bar press) or at irregular intervals. He found that irregularly rewarded behavior was the hardest of all to eradicate. Aha! He stopped there. This was a discovery as big as dog drool. Suddenly, Skinner was able to systematically evoke and explain much of human folly, why we do dumb things even when we're not consistently rewarded, why your best friend hangs over the phone, saliva shining in the corners of her mouth, waiting for that mean boyfriend with an occasional streak of kindness to call, just call. Oh please call! Why perfectly normal people empty their coffers in smoky casinos and wind up in terrible trouble. Why women love too much and men stock-trade on margin. It was all about this thing called intermittent reinforcement and he could show it, its mechanisms, the contingencies of compulsion. And compulsion is huge. It has, no pun intended, dogged us and drowned us since the first person entered Eden. It is huge.

However, Skinner didn't stop there. If he could train rats to press levers, why not train pigeons to, say, play ping-pong? To bowl? What were the limits, he wondered, to how man could shape another being's behavior? Skinner writes about trying to train a bird to peck a dish: "We first give the bird food when it turns its head slightly in the direction [of the dish] from any part of the cage. This increases the frequency of the behavior. . . . We continue by reinforcing positions successively closer to the spot, then by reinforcing only when the head is moved slightly forward, and finally only when the beak makes contact with the spot. In this way, we can build rare, complicated operants which would never appear in the repertoire of the organism otherwise."

Rare, indeed. Using his behavioral methods, Skinner's followers were able to teach a rabbit to pick up a coin in its mouth and drop it into a piggy bank. They also taught a pig to vacuum.

Based on these experiments, he refined his relentlessly reductive philosophy. He began, surrounded by his pecking pigeons, to abhor words like *sensed*, or *feel* or *fear*. There is no fear, just certain galvanic skin responses and involuntary muscle tremblings that emit 2.2 volts of energy. Why didn't we just dismiss him as a tilted radical? Not only because he discovered the first science of behavior. His vision was also boldly, perhaps patriotically optimistic. It denied Americans their coveted autonomy while simultaneously returning it to them all new and improved. Skinner's was a world of extreme freedom wrought through its opposite: conformity. In the Skinnerian scheme, if we only submit to mindless training, we will be rendered biologically boundless, able to learn skills far outside the "repertoire" of our species. If pigeons can play ping-pong, then perhaps humans could learn still more amazing feats. All it takes is the right training, and we step out, over the boundaries of our bodies and their limitations.

Skinner's fame slowly grew. He went on to devise teaching machines, to construct a theory of language acquisition as operant conditioning, to train pigeons as missile guiders in World War II. He wrote a book called *Walden Two* in which he outlined a proposal for a community based on "behavioral engineering," wherein the power of positive reinforcement was used for the scientific control of humans. In Skinner's view, this ideal community would be governed not by politicians, but by benevolent behaviorists armed with candy canes and blue ribbons. He wrote a book called *Beyond Freedom and Dignity*, about which a reviewer wrote, "It is about the taming of mankind through a system of dog obedience schools for all."

Before Skinner could bring to fruition the social implications of his great experiments, he died. He died of leukemia in 1990. Did he realize, at the very end, that the final act of life, which is death, cannot be learned or otherwise overcome?

How can we locate Skinner? His experiments are disturbing in their implications. On the other hand, his discoveries are absolutely significant. They, in essence, illuminate human stupidity, and anything that illuminates stupidity is brilliant.

Jerome Kagan is a contemporary of Skinner's who carries many memories and opinions of his colleague. A professor of psychology at Harvard, Kagan has insights into what sense to make of this man and his place in the twentieth century. I go to see him.

Kagan's office building, William James Hall, is under construction when I arrive, so I have to dodge and wend my way through a concrete maze, above me banners flapping, "Warning. Hard Hat Area." I ride the elevator up. The entire building is in a reverential hush. Deep, deep beneath me, in the bowels of the basement where artifacts are stored, where supposedly some of Skinner's black boxes are encased, jackhammers gnaw through old concrete and I can hear a tiny voice yelling, "Presto."

I get off on floor fifteen. The elevator doors part and before me, as though in a dream, sits a tiny black dog, a toy breed, its mouth a red rent in its otherwise dark fur face. The dog stares and stares at me, some sort of sentry— I don't know. I love dogs, although toys are not my preference. I wonder why they're not my preference. As a child I had a toy dog and it bit me, so perhaps I've been conditioned against them, and I could be reconditioned with rewards so I come to champion the shitzu over the shepherd. In any case, I bend down to pat the little dog, and as though it senses my dislike, it flies into a frenzy, baring a set of impressive and very un-toy-like teeth and snarling as it leaps up to grab my exposed wrist.

"Gambit!" a woman shouts, running out from one of the offices. "Gambit stop that! Oh my god, did he hurt you?"

"I'm fine," I say, but I'm not fine. I'm shaking. I have been negatively reinforced—no, I have been punished. I will never trust a toy again, and I don't WANT that to change. Skinner would say he could change it, but how changeable am I, are we?

Professor kagan smokes a pipe. His office smells like pipe, that semisweet rancid odor of burnt embers. He says with the kind of total assurance I associate with the Ivy League cast, "Let me tell you, your first chapter should not be Skinner. It was Pavlov in the early twentieth century and then Thorndike a decade later who did the first experiments showing the power of conditioning. Skinner elaborated on this work. But his findings can't explain thought, language, reasoning, metaphor, original ideas, or other cognitive phenomena. Nor will they explain guilt or shame."

"What about," I say, "Skinner's extrapolations from his experiments? That we have no free will. That we are ruled only by reinforcers. Do you believe that?"

"Do *you* believe that?" Kagan asks.

"Well," I say, "I don't absolutely rule out the possibility that we are always either controlled or controlling, that our free will is really just a response to some cues that—"

Before I can finish my sentence, Kagan dives under his desk. I mean that literally. He springs from his seat and goes head forward into nether regions beneath his desk so I cannot see him anymore.

"I'm under my desk," he shouts. "I've NEVER gotten under my desk before. Is this not an act of free will?"

I blink. Where Kagan was sitting is just space. Beneath his desk, I hear a rustle. I'm a little worried about him. I think he said to me, over the phone when I asked for the interview, that he had a bad back.

"Well," I say, and suddenly my hands feel cold with fear, "I guess it could be an act of free will or it could be that you've—"

Again, Kagan won't let me finish. He's still under the desk, he won't come up, he's conducting the interview in a duck-and-cover crouch. I can't even see him. His voice rises, disembodied.

"Lauren," he says, "Lauren, there is no way you can explain my being under this desk right now as anything but an act of free will. It's not a response to a reinforcer or a cue. I've NEVER gotten under my desk before."

"Okay," I say.

We sit there for a minute, he down there, I up here. I think I hear that damn dog in the hall, scratching. I'm afraid to go back out there, but I no longer want to be in here. I am caged by contingencies, and so I sit very still.

Kagan, it appears to me, is somewhat dismissive of Skinner's contributions. But certainly there *are* ways in which Skinner's experiments—even if they are derivative—are both currently relevant and helpful in the construction of a better world. In the 1950s and 1960s Skinner's behavioral methods were taken to state asylums and applied to the severely psychotic. Using his principles of operant conditioning, hopelessly schizophrenic patients were able to learn to dress themselves, to feed themselves, each rise of the spoon rewarded with a coveted cigarette. Later in the century, clinicians began using techniques like systematic desensitization and flooding, drawn directly from Skinner's operant repertoire, to treat phobias and panic disorders, and these behavioral treatments are still widely employed and obviously efficacious today. Says Stephen Kosslyn, professor of psychology at Harvard, "Skinner will make a comeback, I predict it. I myself am a real Skinner fan. Scientists are just now making exciting new discoveries that point to the neural substrates of Skinner's findings." Kosslyn explains the evidence that there are two major learning systems in the brain: the basal ganglia, a collection of spidery synapses located deep in the paste of the ancient brain, where habits are grooved, and the frontal cortex, that big rumpled bulge that rose in tandem with our reason and ambition. The frontal cortex, neuro-scientists hypothesize, is where we learn how to think independently, to visualize the future and plan based on the past. It is where creativity and all its surprising swerves originate, but, says Kosslyn, "Only a portion of our cognitions are mediated by this cortex." The rest of learning, says Kosslyn, "a significant amount, is habit driven, and Skinner's experiments have led us to search for the neural substrates of these habits." In essence, Kosslyn is saying, Skinner led scientists to the basal ganglia, he led them down, down into the basement of the brain, where they sifted through neural tangles to find the chemistry behind the pecks and presses and all those conditioned cartwheels we do on the green grass, in the summer.

Says Bryan Porter, an experimental psychologist who applies Skinnerian-based behaviorism to address traffic safety problems, "Of course behaviorism is neither bad nor dead. Skinner's behaviorism is responsible for so many beneficial social interventions. Using behavioral techniques we have been able to reduce dangerous driving, in terms of the number of red lights run, by ten to twelve percent. Also because of Skinner, we know that people respond better to rewards than punishment. Skinner's techniques have been instrumental in helping the huge population of anxiety-disordered people overcome, or extinguish, their phobias. Thanks to Skinner, you know that rewards work far better in the establishment of behavior than punishment. This has huge implications politically, if our government could just absorb that."

My child cries in the night. She wakes soaked in sweat, eyeballs bulging, dreams melting as she comes to consciousness. "Shhhh. Shhhh." I hold her body against mine. Her bedclothes are soaked, her hair a dark mat of pressed curls. I stroke her head, where the fontanels have long since sealed. I stroke the slope of her forehead, where the frontal cortex daily sprouts its exuberant rootwork, and then move my hand down to her taut neck, where I imagine I feel the basal ganglia, its seaweed-like snarls. I hold my child in the night, and outside her bedroom window a dog howls, and when I look, the animal is soap-white in the moonlight.

At first my child cries because she's scared, a series of bad dreams I'm guessing. She's two and her world is expanding with fearful speed. But then, as the nights go by, she cries simply because she longs to be held. She has become habituated to these predawn embraces, to the rocking chair's rhythm while the sky outside is so generously salted with stars. My husband and I are exhausted.

"Maybe we should Skinnerize her," I say.

"We should what?" he says.

"Maybe we should employ Skinnerian principles to break her of her habit. Every time we go to her and pick her up, we're giving her what Skinner would call positive reinforcement. We have to extinguish the behavior by reducing and then eliminating our responses."

My husband and I are having this conversation in bed. I'm surprised by how nimbly my tongue takes in and swirls out the language of B. F. I practically sound like an expert. Speaking Skinnerian is almost fun. Chaos confined. Rest returned.

"So you're suggesting," he says, "that we just let her cry it out." He sounds weary. All parents know this debate.

"No," I say. "Listen. Not cry it out. Put her on a strict rate of reduced reinforcement. The first time she cries, we pick her up for only three minutes. The next time she cries, we only pick her up for two minutes. We could even use a stopwatch." My voice grows excited, or is it anxious? "Then we gradually lengthen the amount of time we allow her to cry. Just very very gradually," I say. "Slowly, we'll extinguish the behavior if we extinguish our responses . . . the contingencies," I say, tracing my hand along the sheet's pattern, a series of green grids, what once looked like country checkerboard but now looks like lab paper.

My husband eyes me, warily I might add. He is not a psychologist, but if he were, he would be of the Carl Rogers school. He has a soft voice, a still softer touch.

"I don't know," he says. "What exactly do you think we'll teach her by doing this?"

"To sleep through the night alone," I say.

"Or," he says, "to realize that when she needs help, we won't respond, that when there's danger real or imagined, we're not there. That's not the worldview I wish to impart."

Nevertheless, I win the debate. We decide to Skinnerize our girl, if only because we need rest. It's brutal in the beginning, having to hear her scream, "Mama mama, papa!," having to put her down as she stretches out her scrumptious arms in the dark, but we do it, and here's what happens: It works like magic, or science. Within five days the child acts like a trained narcoleptic; as soon as she feels the crib's sheet on her cheek, she drops into a dead ten-hour stretch of sleep, and all our nights are quiet.

Here's the thing. And all our nights are quiet. But sometimes now, we cannot sleep, my husband and I. Have we remembered to turn the monitor on? Is the dial up high enough? Did the pacifier break off in her mouth, so she will smother as she is soothed? We stay up, and through the monitor we can sometimes hear the sound of her breathing, like a staticky wind, but not once does her voice break through—not a yelp, a giggle, a sweet sleep-talk. She has been eerily gagged.

She sleeps so still, in her white baby box.

Some of the actual boxes that Skinner used have been archived at Harvard. I go to view them. They are in the basement of William James Hall, still under construction. I have to wear a hard hat, a heavy yellow shell on my head. I go down, down the stairs. There is a moist stink in the air, and black flies buzz like neurons, each one plump with purpose. The walls themselves are porous, and when you press them, a fine white powder comes off in your hands. I pass a worker in hip-high boots, smoking a cigarette, the bright tip sizzling like a cold sore at the corner of his lip. I imagine this cellar is full of rats; they careen around the boxes, their glass-pink eyes, their scaly tails flicking: what freedom!

Up ahead, I see a huge dark stain—or is it a shadow?—on a brick wall. "There they are," my guide, a buildings and grounds person, says and points.

I go forward. Ahead of me in the cellar's dimness, I can make out large glass display cases, and within them some sort of skeleton. Closer up, I see it is the preserved remains of a bird, its hollow, flight-friendly bones arranged to give it the appearance of mid-soar, its skull full of tiny pinprick holes. One of Skinner's pigeons, perhaps, the eye sockets deep, within them a tiny living gleam, and then it goes.

I move my gaze from bones to boxes. It is at this point that I feel surprised by what I see. The bones are in line with this man's ominous mystery, but the boxes, the famous boxes—*these* are the famous black boxes? They are, for starters, not black. They are an innocuous gray. Did I read the boxes were black, or did I just concoct that, in the intersection where fact and myth meet to make all manner of odd objects? No, these boxes are not black, and they are rather rickety looking, with an external spindle graphing device and tiny levers for training. The push pedals are so small, almost cute, but the feeding dishes are a cold institutional chrome. This is what I do: I put my head in. I lift the lid and put my head deep inside a Skinner box, where the smell is of scat, fear, food, feathers, things soft and hard, good and bad; how swiftly an object switches from benign to ominous. How difficult it is to box even a box.

Perhaps, I think, the most accurate way of understanding Skinner the man is to hold him as two, not one. There is Skinner the ideologue, the ghoulish man who dreamt of establishing communities of people trained like pets, and then there is Skinner the scientist, who made discrete discoveries that have forever changed how we view behavior. There is Skinner's data, irrefutable and brilliant, the power of intermittent reinforcement, the sheer range of behaviors that can be molded, enhanced, or extinguished, and then there is Skinner's philosophy, where, I imagine, he earned his dark reputation. These two things perhaps have been mixed up in the public's mind, in my mind certainly, as science and the ideas it spawned melded into a mythical mess. But then again, can you really separate the significance of data from its proposed social uses? Can we consider *just* splitting the atom, and not the bomb and the bones that followed? Is not science indelibly rooted in the soil of social construction, so that the value of what we discover is inextricably tied to the value of the uses we discover for the discovery? Round and round we go. It's a lexical, syntactical puzzle, not to mention a moral one, not to mention an intellectual one of grave import—the idea that science and its data are best evaluated in a box, apart from the human hands that will inevitably give it its shape.

Questions of application as a means of measuring data's worth aside, what are all the mechanisms, so to speak, that contributed to Skinner's infamy? How and why did the bizarre myth of the dead daughter (who is supposedly quite alive), the black boxes, and the robotic scientist take precedence over what I am coming to see should maybe be a more nuanced view of a man who hovered between lyric prose and number crunching, a man who skinny-dipped just after he ran his rats and birds, a man who hummed Wagner, that composer of pure sentiment, while he studied the single reflex of a green frog? How did all this complexity get lost? Surely Skinner himself is partly to blame. "He was greedy," says a source who wishes to remain anonymous. "He made one discovery and he tried to apply it to the whole world, and so he fell over a ledge."

And yet, there's much, much more than greed that turns us off. Skinner, in developing new devices, raised questions that were an affront to the Western imagination, which prides itself on liberty while at the same time harboring huge doubts as to how solid our supposed freedoms really are. Our fears of reductionism, our suspicions that we really may be no more than a series of automated responses, did not, as so many of us like to think, come to prominence in the industrial age. They are way, way older than that. Ever since Oedipus raged at his carefully calibrated fate, or Gilgamesh struggled to set himself free from his god's predestined plans, humans have wondered and deeply worried about the degree to which we orchestrate our own agentic actions. Skinner's work was, among other things, the square container into which those worries, forever resurrected, were poured in the shadow of the twentieth century's new gleaming machines.

Before i leave the Skinner archives for good, I make one more stop, and that's to view the famous baby box in which Skinner's daughter slept for the first two and a half years of her life. The box itself, I learn, has been dismantled, but I see a picture of it, from *Ladies' Home Journal*, which ran an article about the invention in 1945. If you wish to raise your reputation as a scientist, *Ladies' Home Journal* is probably not the best choice of outlets. The fact that Skinner chose to publish his supposed scientific inventions in a second-tier women's magazine speaks of his very poor "PR" skills.

"BABY IN A BOX"

the heading to the article reads, and beneath that there is, indeed, a picture of a baby in a box, a cherubic-looking Deborah grinning, hands plastered on Plexiglas sides. But read further. The baby box, it turns out, was really no more than an upgraded playpen in which young Deborah spent a few hours a day. With a thermostatically controlled environment, it guaranteed against diaper rash and kept nasal passages clear. Because the temperature was so fine-tuned, there was no need for blankets, and so the danger of suffocation, every mother's nightmare, was eliminated. Skinner outfitted his baby box with padding made of special material that absorbed odors and wetness so a woman's washing time was reduced by half, and she was free to use her hands for other pursuits—this in an era before disposable diapers. It all seems humane, if not downright feminist. And then, read still further. By giving the child a truly benevolent environment, an environment with no punishing dangers (if the baby fell down, it wouldn't hurt because the corners were padded to eliminate hard knocks), an environment, in other words, that conditioned by providing pure reward, Skinner hoped to raise a confident swashbuckler who believed she could master her surroundings and so would approach the world that way.

It all seems, without a doubt, good intentioned, if not downright noble, and sets Skinner firmly in humane waters. But then (and there is always a *but then* in this tale), I read the name that others have proposed for his invention: Heir Conditioner. This is either frightening or just plain foolish.

There are thousands upon thousands of "Deborah Skinners" listed on-line, but none of them pan out. I'd like to find her; confirm her status as living. I telephone a Deborah Skinner, author of a cook-book titled *Crab Cakes and Fireflies*, and a four-year-old Deborah, and several disconnected numbers. I call Deborahs in flower shops, Deborahs on treadmills, Deborahs selling real estate and hawking credit cards, but none can claim they know a B. F. Skinner.

No, I don't find Deborah Skinner anywhere in America, nor do I find records of a death in Billings, Montana. But what I do find, in the circuitous, associative way that the Internet works, is her sister, Julie Vargas, a professor of education at the University of West Virginia. I dial.

"I'm writing about your father," I say after I establish that she is an actual offspring. In the background, pots and pans clang. I hear what sounds like a knife—chop chop—and I imagine her, Skinner's other girl, the one who missed the myth, boiling the plainest of potatoes, slicing bright chips of carrots on an old cutting board somewhere where no one can see her.

"Oh," she says, "and what about him are you writing?" There is no doubt I hear suspicion in her voice, an obvious edge of defensiveness.

"I am writing," I say, "about great psychological experiments, and I want to include your father in the book."

"Oh," she says, and won't go further.

"So, I was wondering if you could tell me what he was like."

Chop chop. I hear, on her side, a screen door slam shut.

"I was wondering," I say, trying again, "if you could tell me what you think of—"

"My sister is alive and well," she says. I have not, of course, even asked her this, but it's clear many others have; it's clear the question tires her; it's clear she knows that every query about her family begins and ends at this place, bypassing entirely the work itself.

"I saw her picture on the Web," I say.

"She's an artist," Julie says. "She lives in England. She's happily married. She taught her cat to play the piano."

"Was she close to your father?" I say.

"Oh, we both were," Julie says, and then she pauses, and I can practically feel things pushing against the pause—memories, feelings, her father's hands on her head—"I miss him terribly," she says.

The knife is silent now; the screen door no longer slams, and in the space where those sounds were comes Julie Skinner Vargas's voice, a voice loaded with memory, a kind of nostalgic incontinence, it pours through; she cannot help herself. "He had a way with children," she says. "He loved them. Our mother, well, our mother was—" and she won't finish that sentence. "But our father," she says, "Dad used to make us kites, box kites which we flew on Monhegan, and he took us to the circus every year and our dog, Hunter, he was a beagle and Dad taught him to play hide and seek. He could teach anything anything, so our dog played hide and seek, it was a world," she says, " . . . those kites," she says, "we made them with string and sticks and flew them in the sky."

"So to you," I say, "he was a really great guy."

"Yes," she says. "He knew exactly what a child needed."

"What about," I ask, "How do you feel about all the criticism his work has engendered?"

Julie laughs. The laugh is more like a bark. "I compare it to Darwin," she says. "People denied Darwin's ideas because they were threatening. My father's ideas are threatening, but they are as great as Darwin's."

"Do you agree with all your father's ideas?" I say. "Do you agree with him that we are just automatons, that we have no free will, or do you think he took his experimental data too far?"

Julie sighs. "You know," she says, "if my father made one mistake, it was in the words he chose. People hear the word *control* and they think fascist. If my father had said people were *informed* by their environments, or *inspired* by their environments, no one would've had a problem. The truth about my father," she says, "is that he was a pacifist. He was also a child advocate. He did not believe in ANY punishment because he saw firsthand with the animals how it didn't work. My father," she said, "is responsible for the repeal of the corporal punishment ruling in California, but no one remembers him for that.

"No one remembers," she says, her voice rising—she's angry now—"how he always answered EVERY letter he got while those *humanists*," and she practically spits the word out, "those *supposed humanists*, the I'm okay you're okay school, they didn't even bother to answer their fan mail. They were too busy. My father was never too busy for people," she says.

"No, no, he wasn't," I say, and suddenly I'm a little frightened. She seems a little edgy, this Julie, a little too passionate about dear old dad.

"Let me ask you something," Julie says. I can tell from the tone of her voice that this question is going to be big, pointed; it's going to put me on the spot.

"Can I ask you something?" she says. "Tell me honestly."

"Yeah," I say.

"Have you actually even READ his works like *Beyond Freedom and Dignity*, or are you just another scholar of secondary sources?"

"Well," I say, stumbling, "I've read A LOT of your dad's work, believe me—"

"I believe you," she says, "but have you read *Freedom and Dignity*?"

"Well no," I say. "I was sticking to the purely scientific texts, not the philosophical treatises."

"You can't separate science from philosophy," she says, answering my earlier question. "So do your homework," and now she sounds like any old mother, or aunt, her voice calm, creased with warmth, chop chop, she is back to the carrots, the plain old potatoes. "Do your homework," she says, "and then we'll talk."

That night, I put the baby to bed. I take down the worn, dogeared copy of *Beyond Freedom and Dignity*, the treatise I have associated with other totalitarian texts, the treatise that, like *Mein Kampf*, I have long owned but never really read, and now I begin.

"Things grow steadily worse and it is disheartening to find that technology itself is increasingly at fault. Sanitation and medicine have made the problems of population control more acute. War has acquired a new horror with the invention of nuclear weapons, and the affluent pursuit of happiness is largely responsible for pollution."

Although this was written in 1971, I might as well be reading a speech by Al Gore, or a Green Party mission statement from 2003. It is true that further into the text Skinner says some troubling things like, "By questioning the control exercised by autonomous man and demonstrating the control exercised by the environment, a science of behavior questions the concepts of dignity and worth." But these sorts of statements are buried in a text immensely pragmatic. Skinner is clearly proposing a humane social policy rooted in his experimental findings. He is proposing that we appreciate the immense control (or influence) our surroundings have on us, and so sculpt those surroundings in such a way that they "reinforce positively," or in other words, engender adaptive and creative behaviors, in all citizens. Skinner is asking society to fashion cues that are most likely to draw on our best selves, as opposed to cues that clearly confound us, cues such as those that exist in prisons, in places of poverty. In other words, stop punishing. Stop humiliating. Who could argue with that? Set the rhetoric aside. Do not confuse content with controversy.

The content says, "Our age is not suffering from anxiety but from wars, crimes, and other dangerous things. The feelings are the byproducts of behavior." This statement is the sum total of Skinner's reviled antimentalism, his insistence that we focus not on mind but on behavior. Really it's no different than your mother's favorite saying: actions speak louder than words. According to Skinner—and New Age author Norman Cousins—when we act meanly, we feel meanly, and not vice versa. Whether you agree with this or not, it's hardly antihumanitarian. And later on in the book, when Skinner writes that man exists irrefutably in relationship to his environment and can never be free of it, is he talking about confining chains, as most have interpreted it, or simply the silvery web work that connects us to this and this and that? I saw Jerome Kagan jump under his desk, assuring me he had free will and could exist independently of his environment. Maybe he is acting out of a more problematic tradition, patriarchal and alone. In Skinner's view, we appear to be entwined and must take responsibility for the strings that bind us. Compare this to the current-day feminist Carol Gilligan, who writes that we live in an interdependent net and women realize and honor this. Gilligan, and all of the feminist psychotherapists who followed, claim we are relational as opposed to strictly separate, and that until we see our world that way, and build a morality predicated on this irrefutable fact, we will continue to crumble. From where did Gilligan and Jean Baker Miller and other feminist theorists draw their theories? Skinner's spirit hovers in their words; maybe he was the first feminist psychologist, or maybe feminist psychologists are secret Skinnerians. Either way, we have viewed the man too simply. It seems we boxed him before he could quite box us.

The Struggle for Meaning

Bruno Bettelheim

If we hope to live not just from moment to moment, but in true consciousness of our existence, then our greatest need and most difficult achievement
is to find meaning in our lives. It is well known how many have lost the will
to live, and have stopped trying, because such meaning has evaded them.
An understanding of the meaning of one's life is not suddenly acquired at a
particular age, not even when one has reached chronological maturity. On
the contrary, gaining a secure understanding of what the meaning of one's
life may or ought to be—this is what constitutes having attained psychological maturity. And this achievement is the end result of a long development: at each age we seek, and must be able to find, some modicum of
meaning congruent with how our minds and understanding have already
developed.

Contrary to the ancient myth, wisdom does not burst forth fully developed like Athena out of Zeus's head; it is built up, small step by small step,
from most irrational beginnings. Only in adulthood can an intelligent understanding of the meaning of one's existence in this world be gained from one's
experiences in it. Unfortunately, too many parents want their children's minds
to function as their own do—as if mature understanding of ourselves and the
world, and our ideas about the meaning of life, did not have to develop as
slowly as our bodies and minds.

Today, as in times past, the most important and also the most difficult
task in raising a child is helping him to find meaning in life. Many growth
experiences are needed to achieve this. The child, as he develops, must learn
step by step to understand himself better; with this he becomes more able to
understand others and eventually can relate to them in ways which are mutually satisfying and meaningful.

To find deeper meaning, one must become able to transcend the narrow
confines of a self-centered existence and believe that one will make a significant

contribution to life—if not right now, then at some future time. This feeling is necessary if a person is to be satisfied with himself and with what he is doing. In order not to be at the mercy of the vagaries of life, one must develop one's inner resources, so that one's emotions, imagination, and intellect mutually support and enrich one another. Our positive feelings give us the strength to develop our rationality; only hope for the future can sustain us in the adversities we unavoidably encounter.

As an educator and therapist of severely disturbed children, my main task was to restore meaning to their lives. This work made it obvious to me that if children were reared so that life was meaningful to them, they would not need special help. I was confronted with the problem of deducing what experiences in a child's life are most suited to promote his ability to find meaning in his life, to endow life in general with more meaning. Regarding this task, nothing is more important than the impact of parents and others who take care of the child; second in importance is our cultural heritage, when transmitted to the child in the right manner. When children are young, it is literature that carries such information best.

Given this fact, I became deeply dissatisfied with much of the literature intended to develop the child's mind and personality, because it fails to stimulate and nurture those resources he needs most in order to cope with his difficult inner problems. The preprimers and primers from which he is taught to read in school are designed to teach the necessary skills, irrespective of meaning. The overwhelming bulk of the rest of so-called "children's literature" attempts to entertain or to inform, or both. But most of these books are so shallow in substance that little of significance can be gained from them. The acquisition of skills, including the ability to read, becomes devalued when what one has learned to read adds nothing of importance to one's life.

We all tend to assess the future merits of an activity on the basis of what it offers now. But this is especially true for the child, who, much more than the adult, lives in the present and, although he has anxieties about his future, has only the vaguest notions of what it may require or be like. The idea that learning to read may enable one later to enrich one's life is experienced as an empty promise when the stories the child listens to, or is reading at the moment, are vacuous. The worst feature of these children's books is that they cheat the child of what he ought to gain from the experience of literature: access to deeper meaning and that which is meaningful to him at his stage of development.

For a story truly to hold the child's attention, it must entertain him and arouse his curiosity. But to enrich his life, it must stimulate his imagination; help him to develop his intellect and to clarify his emotions; be attuned to his anxieties and aspirations; give full recognition to his difficulties, while at the same time suggesting solutions to the problems which perturb him. In short, it must at one and the same time relate to all aspects of his personality—and this without ever belittling but, on the contrary, giving full credence to the seriousness of the child's predicaments, while simultaneously promoting confidence in himself and in his future.

In all these and many other respects, of the entire "children's literature"—with rare exceptions—nothing can be as enriching and satisfying to child and adult alike as the folk fairy tale. True, on an overt level fairy tales teach little about the specific conditions of life in modern mass society; these tales were created long before it came into being. But more can be learned from them about the inner problems of human beings, and of the right solutions to their predicaments in any society, than from any other type of story within a child's comprehension. Since the child at every moment of his life is exposed to the society in which he lives, he will certainly learn to cope with its conditions, provided his inner resources permit him to do so.

Just because his life is often bewildering to him, the child needs even more to be given the chance to understand himself in this complex world with which he must learn to cope. To be able to do so, the child must be helped to make some coherent sense out of the turmoil of his feelings. He needs ideas on how to bring his inner house into order and on that basis be able to create order in his life. He needs—and this hardly requires emphasis at this moment in our history—a moral education which subtly, and by implication only, conveys to him the advantages of moral behavior, not through abstract ethical concepts but through that which seems tangibly right and therefore meaningful to him.

The child finds this kind of meaning through fairy tales. Like many other modern psychological insights, this was anticipated long ago by poets. The German poet Schiller wrote: "Deeper meaning resides in the fairy tales told to me in my childhood than in the truth that is taught by life" (*The Piccolomini*, III, 4).

Through the centuries (if not millennia) during which, in their retelling, fairy tales became ever more refined, they came to convey at the same time overt and covert meanings—came to speak simultaneously to all levels of the human personality, communicating in a manner which reaches the uneducated mind of the child as well as that of the sophisticated adult. Applying the psychoanalytic model of the human personality, fairy tales carry important messages to the conscious, the preconscious, and the unconscious mind, on whatever level each is functioning at the time. By dealing with universal human problems, particularly those which preoccupy the child's mind, these stories speak to his budding ego and encourage its development, while at the same time relieving preconscious and unconscious pressures. As the stories unfold, they give conscious credence and body to id pressures and show ways to satisfy these that are in line with ego and super-ego requirements.

But my interest in fairy tales is not the result of such a technical analysis of their merits. It is, on the contrary, the consequence of asking myself why, in my experience, children—normal and abnormal alike, and at all levels of intelligence—find folk fairy tales more satisfying than all other children's stories.

The more I tried to understand why these stories are so successful at enriching the inner life of the child, the more I realized that these tales, in a much deeper sense than any other reading material, start where the child really is in his psychological and emotional being. They speak about his severe inner pressures in a way that the child unconsciously understands and—without belittling the most serious inner struggles which growing up entails—offer examples of both temporary and permanent solutions to pressing difficulties.

FAIRY TALES AND THE EXISTENTIAL PREDICAMENT

In order to master the psychological problems of growing up—overcoming narcissistic disappointments, oedipal dilemmas, sibling rivalries; becoming able to relinquish childhood dependencies; gaining a feeling of selfhood and of self-worth, and a sense of moral obligation—a child needs to understand what is going on within his conscious self so that he can also cope with that which goes on in his unconscious. He can achieve this understanding, and with it the ability to cope, not through rational comprehension of the nature and content of his unconscious, but by becoming familiar with it through spinning out daydreams—ruminating, rearranging, and fantasizing about suitable story elements in response to unconscious pressures. By doing this, the child fits unconscious content into conscious fantasies, which then enable him to deal with that content. It is here that fairy tales have unequaled value, because they offer new dimensions to the child's imagination which would be impossible for him to discover as truly on his own. Even more important, the form and structure of fairy tales suggest images to the child by which he can structure his daydreams and with them give better direction to his life.

In child or adult, the unconscious is a powerful determinant of behavior. When the unconscious is repressed and its content denied entrance into awareness, then eventually the person's conscious mind will be partially overwhelmed by derivatives of these unconscious elements, or else he is forced to keep such rigid, compulsive control over them that his personality may become severely crippled. But when unconscious material *is* to some degree permitted to come to awareness and worked through in imagination, its potential for causing harm—to ourselves or others—is much reduced; some of its forces can then be made to serve positive purposes. However, the prevalent parental belief is that a child must be diverted from what troubles him most: his formless, nameless anxieties, and his chaotic, angry, and even violent fantasies. Many parents believe that only conscious reality or pleasant and wish-fulfilling images should be presented to the child—that he should be exposed only to the sunny side of things. But such one-sided fare nourishes the mind only in a one-sided way, and real life is not all sunny.

There is a widespread refusal to let children know that the source of much that goes wrong in life is due to our very own natures—the propensity of all men for acting aggressively, asocially, selfishly, out of anger and anxiety. Instead, we want our children to believe that, inherently, all men are good. But children know that *they* are not always good; and often, even when they are, they would prefer not to be. This contradicts what they are told by their parents, and therefore makes the child a monster in his own eyes.

The dominant culture wishes to pretend, particularly where children are concerned, that the dark side of man does not exist, and professes a belief in an optimistic meliorism.[2] Psychoanalysis itself is viewed as having the purpose of making life easy—but this is not what its founder intended. Psychoanalysis was created to enable man to accept the problematic nature of life without being defeated by it or giving in to escapism. Freud's prescription is that only by struggling courageously against what seem like overwhelming odds can man succeed in wringing meaning out of his existence.

This is exactly the message that fairy tales get across to the child in manifold form: that a struggle against severe difficulties in life is unavoidable, is an intrinsic part of human existence—but that if one does not shy away, but steadfastly meets unexpected and often unjust hardships, one masters all obstacles and at the end emerges victorious.

Modern stories written for young children mainly avoid these existential problems, although they are crucial issues for all of us. The child needs most particularly to be given suggestions in symbolic form about how he may deal with these issues and grow safely into maturity. "Safe" stories mention neither death nor aging, the limits to our existence, nor the wish for eternal life. The fairy tale, by contrast, confronts the child squarely with the basic human predicaments.

For example, many fairy stories begin with the death of a mother or father; in these tales the death of the parent creates the most agonizing problems, as it (or the fear of it) does in real life. Other stories tell about an aging parent who decides that the time has come to let the new generation take over. But before this can happen, the successor has to prove himself capable and worthy. The Brothers Grimm's story "The Three Feathers" begins: "There was once upon a time a king who had three sons. . . . When the king had become old and weak, and was thinking of his end, he did not know which of his sons should inherit the kingdom after him." In order to decide, the king sets all his sons a difficult task; the son who meets it best "shall be king after my death."

It is characteristic of fairy tales to state an existential dilemma briefly and pointedly. This permits the child to come to grips with the problem in its most essential form, where a more complex plot would confuse matters for him. The fairy tale simplifies all situations. Its figures are clearly drawn; and details, unless very important, are eliminated. All characters are typical rather than unique.

Contrary to what takes place in many modern children's stories, in fairy tales evil is as omnipresent as virtue. In practically every fairy tale good and evil are given body in the form of some figures and their actions, as good and evil are omnipresent in life and the propensities for both are present in every man. It is this duality which poses the moral problem and requires the struggle to solve it.

Evil is not without its attractions—symbolized by the mighty giant or dragon, the power of the witch, the cunning queen in "Snow White"—and often it is temporarily in the ascendancy. In many fairy tales a usurper succeeds for a time in seizing the place which rightfully belongs to the hero—as the wicked sisters do in "Cinderella." It is not that the evildoer is punished at the story's end which makes immersing oneself in fairy stories an experience in moral education, although this is part of it. In fairy tales, as in life, punishment or fear of it is only a limited deterrent to crime. The conviction that crime does not pay is a much more effective deterrent, and that is why in fairy tales the bad person always loses out. It is not the fact that virtue wins out at the end which promotes morality, but that the hero is most attractive to the child, who identifies with the hero in all his struggles. Because of this identification the child imagines that he suffers with the hero his trials and tribulations, and triumphs with him as virtue is victorious. The child makes such identifications all on his own, and the inner and outer struggles of the hero imprint morality on him.

The figures in fairy tales are not ambivalent—not good and bad at the same time, as we all are in reality. But since polarization dominates the child's mind, it also dominates fairy tales. A person is either good or bad, nothing in between. One brother is stupid, the other is clever. One sister is virtuous and industrious, the others are vile and lazy. One is beautiful, the others are ugly. One parent is all good, the other evil. The juxtaposition of opposite characters is not for the purpose of stressing right behavior, as would be true for cautionary tales. (There are some amoral fairy tales where goodness or badness, beauty or ugliness, play no role at all.) Presenting the polarities of character permits the child to comprehend easily the difference between the two, which he could not do as readily were the figures drawn more true to life, with all the complexities that characterize real people. Ambiguities must wait until a relatively firm personality has been established on the basis of positive identifications. Then the child has a basis for understanding that there are great differences between people and that therefore one has to make choices about who one wants to be. This basic decision, on which all later personality development will build, is facilitated by the polarizations of the fairy tale.

Furthermore, a child's choices are based, not so much on right versus wrong, as on who arouses his sympathy and who his antipathy. The more simple and straight-forward a good character, the easier it is for a child to identify with it and to reject the bad other. The child identifies with the good hero not because of his goodness, but because the hero's condition makes a deep positive appeal to him. The question for the child is not "Do I want to be good?" but "Who do I want to be like?" The child decides this on the basis of projecting himself wholeheartedly into one character. If this fairy-tale figure is a very good person, then the child decides that he wants to be good, too.

Amoral fairy tales show no polarization or juxtaposition of good and bad persons; that is because these amoral stories serve an entirely different purpose. Such tales or type figures as "Puss in Boots," who arranges for the hero's success through trickery, and Jack, who steals the giant's treasure, build character not by promoting choices between good and bad, but by giving the child the hope that even the meekest can succeed in life. After all, what's the use of choosing to become a good person when one feels so insignificant that he fears he will never amount to anything? Morality is not the issue in these tales, but rather, assurance that one can succeed. Whether one meets life with a belief in the possibility of mastering its difficulties or with the expectation of defeat is also a very important existential problem.

The deep inner conflicts originating in our primitive drives and our violent emotions are all denied in much of modern children's literature, and so the child is not helped in coping with them. But the child is subject to desperate feelings of loneliness and isolation, and he often experiences mortal anxiety. More often than not, he is unable to express these feelings in words, or he can do so only by indirection: fear of the dark, of some animal, anxiety about his body. Since it creates discomfort in a parent to recognize these emotions in his child, the parent tends to overlook them, or he belittles these spoken fears out of his own anxiety, believing this will cover over the child's fears.

The fairy tale, by contrast, takes these existential anxieties and dilemmas very seriously and addresses itself directly to them: the need to be loved and the fear that one is thought worthless; the love of life and the fear of death. Further, the fairy tale offers solutions in ways that the child can grasp on his level of understanding. For example, fairy tales pose the dilemma of wishing to live eternally by occasionally concluding: "If they have not died, they are still alive." The other ending—"And they lived happily ever after"—does not for a moment fool the child that eternal life is possible. But it does indicate that which alone can take the sting out of the narrow limits of our time on this earth: forming a truly satisfying bond to another. The tales teach that when one has done this, one has reached the ultimate in emotional security of existence and permanence of relation available to man; and this alone can dissipate the fear of death. If one has found true adult love, the fairy story also tells, one doesn't need to wish for eternal life. This is suggested by another ending found in fairy tales: "They lived for a long time afterward, happy and in pleasure."

An uninformed view of the fairy tale sees in this type of ending an unrealistic wish-fulfillment, missing completely the important message it conveys to the child. These tales tell him that by forming a true interpersonal relation, one escapes the separation anxiety which haunts him (and which sets the stage for many fairy tales, but is always resolved at the story's ending). Furthermore, the story tells, this ending is not made possible, as the child wishes and believes, by holding on to his mother eternally. If we try to escape separation anxiety and death anxiety by desperately keeping our grasp on our parents, we will only be cruelly forced out, like Hansel and Gretel.

Only by going out into the world can the fairy-tale hero (child) find himself there; and as he does, he will also find the other with whom he will be able to live happily ever after, that is, without ever again having to experience separation anxiety. The fairy tale is future-oriented and guides the child—in terms he can understand in both his conscious and his unconscious mind—to relinquish his infantile dependency wishes and achieve a more satisfying independent existence.

Today children no longer grow up within the security of an extended family or of a well-integrated community. Therefore, even more than at the times fairy tales were invented, it is important to provide the modern child with images of heroes who have to go out into the world all by themselves and who, although originally ignorant of the ultimate things, find secure places in the world by following their right way with deep inner confidence.

The fairy-tale hero proceeds for a time in isolation, as the modern child often feels isolated. The hero is helped by being in touch with primitive things—a tree, an animal, nature—as the child feels more in touch with those things than most adults do. The fate of these heroes convinces the child that, like them, he may feel outcast and abandoned in the world, groping in the dark, but, like them, in the course of his life he will be guided step by step, and given help when it is needed. Today, even more than in past times, the child needs the reassurance offered by the image of the isolated man who nevertheless is capable of achieving meaningful and rewarding relations with the world around him.

THE FAIRY TALE: A UNIQUE ART FORM

While it entertains the child, the fairy tale enlightens him about himself and fosters his personality development. It offers meaning on so many different levels, and enriches the child's existence in so many ways, that no one book can do justice to the multitude and diversity of the contributions such tales make to the child's life.

This book [*The Uses of Enchantment*] attempts to show how fairy stories represent in imaginative form what the process of healthy human development consists of and how the tales make such development attractive for the child to engage in. This growth process begins with the resistance against the parents and fear of growing up, and ends when youth has truly found itself, achieved psychological independence and moral maturity, and no longer views the other sex as threatening or demonic, but is able to relate positively to it.

In short, this book explicates why fairy tales make such great and positive psychological contributions to the child's inner growth.

If this book had been devoted to only one or two tales, it would have been possible to show many more of their facets, although even then complete probing of their depths would not have been achieved; for this, each story has meanings on too many levels. Which story is most important to a particular child at a particular age depends entirely on his psychological stage of development and the problems which are most pressing to him at the moment. While in writing the book it seemed reasonable to concentrate on a fairy tale's central meanings, this has the shortcoming of neglecting other aspects which might be much more significant to some individual child because of problems he is struggling with at the time. This, then, is another necessary limitation of this presentation.

For example, in discussing "Hansel and Gretel," the child's striving to hold on to his parents even though the time has come for meeting the world on his own is stressed, as well as the need to transcend a primitive orality, symbolized by the children's infatuation with the gingerbread house. Thus, it would seem that this fairy tale has most to offer to the young child ready to make his first steps out into the world. It gives body to his anxieties and offers reassurance about these fears because even in their most exaggerated form—anxieties about being devoured—they prove unwarranted: the children are victorious in the end, and a most threatening enemy—the witch—is utterly defeated. Thus, a good case could be made that this story has its greatest appeal and value for the child at the age when fairy tales begin to exercise their beneficial impact, that is, around the age of four or five.

But separation anxiety—the fear of being deserted—and starvation fear, including oral greediness, are not restricted to a particular period of development. Such fears occur at all ages in the unconscious, and thus this tale also has meaning for, and provides encouragement to, much older children. As a matter of fact, the older person might find it considerably more difficult to admit consciously his fear of being deserted by his parents or to face his oral greed; and this is even more reason to let the fairy tale speak to his unconscious, give body to his unconscious anxieties, and relieve them, without this ever coming to conscious awareness.

Other features of the same story may offer much-needed reassurance and guidance to an older child. In early adolescence a girl had been fascinated by "Hansel and Gretel," and had derived great comfort from reading and rereading it, fantasizing about it. As a child, she had been dominated by a slightly older brother. He had, in a way, shown her the path, as Hansel did when he put down the pebbles which guided his sister and himself back home. As an adolescent, this girl continued to rely on her brother, and this feature of the story felt reassuring. But at the same time she also resented the brother's dominance. Without her being conscious of it at the time, her struggle for independence rotated around the figure of Hansel. The story told her unconscious that to follow Hansel's lead led her back, not forward, and it was also meaningful that although Hansel was the leader at the story's beginning, it was Gretel who in the end achieved freedom and independence for both, because it was she who defeated the witch. As an adult, this woman came to understand that the fairy tale had helped her greatly in throwing off her dependence on her brother, as it had convinced her that an early dependence on him need not interfere with her later ascendancy. Thus, a story which for one reason had been meaningful to her as a young child provided guidance for her at adolescence for a quite different reason.

The central motif of "Snow White" is the pubertal girl's surpassing in every way the evil stepmother who, out of jealousy, denies her an independent existence—symbolically represented by the stepmother's trying to see Snow White destroyed. The story's deepest meaning for one particular five-year-old, however, was far removed from these pubertal problems. Her mother was cold and distant, so much so that she felt lost. The story assured her that she need not despair: Snow White, betrayed by her stepmother, was saved by males— first the dwarfs and later the prince. This child, too, did not despair because of the mother's desertion but trusted that rescue would come from males. Confident that "Snow White" showed her the way, she turned to her father, who responded favorably; the fairy tale's happy ending made it possible for this girl to find a happy solution to the impasse in living into which her mother's lack of interest had projected her. Thus, a fairy tale can have as important a meaning to a five-year-old as to a thirteen-year-old, although the personal meanings they derive from it may be quite different.

In "Rapunzel" we learn that the enchantress locked Rapunzel into the tower when she reached the age of twelve. Thus, hers is likewise the story of a pubertal girl and of a jealous mother who tries to prevent her from gaining independence—a typical adolescent problem, which finds a happy solution when Rapunzel becomes united with her prince. But one five-year-old boy gained quite a different reassurance from this story. When he learned that his grandmother, who took care of him most of the day, would have to go to the hospital because of serious illness—his mother was working all day, and there was no father in the home—he asked to be read the story of Rapunzel. At this critical time in his life, two elements of the tale were important to him. First, there was the security from all dangers in which the substitute mother kept the child, an idea which greatly appealed to him at that moment. So what normally could be viewed as a representation of negative, selfish behavior was capable of having a most reassuring meaning under specific circumstances. And even more important to the boy was another central motif of the story: that Rapunzel found the means of escaping her predicament in her own body—the tresses on which the prince climbed up to her room in the tower. That one's body can provide a lifeline reassured him that, if necessary, he would similarly find in his own body the source of his security. This shows that a fairy tale—because it addresses itself in the most imaginative form to essential human problems and does so in an indirect way—can have much to offer to a little boy even if the story's heroine is an adolescent girl.

These examples may help to counteract any impression made by my concentration here on a story's main motifs, and demonstrate that fairy tales have great psychological meaning for children of all ages, both girls and boys, irrespective of the age and sex of the story's hero. Rich personal meaning is gained from fairy stories because they facilitate changes in identification as the child deals with different problems, one at a time. In the light of her earlier identification with a Gretel who was glad to be led by Hansel, the adolescent girl's later identification with a Gretel who overcame the witch made her growth toward independence more rewarding and secure. The little boy's first finding security in the idea of being kept within the safety of the tower permitted him later on to glory in the realization that a much more dependable security could be found in what his body had to offer him, by way of providing him with a lifeline.

As we cannot know at what age a particular fairy tale will be most important to a particular child, we cannot ourselves decide which of the many tales he should be told at any given time or why. This only the child can determine and reveal by the strength of feeling with which he reacts to what a tale evokes in his conscious and unconscious mind. Naturally a parent will begin by telling or reading to his child a tale the parent himself or herself cared for as a child, or cares for now. If the child does not take to the story, this means that its motifs or themes have failed to evoke a meaningful response at this moment in his life. Then it is best to tell him another fairy tale the next evening. Soon he will indicate that a certain story has become important to him by his immediate response to it, or by his asking to be told this story over and over again. If all goes well, the child's enthusiasm for this story will be contagious, and the story will become important to the parent too, if for no other reason than that it means so much to the child. Finally there will come the time when the child has gained all he can from the preferred story, or the problems which made him respond to it have been replaced by others which find better expression in some other tale. He may then temporarily lose interest in this story and enjoy some other one much more. In the telling of fairy stories it is always best to follow the child's lead.

Even if a parent should guess correctly why his child has become involved emotionally with a given tale, this is knowledge best kept to oneself. The young child's most important experiences and reactions are largely subconscious and should remain so until he reaches a much more mature age and understanding. It is always intrusive to interpret a person's unconscious thoughts, to make conscious what he wishes to keep preconscious, and this is especially true in the case of a child. Just as important for the child's well-being as feeling that his parent shares his emotions, through enjoying the same fairy tale, is the child's feeling that his inner thoughts are not known to his parent until he decides to reveal them. If the parent indicates that he knows them already, the child is prevented from making the most precious gift to his parent of sharing with him what until then was secret and private to the child. And since, in addition, a parent is so much more powerful than a child, his domination may appear limitless—and hence destructively overwhelming—if he seems able to read the child's secret thoughts, know his most hidden feelings, even before the child himself has begun to become aware of them.

Explaining to a child why a fairy tale is so captivating to him destroys, moreover, the story's enchantment, which depends to a considerable degree on the child's not quite knowing why he is delighted by it. And with the forfeiture of this power to enchant goes also a loss of the story's potential for helping the child struggle on his own and master all by himself the problem which has made the story meaningful to him in the first place. Adult interpretations, as correct as they may be, rob the child of the opportunity to feel that he, on his own, through repeated hearing and ruminating about the story, has coped successfully with a difficult situation. We grow, we find meaning in life and security in ourselves by having understood and solved personal problems on our own, not by having them explained to us by others.

Fairy-tale motifs are not neurotic symptoms, something one is better off understanding rationally so that one can rid oneself of them. Such motifs are experienced as wondrous because the child feels understood and appreciated deep down in his feelings, hopes, and anxieties, without these all having to be dragged up and investigated in the harsh light of a rationality that is still beyond him. Fairy tales enrich the child's life and give it an enchanted quality just because he does not quite know how the stories have worked their wonder on him.

NOTES

1. From *The Uses of Enchantment: The Meaning and Importance of Fairy Tales* (New York: Alfred Knopf, 1976).
2. meliorism: A doctrine that the world can be made better by human effort.

What Fairy Tales Tell Us

Alison Lurie

The stories of magic and transformation that we call "fairy tales" (though they usually contain no fairies) are one of the oldest known forms of literature and also one of the most popular and enduring. Even today they are a central part of our imaginative world. We remember and refer to them all our lives; their themes and characters reappear in dreams, in songs, in films, in advertisements, and in casual speech. We say that someone is a giant-killer or that theirs is a Cinderella story.

The fairy tale survives because it presents experience in vivid symbolic form. Sometimes we need to have the truth exaggerated and made more dramatic, even fantastic, in order to comprehend it. (The same sort of thing can occur in other ways, of course, as when at a costume party we suddenly recognize that one of our acquaintances is in fact essentially a six-foot-tall white rabbit, a pirate, or a dancing doll.)

"Hansel and Gretel," for instance, may dramatize the fact that some parents underfeed and neglect their children physically and/or emotionally, while others, like the witch who lives in a house made of cake and candy, overfeed and try to possess and perhaps even devour them. "Beauty and the Beast" may suggest that a good man can seem at first like a dangerous wild animal or that true love has a power to soothe the savage heart. The message may be different for each reader; that is one of the great achievements of the fairy tale, traditional or modern.

For though not everyone knows it, there are modern fairy tales. Though most people think of these stories as having come into existence almost magically long ago, they are in fact still being created and not only in less urbanized parts of the world than our own. Over the last century and a half many famous authors have written tales of wonder and enchantment. In Britain and the United States they have included Nathaniel Hawthorne, Charles

Dickens, Robert Louis Stevenson, Oscar Wilde, H.G. Wells, Carl Sandburg, James Thurber, Bernard Malamud, I.B. Singer, T.H. White, Angela Carter, and Louise Erdrich. Like other authors in other countries (especially France and Germany) they have used the characters and settings and events of the fairy tale to create new and marvelous stories—not only for children, but for adults. The traditional fairy tale was not read from a book but passed on orally from one generation to the next, and its audience was not limited to children. Its heroes and heroines most often are not children but young people setting out to make their fortunes or find a mate, or most often both. Many of these stories were written for readers of all ages, or only for adults. But even when they were principally meant for children, and have child protagonists, these modern tales often contain sophisticated comments and ironic asides directed to the adults who might be reading the story aloud.

The best modern fairy stories, like traditional folk tales, can be understood in many different ways. Like all great literature, they speak to readers of every place and time. They have one message for a seven-year-old and another one, more complex and sometimes more melancholy, for a seventeen-year-old or a seventy-year-old; they may mean one thing to a nineteenth-century reader and another to a twentieth-century one.

George MacDonald's "The Light Princess" (1864), for example, is on the face of it a traditional tale of enchantment. When the princess is born, her parents, in the time-honored manner, fail to invite a wicked witch (who is also the king's sister) to the christening party. As a result, the witch curses the baby with a lack of gravity. This lack manifests itself both physically and psychologically: the princess weighs nothing, and she also is incapable of serious emotions; in contemporary parlance, she is a total airhead. Eventually a prince falls in love with the Light Princess. He is willing to sacrifice his life for her, and when the princess finally realizes it, she too falls in love, and this breaks the enchantment. The prince is restored to life, and they are married and live happily ever after.

A modern reader might come away from this story thinking it says that the best way to grow up fast is to fall in love. To a Victorian reader, however, it would more likely have seemed to be about the proper behavior of women. At the time it was generally considered, as the Light Princess's Queen remarks, a bad thing for a woman to be light-headed and light-minded. Later on the prince who loves her is pleased to discover that when the princess swims in the lake, she is "not so forward in her questions, or pert in her replies. . . . Neither did she laugh so much, and when she did laugh, it was more gently. She seemed altogether more modest and maidenly." Like the ideal Victorian girl, the princess becomes gentle, quiet, and above all serious.

The earliest attempts to create modern fairy tales were tentative. At first, authors merely rewrote the traditional stories of Grimm and Perrault, sometimes in what now seems a ridiculous manner. In 1853 the Grimms' first English illustrator, George Cruickshank, began to publish revisions of the most popular tales from a teetotal point of view. The Giant in his "Jack and the

Beanstalk" turns out to be an alcoholic, and Cinderella's wedding is celebrated by the destruction of all the drink in the Prince's castle.

Meanwhile, other writers were beginning to go beyond revision to compose original tales, often in order to point out an improving moral. The lesson, of course, varied with the convictions of the author. Catherine Sinclair's light-hearted "Uncle David's Nonsensical Story About Giants and Fairies" (1839) suggested that idle and overfed children were apt to be eaten alive, while Juliana Horatia Ewing's "Good Luck Is Better Than Gold" (1882) and Howard Pyle's "The Apple of Contentment" (1886) punished greed and laziness.

Some writers were concerned with more contemporary issues. John Ruskin's famous ecological fable, "The King of the Golden River" (1851), promotes both his political and his aesthetic beliefs. The two wicked older brothers in this story are shortsighted capitalists who exploit both labor and natural resources, turning a once-fertile and dramatically beautiful valley into a barren wasteland. Their moods are so dark and their hearts so hard that it seems quite appropriate that they should eventually be transformed into two black stones, while little Gluck, who appreciates the sublime natural landscape and relieves the sufferings of the poor and disabled, restores the land to beauty and fruitfulness.

In "A Toy Princess" (1877) Mary De Morgan mounts a scathing attack on the ideal Victorian miss. The courtiers among whom her heroine grows up scold her for expressing her feelings and much prefer the artificial doll-princess who never says anything but "If you please," "No thank you," "Certainly," and "Just so." With the help of a good fairy, the real princess escapes from the palace and finds happiness and love in a fisherman's family.

More unsettling, and with a darker ending, is Lucy Lane Clifford's "The New Mother" (1882), which tells of the awful fate of two innocent children who are repeatedly encouraged in naughty behavior by a strange and charming young woman who may be an evil spirit. Eventually the children try their mother's patience so far that she threatens to leave them and send home a new mother, with glass eyes and a wooden tail. Anyone who has ever seen a harassed parent appear to turn temporarily into a glassy-eyed monster— or done so themselves—will understand this story instinctively, and so will parents who have doubts about the moral qualities of their baby-sitters. The author was a good friend of Henry James, and it is possible that "The New Mother" may be one of the sources of *The Turn of the Screw*.

After Perrault and Grimm the greatest influence on the literary fairy tale was Hans Christian Andersen, whose work was first translated into English in 1846. Andersen's early tales were adaptations of those he had heard from his grandmother, with their commonsense pagan fatality overlaid with Christian morality; later he composed original stories that often celebrated the nineteenth-century virtues of stoicism, piety, and self-sacrifice.

Andersen's romantic, spiritual narratives were echoed in the work of Oscar Wilde and Laurence Housman, among many others. Often their tales seem remarkably modern. In Housman's "The Rooted Lover" (1894) the hero is what my students at Cornell would call a post-feminist man. Like the prince in George MacDonald's "The Light Princess," he does not fight giants and dragons, but shows his courage and virtue through patient endurance for the sake of love.

In Wilde's "The Selfish Giant" (1888) Christian morality and myth dominate. The traditional fairy-tale villain of the title is not slain but reformed by a child who turns out to be Christ. Other writers, following Andersen's example, abandoned the usual happy ending of the fairy tale to create stories with an ambiguous or disturbing conclusion, like Robert Louis Stevenson's "The Song of the Morrow" (1894) in which a series of events is endlessly repeated in an almost Kafka-like manner.

Not all nineteenth-century British fairy tales are this serious: many are quietly or broadly comic. There are good-natured burlesques like Charles Dickens's "The Magic Fishbone" (1868) in which a scatty Micawber-like (or Dickens-like) family is saved by the patience and good sense of the eldest daughter; and there are gentle satires of social conformity and cowardice, like Frances Browne's "The Story of Fairyfoot" (1856), which exposes the arbitrary nature of standards of beauty, imagining a kingdom where the larger your feet are, the better-looking you are thought to be. Perhaps the best known of such stories is Kenneth Grahame's "The Reluctant Dragon" (1898), possibly the first overtly pacifist fairy tale. It features a sentimental dragon who writes sonnets and only wishes to be admired by the villagers whom he has terrified; many readers will recognize a common human type.

The fashion for tales that were humorous and satirical as well as (or instead of) uplifting or improving continued into the early twentieth century. E. Nesbit's "The Book of Beasts" (1900) is a lighthearted fable about the magical power of art. The volume that contains this title has pictures of exotic creatures that come alive when the pages are opened. The boy who finds the book releases first a butterfly, then a Blue Bird of Paradise, and finally a dragon that threatens to destroy the country. If any book is vivid enough, this story seems to say, its content will invade our world for good or evil.

For H.G. Wells, magic was allied with, or a metaphor for, science. His rather spooky Magic Shop, in the story of the same name (1903), contains both traditional supernatural creatures, like a small angry red demon, and the actual inventions of the future, including a train that runs without steam.

Other twentieth-century British writers composed more romantic tales. Some, like Walter de la Mare's "The Lovely My-fawny" (1925) and Sylvia Townsend Warner's witty "Bluebeard's Daughter" (1940), have a traditional fairy-story background of castles and princesses, and rebuke old-fashioned faults—in the former case, possessive paternal love; in the latter, curiosity.

Others are set in the contemporary world. John Collier's "The Chaser" (1941), a very short story with a sting in its tale, takes place in modern London; Naomi Mitchison's "In the Family" (1957) is set in a Scotland complete with buses and parish halls—and a fairy woman who warns the hero of a future highway accident.

Often these twentieth-century tales are interesting variations on earlier classics. Lord Dunsany's "The Kith of the Elf-Folk" (1910) is a half-poetic, half-satirical version of Andersen's "The Little Mermaid," with a happier, though rather conservative conclusion. In it a Wild Thing from the marshes ends by rejecting both her newly acquired human soul and a singing career in London. She returns to her former life and companions in the depths of the countryside—as other strange wild young women have sometimes done.

More recently the gifted British writer Angela Carter has become famous for her dramatic retellings of well-known fairy tales. Though her stories are as full of mystery and wonder, they are clearly set in modern times: Bluebeard's castle is connected to Paris by telephone, and in "The Courtship of Mr. Lyon" (1979) Beauty returns to her dying Beast from contemporary London on a train. Her characters too have been subtly updated: her Beast is Mr. Lyon, the awkward, lonely, growling owner of a Palladian villa equipped with politely rather than magically invisible servants. Beauty temporarily abandons Mr. Lyon to become a spoiled urban society girl who "smiled at herself in mirrors a little too often," but later she as well as he is transformed by the power of love. In another version of the same story, "The Tiger's Bride," the hero does not become a handsome prince; instead Beauty is transformed into a tigress by his passionate kisses. The implication is that the magical world is not a thing of the past but may coexist with ours. Perhaps, at any moment, we may enter it.

Some modern British authors of fairy tales, like these, revel in descriptions of exotic or luxurious settings. Others, by contrast, sometimes seem deliberately to choose the drabbest and most ordinary backgrounds, as if to remind us that strange and wonderful things can happen anywhere. Joan Aiken's "The Man Who Had Seen the Rope Trick" (1976) takes place in a dreary English seaside boardinghouse, and T.H. White, in "The Troll" (1935), begins with a similarly pedestrian setting, a comfortable railway hotel in northern Sweden where his hero has gone for the fishing. During his first night there he discovers that the professor in the next room is a troll who has eaten his wife. We accept this, and all that follows, not only because of White's great literary skill but because we know that some men, even some professors, are really trolls, and that some husbands do, psychologically at least, devour their wives (and wives their husbands).

In the nineteenth century it was sometimes suggested that Americans didn't need fairy tales, certainly not new ones. Instead of imaginary wonders we had the natural wonders of a new continent: we had Indians and wild animals instead of sprites and dragons; Niagara Falls and the Rockies instead of enchanted lakes and mountains.

However, Americans were already writing new fairy tales. Sometimes these stories featured old-fashioned props and characters: magic potions and spells, dwarves and witches, princes and princesses. But often they also included contemporary objects and figures: hotels and telephones, mayors and gold miners. And even from the beginning the best American stories had a different underlying message than many of those from across the Atlantic.

The standard European fairy tale, both traditional and modern, takes place in a fixed social world. In the usual plot a poor boy or girl, through some combination of luck, courage, beauty, kindness, and supernatural help, becomes rich or marries into royalty. In a variation, a prince or princess who has fallen under an evil enchantment, or been cast out by a cruel relative, regains his or her rightful position. These stories are full of wicked stepmothers and cruel kings and queens, but they seldom attack the institutions of marriage or monarchy. It is assumed that what the heroine or hero wants is to become rich and marry well. Usually the social system is implicitly unquestioned and remains unchanged; what changes is the protagonist, and what he or she hopes for is to succeed within the terms of this system. What makes American fairy tales different is that in many of them this does not happen. Instead, the world within the story alters or is abandoned. In Washington Irving's "Rip Van Winkle" (1820) Rip falls into a twenty-year sleep and wakes to find that a British colony has become a new nation, in which "the very character of the people seemed changed."

Even if the world does not change, its values are often implicitly criticized. The guests who visit "The Rich Man's Place" (1880) in Horace Scudder's story of that name enjoy the palatial house and grounds but don't express any desire to live there. In Frank Stockton's "The Bee-Man of Orn" (1887) a Junior Sorcerer discovers that an old beekeeper has been transformed from his original shape and sets out to dissolve the enchantment. But as it turns out his original shape (like everyone's) was that of a baby. The Junior Sorcerer restores him to infancy, but when he grows up he does not become a prince, but a beekeeper again—and as before he is perfectly contented.

In American fairy tales there is often not much to be said for wealth and high position, or even for good looks. In Nathaniel Hawthorne's "Feathertop" (1854) a New England witch transforms an old scarecrow into a fine gentleman and sends him out into the world, where he exposes the superficiality and snobbery of the well-to-do. In some ways the story is a democratic version of Mary De Morgan's "A Toy Princess." The scarecrow's vocabulary, like that of the Toy Princess, is very limited, consisting only of phrases like "Really! Indeed! Pray tell me! Is it possible! Upon my word! By no means! O! Ah!" and "Hem," but he is taken by the local people for a foreign nobleman and almost succeeds in winning the heart and hand of a good and beautiful girl. Though both these stories end without any real damage having been done, they are full of the unease we feel in the presence of someone with fine clothes and impenetrably bland good manners.

L. Frank Baum's "The Queen of Quok" (1901) contains a castle and royal personages, but Quok is essentially ruled by common sense and small-town American values. At one point the boy king has to borrow a dime from his chief counselor to buy a ham sandwich. Love of money turns the would-be queen into a haggard old woman, while the insouciant young hero lives happily ever after. And in Baum's "The Glass Dog" (1901) the poor glassblower manages to marry a princess, but she "was very jealous of his beauty and led him a dog's life." The implication of such stories is that an American does not need to become rich or marry up in order to be happy; in fact, one should avoid doing so if possible. Happiness is all around one already, as the boy in Laura Richards's story "The Golden Window" (c. 1904) discovers: his farmhouse already has "windows of gold and diamond" when the setting sun shines on it.

Even further from the traditional pattern are Carl Sandburg's *Rootabaga Stories* (1922), which reflect his love of American tall tales and deadpan humor, as well as his closeness to his pioneer ancestors. The family in his "How They Broke Away to Go to the Rootabaga Country" repeats the experience of many nineteenth-century immigrants to the Midwest. They sell all their possessions and ride to "where the railroad tracks run off into the sky," ending up not in a fairy kingdom but in rich farming country named after a large turnip. "The Story of Blixie Bimber and the Power of the Gold Buckskin Whincher" takes place in what is obviously the early-twentieth-century Midwest, complete with hayrides, band concerts, and steeplejacks. But magic is still potent, and romantic passion is a kind of inexplicable spell. "The first man you meet with an X in his name you must fall head over heels in love with him, said the silent power in the gold buckskin whincher," and Blixie Bimber does, the traditional three times.

Other American fairy tales also take place in a contemporary, unromantic milieu. In Philip K. Dick's "The King of the Elves" (1953), for instance, the future leader of the elves turns out to be an old man in charge of a rundown rural gas station. Anyone, the story says, no matter how mundane his circumstances, may be a magical hero in disguise.

Sometimes American authors used the stock figures of the folktale to criticize contemporary skepticism: James Thurber's famous comic fable "The Unicorn in the Garden" (1939) presents the triumph of a mild visionary over his would-be oppressors: the police, a psychiatrist, and a hostile, suspicious wife who thinks that anyone who sees unicorns is mad.

Some modern American writers have taken the conventions of the folk tale or children's story and turned them upside down, as real life sometimes does. In Richard Kennedy's "The Porcelain Man" (1987) the heroine declines to rescue the enchanted hero, whose only attractive quality is his beauty. Another strange reversal occurs in Ursula Le Guin's "The Wife's Story" (1982), a werewolf tale related by a wolf, which can be read as a brief but terrifying fable about family love, madness, and social prejudice.

Many of the best recent American fairy tales comment on twentieth-century events. In Bernard Malamud's "The Jewbird" (1963) a talking crow flies into the Lower East Side apartment of a frozen-foods salesman and announces that he is fleeing from anti-Semites. To judge by what happens next, he may be one of those immigrant survivors of the Holocaust whom some American Jews, after the Second World War, found burdensome. Donald Barthelme's experimental "The Glass Mountain" (1970) takes off from a traditional story of the same name in Andrew Lang's *The Yellow Fairy Book*, and manages simultaneously to expose the callous ambition of New Yorkers and the formulaic analysis of literary scholars. The mountain he climbs is a skyscraper, and he rejects the princess because she is only "an enchanted symbol." In the late twentieth century American writers also began to compose tales of magic based upon previously untapped folk traditions. Many of Isaac Bashevis Singer's stories, including "Menaseh's Dream" (1968), draw on Jewish folk beliefs and make wise, if disguised, comments on Jewish life, in this case on the power of memory and of family love. Louise Erdrich, in "Old Man Potchikoo" (1989), uses the Native American trickster tale as a starting point for celebration of Dionysian energy.

Several writers, both British and American, have produced fairy tales with a strong feminist slant. Among them are Tanith Lee's "Prince Amilec" (1972), Jay Williams's "Petronella" (1973), and Jeanne Desy's inventive "The Princess Who Stood on Her Own Two Feet" (1982), in which a well-meaning young woman gives up more and more of her natural abilities in order to make her fiancé feel good about himself—a procedure that unfortunately may still be observed in real life. In the end, of course, she rebels and refuses to marry the prince. And in Angela Carter's "Bluebeard" (1979) the heroine is rescued not by her brothers but by her mother, who has already killed a man-eating tiger.

Another interesting example of the genre is Jane Yolen's "The River Maid" (1982). The protagonists of Yolen's poetic fairy tales are often prefeminist: delicate, passive, and either victimized or self-sacrificing or both. But in "The River Maid," though the eponymous heroine remains frail and helpless, the river of which she is the guardian spirit is strong. A greedy farmer dams and diverts the water to enrich his fields, and abducts and rapes the River Maid. The following spring the river rises, washes away the farm, and drowns the farmer. Afterward it can be heard "playing merrily over [his] bones," with a "high, sweet, bubbling song . . . full of freedom and a conquering joy." Women may be imprisoned and abused, the story seems to say, but time and the forces of nature will avenge them.

Today, the fairy tale is often dismissed as old-fashioned, sentimental, and silly: a minor form of literature, appropriate only for children. To readers who have been overexposed to the bowdlerized and prettified cartoon versions of the classic stories, this criticism may seem justified. But any reader who knows the authentic traditional tales, or the many brilliant modern variations on their themes, will realize that fairy tales are not merely childish entertainments set in an unreal and irrelevant universe. Though they can and do entertain children, we will do well to listen seriously to what they tell us about the real world we live in.

NOTES

1. From *Boys and Girls Forever: Children's Classics from Cinderella to Harry Potter* (New York: Penguin, 2003).

Did They Live Happily Ever After? Rewriting Fairy Tales For a Contemporary Audience

Laura Tosi

A long time ago, people used to tell magical stories of wonder and enchantment. Those stories were called Fairy Tales.

Those stories are not in this book. The stories in this book are almost
Fairy Tales. But not quite. The stories in this book are Fairly Stupid Tales.
[. . .] In fact, you should definitely go read the stories now, because the
rest of this introduction just goes on and on and doesn't really say anything. [. . .] So stop now. I mean it. Quit reading. Turn the page. If you
read this last sentence, it won't tell you anything (Scieszka 1992).

We have obviously travelled a long way from the familiar "Once upon a time"
opening: a promiscuous anarchic genre which digests high and low elements,
the fairy tale has undergone a process of textual and social alteration in the
course of the centuries.[2]

The fairy tale, relying on various forms of cultural transmission and ever-
changing ideological configuration for its very existence, has pride of place
in the system of children's literature. Like many children's genres, it is characterized by a much higher degree of intertextuality than general literature.
The term "intertextuality," still relatively recent, may not yet have reached
a definitive formulation (see Kristeva 1970; Genette 1982; Worton 1990;
Clayton and Rothstein 1991. Among Italian contributors see Polacco 1998
and Bernardelli 2000), but in its extended sense, it is an essential term,
defining the intersection of texts or cultural and ideological discourses (see
Segre 1984) within the literature system: as Stephens (1992) has put it

succinctly: "intertextuality is concerned with how meaning is produced at points of interaction" (16). No text exists in isolation from other texts or from social and historical contexts (see Lotman 1980). The initiating and socializing function of children's literature, concerned, among other things, with transmitting the cultural inheritance of values, experiences, and prohibitions, makes it necessary to address an audience whose decoding must rely on the reader's recognition of familiar genres and narratives—hence the value of retelling as a strategy to activate the implied child reader's often partial competency and this reader's aesthetic pleasure of recognition and appreciation. Fairy tales in particular—possibly the first examples of poetic form we confront in life—as part of contemporary (even consumer's) culture, are constantly refashioned, restructured, defamiliarized in modern times, so that they resemble, as Marina Warner says,

> [. . .] an archeological site that has been plundered by tomb robbers, who have turned the strata upside down and inside out and thrown it all back again in any old order. Evidence of conditions from past social and economic arrangements co-exist in the tale with the narrator's innovations: Angela Carter's Beauty is lost to the Beast at cards, a modern variation on the ancient memory, locked into the plot of Beauty and the Beast, that daughters were given in marriage by their fathers without being consulted on the matter. (Warner 1994: xix)

The scholar and common reader alike need a high threshold for tolerance as far as reinterpretation is concerned since even a hasty overview of the rise of the literary fairy tale in Europe reveals further evidence of its hybridity and intertextual nature. As we are often reminded, the fairy tale was not even a genre meant primarily for children. By incorporating oral traditions into a highly literary and aristocratic discourse, the fairy tale dictated and celebrated the standards of *civilité* in the French salons of the seventeenth century (in Italy a century earlier literary fairy tales circulated in the vernacular for an educated audience of upper-class men and women). As Zipes (1983) has written, challenging the assumption that the best fairy tales are universal and timeless:

> The shape of the fairy tale discourse, of the configuration within the tales, was molded and bound by the European civilizing process which was undergoing profound changes in the sixteenth, seventeenth and eighteenth centuries. The profundity of the literary fairy tale for children, its magic, its appeal, is marked by these changes, for it is one of the cornerstones of our bourgeois heritage. As such, it both revolutionized the institution of literature at that time while abiding by its rules. (10, and see Zipes 1999)

Literary appropriation of oral folk tales also characterizes the Grimms' enterprise of collecting traditional folk tales of German origin (see Kamenetsky 1992), which, in translation, had a powerful influence on further developments of the genre. One of the most common misconceptions about the brothers Grimm's method regards their informants: far from being illiterate peasants, as has often been claimed, the Grimms' storytellers belonged to a cultivated middle class which might have been familiar with written, literary versions of folk tales. Any scholar who handles fairy tales (as the Grimms were perfectly aware) must necessarily abandon the idea of a faithful, "original" tale (for example, the myth of an "Ur-Little Red Riding Hood") and take the plunge in the wide sea of folklore variants in different countries or centuries, with diverse historical perspectives and ideological conformations. In our own time, the younger generation is probably best acquainted with the Disney versions of *Snow White* and *Cinderella*, only loosely based on the Perrault and Grimms' plots and characterization, with much simplification and reinforcement of stereotypes of female passivity (see Zipes 1979 and Stone 1975). The wholesale exploitation of fairy-tale and folklore material by the mass media has only recently been studied by critics and provides one of the latest additions to the abundant and heterogeneous body of criticism on the fairy tale.

As a transitional genre, intended for children and adults alike, the fairy tale has been made the object of several critical approaches. These range from the anthropological (for example, in studies of comparative mythologies and recurrent and cross-cultural folktale themes) to the psychoanalytic, of which Bettelheim's (1977) interpretation of the Grimms' tales as significant instruments in helping the process of maturation in a child is probably the best-known, to the formalistic and structuralist methods of classifying folktales in catalogues, or examining individual structural components as functions (see Propp 1928/1968 and Bremond 1977). When we analyze folk or fairy tales from the vantage point of children's literature, then, it is inevitable that we should use an integrated cross-cultural, interdisciplinary approach. In the last few decades, Jack Zipes has focussed critical attention on the social function of fairy tales, thus providing the basis for an ideological critique of dominant cultural patterns in fairy tales, previously perceived as natural, but "which appear to have been preserved because they reinforce male hegemony in the civilization process" (Zipes 1986: 9). Many contemporary rewritings of fairy tales tend to challenge the conservative norms of social behaviour and the implications of gender roles in fairy tales. Feminist critics and writers have collaborated in the critical exposure of fairy tales as narratives voicing, in the main, patriarchal values, both by providing critical readings which investigate the social construction of gender and by rewriting traditional fairy tales in order to produce non-sexist adult and children's versions.

However, the compulsion to retell or rewrite fairy tales in order to subvert historically inscribed ideological meanings should not be considered exclusively a contemporary practice. One only needs to recall the extraordinary flowering of the fairy tale in Victorian England, a flowering which succeeded the well-documented English resistance to fairy tales in the eighteenth century, born out of a combination of Puritan disapproval and a rationalist distrust of the imagination. Fairy tales, as carriers of reformist ideas and social criticism, not only provided Dickens and Wilde, for example, with a symbolic and imaginative form for their protest against the growing alienation of an increasingly industrialized society, they also questioned stereotypical gender roles and patterns (Zipes 1987 and 1999). Tales like MacDonald's *The Light Princess* (1893), a parody of "Sleeping Beauty," or Mary De Morgan's *A Toy Princess* (1877), the story of an unconventional princess who is rejected by her Court in favour of a more docile toy replica, anticipate feminist issues and concerns in their depiction of strong heroines who refuse to conform to the passive female ideal of the age. In Edith Nesbit's *The Last of the Dragons* (1925/1975), for example, the traditional pattern of "prince rescues princess" is satirically reversed. Though familiar with endless tales where princesses, tied to a pole, patiently wait for a prince to rescue them from the dragon ("such tales are always told in royal nurseries at twilight, so the Princess knew what she had to expect"), the heroine objects to this:

"All the princes I know are such very silly little boys," she told her father. "Why must I be rescued by a prince?"

> "It's always done, my dear," said the King, taking his crown off and putting it on the grass, for they were alone in the garden, and even kings must unbend sometimes. [. . .]
> "Father, darling, couldn't we tie up one of the silly little princes for the dragon to look at—and then I could go and kill the dragon and rescue the prince? I fence much better than any of the princes we know." "What an unladylike idea!" said the King, and put his crown on again, for he saw the Prime Minister coming with a basket of new-laid bills for him to sign.
> "Dismiss the thought, my child. I rescued your mother from a dragon, and you don't want to set yourself up above her, I should hope?"
> "But this is the last dragon. It is different from all other dragons." (10)

In the end the strong, fencing princess and the pale weak prince "with a head full of mathematics and philosophy" (10) come to an agreement ("he could refuse her nothing," 12) about the way to handle the dragon, who is easily tamed by the princess and becomes a valuable asset to the court as a sort of scaly aeroplane employed to fly children around the kingdom or to the seaside in summer.

The impact of these protofeminist precedents in fairy-tale tradition should not be underestimated: Jay Williams's "The Practical Princess" and "Petronella" (1978) follow a very similar pattern in their depiction of a brave and assertive princess. Williams's ideal audience includes teenagers and adults; in the second half of the twentieth century the fairy tale, once again crossing the boundary between children's and adult literature, was appropriated by postmodernist and feminist writers like Angela Carter, Anne Sexton and

Margaret Atwood, as a powerful discourse for the representation of gender (see Bacchilega 1997). Fairy tales have also served as structuring devices for both canonical novels (see the *Cinderella* and the *Beauty and the Beast* subtexts in *Jane Eyre*) and for popular romance. Rewritings both for children and adults assume the reader's knowledge of the original tales, thus encouraging the reader to take note of the formal changes which have led to an ideological reorientation of the tales.

In this essay I intend to give a survey (albeit incomplete and partial, given the ever-growing number of fairy-tale adaptations in the English language) of rewriting practices and techniques, although, as mentioned earlier, it is impossible to trace an archetypal "first telling" or version of a particular fairy tale, nor can the critic expect to fix a fairy tale "hypotext." Genette (1982) in his *Palimpsestes*, defines a hypertextual relationship as "toute relation unissant un texte B (que j'appellerai *hypertexte*) à un texte antérieur A (que j'appellerai, bien sûr, *hypotexte*) sur lequel il se greffe d'une manière qui n'est pas celle du commentaire" (11-12).[3] With reference to fairy tales, Genette's concept of the hypotext as a single and identifiable entity needs to be enlarged and renamed as "hypotextual class," which would include all those versions of a single fairy tale that have combined to create the reader's cultural and diegetic construct of that traditional tale in the canon (the hypotextual class of the *Cinderella* tales, for example). Ironically, the constant restructuring and rewriting of fairy tales' hypotextual classes, in order to adapt them to the new social and moral requirements of contemporary audiences, has had the effect of preserving and encoding traditional fairy tales within the canon so that they are still widely read, alongside more challenging and subversive versions (see Tatar 1992).

In an attempt to classify different practices of fairy-tale adaptations, so as to make this abundant and heterogeneous material easier to analyse, I have chosen to discuss three types of fairy-tale rewritings which I have called: a) "morally correct" rewritings; b) postmodernist/metafictional rewritings; c) feminist rewritings. There are several overlappings in the three groups: many adaptations could be grouped indifferently under more than one category as to their ideological orientation and often share formal changes (changes of setting, place and time, focalization—Genette's "transpositions diégétiques,"[4] 341). In the first group, however, I shall discuss primarily rewritings which aim at exposing the presence of an ambiguous morality or a moral gap in the hypotextual class, by superimposing a new ethics of justice and human compassion on traditional tales which reward, for example, acquisitive behaviour. The second group includes tales which emphasise their fictional and conventional status, which leads to a more or less good-natured critique of ideological assumptions about the culture of the child. The third group is probably the most widely studied and includes fairy-tale adaptations which, by breaking established diegetic patterns, like "Princess marries prince," subvert accepted notions of female cultural identity.

Discussions about the ethics or justice of traditional fairy tales are not a recent phenomenon: one only needs to think of the political-ideological appropriation of the Grimms' tales in the Nazi era (Kamenetsky 1992).

Even to the naïve reader it is painfully (or enjoyably) clear that the youngest brother often gets his fortune by chance rather than merit, that valiant little tailors are rewarded for deceit, and that the Giant's seven daughters do not really deserve to die at their father's hand. Many scholarly explanations of fairy or folktale ethics have been provided, from the analysis of the Grimms' own moral outlook to the discussion of the peculiar kind of knowledge about life fairy tales were meant to instil: the value of resourcefulness and risk-taking rather than of traditional morality, and the importance of perseverance. Contemporary retellings have challenged the value system of some traditional fairy tales, which, contrary to popular belief, do not always reward good characters and punish evil ones.

This redressing of the moral balance can be effected by means of a change in the narrating voice and the point of view. In the traditional story "Jack and the Beanstalk," the young boy Jack comes into possession of magic beans which allow him to climb a beanstalk and reach the giant's house. He is fed by the giant's wife who takes pity on the starved boy each time he visits their house. As we all remember, Jack first steals the giant's gold, then the magic hen who lays golden eggs, and ultimately the giant's golden harp.[5] By chopping away at the beanstalk on his way home so that the giant falls to the ground on his head, Jack secures for his mother and himself a wealthy future, with the giant's gold, hen, and harp.

Alvin Granowsky's *Giants Have Feelings, Too* (1996) exposes the ambiguous morality of the tale, which sets greed as the rewarded virtue, by having the giant's wife retell the story:

> I am sure that the rest of you people living down below are very nice. But that boy, Jack, is something else. After I was so kind to him, he stole from us, and he hurt my husband. All because we are giants! That's no reason to take our treasures or to make my husband fall on his head. See what you think. (3)

The giant couple is reframed as good-natured and middle class, with grown-up children, with savings which are a necessity for their old age, and with an innocent love of food, Mrs. Giant being apparently an exceptional cook:

> Then Herbert came in singing "Fe! Fi! Fo! Fum! My wife's cooking is Yum! Yum! Yum! Be it baked or be it fried, we finish each meal with her tasty pies!" (13)

The reaction to Jack's treachery is a common-sense open-hearted discussion between husband and wife:

> "Oh, dear," Herbert said. "We can only hope that the boy's mother will find out what he has done. Surely, she will make him return our things. Maybe she will even return them herself."

> "You're right, Herbert," I said. "When his mother brings back
> our gold and our hen, I'll be here to thank her." (18)

Jack, as we all know, only comes back to collect the giant's last treasure, the golden harp:

> "Stop! You're stealing!" Herbert yelled as he ran after Jack. "Don't
> you know it's wrong to steal?" (22)

The moral at the end of the tale turns into a direct appeal to the reader for sympathy:

> He had no right to take what was ours or to hurt my husband.
> Giants have feelings, you know. You wouldn't hurt a giant's feel-
> ings, would you? (25)

One interesting aspect of this retelling is that both stories are contained in the same book with a "flip me over" system so that the reader can access both versions of the story at the same time (the series is called "Another Point of View") and question, rather than take passively for granted, Jack's real motives for his actions.

Granowsky's adaptations seem very serious when compared with Dahl's inventive and highly irreverent retellings in *Revolting Rhymes* (1982/1984) and *Rhyme Stew* (1989). His version of the story of *Goldilocks and the Three Bears*, in *Revolting Rhymes*, addresses the issue of Goldilocks' infraction of the basic rules of polite behaviour (i.e., entering a home without an invita- tion, touching other people's things, breaking an item of furniture in some- one else's house) which parental figures teach children in order to ease their assimilation into the adult community. The socializing and cautionary func- tion of fairy tales is generally dependent on the transmission of a code of social behaviour and norms from an older voice of experience to a younger audience badly in need of moral and social guidance.

Goldilocks is called in the course of the story "little toad," "little louse," "a delinquent little tot," "a brazen little crook"—graphic and comic expres- sions which, rather than celebrating the cuteness of the little blonde girl, convey adult horror at the misbehaved unrestrained child's invasion of one's personal space. One interesting aspect of this retelling is that Dahl is clearly playing with the figure of his ideal reader—not so much the house-proud bourgeois wife who takes pride in "one small children's dining-chair, Elizabe- than, very rare" smashed by Goldilocks, as the irreverent and playful reader, to whom he addresses one of his characteristic sadistic endings. In this version Big Bear advises Baby Bear to go upstairs and eat his porridge: "But as it is inside mademoiselle, you'll have to eat her up as well" (39).

Among the various kinds of correspondence that the Ahlbergs' *The Jolly Postman* (1986) delivers to fairy-tale characters, there is a repentant letter by Goldilocks, addressed to Mr. and Mrs. Bear, Three Bears Cottage, the Woods, which says:

Dear Mr and Mrs Bear and Baby Bear,

I am very sorry indeed that I cam into your house and ate Baby Bears porij. Mummy says I am a bad girl. I hardly eat any porij when she cooks it she says. Daddy says he will mend the little chair.

Love from
Goldilocks

In one of the next tableaux among the several fairy-tale characters with whom Goldilocks is celebrating her birthday (a little pig, Humpty Dumpty, the magic goose, etc.) Baby Bear has pride of place near the little girl, who has obviously been forgiven. The Ahlbergs' ingenious toy and picture book, which relies on the reader's knowledge of other children's texts, creates an appealing context for a genial twist in the morality of the tale. It is the heroine herself, in her own tentative and childish writing, who condemns her selfish behaviour and promises to mend her ways.

Not all the protagonists of fairy tales, when allowed to speak and give their side of the story, are as convincing or trustworthy. In Scieszka's *The True Story of the Three Little Pigs* (1989) Mr. Wolf's attempt to rehabilitate his good name is only partly convincing:

I'm the wolf. Alexander T. Wolf.
You can call me Al.
I don't know how this whole Big Bad Wolf thing got started, but it's all wrong.
Maybe it's because of our diet.
Hey, it's not my fault wolves eat cute little animals like bunnies and sheep and pigs. That's just the way we are. If cheeseburgers were cute, folks would probably think you were Big and Bad, too.

A contemporary audience, due to environmental awareness, might be willing to concede that wolves eat little pigs as part of the nature food chain and not because they are intrinsically bad. Mr. Wolf's version of the story, however, lays the blame for the destruction of the pigs' houses on the wolf's bad cold and urge to sneeze while he was innocently asking to borrow a cup of sugar for his granny's birthday cake.

Another example of a fairy-tale retelling which, by giving voice to the traditional villain of the piece, attempts to justify his/her actions is Donna Jo Napoli's *The Magic Circle* (1983), marketed to a young adult audience. This prequel, in novel form, to *Hansel and Gretel*, explains the reason for the witch's cannibalistic drive. As the "Ugly One" unfolds the story of her past as a loving mother and blessed healer, the reader learns of the circumstances which led her to be claimed and possessed by devils. The description of her death, which she willingly brings about in order to disobey the demons' order to harm the children, is a tale of liberation and purification from evil.

"A site on which metanarratival and textual processes interact, either to reproduce or contest significance" (Stephens and McCallum 1998: 9), the retold fairy tale on the one hand can distance itself from conventional concepts of morality, perceived as unsuitable or outmoded guidelines for the child's social and moral development, on the other it may suggest a new ethics of compassion and respect for other people's culture and possessions, even extending it, in some cases, to canonically undeserving characters[6] whose motives and actions are defamiliarized in order to be re-encoded in a new system of beliefs.

A second group of fairy tale adaptations includes self-reflexive, often explicitly postmodernist, versions, where make-believe or illusionist conventions are exposed in order to highlight the hypercodification of fairy-tale conventions. In the case of *The Stinky Cheese Man and Other Fairly Stupid Tales*, which opened the present discussion, basic literary conventions are parodied so that the young reader is invited to reflect on what constitutes a book, and the rules that are normally followed by the author, the editor, the publisher etc. In Scieszka's book, essentially postmodernist in its critical and ironic revisiting and disruption of the cultural and literary pattern of the fairy tale, the table of contents falls and squashes all the characters of the first story of the collection ("Chicken Licken"), the dedication is upside down, the "lazy narrator" at some point disappears, leaving a blank page, the little red hen is never given the opportunity to tell her story and the various narratives are constantly interrupted by arguments between the narrator and the characters:

"Now it's time for the best story in the book—my story. Because Once Upon a Time I traded our last cow for three magic beans and . . . hey, Giant. What are you doing down here? You're wrecking my whole story."

"I DON'T LIKE THAT STORY," said the Giant.

"YOU ALWAYS TRICK ME."

"That's the best part," said Jack.

"FEE FI FUM FORY I HAVE MADE MY OWN STORY."

"Great rhyme, Giant [. . .] But there's no room for it. So why don't you climb back up the beanstalk. I'll be up in a few minutes to steal your gold and your singing harp.

"I'LL GRIND YOUR BONES TO MAKE MY BREAD."

"[. . .] And there's another little thing that's been bugging me. Could you please stop talking in uppercase letters? It really messes up the page."

In such a context of textual and narrative instability a number of fairy-tale retellings are defined by parodic hyperrealism and comic dismissal of the magic and romantic element. "The Really Ugly Duckling" grows up to be just a really ugly duck instead of a beautiful swan; the frog lies to the princess about being a handsome prince under a spell (" 'I was just kidding,' said the frog. He jumped back into the pond and the princess wiped the frog slime off her lips. The End"); the Prince, in order to make sure of marrying the girl of his dreams, places a bowling ball under the one hundred mattresses.

"Cinderrumpelstiltskin" in Scieszka's collection furnishes an example of fairy-tale conflation, or, as the Italian educationalist and children's writer Gianni Rodari would call it, a fairy-tale salad, "una insalata di favole" (Rodari 1973/1997: 72): Cinderella, expecting the customary visit of her fairy god-mother to provide her with a dress, glass slippers and a coach to go to the ball, sends Rumpelstiltskin (a character from another Grimms' tale who knows how to spin gold) away ("I am not supposed to talk to strangers," she says), conse-quently missing the opportunity to become rich ("Please don't cry," he said, "I can help you spin straw into gold." "I don't think that will do me much good [. . .] If you don't have a dress, it doesn't really matter"). Scieszka's Cinderella, who obviously intends to be faithful to the traditional version, is not rewarded at the end (the ironic subtitle to the tale is "The girl who really blew it").

Fairy-tale salads, based on the comic coexistence of heterogeneous fairy-tale plots and character types, create playful conflations of traditional fairy tales which are easily recognized by the implied child reader who brings his/her knowledge of the character's familiar traits to bear on the new version. These highly intertextual and metafictional versions work within conventions, casting well-known fairy characters in different settings and story lines or, by contrast, combining two or more plots with the same protagonist. An example of the latter kind of procedure is the conflation of *Red Riding Hood* with *The Three Little Pigs*, both based on the powerful and murderous figure of the wolf. In Dahl's *Revolting Rhymes* (1982/1984) Pig number 3, who has built his house of bricks, but is made nervous by the wolf's huffing and puffing, phones Little Red Riding Hood for help. Having already shot a wolf in her own story earlier in the collection, the resourceful girl can now boast a "lovely furry wolfskin coat," but the ending has an unexpected twist, as the pig makes the mistake of trusting Miss Riding Hood. At the end of the story, not only can she boast of two wolfskin coats, "But when she goes from place to place, / She has a PIGSKIN TRAVELLING CASE" (47).

Similarly, in the already quoted Ahlbergs' *Postman* book; the wolf receives a letter from a law-firm representing the interests of both Little Red Riding Hood and the Three Little Pigs:

> Dear Mr. Wolf
>
> We are writing to you on behalf of our client, Miss Riding-Hood, con-cerning her grandma. Miss Hood tells us that you are presently occupying her grandma's cottage and wearing her grandma's clothes without this lady's permission. [. . .] On a separate matter, we must inform you that Messrs. Three Little Pigs Ltd. are now firmly resolved to sue for damages [. . .]
>
> Yours sincerely,
> Harold Meeney, solicitor

Even in fairy tales which do not deviate from a recognizable story line, characters often show an unusual degree of knowledge of fairy-tale conventions and of their own fictional status. Their awareness of the conventionality of stock situations and the outcome of their expected choices may lead them to question and change the task or the role they are assigned in the story. In Jane Yolen's *Sleeping Ugly* (1997) prince Jojo, who, "being the kind of young man who read fairy tales, [. . .] knew just what to do" (49), decides to devote special consideration to the issue of kissing and thus awakening the three ladies who lie asleep in the cottage, covered in spiderwebs. The most striking woman is the beautiful, albeit cruel, princess, protagonist of many fairy tales: "But Jojo knew that kind of princess. He had three cousins just like her. Pretty on the outside. Ugly within" (59). Prince Jojo decides to let the beautiful sleeping princess lie, so that she is later used as conversation piece or coat hanger, and kisses (and marries) instead plain Jane, blessed with a kindly disposition, with whom he will attain marital bliss if not social elevation or riches.

Fairy-tale characters who are not well informed regarding fairy-tale conventions are often at a disadvantage in contemporary retellings. In Drew Lamm's *The Prog Frince. A Mixed-Up Tale* (1999) the only chance for the heroine to break the spell, as the reader discovers only at the end of the story, is to learn "The Frog Prince" and behave accordingly towards the talking frog. A sensible girl, Jane dismisses tales of the imagination as untrue:

> "Do you read fairy tales?" interrupted the frog, "like the Frog Prince?"
> "No," said Jane. "They don't make sense. And they're not true."
> "What do you dream about?" he asked.
> "I don't," said Jane.
> "What do you do?"
> "I go to school," she said, glaring at the frog.
> "Unfortunate," croaked the frog, and he leapt off Jane's hand.

Only when she is ready to sit and listen to the *The Frog Prince* and therefore begins to grow fond of the frog, does she recover her lost memory and identity as Jaylee, the prince's lover of base descent whom he had to forsake:

> Jaylee blinked. The spell was broken. In front of Jaylee stood the prince. He smiled.
> "I thought the princess had to kiss the frog," said Jaylee.
> "You're not a princess. You had to miss me."
> "Magnificent," said Jaylee. "I'd rather kiss you now, when you are not so green."

In this story the need for familiarity with fairy stories if one is to fulfil one's destiny (even if in a slightly different manner than that suggested in the canonical story) is constantly reasserted.

The comic retelling of *Snow White* in the "Happily Ever Laughter" series (Thaler 1997) has "Schmoe White and the Seven Dorfs" forming a pop group in which Schmoe will play the part of lead singer by virtue of her role in the fairy story:

> "We'll call ourselves 'Schmoe White and the Seven Dorfs,' " said Schmoe.
> "Why do you get top billing?" asked Grouchy.
> "Because if it weren't for me, you wouldn't be in this story," replied Schmoe.

Similarly, in Margaret Atwood's "Unpopular Gals" (1994), the character's self-consciousness as the narrative pivot of the folk tale emerges as the female villain is given a voice:

> The thing about those good daughters is, they're so good. Obedient and passive. Sniveling, I might add. No get-up-and-go. What would become of them if it weren't for me? Nothing, that's what. All they'd ever do is the housework, which seems to feature largely in these stories. They'd marry some peasant, have seventeen kids, and get 'A Dutiful Wife' engraved on their tombstones, if any. Big deal. [. . .] You can wipe your feet on me, twist my motives around all if you like, you can dump millstones on my head and drown me in the river, but you can't get me out of the story. I'm the plot, babe, and don't you ever forget it. (11-12) (See also Gilbert and Gubar's analysis of "Snow White" in *The Mad-woman in the Attic* 1979: 38-39.)

A strong narratorial voice (especially when it is intradiegetic) in fairy-tale adaptations (whether directed to an adult or a child reader) obviously implies that the story is a fictional construct which needs to be told (and retold) in order to exist, and relies on a number of diegetic, linguistic, as well as cultural and moral rules in order to be recognizable as such. In metafictional rewritings for children a form of detachment and the surprise following defamiliarization are encouraged, rather than emphatic alignment with the characters. Adaptations of traditional fairy tales continue to awaken the child reader's sense of wonder and humour through the introduction of new narrative incidents, and highly recognizable characters who, by reflecting on their fictional status, engage in playful alliance with the child reader—the aesthetic pleasure of recognition should not be underestimated.

It is to be noted, however, that child readers do not always tolerate retellings or modifications of their favourite stories. Within contemporary retellings experiments of juxtaposing traditional fairy plot-types with unconventional patterns may serve to dramatize the child's resistance to letting go of the stereotypes of the hypotextual class. The adaptation can turn into a hilarious battleground between orthodoxy and innovation, as in Storr's *Little Polly Riding Hood* (1955/1993). In this version the wolf is unable to assimilate the refashioning of the story of which he is a central character:

> "Good afternoon, Polly," said the wolf. "Where are you going, may I ask?"
> "Certainly," said Polly. "I am going to see my grandma."

"I thought so!" said the wolf, looking very much pleased. "I've been reading about a girl who went to visit her grandmother and it's a very good story."

"Little Red Riding Hood?" suggested Polly.

"That's it!" cried the wolf. "I read it out loud to myself as a bedtime story. I did enjoy it. The wolf eats up the grandmother, and Little Red Riding Hood. It's almost the only story where the wolf really gets anything to eat," he added sadly.

"But in my book he doesn't get Red Riding Hood," said Polly. "Her father comes in just in time to save her."

"Oh, he doesn't in my book!" said the wolf. "I expect mine is the true story, and yours is just invented. [. . .] Where does your grandmother live, Polly Riding Hood?"

"Over the other side of town," answered Polly.

The wolf frowned.

"It ought to be "Through the Wood," " he said. "But perhaps town will do. How do you get there, Polly Riding Hood?"

"First I take a train and then I take a bus," said Polly.

The wolf stamped his foot.

"No, no, no, no!" he shouted. "That's all wrong. You can't say that. You've got to say, 'By the path winding through the trees,' or something like that. You can't go by trains and buses and things. It isn't fair. [. . .] it won't work, [. . .] You just can't say that!" (234-35)

The wolf's unwillingness to adapt to the new story, his blind adherence to the traditional configuration of Little Red Riding Hood, and his refusal to accept major changes in society (like modern means of transport), as well as a more active and assertive version of the tale will lead him to frustration and defeat. The wolf may thus come to embody the young reader's anxiety about unfamiliar retellings of fairy tales, which pose a threat to his/her conventional assumptions and expectations about gender roles and social behaviour.

There is no need to expatiate on the fact that, as educators and psychotherapists have demonstrated, fairy tales do influence the way children conceive the world in terms of power relations, patterns of behaviour, and gender roles.

The third group of fairy-tale adaptations for children I shall be examining shortly, addresses precisely the issue of presenting a non-sexist vision of the world in fairy tales. As Zipes (1986) has remarked: "the political purpose and design of most of the tales are clear: the narratives are symbolical representations of the author's critique of the patriarchal status quo and their desire to change the current socialization process" (xi-xii). In feminist rewritings of canonical fairy tales a tendency to retell princess stories which dispense with marriage-dominated plots and the traditional equation between beauty and goodness can be detected. In both adult and children's modern revisions of princess stories, plots and patterns as well as characterization are subverted and deconstructed in order to reshape female cultural identity into that of an independent, liberated, and self-confident heroine. A new generation of smart princesses can oppose tyrannical or stereotyped role models by assuming active roles or considering alternative options for their self-definition as females: in A. Thompert's *The Clever Princess* (1977) self-fulfilment can be achieved through active involvement in ruling one's kingdom rather than by getting married.

Rewriting *Sleeping Beauty*, the tale that features the most emblematic example of female passivity, can turn into a positive attempt to acculturate women to new rewarding social roles as well as pointing out the value of overcoming ignorance and of intelligent initiative (see Lieberman 1972/1986). Katherine Paterson's *The Wide-Awake Princess* (2000) is given a very precious gift by her judicious fairy godmother, that of being wide-awake all her waking hours in a sleeping world (that is, in a world where greedy and indifferent nobles live in luxury). Throughout the story the value of seeing for oneself (the poverty and unhappiness of the people, for example), the value of being able to assess a situation, and the value of working to spread awareness are constantly reaffirmed. Only by keeping her eyes open while mixing with the people of the kingdom can Princess Miranda form a plan to help her people and regain her rightful place as a queen—a strikingly different model for female behaviour from that of submissive Sleeping Beauty waiting for a brave prince to kiss and wake her (on *Sleeping Beauty* as a literary model for female passivity, see Kolbenschlag 1979).

Cultural autonomy, and a sense of compassion and sisterhood for other girls who embody more conventional prototypes of female passivity, are emphasized in Harriet Herman's *The Forest Princess* (1974), a rewriting of Rapunzel, where the lonely heroine is free to climb up and down the tower by a ladder. After having rescued a prince, she learns of gender differences and spends many happy hours with him. In the neutral setting of the forest they are free to exchange experiences and share the knowledge of the world. Back in the prince's court, however, rigid gender rules are assigned. What is considered praiseworthy in males (reading books, riding horses) is rejected in females, who are forbidden to read and must be suffocated in tight and uncomfortable clothes all day. When the forest princess questions the unfairness of the situation, the Prince defends the status quo:

> "There are so many people here and so many rules. Tell me, prince, why is it that only boys are taught to read in your land?"
> His smile turned into a frown.
> "That is the way it has always been."
> "But you taught me to read."
> "That was in the forest. Things are different here."
> "They don't have to be different. I could teach the girls what you taught me."
> The prince stood up abruptly.
> "Why can't you accept things the way they are?"

As things turn out, because of her outrageous requests, the Princess is forced to leave the castle:

> But if you go to the land of the golden castle today, you will find the boys and girls playing together, reading books together, and riding horses together. For you and I both know that a fairy tale isn't a fairy tale unless everyone lives happily ever after.

The female desire to conform to a pattern of desirability that posits beauty and passivity as the virtues required for marriage is presented as a dilemma in Desy's *The Princess Who Stood On Her Own Two Feet* (1982/1986). The protagonist, in order to subscribe to the prince's patriarchal view of femininity ("haven't you ever heard that women should be seen and not heard?" 42), pretends to be struck mute, as earlier she had feigned not to be able to walk due to a riding accident (the prince seems unable to get over the fact that the princess is much taller than he is). It is through a painful experience of loss that the princess arrives at a new understanding of her self-worth, which results in her meeting a wiser, if shorter, suitor for her hand. Desy's princess story, like *The Forest Princess* and *The Wide-Awake Princess* is aimed at an audience of older children and can therefore explore gender issues in relative depth, but even in some picture books for younger children there is an awareness of sexual stereotyping. In Mike Thaler's *Hanzel and Pretzel* (1997), for example, Pretzel is much more assertive and resourceful than the original Gretel (who, in the Grimms' story displays a worrying tendency to burst into tears at very inappropriate moments). In fact, it is a rejuvenated frightened Hanzel who constantly cries and is jokingly reassured by his cool-tempered sister:

> "Hanzel looked out through the bars and began to cry.
> "Look on the bright side," joked Pretzel.
> "At least we're not lost anymore."

The happy ending is brought about, as in the Grimms' tale, by efficient Pretzel who, after having thrown the witch into a cauldron, flies her brother home on the witch's broom without losing her sense of humour and love for puns.

Babette Cole's *Princess Smartypants* (1986/1996) and *Prince Cinders* (1993) comically reverse fairy-tale plots and culturally determined sexual stereotypes, keeping the text to a minimum and letting pictures convey most of the information regarding the characters. Princess Smartypants, for example, is pictured wearing denim dungarees, and watching horse races with her pet dragons, or brushing her pet giant crocodile with dishevelled hair like a common stable girl. It is only fair that such an informal and sporty princess should not automatically fall in love with smug Prince Swashbuckle who drives a posh sportscar, wears a multi-medalled uniform and flaunts a Clark Gable-type moustache. The end reaffirms the princess's independence and rejects the picture of the narcissistic macho man as the patronizing hero of the piece.

If we agree with the assumption that gender has a cultural character, we should not underestimate the impact of fairy-tale characters or circumstances in the formation of psycho-sexual concepts of the female or male self. The device of the change of sex in *Prince Cinders* is in itself a statement about the nature of male personality when this is culturally determined as a combination of physical strength, lack of sensitive feelings, and contempt for more vulnerable males. Prince Cinders' three hairy brothers, who belong to the same category as Prince Swashbuckle, spend their time at the palace disco with their princess girlfriends while Prince Cinders is left behind to clean up their mess: Cole's highly communicative pictures show the princes' rooms scattered with empty beer cans, football and body building magazines, and cigarette ends. Cinders' wish to be "big and hairy" like his brothers exposes the dominant cultural paradigm of masculinity (based on aggressive and insensitive behaviour) as ridiculous and old-fashioned: when the inexperienced fairy godmother, a teenage school-girl in her grey uniform and tie, performs the necessary magic, he will be turned into a big hairy monkey. After the customary happy ending with the marriage to Princess Prettypenny (who believes Cinders to have scared off the big hairy monster at midnight) the hairy brothers are suitably punished by being turned into house fairies, "and they flitted around the palace doing the housework for ever and ever."

By ridiculing stereotypical and outmoded notions of masculinity and having the fairy fulfil his desires to the letter (for in fairy tales one must really be careful what to wish for), Babette Cole's retelling ironically deconstructs a traditional paradigm of male identity, in order to stress the value of individuality and self-esteem. Even though some ambiguity as to gender roles remains, as Prince Cinders is cast in the conventional role of rescuer, this is one of the few adaptations which addresses the issue of male acculturation into traditional social roles. In retellings which challenge stereotypical sexual and social roles, fairy-tale discourse becomes emancipatory and innovative, rather than a reinforcement of patriarchal culture.

Fairy stories are "elastic": they evolve revealing a process of organic reshaping around a set of core elements in response to historical and cultural influences (see Hearne 1988). Fairy-tale hypotextual classes have survived many adaptations and will outlast many more. The central issue is that, by revitalizing canonical fairy-tale values and conventions, to which they add layers of non-conventional meanings, creative retellings liberate the imaginative and subversive potential of fairy tales in contemporary child culture.

REFERENCES

Ahlberg, J. and A. (1986) *The Jolly Postman or Other People's Letters.* Harmondsworth: Penguin.

Atwood, M. (1994) *Bones and Murder*. London: Virago.

Bacchilega, C. (1997) *Postmodernist Fairy Tales. Gender and Narrative Strategies*. Philadelphia: University of Pennsylvania Press.

Bernardelli, A. (2000) *Intertestualità* Bari: La Nuova Italia.

Bettelheim, B. (1977) *The Uses of Enchantment: The Meaning and Importance of Fairy Tales*. New York: Random House.

Bremond, C. (1977) "The Morphology of the French Fairy Tale: The Ethical Model." In Janson, H. and Segal, D. (eds.) *Patterns in Oral Literature*. Paris, The Hague: Mouton, 50-76.

Clayton, J. and Rothstein, E. (eds.) (1991) *Influence and Intertextuality in Literary History*. Madison: The University of Wisconsin Press.

Cole, B. (1986/1996) *Princess Smartypants*. Harmondsworth: Penguin.

Cole, B. (1993) *Prince Cinders*. Hayes, Middlesex: Magi Publications.

Coover, R. (1973) "The Dead Queen." *Quarterly Review of Literature* XVIII, 3-4: 304-13.

Dahl, R. (1982/1984) *Revolting Rhymes*. Harmondsworth: Penguin.

Desy, J. (1982) "The Princess Who Stood On Her Own Two Feet." in Zipes, J. (ed.) (1986) *Don't Bet on the Prince: Contemporary Feminist Fairy Tales in North America and England*. New York: Routledge, 39-47.

Genette, G. (1982) *Palimpsestes. La littérature au second degré*. Paris: Editions du Seuil.

Gilbert. S.A. and Gubar, S. (1979) *The Madwoman in the Attic: The Woman Writer and the Nineteenth-Century Imagination*. New Haven: Yale University Press.

Granowsky, A. (1996) *Giants Have Feelings, Too*. Austin: Steck-Vaughn.

Hearne, B. (1988) "Beauty and the Beast: Visions and Revisions of an Old Tale: 1950-1985." *The Lion and the Unicorn* 12.2: 74-109.

Herman, H. (1974) *The Forest Princess*. Berkeley: Rainbow Press.

Kamenetsky, C. (1992) *The Brothers Grimm and Their Critics: Folktales and the Quest for Meaning*. Athens: Ohio University Press.

Kolbenschlag, M. (1979) *Kiss Sleeping Beauty Good-bye: Breaking the Spell of Feminine Myths and Models*. San Francisco: Harper and Row.

Kristeva, J. (1970) *Le texte du roman: Approche sémiologique d'une structure discoursive transformationelle*. The Hague, Paris: Mouton.

Lieberman, M.K. (1972) " 'Some Day My Prince Will Come': Female Acculturation through the Fairy Tale." In Zipes, J. (ed.) (1986) *Don't Bet on the Prince: Contemporary Feminist Fairy Tales in North America and England*. New York: Routledge, 185-200.

Lotman, J. (1980) *Testo e Contesto. Semiotica dell'arte e della cultura*. Roma-Bari: Laterza.

Napoli, D.J. (1993) *The Magic Circle*. Harmondsworth: Penguin.

Nesbit, E. (1925/1975) *The Last of the Dragons and Some Others*. Harmondsworth: Penguin.

Paterson, K. (2000) *The Wide-Awake Princess*. New York: Clarion Press.

Polacco, M. (1998) *Intertestualità*. Bari: Laterza.

Propp, V. (1928/1968) *Morphology of the Folktale*. Austin: Texas University Press.

Rodari, G. (1973/1997) *Grammatica della fantasia: Introduzione all'arte di inventare storie*. Torino: Einaudi.

Scieszka, J. (1989) *The True Story of the Three Little Pigs*. Harmondsworth: Penguin.

Scieszka, J. (1992) *The Stinky Cheese Man and Other Fairly Stupid Tales*. New York: Viking.

Segre, C. (1984) "Intertestualità e interdiscorsività nel romanzo e nella poesia." In *Teatro e romanzo*. Torino: Einaudi, 103-108.

Stephens, J. (1992) *Language and Ideology in Children's Fiction*. London and New York: Longman.

Stephens, J. and McCallum, R. (1998) *Retelling Stories, Framing Culture: Traditional Story and Metanarratives in Children's Literature*. New York and London: Garland.

Stone, K. (1975) "Things Walt Disney Never Told Us." In Farrer, C.R. (ed.) *Women and Folklore*. Austin: University of Texas Press, 42-50.

Storr, K. (1955) "Little Polly Riding Hood." In Zipes, J. (ed.) (1993) *The Trials and Tribulations of Little Red Riding Hood*. New York and London: Routledge, 234-38.

Tatar, M. (1992) *Off With Their Heads: Fairy Tales and the Culture of Childhood*. Princeton: Princeton University Press.

Thaler, M. (1997) *Schmoe White and the Seven Dorfs*. New York: Scholastic.

Thaler, M. (1997) *Hanzel and Pretzel*. New York: Scholastic.

Warner, M. (1994) *From the Beast to the Blonde: On Fairy Tales and Their Tellers*. London: Chatto and Windus.

Williams, J. (1978) *The Practical Princess and Other Liberating Fairy Tales*. London: The Bodley Head.

Worton, M. and Still, J. (1990) *Intertextuality: Theories and Practices*. Manchester: Manchester University Press.

Yolen, J. (1981/1997) *Sleeping Ugly*. New York: Putnam and Grosset.

Zipes, (1979) "The Instrumentalization of Fantasy: Fairy Tales, the Culture Industry, and Mass Media." In *Breaking the Magic Spell: Radical Theories of Folk and Fairy Tales*. Austin: University of Texas Press, 93-128.

Zipes, J. (1983) *Fairy Tales and the Art of Subversion: The Classic Genre for Children and the Process of Civilization*. New York: Routledge.

Zipes, J. (1986) *Don't Bet on the Prince: Contemporary Feminist Fairy Tales in North America and England*. New York: Routledge.

Zipes, J. (ed.) (1987) *Victorian Fairy Tales*. New York and London: Methuen.

Zipes, J. (1999) *When Dreams Come True: Classic Fairy Tales and Their Tradition*. London: Routledge.

NOTES

1. From *Hearts of Lightness: The Magic of Children's Literature* (Venice: Universita Ca'Foscari Di Venezia, 2001).
2. By "fairy tales" I mean canonic fairy tales of Western tradition which have always been called by that name even if they do not feature fairy or fairy-tale characters. I am aware of the looseness of the term, which overlaps with very similar genres, like the folk tale, the wonder tale, legends etc.
3. *toute relation . . . du commentaire.* Translation (from the French): Any relationship uniting a text B (which I will call hypertext) with an earlier text A (which I will call, naturally, hypotext), in which the later text is grafted on the earlier text in a manner that isn't that of a commentary.
4. diegetic transpositions: Rewritten narratives.
5. In the English version of the tale, the giant is the villain of the piece. One only needs to remember his "Fee-fi-fo-fum
   I smell the blood of an Englishman
   Be he alive or be he dead
   I'll grind his bones to make my bread."
6. For example, in Robert Coover's retelling of Snow White for an adult audience, "The Dead Queen" (1973), the prince feels sorry for the harsh punishment which is meted out for Snow White's stepmother as he tries, in vain, to kiss her back to life.

Shitty First Drafts

Anne Lamott from Bird by Bird

Born in San Francisco in 1954, Anne Lamott is a graduate of Goucher College in Baltimore and is the author of six novels, including Rosie *(1983),* Crooked Little Heart *(1997),* All New People *(2000), and* Blue Shoes *(2002). She has also been the food reviewer for* California *magazine, a book reviewer for* Mademoiselle, *and a regular contributor to* Salon's *"Mothers Who Think." Her non-fiction books include* Operating Instructions: A Journal of My Son's First Year *(1993), in which she describes her adventures as a single parent, and* Tender Mercies: Some Thoughts on Faith *(1999), in which she charts her journey toward faith in God.*

In the following selection, taken from Lamott's popular book about writing, Bird by Bird *(1994), she argues for the need to let go and write those "shitty first drafts" that lead to clarity and sometimes brilliance in our second and third drafts.*

Now, practically even better news than that of short assignments is the idea of shitty first drafts. All good writers write them. This is how they end up with good second drafts and terrific third drafts. People tend to look at successful writers who are getting their books published and maybe even doing well financially and think that they sit down at their desks every morning feeling like a million dollars, feeling great about who they are and how much talent they have and what a great story they have to tell; that they take in a few deep breaths, push back their sleeves, roll their necks a few times to get all the cricks out, and dive in, typing fully formed passages as fast as a court reporter. But this is just the fantasy of the uninitiated. I know some very great writers, writers you love who write beautifully and have made a great deal of money, and not one of them sits down routinely feeling wildly enthusiastic and confident. Not one of them writes elegant first drafts. All right, one of them does, but we do not like her very much. We do not think that she has a rich inner life or that God likes her or can even stand her. (Although when I mentioned this to my priest friend Tom, he said you can safely assume you've created God in your own image when it turns out that God hates all the same people you do.)

Very few writers really know what they are doing until they've done it. Nor do they go about their business feeling dewy and thrilled. They do not type a few stiff warm-up sentences and then find themselves bounding along like huskies across the snow. One writer I know tells me that he sits down every morning and says to himself nicely, "It's not like you don't have a choice, because you do—you can either type, or kill yourself." We all often feel like we are pulling teeth, even those writers whose prose ends up being the most natural and fluid. The right words and sentences just do not come pouring out like ticker tape most of the time. Now, Muriel Spark is said to have felt that she was taking dictation from God every morning—sitting there, one supposes, plugged into a Dictaphone, typing away, humming. But this is a very hostile and aggressive position. One might hope for bad things to rain down on a person like this.

For me and most of the other writers I know, writing is not rapturous. In fact, the only way I can get anything written at all is to write really, really shitty first drafts.

The first draft is the child's draft, where you let it all pour out and then let it romp all over the place, knowing that no one is going to see it and that you can shape it later. You just let this childlike part of you channel whatever voices and visions come through and onto the page. If one of the characters wants to say, "Well, so what, Mr. Poopy Pants?," you let her. No one is going to see it. If the kid wants to get into really sentimental, weepy, emotional territory, you let him. Just get it all down on paper because there may be something great in those six crazy pages that you would never have gotten to by more rational, grown-up means. There may be something in the very last line of the very last paragraph on page six that you just love, that is so beautiful or wild that you now know what you're supposed to be writing about, more or less, or in what direction you might go—but there was no way to get to this without first getting through the first five and a half pages.

I used to write food reviews for *California* magazine before it folded. (My writing food reviews had nothing to do with the magazine folding, although every single review did cause a couple of canceled subscriptions. Some readers took umbrage at my comparing mounds of vegetable puree with various ex-presidents' brains.) These reviews always took two days to write. First I'd go to a restaurant several times with a few opinionated, articulate friends in tow. I'd sit there writing down everything anyone said that was at all interesting or funny. Then on the following Monday I'd sit down at my desk with my notes and try to write the review. Even after I'd been doing this for years, panic would set in. I'd try to write a lead, but instead I'd write a couple of dreadful sentences, XX them out, try again, XX everything out, and then feel despair and worry settle on my chest like an x-ray apron. It's over, I'd think calmly. I'm not going to be able to get the magic to work this time. I'm ruined. I'm through. I'm toast. Maybe, I'd think, I can get my old job back as a clerk-typist. But probably not. I'd get up and study my teeth in the mirror for a while. Then I'd stop, remember to breathe, make a few phone calls, hit the kitchen and chow down. Eventually I'd go back and sit down at my desk, and sigh for the next ten minutes. Finally I would pick up my one-inch picture frame, stare into it as if for the answer, and every time the answer would come: all I had to do was to write a really shitty first draft of, say, the opening paragraph. And no one was going to see it.

So I'd start writing without reining myself in. It was almost just typing, just making my fingers move. And the writing would be terrible. I'd write a lead paragraph that was a whole page, even though the entire review could only be three pages long, and then I'd start writing up descriptions of the food, one dish at a time, bird by bird, and the critics would be sitting on my shoulders, commenting like cartoon characters. They'd be pretending to snore, or rolling their eyes at my overwrought descriptions, no matter how hard I tried to tone those descriptions down, no matter how conscious I was of what a friend said to me gently in my early days of restaurant reviewing. "Annie," she said, "it is just a piece of *chicken*. It is just a bit of *cake*."

But because by then I had been writing for so long, I would eventually let myself trust the process—sort of, more or less. I'd write a first draft that was maybe twice as long as it should be, with a self-indulgent and boring beginning, stupefying descriptions of the meal, lots of quotes from my black-humored friends that made them sound more like the Manson girls than food lovers, and no ending to speak of. The whole thing would be so long and incoherent and hideous that for the rest of the day I'd obsess about getting creamed by a car before I could write a decent second draft. I'd worry that people would read what I'd written and believe that the accident had really been a suicide, that I had panicked because my talent was waning and my mind was shot.

The next day, I'd sit down, go through it all with a colored pen, take out everything I possibly could, find a new lead somewhere on the second page, figure out a kicky place to end it, and then write a second draft. It always turned out fine, sometimes even funny and weird and helpful. I'd go over it one more time and mail it in.

Then, a month later, when it was time for another review, the whole process would start again, complete with the fears that people would find my first draft before I could rewrite it.

Almost all good writing begins with terrible first efforts. You need to start somewhere. Start by getting something—anything—down on paper. A friend of mine says that the first draft is the down draft—you just get it down. The second draft is the up draft—you fix it up. You try to say what you have to say more accurately. And the third draft is the dental draft, where you check every tooth, to see if it's loose or cramped or decayed, or even, God help us, healthy.

NOTES

1. Lamott says that the perceptions most people have of how writers work is different from the reality of the work itself. She refers to this in paragraph I as "the fantasy of the uninitiated." What does she mean?
2. In paragraph 7 Lamott refers to a time when, through experience, she "eventually let [herself] trust the process – sort of, more or less." She is referring to the writing process, of course, but why "more or less"? Do you think that her wariness is personal, or is she speaking for all writers in this regard? Explain.
3. From what Lamott has to say, is writing a first draft more about the product or the process? Do you agree in regard to your own first drafts? Explain.

Lamott, Anne. "Shitty First Drafts." Language Awareness: Readings for College Writers. Ed. by Paul Eschholz, Alfred Rosa, and Virginia Clark. 9th ed. Boston: Bedford/St. Martin's, 2005: 93-96.

Responding—Really Responding—to Other Students' Writing

Richard Straub

Richard Straub lives on the borders of Tallahassee and teaches courses in writing, rhetoric, and literature at Florida State University. The focus of much of his work is on reading, evaluating, and responding to student writing. He is from Dunmore, Pennsylvania.

Okay. You've got a student paper you have to read and make comments on for Thursday. It's not something you're looking forward to. But that's alright, you think. There isn't really all that much to it. Just keep it simple. Read it quickly and mark whatever you see. Say something about the intro-duction. Something about details and examples. Ideas you can say you like. Mark any typos and spelling errors. Make your comments brief. Abbreviate where possible: *awk, good intro, give ex, frag.* Try to imitate the teacher. Mark what he'd mark and sound like he'd sound. But be cool about it. Don't praise anything really, but no need to get harsh or cut throat either. Get in and get out. You're okay, I'm okay. Everybody's happy. What's the problem?

This is, no doubt, a way of getting through the assignment. Satisfy the teacher and no surprises for the writer. It might just do the trick. But say you want to do a *good* job. Say you're willing to put in the time and effort—though time is tight and you know it's not going to be easy—and help the writer look back on the paper and revise it. And maybe in the process learn something more yourself about writing. What do you look for? How do you sound? How much do you take up? What exactly are you trying to accomplish? Here are some ideas.

HOW SHOULD YOU LOOK AT YOURSELF AS A RESPONDER?

Consider yourself a friendly reader. A test pilot. A roommate who's been asked to look over the paper and tell the writer what you think. Except you don't just take on the role of The Nice Roommate or The Ever-faithful Friend and tell her what she wants to hear. *This all looks good. I wouldn't change a thing. There are a couple places that I think he might not like, but I can see what you're doing there. I'd go with it. Good stuff.* You're supportive. You give her the benefit of the doubt and look to see the good in her writing. But friends don't let friends think their writing is the best thing since *The Great Gatsby* and they don't lead them to think that all is fine and well when it's not. Look to help this friend, this roommate writer—okay, this person in your class—to get a better piece of writing. Point to problems and areas for improvement but do it in a constructive way. See what you can do to push her to do even more than she's done and stretch herself as a writer.

WHAT ARE YOUR GOALS?

First, don't set out to seek and destroy all errors and problems in the writing. You're not an editor. You're not a teacher. You're not a cruise missile. And don't rewrite any parts of the paper. You're not the writer; you're reader. One of many. The paper is not yours; it's the writer's. She writes. You read. She is in charge of what she does to her writing. That doesn't mean you can't make suggestions. It doesn't mean you can't offer a few sample rewrites here and there, as models. But make it clear they're samples, models. Not rewrites. Not edits. Not corrections. Be reluctant at first even to say what you would do if the paper were yours. It's not yours. Again: Writers write, readers read and show what they're understanding and maybe make suggestions. What to do instead: Look at your task as a simple one. You're there to play back to the writer how you read the paper: what you got from it; what you found interesting; where you were confused; where you wanted more. With this done, you can go on to point out problems, ask questions, offer advice, and wonder out loud with the writer about her ideas. Look to help her improve the writing or encourage her to work on some things as a writer.

HOW DO YOU GET STARTED?

Before you up and start reading the paper, take a minute (alright, thirty seconds) to make a mental checklist about the circumstances of the writing, the context. You're not going to just read a text. You're going to read a text within a certain context, a set of circumstances that accompany the writing and that you bring to your reading. It's one kind of writing or another, designed for one audience and purpose or another. It's a rough draft or a final draft. The writer is trying to be serious or casual, straight or ironic. Ideally, you'll read the paper with an eye to the circumstances that it was written in and the situation it is looking to create. That means looking at the writing in terms of the assignment, the writer's particular interests and aims, the work you've been doing in class, and the stage of drafting.

- *The assignment:* What kind of writing does the assignment call (or allow) for? Is the paper supposed to be a personal essay? A report? An analysis? An argument? Consider how well the paper before you meets the demands of the kind of writing the writer is taking up.
- *The writer's interests and aims:* What does the writer want to accomplish? If she's writing a personal narrative, say, is she trying to simply recount a past experience? Is she trying to recount a past experience and at the same time amuse her readers? Is she trying to show a pleasant experience on the surface, yet suggest underneath that everything was not as pleasant as it seems? Hone in on the writer's particular aims in the writing.
- *The work of the class:* Try to tie your comments to the concepts and strategies you've been studying in class. If you've been doing a lot of work on using detail, be sure to point to places in the writing where the writer uses detail effectively or where she might provide richer detail. If you've been working on developing arguments through examples and sample cases, indicate where the writer might use such methods to strengthen her arguments. If you've been considering various ways to sharpen the style of your sentences, offer places where the writer can clarify her sentence structure or arrange a sentence for maximum impact. The best comments will ring familiar even as they lead the writer to try to do something she hasn't quite done before, or done in quite the same way. They'll be comforting and understandable even as they create some need to do more, a need to figure out some better way.
- *The stage of drafting:* Is it an early draft? A full but incomplete draft? A nearly final draft? Pay attention to the stage of drafting. Don't try to deal with everything all at once if it's a first, rough draft. Concentrate on the large picture: the paper's focus; the content; the writer's voice. Don't worry about errors and punctuation problems yet. There'll be time for them later. If it's closer to a full draft, go ahead and talk, in addition to the overall content, about arrangement, pacing, and sentence style. Wait till the final draft to give much attention to fine-tuning sentences and dealing in detail with proofreading. Remember: You're not an editor. Leave these sentence revisions and corrections for the writer. It's her paper. And she's going to learn best by detecting problems and making her own changes.

WHAT TO ADDRESS IN YOUR COMMENTS?

Try to focus your comments on a couple of areas of writing. Glance through the paper quickly first. Get an idea whether you'll deal mostly with the overall content and purpose of the writing, its shape and flow, or (if these are more or less in order) with local matters of paragraph structure, sentence style, and correctness. Don't try to cover everything that comes up or even all instances of a given problem. Address issues that are most important to address in this paper, at this time.

WHERE TO PUT YOUR COMMENTS?

Some teachers like to have students write comments in the margins right next to the passage. Some like to have students write out their comments in an end note or in a separate letter to the writer. I like to recommend using both marginal comments and a note or letter at the end. The best of both worlds. Marginal comments allow you to give a quick moment-by-moment reading of the paper. They make it easy to give immediate and specific feedback. You still have to make sure you specify what you're talking about and what you have to say, but they save you some work telling the writer what you're addressing and allow you to focus your end note on things that are most important. Comments at the end allow you to provide some perspective on your response. This doesn't mean that you have to size up the paper and give it a thumbs up or a thumbs down. You can use the end comment to emphasize the key points of your response, explain and elaborate on issues you want to deal with more fully, and mention additional points that you don't want to address in detail. One thing to avoid: plastering comments all over the writing; in between and over the lines of the other person's writing—up, down, and across the page. Write in your space, and let the writer keep hers.

HOW TO SOUND?

Not like a teacher. Not like a judge. Not like an editor or critic or shotgun. (Wouldn't you want someone who was giving you comments not to sound like a teacher's red pen, a judge's ruling, an editor's impatience, a critic's wrath, a shotgun's blast?) Sound like you normally sound when you're speaking with a friend or acquaintance. Talk to the writer. You're not just marking up a text; you're responding to the writer. You're a reader, a helper, a colleague. Try to sound like someone who's a reader, who's helpful, and who's collegial. Supportive. And remember: Even when you're tough and demanding you can still be supportive.

HOW MUCH TO COMMENT?

Don't be stingy. Write most of your comments out in full statements. Instead of writing two or three words, write seven or eight. Instead of making only one brief comment and moving on, say what you have to say and then go back over the statement and explain what you mean or why you said it or note other alternatives. Let the writer know again and again how you are understanding her paper, what you take her to be saying. And elaborate on your key comments. Explain your interpretations, problems, questions, and advice.

IS IT OKAY TO BE SHORT AND SWEET?

No. At least not most of the time. Get specific. Don't rely on general statements alone. How much have generic comments helped you as a writer? "Add detail." "Needs better structure." "Unclear." Try to let the writer know what exactly the problem is. Refer specifically to the writer's words and make them a part of your comments. "Add some detail on what it was like working at the beach." "I think we'll need to know more about your high school crowd before we can understand the way you've changed." "This sentence is not clear. Were *you* disappointed or were *they* disappointed?" This way the writer will see what you're talking about, and she'll have a better idea what to work on.

DO YOU PRAISE OR CRITICIZE OR WHAT?

Be always of two (or three) minds about your response to the paper. You like the paper, but it could use some more interesting detail. You found this statement interesting, but these ideas in the second paragraph are not so hot. It's an alright paper, but it could be outstanding if the writer said what was really bothering her. Always be ready to praise. But always look to point to places that are not working well or that are not yet working as well as they might. Always be ready to expect more from the writer.

HOW TO PRESENT YOUR COMMENTS?

Don't steer away from being critical. Feel free—in fact, feel obliged—to tell the writer what you like and don't like, what is and is not working, and where you think it can be made to work better. But use some other strategies, too. Try to engage the writer in considering her choices and thinking about possible ways to improve the paper. Make it a goal to write two or three comments that look to summarize or paraphrase what the writer is saying. Instead of *tell-*

ing the reader what to do, *suggest* what she might do. Identify the questions that are raised for you as you reader:

- Play back your way of understanding the writing:
  This seems to be the real focus of the paper, the issue you seem most interested in.
  So you're saying that you really weren't interested in her romantically?
- Temper your criticisms:
  This sentence is a bit hard to follow.
  I'm not sure this paragraph is necessary.
- Offer advice:
  It might help to add an example here.
  Maybe save this sentence for the end of the paper.
- Ask questions, especially real questions:
  What else were you feeling at the time?
  What kind of friend? Would it help to say?
  Do you need this opening sentence?
  In what ways were you "a daddy's little girl"?
- Explain and follow up on your initial comments:
  You might present this episode first. This way we can see what you mean when you say that he was always too busy.
  How did you react? Did you cry or yell? Did you walk away?
  This makes her sound cold and calculating. Is that what you want?
- Offer some praise, and then explain to the writer why the writing works:
  Good opening paragraph. You've got my attention.
  Good detail. It tells me a lot about the place.
  I like the descriptions you provide—for instance, about your grandmother cooking, at the bottom of page 1; about her house, in the middle of page 2; and about how she said her rosary at night: "quick but almost pleading, like crying without tears."

HOW MUCH CRITICISM? HOW MUCH PRAISE?

Challenge yourself to write as many praise comments as criticisms. When you praise, praise well. Think about it. Sincerity and specificity are everything when it comes to a compliment.

HOW MUCH SHOULD YOU BE INFLUENCED BY WHAT YOU KNOW ABOUT THE WRITER?

Consider the person behind the writer when you make your comments. If she's not done so well in class lately, maybe you can give her a pick-me-up in your comments. If she's shy and seems reluctant to go into the kind of personal detail the paper seems to need, encourage her. Make some suggestions or tell her what you would do. If she's confident and going on arrogant, see what you can do to challenge her with the ideas she presents in the paper. Look for other views she may not have thought about, and find ways to lead her to consider them. Always be ready to look at the text in terms of the writer behind the text.

Good comments, this listing shows, require a lot from a reader. But you don't have to make a checklist out of these suggestions and go through each one methodically as you read. It's amazing how they all start coming together when you look at your response as a way of talking with the writer seriously about the writing, recording how you experience the words on the page and giving the writer something to think about for revision. The more you see examples of thoughtful commentary and the more you try to do it yourself, the more you'll get a feel for how it's done.

Here's a set of student comments on a student paper. They were done in the last third of a course that focused on the personal essay and concentrated on helping students develop the content and thought of their writing. The class had been working on finding ways to develop and extend the key statements of their essays (by using short, representative details, full-blown examples, dialogue, and multiple perspectives) and getting more careful about selecting and shaping parts of their writing. The assignment called on students to write an essay or an autobiographical story where they looked to capture how they see (or have seen) something about one or both of their parents—some habits, attitudes, or traits their parents have taken on. They were encouraged to give shape to their ideas and experiences in ways that went beyond their previous understandings and try things they hadn't tried in their writing. More a personal narrative than an essay, Todd's paper looks to capture one distinct difference in the way his mother and father disciplined their children. It is a rough draft that will be taken through one or possibly two more revisions. Readers were asked to offer whatever feedback they could that might help the writer with the next stage of writing.

This is a full and thoughtful set of comments. The responder, Jeremy, creates himself not as a teacher or critic but first of all as a reader, one who is intent on saying how he takes the writing and what he'd like to hear more about:

> Good point. Makes it more unlikely that you should be the one to get caught.
> Great passage. Really lets the reader know what you were thinking.
> Was there a reason you were first or did it just happen that way?
> Would he punish you anyway or could you just get away with things?

He makes twenty-two comments on the paper—seventeen statements in the margins and five more in the end note. The comments are written out in full statements, and they are detailed and specific. They make his response into a lively exchange with the writer, one person talking with another about what he's said. Well over half of the comments are follow-up comments that explain, illustrate, or qualify other responses.

The comments focus on the content and development of the writing, in line with the assignment, the stage of drafting, and the work of the course. They also view the writing rhetorically, in terms of how the text has certain effects on readers. Although there are over two dozen wording or sentence-level errors in the paper, he decides, wisely, to stick with the larger matters of writing. Yet even as he offers a pretty full set of comments he doesn't ever take control over the text. His comments are placed unobtrusively on the page, and he doesn't try to close things down or decide things for the writer. He offers praise, encouragement, and direction. What's more, he pushes the writer to do more than he has already done, to extend the boundaries of his examination. In keeping with the assignment and the larger goals of the course, he calls on Todd in several comments to explore the motivations and personalities behind his parents' different ways of disciplining:

> Maybe you could say more as to why you think your mom is like this.
> Did your dad get into trouble as a kid so he know what it's like? Explain why he reacts as he does.

He is careful, though, not to get presumptuous and make decisions for the writer. Instead, he offers options and points to possibilities:

> Perhaps more on your understanding of why your parents react as they do.
> What other things did you do to get into trouble? Or is it irrelevant?

From start to finish he takes on the task of reading and responding and leaves the work of writing and revising to Todd.

Jeremy's response is not in a class by itself. A set of comments to end all commentary on Todd's paper. He might have done well, for instance, to recognize how much this paper works because of the way Todd arranges the story. He could have done more to point to what's not working in the writing or what could be made to work better. He might have asked Todd for more details about his state of mind when he got caught by the policeman and while he was being held at the police station. He might have urged him more to make certain changes. He might even have said, if only in a brief warning, something about the number of errors across the writing. But this is moot and just. Different readers are always going to pick up on different things and respond in different ways, and no one reading or response is going to address everything that might well be addressed, in the way it might best be addressed. All responses are incomplete and provisional—one reader's way of reading and reacting to the text in front of him. And any number of other responses, presented in any number of different ways, might be as useful or maybe even more useful to Todd as he takes up his work with the writing.

All this notwithstanding, Jeremy's comments are solid. They are full. They are thoughtful. And they are respectful. They take the writing and the writer seriously and address the issues that are raised responsibly. His comments do what commentary on student writing should optimally do. They turn the writer back into his writing and lead him to reflect on his choices and aims, to consider and reconsider his intentions as a writer and the effects the words on the page will have on readers. They help him see what he can work on in revision and what he might deal with in his ongoing work as a writer.

SHARING IDEAS

- What are your experiences with responding to other students' writing? Have you done so in other classes? How did that work out? Were you able to discuss your responses? In small groups or large groups? Which situation did you like best?
- Do you have any papers where others have responded to your writing? Collect one or more and see how the responses stack up against Rick's guidelines. Having read his essay, what would you say your respondent did well and needs to learn to do better?
- In the same way, after everyone in your small group responds to a first paper, go over those papers/responses together in a group and look at what was done and what could be done to improve the quality of responses. In addition, you might try to characterize each of you as a responder: What are your habits? What character/persona do you take on? Would you like to be responded to by the responder you find you are through this group analysis?
- Look at Hint Sheet I in this collection. How do my suggestions for response to student writers sound the same or different from Rick's suggestions? Do we come from the same "school" of responding or do we suggest different approaches? Characterize the differences or similarities you find.
- Rick shows you a responder—Jeremy—and the comments he wrote on Todd's paper. If you were Todd, how would you feel about Jeremy's responses? Do you agree with Rick's analysis of Jeremy's comments? What three or four additional things would you tell Todd about his paper?
- What are your insights into responding? What has worked for you? What do you wish people would do or not do when they respond to your writing? What would make you most inclined to listen to responses and use them to change your work?

How to Write with Style

By Kurt Vonnegut

Newspaper reporters and technical writers are trained to reveal almost nothing about themselves in their writings. This makes them freaks in the world of writers, since almost all of the other ink-stained wretches in that world reveal a lot about themselves to readers. We call these revelations, accidental and intentional, elements of style.

These revelations tell us as readers what sort of person it is with whom we are spending time. Does the writer sound ignorant or informed, stupid or bright, crooked or honest, humorless or playful–? And on and on.

Why should you examine your writing style with the idea of improving it? Do so as a mark of respect for your readers, whatever you're writing. If you scribble your thoughts any which way, your readers will surely feel that you care nothing about them. They will mark you down as an egomaniac or a chowderhead – or, worse, they will stop reading you.

The most damning revelation you can make about yourself is that you do not know what is interesting and what is not. Don't you yourself like or dislike writers mainly for what they choose to show you or make you think about? Did you ever admire an empty-headed writer for his or her mastery of the language? No.

So your own winning style must begin with ideas in your head.

1. FIND A SUBJECT YOU CARE ABOUT

Find a subject you care about and which you in your heart feel others should care about. It is this genuine caring, and not your games with language, which will be the most compelling and seductive element in your style.

I am not urging you to write a novel, by the way – although I would not be sorry if you wrote one, provided you genuinely cared about something.

A petition to the mayor about a pothole in front of your house or a love letter to the girl next door will do.

2. DO NOT RAMBLE, THOUGH

I won't ramble on about that.

3. KEEP IT SIMPLE

As for your use of language: Remember that two great masters of language, William Shakespeare and James Joyce, wrote sentences which were almost childlike when their subjects were most profound. "To be or not to be?" asks Shakespeare's Hamlet. The longest word is three letters long. Joyce, when he was frisky, could put together a sentence as intricate and as glittering as a necklace for Cleopatra, but my favorite sentence in his short story "Eveline" is this one: "She was tired." At that point in the story, no other words could break the heart of a reader as those three words do.

Simplicity of language is not only reputable, but perhaps even sacred. The *Bible* opens with a sentence well within the writing skills of a lively fourteen-year-old: "In the beginning God created the heaven and the earth."

4. HAVE THE GUTS TO CUT

It may be that you, too, are capable of making necklaces for Cleopatra, so to speak. But your eloquence should be the servant of the ideas in your head. Your rule might be this: If a sentence, no matter how excellent, does not illuminate your subject in some new and useful way, scratch it out.

5. SOUND LIKE YOURSELF

The writing style which is most natural for you is bound to echo the speech you heard when a child. English was the novelist Joseph Conrad's third language, and much that seems piquant in his use of English was no doubt colored by his first language, which was Polish. And lucky indeed is the writer who has grown up in Ireland, for the English spoken there is so amusing and musical. I myself grew up in Indianapolis, where common speech sounds like a band saw cutting galvanized tin, and employs a vocabulary as unornamental as a monkey wrench.

In some of the more remote hollows of Appalachia, children still grow up hearing songs and locutions of Elizabethan times. Yes, and many Americans grow up hearing a language other than English, or an English dialect a majority of Americans cannot understand.

All these varieties of speech are beautiful, just as the varieties of butterflies are beautiful. No matter what your first language, you should treasure it all your life. If it happens not to be standard English, and if it shows itself when you write standard English, the result is usually delightful, like a very pretty girl with one eye that is green and one that is blue.

I myself find that I trust my own writing most, and others seem to trust it most, too, when I sound most like a person from Indianapolis, which is what I am. What alternatives do I have? The one most vehemently recommended by teachers has no doubt been pressed on you, as well: to write like cultivated Englishmen of a century or more ago.

6. SAY WHAT YOU MEAN TO SAY

I used to be exasperated by such teachers, but am no more. I understand now that all those antique essays and stories with which I was to compare my own work were not magnificent for their datedness or foreignness, but for saying precisely what their authors meant them to say. My teachers wished me to write accurately, always selecting the most effective words, and relating the words to one another unambiguously, rigidly, like parts of a machine. The teachers did not want to turn me into an Englishman after all. They hoped that I would become understandable – and therefore understood. And there went my dream of doing with words what Pablo Picasso did with paint or what any number of jazz idols did with music. If I broke all the rules of punctuation, had words mean whatever I wanted them to mean, and strung them together higgledy-piggledy, I would simply not be understood. So you, too, had better avoid Picasso-style or jazz-style writing, if you have something worth saying and wish to be understood.

Readers want our pages to look very much like pages they have seen before. Why? This is because they themselves have a tough job to do, and they need all the help they can get from us.

7. PITY THE READERS

They have to identify thousands of little marks on paper, and make sense of them immediately. They have to *read*, an art so difficult that most people don't really master it even after having studied it all through grade school and high school – twelve long years.

So this discussion must finally acknowledge that our stylistic options as writers are neither numerous nor glamorous, since our readers are bound to be such imperfect artists. Our audience requires us to be sympathetic and patient teachers, ever willing to simplify and clarify – whereas we would rather soar high above the crowd, singing like nightingales.

That is the bad news. The good news is that we Americans are governed under a unique Constitution, which allows us to write whatever we please without fear of punishment. So the most meaningful aspect of our styles, which is what we choose to write about, is utterly unlimited.

8. FOR REALLY DETAILED ADVICE

For a discussion of literary style in a narrower sense, in a more technical sense, I commend to your attention *The Elements of Style*, by William Strunk, Jr., and E.B. White (Macmillan, 1979). E.B. White is, of course, one of the most admirable literary stylists this country has so far produced.

You should realize, too, that no one would care how well or badly Mr. White expressed himself, if he did not have perfectly enchanting things to say.